LITHUANIA

ATVIA

BIRŽAI ⊙

ROKIŠKIS ⊙

56°

PANEVĖŽYS ⊙

Sartai

ZARASAI ⊙

Snūdas

UTENA ⊙

ŠVENTOJI ⊙ UKMERGĖ

ŠVENČIONYS ⊙

55°

NERIS

Narutis

VILNIUS

TRAKAI ⊙

NERIS

AŠMENA ⊙

54°

LYDA ⊙

NEMUNAS

U.S.S.R.

AND

LEGEND

———••••——— Boundaries Set by International Agreements

`················` Line Indicating the Portion of Lithuanian Territory Transferred to Byelorussia by the U.S.S.R.

Capital

⊙ Major Cities

Lakes

Rivers

53°

SCALE

10 5 0   10   20   30   40   50

MILES

D1547990

The USSR - German Aggression
Against Lithuania

The USSR-German Aggression Against Lithuania

Edited, with a Foreword and
Introduction by

BRONIS J. KASLAS, Ph.D.

Robert Speller & Sons, Publishers, Inc.
New York, New York 10010
1973

©1973 by Bronis J. Kaslas

Library of Congress Catalog Card No. 72-12230
ISBN 0-8315-0135-9

First Edition

Printed in the United States of America

CONTENTS

The USSR - German Aggression
Against Lithuania

FOREWORD

As this collection of documents is being prepared for publication, the Western World is enjoying an age of rapprochement and nostalgia. West Germany, at a sort of Eastern Locarno with the U. S. S. R. and Poland, has signed a treaty recognizing Poland's western boundaries, thereby settling a long-standing uncertainty. The East and West German governments also concluded their first treaty providing transportation across the closely guarded boundaries and easing the travel of Germans in both directions, and announced that they would continue the negotiations aimed at normalizing relations between the two Germanies.

Greatly enhancing the picture is the American withdrawal from Southeast Asia which seems to have created conditions for a rapprochement between the United States and Communist China after twenty three years of hostility; even as the manuscript of this book was being completed the People's Republic of China was accepted into the membership of the United Nations and a Mao-Nixon meeting was under way in Peking where they reached very important decisions on Taiwan and laid down a favorable atmosphere for cultural and diplomatic cooperation.

Moreover, as this book was being printed President Nixon, crowning a year of extraordinary summitry, met for a week in the Kremlin Palace in Moscow with Leonid Brezhnev, the head of the Communist Party of the U. S. S. R. and other Soviet leaders and reached agreements to curb the nuclear arms race, to prevent naval incidents at sea, to cooperate in space exploration etc, as well as to summon in the near future a European Security conference.

It is natural, meanwhile, for popular opinion to take a wistful look at the past. Undoubtedly, this turning back originated with the youth of the world which has been indiscriminately adopting the trappings of bygone ages in some desperate quest for a vanished arcadia. This general feeling that the past must have been better than the present is having a specific echo in fashion and design as the styles of the Thirties and Forties are increasingly reproduced among us; apparently, the passing of the years between has softened the memory of two of the most anguished decades in recent history.

It is understandable that in a time of easing tensions one is enticed into setting aside the sins of an erstwhile enemy. Peace is so hard to achieve and so sweet to know that further tampering with sensitive areas holds little attraction for most people. Then, as life continues and the participants in the events become nothing but names, it is easy for future generations to consign unpleasant memories to the receding past, especially if they should happen to involve small and faraway nations such as the Baltic States which cannot raise their voices from the tribune of the United Nations or explode their bombs to disturb anyone's peace of mind.

Historians, however, know that nostalgia and expediency are alien to their dispositions, and that serenity will elude them as long as there are questions to ask: For example, in this era when the United Nations (comprising virtually every State in the world) is loudly proclaiming the noblest of principles, why are repressed millions subjected to political and economic bondage? In this era, allegedly characterized by the dissolution of colonialism, why are so many nations nothing more than subjugated territories? The incorporation of Lithuania into the U. S. S. R. was not an isolated event of local significance, but was part of the context of the collaboration of Germany and the Soviet Union in the early stages of the Second World War. As such, it shaped the syndrome which charted the course of the War, and it effected changes in the political contour of Europe as profound as those of the Peace at Westphalia, the Congress of Vienna and the Treaty of Versailles.

Vladimir Petrov, in an article in *Orbis* (11(4), Wint. 68: 1113), writes: "Western historians seem to have lost interest in the Nazi-Soviet collaboration during the 1939-1941 period. . . . This tendency to skirt one of the most momentous developments in modern history is regrettable. A judicious examination of the subject would give us insight into the relations between the two most powerful countries of Europe during the early years of World War II, as well as into the mentality of some of the most powerful leaders of our era." It is earnestly hoped that the present collection of documents will in some way counter this trend.

It is regrettable that the sources available for certain periods may appear limited and inadequate. The Soviet Union has yet to open its archives for our generation; even Soviet historians use Western sources for their information. In preparing this presentation, we think we will reveal some fresh insights, (including the more remote fruits of Soviet research which are not readily available to the English-speaking reader), and that, perhaps for the first time, an effort will have been made to offer the material in a meaningful thematic arrangement as opposed to a purely chronological listing.

From 1939 to 1941, Lithuania was a microcosm of the German-Soviet collaboration; she was more intensely involved than the other Baltic States, Latvia and Estonia, because her land bordered on Germany.

Lithuania became the pawn in a developing relationship between the two major powers which soon revealed their personalities as they carried on negotiations with frank cynicism, making only a token effort at dissemblance. Perhaps they themselves may have failed to realize how clearly their behavior mirrored their true feelings. For example, their wrangling to settle the title to a certain tiny strip (less than three counties) of Lithuania, showed the startling disintegration of German-Soviet friendship as both sides tore at the small objective with disproportionate fervor. Additionally, during personal negotiations with the Lithuanians, (such as at Moscow in October of 1939), Soviet officials completely disregarded the sensibilities of their besieged neighbor and acted with a Machiavellian frankness not to be found in their dealings with the West.

Few would argue against the axiom that mankind should learn from the teachings of history; in practice, however, it seems that no lesson is forgotten as promptly and thoroughly as a bad experience. Over and over, nations repeat their mistakes. The particular fate of Lithuania was not only of interest to her four million countrymen, (one million abroad); this deeply troubled land would be the forerunner of great events spawned by World War II. Importantly, the restoration of Lithuania after the first World War was more than a manifestation of national consciousness. It also meant that the Wilsonian spirit had permeated international politics, the spirit which, beautifully conceived even though only half-heartedly applied, stood for a legitimate desire to create a better world. The later destruction of the Baltic States resulted from the collapse of the system of collective security and the eventual abandonment of Wilsonian ideals, leading, in turn, to the massive deterioration of political morality.

Following the Second World War, it was tacitly conceded that the subjugation of the Baltic nations was an outcome of a disastrous foray into personal diplomacy in which the West negated sound principles of statesmanship with inept negotiatory tactics. When Castlereagh returned from attending the Congress of Vienna, Napoleon expressed astonishment that England had not been rewarded for her leading role in defeating him. Had he been victorious, Napoleon declared, he would have seen to it that England received more compensation for her efforts. But Castlereagh's sacrifice of a narrow national interest, (in this case territorial aggrandizement in Europe), served the world well, inasmuch as it provided an equilibrium which substantially preserved general peace throughout Europe for ninety-nine years. The Western leaders at Yalta and Potsdam continued the tradition of sacrificing their national interests but perhaps they lost sight of Castlereagh's diplomatic reasons for having set the precedent. As it happened, they obtained no reciprocal advantages for themselves or for the other countries of Europe. Indeed, they departed from the meetings with no hope for equilibrium in postwar Europe, and with the seeds of the cold war already sown.

With World War II at an end, Lithuania, just as the rest of Eastern Europe, became a painful and embarrassing problem for the West. But if nothing has been done to solve the problem, neither can it be swept under the rug of time to lie in the dust and rubble like a torn fragment of history. History does not permit us the luxury of a tabula rasa, for nothing and no one can wipe the slate clean of the horrors imprinted there by selfishness and greed.

Many of the world's nations can identify with beleaguered Lithuania and sympathize with her experiences, for there are more small countries than large, and a host of losers for every winner. Even the deprivation of freedom is far from unique, and might, under various conditions, happen to almost anybody. In fact, one must admit that in this age of the development of the technology of control, in the era of the preeminence of the Western democracies and under the U. N. system, more people have lost their freedom than have gained it. Nor is the fact that a given nation small in size is a sufficient reason for dismissing its fate. The empires of the Assyrians and Medes left us with nothing more than diversion for archeologists, while the insignificant tribes of Israel and the tiny city-state of Athens have actually shaped the values of the civilized world.

Perhaps the most compelling reason for compiling this collection of documents on the destruction of a small country through the machinations of great powers is to try to harness the widespread tendency to forget the problem of Lithuania and to turn it ..ito nothing more than an artifact for archeologists to ponder on in future centuries. It is worth noting that an active attempt by politicians to "forget" may be quite a reliable indicator that this particular episode ought to be fully remembered and closely examined. . .

A work of this sort is beyond the capacity of one man to produce. Therefore, this opportunity is gratefully taken to thank those whose assistance has been invaluable: Dr. Jonas Balys, Reference Librarian of the Slavic and Central European Division of the Library of Congress, who freely contributed his help and advice to this effort; Dr. Kestutis Valiūnas, Juozas Audėnas and Jonas Dainauskas, who kindly furnished some important documents; Col. Kazys Škirpa, who shared his extensive personal archives and his even more extensive memory; the Lithuanian Legation in Washington, D. C., its Chargé d'Affaires, Mr. Joseph Kajeckas, and its Counsellor, Dr. Stasys Bačkis, who helped in every way they could; the Lithuanian Encyclopedia, an indispensable reference source; the Lithuanian National Fund (Tautos Fondas) for its support; Wilkes College, and especially its Chancellor, Dr. Eugene S. Farley, its president, Dr. Francis Michelini, and the Chairman of the Division of Social Sciences, Professor David Leach, all of whom provided facilities and moral support while the book was in preparation; the Library of the Hoover Institution of War, Revolution and Peace at Stanford University, and its former Director and Professor Emeritus, Witold Sworakowski, who provided a rich and accessible vein of material; and finally, thank you to a wonderful young assistant, Henry Horbaczewski (Harvard, '72), who, added his dedication and freshness to this quest for truth.

INTRODUCTION

HISTORICAL BACKGROUND OF LITHUANIAN-RUSSIAN RELATIONS

Rivalry of a wholesome nature becomes an incentive for men to attempt greater achievements for the benefit of humankind. But when the contest is allowed to degenerate into aggrandizement by conquest, true peace, order and progress lie as sacrificial offerings on the altar of ruin.

It has perhaps been all but forgotten that competition once pulsed strongly between Lithuania and Russia, flourishing, in fact, to such a degree of intensity that its influence still affects political conditions today. Lithuania has been reduced to a small country of farms, forests and lakes, while Russia has fought her way to a huge empire, yet even now the present is constantly intruded upon by the past when the former was a powerful nation.

The ancient memory of that greatness gives Lithuania the stalwart heritage which sustains her in the struggle for survival. Consistently clinging to survival with her self-respect intact, she stands resolute in the knowledge that she has done her best.

Long centuries of the most intense forms of repression have failed to denationalize her homeland or to strip her consciousness of those possessions which are capable of turning masses of humanity into people — namely, their culture, their religion, and their language.

EARLY PERIOD 1300-1505

Since the fourteenth century, Lithuania was a mighty state stretching all the way from the Baltic to the Black Sea, vigorous, enterprising and with valid plans for the future. She used her strength not to conquer other peaceful peoples or to deprive them of their social and religious treasures, but for the sole purpose of protecting both them and herself against their common enemies. In shielding the beleaguered Slavs from further Tartar invasions, she contributed heavily to the eventual collapse of the Mongol Tribes, nomadic warriors who had reduced Russia to serfdom during the 13th-15th centuries. It was Lithuania's ability to act as the guardian of a vast expanse of Eastern Slav territories, by pushing the frontiers of her own Grand Duchy as far eastward as the Ugra, Oka and Donets Rivers, which resulted in Russia's opportunity to free herself from Mongol hordes. Slowly and methodically consolidating all her domains to emerge as a truly independent political reality as the 15th century drew to its close, Moscow Principality rose up as Lithuania's rival for power on the borderlands of Europe.

Liberated from the Mongol threat, Moscovy cast off the old yoke. But instead of proceeding to advance her unique culture and form of government for the benefit of her people, she began using her energies to absorb as many peoples and as much land as possible.

Ivan the Third began his reign by setting the mood for Moscow's expansion. Toward this end he rejected all expressions of good will from the Lithuanian Grand Duke, Alexander, discarding the solemn pledge he had offered in the Treaty of 1494 to maintain perpetual peace with Lithuania and her people. Five years after the Treaty had been signed, Ivan marched into the Grand Duchy of Lithuania, the act responsible for spawning an imperialist policy.

THE POLISH-LITHUANIAN COMMONWEALTH AND RUSSIA, 1569-1795

In just seventy years, Lithuania found herself in a noose that Russia drew tighter every day. She suffered so severely that she was forced to accept a promise of Polish aid even though the conditions named by Poland undermined Lithuanian statehood. At Lublin, in 1569, Lithuania was compelled to agree to the creation of a Polish-Lithuanian Commonwealth which was to be a dual state presided over by a common ruler and a common Diet or parliament. Lithuanians were induced to accept the dictated Union after two provinces, Podlachia and Volhynia, and later two palatinates, Podolia and Braclaw with Kiev, were annexed by Poles.

Despite the Lithuanian payment of this staggering price, Poland's promise of assistance was fruitless; she herself lost Kiev and the areas east of the Dnieper within 100 years. Poland had been in a choice position to foster the newly born movement for national independence among the Ukrainians, thereby gaining a loyal ally in the South. But she missed this important chance by frustrating their hopes for self-determination, and in 1667, under the terms of the Armistice, and the Treaty of Andrusovo, she abandoned the Ukrainians entirely to Russian domination.

As the 18th century traveled across the world, Russian imperialism traveled with it. Russia resorted to all the classic methods with which we are so familiar today, that of whipping up internal disharmony until utter chaos results, and then presenting herself as the protectress of human rights and a guardian of well-being.

Raging for more than two decades, 1699-1721, the Great Northern War gave Tsar Peter the First one of history's most convenient combinations of circumstances with which to accomplish his expansionist objective. With both Lithuania and Poland overrun by the Swedish troops of Charles the Twelfth, Peter saw a way to achieve domination of the Polish-Lithuanian Commonwealth. Promising Augustus the Second (who functioned as both the King of Poland and the Grand Duke of Lithuania) valuable assistance against the Swedish invader, Peter sent his troops into the two countries. Then, when the Swedish armies were defeated (Charles XII, the "hero king," died in 1718) and Sweden herself had exhausted her resources in fighting the 1700 Alliance composed of Denmark, Prussia, Poland-Saxony and Russia, Peter announced his intention to leave his forces exactly where they were. The Poles and the Lithuanians bitterly protested this highhanded violation of their sovereign rights, but were quelled by intimidation from the rapidly mushrooming Russian sphere. The Diet of 1717 was convened with Moscovite soldiers menacingly surrounding the building, their guns in firing position in the conference halls. Peter's representative, Dolgoruki, swept in and dictated certain demands to the Diet, one of which was an order that the Republic reduce its military personnel to 24,000 soldiers. Under threat of the Russian soldiers, the Diet agreed to the demands in silence. This Parliament is known to history as the "dumb" Diet.

The Great Northern War, which lasted 21 years, ended with the Treaty of Nystadt in 1721. Russia obtained a very important part of the Baltic coast, including Livonia, Estonia, Ingermanland, part of Karelia, Vyborg, the islands of Oesel and Dago.

Thus, with the defeat of Sweden and the conquest of the Baltic coast, Peter had opened Russia's "Window to the West."

From the "Dumb Diet" of 1717, Russia's interference in the domestic affairs of Poland-Lithuania became a permanent pattern of Russia's foreign policy. In 1733, at an Election Diet, she again violated all the constitutional rights of the Polish-Lithuanian Commonwealth by forcing the latter's candidate out of office and substituting a choice of her own: — Lithuanian and Polish electors had legally chosen Stanislas Leszczynski to succeed Frederick Augustus the Second. At once, Russia transformed the new leader's life into a nightmare. She dispatched troops to frustrate his movements and threaten his bodily safety, and Leszczynski was forced to escape to Danzig (Gdansk). Tsarina Anne's General Lascy then summoned a "phantom" Polish-Lithuanian Diet that October, so-called because only a small minority of qualified Polish-Lithuanian deputies attended the call. Shortly thereafter, and in accordance with the desires of Russia and Prussia, this alleged "parliament" (composed of just a handful of voters) proclaimed Frederick Augustus the Third as the new Polish-Lithuanian ruler.

The scene was replayed in 1746, when Frederick II of Prussia and Catherine II of Russia formally agreed that a selected individual would have to receive the sanction of both countries before he could be permitted to ascend the Polish-Lithuanian throne. However, to insure a Russian victory, a foolproof blueprint was drawn: — Kayserling, the Prussian representative, and Repnin, the representative from Moscow, placed Poland and Lithuania under maximum pressure by directing Russian soldiers to maneuver inside their borders and Prussian forces to poise on their outskirts while awaiting the order to attack. Facing possible massacre on their own territories, the Lithuanian and Polish gentry had to accede to the demand of Russia and Prussia that Stanislas Poniatowski be named their new leader.

Three years later, the shrewd Repnin managed to enlist the aid of Charles Radvila, (Lith.: Karolis Stanislovas Radvilas, Pol: Karol Stanislaw Radziwill) a Lithuanian who was at odds with the King and the important politicians of the Republic, to assemble a substantial group of the Lithuanian and Polish gentry at Radom. Repnin said this meeting would consider methods of protecting the exaggerated notions of aristocratic liberty which the Poles had fostered, and which Lithuania had "inherited" at Lublin in 1569. But under Repnin's direction, the meeting considered nothing but Russia herself. In tried and true fashion,

Russian troops were assigned to surround the Radom assemblage so that the pressure would be stifling. Catherine the II of Russia was invoked as the protectress of the Polish-Lithuanian Republic according to Russian plan. When at the General Diet of Warsaw, Lithuanian and Polish members refused to sanction the Radom decision because it had been secured under coercion, Repnin arrested four of these deputies and had them deported to Kaluga. This act, cold-blooded even by Russian standards, set the stage for war between Russia and the Polish-Lithuanian Commonwealth. In 1772, after four bitter years, the war ended with the First Partition.

Russia was more than anxious to absorb all of victimized Poland-Lithuania at once. However, since there were a number of circumstances making it more expedient for her to accept her victory "graciously," she settled for a gradual absorption of the territories. Consequently, Frederick II of Prussia played the pivotal role in the maze of political maneuvers which led to the First Partition. Three years before, he had discussed a plan of partition with Panin, the Russian minister at that time, in return for Russian aid against the Turks. Frederick was friendly with Russia, yet he had also displayed an interest in listening to Vienna's opinions (indicated by two conferences which he held with Joseph II, Maria Theresa's son). For her own part, Vienna was hoping to prevent the expansion of Tsarist domains along the lower Danube, and thereby to stymie the Turkish aggression.

Now, Catherine made a special effort to strengthen the bonds between Russia and Prussia. She extended an invitation to Frederick's brother, Prince Henry, to visit St. Petersburg in July of 1770, and Henry's stay was a prolonged one. When Henry departed from Russia, Catherine abandoned her former interest in the territories of Wallachia and Moldavia, and thus avoided a clash with Austria. The following February, Russia and Prussia signed the first treaty of the partitioning of Poland-Lithuania, and in August, Austria was admitted as the third partner. The three partitioning powers were now ready to divide the spoils.

It was agreed that Russia would occupy the palatinates of Polock, Vitebsk and Mstislavl, the eastern borders of the Lithuanian Grand Duchy and the palatinate of Livonia (Latgale), while Austria would assume possession of Galicia, the southern portion of Poland up to the Vistula. The third member, Prussia, would acquire Polish West Prussia with the exceptions of Thorn (Torun) and Danzig (Gdansk), the lands which formed the link uniting Frederick's East Prussian kingdom with

Brandenburg. In April of 1773 a General Diet of the Republic was summoned by King Stanislas on the demand of Russia, Prussia and Austria. These three partitioning powers stated they were waiting eagerly for the "governing body of Poland-Lithuania" to "ratify" their actions.

Many of the summoned deputies refused to respond. Immediately, Russian and Prussian bribery, treachery and intimidation were carried out on a more ambitious scale than ever before, set into motion under the directing force of Stackelberg, Catherine's ambassador and Repnin's successor. Stackelberg arranged to have a committee of just 30 deputies and senators meet under the most transparent semblance of legality. When additional persons would be required to give approval, or to stamp the measures "adopted," they would merely be corralled at random and forced to do as they were told.

Violent protest lashed helplessly against the Russian tactics as the oppressed Republic raised its agonized voice through the Lithuanian deputy, Thaddeusz Rejtan. Rejtan, representing Naugardukas (Nowogrodek) worked so uncompromisingly to reverse some of Moscow's maneuvers that he became a national hero. But the Polish-Lithuanian Republic had grown too frail to continue opposition and could do no more than delay "ratification" for a brief period. Soon afterward, Russia was successful in wresting an "adoption" of the First Partition from the mourning Republic.

The Russian ambassador Stackelberg, proving himself as skillful at promulgating Russian policy as his predecessors, assumed full charge of the partitioned countries. Neither the King nor the Permanent Council could take any action whatever without first seeking and obtaining Stackelberg's consent. Additionally, his approval would be required before selected individuals could be promoted to higher offices. A few nobles of the Republic saw that they might advance their personal careers if they catered to Stackelberg. Some of them journeyed to St. Petersburg to discuss their interests with Catherine and try to win her intercession in their behalf. Most noteworthy of all the events surrounding the First Partition was Russia's declaration that Poland-Lithuania was enjoying "independence"; in reality, the latter had been lost due to Russian intrigue against the sovereignty which belongs naturally to an independent state.

A rare 4-year interlude followed in which Poland-Lithuania had an opportunity to try to free herself from the shackles of Russian imperialism, a bonanza arising out of the abandonment of the Prussian alliance with Russia by Frederick William II, who had succeeded Frederick the Great. In October 1786, one year before Turkey and Sweden would declare war on Russia, the General Diet of the Polish-Lithuanian Republic met at Warsaw. Remaining in session for four consecutive years, the Diet made every possible effort to accomplish a series of positive reforms. It abolished the use of the principle of unanimity (liberum veto), the free election of kings, and the gentry's right to form confederations opposing the King, thereby eliminating the Polish "notions of liberty and democracy" which Repnin had discussed, and which had only served as another Russian means of encroachment upon the sovereignty of the oppressed peoples. Inspired, and filled with the courage of its convictions, the Diet even formulated a proposal to organize a Polish-Lithuanian army staffed by some 100,000 soldiers, an act which had been strictly forbidden by the Tsarina!

The seeds had been planted with care, but the soil was barren. In July 1791, two months after a new constitution had been adopted, Austria and Prussia entered into an agreement allegedly to "safeguard" the inviolability of the hard-won articles of law, (a step undertaken by both parties to strengthen their positions against Russia). The Russians, busy for four years waging war with Turkey, now concluded peace with that country. Once again, they were free to grind their pressure-tactics into the Polish-Lithuanian state; unhappily, the latter's short respite from the endless manueverings had come to an end.

Russia's next stratagem was brought about through a group of Polish nobles abetted by the Court of St. Petersburg. Creating the Confederation of Targowica while conducting themselves according to Russian wishes, the Polish nobles produced a formal petition requesting "protection" from the Russians (May, 1792). A similar Confederation was formed at the Lithuanian capital of Vilnius, and its constituents announced their alliance with the rebels of Targowica. Catherine promptly assigned troops to Poland and Lithuania, whose many loyal citizens offered impassioned resistance against the invader. Their cause, however, was hopeless from the beginning; in only two months, they had been captured by the Russian machine.

Prussia was eager to share in the booty of the new acquisitions, and suggested that the Second Partitioning of Poland-Lithuania be completed (January 23, 1793). Austria, afraid of losing Prussian support in her fight with France, was gracefully eliminated from the contest through astute political maneuvering on the part of Haugwitz, the Prussian delegate. The result was that Russia annexed the eastern areas of the Grand Duchy of Lithuania, with Minsk and Pinsk, as well as the eastern sections of Poland which included the western Ukraine and parts of Podolia and Volhynia. Prussia gained Polish Danzig, Thorn, Great Poland and part of Mazovia. The Comedy of 1773 (when a Diet had been summoned to "ratify" the deeds of the partitioning powers) was due to be replayed, as now, two decades later, the Confederates of Targowica were ordered to assemble a General Diet of Poland-Lithuania whose members would be commanded to give their "formal sanction" to the Russian and Prussian seizure of their homelands. A number of revolutionist groups which had been deceived by Tsarina Catherine took the retaliatory measure of refusing to convene the Diet. Consequently, Russia convoked the assemblage herself; the Diet met at Gardinas (Grodno), Lithuania, (where every third General Diet of the Republic had convened since 1673).

At this new Diet, only those territories which had escaped seizure on January 23 would even be represented. (The district Diet lines were observed scrupulously so that Russian-Prussian psychology of fear could have the fullest impact on the depressed and sorrowing Diet members.) A new Russian ambassador, Sievers, became the Diet's most powerful personage; even Buchholz, the Prussian delegate, depended upon Sievers to protect the joint interests of their countries.

Sievers found it far from easy to extort "approval" for the Second Partition. It took three months of active misery, including violence performed upon the persons and properties of many deputies, alarming threats that the entire mutilated Republic would be exposed to the plunder and cruelty of Russian soldiers, and vengeful promises that Poland-Lithuania would have its remaining nominal sovereignty torn away, before the exhausted ambassador finally secured the prize of "ratification." After that, the defeated Diet had one more "decision" to render; inasmuch as the army of Poland-Lithuania was limited to only 15,000 soldiers, a so-called "mutual assistance pact" was signed between the Polish-Lithuanian Republic and Russia.

In March 1794, under the great Thaddeus Kosciusko (who was born in Lithuania of a poor but noble family and had won fame for his service to the American colonies in the Revolutionary War) the Republic rose in angry rebellion against its oppressors. It struggled valiantly, although of course in vain, against the numerically larger Russian troops for eight months. More diplomatic maneuvers and intense wrangling followed, (especially between the Partitioning Powers themselves), before Poland and Lithuania were subjected to the Third and Final Partition.

With the Treaty of October 24, 1795, Russia took possession of the Polish-Lithuanian fief of Courland, all that remained of the Lithuanian Grand Duchy east of the Nemunas (Niemen) River up to Brest, and Polish Volhynia. Prussia moved into the Suvalki area of Lithuania west of the Nemunas, and also occupied the Polish lands of western Mazovia and western Galicia along with a strip of Lithuanian territory southwest of Brest.

When Stanislas Poniatowski abdicated a month later, Russia was sated with the realization of uncounted imperialistic schemes.

THE FLAME SPUTTERS 1795-1915

To write a history of Lithuania under the Tsarist regime, (a period of 120 years), is to set down a prolonged series of tragic events.

Lithuania tried in four major revolutions to free herself from the Russian occupation, (1812, 1831, 1863 with the Poles, and 1905). During this entire period, she was constantly exposed to the threat of total annihilation, and subjected to the worst form of oppression which Russian imperialism produced, namely the denationalization of the conquered people.

Because the scourge of the Napoleonic Wars would menace Russia's own sovereignty, Tsar Alexander seemed to be permitting Lithuanian leaders to entertain a vague hope that an autonomous Lithuanian Grand Duchy might actually be restored at some future date. But in the wake of the Napoleonic conflicts Lithuania found herself devastated, depopulated and destined for oblivion through incorporation into the Russian Empire. Alexander, acting as though he were seeking Polish good will, allowed the Poles to operate a Polonization campaign in the Lithuanian capital of Vilnius. He sealed off every avenue of cultural and spiritual growth to the Lithuanians and even ignored their existence. But since the Poles refused to become obedient subjects of St. Petersburg, Lithuania was submitted to Russification instead of Polonization.

The most desperate period in the history of Lithuania now began. Her culture and human rights were disposed of by the Russian machine. The University of Vilnius, in reprisal for the uprising of 1831, was closed in 1832 and its library artifacts and treasures transferred to Russia. The Lithuanian people were persecuted, called "disloyal" without cause, and regularly exiled to the Caucasus or Siberia. If they owned properties the Russians confiscated these for their own officers and colonists. Even the name "Lithuania" and Byelorussia was officially abolished and replaced by a loose territorial description: — "Northwestern Province of Russia".

The ancient Lithuanian statute containing the code of laws by which the Grand Duchy of Lithuania had governed itself since 1529, was cancelled in 1840. National schools were replaced by exclusively Russian schools. In addition to losing their cultural and educational rights and their remaining vestiges of government, the people were deprived of religious freedom, for Russian Orthodoxy was considered to be a leading means of Russification. Special catechisms were published in an attempt to encourage youth to be loyal to the Tsar. These publications even went so far as to claim that the Russian Empire was the "true homeland of Lithuania"! The Russian historian, Karamzin, wrote that the territories seized by his country during the partitions (either by force or by threat of force) had actually been Russian possessions in the first place. These misrepresentations were further compounded by a Russian order that the wearing of national costumes would be strictly forbidden.

A complex system of espionage and intrigue spread throughout all centers of Lithuania. The Lithuanians could not officially use their own language for a period of 40 years (1864-1904): a book written in Lithuanian and printed in proper Latin characters, was treated as a major crime against the government. Many who engaged in the traffic of "contraband literature" in an effort to save their birthrights were either jailed or lost their health as a result of the imprisonment or floggings to which they were sentenced. Whenever the Lithuanians tried to resist, the Russians conducted a massacre as the "cure." Those massacres occurred at Kestaičiai (1886) and at Kražiai (1893) when Lithuanian victims who could not tolerate the closing of their churches by the Russians were brutally slain.

For 120 years Lithuania bore repression the like of which few have suffered and yet the Russians failed to destroy or denationalize this gallant country. Lithuania's bitter struggle, waged against a mighty power she could never hope to match, was an amazing testimonial to courage. Lithuania emerged victorious from the struggle because she preserved her culture, her religion and her language. Assisted by the great democracies, she was a battered figure after World War I, but a living entity and a free one.

At the same time, Russian imperialism was pushing onward. This time the Soviet government proceeded to send their armed forces against exhausted, depleted Lithuania, and against Estonia, Latvia and Poland.

INDEPENDENCE 1918-1930

World War I was the Götterdämerung of the imperial system in Eastern Europe, for the two dominant forces of the preceeding centuries, Germany's "Drang Nach Osten" and Russia's "Window to the West" policy, finally collided. When the reverberations had faded and the dust had cleared, Europe's great empires no longer existed. For the next twenty years, while the war-ruined great powers of Europe rebuilt their strength, the new free nations of the region flourished in the political vacuum.

One would like to speak of the idealism of the Russian revolutionary governments but, from Kerensky to Brezhnev, Russian rulers maintained their Empire. The right of self-determination (proclaimed by no less than Lenin himself) did not apply to Georgia, Kazakhstan, the Ukraine, or the Baltic nations.

Even in the midst of a civil war (1918-1922), the Red Army found enough energy to attack Poland and the Baltic States simultaneously. The latter managed a defense with its own military efforts plus minor support from Britain in the Baltic, and Poland, receiving the main offensive of the Russian attack, was substantially aided by France. In the end the Bolshevik armies were routed, and reality finally dispelled the Russian dream of total supremacy. Realizing that it was now a third-rate power, the Soviet Government turned its chief attention inward and concentrated its energies on the work to be done at home. Between 1920 and 1922, the Russians concluded peace treaties with their Western neighbors. Meanwhile the last Germans in Latvia and Lithuania went home, and there was peace.

The era between the wars could have been described as a pleasant interlude during which the Eastern European countries played out their national ambitions in an atmosphere of unreal complacency. Below the surface, Russia and Germany rebuilt and rearmed. The whole region had been brutally ravaged for six years, and while the erstwhile powers now paused to renew their strength, the emphasis was on reconstruction and development, rather than on power politics.

Lithuania declared her independence in 1918. The original constitution adopted by the Constituent Seimas in 1922, introduced popular democracy on the French model or the multi-party system. In the free elections of the following four years the government moved slowly to the left. When a Socialist-Populist government was voted into power in 1926, the army staged a coup d'état on the pretext of preventing a Communist plot to overthrow the Republic. Claiming that the left was incapable of preserving peace and order within the country, the army installed Antanas Smetona (one of the leaders of the national movement for independence) as president.

At first, Smetona's government was composed of Nationalists (Tauti-ninkai)* and Christian Democrats, but the latter soon decided to withdraw from government. A drift to the right set in, but the trend was halted abruptly in 1929 when Prime Minister Voldemaras (leader of the right wing of the Nationalists) was removed from office. Under Smetona, the pendulum swung back toward the center. A new constitution was adopted in 1938.

At this time, the Lithuanian government could be described as a paternalistic, presidential, one-party system, but with political freedom existing beyond the letter of the law. Economically, she was an agricultural society composed of small farmers. Part of the legacy of Lithuania's former union with Poland was that her native aristocracy had been Polonized; thus, when the laws were enacted to expropriate their vast estates for distribution to the peasantry, no substantial objections were heard. Lithuania had also inherited a legacy from her experience with imperial Russia, that of the absence of a secure middle class. With small farmers comprising the overwhelming majority of the population, large-scale capitalism was no factor. The Lithuanian farmers worked their parcels of land industriously throughout the two decades of independence. At the same time, the nation, always highly literate, reveled in the restoration of its freedom of language and education. By 1939 it was difficult to believe that the Lithuanian nation had been actively suppressed for more than a century.

The focal point of Lithuania's foreign policy for nineteen years was the Polish seizure of Vilnius in 1920, yet another part of the legacy of her union with Poland. Both Pilsudski, the Polish Commander-in-Chief, and Zeligowski, the Polish Commander-in-the-Field, were of the regional gentry (Zeligowski's home was near Vilnius) which had been thoroughly Polonized. Even though they might have eventually been convinced of Lithuania's lack of interest in resuming the union, nothing could cure these leaders of the tendency to be high-handed with their true countrymen, the Lithuanian peasants. Unquestionably, victory over the Soviets had filled Polish heads with dreams of glory, and it was well-known that Pilsudski had hopes for a Polish hegemony in Eastern Europe. Lithuania promptly broke off diplomatic relations with Poland,

*Should not be confused with 'Nazis' or 'Fascists' in Germany or Italy.

and the two countries began to intrigue and squabble over Vilnius, seemingly unaware of Germany's daily strides toward rearmament and the rapidly increasing strength of the U. S. S. R. The "Vilnius Question" also stymied the formation of a Baltic regional association. The original crisis induced Finland to adopt a purely Scandinavian orientation which virtually excluded the Baltic States. Subsequent efforts at forming a smaller association were hampered by Latvia and Estonia, both of whom were understandably reluctant to become involved in the problem.

Relations with Germany were acceptable until 1933 and the rise of Hitler, when an irritating dilemma developed over the city of Klaipėda (Memel). The situation at Klaipėda was a good example of the drawbacks to be expected when statesmanship is purely ethnographic in nature. The city of Klaipėda was Germanized, but the countryside was Lithuanian, and the city itself was Lithuania's only door to the sea. The existence of the Lithuanian hinterland was as economically important to Klaipeda as the possession of a seaport was vital to the nation's well-being, for neither side could prosper in isolation. A 1939 German ultimatum was followed by a compromise: Klaipeda and its surrounding region were ceded to German ownership, but Lithuania retained her economic rights with the creation of a free port zone. Thus, after the signing of the Molotov-Ribbentrop Pact, Lithuania had the small consolation of having been sold down the river out of expediency rather than vindictive ill will. (By 1941, of course, the entire picture had changed.)

During this same period, relations with the U. S. S. R. were satisfactory. Temporarily in a peaceful mood, the Soviet Union was working for internal growth and a climate of good will with its neighbors. Lithuania and Russia signed a peace treaty in 1920, and a non-aggression pact in 1926 which was later extended to 1945. In 1929, both countries subscribed to the Briand-Kellogg Pact, and in 1933 both agreed on Litvinov's "definition of aggression." With Russia steadfastly refusing to recognize the Polish seizure of Vilnius, relations between the two states concerned themselves mainly with the improvement of economic and cultural welfare.

At first, no hypocrisy was detectable in the Russian atmosphere of friendliness. The mood of "Socialism in one country" discouraged and even discredited militaristic expansionists. The Soviet Foreign Commissar, M. Litvinov, soft-spoken, Jewish, cosmopolitan and married to an Englishwoman, was genuinely more comfortable in a climate of peace and reason, and he negotiated with much more enthusiasm than might be expected from a Russian statesman. It was only the unfortunate failure of his collective security policy at Munich which returned the great-Russian chauvinists to their former preeminence.

Thus, as the Thirties drew to a close, the Baltic countries had no way of knowing whether the rosy glow with which they were viewing the world was a reflection of the dawn or of the sunset of freedom in Eastern Europe.

ANGLO-FRANCO-RUSSIAN NEGOTIATIONS 1939

Although they made efforts from mid-April to the end of July in 1939, the British, French and Soviet governments were unable to conclude successful negotiations for a mutual alliance to halt the course of German aggression in Eastern Europe.

The British and French guarantees to Poland had been a grand gesture but a hollow one; since no major change in leadership had occurred, the Munich psychology still hovered over London and Paris. As a result, Britain and France had a commitment in a remote part of Europe which they were unwilling to provide with immediate support by opening a second front, and which they were unable to defend by direct means. Far from being a deterrent, the unrealistic guarantee only encouraged greater defiance on Poland's part, and increased the likelihood of war with Germany. Nor could the guarantee ever become meaningful as a deterrent unless Russia were actively involved.

Fully aware of her important position in French and British policy, Russia could dictate her own terms. What she wanted, essentially, was a free hand in the countries along her borders, including the right of military intervention at her discretion, such as when, for example, a border country was threatened by direct or "indirect" German aggression. A long list of items could be found under the heading "indirect aggression," for as little as a change of government policy to a new one less favorable to the U. S. S. R. would be interpreted as an indirect means of aggression. France expressed willingness to accept this formula, but England was reluctant. The border countries involved, of course, protested strongly.

The problem was strictly one of good will. A similar British and French attitude toward Belgium, the Netherlands, Luxembourg and Switzerland was accepted uneventfully, since none of the countries concerned feared that Britain and France could be seeking a pretext for intervention and annexation. On the other hand, the French and British perceived that the Soviet Union had legitimate security interests in the Baltic States and Poland, but it was widely held that the U. S. S. R. would use the first available pretext to accomplish the subversion of its neighbors. Though the British were prepared to concede a great deal, they could not agree with the Soviet definition of "indirect aggression," and negotiations dragged on interminably. Finally, on August 23, 1939, the U. S. S. R. signed the Molotov-Ribbentrop Pact which provided it with carte blanche in Eastern Europe.

Ironically, in 1944-45, when it became apparent that the German threat would lie dormant for some time after World War II, Great Britain and the United States were willing to concede the Soviets much more than they had asked for in 1939.

LITHUANIA IN THE FOURTH PARTITION 1939-1941

From the 16th to the 18th centuries Russia had been determined to conquer Lithuania. In the 19th century she had decided upon a campaign which was supposed to result in the denationalization of the smaller country. Having failed to achieve her desire in 300 years, it may be declared that Soviet Russia, in the 20th century, has dedicated herself to the total eradication of the Lithuanian state and will stop at nothing to realize this long-standing ambition.

All those who played leading parts in the tragedies of the Partitions during the 18th century, and in the intensification of Lithuanian suffering during the 19th century, extended their roles to the period from 1939 to 1941. As they had before, Germany and Russia plotted the destruction of Eastern Europe.

Using threats of force, the Germans successfully removed Lithuania's single seaport Klaipėda (Memel) from her in March 1939. Undoubtedly it was the mutual distrust existing between Germany and Russia which painted the backdrop against which these two powers entered into a partnership. On August 23 they signed a nonaggression pact; a secret proviso was attached to the treaty stipulating the division between them of the Baltic areas and Poland.

Losing no time, the partners began carrying out a foolproof plan on September 1. Germany made the initial move by invading Poland from the west, and on September 17, Russia invaded Poland from the east.

It was now necessary to draw up another treaty, which the two powers signed quickly. This pact would determine exactly how Poland should be divided between these conquerors, and also which segments of the Baltic coast should become "German" and which "Russian." On

October 10, 1939, Russia devised a new list of penalties for Lithuania if she refused to enter a "mutual assistance pact" which would permit the Russians to establish air bases and maintain garrisons of soldiers inside her borders (as had already been done in Estonia and Latvia). Russia then offered a "sign of friendship" to the beleaguered Lithuanians by returning to them one-third of the Vilnius territory which she had annexed illegally in 1795, and had been forced to relinquish in 1920. This land was never justly hers under any circumstances, and in 1939 it was not hers either to withold or to return. On May 25th, 1940, she accused the Lithuanian government of abducting Russian soldiers stationed on Lithuanian soil. "It cannot be denied", wrote Commissar Molotov in an irate note to the Lithuanian Government, "that desertion of our soldiers is organized by the Lithuanian government which draws Soviet men into espionage . . " . Moscow had no way of substantiating this fabrication, but that did not prevent her from adding another ridiculous claim, namely, that the Baltic republics of Lithuania, Latvia and Estonia had formed a secret military alliance with which they were preparing aggression against the U. S. S. R., and that the latter would have to "protect" herself against the military conspiracy threatening her safety. No effort was made to prove this statement because of its farcical nature. At a few minutes before midnight on June 14, 1940, Mr. Molotov presented the Lithuanian Foreign Minister, Juozas Urbšys, with an ultimatum which would expire in just nine hours. The terms of the ultimatum (which had to be decided one way or the other by 9 o'clock on the morning of the next day) required that General Kazys Skučas, Minister of the Interior, and Augustinas Povilaitis, Director of State Security, be prosecuted at once for "provoking a conflict between Lithuania and Russia." The ultimatum demanded additionally that a new government be formed immediately which would be "acceptable to Moscow," and it also directed Lithuania to provide free passage into her territory for Soviet troops. Tsarist Imperialism in the 18th century had sought to maintain Russian armies in Poland-Lithuania, to elect the individual who would rule the Republic, and to draft the legislation that would govern it. Since 20th century Moscow's policy was identical to that envisaged one hundred and fifty-five years earlier, it cannot be said that any basic differences ever existed. The single motive of the Russian rulers, whether ancient or modern, has been to grind up as many people and as much territory as possible, regardless of the amount of unjust pressure employed in the process.

Faced with a tense night of discussion and deliberation, Lithuanian

President Antanas Smetona met with his Cabinet in an extraordinary session to find some way of coping with Russia's demands in a few hours. The nervous Cabinet members had to try to dissolve the boil of the crisis, preserve Lithuanian independence, and emerge intact from the dangerous situation. To accomplish this task, they proposed that the democratic and courteous, humanitarian gentleman Stasys Raštikis, assume leadership of the new government. The Soviets, of course, interested only in Lithuania's unconditional obedience, vetoed this logical proposal. The question then arose: If Lithuania could not retain her independence, how were the terms of the Russian ultimatum to be carried out in a legal manner?

By noon (June 15) Soviet troops began streaming into Lithuania to occupy Kaunas, Vilnius, Raseiniai, Siauliai, and Panevežys. Lithuania knew that if she offered armed resistance, the tremendous Russian military strength would destroy even the barest semblance of political freedom and this was a dread climax which she had to avoid at any price. That same day, Deputy Commissar of Foreign Affairs De-kanozov, accompanied by the Russian envoy to Lithuania, Pozdniakov, arrived at Kaunas prepared to play out an updated version of the same tragicomedy performed by their counterparts in 1795.

The Soviets found a journalist, Justinas Paleckis, to name as the "Prime Minister of the Lithuanian Republic." Paleckis' "cabinet" consisted of radicals who offered the besieged nation their treasonous concepts. To start with, all organizations and political parties were declared illegal; a communist faction, which had never had a membership of more than two thousand, was reactivated and furnished with the necessary means for supremacy. The Lithuanian National Diet (Seimas) was eliminated, and "elections" ordered to create a new parliament. While mass arrests of Lithuanians accused of loyalty to Lithuania were taking place, a single-column roster of candidates for the parliament was drawn up by the Russian authorities. To be eligible for candidacy, an individual had to be nominated by popular assemblies under the guidance and control of the communist party.

The so-called "elections" were scheduled for July 14th. Voting was compulsory, though there was no choice between parties or principles. Citizens were warned that failure to obtain balloting stamps on their passports (as proof of having voted) would be interpreted as sabotage and dealt with accordingly. The elections were marked by a total lack of organization because Russia had not bothered to arrange for the details of proper registration for eligible voters. In the ensuing disorder, some voters managed to deposit blank ballots as a sign of their protest. Instances were recorded in which foreign persons visited the polls to cast votes. No attempt whatever was made to count ballots.

The Russians announced an incredible 99.19% victory in Lithuania. (Someone had been astute enough to subtract .81% from the figure; Russian-style elections generally showed a 100% pro-Soviet result.) Seventy-nine "Representatives" were now deputies to the new Seimas of Lithuania. (Events similar to these had already occurred in Latvia and Estonia.)

Working quickly, the new Diet convened at Kaunas on July 21st. In the 18th century, Dolgoruki had directed the proceedings; in the 20th, Ambassador Dekanozov was the leading force. It was reported that the Diet had "unanimously" (not one vote was taken) decided to request Russia to "accept" Lithuania into the "family of Soviet Republics." Here were the Diets of Ratification to "sanction" the First and Second Partitions of Poland-Lithuania, as well as the "Dumb Diet" of 1717, dressed in modern clothing.

As was to be anticipated, Russia went through the motions necessary to conceal her aggression under a thin cloak of legality. She may even have reasoned that she had been clever enough to convince the world that the patriotic Lithuanians had decided to become Soviet citizens.

Given the history of the Baltic nations, Lithuania, Latvia and Estonia were incapable of accepting the "benevolent" Russian regime on their streets or in their hearts and homes. To subjugate the country, Russia inaugurated a reign of terror just as she had in bygone days. She dragged 34,260 Lithuanians into cattle cars and deported them to Siberia, the Arctic regions and other wastelands. To destroy systematically the Lithuanian spirit she separated families, cut off Red Cross assistance, and executed any former government official or other prominent person who had ever manifested the slightest disapproval of her policies. With great care, she devised detailed plans for a massive transplantation of Baltic peoples into faraway Russian regions.

The Russo-German Alliance of August 23rd, 1939, was voided on June 22nd, 1941, when Hitler's armies invaded the U. S. S. R. It had endured less than two years.

THE GERMAN OCCUPATION 1941-1944

It would be misleading if this study attempted to disassociate Lithuanian resistance to Germany from Lithuanian resistance to Russia. The facts tell us that Lithuanian resistance was a movement of national liberation, directed, of course, against the invader who happened to be in possession of the country. In reality, however, Lithuania did not discriminate between the ideological shades of difference marking the two separate invading powers. Inasmuch as both consistently confused objective reality with ideological illusion, neither Germany nor Russia ever understood or appreciated the true nature of Lithuanian resistance.

Germany was intimately connected with Lithuania's first loss of independence in 1940, followed by Soviet occupation and annexation. It was only because of the German agreement with the Soviets that the latter had dared to move against the Baltic States, and it was only the temporary German "disinterest" which had secured the Russian position in Lithuania. Therefore, it was not at all surprising that organized Lithuanian resistance abroad should begin in Berlin, the true center of action. About one thousand prominent Lithuanians had escaped the Soviet occupation of June-July, 1940, and a number of these had settled in the German capital, where they found a dynamic and resourceful leader in the Lithuanian Minister, Col. Kazys Škirpa. On November 17th, 1940, this group launched the Lithuanian Activist Front, an organization which Col. Škirpa defined in these words: —

> "The plan for a more determined unification of our national efforts was not born on November 17th, 1940, when the nucleus of LAF was formed. It was born much earlier, in July. . . . The plan was not given to me by any outsider. It was a natural development from the news that the Moscow-Berlin Pact might suddenly explode and that there were hopes of reestablishing the sovereignty of the Lithuanian State without waiting for a further opportunity. . . . Generally there was adherence, to the determination not to beg anything from Hitler's Germany, but only to prepare properly for the reestablishment of Lithuania's independence and state sovereignty through a national uprising while utilizing the destruction of the Moscow-Berlin Pact."

Moscow's negative interpretation of these developments is summed up succinctly in the title of the documentary history, "Nacionalistu Talka Hitlerininkams". (The Nationalists, Accomplices of the Hitlerites). Nevertheless, subsequent events seemed to substantiate Col. Škirpa's explanation.

Liaison was established between the Lithuanian Activist Front in

Berlin and guerrillas in Lithuania during the winter and early spring of 1941, and by March 24, directives for the insurrection were issued: —

> "The signal for the uprising will be the moment when the German army crosses the Lithuanian border and attacks the Russian army. . . . In any event, the true signal will be the German crossing of the border. As long as this shall not have occurred, do not follow any orders, in order to avoid provocation.

> If we were not able to reach an agreement with the Germans concerning the formation of a new government. .we would have to recognize that the Germans have aggressive plans against Lithuania.

> Even in this case we should not abstain from revolt. It should be carried out as planned. The government should then be proclaimed by (the) Vilnius Central Committee so that (the) Germans would again be faced with an accomplished fact."

Despite massive deportations by the Soviets from June 13 through 15, 1941, the insurrection took place according to plan. On the night of June 22nd, LAF guerrillas attacked communications centers in Kaunas, and began broadcasting from the radio station on the following morning. At the same time, Lithuanian units in the Red Army revolted, and the disintegrating Soviet forces came under heavy attack. Of the 90 to 100,000 Lithuanians who took part in this insurrection, between four and five thousand were slain. On June 23rd, before the German Armies had been able to reach Kaunas, the Lithuanian capital had proclaimed a Provisional Government and, on June 25th, had conducted its first Cabinet meeting.

The Germans might have been surprised by the Lithuanian insurrection, but their sole reaction when it was over was acute embarrassment. Any hope of cooperation between the new Provisional Government and the German occupying forces was doomed by the radically divergent motives pursued by each side. The Lithuanians insisted on political independence, or at the least, formal sovereignty, while the project of the Germans was to create an "Ostland", or German province on the Baltic Sea. The coat-of-arms of the Teutonic Order was revived, a special Reich Ministry for eastern territories duly organized under Alfred Rosenberg, and German colonists dispatched to the Baltic States. Germany pursued this policy even when it became evident that there would be a shortage of German personnel, and that if the civil administration ("Zivilverwaltung") were to be fully staffed, natives would have to be employed. Naturally, the Germans and the Lithuanians would never work together except in a climate of mutual distrust. But worst of all the effects of the German occupation was the transfer to the Reich of state property belonging to the former Baltic governments, including any properties which had been nationalized by the Soviets. Through this despicable tactic, Lithuanian farmers not only ceased to own their land, but occupied it by the "grace of the Reich."

The Germans did not recognize the Lithuanian Provisional Government at Kaunas, and would not permit Col. Škirpa, who had been selected Prime Minister, to leave Berlin. General Stasys Raštikis, the Minister of Defense, was soon brought from Berlin to Lithuania, but if the German tacticians thought that Raštikis would be servile to the Reich, they were soon to be disappointed.

When the Lithuanians were commanded by the occupation to disband the Provisional Government, they adjourned *sine die* on August 5th, 1941, under protest. First the Lithuanian Activist Front, and then the Lithuanian Nationalist Party were dissolved, leaving Lithuania with not even a puppet political organization.

At this point, the German conquerors launched their occupation in earnest. Beginning in September, Lithuanian Jewry was exterminated. Lithuanian citizens were subjected to confiscations, deportations and executions. According to Soviet sources, 300,000 Lithuanians were killed by the Germans during three years of occupation.

Underground organizations were formed in the captive country. Resistance would have been more formidable except for the frustration inherent in weakening the German war effort only to aid the U. S. S. R. Nevertheless, the underground was united under the Supreme Committee for the Liberation of Lithuania in November 1943 and, despite the clear odds against it, succeeded in making clear to the Germans and the Soviets the Lithuanian national will for political freedom. Some startling tactical achievements were enjoyed, such as a successful boycott of a German attempt to conscript an SS division composed of Lithuanians.

In March 1944, with Soviet armies marching on Lithuania, a compromise agreement was drawn up. The Lithuanians accepted the order to form a territorial Defense Corps containing fourteen battalions (11,550 soldiers) under the command of General Povilas Plechavičius, but the failure of this attempt was caused by bad faith. The recruitment was so successful that the alarmed Germans tried to transfer the Lithuanian volunteers into SS units. When the volunteers resisted, German troops attacked the Lithuanian detachments, arresting the officers and disarming the soldiers, an act which ended the last attempt at Lithuanian-German cooperation in the war with the U. S. S. R.

On July 7, 1944, Soviet armies crossed the Lithuanian border. Vilnius fell on July 13, Kaunas on August 1. On October 23, the Soviets reached the Baltic.

SECOND SOVIET OCCUPATION 1944-1952

Lithuania's resistance to the second Soviet occupation is best defined as a struggle for national liberation, since no cause of lesser proportions could have explained the intensity of her efforts in the face of insurmountable disadvantages. Feeding on the obstinacy of courage, her guerrillas managed to survive for a long time despite massive Soviet campaigns to exterminate them. Several misunderstandings contributed to the continuation of the bloody strife.

For example, neither the Soviets nor the Lithuanian guerrillas had been able to ascertain the true position of the West. The Lithuanians expected conflict to break out between the West and the U. S. S. R. at any moment; the Soviets suspected that the West was really aiding the Lithuanian guerrillas.

The fact is that, even more so than in the case of Hungary in 1956, some of the moral responsibility for death and destruction must fall on the West, both for policy statements which lacked substance (such as the Atlantic Charter), and for the campaign of inflammatory propaganda, entirely unconnected to actual policy, which was conducted after 1947. Of course, even if the West had candidly announced that it was accepting the status quo in Eastern Europe, this would not have precluded Lithuanian resistance. Perhaps accommodation would have been possible if the Soviets either imposed communization with a retention of formal sovereignty, or ran a simple military occupation which would have created little change in the affairs of the citizenry. But in the face of Soviet ideological imperialism, caused no doubt by a genuine confusion between their roles as conquerors and social revolutionaries, the Lithuanians found armed resistance unavoidable.

With the experiences of the German invasion behind them, the Lithuanians were prepared when the second Soviet occupation occurred. The fiasco of the Territorial Defense Corps. which the Germans had trained and armed and then attacked, had left sizable groups of organized soldiers hiding in the forests.

The Soviet government had not learned anything new. They immediately reinstated the terror and Sovietization measures of 1940-41, driving many people to join the cadre of a guerrilla army. Demonstrating the absence of insight, the Soviets called these guerrilla groups "Hitlerite" or "Bourgeois-Nationalist" bands. The first concept resulted from their lack of willingness to distinguish between ideology and nationalism, to perceive that the Lithuanians were fighting for their lives independently, and certainly not as an extension of the German war effort. Undoubtedly, the guerrillas were nationalist. But the misunderstanding here was that times had changed since prewar days when the difference in the standard of living between Russia and Lithuania had been so great. According to Soviet opinion, most of the Lithuanian population still qualified as bourgeoisie, but this opinion showed a lack of perception. Obviously, the Lithuanian guerrillas would never have survived as long as they did (1944-1952) if they had enjoyed anything less than almost universal popular support. Moreover, by attacking the Church, liquidating all elements of the national independence system and announcing reprisals against the families and friends of actual guerrillas, the Soviets forced many citizens into armed resistance.

The guerrillas operated mainly in small groups, though their territorial organizations were fairly large and complex. An extensive underground press flourished, and broad political fronts such as the Lithuanian Freedom Fight Movement (LLKS) operated vigorously. In its fight to halt the Sovietization of Lithuania, the underground carried out the physical extermination of local Communist Party organizations. The other major aspect of this armed struggle was the underground's battle for survival against the Soviet security forces which had been sent to eradicate them.

The Lithuanian underground conducted two offensives. The first, from 1945 to 1947, resisted all aspects of Sovietization. In 1947, a growing sense of disillusionment with the West's commitment to anti-Communism coupled with a Soviet amnesty, led to a reduction in guerrilla activity. In 1948, when the Soviets resumed collectivization, the underground launched a last, desperate offensive in the bloody battle for freedom. With the success of forcible collectivization, the guerrillas were effectively deprived of material support from the peasantry. The guerrilla movement subsided in 1952, and a general amnesty was issued in 1955. Individual guerrillas were being killed as late as 1959, and at the present writing, old cases are still being exhumed for trial in violation of the amnesty.

Armed resistance had ended, and the intensity of the struggle could be seen in the casualty lists — 25,000 to 50,000 guerrillas dead. An army of 25,000 to 40,000 men had been maintained in the field for seven years, and the dead personnel represented 1% to 2% of the population of this occupied country.

The Soviets had understood the threat of the guerrillas, rough-hewn men who placed the welfare of their country far above their own. The conquerors had expended a great deal of effort to crush their Lithuanian enemies. Besides eight divisions of the regular army garrisoned in Lithuania to serve as supporting troops, the Soviets employed some 100,000 security troops consisting of MVD and MGB units and local "istrebiteli" to do the actual fighting. The Soviet military commander was General Kruglov who succeeded Beria in 1953. Kruglov took orders from a special "Organizational Bureau for Lithuania of the Central Committee of the Communist Party," headed by Mikhail Suslov in Moscow. Soviet casualties, of both the security forces and the Communist Party activists, exceeded 80,000.

The Lithuanian struggle against the second Soviet occupation had been indescribably tragic from the onset. It was longer, more violent and, if possible, characterized by even greater despair than the well-publicized Hungarian revolt. The second Soviet invasion has left the Lithuanian people indelibly scarred.

The reasons for Soviet writers having neglected to chronicle this period are of course obvious. But the fact that the West has ignored it too is painful to accept and difficult to understand.

EPILOGUE

The period of de-Stalinization brought a measure of relief to Lithuania, though the anguish of her history showed itself in continuing tensions. Soviet officials declared they had discovered treasonable tendencies among Lithuanian citizens toward "national communism." In 1959 a retaliatory purge was carried out.

Still, the Khrushchev era was notable for its thaw and for the relaxation of political terror, and at long last the old, cold atmosphere seemed to have lost its imperviousness to change. Most importantly, the political easement led to a national cultural flowering; many new publications in the Lithuanian tongue acted as balm on the wounds of the intellectually starved country.

The Brezhnev regime represented a partial return to Stalinist thinking. *Pravda* accused Lithuanians of harboring "bourgeois nationalist" tendencies. Cultural administrators were purged, the security police assumed prominent positions. The Lithuanians responded to the new pressures with a wave of defection attempts which embarrassed Moscow. For instance, in October 1970, two Lithuanians successfully highjacked a Russian plane into Turkey, and in December of the same year a Lithuanian sailor defected to the United States, only to be returned to Soviet custody, allegedly to avoid jeopardizing a fishing agreement. A massive Lithuanian revolt broke out in May, 1972.

But the problem of the Baltic nations goes deeper than mere ideology. Lithuania, Latvia and Estonia have established traditions of clearly realized national identities and political independence. It is the "great Russian chauvinists," as Stalin put it, who refuse to concede these countries any part of their national aspirations. The Baltic struggle, then, does not ask the relatively simple question of whether or not these suffering nations shall be democratic or authoritarian, capitalist or socialist, neutral or allied to the Soviet Union. Transcending any such categories, it is a grim and bloody battle for national survival against the looming bulk of the U. S. S. R.

The Soviet Union has an imposing name, but in many respects the name stands only for the original Empire. Whenever Stalin made a statement of foreign policy, it might have been Peter the Great who was speaking. Also, all Russification tactics promulgated by the Soviets implicitly echoed Alexander III. Without perceptiveness or imagination, and inflexibly bound to centuries old basic thinking, the Soviets continue to hammer out the *drang nach Westen* policy in this precarious corner of Europe.

It should be understood that the nationalism toward which a number of Asian and African countries are presently groping, has a long, genuine, vital history in the Baltic states. If the world is witnessing a wave of national liberation for nations which will be novices, there is no doubt that the Balts, with the pattern of political independence molding their very origins, are capable of participating in the rising tide with total logic and complete realism.

Meanwhile, Baltic countries are still climbing uphill to regain their independence of which a stronger power has unfairly deprived them.

They can only hope that they too will derive some benefit from the self-determination springing up in many places throughout our planet, for it is they who have suffered so severely for the cause of political freedom.

ANALYTICAL TABLE OF CONTENTS

CHAPTER IV PRINCIPLE OF NONRECOGNITION OF THE USE OF FORCE AND CONQUEST IN INTERNATIONAL RELATIONS

CHAPTER I
LITHUANIAN-RUSSIAN RELATIONS 1918-1939

No. 1

Declaration of Independence of Lithuania

The Council of Lithuania in its meeting on February 16, 1918, voted unanimously to address the governments of Russia, Germany, and other states with the following declaration:

The Council of Lithuania, as sole representative of the Lithuanian nation, in conformity with the recognized right to national self-determination, and in accordance with the resolution of the Lithuanian Conference held in Vilnius* from September 18 to 23, 1917, hereby proclaims the restoration of the independent State of Lithuania, founded on democratic principles, with Vilnius as its capital, and declares the termination of all ties which formerly bound this State to other nations.

The Council of Lithuania also declares that the foundation of the Lithuanian State and relations with other countries will be finally determined by a constituent Seimas [Assembly], democratically elected by all the people of Lithuania.

The Council of Lithuania in informing the Government of [country addressed] to this effect kindly requests recognition of the independent State of Lithuania.

Vilnius, February 16, 1918

Signed:

S. Banaitis   P. Klimas   K. Saulys   J. Vailokaitis

---

*Russian Vilna, Polish Wilno.

Dr. J. Basanavičius Donatas Malinauskas J. Šernas

M. Biržiška   Vl. Mironas   A. Smetona   J. Vileišis

K. Bizauskas   S. Narutavičius   J. Smilgevičius

P. Dovydaitis   Alfonsas Petrulis   J. Staugaitis

S. Kairys   Dr. J. Šaulys   A. Stulginskis

No. 2

Acts of the Lithuanian National Council and Resolution of the Constituent Seimas

a. *The basic Principles of the Provisional Constitution of the Lithuanian state, adopted by the State Council on November 2, 1918.** *

Until the Constituent Seimas shall determine the form of Government and the Constitution, the Lithuanian National Council, representing the sovereign power (suprema potestas) of Lithuania, hereby establishes the Provisional Government of Lithuania on the following provisional constitutional foundations:

I. *General Matters*

1. The supreme provisional organs of the state are.
   A) The Council of State;
   B) The Presidium of the Council of State (III, 9) with the Cabinet of Ministers.
2. The seat of the supreme government is the Capital of the Lithuanian State, Vilnius.
3. Laws shall be initiated by the Council of State and the Cabinet of Ministers.

• • •

II. *The Council of State*

5. The Council of State considers and enacts provisional laws and concludes treaties with foreign states.

---

*Lietuvos Aidas, Nov. 13, 1918, No. 130.

• • •

III. *The Provisional Powers of the Presidium of the Council of State*

9. Until a separate supreme organ of government is established its powers shall be invested in the presidium of the Council of State, composed of an ad hoc president and two vice-presidents.**
10. The provisional executive power of the presidium shall be exercised through the Cabinet of Ministers responsible to the Council of State.

• • •

V. *The Fundamental Rights of Citizens*

22. All the citizens of the state are equal before the law, regardless of sex, nationality, religion, or class. There are no class privileges.
23. Safety of person, residence, and property are guaranteed, as well as freedom of religion, press, assembly, and association if their purposes and means are not contrary to the laws of the state. Assemblies of armed persons are prohibited.

• • •

VI. *The Constituent Seimas*

26. The Provisional Government enacts and promulgates the law for the election of a Constituent Seimas.
27. The Constituent Seimas is to be elected on the basis of a universal, equal, direct, and secret election.

b. *The first cabinet, approved by the Council of State on November 11, 1918.* *

The Presidium of the Council of State requested Prof. Augustinas Voldemaras to form the first cabinet of Lithuania. The Coalition Cabinet, approved by the Council of State on November 11, 1918, consisted of the following:

---

*For details on the Lithuanian Cabinet of Ministers see Lietuviu Enciklopedija (The Lithuanian Encyclopedia), Vol. XV, pp. 353-356.

**An amendment was adopted on March 4, 1919:

Until the Constituent Seimas meets and decides the form of government and the constitution, the president of the state shall be elected by the Council of State (Art. 6).

The executive power of the state is invested in the president and will be exercised by the Cabinet of Ministers responsible to the Council of State (Art. 8).

Antanas Smetona was then elected the first president of Lithuania on April 4, 1919.

Prof. Augustinas Voldemaras, Prime Minister and Minister of Foreign
Affairs

Atty. Vladas Stašinskas, Minister of the Interior and Minister of
Public Works and Welfare

Atty. Petras Leonas, Minister of Justice

Atty. Martynas Yčas, Minister of Finance and Minister of Communications

Juozas Tubelis, Minister of Agriculture and Minister of Natural
Resources

Jonas Yčas, Minister of Education

Jokubas Vygodskis, Minister of Jewish Affairs

Juozas Voronko, Minister of Byelorussian Affairs

Col. Mykolas Velykis, Minister of Defense

c. *Resolution of the Constituent Seimas adoptea* **unanimously****

The Constituent Seimas of Lithuania, expressing the will of the
people of Lithuania, hereby proclaims the restoration of the Lithuanian
state as a democratic republic, within its ethnic boundaries and free
from all political ties which formerly had existed with other states.

Kaunas, May 15, 1920

No. 3

Treaty of Peace between Lithuania and the Russian Socialist
Federal Soviet Republic

[2]Translation

*No. 94. — Peace treaty between Lithuania and the Russian Socialist
Federal Republic, and Protocol, signed at Moscow on July 12, 1920.*

RUSSIA on the one part and LITHUANIA on the other part, being guided by a
firm desire to establish, on the principles of right and justice, lasting

---

[1]Not reproduced.

[2]Translated by the Secretariat of the League of Nations.

Translation communicated by His Britannic Majesty's Foreign Office.

**The date of the election of the Constituent Seimas was set by the president of the republic on
April 14-15, 1920. It met on May 15, 1920 in Kaunas.

foundations for future relations, guaranteeing to both countries and their peoples all the benefits of peace and good neighbourship, have decided to enter into negotiations for such purpose and have appointed as their representatives to this end:

THE GOVERNMENT OF THE RUSSIAN ·SOCIALIST FEDERATED SOVIET RE-PUBLIC: — Adolf Abramovitch Joffe, Julian Josephovitch Marchlevski, and Leonid Leonidovitch Obolenski; *and* THE GOVERNMENT OF THE LITHUANIAN DEMOCRATIC. REPUBLIC: — Thomas Narusevicius, Peter Klimas, Simon Rozenbaum, Josef Vailokaitis, and Witovt Rackauskas.

The said representatives having mutually produced their powers, which were found drawn up in proper form and in due order, agreed as follows: —

Article 1.

Proceeding from the right, proclaimed by the Russian Socialist Federated Soviet Republic, of all nations to free self-determination up to their complete separation from the State into the composition of which they enter, Russia recognises without reservation the sovereign rights and independence of the Lithuanian State, with all the juridical consequences arising from such recognition, and voluntarily and for all time abandons all the sovereign rights of Russia over the Lithuanian people and their territory.

The fact of the past subjection of Lithuania to Russia does not impose on the Lithuanian nation and its territory any liabilities whatsoever towards Russia.

Article 2.

The State frontier between Russia and Lithuania proceeds:

Commencing from the point of the junction of the Gorodnianka river with the Bobr river at 2 versts on the east of the Tsharnylias village along the Gorodnianka small stream between the village of Khmelniki and Khmelevka and the villages of Levki and Olsha; from there along the dried-up watercourse to the southern side of the village of Veselovo; from there along the unnamed tributary of the small stream Kamennaya to the junction of this tributary with the aforesaid small stream Kamennaya at a distance of about a verst from the village of Veselovo. Farther, up the flow of the small stream Kamennaya for a distance of about one verst; from there along the driedup watercourse roughly in the direction of the eastern side of the village of Nerasnaya right up to the source of the unnamed tributary of the small stream Siderka; farther, along this tributary to its confluence with the small stream Siderka at a distance of about one verst from the village of Siderka; from there along the flow of the Siderka (Siderianka) small stream, between the villages of Shestaki and Siderka, past the town of Sidra, between the villages of Yuashi and Ogorodniki, past the village of Beniashi, past the village of Litvinka, between the villages of

Zveriany and Timani up to the village of Lovtshiki; from there along the dried-up watercourse in the direction of the southern outskirts of the village Volkusha; from there to the northern side of the village of Tshuprinovo; farther up the elevation with the trigonometric point 108.0, which is at a distance of about one verst on the south of the village of Novodeli; farther, in a direction towards the northern side of the environs of Toltshi, at a distance of roughly one verst on the north of same; from there in a direction towards the southern side of the village of Dubovaya; farther, along the small stream Indurka, past the village of Luzhki, past the town of Indura, past the village of Prokopitshi, past the village of Belevo; farther, along the small stream Lashanka, past the village of Bobrovniki, and farther, along this small stream to its junction with the small stream Svislotsh. Farther, along the small stream Svislotsh up to its junction with the Neman river; from there along the Neman river to the mouth of the Berezina river along the Berezina, Islotsh and Volozhinka rivers along the western side of the town of Volozhin and along the northern side of the villages of Brilki, Burlaki and Polikshovstshizna; from there to the north-east along the eastern side of the villages of Melashi and Gintovtshizna (Menzhikovtshizna) at about one verst from them; farther, towards the north-east in the direction of the western side of the town of Kholkhlo at a distance of about one verst from the same; farther, towards the western side of the village of Sukhonarovstshizna at a distance of about one verst from it. From there the frontier turns north-east towards the western side of the village of Berezovtzy at a distance of about one verst from it; farther, towards the north-east in the direction of the western side of the village of Vaskovtzy; from there in the direction of the western side of the village of Lialkovtshizna at a distance of about one verst from it; from there it turns to the north towards the western side of the village of Kulevshizna, and from there to the north between the villages of Dreni and Zherlaki; from there to the north-west along the eastern side of the village of Garavina and the western side of the village of Adamovitchi; farther, towards the eastern side of the village of Myslevitchi; farther, along the eastern side of the village of Bukhovsttshina, towards the station of Molodetshno, crossing the railway junction in such a manner, that the Vilno-Molodetshno-Lida railway line remains in Lithuanian territory, and the Vileika-Molodetshno-Minsk railway line in Russian territory; from there along the small stream Bukhovka to its junction with the small stream Usha; along this small stream Usha to the village of Usha; from there it turns north-east and passes along the dried-up watercourse on the western side of the villages of Slobodka, Dolgaya and Prenta; from there along the small stream Narotch, and near the village of Tsheremstshitza, at a distance of about one verst from the same, it turns northward and passes along the eastern shore of the Bliada lake; at a distance of about one verst from same it proceeds northward across the Miastra lake, and upon issuing from this lake, along the dried-up watercourse between the village of Pikoltzy on the western side, and the village of Mintshaki on the eastern side; farther, northward and on the western side of the village of Volotshek at a distance of about one verst from it; from there northward across the Madziol lake to the western side of the village of Pshegrode at a distance of about one verst from same; from there towards the source of the Miadzelka small stream, and along this small stream to its junction with the Disna river; from there the frontier proceeds along the dried-up watercourse north-eastward towards the western side of the village of Borovyia, at a distance of about one verst from the same; farther, north-eastward in a direction across the Mikhalishki lake; farther, along the small stream Nistshenka to the parallel of the Ozyraitzy lake, to the western edge of the Repistshe lake, to the western outskirts of Zamoshie; to the Zolva lake; along the small stream Zolvitza, across the Dryviaty lake to the Tzno lake and Neslizha lake; farther, northward across the Nedrovo lake, and from this lake along the Druika river to its intersection with the boundary line of the province of Kovno; farther, along the boundary line of the province of Kovno, and, farther, to the Western Dvina river near the Shafranovo farm.

REMARK 1

The frontier line between Lithuania and Poland, and between Lithuania and Latvia, will be fixed by arrangement with these States.

REMARK 2.

The State frontier between the two contracting parties shall be established *in situ*, and the frontier marks shall be fixed by a mixed commission having an equal number of representatives on both sides. In establishing the frontier *in situ* the mixed commission shall be guided by ethnographic and economic features, keeping as far as possible to the natural lines of division, and inhabited points shall as far as possible enter wholly into the composition of one State. In those cases where the frontier is carried along lakes, rivers and canals, it shall pass through the middle of these lakes, rivers and canals, unless otherwise provided for in this treaty.

REMARK 3.

The frontier herein described has been delineated in red line on the map hereto annexed[1].

In the event of any disagreement between the map and text, the text shall be the deciding factor.

REMARK 4.

The artificial diversion of water from the frontier rivers and lakes, causing a lowering of the average level of the water of same, is not permitted.

The order and conditions of navigation and fishing in these rivers and lakes shall be determined by a special arrangement, and fishing may only be carried on by means which do not exhaust the fishing resources.

Article 3.

The conditions relating to the protection of the frontier, as also custom-house and other questions connected therewith, will be regulated by a separate agreement between the contracting parties after the occupied localities dividing Lithuania and Russia shall have been freed of occupation.

Article 4.

Both contracting parties undertake: —

(1) Not to permit on their territory the formation and sojourn of the Governments, organisations or groups, who have for their object armed warfare against the other contracting party. Similarly not to permit within their territories the recruiting and mobilisation of effectives for the armies of such Governments, organisations or groups, and the sojourn of their Governments and officials.

(2) To prohibit those countries who are *de facto* in a state of war with the other of the contracting parties, and also organisations or groups, who have as their object armed warfare against the other contracting party, the importation into their ports and the transport through their territories of all that may be made use of against the other contracting party, such as: armed forces, military equipment, technical war supplies and artillery, commissariat, engineering and flying materials.

Article 5.

In the event of international recognition of the permanent neutrality of Lithuania, Russia on its part undertakes to conform to such neutrality and to participate in the guarantees for the maintenance of same.

Article 6.

Persons resident at the date of the ratification of this treaty within the confines of Lithuania, who themselves or whose parents have permanently resided in Lithuania, or who were registered with the rural, municipal or corporate bodies in the territory of the Lithuanian State, and also persons, who prior to 1914 were residing in the territory of the same State for not less than the last ten years and had a permanent occupation there, excepting former civil and military officials not of Lithuanian origin and the members of their families, shall *ipso facto* be considered citizens of the Lithuanian State.

Persons of the same category, residing at the time of the ratification of this treaty in the territory of a third State, but not naturalised there, are equally considered to be Lithuanian citizens.

However, all persons who have attained the age of 18 years and are resident in the territory of Lithuania, are entitled within the period of one year from the date of the ratification of this treaty to declare their wish to opt for Russian citizenship, and their citizenship shall extend to the children under 18 years of age and to the wife, if no other arrangement has been made between the husband and wife.

Similarly, persons residing in the territory of Russia and coming under the first paragraph of this article, may within the same period and on the same conditions opt for Lithuanian citizenship.

Those who have made a declaration of optation and also those who follow their citizenship, shall retain their rights to personal and real property within the limits of the laws in force in that State in which they reside, but must within a year from the date of handing in the declaration leave its confines, they being entitled to realise all their property or to take the same away with them.

REMARK 1.

For persons residing in the Caucasus and Russia in Asia, the periods indicated in this article for lodging the declarations, and also for departure, are extended by one year.

REMARK 2.

The rights of optants indicated in this article shall be enjoyed by those citizens also who prior to and during the world war were resident in the territory of one side, but at the moment of the ratification of this treaty reside in the territory of the other.

Fugitives, with regard to their property which they were unable to take out of the country under the re-evacuation of Fugitives Treaty of the 30th June, 1920, enjoy the same rights as are provided for in this article in regard to optants, but only in so far as they do prove that such property belongs to them and was at the time of the re-evacuation in their actual possession.

Article 7.

Fugitives of both contracting parties, who desire to return to their country of origin, shall be returned to such country at the earliest possible date.

The order and conditions of re-evacuation are to be established by arrangement between the Governments of the contracting parties.

Article 8.

Both contracting parties mutually renounce all accounts whatsoever arising from the fact of Lithuania having in the past belonged to the past Empire of Russia, and acknowledge that State property of various denominations, existing on the territory of either of them, constitutes the inalienable property of the respective State. However, if property thus belonging to Lithuania has been removed from its territory after the 1st August, 1914, by a third State, the right of claiming same passes to the Lithuanian State.

To the Lithuanian State are transferred all the claims of the Russian Treasury burdening properties situated within the Lithuanian State, and also all claims against Lithuanian citizens, but only for the amounts not liquidated by counter-claims subject to acceptance in payment on account.

REMARK.

The right of claiming from small peasants their debts to the former Russian Peasants' Land Bank and others, now nationalised Russian land banks, and also the right of claiming the debts due to the former Russian Noblemen's Land Bank and others, now nationalised Russian land banks, secured on landed estates, in the event of such estates passing into the possession of small and landless peasants, are not transferred to the Lithuanian Government, but are considered cancelled.

The documents and deeds, in proof of the titles referred to in this article, shall be delivered by the Russian Government to the Lithuanian Government as far as they are actually in the possession of the former. In the event of it being impossible to effect this within the period of one year from the date of the ratification of the present treaty, such documents and deeds shall be deemed to be lost.

Article 9.

(1) The Russian Government shall return at its expense to Lithuania, and shall hand over to the Lithuanian Government, the libraries, archives, museums, objects of vertu, educational supplies, documents, and other property of educational establishments, scientific, governmental, religious, communal and professional institutions, in so far as the said objects have been removed beyond the limits of Lithuania during the world war of 1914-1917, and which actually are or shall prove to be in the keeping of the governmental or communal establishments of Russia.

As regards the archives, libraries, museums, objects of vertu, and documents, which are of material, scientific, artistic, or historical value to Lithuania, and had been removed from the confines of Lithuania to Russia prior to the world war of 1914-1917, the Russian Government agrees to return the same to Lithuania, in so far as their elimination may not cause serious deficiencies in the Russian archives, libraries, museums, picture galleries, in which they are kept.

The questions relating to such elimination are to be dealt with by a special mixed commission of an equal number of members of the two contracting parties.

(2) The Russian Government shall return at its expense, and shall hand over to the Lithuanian Government, all the judicial and governmental dossiers, judicial and governmental archives, including amongst these also the archives of senior and junior notaries, the archives of mortgage registries, the archives of the Consistorial Departments of all confessions, the archives and plans of the surveying, land-establishment, forestal, railway, roadway, postal and telegraphic and other offices, the plans, drawings, maps and, generally, all the material of the topographical section of the military district of Vilno, removed during the world war of 1914-1917 from the confines of Lithuania, in so far as they refer to the territory of the Lithuanian State; the archives of the local branches of the noblemen's and peasants' banks, of the branches of the State bank and of all other credit, co-operative, mutual assurance establishments; also the archives and affairs of private establishments of Lithuania in so far as all the said objects actually are or shall prove to be in the keeping of governmental or communal establishments of Russia.

(3) The Russian Government shall return at its expense, and shall hand over to the Lithuanian Government for delivery to whomsoever it may concern, all kinds of title deeds, such as: purchase and mortgage deeds, agreements of lease, all kinds of cash securities, etc. including amongst these books, papers and documents required to effect settlements, and, generally, documents which are of importance for determining the ownership and legal titles of Lithuanian citizens, and which have been removed from the confines of Lithuania during the world war of 1914-1917, as far as the same actually are or shall prove to be in the keeping of governmental or communal establishments of Russia. In the event of their not being returned within two years from the date of the ratification of this treaty, such documents shall be deemed to be lost.

(4) As regards parts of the archives of the central establishments which relate to the territory of Lithuania and which are subject to elimination, there is to be a special arrangement, for which purpose a mixed commission of an equal number of members of the two contracting parties is to be appointed.

Article 10.

(1) The Russian Government shall return at its expense, and shall hand over to the Lithuanian Government for delivery to whomsoever it may concern, the property of communal, benevolent, culture, educational establishments, and also the bells and utensils of churches and places of worship of all denominations which have been evacuated during the world war of 1914-1917, in so far as the said objects actually are or shall prove to be in the keeping of the governmental or communal establishments of Russia.

(2) *(a)* As regards the payments in savings banks, deposits, guarantees and other amounts paid into the former Russian governmental and judicial establishments, as far as such payments and amounts belong to citizens of Lithuania,

(b) as regards deposits or amounts of various descriptions paid into the branches of the State bank and into the nationalised and liquidated credit establishments, and their branches, in so far as such deposits and amounts belong to citizens of Lithuania, the Russian Government binds itself to admit to the Lithuanian citizens all those rights which at the time were admitted to all Russian citizens, and, therefore, grant permission to Lithuanian citizens, who in consequence of the occupation were not able to make use at the time of these their rights, to make use of the same now and to receive compensation for their claims in paper money values which have currency in the Russian Republic at the time such compensation is paid, and at the rate of exchange of the paper rouble existing on the internal money market at the time of the final occupation of Lithuania, that is, on the 1st September, 1915.

As regards securities and properties now kept, and which have been kept, at the offices of the banks and in their safes, as far as such securities and properties belong to citizens of Lithuania, the conditions set out in the first paragraph of this clause are to apply.

The sums, securities and properties mentioned in this article are to be handed over to the Lithuanian Government for delivery to whomsoever it may concern.

(3) The Russian Government shall return at its expense, and hand over to the Lithuanian Government the funds which are intended for the endowment of stipends for the educational establishments of Lithuania and for the Lithuanian citizens in the educational establishments in Russia.

(4) As regards payment of Russian monetary assignats, securities, governmental or state-guaranteed, and also private securities issued by companies and institutions, the undertakings of which have been nationalised by the Russian Government and which are circulating within the confines of Lithuania, and also as regards satisfaction of claims by Lithuanian citizens against the Russian Exchequer and against the nationalised institutions, Russia binds herself to allow Lithuania and Lithuanian citizens all those privileges, rights and preferences which are directly or indirectly granted by her or which may be granted to any third State or to its citizens, companies and institutions.

In the event of the securities and title deeds not being available, the Russian Government expresses its willingness, in the case of the application of this clause of this article, to recognise as the holders of the securities and others those who submit adequate proofs of the evacuation of the papers belonging to them during the war.

Article 11.

(1) The Russian Government shall return to the Lithuanian Government, for delivery to whomsoever it may concern, the property of Lithuanian citizens or partnerships, companies and joint stock companies, the majority of the stock or shares of which at the time of the promulgation of the respective decrees of nationalisation by the Russian Government, belonged to Lithuanian citizens, and which had been evacuated during the world war of 1914-1917, in so far as such property actually is or shall prove to be in the keeping of the Russian Government.

REMARK.

The present clause does not apply to funds, deposits and securities in the care of the branches of the State Bank or private banks, credit establishments and savings banks in the territory of Lithuania.

(2) As regards the railway rolling stock and telegraph and telephone installations, as well as all the equipment of the railway shops evacuated into Russia during the world war of 1914-1917, Russia agrees to make good to Lithuania part of these at a rate corresponding to the local requirements of the Lithuanian State, and making allowance for the general lowering of the tone of the economic life.

In order to exactly determine the amount of the said replacement, a mixed commission consisting of an equal number of members of the two contracting parties shall be appointed immediately upon the ratification of the present treaty.

REMARK.

The replacement of railway rolling stock and telegraph and telephone installations and railway shop plant due to the occupied territory of Lithuania can only commence after the same has been relieved from occupation.

(3) For the purpose of carrying out the conditions set forth in Articles 8, 9, 10 and 11 of the present Treaty, the Russian Government undertakes to supply the Government of Lithuania with all the particulars and data referring thereto and to give every possible assistance in tracing returnable property, archives, documents, etc. The more detailed arrangement of the questions arising in connection with this subject shall be entrusted to a special mixed commission consisting of an equal number of members of the two contracting parties.

Article 12.

The Russian Government taking into consideration that during the world war Lithuania has been almost entirely ruined, and that Lithuanian citizens are deprived of the possibility even of re-establishing their homesteads, their partly destroyed and gutted buildings, owing to the destruction of the forests of Lithuania, expresses its willingness:

(1) To release Lithuania from responsibilities in regard to the debts and any other liabiiities of Russia, including such as have resulted from the issue of paper money, treasury notes, bonds, series and certificates of the Russian Treasury in connection with the foreign and internal loans of the Russian State, guarantees to sundry institutions and undertakings, and the guaranteed loans of same, etc. All such claims of creditors of Russia for the share relating to Lithuania shall only be directed against Russia.

(2) In the localities nearest to the frontiers of Lithuania and as near as possible to rivers down which timber can be floated, and to railways, to grant to the Lithuanian Government the right to cut timber over an area of 100,000 dessiatins with a gradual allocation during the period of twenty years of timber-cutting areas in accordance with the plans of the Russian Forestal Department. The fixing of the detailed conditions of the cutting of timber is left to a mixed commission consisting of an equal number of members of both contracting parties.

(3) To give to the Lithuanian Government 3,000,000 roubles in gold within the period of one month and a half from the date of the ratification of this treaty.

Article 13.

(1) The contracting parties agree to commence within the earliest possible time after the ratification of the present treaty, negotiations for the conclusion of trading and transit conventions.

(2) The principle of the most-favoured nation shall be the basis of the trading convention.

(3) The following principles shall form the basis of the transit convention:

(a) Goods passing in transit through the territory of one of the contracting parties shall not be subject to any import dues or taxes.

(b) The freight rates for goods in transit shall not be higher than the freight rates for similar goods of local destination.

REMARK.

Prior to the commencement of normal conditions, mutual transit traffic between Russia and Lithuania shall be regulated by the same principles. Other conditions in reference to the transit trade shall be fixed by special temporary agreements.

(4) The Russian and Lithuanian commercial fleets shall mutually make use of the harbours of the contracting parties on equal rights.

(5) Property left after the death of a citizen of one of the contracting parties on territory of the other shall be handed *in toto* into the charge of the consular or respective representative of the country to which the testator belonged, to be dealt with by the same in accordance with the laws of such country.

Article 14

The diplomatic and consular relations between the contracting parties shall be established immediately after the ratification of the present treaty. Upon the ratification of the present treaty the parties shall proceed with the making of a Consular Convention.

Article 15.

Upon the ratification of this treaty the Russian Government shall release Lithuanian citizens and those opting Lithuanian citizenship, and the Lithuanian Government shall release Russian citizens and those opting Russian citizenship of military and civil classes from penalties in connection with all political and disciplinary actions. However, if judgments have as yet not been given in such cases, the proceedings in connection with the same shall be stopped.

Persons who commit the aforesaid acts after the ratification of this treaty shall not enjoy this amnesty.

Persons condemned by a criminal court for acts not coming under the amnesty shall be returned to their country of origin after serving sentence. However, in the event of judgment in cases of such description not being given prior to the expiration of one year from the date of the accused being charged, he shall on the expiration of this period be handed over to the home authorities with all the proceedings relating thereto.

In connection therewith both contracting parties also release their own citizens from punishment for acts committed by them prior to the ratification of the present treaty for the benefit of the other party.

Article 16.

In dealing with the present treaty the two contracting parties shall take into consideration the fact of their never having been in a state of war one with the other and that Lithuania as a region of military operations during the world war of 1914-1917 has particularly suffered from the latter. Therefore, all the conditions of the present treaty can in no way serve as a precedent for any third country. On the other hand, should one of the contracting parties allow a third country or the citizens thereof special privileges, rights and preferences, the same shall without special agreement also extend to the other party or to the citizens thereof.

REMARK.

The contracting parties, however, shall not prefer any claims to preferential rights which one of them may grant to a third country united to it by custom house or any other union.

Article 17.

The settlement of questions of a public-legal and private-legal description arising between the citizens of the contracting parties, and also the adjustment of any separate points between the two countries, or between the countries and citizens of the other party, shall be effected by a special mixed commission of an equal number of members of the two parties, appointed immediately upon the ratification of the present treaty, the composition, powers and duties of which shall be fixed by an instruction, to be agreed upon between the two contracting parties.

Article 18.

The present treaty is drawn up in the Russian and Lithuanian languages. In its reading both texts are to be considered authentic.

Article 19.

The present treaty is subject to ratification.

The exchange of the letters of ratification is to take place at Moscow.

Wherever the time of the ratification of the treaty is mentioned in the present treaty, this applies to the time of the mutual exchange of the letters of ratification.

In witness whereof the representatives of both parties have set their hands to the present treaty and have affixed their seals thereto.

The original was drawn up in duplicate and executed in the city of Moscow on the twelfth day of July, one thousand nine hundred and twenty.

[1] TRANSLATION.

PROTOCOL.

The signatories of the present Protocol met on October 14th, 1920, at Moscow, in the offices of the Commissary of the People for Foreign Affairs, in order to exchange the instruments of ratification of the Peace Treaty, between Russia on the one hand and Lithuania on the other, which was signed at Moscow on July 12th, 1920, in accordance with Article 19 of that Treaty.

---

[1] Translated by the Secretariat of the League of Nations.

After presentation of the instruments of ratification, which were found to be in good and due form, the two Parties satisfied themselves that the contents were identical and the exchange of ratifications took place. In testimony whereof the undersigned have drawn up this Protocol and have thereto affixed their hand and seal.

This Protocol is drawn up in duplicate.

(Signed) J. BALTRUŠAITIS.
(Signed) L. KARACHAN.

Editor's comment: By the Treaty of Peace with Russia, Lithuania regained the title to the ethnic territory which she had lost to Russia by virtue of the partitions of the Polish-Lithuanian Commonwealth. Similar treaties were signed with Finland, Latvia, Estonia and Poland.

In Russian foreign policy, the provisions of the treaty were the logical extension of the Declaration of the Soviet Government on the Right of Self-Determination of Nationalities and of Decree #64 of the Council of People's Commissars of August 29, 1918, signed by Lenin, Karakhan and Bruyevich, which stated: "All agreements and acts concluded by the Government of the former Russian Empire with the Governments of the Kingdom of Prussia and the Austro-Hungarian Empire referring to the partitions of Poland are irrevocably annulled by the present decree, since they are contrary to the principle of the self-determination of peoples and to the revolutionary-legal conceptions of the Russian people. . ."

No. 4

Note of the Soviet Commissar for Foreign Affairs, Chicherin, to the Lithuanian Minister in Moscow, Baltrušaitis.

People's Commissar of Foreign Affairs

January 30, 1921
No. 1/156
Moscow, 2nd Chamber of Soviets
Tel. No. 302-65 Kremlin

Sir:
I have the honor of requesting that you bring the following to the attention of your government:

The Russian government cannot view without concern the disturbance reigning in Vilnius and its district which, by the treaty concluded
on July 12, 1920 between Russia and Lithuania, was to belong to the
latter. At the moment in which the Polish general Zeligowski occupied
Vilnius with the aid of several Polish units, and when officers and
soldiers belonging to counter-revolutionary units, hostile to the Russian
Republic, began to flow into Vilnius and its district, the Russian
government addressed on this subject a protest to the Polish government, making it responsible for the possible consequences of the
agitation of Zeligowski and his detachments. At the same time,
however, the Russian government cannot fail to draw the attention of
the Lithuanian government to its international duties concerning
Vilnius and its districts. According to the treaty concluded July 12, 1920
between Russia and Lithuania, the Russian government has the right to
demand of the Lithuanian government that the latter take all measures
within its power to put an end to the state of affairs in that region, which
presents a menace to the security of the Soviet Republics. I believe it is
necessary to emphasize that the preliminary treaty concluded October
12 at Riga between Russia and Poland does not in any way annul the
Russo-Lithuanian treaty of July 12, nor diminish its force. The first
article of the preliminary treaty, concluded on one side by Russia and
the Ukraine, and on the other by Poland, provides that the question of
assignment of territories disputed by Poland and Lithuania, whether to
one state of the other, is to be resolved only by Poland and Lithuania.
This decision stems from the fact that the Russian Republic has ceded its
sovereign rights in that which concerns Vilnius and its district, but it
does not mean by any means that the Russian government should
remain passive in the face of the state of affairs which reigns in Vilnius,
if that constitutes a menace to its security. Insofar as the question of the
assignment of the above-mentioned territories has not been resolved by
means of a treaty between Lithuania and Poland in favor of the latter,
the sovereign power in Vilnius and its district belongs to Lithuania, to
which it was transferred by the Russo-Lithuanian treaty. The Russian
government, then, has the right to demand of the Lithuanian government that it take all measures to put a stop to that state of affairs in
which that city has become the source of the concentration of military
adventurers and counter-revolutionary elements, who find there the
opportunity to prepare their acts of aggression against the Soviet
Republics.

The Russian government has learned, among other things, that a group of states called the "League of Nations" plans again to send international military units to Vilnius. The Russian government draws the attention of the Lithuanian government to the fact that the appearance of such units in Vilnius could not be considered compatible with the provisions of the Russo-Lithuanian treaty. No treaty exists between the so-called League of Nations and the Russian Republic, and given the continuation of hostilities between several of the states taking part in the so-called League of Nations and the Soviet government, such units would be considered as hostile groups by the Russian government.

We express, consequently, the firm hope that the Lithuanian government will not permit the appearance in Vilnius of such units, whose presence in that city would be considered by the Russian government as an act unfriendly to Russia, presenting a menace to the security of the Soviet Republics. The Russian government expresses the conviction that the Lithuanian Government will take all the measures at its disposal to put a stop to that state of affairs in Vilnius which is incompatible with the treaties already concluded, and will not permit the appearance in the city of the above-mentioned international units.

I take advantage of this occasion, Sir, to beg you to accept the assurance of my deepest consideration and devotion.

(signed) George Chicherin
People's Commissar of Foreign Affairs

Editor's comment: In the fall of 1920 the Bolshevik offensive against Poland was in full retreat, and the victorious Polish Army swept through the eastern regions, seizing large sections of Byelorussia and the Ukraine.

The Poles also seized Lithuanian territory. When the Polish Army reached the Lithuanian frontier of July 12, 1920 it simply continued its advance. Negotiations were initiated at Suwalki, and the French prevailed upon the Poles to stop. On October 7, a treaty was concluded which involved a border revision favorable to the Poles. The treaty was to take effect on October 9, but on October 8, a Polish division "revolted" and advanced into Lithuania, capturing the capital, Vilnius. Zeligowski then proclaimed the Central Lithuanian Republic, which was incorporated into Poland in 1922.

Lithuania took its case to the League of Nations, which proposed a plebiscite to determine the preference of the Vilnius population. The plebiscite was to be administered by an international force sent by the

League. Needless to say, the U. S. S. R., which still had vivid memories of Allied interventionary forces on its own territory and which still feared an international crusade to stamp out the revolution, protested vehemently. In doing so the Soviets may well have preserved the Lithuanians' legal claim to Vilnius.

No. 5

Note of the Polish Government to the Lithuanian Government

July 4, 1920   WARSAW, 1171 187.
                                                                    4-7 20-16

To the Minister of Foreign Affairs of the Lithuanian Republic at Kovno.

Mr. Minister:

I have the honor to bring to the knowledge of your Excellency that the Polish Government has decided to recognize the Constituent Assembly of Lithuania and the Government placed in power by said Assembly as independent organizations *de facto*. Desiring to give at the same time practical testimony as to the sentiment which the Polish Nation has always entertained toward your country, sentiments which the past relations of the two Nations, so closely allied, will I hope serve to expand and strengthen, the Polish Government declares it is ready on its part to enter into friendly relations with the Lithuanian Government. The Polish Government believes that the application of principles of justice and equity in all the relations between the two countries and toward the national minorities of each other will form the most secure basis for this friendship.

I take this opportunity to present to you, Mr. Minister, the assurance of my high consideration.

(Signed) Minister of Foreign Affairs Sapieha.
4020

Editor's comment: It is worth noting that July, 1920, was a black month in the history of Poland. The Polish campaign against Russia had backfired, and in July the Poles found themselves pushed back to the suburbs of Warsaw. This in part explains the conciliatory tone of the Polish recognition. However, plans for a restoration of the Polish-

Lithuanian Commonwealth, or at least a federation involving Lithuania, were still very much alive in Poland. Thus *de jure* recognition was delayed, and various military measures were initiated against Lithuania in the hope of forcing a union. The Lithuanians, neither enraptured by the idea of cultural assimilation into Poland and the disappearance of the Lithuanian nation, nor encouraged by the crudity and tactlessness of the Polish overtures, resisted.

However, in all fairness, it should be pointed out that the cordiality expressed in the Polish note is not pure hypocrisy. Three hundred years of co-existence between Poland and Lithuania had produced very close ties. For example, Pilsudski himself came from an undisputably Lithuanian family and was born not far from Vilnius. His brother, Bronislovas, was the president of the Lithuanian Council in Switzerland. Stanislovas Narutavičius signed the Lithuanian Declaration of Independence; his brother, Gabriel Narutowicz, was elected President of Poland in 1922. Eustace Sapieha, the Polish Foreign Minister who signed the Note of Recognition, came from an old Lithuanian aristocratic family. Lucian Zeligowski, the Polish General who seized Vilnius, was born in Ašmena in the Vilnius region. The examples are endless. The patronizing attitude of these polonized Lithuanians toward their former country is abundantly evident, but it cannot be denied that it was mixed with a certain degree of sentimental attachment.

No. 6

The U. S. Secretary of State, Hughes, to the U. S. Commissioner in Riga, Young

860.n.01/52a: Telegram
The Secretary of State to the Commissioner at Riga (Young)

WASHINGTON, July 25, 1922, 4 p.m.

Advise Foreign Offices of Estonia, Latvia and Lithuania as nearly at the same time as possible on the morning of July 28, that the United States extend to each full recognition. The fact will be communicated to the Press at Washington for publication in the morning papers of July 28, and the following statement will be made:

The Governments of Estonia, Latvia and Lithuania have been recognized either de jure or de facto by the principal Governments of Europe and have entered into treaty relations with their neighbors.

In extending to them recognition on its part, the Government of the United States takes cognizance of the actual existence of these Governments during a considerable period of time and of the successful maintenance within their borders of political and economical stability.

The United States has consistently maintained that the disturbed conditions of Russian affairs may not be made the occasion for alienation of Russian territory, and this principle is not deemed to be impinged by the recognition at this time of the Governments of Estonia, Latvia and Lithuania which have been set up and maintained by indigenous population.

Pending legislation by Congress to establish regular diplomatic representation Mr. Young will continue as Commissioner of the United States and will have the rank of Minister. Request from respective Governments temporary recognition pending formal application for exequatures of John P. Hurley, Charles H. Albrecht, and Clement S. Edwards, consuls at Riga, Reval and Kovno, respectively.

Signed: Hughes.

No. 7

Data of the Recognition of Lithuania, de facto and de jure, by the Sovereign States of the World

March 23, 1918:	Germany, de jure
August 22, 1919:	Norway, de facto
November 8, 1919:	Latvia, de facto
November 17, 1919:	Finland, de facto
May 11, 1920:	France, de facto

July 4, 1920:   Poland, de facto

March 10, 1921:   Estonia, de facto

March 14, 1921:   Argentina, de jure·

May 5, 1921:   Mexico, de facto

August 19, 1921:   Switzerland, de facto

September 4, 1921:   Norway, de jure

September 22, 1921:   Lithuania admitted to the League of Nations

September 28, 1921:   Sweden, de jure

September 30, 1921:   Denmark, de jure

October 6, 1921:   The Netherlands, de jure

October 14, 1921:   Finland, de jure

December 9, 1921:   Brazil, de jure

January 5, 1922:   Czechoslovakia, de jure

May 9, 1922:   Venezuela, de jure

May 23, 1922:   Greece, de jure

May 29, 1922:   Chile, de jure

June 14, 1922:   Bolivia, de jure

July 13, 1922:   The Conference of Ambassadors (England, France, Italy, Japan), de jure

July 27, 1922:   Spain, de jure

July 28, 1922:   United States of America, de jure

November 1, 1922:   Iceland, de jure

November 10, 1922:   The Holy See, de jure

December 27, 1922:   Belgium, de jure

December 28, 1922:   Panama, de jure

January 5, 1923:   Costa Rica, de jure

January 30, 1923:   Siam, de jure

February 5, 1923:   Peru, de jure

February 9, 1923:   Paraguay, de jure

February 12, 1923:   China, de jure

February 13, 1923:   Liberia, de jure

February 26, 1923:   Guatemala, de jure

May 11, 1923:   Cuba, de jure

August 11, 1923:   Persia, de jure

November 6, 1923:   Equador, de jure

February 7, 1924:   Austria, de jure

August 21, 1924:   Roumania, de jure

November 3, 1924:   Bulgaria, de jure

Editor's comment: It is worth noting that there were no recognitions of Lithuania, either *de facto* or *de jure,* between July 4, 1920 and March 10, 1921, and in fact until the admission of Lithuania to the League of Nations in late September 1921, only two states had recognized Lithuania *de jure,* although Lithuania had been independent for more than two years.

Lithuania's recognition problems stemmed mainly from her chronic conflict with Poland. Poland still had ambitions of reactivating the Lublin Union of 1569 and of presiding over a power bloc from the Baltic to the Black Sea. More importantly, in October, 1920, Poland had seized and incorporated Vilnius and the Vilnius region, i.e., Lithuania's capital and 33,000 square kilometers of her territory. The result was the complete breakdown of relations between Poland and Lithuania for eighteen years. At the time (1920), Poland enjoyed great popularity among the Western Powers, especially France, which hoped that a great Poland would be the bulwark both of the "cordon sanitaire" against the USSR, and of the French two front encirclement of Germany — thus Polish opposition seriously hampered Lithuania's attempts to gain recognition.

No. 8

Treaty of Nonagression between Lithuania and the Union of Soviet Socialist Republics.[1]

[2]Translation.

No. 1410. — Treaty of nonaggression between the Republic of Lithuania and the Union of Soviet Socialist Republics. Signed at Moscow, September 28, 1926.

THE PRESIDENT OF THE LITHUANIAN REPUBLIC, of the one part, and THE CENTRAL EXECUTIVE COMMITTEE OF THE UNION OF SOCIALIST SOVIET REPUBLICS, of the other part, being convinced that the interests of the Lithuanian people and of the peoples of the Union of Socialist Soviet Republics demand constant co-operation based on mutual confidence, have agreed, in order to contribute to the best of their ability to the maintenance of universal peace, to conclude a treaty with a view to strengthening the friendly relations existing between them, and to this end have appointed as their Plenipotentiaries:

THE PRESIDENT OF THE LITHUANIAN REPUBLIC: Mykolas Sleževičius, Prime Minister and Minister of Justice, Acting Minister for Foreign Affairs of the Lithuanian Republic; and Jurgis Baltrušaitis, Envoy Extraordinary and

---

[1]Communicated by the Permanent Delegate of Lithuania accredited to the League of Nations.
[2]Translated by the Secretariat of the League of Nations.

Minister Plenipotentiary of the Lithuanian Republic accredited to the Union of Socialist Soviet Republics; and THE CENTRAL EXECUTIVE COMMITTEE OF THE UNION OF SOCIALIST SOVIET REPUBLICS: Georges Tchitcherine, Member of the C. E. C. of the Union of Socialist Soviet Republics, People's Commissary for Foreign Affairs; and Serge Alexandrovsky, Plenipotentiary Representative of the Union of Socialist Soviet Republics in Lithuania;

Who having met at Moscow and exchanged their full powers found in good and due form, have agreed upon the following provisions:

Article 1.

The relations between the Union of Socialist Soviet Republics and the Lithuanian Republic shall continue to be based on the Treaty of Peace between Lithuania and Russia, concluded at Moscow on July 12, 1920. all the provisions of which shall retain their force and inviolability.

Article 2.

The Lithuanian Republic and the Union of Socialist Soviet Republics undertake to respect in all circumstances each others sovereignty and territorial integrity and inviolability.

Article 3.

Each of the two Contracting Parties undertakes to refrain from any act of aggression whatsoever against the other Party.

Should one of the Contracting Parties, despite its peaceful attitude, be attacked by one or several third Powers, the other Contracting Party undertakes not to support the said third Power or Powers against the Contracting Party attacked.

Article 4.

If, on the occasion of a conflict of the type mentioned in Article 3, second paragraph, or at a time when neither of the Contracting Parties is engaged in warlike operations, a political agreement directed against one of the Contracting Parties is concluded between third Powers, or a coalition is formed between third Powers with a view to the economic or financial boycott of either of the Contracting Parties, the other Contracting Party undertakes not to adhere to such agreement or coalition.

Article 5.

Should a dispute arise between them, the Contracting Parties undertake to appoint conciliation commissions, if it should not prove possible to settle the dispute by diplomatic means.

The composition of the said commissions, their rights and the procedure they shall observe shall be settled in virtue of a separate agreement to be concluded between the two Parties.

Article 6.

The present Treaty is subject to ratification, which must take place within six weeks of the date of its signature.

The exchange of the instruments of ratification shall take place at Kovno.

The present Treaty has been drawn up in Lithuanian and Russian.

As regards interpretation, both texts shall be considered as authentic.

Article 7.

The present Treaty shall enter into force on the date of the exchange of the instruments of ratification and shall remain in force for five years, except Articles 1 and 2, the duration of the validity of which is not limited.

The validity of the present Treaty shall be prolonged automatically, on each occasion for one year, until either of the Contracting Parties expresses, at least six months before the expiration of the Treaty, the desire to enter upon negotiations regarding the future form of political relations between the two States.

In faith whereof, the Plenipotentiaries have affixed to the present Treaty their autograph signatures, and their seals.

The original has been done and signed in duplicate at Moscow the twenty-eighth day of September, One thousand nine hundred and twenty-six.

(L.S.) (Signed) Mykolas Sleževičius.

(Signed) Jurgis Baltrušaitis.

(L.S.) (Signed) G. V. Tchitcherine.

(Signed) Serge Alexandrovsky.

[1] Traduction.

No. 2859. — Protocol renewing the treaty of non-aggression between Lithuania and the Union of Soviet Socialist Republics of September 28, 1926. Signed at Moscow, May 6, 1931.

THE PRESIDENT OF THE LITHUANIAN REPUBLIC AND THE CENTRAL EXECUTIVE COMMITTEE OF THE UNION OF SOVIET SOCIALIST REPUBLICS,

Considering that the Treaty between the Republic of Lithuania and the

---

[1] Translated by the Secretariat of the League of Nations, for information.

Union of Soviet Socialist Republics, signed at Moscow on September 28th, 1926, has effectively helped to strengthen and develop friendly relations between the two States and to consolidate peace in Eastern Europe,

And being desirous of further strengthening and developing their mutual relations, which are inspired with a spirit of peace and sincere friendship,

Have decided to prolong the validity of the said Treaty, and have to that end appointed as their Plenipotentiaries:

THE PRESIDENT OF THE LITHUANIAN REPUBLIC: Jurgis Baltrušaitis, Envoy Extraordinary and Minister Plenipotentiary of the Lithuanian Republic at Moscow; THE CENTRAL EXECUTIVE COMMITTEE OF THE UNION OF SOVIET SOCIALIST REPUBLICS: Maxim Litvinov, Member of the Central Executive Committee of the Union of Soviet Socialist Republics, People's Commissary for Foreign Affairs;

Who, having exchanged their full powers, found in good and due form, have agreed on the following provisions:

Article 1.

The Treaty concluded between the Lithuanian Republic and the Union of Soviet Socialist Republics at Moscow on September 28, 1926, together with the notes of the Governments of Lithuania and the Union of Soviet Socialist Republics annexed thereto, shall be deemed to be prolonged for a period of five years from the date of expiry of the said Treaty. Unless either of the Contracting Parties informs the other, six months before the expiry of this period, of its desire to enter upon negotiations regarding the future form of the political relations between the two States, the Treaty shall be regarded as being automatically prolonged on each occasion for one year.

Article 2.

The present Protocol is drawn up in the Lithuanian and Russian languages. For its interpretation both texts shall be deemed authentic. The Protocol shall be ratified as soon as possible. It shall come into force on the date of the exchange of ratifications, which shall take place at Kaunas.

In faith whereof the above-mentioned Plenipotentiaries have signed the present Protocol and thereto affixed their seals.

Done at Moscow, in duplicate, May 6, 1931.

Jurgis Baltrušaitis.
Litvinov.

Editor's comment: The Treaty provides that neither party will commit any act of aggression against the other, nor will it support such an act by a third party. This Treaty, thus, would also make it illegal for one of the contracting parties to enter into secret or open agreements with a third party directed against the independence or territorial integrity of the other signatory. The Treaty was renewed by a protocol on May 6. 1931, and again on April 4, 1934.

No. 9

Letter of G. V. Chicherin, Soviet Commissar for Foreign Affairs, to Mykolas Sleževičius, Prime Minister and acting Foreign Minister of Lithuania.

Moscow, September 28, 1926.

Your Excellency,

On to-day's date you have addressed to me a Note to the following effect:

"(1) The two Governments have examined the questions of principle which are bound up with Lithuania's membership of the League of Nations. As regards this question the Lithuanian Government, both during the negotiations for the conclusion of the Treaty, and at the time of its signature, was guided by the conviction that the principle adopted by the Parties in Article 4 of the Treaty and relating to non-participation in any political agreements directed against one of the Contracting Parties which might be concluded between third Powers, cannot in any way hinder Lithuania's execution of the obligations laid up on her by the Covenant of the League of Nations.

"(2) The Lithuanian Government is convinced that Lithuania's membership of the League of Nations cannot constitute an obstacle to the friendly development of the relations between Lithuania and the Union of Socialist Soviet Republics.

"(3) At the same time the Lithuanian Government considers that in view of Lithuania's geographical situation, the obligations laid upon her by her membership of the League of Nations—an Institution whose fundamental purpose is to settle international disputes in a peaceful and equitable manner—cannot constitute an obstacle to the Lithuanian nation's aspirations towards neutrality, which is the policy best suited to her vital interests."

In conformity with my Government's instructions, I have the honour to inform you that the Government of the Union takes due note of the above declaration.

I have the honour to be, etc.

(Signed) Georges Tchitcherine.

Monsieur Mykolas Sleževičius,
Prime Minister and Minister of Justice, Acting Minister for Foreign Affairs of the Lithuanian Republic.

Editor's comment: The U. S. S. R. was not at this time a member of the League of Nations, and did not join it until September 18, 1934. Since the relations between the U. S. S. R. and the League, or its more important members, were not friendly, Lithuania, under Article 4 of the Nonaggression Treaty, felt under obligation to inform the Soviets on its membership in the League.

No. 10

Letter of G. V. Chicherin, Soviet Commissar for Foreign Affairs, to Mykolas Sleževičius, Prime Minister and acting Foreign Minister of Lithuania.

Moscow, September 28, 1926.

Your Excellency,

On the occasion of the signature on today's date of the Treaty between the Union of Socialist Soviet Republics and the Lithuanian Republic, I have the honour to inform you of the following:

> The Government of the Union, being guided as always by its desire to see the Lithuanian nation, like all other nations, independent—a desire which the Government of the Union of Socialist Soviet Republics has on several occasions expressed in its declarations—and in conformity with the Note addressed by the Soviet Government on April 5, 1923, to the Polish Government, and with the good-will with which the public opinion of the workers of the Union of Socialist Soviet Republics follows the destinies of the Lithuanian nation, declares that the *de facto* violation of the Lithuanian frontiers committed against the will of the Lithuanian nation has not shaken its attitude with regard to the territorial sovereignty defined in Article 2 of the Treaty of Peace,

concluded between Russia and Lithuania on July 12, 1920, and in
the Note annexed to the said Article.

I have the honour to be, etc.

(Signed) Georges Tchitcherine.

Monsieur Mykolas Sleževičius,
   *Prime Minister and Minister for Foreign Affairs of the Lithuanian
   Republic.*

Editor's comment: The last point of the letter refers to the Polish
occupation of the city and district of Vilnius on October 9, 1920, after
the signing of the Soviet-Lithuanian Peace Treaty of July 4, 1920, in
which the U. S. S. R. recognized Lithuanian frontiers which included
the Vilnius region. The Soviet Government adopted a policy of
nonrecognition of the Polish occupation of Vilnius which was never
publicly abandoned in the period 1920-1940, a fact which Molotov
conveniently forgot to mention both in his political bargaining with the
Germans in 1939, and in imposing Soviet military bases on Lithuania
as a condition for the return of Vilnius during the negotiations leading
to the Soviet-Lithuanian Mutual Assistance Pact of October 10, 1939.

No. 11

Protocol Renewing the Nonaggression Treaty of September 28, 1926

[1] Translation.

*No. 4315. — Protocol renewing the Treaty of Non-Aggression of
September 28th, 1926, between Lithuania and the Union of Soviet
Socialist Republics. Signed at Moscow, April 4th, 1934.*

THE CENTRAL EXECUTIVE COMMITTEE OF THE UNION OF SOVIET SOCIALIST
REPUBLICS and THE PRESIDENT OF THE REPUBLIC OF LITHUANIA;
   Being desirous of providing as firm a basis as possible for the development of
the relations between their countries;
   Being desirous of giving each other fresh proof of the unchangeable character
and solidity of the peaceful and friendly relations happily established between
them;

---

[1] Translated by the Secretariat of the League of Nations, for information.

Actuated by the desire to contribute to the consolidation of world peace and to the stability and peaceful development of international relations in Eastern Europe;

And noting that the conclusion of the Treaty of September 28th, 1926 between the Union of Soviet Socialist Republics and Lithuania, and its prolongation in 1931 have had a beneficial influence on their relations and on the solution of the above-mentioned problems;

Have decided to sign the present Protocol and have for this purpose appointed as their Plenipotentiaries:

THE CENTRAL EXECUTIVE COMMITTEE OF THE UNION OF SOVIET SOCIALIST REPUBLICS: Maxime Maximovitch Litvinoff, Member of the Central Executive Committee of the Union of Soviet Socialist Republics, People's Commissary for Foreign Affairs; THE PRESIDENT OF THE REPUBLIC OF LITHUANIA: Jurgis Baltrušaitis, Ambassador Extraordinary and Minister Plenipotentiary of the Republic of Lithuania at Moscow;

Who, having communicated their full powers, found in good and due form, have agreed on the following provisions:

Article 1.

In modification of Article 1 of the Protocol signed at Moscow on May 6th, 1931, the Treaty of September 28th, 1926, concluded between the Union of Soviet Socialist Republics and the Lithuanian Republic, together with the two annexed notes of the Government of the Union of Soviet Socialist Republics and of the Lithuanian Republic, shall be deemed to be prolonged until December 31st, 1945.

Article 2.

The present Protocol is drawn up in duplicate, in the Russian and Lithuanian languages, both texts being equally authentic. It shall be ratified as soon as possible and the instruments of ratification shall be exchanged between the High Contracting Parties at Kaunas.

The present Protocol shall come into force on the date of the exchange of the instruments of ratification.

In faith whereof the above-mentioned Plenipotentiaries have signed the present Protocol and have thereto affixed their seals.

Done at Moscow in duplicate, in the Russian and Lithuanian languages, this 4th day of April, 1934.

(L.S.) (Signed) M. Litvinoff.
(L.S.) (Signed) J. Baltrušaitis.

Editor's comment. This document proves that the nonaggression treaty

After signing the Pact of September 23, 1939 Stalin and Ribbentrop "cordially" shook hands.

was still in effect in 1939-1940, during the Soviet annexation of Lithuania.

No. 12

Protocol between Estonia, Latvia, Roumania, Poland, and the USSR Declaring Adherence to the Briand-Kellogg Pact of August 27, 1928.

[1] Traduction. — Translation.

No. 2028. — Protocol[2], signed at Moscow, February 9, 1929, between Estonia, Latvia, Poland, Roumania and the Union of Soviet Socialist Republics for the immediate entry into force of the Treaty of Paris of August 27, 1928, regarding renunciation of war as an instrument of national policy.

French official text communicated by the Polish Delegate accredited to the League of Nations and the Estonian Minister for Foreign Affairs. The registration of this Protocol took place June 3, 1929.

THE GOVERNMENT OF THE ESTONIAN REPUBLIC, THE PRESIDENT OF THE LATVIAN REPUBLIC, THE PRESIDENT OF THE POLISH REPUBLIC, HIS MAJESTY THE KING OF ROUMANIA AND THE CENTRAL EXECUTIVE COMMITTEE OF THE UNION OF SOVIET SOCIALIST REPUBLICS, being desirous of promoting the maintenance of peace between their respective countries and for this purpose of putting into force without delay, between the peoples of those countries, the Treaty for the renunciation of war as an instrument of national policy, signed at Paris on August 27, 1928, have decided to achieve this purpose by means of the present Protocol and have appointed as their Plenipotentiaries:

THE GOVERNMENT OF THE ESTONIAN REPUBLIC: M. Julius Seljamaa, Estonian Envoy Extraordinary and Minister Plenipotentiary at Moscow; THE PRESIDENT OF THE LATVIAN REPUBLIC: M. Charles Ozols, Latvian Envoy

---

[1] Translated by the Secretariat of the League of Nations, for information.
[2] Deposit of ratifications:
Latvia, March 5, 1929.
Estonia, March 16, 1929.
Poland, March 30, 1929.
Roumania, March 30, 1929.

Extraordinary and Minister Plenipotentiary at Moscow; THE PRESIDENT OF
THE POLISH REPUBLIC: M. Stanislav Patek, Polish Envoy Extraordinary and
Minister Plenipotentiary at Moscow; HIS MAJESTY THE KING OF ROUMANIA:
M. Charles A. Davila, His Majesty's Envoy Extraordinary and Minister
Plenipotentiary at Warsaw and THE CENTRAL EXECUTIVE COMMITTEE OF THE
UNION OF SOVIET SOCIALIST REPUBLICS: M. Maxime Litvinoff, Member of the
Central Executive Committee, People's Commissar for Foreign Affairs *ad
interim,*

Who, having communicated their full powers, found in good and due form,
have agreed as follows:

Article 1.

The Treaty for the renunciation of war as an instrument of national policy,
signed at Paris on August 27, 1928, a copy of which is attached to the present
Protocol as an integral part of that instrument, shall come into force between
the Contracting Parties after the ratification of the said Treaty of Paris of 1928
by the competent legislative bodies of the respective Contracting Parties.

Article 2.

The entry into force in virtue of the present Protocol, of the Treaty of Paris of
1928 in reciprocal relations between the Parties to the present Protocol shall be
valid independently of the entry into force of the Treaty of Paris of 1928 as
provided in Article III of the last named Treaty.

Article 3.

1. The present Protocol shall be ratified by the competent legislative bodies
of the Contracting Parties, in conformity with the requirements of their
respective constitutions.

2. The instruments of ratification shall be deposited by each of the
Contracting Parties with the Government of the Union of Soviet Socialist
Republics within one week of the ratification of the present Protocol by the
respective Parties.

3. As from the date of the deposit of the instruments of ratification by two of
the Contracting Parties, the present Protocol shall come into force between
those two Parties. In reciprocal relations between the other Contracting Parties
and the States for which it has already come into force, the Protocol shall come
into force as and when their instruments of ratification are deposited.

4. The Government of the Union of Soviet Socialist Republics shall
immediately notify the deposit of the several ratifications to all the signatories
to the present Protocol.

Article 4.

In order to give effect to Article I of the present Protocol, each of the High Contracting Parties, after ratification by its legislative bodies of the Treaty of Paris of 1928, shall immediately notify the Government of the Union of Soviet Socialist Republics and all the other Parties to the present Protocol, through the diplomatic channel.

Article 5.

The present Protocol shall be open for the accession of the Governments of all countries. Notification of final accession shall be made in the name of the Government of the Union of Soviet Socialist Republics, which shall duly notify all the other Parties to the present Protocol. Immediately on receipt of such notification of accession, the present Protocol shall be put into force in reciprocal relations between the acceding State and all the other Parties to the present Protocol.

Article 6.

The entry into force, in virtue of the present Protocol, of the Treaty of Paris of 1928, in reciprocal relations between the acceding State and all the other Parties to the said Protocol, shall be effected in the way laid down in Article IV of the Protocol.

Article 7.

The present Protocol has been drawn up in a single copy, an authentic copy of which shall be communicated by the Government of the Union of Soviet Socialist Republics to each of the signatory or acceding States.

In faith whereof the above-mentioned Plenipotentiaries have signed the present Protocol and have affixed their seals thereto.

Done at Moscow, February 9, 1929.

(L.S.) (Signed) Jul. Seljamaa.
(L.S.) (Signed) C. Ozols.
(L.S.) (Signed) St. Patek.
(L.S.) (Signed) Davila.
(L.S.) (Signed) Maxime Litvinoff.

ANNEXE[1].

Editor's comment: Sixty-three States adhered to the Briand-Kellogg Pact before the outbreak of World War II. The validity of the treaty in

---

[1] The Annexe is a copy of the Briand-Kellogg Pact. See Document 202 for the text.

international law was confirmed by the International Military Tribunal at Nuremburg, of which the U. S. S. R. was a prominent member, when it judged violations of the Pact to be international crimes against peace.

No. 13

Convention for the Definition of Aggression between Lithuania and the USSR

[1]Translation.

No. 3405 — Convention[2] *between Lithuania and the Union of Soviet Socialist Republics for the definition of aggression — signed at London, July 5th, 1933*

French official text communicated by the Lithuanian Minister for Foreign Affairs. The registration of this Convention took place April 16th, 1934

The President of the Republic of Lithuania and the Central Executive Committee of the Union of Soviet Socialist Republics;

Being desirous of consolidating the peaceful relations existing between their countries;

Mindful of the fact that the Briand-Kellogg Pact, of which they are signatories, and likewise the Pact of Non-Aggression concluded between them at Moscow on September 28th, 1926, prohibit all aggression;

Deeming it necessary, in the interest of the general security, to define aggression as specifically as possible, in order to obviate any pretext whereby it might be justified;

And noting that all States have an equal right to independence, security, the defense of their territories and the free development of their institutions;

And desirous, in the interest of the general peace, to ensure to all peoples the inviolability of the territory of their countries;

And judging it expedient, in the interest of the general peace, to bring into force as between their countries precise rules defining aggression, until such time as those rules shall become universal;

---

[1]Translated by the Secretariat of the League of Nations, for information.
[2]The exchange of ratifications took place at Moscow, December 14th, 1933.

Have decided, with the aforesaid objects, to conclude the present Convention and have duly authorised for that purpose:

The President of the Republic of Lithuania:

Mr. Vaclovas Sidzikauskas, Envoy Extraordinary and Minister Plenipotentiary in London;

The Central Executive Committee of the Union of Soviet Socialist Republics: Mr. Maxime Litvinoff, People's Commissar for Foreign Affairs:

Who have agreed upon the following provisions:

Article 1.

Each of the High Contracting Parties undertakes to accept in its relations with the other Party, from the date of the entry into force of the present Convention, the definition of aggression framed by the Committee on Security Questions of the Conference for the Reduction and Limitation of Armaments, following on the Soviet delegation's proposal.

Article 2.

Accordingly, the aggressor in an international conflict shall, subject to the agreements in force between the parties to the dispute, be considered to be that State which is the first to commit any of the following actions:

(1) Declaration of war upon another State;

(2) Invasion by its armed forces, with or without a declaration of war, of the territory of another State;

(3) Attack by its land, naval or air forces, with or without a declaration of war, on the territory, vessels or aircraft of another State;

(4) Naval blockade of the coasts or ports of another State;

(5) Provision of support to armed bands formed in its territory which have invaded the territory of another State, or refusal, notwithstanding the request of the invaded State, to take in its own territory all the measures in its power to deprive those bands of all assistance or protection.

Article 3.

No political, military, economic or other considerations may serve as an excuse or justification for the aggression referred to in Article 2 (for examples, see Annex).

Article 4.

The present Convention shall be ratified by the High Contracting Parties in conformity with their national laws.

It shall come into force immediately after the exchange of the instruments of ratification, which shall take place at Moscow.

In faith whereof the above-mentioned Plenipotentiaries have signed the present Convention and have thereto affixed their seals.

Done in London in two copies, in French, July 5th, one thousand nine hundred and thirty-three.

(s) Vaclovas Sidzikauskas.

(s) Maxime Litvinoff.

ANNEX TO ARTICLE 3 OF THE CONVENTION RELATING TO THE DEFINITION OF AGGRESSION

The High Contracting Parties signatories of the Convention relating to the definition of aggression,

Desiring, subject to the express reservation that the absolute validity of the rule laid down in Article 3 of that Convention shall be in no way restricted, to furnish certain indications for determining the aggressor,

Declare that no act of aggression within the meaning of Article 2 of that Convention can be justified on either of the following grounds, among others:

A. *The internal condition of a State:*

E. g., its political, economic or social structure; alleged defects in its administrations; disturbances due to strikes, revolutions, counter-revolutions or civil war.

B. *The international conduct of a State:*

E. g., the violation or threatened violation of the material or moral rights or interests of a foreign State or its nationals; the rupture of diplomatic or economic relations; economic or financial boycotts; disputes relating to economic, financial or other obligations towards foreign States; frontier incidents not forming any of the cases of aggression specified in Article 2.

The High Contracting Parties further agree to recognize that the present Convention can never legitimate any violations of international law that may be implied in the circumstances comprised in the above list.

(s) V. Sidzikauskas.

(s) Maxime Litvinoff.

CHAPTER II

LITHUANIAN-USSR RELATIONS DURING WORLD WAR II, 1939-1945

A. THE GERMAN-SOVIET PARTITION PLOT

No. 14

Memorandum of the Lithuanian Foreign Minister, Urbšys, to Lithuanian Diplomatic Missions in Europe

Ministry of Foreign Affairs   KAUNAS, *May 11, 1939*
No. 469/sl   *Secret*

1. To the Envoy of Lithuania in Moscow
2.   "   "   "   "   " Tallin
3.   "   "   "   "   " Stockholm
4.   "   "   "   "   " Berlin
5.   "   "   "   "   " Paris
6.   "   "   "   "   " London
7.   "   "   "   "   " Warsowie
8.   "   "   "   "   " Ryga
9.   "   "   "   "   " Roma
10. Copy to the Chief of Military Staff

Some time ago, when tension between Germany and Poland increased, there were certain cases where foreign diplomatic representatives in their private conversations with our diplomatic representatives had alluded to the fact that Lithuania, taking advantage of an opportunity, might bring up its territorial demands. For instance, the Poles talk about an opportunity of recovering Klaipeda (Memel) or eventually a part of East Prussia, and the Germans and Russians — about giving back the region of Vilnus.

It is quite possible that the purpose of such allusions, from the reaction of our diplomatic representatives, were to check the attitude of the Government or of our public opinion on these questions or to extract careless statements which could be used to influence our relations with one or another State.

In any case, it is clear that the present dangerous situation imposes upon us a particular duty of caution. Therefore, such allusions should be answered so clearly that there can be no doubt that the basic point of the Lithuanian policy and its attitude is strict neutrality which we are firmly determined to defend in any situation and on any question.

Please give instructions in this sense to the members of your legation.

J. URBŠYS
Minister of Foreign Affairs.

Editor's comment: The memorandum is a clear refutation of any rumors that Lithuania would take advantage of the tension and confusion of the international situation to advance any genuine or imagined territorial claims, and a clear instruction to Lithuanian diplomats to dispell any misconceptions to that effect. The basic principles of Lithuania's foreign policy remained based on strict neutrality.

No. 15

Lithuanian Neutrality Law.

Article I

§1. Warships of belligerents are accorded admission to the ports and other territorial waters of Lithuania with the reservation of the following restrictions and conditions.

§2. Warships of belligerents are prohibited access to those ports and maritime areas which have been declared naval stations or which belong to the protected zones of coastal defense installations.

Warships of belligerents are equally prohibited access to those inland waters to which entrance is barred, whether by underwater mines or by other means of defense.

By inland waters of Lithuania, the present law understands ports, entrances to ports, gulfs and bays, as well as the waters surrounding and on the mainland side of those Lithuanian islands, islets, and reefs which are not permanently submerged.

Navigation or sojourn within Lithuanian territorial waters is prohibited to the armed war-submarines of belligerents.

This prohibition is not always applicable to submarines forced by the condition of the sea or by damages to penetrate the prohibited waters and which indicate by means of an international signal the cause of their presence in these waters. The said submarines are obliged to quit the forbidden waters as soon as the reason for which they have penetrated them has ceased. Within Lithuanian territorial waters the submarines are to have their national flag hoisted at all times, and to navigate on the surface.

The President of Lithuania reserves the right to prohibit, in case of special circumstances, in order to safeguard the sovereign rights and preserve the neutrality of Lithuania in observance of the general principles of international law, entrance to Lithuanian ports or other determined zones of Lithuanian territorial waters other than those to which access is prohibited by the dispositions stated above.

The President of Lithuania also reserves for himself the right to prohibit access to Lithuanian ports and anchorages to those warships of belligerents which have neglected to conform to prescriptions issued by the competent Lithuanian authorities or which have violated the authority of Lithuania.

§3. Corsairs are never permitted to enter Lithuanian ports or to sojourn in Lithuanian territorial waters.

It is also prohibited for the armed commercial vessels of belligerents, if the armament is designed for any purpose other than their defense, to enter Lithuanian ports or to sojourn within Lithuanian territorial waters.

§4. Warships of belligerents are prohibited from remaining in Lithuanian ports or anchorages, or within other territorial waters of Lithuania, longer than twenty-four hours, unless for reasons of damages or running aground, or the reason of the condition of the sea, or for the reasons foreseen below in paragraphs 3 and 4. In those cases, they are to leave as soon as the cause of the delay has ceased. In case of repairs or running aground, the competent Lithuanian authority shall fix a time limit which shall be judged sufficient for the repair of the damages or refloatation of the vessel. Prolongation of sojourn for more than 24 hours will not always be granted if it is obvious that the vessel cannot be made navigable within a reasonable period, or when its damages have been caused by an act of war of the enemy.

The above dispositions concerning the limitation of sojourn do not apply to warships employed exclusively on religious, scientific, or humanitarian missions, nor to military-hospital-ships.

The maximum number of warships of one belligerent power, or of several allied belligerent powers, admitted to sojourn at the same time in one Lithuanian port or anchorage, or the ports or anchorages of the same coastal district of Lithuania, when the coast shall have been divided into districts for this purpose, is two.

If warships of two belligerent parties sojourn in a Lithuanian port or anchorage at the same time, 24 hours must elapse between the departure of one belligerent vessel and that of the other, the order of departures being determined by the order of arrivals, unless the vessel which arrived first would be in a category in which extension of sojourn is admissible.

The warship of a belligerent cannot leave a Lithuanian port or anchorage in which there is a commercial vessel flying the flag of an adversary less than twenty-four hours after the departure of the said commercial vessel. The competent authorities shall regulate the departures of commercial vessels in order to avoid prolonging without necessity the sojourns of warships.

§5. In Lithuanian ports or anchorages, the warships of belligerents cannot repair their damages more than is indispensable for the safety of navigation, and they cannot augment their military power in any way. For the repair of damages obviously caused by acts of war of an adversary, they cannot have recourse to any aid which the warships would procure from Lithuanian territory. The competent Lithuanian authorities shall determine the nature of the repairs to be made. The repairs shall be made as quickly as possible, and in observance of the terms expressed in §4 paragraph 1.

Warships of belligerents are forbidden to use Lithuanian ports or other Lithuanian territorial waters to augment their military provisions or their armament, or to complete their crew.

Warships of belligerents cannot provision themselves in Lithuanian ports or anchorages except to complete their normal peacetime provisioning.

In Lithuanian ports and anchorages, the warships of belligerents will be subject to, as far as concerns the reprovisioning of fuel, to the same regulations as other foreign ships. They will not be able to take on at any time more than the amount of fuel necessary to reach the nearest port of their own country, and in no case a quantity necessary to fill their properly termed storerooms or fuel tanks. After having taken on fuel in a port or anchorage of Lithuania, they cannot renew their provisioning in its ports or anchorages before the expiration of a term of three months.

§6. Warships of belligerents are obliged to use pilots certified by Lithuania in Lithuanian territorial waters under the same rules which applied to them, or which apply to warships in times of peace; otherwise they are not permitted to use such a pilot except in case of distress, or to escape a danger of the sea.

§7. It is prohibited to bring prizes of a foreign country into a Lithuanian port or anchorage except in the case of unseaworthiness, bad conditions of the sea, or lack of fuel or of provisions. Any prize brought into a Lithuanian port or anchorage for one of the above mentioned reasons is obliged to depart as soon as that reason has ceased to apply.

No prize court may be set up by a belligerent, either on Lithuanian soil or on a ship in Lithuanian territorial waters. The sale of prizes in a Lithuanian port or anchorage is also forbidden.

§8. The military aircraft of belligerents, with the exception of aerial ambulances and the aircraft carried on board warships, shall not be admitted on Lithuanian territory.

Aircraft transported on warships of belligerents are prohibited from leaving these warships as long as they find themselves in Lithuanian territorial waters.

§9. The warships and military aircraft of belligerents are obliged to respect the sovereign rights of Lithuania and to abstain from all acts contrary to her neutrality.

They are prohibited within the Lithuanian territorial limits from all hostile acts, included in this being the accosting, boarding and capture of ships or airplanes, whether neutral or belonging to an adversary. Any ship or airplane which has been captured is to be released immediately, together with its officers, crew, and cargo.

§10. Sanitary regulations, pilotage regulations, customs, navigation, air traffic, port and police regulations are to be strictly observed.

§11. Belligerents are prohibited from making Lithuanian territory a base for military operations against an adversary.

§12. Belligerents and persons in their service are prohibited from installing or employing on Lithuanian territory radio transmitter stations or other apparatus designed to be used for communication with belligerent military, naval, or air forces.

Belligerents are prohibited from employing their mobile radio transmitters on Lithuanian territory, whether belonging to armed forces or not, for the transmission of communications, except in case of distress or for communication with the Lithuanian authorities through the intermediary of a Lithuanian radio station, terrestrial or coastal, or a radio station installed on board a ship belonging to the Lithuanian navy.

§13. It is prohibited for anyone to make observation from an airplane in Lithuanian territory or to gather through any other procedure information concerning the movements, operations, or defense works of a belligerent with the aim of aiding the other belligerent.

§14. Belligerents are prohibited from establishing fuel depots, whether on Lithuanian soil, or on ships stationed in her territorial waters.

It is prohibited for ships or airplanes travelling with the obvious purpose of supplying fuel or other provisions to combatant forces of belligerents to take on in Lithuanian territory any quantity of these exceeding that necessary for their own needs.

§15. It is prohibited to equip or arm on Lithuanian territory any ship destined to be employed to cruise or co-operate in military operations against one of the belligerents. It is equally prohibited for any ship having been earmarked for one of the above mentioned objectives and having been adapted, in whole or part, on the territory of Lithuania to the usages of war, to quit this territory.

It is prohibited for any airplane in the process of perpetrating an attack on a belligerent, or carrying apparatus or material the mounting or utilization of which would enable it to perpetrate an attack, to leave Lithuanian territory, if there is reason to believe that it is going to be used against a belligerent power. It is equally prohibited to execute work designed to prepare it for the above-mentioned purposes on an airplane.

Article II

The present law does not affect the rights and obligations stemming from international accords.

Article III

The dispositions of the present law will come into effect by the decision of the President of the Republic, from the date and in the measure determined by him.

Act of the President of the Republic of Lithuania concerning the coming into force of the dispositions of the Law Regulating Neutrality.

Basing myself on Article 3 of the law of January 25, 1939 containing the regulation of neutrality, I proclaim the following:

1.-The Republic of Lithuania remains neutral in the war which has just broken out between the foreign powers.

2.-All those actions which, in conformity with the general rules recognized by the right of nations, carry impairment of this neutrality are prohibited on the territory of the Republic of Lithuania.

3.-In order to safeguard the neutrality of the Republic of Lithuania, the dispositions of the law containing the regulation of neutrality come into effect from September 1, 1939 in regard to all the belligerent powers.

Kaunas, September 1, 1939, No. 1000

(signed) A. SMETONA

President of the Republic

(signed) J. Černius

Chairman of the Council of Ministers (Prime Minister)

Editor's comment: The policy of neutrality adopted by the Baltic States, individually and collectively, in World War II was nothing new in their international relations. For example, Article 5 of the Treaty of Peace between Russia and Estonia [Lithuania] of February 2 [July 12], 1920 provides that "should the perpetual neutrality of Estonia [Lithuania] be internationally recognized, Russia undertakes to respect such neutrality and to join in guaranteeing it." Once the collective security system had been founded under the Covenant of the League of Nations, the Baltic States increasingly manifested their interest in neutral status.

Thus, under the pressure of the tense international situation of the late thirties, the Baltic States in November of 1938 mutually agreed on a policy of neutrality based on laws modelled on the neutrality laws of the Scandinavian countries. The laws were passed by the national legislatures: the Estonian on December 6, 1938; the Latvian on December 21; the Lithuanian on January 25, 1939. On September 1, 1939, President Smetona of Lithuania issued a proclamation to the Lithuanian people appealing for unity and discipline in the observance of the country's neutrality law in the war, and declared that the Law of neutrality had come into force. Latvia and Estonia did the same.

In view of the Russian pledge in the peace treaties, and of the German pledge not to resort to violence against Lithuania, contained in Article 4 of the German-Lithuanian Treaty of March 22, 1939, the Baltic States hoped that the two powers would respect their neutrality and political freedom.

No. 16

Treaty of Nonaggression Between Germany and the Union of Soviet Socialist Republics

The Government of the German Reich and the Government of the Union of Soviet Socialist Republics desirous of strengthening the cause of peace between Germany and the U.S.S.R., and proceeding from the fundamental provisions of the Neutrality Agreement concluded in April 1926 between Germany and the U. S. S. R., have reached the following agreement:

Article I

Both High Contracting Parties obligate themselves to desist from any act of violence, any aggressive action, and any attack on each other either individually or jointly with other powers.

Article II

Should one of the High Contracting Parties become the object of belligerent action by a third power, the other High Contracting Party shall in no manner lend its support to this third power.

Article III

The Governments of the two High Contracting Parties shall in the future maintain continual contact with one another for the purpose of consultation in order to exchange information on problems affecting their common interests.

Article IV

Neither of the two High Contracting Parties shall participate in any grouping of powers whatsoever that is directly or indirectly aimed at the other party.

Article V

Should disputes or conflicts arise between the High Contracting Parties over problems of one kind or another, both parties shall settle these disputes or conflicts exclusively through friendly exchange of opinion or, if necessary, through the establishment of arbitration commissions.

Article VI

The present treaty is concluded for a period of ten years, with the proviso that, in so far as one of the High Contracting Parties does not denounce it one year prior to the expiration of this period, the validity of this treaty shall automatically be extended for another five years.

Article VII

The present treaty shall be ratified within the shortest possible time. The ratifications shall be exchanged in Berlin. The agreement shall enter into force as soon as it is signed.

Done in duplicate, in the German and Russian languages.

Moscow, August 23, 1939.

For the Government	With full power of the
of the German Reich:	Government of the U. S. S. R.:
v. Ribbentrop	V. Molotov

Editor's comment: In the British-Soviet negotiations of August 1939, the British had refused to grant the U.S.S.R. the right of arbitrary intervention and military transit in the Baltic States in return for an Anglo-Soviet defensive alliance. On August 14, Ribbentrop proposed by wire to fly to Moscow "to lay the foundations for a final settlement of German-Russian relations." The Russians accepted, and Ribbentrop flew to Moscow and signed the Russo-German nonaggression pact on

August 23. The public announcement of the pact made no mention of the secret protocol signed the same day (Document No. 17).

This pact was probably the most dramatic reversal of alliances, and the greatest diplomatic bombshell of the century, if not of history. The Nazis and the Communists — two irreconcilable ideological enemies — declared that they had settled their differences and agreed to live at peace with one another.

No. 17

Secret Protocol to the Russo-German Nonaggression Pact of August 23, 1939

Secret Additional Protocol

On the occasion of the signature of the Nonaggression Pact between the German Reich and the Union of Socialist Soviet Republics the undersigned plenipotentiaries of each of the two parties discussed in strictly confidential conversations the question of the boundary of their respective spheres of influence in Eastern Europe. These conversations led to the following conclusions:

1. In the event of a territorial and political rearrangement in the areas belonging to the Baltic States (Finland, Estonia, Latvia, Lithuania), the northern boundary of Lithuania shall represent the boundary of the spheres of influence of Germany and the U. S. S.R. In this connection the interest of Lithuania in the Vilna area is recognized by each party.

2. In the event of a territorial and political rearrangement of the areas belonging to the Polish state the spheres of influence of Germany and the U. S. S. R. shall be bounded approximately by the line of the rivers Narew, Vistula, and San.

The question of whether the interests of both parties make desirable the maintenance of an independent Polish state and how such a state should be bounded can only be definitely determined in the course of further political developments.

In any event both Governments will resolve this question by means of a friendly agreement.

3. With regard to Southeastern Europe attention is called by the

Soviet side to its interest in Bessarabia. The German side declares its complete political disinterestedness in the areas.[34]

4. This protocol shall be treated by both parties as strictly secret.

Moscow, August 23, 1939.	Plenipotentiary of the
For the Government	Government of the U. S. S. R.:
of the German Reich:	V. MOLOTOV
v. RIBBENTROP	

Editor's comment: It was inconceivable for the Germans to abandon the Baltic States completely. Lithuania was retained by Germany, and was later used very effectively by the Germans to extract concessions from the U.S. S. R.

Once the spoils in Poland and the Baltic States had been theoretically divided and Russia's neutrality assured, Hitler was convinced that he could attack Poland to effect the partition. He may have thought that Britain, having lost Russia's support, would now withdraw its pledge to Poland, enabling him to dispose of Poland and the Baltic area with no further consequences.

No. 18

The German Foreign Minister, Ribbentrop, to the German Legation in Kaunas

Telegram

MOST URGENT   BERLIN, August 29, 1939—3:45 a.m.

No. 114   e.o Pol. II . . . g. Rs.

Drafting Officer: Senior Counsellor Rintelen.

In view of the sharp deterioration in the whole political situation resulting from Poland's behaviour, it appears necessary that you should at once make to the Government to which you are accredited, the following statement which clarifies the attitude that we shall observe

---

[34] The German text of this article of the Protocol is as follows: "Hinsichtlich des Südostens Europas wird von sowjetischer Seite das Interesse an Bessarablen betont. Von deutscher Seite wird das völlige politische Desinteressement an diesen Gebieten erklärt."

For a statement by the Reich Foreign Minister concerning the discussion of these subjects at the time of the conclusion of the Nonaggression Pact, see Ribbentrop's memorandum for Hitler of June 24, 1940.

towards Lithuania, and that which we, on our side, expect from Lithuania, should it ultimately prove impossible to avoid hostilities.

We are determined to abide unconditionally by our assurance under the German-Lithuanian Treaty on Memel of March 22 last, by which we shall in no circumstances resort to force against Lithuania. We naturally expect in return that in any conflict Lithuania will observe a completely unimpeachable neutrality towards us. This would, in particular, include Lithuania refusing to tolerate any possible infringement of her neutrality by a third party, but, should such occur, resisting it with all means at her disposal. Should, contrary to our expectations, Lithuania's attitude, in the event of such an infringement of her neutrality by a third Power, be other, or should Lithuania, in such an eventuality, find herself so placed as to be unable to maintain her neutrality, then we should naturally be obliged to safeguard our interests in such a way as the resulting situation required.

You should make this declaration in a clear but markedly friendly form. In so doing you should state that we were aware that, particularly in Lithuania, we would meet with the utmost understanding for the way we are placed in the German-Polish conflict. Just as we, by the imposed Peace Dictate of Versailles, have had the purely German city of Danzig and the Corridor torn from us, so too the Lithuanian people have been cheated out of the realization of their aspirations to Vilna, stolen by a Polish *coup*, through the attitude adopted towards Lithuania by Poland and the League of Nations in this question. Now that, thanks to the recently concluded German-Russian Non-Aggression Pact, the way is open to a fundamental change in the general political situation in Eastern Europe, we attach importance to expressing the hope that, within the framework of this new situation, German-Lithuanian relations will be allowed to continue to develop along friendly lines.

As to what concerns certain difficulties in the present situation which Lithuania may experience in connection with German security measures on the German-Lithuanian frontier, we will endeavour, in applying these measures, to take Lithuanian requirements into account as fully as possible, particularly in respect of traffic through the port of Memel. Please report by telegram on action taken.

Ribbentrop

Editor's Comment: Ribbentrop is hoping to use Lithuania as a "buffer" between the Soviet and German zones of influence. Since Lithuania would, under the Secret Protocol of August 23, certainly remain part of the German sphere, claiming Vilnius for Lithuania, would, of course, mean increasing the German zone, and under those circumstances, would be in the German interest.

No. 19

The German Minister in Kaunas, Zechlin, to the German Foreign Ministry

Telegram

No. 73 of August 29 Kovno, August 29, 1939—5:52 p.m.
Received August 29—8:50 p.m.
Pol. II 3085.

With reference to your telegram No. 114 of August 29.

As instructed, I today told the ... (group mutilated) Minister President and Foreign Minister Bizauskas [*sic*],* in very friendly but unequivocal terms that, in accordance with the Treaty of March 22, Germany would in no circumstances resort to force against Lithuania. Germany, however, expects Lithuania to observe absolutely unimpeachable neutrality which also means that she would resist with all available means any violation of her neutrality by a third party. If, contrary to expectations, Lithuania adopted a different attitude or was unable to maintain her neutrality, Germany would also safeguard her interests as the situation demanded. At the same time I stated Germany's reasons for expecting special understanding from Lithuania for her attitude in the present conflict.

Bizauskas expressed his satisfaction and his sincere thanks for the statement; he could only repeat, as the Lithuanian Government had often declared, that Lithuania would pursue a policy of strictest neutrality and would resist with all means in her power any violation of her neutrality by a third party. Lithuania was adopting this attitude in her own particular interests, for she fully realized the consequences which any other attitude would incur for the country. I urgently request [*sic*]. According to what Bizauskas said, although Poland had previously made a statement regarding respect for Lithuania's neutrality, she had so far not done so in the present crisis.

---

*Kazys Bizauskas, Deputy Minister President.

Bizauskas also expressed his thanks for Germany's intention to take Lithuanian wishes into consideration in any difficulties arising in Memel or on the German-Lithuanian frontier. However, no complaints on this subject have so far become known to him or to the Legation.

Bizauskas said that the German-Russian Treaty has been welcomed here as a valuable contribution to the pacification of Eastern Europe.

ZECHLIN

Editor's comment: It seems that on August 29, 1939, the Lithuanian Government did not yet know of the Secret Protocol annexed to the German-Soviet Nonaggression Pact which divided Eastern Europe and the Baltic States between the U. S. S. R. and Germany. Thus, the Nonaggression Pact as such did not appear to the Lithuanian Government to be harmful or a cause for immediate concern. The failure of the Anglo-Soviet negotiations had been viewed by the Lithuanian Government as a serious blow to collective security, which was felt to be the only solution for preventing war and assuring the survival of the small countries of Europe.

No. 20

The State Secretary of the German Foreign Ministry, Weizsäcker, to the German Legation in Kaunas

Telegram

MOST URGENT   BERLIN, August 29, 1939.
No. 115   [Pol. II 1114 g. Rs.]

With reference to our telegram No. 114.

The Foreign Minister asks you to sound the Lithuanian Government cautiously as to whether they would be prepared to stage some kind of demonstration on the Polish frontier, perhaps by means of troop concentrations.

WEIZSÄCKER

Editor's comment: In the opinion of the Germans, the Lithuanian desire for Vilnius could be exploited by involving Lithuania in a military adventure against Poland. Germany also hoped by this means to enhance its own territorial gains in Lithuania by precluding any possible Soviet penetration into the Vilnius region.

No. 21

The State Secretary of the German Foreign Ministry, Weizsäcker, to the German Legation in Kaunas.

Telegram

No. 120 BERLIN, August 30, 1939—9:15 p.m.

zu Pol. II 3085.

Drafting Officer: Senior Counsellor von Rintelen.

With reference to your telegram No. 73 of August 29.

In conversations with the Lithuanian Government you are requested to express still more clearly than has already been done, on the basis of our telegram No. 114, our sympathies with Lithuanian aspirations to the Vilna area, and to state the view that, in the event of a territorial rearrangement taking place between Germany and Poland, any Lithuanian claims to the Vilna area might also to a large extent be taken into consideration.

WEIZSÄCKER

No. 22

The German Minister in Kaunas, Zechlin, to the German Foreign Ministry

Telegram

No. 76 of August 31 KOVNO, August 31, 1939—9:06 p.m.

Received August 31—11 p.m.

Minister President Černius has stated in a speech to Lithuanian journalists that Lithuania would preserve her neutrality and defend Lithuanian territory against any aggressor with all her means. The necessary military measures for safeguarding her neutrality had been taken. The entire Lithuanian press underlines the determination to remain neutral, and the German move is mentioned with special satisfaction. In fact the press in general has also taken up a neutral attitude, apart from a few deviations which I have raised with the Foreign Ministry.

In so far as there is any concern here about violation of Lithuanian neutrality, it is directed against Poland, as no Lithuanian-Polish non-aggression pact exists and no official Polish statement on respecting

Lithuanian neutrality has as yet been made during the present crisis. This, however, according to rumours current here, seems to be expected tomorrow. As General Rastykis has informed the Military Attaché in the strictest confidence, the military measures taken consist almost exclusively of troop reinforcements along the Polish frontier, whereas only very few formations have been brought up to war-time strength along the German frontier. However, the strictest secrecy is being observed regarding this, as it is desired to avoid any outward demonstration against Poland. Bizauskas, too, to whom in accordance with your telegram No. 115 (Pol. II 1114 g. Rs.) I suggested demonstrative action along the Polish frontier in view of the Polish attitude up to the present, avoided discussion on it and confined himself to replying that Rastykis had informed the Military Attaché in strict confidence of the Lithuanian measures. The Government at present are all the less inclined to take action against Poland because, while on the one hand one section of public opinion entertains the hope of acquiring Vilna, another section, also within the Government, inclines, if not actually towards Poland, in any case towards Britain and France. I shall continue to work in the sense of your telegrams No. 115 of August 29 and No. 116 of August 30.

ZECHLIN

Editor's comment: The German Minister's characterization of Lithuanian attitudes is quite realistic. In her foreign policy, Lithuania espoused the principles of the Covenant of the League and the Briand-Kellogg Pact, and as a small nation, did not ally herself with any great power.

No. 23

The German Minister in Kaunas, Zechlin, to the German Foreign Ministry

Telegram

No. 130 of September 13   KAUNAS, September 13, 1939—3:35 p.m.
                               Received September 13—5:35 p.m.

With reference to your telegrams Nos. 177 and 189.

The Military Attaché talked to Commander in Chief Raštikis again this morning, after having tried several times to approach him. Commander in Chief Raštikis apologized in the first place for the fact that a conversation between the President and me had not yet taken place. However, the Polish Minister here had for several days been pressing for an interview with the President, which the latter had refused up to now. Therefore he, Raštikis, asked me to refrain from calling on the President and instead to call on Minister President Černius privately. I will see the Minister President tomorrow. Regarding the Vilna question, the Commander in Chief stated that Lithuania's interest in the Vilna territory was as great as ever and that Lithuania still considered it Lithuanian territory today from both juridical and ethnic points of view. However, if Lithuania should openly abandon her neutrality at the present time this would greatly handicap her. He indicated that strong pressure was also being placed on Lithuania by England and France not to give up her neutrality in any circumstances. Moreover, as I have heard from other sources, the Soviet Union also seems to be working here in the same direction.

ZECHLIN

Editor's comment: The U. S. S. R. would naturally put pressure on Lithuania to remain neutral, that is, not to move into Vilnius. Having been assured of the Vilnius region under the secret protocol of August 23, 1939, even though Lithuanian rights in the region had been recognized, the Soviet Government itself probably had a plan to occupy Vilnius and subsequently to use it both as bait for luring Lithuania into a closer association with the U. S. S. R. and as a pacifier for Lithuanian public opinion.

No. 24

The German Minister in Kaunas, Zechlin, to the German Foreign Ministry

Telegram

KAUNAS, September 14, 1939—9:00 p.m.

No. 133 of September 14   Received September 14—11:25 p.m.

With reference to my telegram No. 130 of September 13.

I again explained our viewpoint in the Vilna question to Minister President Černius (several groups apparently missing) which was of a private nature, and pointed out that the rapidly approaching collapse of Poland made a decision imperative. Moreover, an advance of German troops could lead to an early occupation of the Vilna territory by us.

Černius, similar to Raštikis, declared that Lithuania could not emerge from her neutrality at the moment, but that she regarded the Vilna region as a territory "occupied" by Poland, which juridically and ethnically belonged to Lithuania. Armed action by Lithuania was not being considered at the moment. He hoped to arrive at a solution of the problem by registering Lithuanian claims at a possible peace conference or by having the Lithuanian population of the Vilna territory declare for joining Lithuania. He himself admitted, however, that the Lithuanians in the Vilna territory were still oppressed by Poland and were hardly in a position for that, while apparently nothing is being done here in this direction. I will continue my efforts to influence the Government.

ZECHLIN

Editor's comment: Even at this late date, on the eve of the collapse of Poland and under the threat that "an advance of German troops could lead to an early occupation of the Vilna territory by [Germany]", Lithuania remained neutral. Such a firm attitude could only be the result of the firm conviction that there was no place for the use of force in Lithuania's international relations.

No. 25

The Secretariat of the German Foreign Minister to the German Legation in Kaunas

Telegram

MOST URGENT   [BERLIN,] September 16, 1939—7:45 p.m.
No. 219 of September 16   e. o. RM 480.

Teletype from special train Heinrich, September 16 (received 2 p.m.). For Minister Zechlin.

The Foreign Minister asks that you now drop the subject of Vilna; please do not respond should it be taken up again by Lithuania, but rather cut short any conversation on the subject.

SCHMIDT

Editor's comment: At 6:00 PM, September 16, Molotov informed Schulenburg, the German ambassador in Moscow, that Soviet intervention in Poland was imminent. A joint Russo-German communique was in preparation at the time and was published on September 18, declaring that the actions of Soviet and of German troops in Poland were in no way contrary to the interests of Germany or the U. S. S. R. and in no way contradicted the spirit or the letter of the nonaggression treaty concluded between Germany and the U. S. S. R. On the same day, Soviet troops entered Vilnius.

Under the circumstances, the German plan to pressure Lithuania into attacking Poland became obsolete.

No. 26

The German Ambassador in Moscow, Schulenburg, to the German Foreign Ministry

Telegram

MOST URGENT   Moscow, September 16, 1939—10:20 p.m.
TOP SECRET   Received September 17—6:00 a.m.
No. 371 of September 16

With reference to your telegram No. 360 of September 15.

I saw Molotov at 6 o'clock today and carried out instructions. Molotov declared that military intervention by the Soviet Union was imminent—perhaps even tomorrow or the day after. Stalin was at present in consultation with the military leaders and he would this very night, in the presence of Molotov, give me the day and hour of the Soviet advance.

Molotov added that he would present my communication to his Government but he believed that a joint communiqué was no longer needed; the Soviet Government intended to justify its procedure as follows: The Polish State had disintegrated and no longer existed; therefore, all agreements concluded with Poland were void; third powers might try to profit by the chaos which had arisen; the Soviet Union considered itself obligated to intervene to protect its Ukrainian and White Russian brothers and make it possible for these unfortunate people to work in peace.

The Soviet Government intended to publicize the above train of thought by the radio, press, etc., immediately after the Red Army had crossed the border, and at the same time communicate it in an official note to the Polish Ambassador here and to all the missions here.

Molotov conceded that the projected argument of the Soviet Government contained a note that was jarring to German sensibilities but asked us in view of the difficult situation of the Soviet Government not to stumble over this piece of straw. The Soviet Government unfortunately saw no possibility of any other motivation, since the Soviet Union had heretofore not bothered about the plight of its minorities in Poland and had to justify abroad, in some way or other, its present intervention.

In conclusion, Molotov urgently asked for an explanation of what was to become of Vilna. The Soviet Government absolutely wanted to avoid a clash with Lithuania and would therefore like to know whether some agreement had been reached with Lithuania regarding the Vilna region, particularly as to who was to occupy the city.

SCHULENBURG

Editor's comment: Aware of the German pressure on Lithuania to take Vilnius by force, the Soviets wished to consult Germany in this matter, especially since Soviet troops were ready to march into Poland. Since Lithuania persisted in remaining neutral, Ribbentrop informed Zechlin (Document No. 25) to "drop the subject of Vilnius."

No. 27

Note of the Soviet Commissar for Foreign Affairs, Molotov, to the Estonian Minister in Moscow

Mr. Envoy,

In transmitting to you the enclosed note dated September 17, 1939 of the Government of the Union of Soviet Socialist Republics addressed to the Polish Ambassador in Moscow, I have the honor under instructions from my Government to declare to you that the Union of Soviet Socialist Republics will pursue a policy of neutrality in the relations between the Union of Soviet Socialist Republics and Estonia.

Accept, Mr. Envoy, the assurances of highest esteem.

Peoples Commissar for Foreign Affairs
of the U. S. S. R.
(Signed) V. Molotov

September 17, 1939

Envoy Extraordinary and
Minister Plenipotentiary of Estonia
Mr. Rei

Estonian Mission
Moscow

Editor's Comment: According to the testimony of members of the Lithuanian Legation in Washington, an identical note was submitted to the Lithuanian Minister in Moscow (Natkevičius). We publish the Estonian note as a substitute. The Soviet Government, of course, did not inform them of the terms of the Secret Additional Protocol of August 23.

No. 28

Letter of the Soviet Commissar for Foreign Affairs, Molotov, to the Polish Ambassador in Moscow.

Mr. Ambassador:

The Polish-German War has revealed the internal instability of the Polish State. During 10 days of military operations Poland has lost all its industrial regions and cultural centers. Warsaw as the capital of Poland no longer exists. The Polish Government has scattered and gives no signs of life. This means that the Polish State and its Government factually have ceased to exist. By this fact in itself treaties concluded between the Union of Soviet Socialist Republics and Poland have lost their validity. Left to shift for itself and left without leadership Poland has become a convenient field for all kinds of eventualities and unforeseen contingencies which may constitute a threat to the Union of Soviet Socialist Republics. Therefore having been heretofore neutral the Soviet Government can no longer adopt a neutral attitude to these facts. The Soviet Government can also not be indifferent to the fact that the consanguine Ukrainians and White Russians living on the territory of Poland who have been left to the whim of fate should be left defenseless. In view of this situation the Soviet Government has issued instructions to the High Command Red Army to give the order to its forces to cross the Polish frontier and take under their protection the life and property of the population of Western Ukraine and Western White Russia.

At the same time the Soviet Government intends to take all measures in order to extricate the Polish people from the illfated war into which they have been led by their unwise leaders and to give them the possibility of living a peaceful life.

Accept, et cetera.

Peoples Commissar for Foreign
Affairs of the U. S. S. R.

September 17, 1939.   V. Molotov

Ambassador Extraordinary and
Plenipotentiary of Poland

Embassy of Poland
    Moscow

No. 29

The German Foreign Minister, Ribbentrop, to the German Embassy in Moscow

Telegram

No. 399 of September 21   BERLIN, September 21, 1939.
                                        RAM 487.

According to a Russian Army communiqué Vilna has been occupied by Russian troops. In our agreement, Lithuania's interest in this area was recognized by both sides. We therefore assume that it is understood that in the final territorial reorganization in the East the Vilna area will be awarded to Lithuania in a form still to be arranged between us. I answered an informal inquiry by the Lithuanian Government a few days ago to the effect that we had no objection to an incorporation of the Vilna area into the Lithuanian national territory and that we had reason to believe that Russia took the same position. Naturally I did not hint in any way at the existence of secret agreements with Russia.

In your next conversation with MM. Molotov and Stalin please bring up this point in a friendly way and clarify it.

RIBBENTROP

Editor's comment: The award of Vilnius to Lithuania was made in Article 1 of the Secret Additional Protocol of August 23, 1939. German interests are involved here. Being a part of the German sphere of interest under the secret protocol, Lithuania, together with Vilnius, would eventually, in one form or another, become part of the German sphere and extend the German "Lebensraum" by several thousand square kilometers. There is some question how large the territory under discussion actually was. By the peace treaty of July 4, 1920, the Vilnius region, that is, the territory seized by Poland in 1920, was 32,441 km.[2] The Soviets never repudiated the Lithuanian frontier established by that treaty; nevertheless, the "Vilnius region" which they transferred to Lithuania by the Treaty of October 10, 1939 was only 6,880 km². Germany, had it been negotiating for a Lithuania within its sphere of influence, would certainly have demanded the larger area, and the Soviets would have been more willing to accommodate the Reich than a tiny Lithuania already within their own zone of control.

The documents show clearly that as of this date (September 21, 1939), the Secret Protocol of August 23 was still secret, i.e., its terms had not been revealed to Lithuania. The secrecy facilitated the dealings of the two great powers, since it kept alive the hopes of the Baltic peoples that they would be left alone in their neutrality, thus paralyzing their will to resist.

No. 30

The German Ambassador in Moscow, Schulenburg, to the German Foreign Ministry

Telegram

URGENT　　　　　　　　　Moscow, September 22, 1939—11:03 p.m.
No. 412 of September 22　　　　　Received September 23—2:15 a.m.

With reference to telegram No. 399 of September 21.

Molotov told me today that the Soviet Government will adhere to the agreements reached on the Vilna question but does not believe that the time is ripe for discussing details. He had made a statement to the same effect to the Lithuanian Minister, too, adding that the Soviet Union would not be forgetful of Lithuania.

Molotov indicated that the Vilna question was part of the entire

Baltic-complex, and that it would have to be taken into account in the final settlement.

SCHULENBURG

Editor's comment: The Soviet Government was evidently making preparations to proceed with the first step of the "final settlement" of the "entire Baltic complex", the introduction of Soviet military bases in the Baltic region. "The final settlement" became a very complex problem for the Soviets because Lithuania had been excluded from their zone of influence by the secret protocol of August 23, 1939. Returning Vilnius to Lithuania at this time would, in effect, be a major concession to Germany with no *quid pro quo*.

No. 31

Outline of a Proposed Defense Treaty Between the German Reich and the Republic of Lithuania

September 20, 1939.

The Government of the German Reich and the Lithuanian Government, in view of the general political situation in Europe and in order to guarantee the interests of the two countries, which complement each other in every respect, have agreed as follows:

Article I

Without prejudice to her independence as a state, Lithuania stands under the protection of the German Reich.

Article II

In order that this protection may be realized, Germany and Lithuania are concluding a military convention with each other.

Article III

The two Governments shall enter into negotiations with each other at once for the purposes of establishing a close and comprehensive economic relationship between the two countries.

Substance of the Military Agreement

1. The strength, distribution, and equipment of the Lithuanian Army shall be regularly determined in close agreement with the High Command of the Wehrmacht.

2. For the practical execution of provision 1, a permanent German military commission shall be dispatched to Kaunas.

Editor's comment: Now that Germany was assured of the acquisition of Lithuania by the secret protocol of August 23, 1939, it was preparing to incorporate Lithuania into the German protectorate system.

No. 32

Memorandum of the Lithuanian Foreign Minister, Urbšys, to the Lithuanian Minister in Berlin, Škirpa

[Translation from Lithuanian]

TO MINISTER K. ŠKIRPA

In the session held on September 22, 1939 in which you participated the following principles of our policy were established:

1. Lithuania wishes and is firmly determined to maintain fully good neighbour relations with Germany. The recent events in East Europe did not change this attitude of Lithuania.

2. Lithuania, in the presence of actual war and after a sober estimate of her own forces, decided to maintain her neutrality. She will also maintain this attitude in the future. Her neutrality means the determination to be a free and independent State.

3. In accordance with this policy, Lithuania wishes to maintain and is maintaining at the present time good relations with all States, especially with neighbouring States.

4. Lithuania has some unrealized national aspirations, but she seeks their realisation only by peaceful measures. This was confirmed recently by a public statement of the Council of Ministers.

5. Lithuania is grateful to Germany for its recently expressed approval of Lithuanian aspirations.

These principles were established in connection with the invitation of the Reich Foreign Minister addressed to me to visit him. I informed Mr. Zechlin about these principles on September 22, 1939.

J. URBŠYS.

KAUNAS, *September 23, 1939.*

Editor's comment: Still ignorant of its role in the power politics of Germany and the U. S. S. R., Lithuania again bravely restated the basic principles of its foreign policy without committing itself to either side and reiterated its "determination to be a free and independent state."

No. 33

The German Minister in Kaunas, Zechlin, to the German Foreign Ministry

Telegram

MOST URGENT   KAUNAS, September 22, 1939—8:45 p.m.
No. 157 of September 22   Received September 22—11:30 p.m.

With reference to my telegram No. 155 of September 21.

Along with Urbšys' reply that he was extremely grateful for the Reich Foreign Minister's invitation to come to Danzig and would accept it, he also made political statements, obviously the result of the previous deliberations, as follows: Lithuania in the present situation wished to continue to cultivate friendly relations with her neighbors and particularly with Germany. She also wished to continue her policy of neutrality, and to emerge free and independent from the present difficult international situation. Her goal was to enjoy good relations with all other states, too, but she gave primary emphasis to her relations with her neighbors. Lithuania had national aspirations, but, as Minister President Černius had recently declared (see telegram No. 150), she wished to achieve them by peaceful means.

Finally he asked that the thanks of the Lithuanian Government be conveyed to the German Government for the understanding that it had recently shown for Lithuania's national demands.

Presumably these are also the (group garbled) that Urbšys received for tomorrow's visit to Danzig.

ZECHLIN

Editor's comment: By now, Germany was planning to present Lithuania with the Defense Treaty, making it truly a part of Germany's sphere of influence, and was sounding out the attitudes of the Lithuanian Government with this in mind. Lithuania's answer, again, was unequivocal.

No. 34

The German Ambassador in Moscow, Schulenburg, to the German Foreign Ministry

Telegram

MOST URGENT   Moscow, September 25, 1939—10:58 p.m.

TOP SECRET   Received September 26—12:30 a.m.

No. 442 of September 25

Stalin and Molotov asked me to come to the Kremlin at 8 p.m. today. Stalin stated the following: In the final settlement of the Polish question anything that in the future might create friction between Germany and the Soviet Union must be avoided. From this point of view, he considered it wrong to leave an independent residual Poland. He proposed the following: From the territory to the east of the demarcation line, all the Province of Lublin and that portion of the Province of Warsaw which extends to the Bug should be added to our share. In return, we should waive our claim to Lithuania.

Stalin designated this suggestion as a subject for the forthcoming negotiations with the Reich Foreign Minister and added that, if we consented, the Soviet Union would immediately take up the solution of the problem of the Baltic countries in accordance with the Protocol of August 23, and expected in this matter the unstinting support of the German Government. Stalin expressly indicated Estonia, Latvia, and Lithuania, but did not mention Finland.

I replied to Stalin that I would report to my Government.

SCHULENBURG

Editor's comment: The Soviet plan for a "final settlement" of the "entire Baltic Complex", i.e., the incorporation of the whole area into the U.S.S.R., could be realized only if Lithuania were within the Soviet zone. In view of the importance of the matter to Russia, Stalin made the proposals personally. They amounted to a basic revision of the secret protocol of August 23, and gave rise to most intense bargaining.

No. 35

Memorandum of the Director of the Political Department of the German Foreign Ministry, Woermann

BERLIN, September 28, 1939.

The Lithuanian Minister called on me today in considerable anxiety and wished to know whether negotiations were being conducted in Moscow regarding Lithuania or any of the Baltic states. He referred to the conversation with the Reich Foreign Minister, in which the latter had promised him that Germany would take a sympathetic attitude toward Lithuanian aspirations, and he referred also to the willingness of Foreign Minister Urbšys to come to Germany in response to the invitation addressed to him. I told the Minister that I did not know whether Lithuania was being discussed in Moscow. I had reports only on the negotiations between Estonia and the Soviet Union, that would doubtless lead to certain military privileges for the Soviet Union in Estonia. In reply to a further question on this point, I said that I did not know whether the Soviet Union was contemplating something similar for Latvia. I told M. Škirpa, as I did other envoys, that Germany had no part in the negotiations of the Soviet Union with Estonia, but, that, on the contrary, this was a purely Soviet-Estonian matter.

WOERMANN

Editor's comment: Considering that intense negotiations (concluded that day) had been carried on for the last three days specifically concerning the cession of Lithuania to the U. S. S. R., this German statement was obviously a deliberate attempt to mislead the Lithuanians and quiet their suspicions.

The U. S. S. R. was already negotiating with Estonia, providing an indication of what was to happen to the Baltic States.

No. 36

Secret Additional Protocol to the German-Soviet Nonaggression Pact of August 23, 1939

MOSCOW, September 28, 1939.

The undersigned plenipotentiaries declare the agreement of the

Government of the German Reich and the Government of the USSR upon the following:

The Secret Additional Protocol signed on August 23, 1939, shall be amended in item 1 to the effect that the territory of the Lithuanian state falls to the sphere of influence of the USSR, while, on the other hand, the province of Lublin and parts of the province of Warsaw fall to the sphere of influence of Germany (cf. the map attached to the Boundary and Friendship Treaty signed today). As soon as the Government of the USSR shall take special measures on Lithuanian territory to protect its interests, the present German-Lithuanian border, for the purpose of a natural and simple boundary delineation, shall be rectified in such a way that the Lithuanian territory situated to the southwest of the line marked on the attached map falls to Germany.

Further it is declared that the economic agreements now in force between Germany and Lithuania shall not be affected by the measures of the Soviet Union referred to above.

For the Government	By authority of the
of the German Reich:	Government of the USSR:
v. Ribbentrop	W. Molotow

Editor's comment: Stalin's insistence on this territorial shift indicates the strategic and political importance which the Soviet Government attached to Lithuania. Germany's agreement to compromise on such a vital question indicates that Germany was willing to accommodate the Soviet Government even at the cost of sacrificing other German interests, at least for the time being while the situation on the Eastern Front was still unsettled and the Western Front was at a standstill. A clever German ploy was the creation of the "Lithuanian Strip," a piece of Southwestern Lithuania to which Germany retained the title. This was a string attached to the Soviet possession of Lithuania for which the Soviets would have to pay dearly.

No. 37

German-Soviet Boundary and Friendship Treaty of September 28, 1939

The Government of the German Reich and the Government of the U. S. S. R. consider it exclusively their task, after the collapse of the former Polish state, to re-establish peace and order in these territories and to assure to the peoples living there a peaceful life in keeping with their national character. To this end, they have agreed upon the following:

Article 1

The Government of the German Reich and the Government of the U. S. S. R. determine as the boundary of their respective national interests in the territory of the former Polish state the line marked on the attached map, which shall be described in more detail in a supplementary protocol.

Article 2

Both parties recognize the boundary of the respective national interests established in Article 1 as definitive and shall reject any interference of third powers in this settlement.

Article 3

The necessary reorganization of public administration will be effected in the areas west of the line specified in 1 by the Government of the German Reich, in the areas east of the line by the Government of the U. S. S. R.*

Article 4

This treaty shall be ratified and the ratifications shall be exchanged in Berlin as soon as possible. The treaty becomes effective upon signature.

Done in duplicate, in the German and Russian languages.

For the Government of the German Reich:	By authority of the Government of the U. S. S. R.
J. RIBBENTROP	V. MOLOTOV

Confidential Protocol

*   The Government of the U. S. S. R. shall place no obstacles in the way of Reich nationals and other persons of German descent residing in the territories under its jurisdiction, if they desire to migrate to Germany or to the territories under German jurisdiction. It agrees that such removals shall be carried out by agents of the Government of the Reich in cooperation with the competent local authorities and that the property rights of the emigrants shall be protected.

A corresponding obligation is assumed by the Government of the German Reich in respect to the persons of Ukrainian or White Russian descent residing in the territories under its jurisdiction.

Moscow, September 28, 1939.   By authority of the
  For the Government   Government of the U. S. S. R.:
  of the German Reich: W. MOLOTOW
    J. RIBBENTROP

No. 38

Declaration of the Government of the German Reich and the Government of the USSR

Moscow, September 28, 1939

After the Government of the German Reich and the Government of the USSR have, by means of the treaty signed today, definitely settled the problems arising from the disintegration of the Polish state and have thereby created a firm foundation for a lasting peace in Eastern Europe, they mutually express their conviction that it would serve the true interest of all peoples to put an end to the state of war existing at present between Germany on the one side and England and France on the other. Both Governments will therefore direct their common efforts, jointly with other friendly powers if occasion arises, toward attaining this goal as soon as possible.

Should, however, the efforts of the two Governments remain fruitless, this would demonstrate the fact that England and France are responsible for the continuation of the war, whereupon, in case of the continuation of the war, the Governments of Germany and of the USSR shall engage in mutual consultations with regard to necessary measures.

For the Government   By authority of the
of the German Reich: Government of the USSR:
  v. Ribbentrop   W. Molotov

No. 39

Protocol to the German-Soviet Boundary and Friendship Treaty of September 28, 1939.

Moscow, October 4, 1939

The undersigned, being duly empowered thereto by the German Government and the Government of the USSR, pursuant to article I of the Boundary and Friendship Treaty concluded in Moscow on September 28, 1939, between Germany and the USSR, have agreed upon the following:

I

The boundary line between the respective national interests in the territory of the former Polish state shall have the following course:

Beginning at the point located on the Igorka River at the mouth of a nameless brook which comes before the village of Pschetok and which ·flows into the Igorka River at a distance of about 2,300 metres northeast of the intersection of this river with the Shondowy-Kopzewo road, the boundary shall run in a southwesterly direction, on a straight line to be determined, to the point located on the Tschernaja Gantscha River opposite the northwestern edge of the village of Shondowy.

Thence the boundary ascends along the Tschernaja Gantscha River to the mouth of the Marycha River. From this mouth the boundary shall follow a southwesterly direction, on a straight line to be determined, to the northern shore of Jedryno Lake. Thence the boundary shall follow a straight line to be determined to the point located opposite the mouth of the Wolkushanka River on the Tschernaja Gantscha River, and further, ascending this latter river, to the point lying south of the village of Ostrynske. Thence the boundary shall run at first in a southwesterly and then in a northwesterly direction along the ravine to its northwestern end and then, on a straight line to be determined, running in a northwesterly direction to the point lying at the northeastern edge of the village of Tscharny Brud. From here the boundary shall run in a northwesterly direction, on a straight line to be determined, to the railroad bridge across the Blisna River at the northern edge of the village of Schtschebra so that the village of Schtschebra shall be on the

USSR side and the village of Blisna on the German side. Continuing the boundary shall descend the Blisna River to the junction of the roads Suwalki-Schtschebra II and Ratschki Schtschebra II, so that the fork of the road and the village of Schtschebra II, shall remain on the German side and the village of Schtschebra I on the USSR side.

Thence the boundary shall continue in a northwesterly direction, on a straight line to be determined, to a point located north of the village of Topilowka and then shall bend slightly in a southwesterly direction and run, on a straight line to be determined, to a point located on the former Russo-German Reich border, which is located at a distance of about 900 metres southwest of the village of Pruska Mala, which shall remain on the German side.

Thence the boundary shall continue generally in a south-westerly direction along the former Russo-German border up to the point where the latter intersects the Pissa River.

Thence the aforesaid boundary shall descend along the Pissa River to its confluence with the Narew River and then descend this river to the mouth of a nameless brook which flows into the Narew River between the town of Ostrolenka and the village of Ostrowa. Thence the boundary shall ascend the brook to the eastern edge of the village of Lawy (South). From the eastern edge of the village of Lawy (South), the boundary shall continue in a southeasterly direction, on a straight line to be determined, to the southern edge of the village of Sussk, and continue, also on a straight line to be determined, to a point situated on the Troschyn-Rabendy road approximately 400 metres southwest of the edge of the village of Troschyn. Thence the boundary runs in a south-southeasterly direction, on a straight line to be determined, to the crossroads south of the village of Stylengi and then shall turn towards the southeast and continue, on a straight line to be determined, to a point on the Osh River south of the village of Butschin, so that this village shall remain on the USSR side, and the village of Saoshe on the German side.

Thence the boundary shall ascend the Osh River to a tributary on the left which flows into the Osh River between the villages of Sokolowo and Rogowek, then along this tributary to a point located 1,200 metres east of the village of Malinowa-Stare. Thence the boundary shall continue in a southeasterly direction, on a straight line to be determined, to a point on the Ostruw-Masowezka-Schabikowo road, approximately 700 metres south of the brick works, so that the Salesze estate, the village of Lubejewo-Nowe and the aforesaid brick works shall be on the

USSR side; the village of Salesze, the village of Pshiimy and the village of Lubejewo on the German side.

Thence the boundary shall continue in a southeasterly direction, on a straight line to be determined, up to a point on the Brotschisko River, approximately 500 metres northwest of the western edge of the village of Nowa Zolotorija, so that the village of Ugnewo shall remain on the German side.

Thence, the boundary shall continue in a southeasterly direction, on a straight line to be determined, to a point on the road, approximately 350 metres south of the village of Petzki.

Thence the boundary shall run in a southeasterly direction to a point on the Sapadnyi Bug River approximately 1,500 metres east of the edge of the village of Nadbushne.

Thence the boundary shall ascend the Sapadnyi Bug River to the mouth of the Solokija River.

From the mouth of the Solokija River, the boundary shall run along this river to a point located opposite the north-western edge of the village of Ugnuw.

Thence the boundary shall continue in a northwesterly direction, on a straight line to be determined, to the southern edge of the village of Chodywantze, so that the village of Pschedno and the village of Nowossjulki shall remain on the USSR side and the village of Mysljatin and Chodywantze on the German side.

Thence the boundary shall continue in a northwesterly direction, on a straight line to be determined, to a point located approximately 1,300 metres north of the northeast edge of the village of Shurawze.

Then the boundary shall continue in a southwesterly direction, on a straight line to be determined, to a point located on the Krinitza Brook, opposite the southeastern edge of the village of Shilka.

Thence the boundary shall continue in a southwesterly direction, on a straight line to be determined, to the southeastern edge of the village of Bshesina, then the boundary shall continue in a southwesterly direction, on a straight line to be determined, to a point approximately 800 metres northwest of the village of Pisuny.

Thence the boundary shall continue in a southwesterly direction, on a straight line to be determined, up to Luwtscha Brook and shall reach this brook opposite the southwestern edge of the village of Garby and thence shall ascend along this brook up to the Sigly farm.

Thence the boundary shall continue in a southwestern direction, on a straight line to be determined, to a point on the Gnoinik Brook opposite the southeastern edge of the village of Gorajetz and shall then descend this brook to its intersection with the Gorajetz-Zetschanuw road.

Thence the boundary shall continue in a southwesterly direction, on a straight line to be determined, to the eastern edge of the village of Zetschanuw.

Thence the boundary shall continue in a southwesterly direction, on a straight line to be determined, to the western edge of the village of Dachnuw, so that the Novy farm shall remain on the German side.

Thence the boundary shall continue in a southwesterly direction, on a straight line to be determined, to the southeastern edge of the village of Futory and thence approximately westward, on a straight line to be determined, to a point on the northwestern edge of the village of Sabjala, so that the Ljatoschin farm and the village of Uschkowtze shall remain on the USSR side.

Thence the boundary shall continue in a northwesterly direction, on a straight line to be determined, to a point on the Pschikopa Brook opposite the northwestern edge of the village of Dobtscha, so that the village of Milkuw shall remain on the USSR side and the village of Degelnja on the German side.

Thence the boundary descends the course of the Pschikopa Brook to its confluence with the Pschiluben River and then follows this river downstream to its confluence with the San River.

Thence the boundary shall ascend the course of the San River to its source, so that the Sjanki and Ushok railroad stations shall remain on the USSR side.

Note 1: At nonnavigable rivers and brooks the boundary line shall be the middle of the main branch of such rivers and brooks. At navigable rivers, the boundary line shall be the middle of the main channel of navigation.

Note 2: Those portions of the boundary which have been determined by lines to be agreed upon, shall be defined in detail at the demarcation of the boundary. [. . .].

II

The boundary line determined in section I of this Protocol shall be marked on the ground by a mixed German-Russian commission.

The commission shall erect boundary monuments, prepare a detailed description of this line and enter it on a map to the scale of 1:25,000.

This commission shall commence its work on October 9 of this year.

The description of the course of the boundary prepared by the foregoing commission and a map of this line shall be confirmed by both Governments.

III

This Protocol, which is subject to ratification, takes effect immediately upon signature. The exchange of ratification shall take place in Berlin within the shortest time possible.

This Protocol has been done in four copies, of which two are in the German and two in the Russian language, both texts being equally authentic.

Signed in Moscow, on October 4, 1939.

By authority of the   For the Government
Government of the USSR: of the German Reich:
   W. Molotov   F. Schulenburg

No. 40

The German Ambassador in Moscow, Schulenburg, to the German Foreign Ministry

Telegram
MOST URGENT   Moscow, October 3, 1939—7:04 p.m.
TOP SECRET   Received October 3—11:10 p.m.
No. 463 of October 3

Molotov summoned me to his office at 2 p.m. today, in order to communicate to me the following:

The Soviet Government would tell the Lithuanian Foreign Minister, who arrives today, that, within the framework of an amicable settlement of mutual relations (probably similar to the one with Estonia), the Soviet Government was willing to cede the city of Vilna and its environs to Lithuania, while at the same time the Soviet Government would let Lithuania understand that it must cede the indicated portion of its territory to Germany. M. inquired what formal procedure we had in mind for carrying this out. His idea was the simultaneous signing of a Soviet-Lithuanian protocol on Vilna and a German-Lithuanian protocol on the Lithuanian area to be ceded to us.

I replied that this suggestion did not appeal to me. It seemed to me more logical that the Soviet Government should exchange Vilna for the strip to be ceded to us and then hand this strip over to us. M. did not seem quite in accord with my proposal but was willing to let me ask for the viewpoint of my Government and give him a reply by tomorrow noon.

Molotov's suggestion seems to me harmful, as in the eyes of the world it would make us appear as "robbers" of Lithuanian territory, while the Soviet Government figures as the donor. As I see it, only my suggestion can be considered at all. However, I would ask you to consider whether it might not be advisable for us, by a separate secret German-Soviet protocol, to forego the cession of the Lithuanian strip of territory until the Soviet Union actually incorporates Lithuania, an idea on which, I believe, the arrangement concerning Lithuania was originally based.

SCHULENBURG

Editor's comment: The wrangling over the transfer of the Lithuanian Strip threatened to upset the whole German-Soviet Baltic deal. Having divided Lithuania by the secret protocol of September 28, and having ceded the Lithuanian Strip to Germany, Molotov very cleverly offered the suggestion that Germany obtain actual possession of the strip by means of a treaty with Lithuania. In this way, the U. S. S. R. could wash its hands of any responsibility for the transaction. Schulenburg rejected the offer, fearing to injure Germany's reputation "in the eyes of the world," as if that reputation had been very high in October, 1939.

No. 41

The German Foreign Minister, Ribbentrop, to the German Ambassador in Moscow, Schulenburg

Telegram

TOP SECRET   BERLIN, October 4, 1939.
No. 488

With reference to your telegram No. 463.

I, too, consider inopportune the method Molotov suggested for the cession of the Lithuanian strip of territory. On the contrary, please ask Molotov not to discuss this cession of territory with the Lithuanians at present, but rather to have the Soviet Government assume the obligation *toward Germany* to leave this strip of territory unoccupied in the event of a posting of Soviet forces in Lithuania, which may possibly be contemplated, and furthermore to leave it to Germany to determine the date on which the cession of the territory should be formally effected. An understanding to this effect should be set forth in a secret exchange of letters between yourself and Molotov.

REICH FOREIGN MINISTER

[Notes:] As directed by the Reich Foreign Minister, this telegram is being dispatched *at once* with his signature. GAUS, October 4.

I telephoned the contents of the telegram in veiled language at 11 a.m. to Count Schulenburg. He fully understood the instruction. G[AUS], October 4.

Editor's comment: Ribbentrop, of course, agreed with Schulenburg's recommendation (cf. Document No. 40) that the transfer of the Lithuanian Strip to Germany be made the responsibility of the U. S. S. R. One can see from the Joint Proclamation of September 28 (Document No. 38) that Germany still had some hopes that Britain and France would overlook the recent destruction of Poland and make peace. It made no sense for Germany to aggravate the international situation further by forcing Lithuania, perhaps even by use of arms, to relinquish as insignificant a piece of territory as the Lithuanian Strip.

No. 42

The German Ambassador in Moscow, Schulenburg, to the German Foreign Ministry

Telegram

MOST URGENT   Moscow, October 5, 1939—12:10 a.m.

TOP SECRET   Received October 5—4:55 a.m.

No. 470 of October 4

With reference to my telegram No. 463 of October 3.

Immediately after Under State Secretary Gaus' first telephone call, I transmitted to Molotov this morning the request not to divulge to the Lithuanian Foreign Minister anything regarding the German-Soviet understanding concerning Lithuania. M. asked me to see him at 5 p. m. and told me, that, unfortunately, he had been obliged yesterday to inform the Lithuanian Foreign Minister of this understanding, since he could not, out of loyalty to us, act otherwise. The Lithuanian delegation had been extremely dismayed and sad; they had declared that the loss of this area in particular would be especially hard to bear since many prominent leaders of the Lithuanian people came from that part of Lithuania. This morning at 8 a. m., the Lithuanian Foreign Minister had flown back to Kaunas, intending to return to Moscow in 1 or 2 days.

I said that I would immediately notify my Government by telephone, whereupon I called Herr Gaus. An hour later Molotov informed me that Stalin *personally* requested the German Government *not* to insist *for the moment* upon the cession of the strip of Lithuanian territory.

SCHULENBURG

Editor's comment: Since the Soviet design to incorporate Lithuania into the U. S. S. R. was not yet known, and the Lithuanian Government still retained the hope that territorial integrity would be preserved, the cession of the Strip to Germany would have appeared to Lithuania only as a terrible blow to the country's heritage — the abandonment of the cradle of the Lithuanian national renaissance. This would have greatly undermined Soviet credibility and prestige, and destroyed any confidence which the Russians might hope to preserve in the minds of the Lithuanian people.

No. 43

The German Foreign Minister, Ribbentrop, to the German Ambassador in Moscow, Schulenburg

Telegram

VERY URGENT   BERLIN, October 5, 1939—3:43 a.m.
STRICTLY SECRET   Received Moscow, October 5, 1939—11:55 a.m.
No. 497 of October 4

Referring to today's telephonic communication from the Ambassador.

The Legation in Kaunas is being instructed as follows:

1) Solely for your personal information, I am apprising you of the following: At the time of the signing of the German-Russian Non-Aggression Pact on August 23, a strictly secret delimitation of the respective spheres of influence in Eastern Europe was also undertaken. In accordance therewith, Lithuania was to belong to the German sphere

of influence, while in the territory of the former Polish state, the so-called four-river line, Pissa-Narew-Vistula-San, was to constitute the border. Even then I demanded that the district of Vilna go to Lithuania, to which the Soviet Government consented. At the negotiations concerning the Boundary and Friendship Treaty on September 28, the settlement was amended to the extent that Lithuania, including the Vilna area, was included in the Russian sphere of influence, for which in turn, in the Polish area, the province of Lublin and large portions of the province of Warsaw, including the pocket of territory of Suwalki, fell within the German sphere of influence. Since, by the inclusion of the Suwalki tract in the German sphere of influence a difficulty in drawing the border line resulted, we agreed that in case the Soviets should take special measures in Lithuania, a small strip of territory in the southwest of Lithuania, accurately marked on the map, should fall to Germany.

2) Today Count von der Schulenburg reports that Molotov, contrary to our own intentions, notified the Lithuanian Foreign Minister last night of the confidential arrangement. Please now, on your part, inform the Lithuanian Government, orally and in strict confidence, of the matter, as follows:

As early as at the signing of the German-Soviet Non-Aggression Pact of August 23, in order to avoid complications in Eastern Europe, conversations were held between ourselves and the Soviet Government concerning the delimitation of German and Soviet spheres of influence. In these conversations I had recommended restoring the Vilna district to Lithuania, to which the Soviet Government gave me its consent. In the negotiations concerning the Boundary and Friendship Treaty of September 28, as is apparent from the German-Soviet boundary demarcation which was published, the pocket of territory of Suwalki jutting out between Germany and Lithuania had fallen to Germany. As this created an intricate and impractical boundary, I had reserved for Germany a border correction in this area, whereby a small strip of Lithuanian territory would fall to Germany. The award of Vilna to Lithuania was maintained in these negotiations also. You are now authorized to make it known to the Lithuanian Government that the Reich Government does not consider the question of this border revision timely at this moment. We make the proviso, however, that the Lithuanian Government treat this matter as strictly confidential. End of instruction for Kaunas.

I request you to inform M. Molotov of our communication to the Lithuanian Government. Further, please request of him, as already indicated in the preceding telegram, that the border strip of Lithuanian territory involved be left free in the event of a possible posting of Soviet troops in Lithuania and also that it be left to Germany to determine the date of the implementing of the agreement concerning the cession to Germany of the territory involved. Both of these points at issue should be set forth in a secret exchange of letters between yourself and Molotov.

RIBBENTROP

Editor's comment: This document reveals the sinister way in which the two powers treated their small, neutral neighbor, carving up its territory, wrangling over the spoils, and covering their actions by hypocritical declarations.

At this date the Lithuanian Government was not actually aware of the details of the secret protocols of August 23 and September 28. The U.S.S.R. had informed the Lithuanian Government of the Strip arrangements, however, and Zechlin was forced to declare that Germany would not demand the Strip from Lithuania for the time being. Germany thought this would make Lithuania very happy, since it involved not only preserving its territorial integrity, but also the cradle of the Lithuanian national renaissance.

No. 44

The German Minister in Kaunas, Zechlin, to the German Foreign Ministry

Telegram

MOST URGENT   KAUNAS, October 5, [1939]—7:55 p.m.
No. 175 of October 5   Received October 5—10:30 p.m.

With reference to telegram No. 252 of October 5 [4]

Bizauskas sent for me today even before I could ask for an appointment with the Foreign Minister as instructed in telegram No. 252; he first made excuses for M. Urbšys, who was completely occupied today with continuous discussions in the Cabinet and therefore unfortunately could not speak with me himself. He then informed me that Molotov had told Urbšys that Germany had laid claim to a strip of Lithuanian territory, the limits of which included the city and district of Naumiestis and continued on past the vicinity of Mariampolè. This had made a deep and painful impression on Lithuania, and Urbšys had flown back to Kaunas partly because of this information, which he had not wished to transmit by telephone.

The Lithuanian Government has instructed Škirpa to make inquiries in Berlin.

I told him that in the Moscow discussions on the delimitation of the German and Soviet spheres of interest, the Reich Foreign Minister had advocated giving the Vilna area to Lithuania and had also obtained the Soviet Government's agreement in the matter. While Lithuania had the prospect of such a great increase in territory a difficult and impracticable boundary in the vicinity of the Suwalki tip had come into existence because of the German-Soviet border division. Therefore the idea of a small border rectification at the German-Lithuanian frontier had also emerged in the course of these negotiations; but I could inform him that the German Government did not consider the question pressing. Bizauskas received this information with visible relief and asked me to transmit the thanks of the Lithuanian Government on this score to the Reich Government. Furthermore he asked on his part that the matter be kept strictly secret, which I promised him.

I might add that since the fixing of the German-Soviet frontier became known, political quarters here have had great hopes of obtaining the Suwalki tip from Germany

ZECHLIN

Editor's comment: Zechlin's communication to the Lithuanian Government that "only the idea of a small border rectification. . . emerged" from the discussions in Moscow is a gross misrepresentation of the secret protocol of September 28, by virtue of which Lithuania was exchanged with the U. S. S. R. for two Polish provinces, and the Lithuanian Strip was retained by Germany.

No. 45

Memorandum by the State Secretary of the German Foreign Ministry, Weizsacker

SECRET
St.S. No. 786

BERLIN, October 5, 1939.

The Lithuanian Minister called on me this evening in order, as was expected, to inquire about German claims to a strip of land in southwestern Lithuania. M. Škirpa, however, even when he entered, had a friendlier appearance than was to be expected. For Minister Zechlin had in the meantime delivered information in Kaunas as instructed, so that I did not need to go any further into the questions put by M. Škirpa. I restricted myself to a brief mention of today's telegraphic instructions to Herr Zechlin. Since M. Škirpa expressed to me the satisfaction of his Government that we had withdrawn our claim, I stressed that the announcement of our needs was "not at the moment pressing." (It is noteworthy that M. Škirpa knew and traced exactly on the map of Poland that happened to be spread out before us the line agreed upon by us in our secret protocol with the Russians.)

The Minister then gave the further information that the Russians expected to get an assistance pact with Lithuania as well as permission to station Russian garrisons, at the same time agreeing in principle to the joining of Vilna and environs to Lithuania. M. Škirpa asked me if I had any ideas or suggestions to give in this regard. I stated that I was not informed and added that in connection with our negotiations in Moscow German interests had not been claimed beyond the Russo-German boundary line in the east known to M. Škirpa.

In conclusion the Minister asked to be given any possible suggestions. Herr Urbšys was still remaining in Kowno today and tomorrow; he himself—Skirpa—was at the disposal of the Reich Foreign Minister at any time.

WEIZSÄCKER

Editor's comment: Mr. Škirpa "expressed satisfaction" and "had a friendlier appearance than expected" not because he agreed with the outrageous territorial deal over his country, but simply because he did not know of the role assigned to Lithuania by the secret protocols of August 23 and September 28. Weizsäcker's remark that German claims to the Lithuanian Strip were *"not at the moment pressing"* should have been realistically interpreted by Škirpa to mean that Germany had withdrawn its claim as a matter of temporary expediency—in fact, so as not to risk the exposure of the secret arrangements with Russia to Lithuania and the world.

No. 46

The German Foreign Minister, Ribbentrop, to the German Ministers in Tallinn, Riga and Helsinki

Telegram

MOST URGENT BERLIN, October 7, 1939.
(1) To Tallinn, No. 257
(2) To Riga, No. 328
(3) To Helsinki, No. 318

Exclusively for the Minister personally.

Supplementing our telegrams No. 241 to (1), No. 303 to (2) and No. 305 to (3), I am communicating the following to you in strict secrecy and for your personal information only:

During the Moscow negotiations with the Soviet Government the question of delimiting the spheres of interest of both countries in Eastern Europe was discussed in strict confidence, not only with reference to the area of the former Polish state, but also with reference to the countries of Lithuania, Latvia, Estonia, and Finland. At the same time the delimitation of the spheres of interest was agreed upon for *the eventuality of a territorial and political reorganization in* these areas. The borderline fixed for this purpose for the territory of the former Polish state is the line designated in article 1 of the German-Soviet Boundary and Friendship Treaty of September 28 and publicly announced. Otherwise, the line is identical with the German-Lithuanian frontier. Thus it follows that Lithuania, Latvia, Estonia, and Finland do not belong to the German sphere of interest in the sense indicated above.

You are requested to refrain, as heretofore, from any explanations on this subject.

THE FOREIGN MINISTER

Editor's comment: The document clearly reveals the partition of the Baltic area between Germany and Russia. The inclusion of Finland in the Baltic bloc ceded to the Soviet sphere is also clearly shown.

Ribbentrop's pronouncement that "the delimitation of the spheres of interest was agreed upon for the eventuality of a territorial and political reorganization in these areas" is a strong indication that in the process of implementing the agreements, the eventual Sovietization of the countries involved was understood and expected by both parties.

No. 47

Note of Chairman of the Council of People's Commissars of the USSR, Molotov, to the German Ambassador in Moscow, Schulenburg.

SECRET   MOSCOW, October 8, 1939.

MR. AMBASSADOR: I have the honor hereby to confirm that in connection with the Secret Additional Protocol, concluded on September 29 [*28*], 1939, between the U. S. S. R. and Germany, concerning Lithuania, the following understanding exists between us:

1) The Lithuanian territory mentioned in the Protocol and marked on the map attached to the Protocol shall not be occupied in case forces of the Red Army should be stationed [in Lithuania];

2) It shall be left to Germany to determine the date for the implementing of the agreement concerning the cession to Germany of the above-mentioned Lithuanian territory.

Please accept, Mr. Ambassador, the expression of my highest consideration.

W. MOLOTOW

Editor's comment: Under the provisions of the secret protocol of September 28, Germany considered itself to have sovereignty over the Lithuanian Strip. The introduction of Soviet troops into the area would have been viewed by Germany as a violation of both the secret protocol of September 28, and the Nonaggression Pact of August 23, and could have provoked a serious conflict between the two powers.

No. 48

Excerpts from Statements by Urbšvs, Molotov and Stalin Pertaining to the Negotiation of the Soviet-Lithuanian Mutual Assistance Pact of October 10, 1939.

Urbšys:
Oct. 7,

In order to make the Lithuanian point of view clearer, let me go back a little into the past. At first, we shall point out that Lithuania is not a new entity, but is a nation which in the past was independent and one which never lost its longing for liberty. Under the Tsarist regime, the liberty of the Lithuanian nation was restricted; printing was banned, and non-Lithuanians in Lithuanian territory were favored by the Russian authorities. When the Revolution broke out, the situation changed in the sense that this movement had raised the principle of the self-determination of nations. By virtue of this principle, we concluded the Treaty of Peace in 1920. In the Treaty we can read that it was concluded freely and for all time (na vechnyie vremena). Thus, we should consider it as a logical result of freedom of self-determination by the two parties. Such a friendly and free conclusion of the Treaty of Peace inaugurated Lithuanian-Soviet relations which from the conclusion of that Treaty up to now were very good. The Soviet attitude toward Lithuania contributed much toward maintaining good and friendly relations. The Soviet Union never infringed upon Lithuanian internal affairs. She never caused us any trouble in foreign relations rather, to the contrary, she helped us much. Therefore, there is in Lithuania an abundance of friendly and favorable sentiments toward the Soviet Union. The ideas, propagated by the Soviet leaders on the peaceful intercourse of nations, based on right and justice, were always close to us.

However, the mutual-assistance pact proposed by the Soviet Union, would, in the opinion of the Lithuanian Government, infringe upon the traditional friendly relations and sow mistrust between the two States. The establishment of foreign troops in our land in time of peace would depress our nation and would make their attitude hostile toward the Soviet Union. The nation would not comprehend the establishment of the Soviet bases except as a military occupation of Lithuania. To station a Soviet army on Lithuanian territory would infringe upon the independence of Lithuania. That would create a source of permanent misunderstanding between the Soviet army and the Lithuanian civilian population. The lodging and maintenance of such an army, under present conditions, would create problems not easily solved. From the international point of view, the presence of Soviet troops in Lithuania would degrade Lithuania to a vassal state. Therefore, the Government of Lithuania proposes a mutual-assistance pact, which will not only satisfy the requisites of Lithuanian security, but which will permit it to maintain its neutrality.

Molotov:
Oct. 7,

Gentlemen, Lithuania should not forget under what conditions

Europe is now living. The present war has not unfolded entirely; it is difficult to forecast its repercussions and, therefore, the Soviet Union considers its security. We do not know what can happen in the West. The Germans can turn against us, if they would win the war. The aims of England are not clear either, if Germany should lose. You should not forget that Lithuania has a long frontier with Germany and that Lithuania should not look thoughtlessly upon its defense. Lithuania wishes to separate itself from Latvia and Estonia in regard to the security of the Soviet Union, but I should point out that Lithuania is much more important to the Soviet Union than Latvia and Estonia.

Stalin:
Oct. 8,

In any case we consider the creation of military bases on Lithuanian territory as a symbolic gesture. They can only be the most precious element in the service of Lithuanian security. If your Government is frightened at the figure of 34,000 soldiers of the Red Army, we can make concessions by asking for bases for 20,000 men * * * only. If Lithuania had fallen under German rule, she would without a doubt have become a German protectorate, whereas we respect the independence of the Lithuanian State. We are disposed to defend its territorial integrity.

Editor's comment: The new assurances of Soviet good intentions and respect for Lithuania's independence by Molotov and Stalin found the Lithuanians eager to be duped, since Soviet goodwill was Lithuania's only hope for maintaining independence. The military bases imposed on Estonia and Latvia were used as a means of coercion against Lithuania, which was told not to isolate herself, but to follow her sister Baltic Republics, especially as Lithuania was "much more" important to the security of the Soviet Union than Latvia or Estonia. The emphasis on the importance of Lithuania to Soviet security explains the reasons for Stalin's insistence on the exchange of Lithuania for the Polish provinces of Lublin and Warsaw. The Soviet Government foresaw Lithuanian resistance, and for this reason solicited and obtained military bases from the more isolated and vulnerable Estonia and Latvia first, using them to provide more pressure on Lithuania.

No. 49

Treaty on the Transfer of Vilnius and Soviet-Lithuanian Mutual Assistance

10 *October* 1939   *Mirovoe Khoziaistvo,* 1939, 10, p. 5

The Presidium of the Supreme Soviet of the USSR on the one side, and the President of the Lithuanian Republic on the other,

For the purpose of developing the friendly relations established by the peace treaty of 12 July 1920, based on the recognition of independent State existence and of non-intervention in the internal affairs of the other party;

Recognizing that the peace treaty of 12 July 1920, and the pact on non-aggression and the peaceful settlement of conflicts of 28 September 1926, continue to provide a firm basis for their mutual relations and undertakings;

Convinced that it is in the interests of both contracting parties to define the exact conditions of ensuring mutual security and to make a just settlement of the question to which State the city of Vilna and the Vilna region (unlawfully wrested from Lithuania by Poland) belong;

Have found it necessary to conclude the following treaty on the transfer of the city of Vilna and the Vilna region to the Lithuanian Republic and on mutual assistance between the Soviet Union and Lithuania, and have appointed for this purpose as their plenipotentiaries;

The Presidium of the Supreme Soviet of the USSR: V. M. Molotov, Chairman of the Council of People's Commissars and People's Commissar for Foreign Affairs;

The President of the Lithuanian Republic: Jouzas Urbšys, Minister for Foreign Affairs; who, having presented their credentials, which were found to be drawn up in due form and proper order, agreed on the following:

Article I

For the purpose of consolidating the friendship between the USSR and Lithuania, the city of Vilna and the Vilna region are transferred by the Soviet Union to the Lithuanian Republic and included in the territory of the

Lithuanian State, the frontier between the USSR and the Lithuanian Republic being established in accordance with the map appended hereto, which frontier shall be specified in more detail in a supplementary protocol.

Article II

The Soviet Union and the Lithuanian Republic undertake to render each other every assistance, including military assistance, should Lithuania be attacked or in danger of attack, or should the Soviet Union be attacked or in danger of attack through Lithuanian territory by any European Power.

Article III

The Soviet Union undertakes to render the Lithuanian army assistance in armaments and other military equipment on favourable terms.

Article IV

The Soviet Union and the Lithuanian Republic undertake jointly to protect the State frontiers of Lithuania, for which purpose the Soviet Union is granted the right to maintain at its own expense, at points in the Lithuanian Republic to be established by mutual agreement, Soviet land and air armed forces of strictly limited strength. The exact locations of these troops and the boundaries within which they may be quartered, their strength at each particular point, and also all other questions of an economic, administrative, or jurisdictional character, and other questions arising in connection with the presence of Soviet armed forces on Lithuanian territory under the present treaty, shall be regulated by special agreements.

The sites and buildings necessary for this purpose shall be allotted by the Lithuanian Government on lease at a reasonable price.

Article V

In the event of the danger of an attack on Lithuania or on the USSR through Lithuanian territory, the two contracting parties shall immediately discuss the resulting situation and take all measures found necessary by mutual agreement to secure the inviolability of the territories of the contracting parties.

Article VI

The two contracting parties undertake not to conclude any alliance or to participate in any coalition directed against either of the contracting parties.

Article VII

The coming into force of the present treaty shall not affect in any way the sovereign rights of the contracting parties, in particular their State organization, economic and social system, military measures, and the principle of nonintervention in internal affairs generally. The locations of the Soviet land and air armed forces (article III of the present treaty) remain in all circumstances a component part of the territory of the Lithuanian Republic.

Article VIII

The provisions of the present treaty concerned with undertakings for mutual assistance between the USSR and the Lithuanian Republic (articles II to VII) shall remain in force for fifteen years, and, unless one of the contracting parties finds it necessary to denounce the provisions of this treaty established for a specified term one year prior to the expiration of that term, they shall automatically continue in force for the next ten years.

Article IX

The present treaty comes into force upon exchange of instruments of ratification. Exchange of these instruments shall take place in Kaunas within six days from the day of signature of this treaty.

The present treaty is made in two originals, in the Russian and Lithuanian languages, at Moscow, 10 October 1939.

V. MOLOTOV

JUOZAS URBŠYS

Editor's comment: It should be noted here that, in spite of plans to incorporate Lithuania, Latvia and Estonia into the U.S.S.R., the Soviet Government still declared in the mutual assistance pact that the Treaty of Peace of July 12, 1920 and the Nonaggression Treaty of September 28, 1926 "continue[d] to provide a firm basis for their [the U.S.S.R.'s and Lithuania's] mutual relations and undertakings." Meanwhile, by the secret agreements of August 23 and September 28, 1939, the U.S.S.R. and Germany undertook to divide the country. The introduction of military bases and personnel on Lithuanian territory is the obvious first step in the incorporation of Lithuania into the U.S.S.R.

No. 50

Protocol Between Lithuania and the USSR of October 27, 1939

In accordance with the Protocol concluded October 27, 1939 by virtue of the Treaty on the Return of Vilnius and the Region of Vilnius to the Republic of Lithuania and of Mutual Assistance between Lithuania and the USSR of October 10, 1939, the Russo-Lithuanian frontier follows the following line: from the point of the former Latvo-Polish frontier, a point located on the western edge of the village of Liudvinavas, the frontier runs in an agreed upon straight line to the south as far as the lake of Druksisi (Drysviaty), and west as far as the extremity of the island of Sosnovecas, leaving on the Soviet side of it the village of Nurvenai (Nurvianca) and the island of Sosnovecas, and on the side of the Republic of Lithuania the property of Nistauciai (Mistovce) and the property of Sorbaline.

From the south-western extremity of the island of Sosnoveca, the frontier turns slightly to the south-west and follows the straight line agreed upon as far as the mouth of the river Druksisi (Drysviata).

From there the frontier is traced by the Druksisi (Drysviata) as far as the mouth of the river Apvardele (Opivardka) and further it follows the Apvardele (Opivardka) to its source in lake Apvarda (Opivarda).

From there the frontier follows a straight line through lake Apvarda (Opivarda) to the point of its junction with lake Zilma, and then it follows the line of the junction of the two lakes to lake Zilma.

From the north-west extremity of lake Zilma, the frontier follows the agreed upon straight line in a south-west direction to lake Alksna (Olksna) cutting lake Zilma and leaving the village of Vilnoki on the side of the USSR, and on the Lithuanian side the village of Nagenai.

From the eastern extremity of lake Alksna the frontier follows a straight line north-west to the north-western extremity of the lake.

From there the frontier turns south-west and follows the agreed upon straight line to the south-eastern edge of the village of Cizunai, leaving the village on the Lithuanian side and the villages of Alksna (Olksna) and Alksnaite (Olksnaitis) on the side of the USSR.

From the south-eastern edge of the village of Cizunai, the frontier follows the agreed upon straight line in a south-west direction to the mouth of the river Disna (Dzisnos), cutting the lake of Disna and the lake of Disnelis (Dzisnisce) and leaving the village of Dailidai on the Lithuanian side.

From the mouth of the river Dzisna the frontier ascends the river to the mouth of a nameless stream which flows into the said river approximately 1500 meters to the south-east of the village of Navikai, leaving the village on the Lithuanian side, then the frontier follows the stream to its source south-east of the village of Jurgeliškiai.

From there the frontier follows the line agreed upon to the south-western shore of lake Seminas (Semino), to the mouth of a nameless stream which flows into this lake, and further it ascends this stream to the north-west extremity of the village of Degutiškiai II, leaving lake Seminas, and the villages of Pleniškiai, Seniškiai II and Degutiškiai II on the side of the USSR, and the villages of Jurgeliškiai, Paukštai, Seniškiai I and Kutnikai (Chutniki) on the Lithuanian side.

From the north-western extremity of the village of Degutiškiai II, the frontier follows the agreed upon straight line in a south-west direction to the north-western extremity of the village of Kuciškiai, leaving that village on the side of the USSR and the village of Beciskiai on the Lithuanian side.

From there the frontier follows the straight line agreed upon in a south-west direction to the south-west shore of lake Verkštis, leaving on the side of the USSR the village of Pekarskiai.

From there the frontier follows the agreed upon straight line in a south-west direction to a nameless lake found approximately 600 meters south-east of the northern extremity of the village of Becenai.

From that lake the frontier runs in a south-west direction through the lake to an unnamed lake located at the northern extremity of the village of Velioniai (Veliance).

From the northern extremity of the lake, the frontier runs in a south-west direction to the eastern edge of the villages of Zuikiškis, Soboliškis and Kozilinas, and on the side of the USSR, the village of Poniziškiai and the property situated 1 kilometer south-west of the village of Poniziškiai.

From the village of Kozičinas, the frontier follows the agreed upon straight line towards the south to the source of the unnamed stream located 1000 meters north of Velka-Ves, leaving the village of Žydeliai on the Lithuanian side, and the village of Rimošiai on the side of the USSR.

Then the frontier follows the nameless stream found to the west of the village of Velka-Ves and further follows the agreed upon straight line in a south-west direction to the village of Novosiullai, leaving the villages of Samine and Novosiulkai on the Lithuanian side, and the villages of Velka-Ves, Bojary and Rusališki on the side of the USSR.

From there the frontier runs in a south-west direction bordering the eastern edge of the village of Novosiulkai and the eastern edge of the village of Mankuškiai, toward the north-eastern edge of the village of Pliaškiai, leaving the village of Kučiai on the side of the USSR and the village of Mankuškiai on the side of Lithuania.

From the village of Pliauškiai, the frontier follows the agreed upon straight line in a south-west direction, to the north-west edge of the village of Paskanai, leaving the villages of Verekale, Brzezniakai and Paskanai on the side of the USSR, and the village of Pliauskiai and the property of Druscenai (Drusciany) on the Lithuanian side.

From the village of Paskane, the frontier follows the agreed upon straight line towards the south-western edge of the village of Romalduvka, leaving the villages of Azuraistis and Mezoniai on the side of the USSR and the villages of Senadvaris and Boguciškiai on the Lithuanian side.

Further, the frontier follows the agreed upon line to the south-west, bordering on the eastern edge of the village of Kisieliškiai toward the northern extremity of Voickunai, leaving the villages of Matusenai (Matusiance), Sakaliai, Masliaskiai and Antesorai on the side of the USSR, and the villages of Lisieliškiai, Elkiškiai and Rudališkiai on the Lithuanian side.

Then the frontier follows the northern edge of the village of Voickunai, the eastern edge of the village of Pasoze, and further, toward the south, the river Edunka, leaving Vockuni and Pasoze on the side of the USSR.

From there the frontier ascends the river Edunka to its intersection with the Pabrade-Švenčionys road.

Departing from this road, the frontier follows the straight line agreed upon in a south-west direction to a nameless lake found near the village of Perkiai, leaving the village of Merancai and the nameless lake on the side of the USSR, and the village of Perkiai on the Lithuanian side.

From the above mentioned lake the frontier follows the agreed upon line in a south-west direction toward the source of the river Belosanka; further, it descends this river to the point where it flows into the river Neris (Vilija) and it descends the latter to the northern extremity of the village of Iseriškiai, leaving that village on the side of the USSR.

Then the frontier follows the agreed upon straight line southward to the village of Kotluvka and then in the direction of the village of Novosiulkai, leaving the villages of Minduciškiai and Bolovikine on the Lithuanian side, and on the side of the USSR the villages of Kotluvka and Novosiulka.

From the village of Novosiulka the frontier turns slightly toward the south-east and, following the straight line agreed upon, it heads in the direction of the river Vileika toward the northwest of the mouth of the river Krasnoborka, leaving the villages of Jazava I and Jazava II on the Lithuanian side.

From there the frontier follows the river Vileika to the point where it intersects the Šumskas-Chudzieniškiai road, and further the frontier follows the agreed upon straight line in a south-west direction to the south-western extremity of the village of Kurganai, leaving that village on the Lithuanian side and the village of Kimenai on the side of the USSR.

From the village of Kurganai the frontier descends in a south-west direction to the north-western extremity of the village of Dainavale (Dainuvka), leaving the villages of Bajorai and Dainuvka on the side of the USSR, and the village of Dainava on the Lithuanian side.

From the village of Dainuvka the frontier follows a nameless stream to the point where it flows into the river Merkys, leaving the villages of Pablieniai, Skujai and Grigi-Dalne on the side of the USSR, and the property of Dvorcai and the village of Grigi-Zabenske on the Lithuanian side.

From there the frontier is traced by the river Merkys to the north-west extremity of the village of Sailiukai, then it follows the agreed upon straight line in a south-west direction to the eastern extremity of the village of Jankunai, leaving the latter village on the Lithuanian side.

From the village of Jankunai the frontier turns to the south-west and follows the straight line agreed upon to the south-east extremity of the village of Smaguriai, leaving that village on the Lithuanian side.

From the village of Smaguriai the frontier descends through a nameless stream to the north-western extremity of the property which is found there, and then follows the agreed upon straight line along its eastern side in a south-west direction to the eastern extremity of the village of Paskuvscizna, leaving the property in question and the village of Zalamanka on the side of the USSR, and the villages of Brusnica and Paskuvscizna on the Lithuanian side.

From there the frontier descends through a nameless stream to the point where it flows into the river Bezé; then it runs in a south-west direction following the agreed upon straight line to the south-eastern extremity of the village of Kaniukai, leaving that village on the Lithuanian side.

From the village of Kaniukai the frontier follows the ditch in a south-west direction, then it follows the agreed upon straight line to the south-eastern extremity of the village of Malakune, leaving that village on the Lithuanian side.

From this village the frontier ascends the river Solnica to the point where it touches on the settlement of Mackiškiai, leaving the property of Kuziai, the village of Jundziliškiai, and the property of Mackiškiai on the side of the USSR, and the property of Narkuškiai and the settlement of Mackiškiai on the Lithuanian side.

From the settlement of Mackiškiai the frontier runs in a south-west direction to the point where the river Dzitva touches the property of Bratemeza.

From the property of Bratemeza the frontier descends the river Dzitva to the point where it intersects the Eišiškiai-Sakaučiai road.

From there the frontier follows the straight line agreed upon toward the west, to the point of junction with the river Versovka, a point found approximately 1300 meters south-west of the village of Dumble, and then the frontier descends this river to the mouth of the river Kapkunka and ascends the latter to a point found approximately 800 meters northwest of the village of Stamerovscizna.

From there the frontier follows the agreed upon line in a south-west direction to the point of junction with a nameless stream, a point found approximately 400 meters to the north-west of the property of Grisaniskiai, leaving the villages of Stamerovscizna, Smilgine, Kaniauka and the property of Grisaniškiai on the side of the USSR, and the villages of Pasiškiai, Milekancai and the property of Klencai on the Lithuanian side.

Further, the frontier follows a nameless stream to the southern extremity of the village of Guta.

From the Village of Guta the frontier follows the agreed upon straight line in a south-west direction, to the point found near the river Ula approximately 1800 meters to the south-east of the village of Kaceta.

From there the frontier follows the river Ula to the point where it flows into the river Merkys (Merecamka), then it runs in a generally western direction along the former Polish-Lithuanian administrative line to the point of junction with the river Igorka approximately 2300 meters north-east of the point where this river cuts the rural road Zendovai-Kapčiamiestis.

Note 1. On the non-navigable rivers and streams, the frontier passes through the bed of the principle branch of these rivers and streams.

Note 2. The agreed upon lines of the frontier in the points indicated above will be established at the moment of determination of the frontier.

Note 3. The line of the frontier fixed by the protocol is indicated in black on the attached map, on a scale of 1:100,000.

The line of the frontier will be determined on the spot by a mixed Soviet-Lithuanian commission. The commission will determine the markings designating the frontier, establish a detailed description of this line and draw it on a map of the scale 1:25,000. The commission will begin its work on November 1, 1939. The detailed description of the frontier established by the above-mentioned commission and the map of the line of the frontier are to be approved by the two governments.

This protocol modifying Article 2 of the Russo-Lithuanian Treaty of July 12, 1920 and coming into force on the date of signature, must be ratified. This protocol is executed in the Lithuanian and Russian languages, and both texts are valid.

Done in Moscow, October 27, 1939.

Editor's comment: The protocol raises some interesting questions about the legal side of the Vilnius transaction. By the Treaty of Peace of July 12, 1920, the U. S. S. R. had recognized the sovereignty of Lithuania over a territory of 88, 111 km.² In October, 1920, Poland seized 33, 441 km.² of this territory, including Vilnius, the capital of Lithuania. The Soviet Government refused to recognize this coup de force at the time, and reiterated its position at the signing of the nonaggression pact of September 28, 1926. In fact, even the Mutual Assistance Treaty of October 10, 1939 cited the Treaty of Peace of 1920 as the basis for Soviet-Lithuanian relations. It would seem incontrovertible, then, that from the Soviet legal point of view, Lithuania retained sovereign rights over the entire area.

Yet, by the Mutual Assistance Treaty of October 10, the U. S. S. R. returned only 6,880 km.² to Lithuania. Simple arithmetic shows that this leaves 26, 561 km.², in other words, three-quarters of the Vilnius region, unaccounted for. Since the U.S. S. R. had never recognized the alienation of this territory from Lithuania, it is difficult to see on what grounds, other than force of arms, the Soviet Government justified its retention of the territory.

Secondly, the Soviet justification for the presence of the Red Army in the territory was based on the disintegration of the Polish State. However, if the Vilnius region was never part of the Polish State, this would not apply. Certainly there can be no question of the Lithuanian State having disintegrated if the U.S.S.R. was soliciting its assistance, and returning a part of the territory to its control. In fact, it is virtually impossible to find any explanation which would cover the territory retained and exclude the territory returned. Thus, it is impossible to find any legal basis for the continued presence of Soviet troops in the Vilnius region, or for the incorporation of a significant part of that territory into the Byelorussian SSR. The Soviet Government itself never attempted to justify, or even explain, this glaring contradiction. Of course, force of arms is not an ineffective justification; the question was never raised.

No. 51

Decree of the Supreme Soviet of the U. S. S. R.

For the approval of the proposition of the Presidium of the Supreme Council of the Byelorussian Soviet Socialist Republic and of the Presidium of the Supreme Council of the Lithuanian Soviet Socialist Republic, the proposition concerning the line of the frontier between the Byelorussian SSR and the Lithuanian SSR (going from north to south):

The new frontier follows the line of the existing frontier between the Byelorussian SSR and the Lithuanian SSR from the intersection of the frontiers of the Byelorussian, Latvian and Lithuanian SSRs to the point where it intersects the south-east bank of lake Opivarda.

Further, the frontier will follow the south-west bank of lake Opivarda in the direction of lake Prute, attributing the hamlets of Mozveliškis and Syviškis to the Lithuanian SSR and the hamlets of Peski to the Byelorussian SSR.

Afterwards, it follows the north-east bank of Lake Pruta, the east and south bank of lake Giluta, in the direction of lake Gulbine, leaving the hamlets of Bitiuny, Maniuki and Bezeniški to Byelorussia.

Further it follows the south-east bank of lake Gulbine to the river Disna, giving the hamlets of Patiuny, Smilgniski, Triciuny, Strilungi, Meleski, Romeiki, Smele, Pagranicne, Niviki, and Podisna to the Lithuanian SSR.

Afterwards it follows the river Disna to the mouth of the river Bitvita, and follows that river to the mouth of the river Medelka.

Then it runs from the settlement of Grigelevcina to the river Carny Rucaj, leaving the hamlets of Rimaldiški, Spijatiški, Carny Rucaj, and Grigelevščina to the Lithuanian SSR.

Afterwards it follows the river Čarny Rucaj to its source in the direction of the hamlet of Gelotylcy, leaving it on the side of the Byelorussian SSR, and then directs itself toward the hamlets of Romaniuny, Jakeli, Jankovici, Milikuci, Liachovici and Novyje Godutiški to the line of the Postavy-Godutiski railway, leaving these hamlets to the Lithuanian SSR.

Further it follows the direction of the hamlets of Godutiški, Eiciški, Regizevka, Bergelata, Gudeliški, Golosiški, Neveriški, Vygary, Visokie, Rinkiany, Kaptaruny, Kobylininkiški, Velicki, and Zaki, leaving them to the Byelorussian SSR.

Afterwards, it takes the direction of the hamlets of Azuruiste, Pepelyny, Obmanka, Rikovscina, Baltrutiski, Janovo, Zbaniški, Moskovščina, Dovjaciški, Labiny and Zalenki, leaving them to the Lithuanian SSR.

Then it follows the Peleka-Rudnia road in the direction of the hamlets of Popelisce, Velikajaves and Ustra, leaving them to the Byelorussian SSR.

Then it takes the direction of the hamlets of Povelnia, Ropeja, Eneraliski, Pordmerance, and Okolenia, leaving them to the Lithuanian SSR, and then it follows the existing frontier between the Byelorussian SSR and the Lithuanian SSR to the hamlets of Lezva and the Ašmena region of the Byelorussian SSR, leaving them to the Byelorussian SSR.

Further it follows the direction of the hamlets of Diaki, Luksany, Bekiany and Dainuvka, leaving them on the side of the Byelorussian SSR, and afterwards it follows the direction of Koktiški, Krupiški, Stitily, Jeninovo Antoniški, Luskiniški, Noviny, Bobromysl, Gevele, and Dovliany, leaving them to the Lithuanian SSR.

Afterwards the frontier goes towards the south-west to the river Podovinka and follows that river to the hamlet of Podokule, leaving it to the Lithuanian SSR.

Then it passes between the hamlets of Vaskele and Nacuki, to the river Gavja, and follows the river to the hamlet of Gudele, leaving it to the Lithuanian SSR.

Further it takes the direction of the hamlets of Dobrovole, Rudevščina, Rudniuny, and Krakuny, leaving them to the Byelorussian SSR, and runs in the direction of the hamlets of Dombrovščina. Zisma, Dolina Vtorja, Dolina Pervaja, Doveniški, Sareicany, Bociany, Stolgany, Podvarance, Michališki, Stoki, and Petraski, leaving them to the Lithuanian SSR.

Afterwards it takes the direction of the hamlets of Taurele, Kukliski, Katrinovscina, Podogute, Dagutka, and Loyce, leaving them to the

Byelorussian SSR, and then it follows the direction of the hamlets of Milvidy, Pomurovanka, Tribance, Bolsaja Posolca, Juzefove, and Malaja Posolce, leaving them to the Lithuanian SSR.

Then it follows the line of the existing frontier between the Byelorussian SSR and the Lithuanian SSR to the hamlet of Rakutiniški, of the Radune region of the Byelorussian SSR, leaving that hamlet to the Byelorussian SSR.

Afterwards it directs itself south-westward to the river Ponocka, leaving the hamlets of Šilgine and Strazuny to the Lithuanian SSR, and then takes the direction of the hamlets of Beliunce, Mickance, Puzele, Kucevice, Naca, and Ginele, leaving them to the Byelorussian SSR.

Then it follows the limits of the cultivated land of the hamlet of Kovalka to the east towards the main body of the forest, and follows the limits of the main body of the forest to the river Ponocna, following that river to the river Poliesa, and leaving the hamlet of Kovalki to the Lithuanian SSR.

Then, from the mouth of the river Ponocna, the frontier runs in the direction of the hamlets of Bolboty and Raki, leaving them to the Lithuanian SSR, and afterwards it touches on lake Motara, leaving the hamlets of Jalki, Ryski and Romanovo to the Byelorussian SSR.

Then, cutting lake Motara, the frontier follows a nameless river to the river Kotra and follows the Kotra to the hamlet of Zasada, leaving it to the Lithuanian SSR; further the frontier directs itself to the west, to the south shore of lake Gruda, and afterwards it follows the south shore of lake Gruda near the hamlet of Uzberze, leaving it to the Byelorussian SSR, and afterwards it proceeds toward the south-west near the river Kusenko.

Further the frontier follows the Kusenko to the Lichace-Privalka road to the cultivated land of the hamlet of Privalka, and then it passes between the hamlets of Privalka and Sandrubra to the existing frontier between the Byelorussian SSR and the Lithuanian SSR, leaving the hamlet of Sandrubra to the Lithuanian SSR.

Further, the frontier follows the existing frontier between the Byelorussian SSR and the Lithuanian SSR.

The President of the Presidium
of the Supreme Council of the USSR
(signed) M. Kalinin

The Secretary of the Presidium
of the Supreme Council of the USSR
(signed) A. Gorkin

Moscow, the Kremlin, November 6, 1940

Editor's comment: This decree, approving the protocol between the Lithuanian and Byelorussian S.S.R.s, established the final eastern frontier of Lithuania. The revision gave the Lithuanian S.S.R. an additional 1,022 sq. mi. and 82,000 inhabitants, a fragment of the original Vilnius region, seized by Poland from Lithuania in 1920 and by the U.S.S.R. from Poland in 1939.

No. 52

The U. S. Minister in Kaunas, Norem, to the U. S. Secretary of State, Hull

[Extracts]

No. 590 (Diplomatic)   KAUNAS, October 13, 1939.
[Received November 6.]

SIR: I have the honor to report that today, October 13, at 1 p. m. I had a most interesting interview with Mr. Bizauskas, Vice Prime Minister, in which he recounted the experiences of the Lithuanian delegation in the Soviet capital and told of the discussions leading up to and following the actual signing of the Pact. Mr. Bizauskas spoke very freely and seemed quite happy over the whole affair. I gathered the impression that the Lithuanian Government regards the present conditions of Russo-Lithuanian relations in a satisfactory light.

. . . .

Mr. Bizauskas went on to say that the Lithuanian delegation was greeted in a friendly manner. The negotiations began with Stalin and Molotov apparently unwilling to treat too kindly and insistent that their demands be immediately met. The Lithuanian delegation surprised them with an agreement that defensive action was a wise policy and proposed to cooperate with them in this regard. This move resulted in the inclusion of article three and a changing of some wording in the fourth and fifth articles. Apparently the return of the Vilna Territory to Lithuania had been agreed upon by the Russians in order better to justify their entrance into Poland. Lithuania in accepting the return of the disputed area from Russia also made good her avowed intent to accept the region should it be offered by Russia. This is the second time she has accepted the region from Russia.

Mr. Bizauskas added a comment that was very interesting and he added that he did so in strictest confidence. They discovered shortly after the conference began in Moscow that originally they had been included in the German "sphere of influence." However, Germany had seen fit to trade Lithuania and the region of Latvia as far north as Riga in this matter of influence spheres in exchange for the territory of Poland between the Bug and the Vistula rivers or roughly the area represented as a difference in the two demarcation lines. On being apprised of this, the Lithuanian delegation set their course and fully cooperated with the Russian Government. In return for their full cooperation, they are assured the full right of sovereignty. Mr. Bizauskas added, with a shrug: "Of course, one cannot be too sure of anything in these days".

The return of the city of Vilna, long regarded as the capital of Lithuania, and other portions along the border was considered a definite gain for the country although an immediate exploitation is out of the question since the mobilization of the Poles and the occupation by the Russians has left the territory in a state of need. The Lithuanians have gathered stores of grain and other necessary supplies which will be rationed to the needy when occupation by Lithuanian forces is effected. This procedure will most likely be begun on Monday or Tuesday of next week following the exchange of signed agreements. The Lithuanian occupational army will advance into specified zones leaving a sealed border behind. The occupation will be gradual and thorough.

. . . .

The withdrawal of Germans from the Baltic States did not meet with the approval of the Russian Government who lodged à strong protest with the German Embassy at Moscow charging an attempt to prejudice their move in the Baltic States.

While not seeking to justify the Russian action in the Baltic States nor excusing their taint of Communism, I believe we are today facing the problem of a strong nationalistic Russia which is determined to strengthen her position in Europe and Asia.

Respectfully yours,

Owen J. C. Norem

Editor's Comment: Mr. Bizauskas was noted for his optimism in dealing with the Soviet government. At a briefing of Lithuanian intellectuals in October-November 1939 (which the editor of this volume attended), Mr. Bizauskas stated that during the reception after the signing of the treaty Stalin had pulled him by the sleeve to a quiet corner, put his arm around Bizauskas' shoulder, pointed out Molotov, and said:

"We other nationalities should stick together against the great-Russian chauvinists like Molotov. If I was not here to protect you, you would be swallowed up by the great Russians or Germans." (Stalin himself, of course, was a Georgian; Georgia had been absorbed by the USSR in 1922.)

The hypocrisy of Stalin became evident when, thirteen months later in November of 1940, Mr. Bizauskas was arrested by the Russian secret police. Stalin did nothing to protect Mr. Bizauskas from the "great-Russian chauvinists" and save him from a cruel death in Soviet exile.

No. 53

The German Minister in Kaunas, Zechlin, to the German Foreign Ministry

Telegram

MOST URGENT   KAUNAS, October 14, 1939—9:08 p.m.

No. 185 of October 14   Received October 15—2:45 a.m.

Foreign Minister Urbšys, on whom I called today following his return from Moscow, gave me rather detailed information of a strictly confidential nature on his Moscow negotiations.

First he emphasized that the rumors circulating abroad to the effect that Lithuania intended to request Memel and the Suwalki corner from Germany were entirely false. Lithuania had no such thought; on the contrary, she was very much interested in continuing to foster, insofar as the changed circumstances permitted, friendly relations with Germany in general, but especially in the economic and the cultural field. To be sure, he could only tell me this confidentially and asked that I transmit it to Berlin in the same manner, since he had noted in Moscow a certain distrust with reference to alleged German intentions in Lithuania. Especially in all Lithuanian objections against Russian wishes for garrisons, the Russians suspected that it was a case of German prompting. I thereupon told him I was convinced that it was also the desire of the Reich Government to continue to foster relations with

Lithuania, but it was, of course, out of the question that Germany should in any way oppose or interfere with Soviet Russia's political interests. Concerning the Moscow negotiations, Urbšys said that in general they took place in an amicable atmosphere. He had been able to defend the Lithuanian viewpoint without restriction and to present all arguments. Only toward the end had the Russians become impatient. Stalin and Molotov had also repeatedly remarked on German-Russian relations and had described them as being very good and friendly. They had also paid high tribute to the Reich Foreign Minister himself. Specifically Urbšys stated the following:

1. Stalin and Molotov had repeatedly stated that the Soviet Union did not wish any sovietization of Lithuania. He had been especially pleased that Stalin had repeated this at the farewell banquet in the presence of many members of the Soviet Government. Urbšys had interpreted this as a directive to the various People's Commissariats.

2. In the Vilna question the Soviet Government had drawn the frontier "with a firm hand," as Urbšys expressed it. No extensive changes had been possible, and objections had been dismissed with the statement that the Soviet Union did not need to give Lithuania any part of the Vilna area. The Lithuanian center Swieciany remained on the Soviet side for strategic reasons, Urbšys thought, since the Soviet Union had evidently been interested in fixing the frontier as close to the Vilna-Daugavpils railway line as possible. The Soviet Government had especially urged that the territory to be ceded be taken over quickly. Lithuanian troops will march in on October 16.

3. By far the most difficult question had concerned the Russian requests for garrisons. The Soviet troops had been fixed at 20,000 men. Vilna would have a Russian garrison until it had really become the Lithuanian capital. Then the city would be evacuated by the Soviet troops. With this exception, Soviet troops are not to be stationed in the larger cities and industrial centers. The Lithuanian delegation had attempted to have further details regarding the garrisons settled at once in Moscow, because the Estonian experience had shown that it was more difficult to negotiate with the military commission. This had, however, been rejected for technical reasons. The Soviet Union had reserved the right to designate an unlimited number of strategic points for Russian garrisons. The details of the billeting were Lithuania's concern. Geographically these points have not yet been fixed; in the course of the negotiations, however, reference had been made to the area between Palanga and Kretinga and the road between Tilsit and Riga.

4. As long as he was in Moscow, no negotiations had been carried on concerning the economic question, but Norkaitis had remained in Moscow for this purpose. In a conversation with Molotov, Urbšys had stressed that Lithuania was especially interested in continuing her full volume of trade with Germany because of the free-port zone in Memel, the settlement resulting from the evacuation of the Memel area, and the good prices paid by Germany. He had further pointed out that Lithuania had so far received the worst prices for her products in the Soviet Union; Molotov had promised to look into this matter. Details on the economic negotiations will not be known until Norkaitis returns from Moscow.

In connection with the foregoing Urbšys did not hide his concern about future developments but he also emphasized that Lithuania would still work in the future to the utmost for her independence; and in conclusion he requested once more that all this information be kept strictly confidential.

ZECHLIN

Editor's comment: The Lithuanian Foreign Minister, Urbšys, as well as Bizauskas, was under the influence of pledges by the Soviets to respect Lithuanian sovereignty, and rather naively hoped to convince Germany that neutral friendship between Germany and Lithuania was still possible, unaware of the firmness of the Russo-German agreement to partition Eastern Europe. Zechlin made it clear when he said: "It was out of the question that Germany should in any way oppose or interfere with Soviet Russia's political interests." However, the Baltic Governments interpreted the term "Russia's political interests" to mean that the Baltic States would not be allowed to join any bloc hostile to the U. S. S. R. and had to officially support the Soviets under all circumstances. They did not anticipate that this would mean the destruction of their independent political, social, economic and cultural existence.

No. 54

The U. S. Minister in Kaunas, Norem, to the U. S. Secretary of State, Hull

No. 601 (Diplomatic)   KAUNAS, October 21, 1939.
                                              [Received November 14.]

SIR: I have the honor to report that on Friday, October 20, I called upon the Lithuanian Foreign Minister, Mr. Juozas Urbšys, and discussed the various problems arising from the general war situation and the Russian-Lithuanian relations.

Mr. Urbšys began by stating that Finland seemed to have determined upon a course of resistance that did not promise to help the generally bad situation in this part of the world. He stated also that Germany's interest in Finland was something to speculate about and surely the Aaland islands were of great importance to her. If Germany and Russia were to come to grips over a misunderstanding on the extent of their spheres of influence, Lithuania might find itself being overrun with an invading host.

Her ally Russia seemed to be moving from one point to another with care and no haste. The various problems connected with the turning over of the Territory had not been solved and the Russians had given no indication that it would be turned over at a definite date. It was thought likely that on either Monday or Tuesday, the various questions would be settled and the final disposition of boundaries, etc. made. 30,000 Lithuanian troops are ready to march.

Mr. Urbšys told me that he expected the Military Commission would leave Moscow on Friday or Saturday evening in their special railway car. Discussions will be carried on at Kaunas between the Russian and Lithuanian Commissions and settlement will be made concerning aerodromes, barracks for the Russian garrison, etc.

The Foreign Minister told me confidentially that the Lithuanian Government found little joy in the prospect of the Russian garrison and have no guarantee that they will leave when a general European Peace might be arrived at. He thinks that they may prefer to stay on in the country. Article One of the recently signed pact was the only article in which Lithuania could find genuine joy. The other articles were in the pact because the Russians insisted upon them.

In this connection I might state that several leading citizens have approached me to say that they appreciated our consideration in hanging out the American flag on October 11, which date the Lithuanians chose to commemorate the return of their beloved Vilna I mentioned to them that ironically enough our flag was hung in honor of a Polish citizen who rendered a service to America, Count Pulaski.

The Lithuanian Government has received various reports and rumors that during the past week the Russians have engaged in a systematic despoiling of the Territory ceded. They are removing machinery from the manufacturing places, etc. I asked whether the Lithuanian Government contemplated entering a protest against this procedure and Mr. Urbšys answered with a question: What is there to do? They had approached the central government in Moscow on hearing the first reports of Russian pilfering and had been referred to one of the Soviet Republics near Vilna, presumably the White Russian Republic. Although the Lithuanian government had understood that the Territory would be handed over "as is", they do not feel that they can effectively protest. In short, they shall be happy to get back the soil of Vilna and the adjacent portions of the grant.

Mr. Urbšys mentioned that the commission which was left in Moscow to work out the details of the border signed by Mr. Molotov and himself had not as yet reported. He thought it likely that their report might arrive on Saturday or Sunday.

Though the unexpected delay has evidently caused some speculation on the part of the Lithuanian Government and given consternation to the large group of newspaper men who had gathered for the occasion, I think it is merely one of those things to be marked as Russian haste. As Mr. Urbšys pointed out, the Lithuanians must wait upon the invitation of the Russian government and move in with due caution to avoid troop clashes.

Respectfully yours, OWEN J. C. NOREM

Editor's comment: The Treaty on the Transfer on Vilnius to Lithuania did not specify the exact date on which the transfer was to be effected or the boundaries of the territory to be transferred. The exact boundaries were determined by the Soviet-Lithuanian Protocol of October 27, 1939. Although the preamble of the Treaty of October 10 stated that "The Peace Treaty of July 12, 1920 and the Pact of Non-aggressionn. . . .continue to provide a firm basis for their mutual relations and undertakings", it was already apparent that the U. S. S. R. did not intend to comply with the boundaries set forth in the Treaty of Peace of· July 12, 1920. Although Mr. Urbšys did not know the exact territory which Lithuania would receive, he was already aware of large tracts of land which Lithuania would not receive. Thus, it is understandable that· Mr. Urbšys should show nervousness over Soviet intentions.

No. 55

The U. S. Minister in Kaunas, Norem, to the U. S. Secretary of State, Hull

[Extracts]

No. 606 (Diplomatic)   KAUNAS, October 27, 1939.

[Received November 25.]

SIR: I have the honor to report that on Thursday morning, October 26, 1939, I called upon the Lithuanian Prime Minister to determine the exact status of the Vilna question and to obtain information, if possible, of the present negotiations with the Russian Commission. On Friday, October 27, I called upon Vice Prime Minister, Mr. Kazys Bizauskas.

The Prime Minister was apparently very anxious to give information on all questions and began by outlining the work of the Lithuanian negotiations with the Russians in connection with the Vilna Territory. He stated that the delay of occupation was due to the aggravating Russian habit of procrastinating on smaller matters rather than due to any time element needed to thoroughly exploit the territory as many thought. That the partial despoiling of the territory has been effected cannot be denied and presumably we shall find a territory in sore need. (I have been invited by the Lithuanian authorities to make a surveying trip on Sunday, October 29, together with the Lithuanian Red Cross and have accepted. We leave at 5 a. m. and plan to spend the day in Vilna.)

The placing of Russian forces within the Lithuanian boundaries is certainly not too agreeable to the Lithuanians and they refer with a sorry smile to the peculiar situation of soon having two foreign armies, Russian and Polish, as their guests. When the Russians suggested that a garrison be placed at Kaunas, the Lithuanians objected. However, it was agreed that for the time being Russian troops shall be stationed near Vilnius. The other places have not been agreed upon and General Jonas Cernius, the Prime Minister, told me that the Lithuanian hope was to reduce the number of garrison places. He added that throughout the negotiations, the Russian Commission has been most congenial and apparently has very little interest where the troops are to be placed. They arrived without instructions or preconceived notions about desirable places. For this reason, the Lithuanians have been able to feel that the negotiations are being well conducted in every way excepting the time element.

On Friday I interviewed the Vice Prime Minister, Mr. Bizauskas, who told me that agreement had been reached on the various matters holding up the movement of troops and that for the next few days, the Lithuanian forces would follow the Russian units very closely. Not a great deal of territory will separate the two forces. The alleged Latvian effort to dump undesirable Polish refugees upon the Lithuanians will be thwarted by careful sealing, post by post, of the portion bordering upon Latvia. The Lithuanian troops began their march at 7 a. m. today, October 27.

Mr. Bizauskas told me that the new Governor of the Territory would most likely be Mr. Antanas Merkys, the present Mayor of Kaunas, who will be granted a leave of absence for the temporary post.

. . . .

In speaking of the German influence in Lithuania, Mr. Bizauskas stated that the organizations such as the Kulturverband would of course be very active with their lists and would urge all Germans to leave. The Lithuanian government will not attempt to deter them except to make certain restrictions of amounts of property, etc. that can be legally taken out of the country. He thought the Germans would soon begin their big offensive on the western front and possibly march through Belgium and Holland. He added another note that has caused me a great deal of speculation: "perhaps they will await cold weather so that they can march across Holland".

Mr. Bizauskas related one account that had come into his office from the Vilna Territory which told of how the women had slept in the factories to keep their machinery from being looted by the Russian soldiers.

Respectfully yours,

OWEN J. C. NOREM

No. 56

Letter of the Prime Minister of Lithuania, Černius, to the Chairman of the Council of the People's Commissars of the Soviet Union, Molotov

Dear Sir,

At this moment, as the Army of Lithuania marches into her ancient capital, Vilnius, the people and Government of Lithuania are filled with sentiments of sincere gratitude towards the peoples and Government of the Soviet Union for the active support which they have always given the Lithuanian nation in its struggle in the field of international relations for freedom and independent life, and for the return to them of their ancient capital — the cradle of their state and the witness of their glorious past.

The Soviet Union has promised this to us in accordance with the Mutual Assistance Treaty between Lithuania and the Soviet Union of October 10, and accordingly, the Soviet Union returns Vilnius to the nation's protection, and the entrance of the Lithuanian Army into the city clearly proves it.

I beg you, sir, to accept this expression of deep gratitude from the Lithuanian nation and Government and to communicate this gratitude to the peoples of the Soviet Union, their leader Stalin, and the entire Soviet Government.

October 28, 1939   Jonas Černius
                                    Prime Minister of Lithuania

To

     Mr. V. Molotov
     People's Commissar for Foreign Affairs
     Moscow

No. 57

The U. S. Consul in Riga, Packer, to the U. S. Secretary of State Hull

RIGA, November 7, 1939—8 p.m.
[Received 9:20 p.m.]

301. Foreign Office official informs me that (1) Lithuanians actually asked Soviet Government for Vilna and requested that Oszmiana be included in territory ceded [by] Soviet, rejection of latter presumably being because of important leather and lumber industries situated there; (2) that Latvian Consul in Vilna who has just been here stated that during Soviet occupation of city there was extensive evacuation to Soviet Union of metal materials, doors and frames, window frames, et cetera, and that numbers of Polish officers and landlords were evacuated.

PACKER

Editor's comment: It is no secret that the Polish territory occupied by the Soviet Army after September 17, 1939 was stripped of industry, valuables, and useful or important people, who were deported to the Soviet Union. Upon reoccupying the territory, the Lithuanian Government was forced to deliver an extensive food supply, to save the people from actual starvation.

No. 58

Statement of the People's Commissar for Foreign Affairs, Molotov, to the Supreme Soviet

Comrade Deputies:

There have been important changes in the international situation during the past two months. This applies above all to Europe. . . .

First, mention should be made of the changes that have taken place in the relations between the Soviet Union and Germany. Since the conclusion of the Soviet-German nonaggression pact on August 23, an end has been put to the abnormal relations. . . . Instead of the enmity that was fostered in every way by certain European powers, we now have . . . friendly relations between the USSR and Germany. Further improvement of these new relations, good relations, found its reflection in the German-Soviet treaty on amity and frontier signed in Moscow September 28.

This radical change in relations between . . . the two biggest States in Europe, was bound to have its effect on the entire international situation. Furthermore, events have entirely confirmed the estimate of the political significance of the Soviet-German rapprochement given at the last session of the Supreme Soviet.

Second, mention must be made of . . . the defeat of Poland in war and the collapse of the Polish State. The ruling circles of Poland boasted quite a lot about the "stability" of their State and the "might" of their army. However, *one swift blow to Poland, first by the German Army and then by the Red Army, and nothing was left of this ugly offspring of the Versailles treaty.* . . .

The war between Germany and Poland ended quickly owing to the utter bankruptcy of the Polish leaders. As we know, neither the British nor the French guarantees were of help to Poland. . . .

We know . . . that . . . such concepts as "aggression" and "aggressor" have acquired a new concrete connotation, a new meaning. . . . Today, . . . Germany is in the position of a State that is striving for the earliest termination of the war and for peace, while Britain and France . . . are in favor of continuing the war and are opposed to the conclusion of peace. . . . Everybody realizes that there can be no question of restoring the old Poland.

It is, therefore, absurd to continue the present war. . . . Although the governments of Britain and France understand this they do not want the war stopped and peace restored. . .

The ruling circles of Britain and France have been lately attempting to depict themselves as champions of the democratic rights of nations against Hitlerism; and the British Government has announced that its aim in the war with Germany is nothing more or less than "the destruction of Hitlerism." It amounts to this, that the British, and with them the French supporters of the war, have declared something in the nature of an "ideological" war on Germany, reminiscent of the religious wars of olden times. . . . It is back to the Middle Ages, to the days of religious wars, superstition and cultural deterioration that the ruling classes of Britain want to drag us? .

. . . But there is absolutely no justification for a war of this kind. One may accept or reject the ideology of Hitlerism as well as any other ideological system; that is a matter of political views.

But everybody would understand that an ideology cannot be destroyed by force, that it cannot be eliminated by war. It is, therefore, not only senseless but criminal to wage such a war as the war for "the destruction of Hitlerism," camouflaged as a fight for "democracy." And, indeed, you cannot give the name of a fight for democracy to such action as the banning of the Communist party in France, arrests of the Communist Deputies in the French Parliament, or the curtailment of political liberties in England or the unremitting national oppression in India, etc. . . . It is the fear of losing world supremacy that dictates to the ruling circles of Great Britain and France the policy of fomenting war with Germany. . . .

Subsequent events fully confirmed that the new Soviet-German relations are based on the firm foundation of mutual interests. . . . The German-Soviet treaty on amity and the frontier . . . concluded at the end of September, has consolidated our relations with the German State. . . We have always held that a strong Germany is an indispensable condition for a durable peace in Europe.

It would be ridiculous to think that Germany could be "simply put out of commission" and struck off the books. The powers that cherish this foolish and dangerous dream ignore the deplorable experience of Versailles . . . may end in disaster for them.

. . . Today our relations with the German State are based on our friendly relations, on our readiness to support Germany's efforts for peace. . . .

I shall now pass to our relations with the Baltic countries. As you know, important changes have taken place in this sphere as well.

The relations of the Soviet Union with Estonia, Latvia and Lithuania are based on peace treaties concluded with the respective countries in 1920. By these treaties Estonia, Latvia and Lithuania became independent States, and ever since then the Soviet Union has invariably pursued a friendly policy toward these newly created small States.

This was the reflection of a radical difference between the policy of the Soviet Government and the policy of Tsarist Russia, which brutally oppressed the small nations, denied them every opportunity of independent national and political development and left them with the most painful memories of it.

It must be admitted that the experience of the past two decades of the development of Soviet-Estonian, Soviet-Latvian and Soviet-Lithuanian friendly relations created favorable conditions for the further consolidation of political and all other relations between the USSR and its Baltic neighbors. This has been revealed, too, in the recent diplomatic negotiations with representatives of Latvia, Estonia and Lithuania and in treaties that were signed in Moscow as a result of these negotiations.

As you know, the Soviet Union has concluded pacts of mutual assistance with Estonia, Latvia and Lithuania that are of major political significance. The principles underlying all these pacts are identical. They are based on mutual assistance between the Soviet Union, on the one hand, and Estonia, Latvia and Lithuania, on the other, and they include military assistance in case any of these countries are attacked. . . .

The Pacts with the Baltic States in no way imply the intrusion of the Soviet Union in the internal affairs of Estonia, Latvia and Lithuania, as some foreign interests are trying to make believe. . . . These pacts are based on *mutual respect for the political, social and economic structure of the contracting parties,* and are designed to strengthen the basis for peaceful, neighborly cooperation between our peoples. *We stand for the scrupulous and punctilious observance of pacts on a basis of complete reciprocity,* and we declare that *all nonsense about sovietizing the Baltic countries* is only to the interest of our common enemies and of all anti-Soviet provocateurs. . . .

The principles of Soviet policy toward small countries have been demonstrated with particular force by the treaty providing for the transfer of the city of Vilnius and the Vilnius region to the Lithuanian Republic. Thereby the Lithuanian State, with its population of 2,500,000, considerably extends its territory, increases its population by 550,000 and receives the city of Vilnius, whose population is almost double that of the present Lithuanian capital.

The Soviet Union agreed to transfer the city of Vilnius to the Lithuanian Republic not because Vilnius has a predominantly Lithuanian population. No, the majority of the inhabitants of Vilnius are non-Lithuanian. But the Soviet Government took into consideration the fact that the city of Vilnius, which was forcibly wrested from Lithuania by Poland, ought to belong to Lithuania as a city with which are associated on the one hand the historical past of the Lithuanian State and on the other hand the national aspirations of the Lithuanian people.

It has been pointed out in the foreign press that there has never been a case in world history of a big country's handing over such a big city to a small State of its own free will. All the more strikingly, therefore, does this act of the Soviet State demonstrate its good will. . . .

Our relations with Finland are of a special character . . . none but the Soviet Government in Russia could tolerate the existence of an independent Finland at the very gates of Leningrad. . . .

I must, however, inform you that even the President of the United States of America considered it proper to intervene in these matters, which one finds it hard to reconcile with the American policy of neutrality. . . . One might think that matters are in better shape between the United States and, let us say, the Philippines or Cuba, who have long been demanding freedom and independence from the United States and cannot get them, than between the Soviet Union and Finland, who has long ago obtained both freedom and political independence from the Soviet Union. . . .

/*Pravda",* Moscow, November 1, 1939./

Editor's comment: There are some indications that Molotov may not have made his assurances in the best of faith. There exists, for instance, a map labelled "THE GENERAL STAFF OF THE RKKA [Workers' and Peasants' Red Army]/Scale 5 kilometers in one centimeter/VILNO". In the upper left-hand corner of the map, the inscription reads: "LITH. SSR, LATV. SSR and B[yelorussian]SSR/First Edition, 1939", and above that, on the margin, the territory is labelled: "Lithuanian SSR". Admittedly, a General Staff of a large power has contingency plans for all sorts of eventualities, but it seems much more likely, in this case, that the Soviet General Staff was already preparing for a certainty.

In fact, the Baltic States had to contend not with the strategic thinking of the Soviet General Staff, but of Stalin himself. Stalin had a Nineteenth Century concept of strategy, and a Nineteenth, if not Eighteenth Century concept of geopolitics, but he was dangerous to contradict. It is well known that Stalin placed great emphasis on meeting the enemy outside Russia's borders, so that the destructive fighting would occur in someone else's country. He had originally demanded territorial concessions from Finland to protect Leningrad from an attack by the German fleet through the Gulf of Finland. The Baltic States, however, had to content not only with this, but with territorial demands derived from Ivan the Terrible and Peter the Great.

In 1967, the Soviets published a book, *Teheran, Yalta, Potsdam; sbornik dokumentov,* which contains a revealing comment by Stalin:

"Russians have no ice-free [nezamerzayushchikh] ports on the Baltic Sea. Therefore, Russians would need ice-free ports at Königsberg and Memel, as well as a corresponding part of the territory of East Prussia. All the more as historically these are Slavic lands from times immemorial. If the English will agree to hand over to us the mentioned territory. . ."

The reasoning is very similar to that of the Ribbentrop-Molotov pact. We have every indication that Stalin's thinking was not developed overnight, or even after March, 1940. One does not have to be an "anti-Soviet provocateur", then, to conclude that, in spite of the "mutual respect for the political, social, and economic structure of the contracting parties" and the "scrupulous and punctilious observance of the pacts on a basis of complete reciprocity", the Baltic States were living on borrowed time.

No. 59

Extracts from a Speech of the People's Commissar for Foreign Affairs, Molotov, to the Supreme Soviet

March 29, 1940

After the experience of half a year which has passed since the conclusion of Mutual Assistance Pacts with Estonia, Latvia, and Lithuania, it is possible to draw definitive and positive conclusion regarding the treaties with the Baltic countries. It must be admitted that the pacts of the Soviet Union with Estonia, Latvia, and Lithuania have furthered the consolidation of the international position of the Soviet Union as well as of Estonia, Latvia, and Lithuania. Despite the intimidation practiced by imperialistic circles, hostile to the Soviet Union, the national independence of Estonia, Latvia, and Lithuania and their autonomous policies have in no way suffered, while the economic relations of these countries with the Soviet Union have undergone considerable expansion. The execution of the pacts with Estonia, Latvia, and Lithuania is proceeding satisfactorily and creating prerequisites for a further improvement of relations between the Soviet Union and these states.

B. OCCUPATION AND INCORPORATION

No. 60

Note of the Soviet Government to the Lithuanian Government

May 25, 1940

According to the report of Mr. Pozdniakov, two more soldiers of the Red Army — Nosov and Shmavgonets — recently disappeared from the Soviet military bases in Lithuania. We are sure that disappearances of Soviet soldiers were brought about by persons under the protection of the Lithuanian authorities. These persons give them drink, involve them in criminal activities, and after that, prepare the way for their desertion or destroy them. The Soviet Government considers such action of the Lithuanian authorities as provocative toward the Soviet Union which may have serious consequences. The Soviet Government proposes to the Lithuanian Government to halt such provocative action to take the necessary steps immediately to search for the Soviet soldiers who disappeared and to transfer them to the military authorities of the Soviet bases in Lithuania. The Soviet Government hopes that the Lithuanian Government will take the necessary measures to comply with the Soviet proposals and will not force it to take other measures.

Editor's comment: There had been stories circulating in the Soviet Union of Soviet soldiers having been kidnapped in Lithuania, but no official pronouncements. When, on May 14, 1940, the Lithuanian Minister in Moscow, Natkevičius, informed the Soviet Commissariat of Foreign Affairs that the soldier Butaev had commited suicide, the only response was a request, made the next day, that the body be transferred to the appropriate Soviet military authorities in Lithuania. Thus, the note of May 25 came as a complete surprise. Nevertheless, the Soviets worded their note in such a way ("two more soldiers . . . recently disappeared") as if to make it seem that this was part of a long-standing dispute. No doubt this was for propaganda value, a concession to sympathizers abroad who would be happy with any excuse for this violation of the U. S. S. R.'s treaty obligation to submit all disputes to arbitration.

Since the incorporation of Lithuania was only a matter of time anyway, the Soviet Government decided that the convenient time was now. The German armies had scored tremendous successes in the West. By May 30, 1940, Norway, Denmark, Holland, Luxembourg, Belgium, and Northern France had been conquered by the Germans, and the British and French armies were surrounded and in the process of being evacuated through Dunkirk. While the German armies were still engaged in the West, the Soviet Government decided to proceed with the incorporation of Lithuania, Latvia and Estonia.

In spite of the Soviet-German agreements for the partition of Eastern Europe, the U. S. S. R. dared to proceed with the implementation of the agreements only when the German armies were engaged elsewhere. Such a moment was late May of 1940, when Germany was deeply involved in France.

No. 61

Note of the Lithuanian Government to the Soviet Government

May 26, 1940

The Chairman of the People's Commissars and the Commissar for

Foreign Affairs, Mr. Molotov, declared in a written communication to the Minister Plenipotentiary of Lithuania, Mr. Natkevičius, that the Soviet Government definitely knows that certain persons, enjoying the protection of the Lithuanian authorities, tempted the Soviet soldiers to commit criminal acts and then helped them to desert or did away with them.

The Government of Lithuania has the honor to ask the Government of the Soviet Union to furnish evidence which would accelerate and facilitate the investigation, especially to indicate the persons and authorities which Chairman Molotov had in mind in his statement. The Government of Lithuania gave the order to search energetically for two soldiers mentioned in the statement of Chairman Molotov, and, if they were found, to arrest them and to deliver them to the military authorities of the Soviet bases in Lithuania.

Editor's comment: Lithuania was sincerely appreciative of the return of Vilnius, and proud of her past relations with the U. S. S. R. The Lithuanian Government, people, and press avoided anything which might displease the Soviet Union. There was no political grievance behind the accusations.

The Soviets' determination to use the alleged disappearances of Soviet soldiers from the bases in Lithuania to implement the German-Soviet agreements for the partition of Eastern Europe was irrevocable.

We note that the Soviets began by accusing persons under the protection of Lithuanian authorities, then proceeded to accuse the Lithuanian authorities, then the Lithuanian Government itself, apparently on the principle that the magnitude of the accusation should be inversely proportional to the seriousness of the evidence.

No. 62

Note of the Lithuanian Government to the Soviet Government

May 28, 1940

In addition to the statement of May 26, the Government of Lithuania has the honor to inform the Government of the Soviet Union that it had appointed a special commission for investigation of the charges made against the agencies of the Lithuanian Government and their officials.

The commission consists of: Mr. Brazinskas, prosecutor of the District Court of Vilnius, Mr. A. Jakobas, legal adviser of the Ministry of the Interior, and Lieutenant Colonel Korla, examining magistrate of the Military Court.

The Government of Lithuania, informing the Government of the Soviet Union on the appointment of this commission, repeats its request for information to expedite its investigation.

The two soldiers of the Red Army mentioned by the Chairman of the People's Commissar and Commissar for Foreign Affairs, Mr. Molotov, were named Nosov and Shmavgonets. Shmavgonets had been returned to his unit on information supplied by the Deputy Commissar for Defense, Loktionov. He was with another soldier, Pisarev, who was not mentioned by the People's Commissar, Mr. Molotov. The Lithuanian Government did not know from other sources about Pisarev's disappearance from the Soviet bases in Lithuania.

In the opinion of the Lithuanian Government, it would be useful in the investigation of this case if both soldiers of the Red Army, who returned to their units, could testify before the above-mentioned commission, and also could indicate, where they were kept if they could recognize the place as stated in their depositions during the period from their disappearance until their return to their military units.

The Government of Lithuania expresses its agreement that the representative of the Soviet Military Command stationed in Lithuania should take part in the investigation of the above-mentioned soldiers of the Red Army and establish the places where they were kept. According to the information of the Soviet Minister in Lithuania, Mr. Pozdniakov, and Deputy Commissar for Defense, General Loktionov, there is one more soldier of the Red Army who is missing from his unit, namely, Shumov.

In order to search for him the Government of Lithuania asks for the following information: from which military unit he had disappeared; when he disappeared; his first name and the name of his father; special identification marks, and his photograph, if possible.

Editor's comment: The seriousness with which the Lithuanian Government undertook the investigation would indicate that it was acting in good faith, still hopeful that it was not dealing with a fabricated incident. Coversely, the repeated refusal of the Soviet Government to permit even minimal co-operation with the investigative effort would indicate that the Soviet accusations were a question of policy, and the Soviets had not the least interest in whether they corresponded with the facts.

A special commission of Lithuanian jurists under the supervision of the Minister of Justice, Antanas Tamošaitis, a law professor known for his socialist leanings, was carefully selected to verify the Soviet accusations. The commission found no evidence to support the Soviet accusations, but, on the contrary, every indication that the Soviet soldiers had deserted of their own volition. Prof. Tamošaitis was arrested by the Soviet occupation army in July, 1940, and tortured to death in Kaunas prison.

No. 63

Telegram of the Lithuanian Foreign Minister, Urbšys, to Lithuanian Diplomatic Missions Abroad

121 SS Kaunas 57224/2232/1801 Etat   May 30, 1940

So far the Russians have refused our repeated proposals, both oral and written, to either allow us to interrogate the formerly kidnapped soldiers or inform us of their own findings, which may facilitate the investigation of their accusations. While demanding that we find and deliver their soldiers to them, they give no detailed information about them, information which could facilitate locating them. For these reasons, and in hope of easing the tension which is arousing great concern in the country, I offered today to go to Moscow for mutual clarifications of what happened, but have received no answer. Otherwise, there are no other disquieting signs. In Estonia and Latvia everything is quiet except that Pravda has attacked Estonia for being pro-English. This attack, as well as the Soviet rebuttal to the English concerning the sending of Cripps, should be considered a friendly gesture toward Germany, in order to distract German attention from their designs in the Baltic.

If a catastrophe occurs here, then consider Lozoraitis as the chief of the residual diplomatic representations abroad, Klimas as his first deputy, and Šaulys the second.

Receives: Berlin, Rome, Paris, London, Washington, Stockholm.

signed: Urbšys
288

Editor's comment: This document is the authorization for the subsequent organized activity of the Lithuanian diplomatic corps, such as the Lithuanian National Committee formed in May 1941.

No. 64

Letter of President Smetona of Lithuania to M.I. Kalinin, Chairman of the Presidium of the Supreme Soviet of the U.S.S.R.

June 10, 1940

The Most Honorable CHAIRMAN OF THE PRESIDIUM OF THE SUPREME SOVIET:

I learned that the Chairman of the Council, of the Soviet Union's People's Commissars and Foreign Commissar, Mr. Molotov, stated to the Prime Minister of the Lithuanian Republic, Mr. Merkys, at the present time on a visit to Moscow, some doubts as to the Lithuanian Republic's public or secret commitments with some states that could be incompatible with the policy of Lithuania toward the U. S. S. R.

Wishing to disperse all possible doubts about the policy of the Republic of Lithuania toward the U. S. S. R., I hasten to assure you that there can be no doubt whatsoever concerning the relations of the Republic of Lithuania with the Soviet Union, because those relations are very clear, having been determined by treaties, beginning with the Treaty of July 12, 1920, the Nonaggression Treaty of September 28, 1926, and by traditions of loyalty and friendship which have been tested through many years.

As a matter of fact, from the Treaty of July 12, 1920, until the Treaty of October 10, 1939, by which Lithuania's eternal capital, Vilnius, was returned to her and Lithuania's security was strengthened by the Mutual Assistance Pact. Lithuania on every occasion collaborated with the U. S. S. R. in international policies of peace, security, and honoring of treaties. The treaty of October 10, 1939, especially cleared up and settled relations between the two states which have been based upon traditional friendship and confidence. The Government of the Republic of Lithuania and myself have always made, are making now, and will continue to make efforts to execute this treaty in the most loyal way.

Therefore, on this occasion I have the honor once again to assure the Government of the U. S. S. R. through you that the Government of the Republic of Lithuania and I by no means intended to enter into any public or secret commitments with any other state because that would be incompatible with existing treaties and traditions of long standing of real friendship between our countries.

Permit me to add that not only the Government of the Republic of

Lithuania and I, but also the entire Lithuanian nation appreciate very much the present conditions of peace in our country which are so closely connected with the whole peace policy of the U. S. S. R., the expression of which is the Treaty of Mutual Assistance concluded by our countries.

Firmly believing in the continuation of the tested friendship of the U. S. S. R. in regard to Lithuania, I can on my part give assurance in the name of all Lithuania that for such friendship Lithuania will know how to repay the Soviet Union.

A. SMETONA.
President of the Lithuanian Republic.

MR. M.I. KALININ,
  Chairman of the Presidium of the Supreme Soviet,
        Moscow, Kremlin.

Editor's comment: President Smetona's assurance that there was no hostile alliance directed against the U. S. S. R. between Lithuania and any other state was confirmed afterwards. During and after the war, the relevant archives became available, and no evidence of any anti-Soviet agreement involving Lithuania was revealed. The very idea of Lithuania acting on aggressive intent against the U. S. S. R. is absurd, of course, and even had she been interested no other major power with the possible exception of Japan would have been so much as interested. Under the circumstances, it would require very strong evidence indeed to make a case for the idea being admissible. Since there is no evidence at all, the Soviet accusation can be correctly viewed as pure fabrication.

No. 65

Memorandum by the Director of the Political Department of the German Foreign Ministry, Woermann

BERLIN, May 30, 1940.

On instructions from his Government the Lithuanian Minister called on me today to discuss the step taken by the Soviet Government regarding Lithuania (already known here through DNB from Tass report put out from Moscow on May 29).

M. Škirpa related the facts as follows:

On May 25 Molotov drew the attention of the Lithuanian Minister to several instances which had occurred involving the disappearance in Lithuania of members of the Soviet Russian Army. Molotov demanded immediate measures for the prevention of these provocative acts, and expressed the hope that the Lithuanian Government would take appropriate steps so that the Soviet Union for her part would not have to take action. M. Molotov handed the Minister a written statement to this effect.

The Lithuanian Government replied after a few days by a note in which it stated its willingness to take the necessary steps at once.

On May 28 Loktionov, Deputy Commissar for National Defense, who has general charge of matters affecting Soviet troops in the Baltic States, arrived in Kaunas. On May 30 he called on the Lithuanian Foreign Minister and mentioned the two cases referred to in the Tass report, according to which two Russian soldiers had disappeared and had later returned, as well as a third case, in which a Soviet soldier had disappeared and on being apprehended by the Lithuanian authorities, had committed suicide. The Lithuanian Foreign Minister expressed his readiness to make a joint investigation of the cases at once. The Deputy Commissar replied, however, that he had only been instructed to carry out investigation in the cases himself; the rest was then a matter for his Government.

M. Škirpa did not present a definite request in raising the matter. He expressed concern, however, lest some other designs of the Soviet Government might be behind these Russian demands, especially in view of the publicity given them in very strong language by both radio and press. He asked whether we had any indications of this, to which I replied in the negative. I told the Minister that, so far, we only knew of the incident through the Tass report. Should we receive reports from our Embassy in Moscow and our Legation in Kaunas containing new aspects, I would inform him.

M. Škirpa took advantage of this opportunity to make the request, which he had done once before, to be informed about the background of the Russian demands on the Baltic States which had been put forward shortly after the conclusion of the German-Soviet Russian Treaty. He added that he was doing this without instructions from his Government. I told him that I had no knowledge of the events myself.

WOERMANN

Editor's comment: Even at the late date of May 30, 1940, the Lithuanian Government did not know of the German-Soviet arrangement establishing zones of influence in Eastern Europe, which was the basis of the impending Soviet moves to incorporate the Baltic States.

The German Foreign Minister, of course, could not reveal the designs of the Soviet Government in its actions against Lithuania, and Under-Secretary Woermann could only deny any knowledge of the background of the Russian demands on the Baltic States.

No. 66

Communique of the People's Commissar for Foreign Affairs of the U.S.S.R., Molotov

ON PROVOCATION BY THE LITHUANIAN AUTHORITIES

COMMUNIQUE OF THE PEOPLE'S COMMISSAR FOR FOREIGN AFFAIRS, MAY 30, 1940

Recently there have been many disappearances of soldiers from Soviet military bases located on Lithuanian territory under the Soviet-Lithuanian Treaty of Mutual Assistance. From information gathered by the N. K. I. D. (People's Commissariat for Foreign Affairs) it appears that these disappearances have been arranged with the support of the Lithuanian Government.

In one case, for instance, a tank driver of the 10th Tank Brigade, one Shmavgonets, disappeared from his military unit on May 18 and came back on May 26. Shmavgonets reported to the command that on May 18 he was kidnapped and transported to an unknown house where he was held in the basement for 7 days. For several days Shmavgonets did not get anything to eat or drink. The kidnappers, using violence and threats, tried to obtain information on the tank brigade and its armament. On the night of May 25 Shmavgonets was blindfolded, taken out of the town and released.

Pisarev, a tank driver of the same tank brigade, disappeared on May 24 and came back on May 27. Pisarev disclosed that on the evening of May 24 when he was in the truck park of the brigade (the park is situated in the yard of a military station of a Lithuanian infantry regiment) he was attacked by 6 persons. The attackers gagged him, put a bag over his head, led him away in an unknown direction to a basement, where he spent 3 days without water and food. The kidnappers, using violence, interrogated Pisarev on the situation of the brigade, especially where it was to be transferred. Pisarev succeeded in escaping through a sewer main.

The outward appearance of both Red Army men, Pisarev and

Shmavgonets, was marked particularly by fatigue and exhaustion attesting to the harsh treatment which they had undergone.

Furthermore, there was the case of Junior Commanding Officer Butaev, who disappeared from his military unit in February of this year. The Lithuanian authorities in Vilna, who were requested by the Red Army command to search for Butaev, informed the Red Army authorities that Butaev had committed suicide when they attempted to arrest him. In this case the Lithuanian authorities explained that death occurred from a bullet in the mouth, but an examination of the corpse established that the wound was in the area of the heart. There were other contradictions in the information given by the officials of Lithuania.

There were two more cases involving the disappearance of Soviet soldiers in Lithuania.

On May 25 of this year the People's Commissar for Foreign Affairs, Mr. V. M. Molotov, stated in the name of the Soviet Government through the Lithuanian Minister in Moscow, Mr. Natkevičius, that the Soviet Government considered that the attitude of the Lithuanian authorities toward the U. S. S. R. was provocative and would involve grave consequences. The Soviet Government demanded that the Lithuanian Government take the necessary steps to halt immediately these provocative actions and to search for the Soviet soldiers who had disappeared. The Soviet Government expressed its hope that the Lithuanian Government would accept the Soviet proposals and would not force it to take other measures.

Editor's comment: The fact that the Soviet Government refused to participate in the Lithuanian investigating commission, but, without the benefit of an investigation, arrived at its own conclusions, which exactly fitted the needs of their developing Baltic policy suggests that with the elimination of British forces from the continent at Dunkirk, which made prolonged German involvement in the West unlikely, the Soviets felt that there was no time to lose in implementing the secret agreements of August 23 and September 28, 1939.

No. 67

Memorandum by the Director of the Political Department of the German Foreign Ministry, Woermann, Transmitted on June

13 to the German Diplomatic Missions in Moscow, Helsinki, Kaunas, Riga, Tallinn and Stockholm, and to the Government General of Occupied Poland

BERLIN, June 11, 1940.

The Lithuanian Minister called on me today to inform me of the further progress of the discussions with the Soviet Union. After the Soviet Union had raised the question of the safety of the Soviet garrisons in Lithuania and had rejected the suggestion for a mixed commission to investigate the incidents, the Lithuanian Government had of its own accord taken a series of measures which it thought would satisfy the Soviet Union. It might perhaps be admitted that relations between the Soviet garrisons and the Lithuanian population had earlier been treated too casually. Restrictive and control measures had now been taken, and many arrests and house searches made, etc. It was known that no reply was received to the Lithuanian suggestion of sending the Foreign Minister to Moscow. It was, therefore, all the more surprising that not the Foreign Minister but Minister President Merkys was summoned to ·Moscow.

On June 7 Merkys had had his first conversation with Molotov. The latter had reproached him severely regarding the safety of the Soviet garrisons and in this connection presented a great many details of incidents. Molotov had in particular maintained persistently that Butayev, a member of the Red Army, who according to Lithuanian reports had committed suicide, had been shot by Lithuanians. He had expressed his dissatisfaction very plainly and stressed that the Lithuanian Ministry of the Interior was not equal to its task.

In a subsequent conversation on June 9, Molotov had brought up questions of foreign policy, which had increased Lithuanian fears regarding the course of the conversations. Molotov had maintained that a military alliance existed between the three Baltic States and as proof had referred to the frequent meetings of the chiefs of staff of the three countries and to other frequent conferences between Baltic personalities. Merkys had replied that there existed neither secret nor open agreements which could violate the letter or the spirit of the Agreement of October 10, 1939. There was the old political treaty between the Baltic States but no military alliance. Merkys had then himself expressed the wish to invite the Foreign Minister to the conversations. The latter had arrived in Moscow yesterday afternoon. M. Škirpa had not yet received any more recent reports. From the standpoint of protocol, everything had taken place in very polite form.

The Lithuanian Government still did not know what the intentions of the Soviet Union might be. The Lithuanian Government was prepared to do even more for the safety of the garrisons than it had done so far. If the Soviet Union now made broader political or military demands, the responsibility could not fall upon the Lithuanian Government. Thus far, the subject of Lithuania's relations with Germany had not been discussed during the foreign policy conversations. However, it was no doubt to be expected that the Soviet Union would raise questions in this respect, too. Here I interjected that there was nothing in German-Lithuanian relations which was not or should not be known by the Soviet Union.

M. Škirpa asked whether we had not instructed our Ambassador in Moscow to make inquiries. I replied in the negative and avoided further discussion of the matter with the remark that our Ambassador would certainly make a report of his own accord.

WOERMANN

Editor's comment: Even at this critical moment, Mr. Škirpa, did not attempt to solicit any German support for Lithuania. Woermann also clearly stated that "there was nothing in German-Lithuanian relations which was not known or should not be known to the Soviet Union."

No. 68

Soviet Ultimatum to Lithuania

June 14, 1940, 11:50 P. M.

As a result of the recent exchange of views which took place in Moscow between the Chairman of the People's Commissars of the U. S. S. R. and the Prime Minister of Lithuania, Mr. Merkys, and also with the Minister of Foreign Affairs in Lithuania, the Soviet Government considers the following facts as established:

1. For some months a series of kidnappings of Soviet soldiers from the military bases established in Lithuanian territory under the Soviet-Lithuanian Mutual Assistance Pact, and the torturing of them in order to get secret military information on the Soviet State has been taking place in Lithuania. It is established that the soldier Butaev was not only

kidnapped but also murdered by the Lithuanian police after the Government of the Soviet Union presented the demand of extradition. Two kidnapped Soviet soldiers, Pisarev and Shmavgonets, succeeded in escaping from the Lithuanian police, who kidnapped and tortured them. Shutov, a soldier kidnapped in Lithuania, was not found until now. By these actions taken against the Soviet troops in Lithuania, the Lithuanian authorities tried to make unbearable the presence of Soviet troops in Lithuania.

This is proved also by such incidents, now frequently occurring, as numerous arrests and the sending to labor camps Lithuanian citizens who served the Soviet units — workers in dining rooms, laundresses, etc. — and also by the mass arrests of the workers and technicians, engaged in building of barracks for the Soviet troops. Those unprovoked and unrestrained repressions against the Lithuanian citizens, engaged in service for the Soviet troops, were intended not only to make impossible the residence of Soviet troops in Lithuania, but also to create a hostile attitude in Lithuania toward the Soviet troops and to prepare aggression against the Soviet military units. All these facts show that the Lithuanian Government is wantonly violating the Treaty of Mutual Assistance concluded with the Soviet Union, and is preparing aggression against the Soviet garrisons, established in accordance with this Treaty.

2. Immediately after the conclusion of the Mutual Assistance Pact between Lithuania and the U. S. S. R., the Lithuanian Government entered into a military alliance with Latvia and Estonia, transforming the so-called Baltic Entente, which was formerly a military alliance only between Latvia and Estonia, into a triple military alliance. The Soviet Government considers as established that this military alliance was directed against the Soviet Union. In connection with the entrance of Lithuania into this military alliance, the relations between the military staffs became closer and were kept secret from the U. S. S. R. It is known that in February 1940 there was established a printed organ of this military Entente, "Revue Baltique," published in English, French, and German.

All these facts prove that the Lithuanian Government brutally violated the Soviet-Lithuanian Pact of Mutual Assistance which had forbidden either to conclude "any alliance or to take a part in coalitions directed against contracting parties" [Section 4 of the Treaty].

All these violations of the Soviet-Lithuanian Pact and the hostile action of the Lithuanian Government toward the U. S. S. R. took place irrespective of an exclusively well-disposed and in reality a pro-

Lithuanian policy of the Soviet Union toward Lithuania, which [The Soviet Union], as it is well known, on its own initiative, ceded the city of Vilnius and its region to Lithuania.

The Soviet Union considers that the present situation cannot be continued. The Soviet Government considers it necessary and urgent:

1. That the Minister of the Interior, Skučas, and the Director of the Department of the Security, Povilaitis, be immediately delivered to the judicial authorities and tried as directly guilty of acts of provocation committed against the garrisons of the Soviet Union in Lithuania.

2. That a Government be immediately formed in Lithuania capable of assuring and determined to assure the proper fulfilment of the Treaty of Mutual Assistance between the Soviet Union and Lithuania and to suppress firmly the enemies of this Treaty.

3. That a free entry into the territory of Lithuania be immediately assured for units of the army of the Soviet Union which will be stationed in the most important centers of Lithuania and which will be sufficiently numerous to assure the enforcement of the Treaty of Mutual Assistance between the Soviet Union and Lithuania and to put an end to acts of provocation directed against the garrisons of the Soviet Union in Lithuania.

The Soviet Government considers that the fulfilment of these demands is a basic condition without which the Soviet-Lithuanian Treaty of Mutual Assistance cannot be carried out honestly and in good faith.

The Soviet Government will wait for the answer of the Lithuanian Government until 10 a.m. of June 15. The failure to respond at the established time will be considered as a refusal to carry out the above mentioned demands of the Soviet Union.

Editor's comment: On June 14 the Germans entered Paris and simultaneously breached the Maginot Line. It was becoming evident that the German military involvement on the Western front might end at any time and their attention might turn to the East.

While German forces were still in France, the Soviet government thought this moment advantageous to advance into the Baltic region and handed their ultimatum to Lithuania.

The Soviet Ultimatum should be considered as the final stage of a series of Soviet actions to bring about the "final settlement of the entire Baltic complex" (cf. Document N.30) under the secret protocols of August 23 and September 28, 1939. Thus, the basis for the ultimatum is not to be found in Soviet-Lithuanian but in German-Soviet relations, starting with the Nonaggression Pact of August 23, 1939 and continuing through 1940, while Poland, the Baltic area, and Roumania were divided between the two powers in a series of agreements. The three Baltic republics, Estonia, Latvia and Lithuania, whose combined populations barely reached six million, could hardly be expected to threaten their giant neighbor, especially since they had been living under the watchful eyes of the Soviet garrisons in their countries since October 1939. Thus, the ultimatum was not designed to put an end to harm done by the Baltic States to the Soviet Union, but to justify subsequent Soviet actions to implement the secret agreements of 1939 in the eyes of the world.

The accusations made in the ultimatum were refuted by the report of the Lithuanian investigating commission (cf. Document 70) and by the letter of the President of Lithuania to the Chairman of the Presidium of the Supreme Soviet (Document 64). Their statements were confirmed by research in the materials made available after World War II.

In conclusion, we may say that the execution of the ultimatum by the U. S. S. R. was a case of simple aggression against Lithuania, in complicity with Germany, in clear violation of the League Covenant, the Nonaggression Treaty of 1926, and the Briand-Kellogg Pact of 1928. Lithuania after June 15, 1940 should be considered as territory under military occupation. All political and administrative acts of the organs in power should be held as acts of the Soviet occupational administration, and in no way representative of the will of the Lithuanian people.

No. 69

The Order of the Lithuanian Chief of Staff

KAUNAS, June 15. Elta.

The Chief of Staff, General Vitkauskas, on June 15 of this year, issued the following order:

1. The Lithuanian government having acceeded to the demands of the government of the USSR on establishing new Soviet military bases in Lithuania, on June 15, at 3 P. M. units of the Soviet army began to march across the border into the interior of the country.

I hereby order:

(1). The Soviet army is to be accorded all the rules of courtesy and friendship such as were accorded to this army previously. . . .

No. 70

What Were Moscow's Accusations Against Lithuania?

[The note of the Lithuanian weekly "Tevyne:" (published in New York issues No. 30-August 20, 1965, No. 31-August 27, 1965, No. 32-September 3, 1965)

We publish here the article of the jurist Juozas Brazinskas. This gives a clear picture of how Soviet Russia provoked difficulties and complications in her preparations for the occupation of Lithuania. Juozas Brazinskas was then the attorney general of the district court of Vilnius, and as the representative of the Ministry of Justice, presided over the commission investigating the events connected with soldiers of the Soviet Red Army.]

Disquieting Rumors.

In May 1940 I listened to Radio Moscow broadcasts about the mass meeting of workers in which the announcer, after having explained to the listeners about alleged kidnappings and murders of soldiers of the Red Army stationed in Lithuania, proposed to send petitions to the government demanding that similar occurrences be stopped.

Soviet Note.

On May 25, 1940, the Soviet Commissar of Foreign Aifairs, V. Molotov, handed the Lithuanian Minister in Moscow, Ladas Natkevičius, a note in which it was revealed that according to information in possession of the Soviet government, certain persons, under the protection of the organs of the Lithuanian government, intoxicated Soviet soldiers, induced them to commit crimes, and after that prepared their desertion and murder.

The Soviet government considered such conduct by the Lithuanian organs a provocation of the Soviet Union and proposed to the government of Lithuania that such provocative actions, undertaken by agents known to the government of Lithuania, be stopped, and that measures be taken to find the missing Soviet soldiers and to deliver them to the headquarters of the Soviet bases in Lithuania without delay. The Soviet government hoped that the Lithuanian government would take all steps to satisfy these proposals and would not compel the Soviet government to use other means.

Commission of Investigation.

On May 27, 1940, the Lithuanian Council of Ministers, having heard the report of the foreign minister, J. Urbšys, on the note of the Foreign Commissar of the Soviet Union, Molotov, decided to thoroughly investigate the events mentioned in the note and decided to form a special commission of which I was appointed the chairman, I, Juozas Brazinskas, district attorney of the court of Vilnius, as the representative of the Ministry of Justice. The members of the commission were the representative of the Ministry of Defense and investigator of important cases, Lt. Col. Korla, and the representative of the Ministry of the Interior, the legal advisor, Antanas Jakobas.

As material to initiate the investigation, we were submitted a copy of the Soviet note and the verbal declaration of the representative of the Commissariat of War of the USSR, General Loktionov, as recorded in writing by the Foreign Minister, Urbšys. The contents of the notes by Minister Urbšys were as follows:

"On May 28 the Deputy Commissar of War of the U. S. S. R., General Loktionov, visiting the Minister of Foreign Affairs, Urbšys, in Kaunas, said the following: 'While on routine inspection of the three bases of the Red Army in Naujoji Vilnia (in Russian known as Novaia Vileika), he learned that a soldier of the Red Army, a driver in the tank brigade, Shmovgonets, disappeared from his unit on May 18, and returned to it only on May 26. Shmovgonets reported to his superiors that on May 18, while his unit was leaving Vilnius, he realized that he had forgotten some of his belongings in the barracks; having retrieved his belongings, he was on his way to his unit, which already was beyond the limits of the barracks. At the eastern gate of the barracks he was attacked by three men in civilian clothes, men unknown to him. The men put a sack on his head, led him in an unknown direction, and threw him into a cave. He remained in this cave, without food, for a long time. From the gurgling of water he understood that he was near a sewer line or aqueduct pipe. He conceived an escape. He penetrated the aqueduct pipe, and by roaming in the pipes after a long period, he climbed out in an unknown part of the city. It was very early in the morning. Here he met a woman who explained to him that he was close to the railroad station

According to Loktionov another soldier, Pisarev, also told that he was kidnapped by some unknown persons on the street on May 24, 1940, put into an automobile driven in an unknown direction, and was thrown into a cave. The unknown persons conversed among themselves in Polish, threatened to shoot him, demanded that he tell them the composition of the tank brigade, about their armaments and exact location. After holding him in this cave more than two days and two nights, the unknown persons blindfolded him at night, put him into an automobile again, and drove in an unknown direction and released him beyond the city limits, from which point, on May 27, he returned to his unit.

General Loktionov added that both soldiers looked very exhausted and tortured and had to be hospitalized. Besides, General Loktionov declared, the Soviet government does not believe that the deserter from the Naujoji Vilnia garrison, soldier Butaev, killed himself; on the contrary, there are undisputable proofs that Butaev was harbored by agents of the Lithuanian government, and only when this hiding became dangerous, they created conditions for Butaev to flee and shot him down in flight.

On May 29, Tass, the News Agency of the U. S. S. R., presented the cases of Shmovgonets and Pisarev in another light, namely that Pisarev freed himself through the aqueduct pipes, while Shmovgonets was conducted blindfolded to a suburb and released there. Tass also recounted the incident of the soldier Butaev. According to Tass, Butaev disappeared from his unit in February of 1940. Responding to the request of Red Army Headquarters to find Butaev, the organs of the Lithuanian government informed them that Butaev shot himself on May 12 when an attempt was made to arrest him, and that the death occurred from a revolver shot into his mouth. However, after the examination of the body it was determined that the wound was in the area of the heart. Besides, other declarations by Lithuanian officials allegedly contradicted themselves. According to Tass, there had been other cases in which Soviet soldiers disappeared.

The Chairman of the Cabinet of Ministers of Lithuania, Antanas Merkys, assured the Chairman of the Commission that all steps had been taken that representatives of the Soviet government be participants in the investigation of the case.

In the first place, the Commission. through liaison officers, Gen. Černius and Col. Skorulis, addressed itself to the headquarters of the Soviet Army stationed in Lithuania with the request that the soldiers mentioned by General Loktionov be jointly questioned, also that the locations of the alleged kidnappings be examined, and so forth.

However, they received the answer that it could not be done without permission from Moscow. Then, the same request was directed to the Soviet Legation in Kaunas, but no answer was received from there either.

The Case of Butaev.[1]

When the Commission began its work, the investigation of the case of Butaev was already finished. The Commission, after consulting the investigation material, for the purpose of objectivity and detail, reexamined all the witnesses already investigated, as well as new witnesses, and after having received all the correspondence concerning the search for Butaev from the Army and organs of the administration, found the following circumstances to be true:

In December 1939 the Red Army soldier who called himself Political Leader (Politruk) Butaev, began visiting the offices of the Lithuanian local government in Naujoji Vilnia. Most of his visits were to the local police precinct. The chief of the local police precinct (it seems to me his name was Vasiliauskas) was clearly given to understand that Butaev desired some refreshments. Butaev thus also became acquainted with the local head of the security police and through him with counter-intelligence agents. Butaev boasted of his great power and influence among other soldiers on the Soviet bases, trying to prove it by improper excesses, however revealing nothing about the Red Army or the Soviet way of life in general. Persons in contact with Butaev were under the impression that he was sent purposely to talk with employees of the Lithuanian government in order to test whether these would not try to extort some information from Butaev on the questions in which they were interested; for this reason, they were very careful with him. This opinion was also based on the fact that Butaev roamed beyond the limits of the Soviet base not only all day, but also in the late evenings and even through the night, and the Red Army commanders seemed to be avoiding a meeting with Butaev.

Under such circumstances, events continued for two months. These contacts with Butaev began to annoy Lithuanian officials and they tried not to meet him. Then Butaev tried to intrigue them with veiled ambiguous phrases and suspicious conduct and to show them that he

---

[1] Vytautas Aleksandras Račkauskas, who in 1940 was the assistant district attorney for the district court of Vilnius, thus the immediate subordinate of Brazinskas, also worked on the investigation and published his recollections in the Lithuanian weekly DIRVA (Cleveland), no. 67-69, June 10-13-15, 1960. Račkauskas reports that Butaev's given name was Dzhebal, i.e., he was Georgian.

had something very important to tell, but he said he needed proper conditions for it, namely something to drink. The drinking took place a couple more times, and during these drinking parties Butaev acted as if he knew a lot. However, he told nothing of importance, and nobody questioned him about the Soviet bases.

In the beginning of March, 1940, the organs of the Lithuanian government received a letter from the commander of the Soviet base in Naujoji Vilnia in which they were requested to find the deserter Junior Commander Butaev. Only then did those Lithuanian officials in contact with Butaev learn that he was a deserter. However, by this time Butaev had already disappeared from Naujoji Vilnia.

After the search for Butaev was initiated, Police received information that Butaev was a frequent visitor of a citizen of Naujoji Vilnia. A search of the house was made but Butaev was not found. However, during the interrogation it was revealed that Butaev, through certain persons of Polish nationality in Naujoji Vilnia and the city of Vilnius, established contacts with French intelligence agents and was giving them information. Some of these people were arrested and brought to trial for espionage.

After a prolonged and unsuccessful search for Butaev, his whereabouts were discovered at the beginning of May: information was received that a Red Army soldier, dressed half in civilian clothes, was a frequent visitor to a house in the section of Rasai, a suburb of Vilnius. The police organized observation of the house and became convinced that the visitor was in fact the soldier Butaev. His arrest was ordered, and detectives were sent for the purpose. When police agents finally were certain that Butaev was in the house under surveillance, in order to avoid resistance, they decided to wait until he left the house, because it was daytime, and there was no danger that Butaev might escape.

When Butaev came out of the house, the police agents ordered him to put his hands up, and asked for his name, but Butaev, acting as if he wanted to show his papers, pulled out a pistol, and after firing a shot at the agents, started to run. Having run a good distance and realizing that he was pursued and would not be able to escape, he shot himself.

The body was not moved, and the information was immediately given to high police officials, and also to the representatives of the Red Army who soon arrived at the scene of the event. The Soviets sent a Colonel and three First Lieutenants, among them one political leader (politruk), one prosecutor, and one physician. About three hundred meters from the houses lay a male body in a dark green civilian suit. The body lying face down, head turned slightly to the left, and foamy blood was coming from his mouth. By his side lay a 7 mm pistol.[2]

From footprints left in the plowed field it was evident that the man had been running. After a search of his person, a wallet and personal papers were found, the proprietor of which was Butaev. The documents and the wallet were taken by the Soviet colonel, who also took the pistol from the side of the body. The police inspector Aleksandras Mauragis offered to identify the weapon in the laboratory of the criminal police to determine if Butaev had been killed by the same weapon, since the bullet seemed to rest in the body, but the Soviet colonel answered that he had no doubt that Butaev shot himself.

This event occurred at 10:00 A. M., May 12, 1940, in the Vilnius suburb Lipuvka. Since that day was the first day of Pentecost, many people gathered at the scene of the event and comments started, whether the fugitive shot himself or someone else shot him. The majority of the people thought that he shot himself, but there were those in the crowd who thought the man was shot. These opinions of the crowd were also heard by the representatives of the Red Army, and this is where the versions arose that he had shot himself through the mouth and other contradictions about which Tass wrote in its telegram.

Not only representatives of the Lithuanian police but the representatives of the Red Army were convinced on the spot that Butaev had shot himself, and not through the mouth but through the heart because the pistol beside the body proved that this was the pistol which had just been fired, and there were even powder burns on the jacket on the body.

The body of Butaev was taken to the hospital and the Vilnius city coroner, Dr. Kauza,[3] a participating investigator of the court, Poskus, and three doctors of the Red Army, namely Colonels Fesko, Osmolovsky, and Zubarev, determined that there was only one gunshot wound on Butaev's body, from the front into the chest into the area of the heart. And there were the signs of burns in the area of the heart on the jacket of the deceased.

The autopsy report and opinions of the experts were drafted and recorded jointly by Dr. Kauza, Investigator Poskus, and the Red Army

---

[2] For technical accuracy: Račkauskas more correctly identifies the pistol as a 6. 35 mm. It should be pointed out that this is a very small pistol (.25 caliber), and would thus make a very small wound so that it would not be immediately obvious whether Butaev had shot himself through the mouth or heart.

[3] According to Račkauskas, after the Soviet invasion, the People's Commissar of Health, Kogan, accused Dr. Kauza of deliberately falsifying the results of the autopsy. Kauza was then deported to Siberia, from which he never returned.

physicians Fesko, Osmolovsky, and Zubarev, though the latter three wished to sign neither the autopsy report nor the opinions, explaining that they were ordered only to participate in and observe the actions of the organs of the Lithuanian government.

Thus, on the basis of the autopsy and all the circumstances of the case, it was categorically determined that Butaev shot himself.

The investigation and interrogations were supervised by the assistant district attorney of the district court of Vilnius, Rackauskas.[4]

The "Kidnapping" of Shmovgonets.

Upon the request of the investigating commission, the Lithuanian liaison officers with the Red Army, Col. Skorulis and Gen. Černius, visited the commander of the Soviet base in Naujoje Vilnia several times, requesting permission for the commission to question and investigate Shmovgonets, or at least an indication of his first name, so that he could tell them his first name in person and describe in detail the circumstances of his kidnapping and his deliverance and indicate the exact spot of his kidnapping. Always, however, they received the same answer: "We can do nothing without Moscow."

In the meantime, alarming information communications were being received from the Lithuanian minister and the Lithuanian military attaché in Moscow that in Moscow there was a very aggressive attitude toward Lithuania and if the guilty parties of the alleged kidnappings were not found, a great calamity would occur.

Extreme measures were thus taken and massive investigations were made of all suspect persons in the region of Vilnius-Rasai where Butaev had hidden and also in the area of Šnipiškiai where the Soviet tank brigade was stationed and where the alleged kidnapping of the Red Army soldier Shmovgonets allegedly took place.

These measures, however, produced nothing positive. Then, upon the request of the investigating commission, the criminal and security police sent as many agents as they could into the area of Šnipiškiai and they were ordered to unofficially check all the houses and taverns which soldiers of the Red Army might have visited.

After a certain time, unexpectedly, an agent of the criminal police, Dimavičius,[5]obtained information, that in one of the Šnipiškiai houses

---

[4]See footnote 1. There are several minor discrepancies of detail in the two accounts, covered in the footnotes. For Račkauskas' reaction to the Brazinskas account, see the affidavit attached to the document.

[5]According to Račkauskas, Dimavičius was summoned to the N. K. V. D. (Soviet secret police) headquarters in Vilnius soon after the Soviet invasion and never seen again.

close to the barracks one Soviet soldier was a frequent visitor. He visited not only when the Soviet tank brigade was stationed there, but also later, when the brigade moved out.

The house was searched, and from the interrogation of the residents of the house, it became clear that one soldier of the Red Army used to come to the house to see one of the residents, Miss Julia[6] Savickas. Savickas told about a Soviet soldier known as Kolia (in Russian the diminutive of the full name Nikolai is Kolia), who left her his picture with the signature "Shmov."[7] Since this was an unexpected discovery, a message was directed to the command of the Soviet base with the request to send its representative to listen to Julia Savickas. But this time too the answer was the same as always: "We can do nothing without Moscow."

The criminal police of Vilnius as well as the investigating commission, now realizing that the Soviets had no interest in the commission, and on the contrary, were creating all sorts of obstructions and ignoring our efforts to clarify this case, undertook further measures by using all precautions. Not to arouse suspicion that Julia Savickas was forced to give testimony or did it unconsciously, during her interrogation by the criminal police the following persons were invited to witness the questioning: the rector of Vilnius University, Mykolas Biržiška; the assistant district attorney of the Vilnius district court, Ignas Navickas; the gymnasium director Dr. Marija Krasauskas; and the director of the high school, Vokietaitis.

While all those invited were present at the interrogation, Julia Savickas stated as follows: "During the stationing of Soviet tanks at the barracks of Šnipiškiai, I used to go often with my girlfriends and boyfriends to gather faggots and take them home. When I was passing through the yard of the tankists, I was approached by one of them several times. Once he invited me into his machine, where we could talk for a longer time. Afterwards, the tankist, named Kolia, started to visit me in my home, even though my mother and stepfather were unhappy with these visits. I cannot tell how long he visited me, but not too long.

One day a truck stopped by our house and the Red Army soldiers threw me a pair of shoes. This provoked some jealousy among my neighbors. The same evening Kolia came and said his unit was leaving

---

[6] Račkauskas recalls the name as Jadwiga. He reports that she was summoned by the N. K. V. D. at the same time as Dimavičius (see footnote 5), and also never seen again.

[7] Račkauskas recalls the name as "Shmorgonets." It must be remembered that he saw it in Cyrillic script and r *(p)* is very similar to v *(b)*.

for somewhere else and he was disgusted and tired of his military service and had decided not to go with his unit. He asked if I agreed to hide him in my house.

I was very scared, but when asked by my beloved, I began to vacillate. That night Kolia did not return to his barracks and left me only very early in the morning. During the day, officials of the Red Army came to my house looking for Kolia, but I explained to them that there was no soldier in this house, and they believed me and left.

Thus, Kolia hid himself for several days; he came to my house late in the evening and left early in the morning. Where he hid himself I really did not know. He used to tell me that he hid in a ditch in the forest beyond Žverynas all day. Each morning I provided him with food. After a few days Kolia and I began to doubt that we would be successful in hiding like this for very long because he said he attracted the attention of people to himself. We both began deliberating on a solution.

I proposed that Kolia flee to his home in Russia, and if he was caught crossing the border, he could explain that he did not intend to desert from the army, that he only intended to return home temporarily to see his family, whom he had not seen for three years and for whom he was very lonely.

Kolia rejected this plan because if he were caught, he would be shot, there being no other penalties for desertion from the Red Army. Kolia then offered this plan. He would return to his unit and explain that he had forgotten his belongings in the barracks and when he returned with his belongings, the unit had already left. Until he found the unit, several days elapsed.

At first, I consented to his plan and I even went to the Lithuanian soldiers to ask where the Russian tankists were gone, but later I rejected Kolia's thoughts because it seemed to me nobody would believe such an explanation. I then suggested that Kolia return to his unit, go to the command, and explain as follows: When the tank brigade was leaving Šnipiškiai, he forgot his belongings. When he was returning with his belongings, close to the eastern gate of the barracks, three men unknown to him attacked him, put a sack over his head, took him and threw him into a cave. He remained in the cave for a long time and felt that there were water pipes not too far away. Then he lowered himself into the pipe, walked through it, and came up into an unknown part of the city very early one morning. Here he met a woman who explained to him that he was not too far from the railroad station. Then he would go to Naujoji Vilnia because he didn't know where his unit was stationed yet.

He agreed to this proposed plan, took his farewells from me, and then left."

The criminal police took minutes of the testimony of Julia Savickas, and Julia Savickas signed it. Julia also left Kolia's photograph to be attached to the testimony, signed on the other side "Nikolai Shmovg." "Nikolai" and "Shmovg" were written very clearly, the ending of the name was not clear, but from the lines and turnings of the script it was possible to establish beyond doubt that this was Shmovgonets.

It is proper to clarify here why Julia Savickas was investigated not by the investigating commission but by the criminal police. The reason is that when the police found Savickas, and on the following day, I, (Brazinskas — ed.), and the members of the commission had gone to Kaunas. This fact can be confirmed by Jonas Talala,[8] assistant district attorney of the district court of Vilnius and my assistant.

After the investigating commission received the records of the Vilnius criminal police on the Savickas testimony, the investigating commission invited Miss Savickas to appear. Here she was reinvestigated and reinterrogated. She was questioned through a Polish interpretor. Miss Savickas told all that she had told the criminal police, and she added that Kolia's belongings were hidden in her home, that is his overcoat, books, and footwear, which he had hidden in her stepfather's cellar, fearing a house search.

Julia also told us what kind of newspapers she had used to wrap Kolia's food in when he was in hiding. Then the police made a search of Julia Savickas' residence, where they found a Red Army overcoat with a signature on the inside very similar to the signature "Shmovg" on the photograph, as well as three military service manuals and puttees. In the woods where Kolia said he had hidden were found remnants of pieces of wrapping paper. Upon presentation of these remnants to Julia Savickas, she confirmed that these were the same papers in which she used to wrap food for Kolia when he went hiding.

The testimony of Julia Savickas was also confirmed by other witnesses. One of them saw a disorderly dressed and stained Red Army soldier of the appearance of Shmovgonets as described by Miss Savickas walking from Žverynas for two evenings in a row. The other witness saw a Red soldier walking out of Julia Savickas yard early one morning. All this testimony totally corresponded to that of Julia Savickas.

---

[8]Jonas Talalas also survived the Soviet occupation. See his affidavit, attached to the document.

Not being satisfied with all the results of the investigation, the investigating commission also tried to clear the other alleged circumstances of the kidnapping of Shmovgonets, and learned the following. The Soviet tank brigade was stationed in the Vilnius Šnipiškiai barracks beside a Lithuanian infantry regiment. The Soviet command was very concerned that no strangers penetrate the area of the barracks, and for this purpose the entire barracks area was lined with sentinels. Since one could get to the Lithuanian barracks only by passing the Soviet sentinels, the Lithuanian soldiers had to be provided with special permits with their pictures on them, and were allowed to pass only by identifying themselves to the Soviet guards. The Lithuanian regiment's guards were posted only in the interior of the barracks area. However, on the day the Soviet tank unit was moving out of Šnipiškiai barracks, the Lithuanian regiment commander, Colonel Šurkus, gave orders to double the guards, and they were posted not only inside the barracks but also beyond the fences of the barracks. According to the statement of Colonel Šurkus, on the day of the alleged kidnapping of the Soviet soldier Shmovgonets or on any other day, he did not receive any reports of any such event in the area of the barracks.

The commission obtained a map of the Snipiškiai garrison area with the places where the Lithuanian regiment had posted its guards specifically marked. The commission went to those places and inspected not only the eastern gate area but other areas as well and became convinced that there was a guard stationed close to the eastern gate where the alleged kidnapping of Shmovgonets took place, and from the guard's station a broad area was clearly visible, especially the place where the controls of the aqueduct pipe were located.

The commission became convinced that the door opening of the control pipe had been locked, and the key had been in the possession of the proper employee. It would be completely impossible to throw a man into the pipe, even without his resistance, and if by any miracle it succeeded, the guard would beyond any doubt see the event. Beyond the eastern gate of the barracks was a wide field. The nearest buildings are very distant and there were no aqueduct pipes there because the barracks had their own water supply system.

The commission also verified the blueprints of the aqueduct of the city of Vilnius and those of the sewer system and after hearing the opinions of experts, became convinced that there were no sewer pipes at all in the Šnipiškiai suburb because it was separated from the center of the city by the river Neris. But even if such pipes had existed there, only a man of diseased imagination could be convinced that a man could travel in these pipes for five kilometers and would reappear in daylight unhurt and sound.

According to the Soviet assertions, Shmovgonets was kidnapped on May 18 and returned only on May 26. That means that according to General Loktionov he was in the water or sewer pipes without food or water and in darkness for almost eight days and, while travelling for five kilometers, was still able to free himself.

The "Kidnapping" of Pisarev.

In spite of repeated requests by the commission for at least some information concerning the kidnapping of Pisarev, according to which it would be possible to find the end of thread, the Soviet command was only giving the usual reply: "We can do nothing without Moscow." Thus, the commission could learn nothing in this case.

The commission obtained no information whatsoever about the kidnappings of other soldiers of the Red Army.

Interruption of the Investigation.

About June 10, the Lithuanian Prime Minister, Antanas Merkys, was called to Moscow. Leaving, he took with him the reports of the investigating commission, the originals of some of the documents, and enlarged photographs of Shmovgonets with his signature.

Antanas Merkys, as well as the persons accompanying him, especially those who were informed about the results of the investigation, were convinced that it would be possible to convince the Soviet government that the accusations against the Lithuanian government had no basis. However, as we later learned, Molotov only laughed at our efforts.

When Merkys returned from Moscow, orders were given to stop the investigations of the commission and to make only a summary of its work. The reason for this instruction quickly became clear. On June 16 the Soviet Red Army crossed the Lithuanian border and occupied Lithuania.

All the investigation material was transferred to the Ministry of Justice.

Conclusions.

1. There is reason to think that Red Army soldier Butaev was purposely sent to officials of the Lithuanian government for

provocative purposes to test if they would not try to collect information about the Soviet bases from him. When Butaev liked the constant hospitality and when consequently he was most likely engaged by regular French intelligence agents, he felt unsafe among his own and deserted from the Red Army. Only then a search for him was undertaken because otherwise it would be difficult to justify such carelessness of the Soviet leadership for Butaev spent entire days and nights for over two months roaming through the town of Naujoje Vilnia while the Soviet military discipline does not allow that.

Butaev certainly killed himself. His suicide and the circumstances aroused no doubt even in the representatives of the Soviet bases, and the suicide was confirmed by three physicians of the Soviet army, physicians participating in the examination of the body, the autopsy, and in the drafting and writing of opinions on this autopsy.

2. The "kidnapping" of the Red Army soldiers Shmovgonets and Pisarev and their "deliverance" was invented from the beginning to the end. It is true that there was information that certain soldiers of the Red Army deserted, as happens in other armies; nevertheless, the command of the Red Army addressed itself only once to the Lithuanian government to find Butaev, and he was found. Thus, the allegations that desertions, intoxications, and murders were executed by persons under the auspices of the Lithuanian government have no basis in fact whatsoever.

Appendix I to Doc. No. 70

Appendix II to Doc. No. 70

I have read the testimony of Juozas Brazinskas, former district attorney for the District Court of Vilnius and chairman of the special commission investigating the alleged kidnapping of Soviet soldiers in Lithuania in 1940, contained in the August 20 and 27 and September 3, 1965 issues of TEVYNE.

I participated in the proceedings of the investigation and was acquainted first hand with the work of the Commission and with its report, and I certify that the account of Mr. Brazinskas is in its essentials an accurate and correct account of the findings of the Commission.

I also certify that in all my previous public statements on the findings of the aforementioned investigation I have agreed essentially and substantially with the account of Mr. Brazinskas.

(signed)

Vytautas Aleksandras Račkauskas

(date) July 10th, 1971
(signed) Jonas Talalas on Nov. 21, 1971

The originals of this affidavit and that of Talalas are on deposit in the Hoover Library, Stanford, California.

Editor's comment: It is unfortunate that we are not able to produce the actual report of the Special Investigating Commission, considering the grave consequences of the Soviet charges. The actual report of the Commission was delivered to the Soviet Foreign Minister in Moscow and a copy deposited in the files of the Ministry of Justice of Lithuania in Vilnius.

Fortunately, Juozas Brazinskas, former District Attorney for the District Court of Vilnius and Chief of the Investigating Commission, survived the events and published his account. We are reproducing his account, with affidavits from the two assistant district attorneys who were his staff investigators, as a substitute for the unavailable commission report. We feel that this, under the circumstances, may be an adequate substitute.

No. 71

Latvian Telegraphic Agency Bulletin

LTA (Latvian Telegraphic Agency), Riga, June 15, 1940. — The official announcement of the Soviet agency *Tass* regarding the liquidation of the Soviet-Lithuanian conflict states, among other things, that Lithuania had entered into a secret military alliance with Latvia and Estonia, thereby turning the Baltic Entente into a military alliance of the three States. The Latvian Telegraphic Agency is authorized to announce that this statement does not coincide with actuality, as Lithuania has not joined the military treaty signed between Latvia and Estonia on November 1, 1923, and that no other military agreement exists between the three Baltic States.

No. 72

Affidavit by the Former Lithuanian Minister of Defence Musteikis, and of Agriculture, Audenas, and of the Former Secretary General of the Cabinet, Mašalaitis

We certify that to the best of our knowledge, after the conclusion of the Mutual Assistance Treaty with the Union of the Soviet Socialist Republics of October 10, 1939, the Lithuanian Government neither entered into political or military alliances nor concluded any open or secret treaties with other states which were contrary to the provisions of the Mutual Assistance Treaty of October 10, 1939, or endangering security of the U. S. S. R.

Neither the Lithuanian Government nor the General Staff of the Lithuanian Armed Forces conducted any secret or open military negotiations with any foreign state in violation of the spirit or letter of the Mutual Assistance Treaty with the U. S. S. R.

The Lithuanian Government observed strictly its declared neutrality in the Second World War.

In testimony whereof, we, Kazys Musteikis, Minister of Defense (1938-1940), Juozas Audenas, Minister of Agriculture (1939-1940), both the surviving members of the Lithuanian Government, and Vincas Masalaitis, Secretary General of the Lithuanian Cabinet of Ministers, have hereunto subscribed our names in the presence of a Notary Public this day of February, 1971

     Kazys Musteikis   Juozas Audenas   Vincas Mašalaitis

No. 73

Declaration of the Former Foreign Minister of Lithuania, Lozoraitis

March 30, 1971

I hereby declare that, before and after the conclusion of the Mutual Assistance Treaty with the Union of the Soviet Socialist Republics of October 10, 1939, the Lithuanian Government neither entered into political or military alliances nor concluded any open or secret treaties with other states which were contrary to the provisions of the Mutual Assistance Treaty of October 10, 1939, or endangering security of the U. S. S. R.

Neither the Lithuanian Government nor the General Staff of the Lithuanian Armed Forces conducted any secret or open military negotiations with any foreign state in violation of the spirit or letter of the Mutual Assistance Treaty with the U. S. S. R.

The Lithuanian Government observed strictly its declared neutrality in the Second World War.

Stasys Lozoraitis,
Chief of the Diplomatic Service
of Lithuania,
former Minister of Foreign Affairs

No. 74

Article by the Prime Minister of Lithuania, Antanas Merkys, in the February, 1940 Issue of Revue Baltique: "Baltic Collaboration and Lithuanian Public Opinion"

The idea of collaboration among the Baltic Nations is older in Lithuania than the very independence of the Lithuanian State, restored following the war of 1914-1918. This idea is based on the kinship existing between the Latvians and Lithuanians, and on the ties of traditional sympathy which unite the Lithuanian and Estonian nations. It is based equally on the geopolitical situation of the lands inhabited by the three nations and by their common thirst for liberty, which derives from the political maturity of the Baltic nations and their high cultural level, which was affirmed with so much force during the great war.

The collaboration of Lithuanians, Latvians, and Estonians, as understood by the Lithuanian nation, has always manifested itself in the realm of politics and even more so in the realm of culture. After the three nations had recovered their sovereignty, and at the same time their economic independence, this collaborating equally included the field of economics.

The Lithuanian nation followed with great interest each stage of the political struggle of their Baltic friends, and each one of their cultural advances. It desired slightly closer ties to unite the representatives of these nations in the Russian Duma. This is why it rejoiced when the rapprochement of Lithuanians, Latvians, and Estonians began to manifest itself intensively when the cannons of the great war rang out again announcing the dawn of the political liberty of the Baltic nations. But it is evident that one could not dream of realizing full Baltic collaboration until after the Baltic nations had recaptured their political liberty and were constituted as independent states.

Like all grand ideas, that of collaboration among the Baltic countries has experienced a series of cycles and crises, and it has met with a great number of enthusiasts and skeptics in all three countries, both types having retarded its definitive triumph. Thus, one recalls, they began to initiate and propagate the idea of a Latvian-Lithuanian republic, an idea based on the ties of blood existing between the two nations; they also envisaged a complete fusion of the Lithuanian and Latvian languages, the creation of a political confederation which was to include at first only Lithuania, Latvia, and Estonia, and later to develop until it included Finland and a thousand other things. . .On the other hand, there were people, even among the most influential, who doubted the possibility and the interest of a closer collaboration among the Baltic states, and who were partisans of either a complete political isolation for their states, or else of a rapprochement with one or another of the great European powers. The realization of the idea of collaboration was slowed as well by poorly understood national ambitions appearing here or there, by prejudices, differences of religion, and the different political and social consequences in each state as a result of long foreign domination.

The idea of Baltic collaboration also encountered other difficulties no less serious. Soon after the beginning of the recovery of its independence, Lithuania considered itself in a state of war with Poland, which had seized her historic capital, Vilnius. Under these conditions, Lithuanian public opinion categorically opposed any idea of extending the Baltic collaboration to Poland; at the same time, Finland, which inclined more and more toward the Scandinavian states, adhered to the so-called nordic bloc. Finally, Latvia and Estonia hesitated to attach themselves too closely to Lithuania, which, besides its conflict over Vilnius, had certain difficulties with what is called the Memel Question. The Pact signed in Geneva on September 12, 1934, by which the Entente of Baltic states was created, recognized these questions as particular problems which should be excluded from the common problems interesting all three states. Because of the exclusion of these particular problems, Lithuanian public opinion concluded that Baltic solidarity was not yet complete. And yet, with great enthusiasm she hailed the formation of the Baltic Entente, publicly proclaimed in Geneva, and participated in the periodical conferences of the foreign ministers of the Baltic states, the alliance of the Baltic press, and all the series of manifestations of Baltic solidarity in which she saw the realization of an important step in the true solidarity of the Baltic nations.

The economic crisis of last September and the beginning of the European conflagration proved the identity of the destiny of the Baltic states and the necessity for them to live with closer ties in order to be able to accomplish a positive action in the Baltic region and to assure their independence. The political obstacles to a full Baltic collaboration have now disappeared, and, on the contrary, an ample field for sincere collaboration offers itself. Today, that collaboration equally embraces the economic domain. As a consequence of the Conference of the Foreign Ministers of the Baltic States which was held in Tallinn, it is expected that the economic consultations which took place at Riga and Kaunas will give practical results which will be useful to the economies of the three countries and for the well-being of their inhabitants.

Great labors still await the governments and populations of the three states in the realm of cultural collaboration. The common joining of the richness of their cultures will create among the Lithuanians, Latvians, and Estonians a profound alliance of hearts and spirits which will resist all trials.

The collaboration of Lithuania, Latvia, and Estonia is today a reality. It has been cemented by the events of the recent past and by the spectacle of calamity which bursts out everywhere. The task of the governments is to develop and deepen the collaboration. The Baltic alliance should pursue a constructive policy of peace, and, at this moment, of neutrality. It should be a factor of liberty and progress in the Baltic lands, which have been sprinkled so plentifully with the blood of our ancestors. The immediate task incumbent upon the populations of the three states is equally important. It falls upon them to prove their activity, initiative, and dynamism in all these fields. As far as the Lithuanians are concerned, joyfully and filled with hope they are ready to accomplish their task and take up their part in Baltic solidarity.

I am happy that a common organ of the press has been created, which will be, I am certain, not only the instrument of the development of Baltic collaboration, but even more the living symbol of the firm solidarity of the three Baltic states.

Editor's comment: We are extremely fortunate to be able to include in our collection this rare but significant article. The Soviet Government felt so threatened after reading it, that it felt compelled, in self-defense, to invade and annex the Baltic States.

On June 9, 1940, the Lithuanian Prime Minister, was in Moscow, attempting to somehow resolve the dispute with the Soviets, that is to say, the Soviet dispute with Lithuania, over the alleged kidnapping of Soviet soldiers stationed in Lithuania. In the middle of an interview, Molotov suddenly accused Lithuania of joining a military alliance contrary to the Mutual Assistance Pact of October 10, 1939. To follow the report of the Lithuanian Minister in Moscow (L. Natkevičius to J. Urbšys. No. 244. Secret. Confidential. Moscow, June 10, 1940):

Mr. Molotov, having mentioned several of Pozdniakov's reports, attacked Lithuania because the latter was organizing a Baltic military alliance against the Soviets [skolachivaet voiennyi baltiiskii soiuz]. Molotov read a translation from the Revue Baltique no. 1, where it was stated that after the Klaipeda [Memel] and Vilnius [Vilna] questions were solved there would be no obstacles whatsoever for complete Latvian, Lithuanian and Estonian collaboration. What does this mean? Previously, there was no such complete collaboration. Now it only remained to conclude a military convention and such collaboration would be complete. In the meantime, Mr. Merkys *did not utter a single word* about the Soviet Union, which was also a Baltic State. . . .

Molotov answered: "One should not be naive. We know what complete collaboration means. You already have a military convention with the Estonians and Latvians."

In the ultimatum, the Soviet Government again stated:

"Immediately after the conclusion of the Mutual Assistance Pact between Lithuania and the U.S.S.R., the Lithuanian Government entered into a military alliance with Latvia and Estonia, transforming the so-called Baltic Entente, which was formerly a military alliance only between Latvia and Estonia, into a triple military alliance. The Soviet Government considers it as established that this military alliance was directed against the Soviet Union. In connection with the entrance of Lithuania into this military alliance, the relations between the military staffs became closer and were kept secret from the U.S.S.R. It is known that in

February, 1940, there was established a printed organ of this military entente, "Revue Baltique", published in English, French, and German."

Merkys, the author of the article, was arrested by the Soviet occupation forces very soon after the invasion in June, 1940, and deported to the U. S. S. R. He was never allowed to return, and died in the Soviet Union in 1955. The reader now has a chance to see for himself the article which so greatly disturbed the Government of the U. S. S. R.

No. 75

The German Minister in Kaunas, Zechlin, to the German Foreign Ministry

Telegram

MOST URGENT   KAUNAS, June 15, 1940 — 1:00 p.m.
No. 94 of June 15   Received June 15 — 6:40 p.m.

Yesterday morning Molotov handed Urbšys a 9-hour ultimatum beginning at midnight consisting of the following three points:

1. Skučas, Minister of the Interior up to now, and Povilaitis, hitherto head of the Security Department, to be put on trial.

2. The Lithuanian Government to be reconstructed on a pattern acceptable to the Soviet Government.

3. The Soviet Union to have complete freedom regarding the number and disposition of its troops in Lithuania.

This morning, after a conference lasting 8 hours, the Lithuanian Cabinet decided to accept the ultimatum. The Cabinet has resigned. The reconstruction of the Cabinet has been entrusted to General Raštikis who has suggested to the Soviet Government that he should come to Moscow for negotiations there on points 2 and 3. Internal considerations in Lithuania are primarily responsible no doubt for the choice of Raštikis (his great following in the Army; after Merkys' exit the only personage who could be considered). Notwithstanding this, information reached the Legation some time ago that he was not unpopular with the Soviets either. Vitkauskas, a former army commander, has been selected for the post of Minister of War. Furthermore there is the possibility that the President will resign, as he feels he is not acceptable to the Soviet Union.

ZECHLIN

Editor's comment: The suggestion of Raštikis, a soft and tactful man, but an unquestionable patriot, was a last gesture by Lithuania to prove her willingness to accommodate. The Soviets rejected him. They would accept only a man of unreserved loyalty to Moscow, who would not hinder the "final solution of the entire Baltic complex."

No. 76

Memorandum by an Official of the Press Department of the German Foreign Ministry

June 15, 1940.
PXIL

At 4:25 p.m. Minister Zechlin stated by telephone that the Soviet Russian Government considered the Lithuanian acceptance of today's ultimatum inadequate, and allowed its troops to cross the Soviet-Lithuanian frontier at 3 p.m. The Lithuanian troops have orders not to offer resistance. As the manner in which the invasion is taking place is not yet known, more precise information cannot as yet be given. For the time being only certain places are to be occupied, to wit, Kaunas, Raseiniai, and Felsche (? here Telschi [*Telšiai*] is obviously meant). The line west of the Memel is apparently not being occupied.

The mood of the Lithuanians can be described as perfectly calm, because neither press, nor radio is publishing anything about the invasion.

Editor's comment: The line west of the River Nemunas was not occupied by the Soviets, as per the agreement between the two powers.

No. 77

Memorandum by the Director of the Political Department of the German Foreign Ministry, Woermann

BERLIN, June 15, 1940

The Lithuanian Minister called on me this afternoon in order to find out what we knew about the events in Lithuania. His own information tallied with the reports of the Lithuanian telegraph agency and the reports at hand from Moscow. The only new item was that the Soviet

Russian Government had also turned down a Raštikis Government. It was not yet certain who would now be entrusted with the formation of a government. A high official of the Soviet Russian Foreign Commissariat had arrived in Kaunas together with the Soviet Minister in Lithuania who had returned from Moscow.

The Lithuanian Minister then inquired very cautiously whether the German Government had defined its attitude in any way toward the events or whether such might be expected. I replied that, of course, this had not yet been done. I was not aware whether it was to be expected at all.

WOERMANN

Editor's comment: G. V. Dekanozov was sent to Kaunas to oversee the process of incorporation. The German-Soviet agreements having solved the territorial partition only in principle, the mode and form or status the Baltic republics would assume was not known to the Germans. Since the Soviet presence in the Baltic countries deeply affected German interests in the Baltic area, it is not surprising that the Germans keenly followed the events in the Baltic area, even though Soviet actions in one form or another had been expected by Berlin.

No. 78

The Lithuanian Foreign Minister, Urbšys, to the Lithuanian Government

[Translation from "Lietuvos Aidas" of June 16, 1940
— No. 281/5490]

TELEGRAM FROM MINISTER URBŠYS JUNE 15TH 2 PM, 1940

The Minister for Foreign Affairs of Lithuania Urbšys about 2 PM of June 15th sent the following telegram from Moscow:

"The Chairman of the Council of the People's Commissars of the Soviet Union and the Commissar of Foreign Affairs Molotov has presented me the following demands: '1/The armed forces of the Soviet Union shall cross the Lithuanian border at 3 Pm of June 15th at the following places — Eišiškes, Druskininkai, railway station of Guda-gojus, Druskininkeliai, Dukštas and Pabrad; 2/Separate detachments of the Soviet army crossing the border shall enter Vilnius, Kaunas, Raseiniai, Panevezys and Šiauliai; 3/Other points of distribution of the army of the Soviet Union shall be determined by agreement by General

Pavlov representing the Soviet Union and General Vitkauskas representing Lithuania; 4/ Gen. Pavlov and Gen. Vitkauskas shall meet in the railway station of Gudagojus at 8 PM of June 15th; to avoid unnecessary conflicts and misunderstandings the organs of the Lithuanian government shall immediately order the population and the armed forces not to interfere with the movements of the army of the Soviet Union in Lithuanian territory'".

The above translation of the telegram from the Minister for Foreign Affairs is a true interpretation into the English language of the demands dictated on June 15, 1940 by the Bolshevists in connection with the occupation of Lithuania

(Signed) K. Musteikis.

K. MUSTEIKIS.

No. 79

The German Minister in Kaunas, Zechlin, to the German Foreign Ministry

Telegram in code
Kaunas, June 16, 1940 — 6:30 p.m.
Received June 16, 1940 — 7:55 p.m

No. 96 of June 15, 1940
Most Urgent

For confirmation of telephone message to Press Department.

The Soviet Government rejected Rastikis as candidate for prime minister and informed that Soviet army units will enter Lithuania today at 3:00 p.m. The Lithuanian army will not resist. According to an announcement by radio Kaunas, the Soviet army will be welcomed at the border by a higher officer of the Lithuanian army. It seems that only a certain number of places will be occupied at first: Vilnius, Kaunas, Raseiniai, Panevezys and Siauliai. However, at a meeting between Lithuanian and Russian military authorities tonight an agreement should be made about the occupation of other localities. Until now nothing has been announced about occupation of localities west of the Nemunas. The Russian Minister Pozdniakov has just arrived with another Soviet commissar who will decide about the formation of a new government.

Zechlin

Editor's comment: Lithuania's occupied status under the sovereign power of the U. S. S. R. is indicated by the arrival of Dekanozov, Deputy Foreign Commissar, with the Soviet troops to decide on the new government of Lithuania. Nor can there be any doubt that Pozdniakov, the Soviet Minister in Kaunas, interfered in Lithuanian domestic affairs drastically in excess of what is acceptable for the diplomatic representative of a foreign country. When a foreign army accompanied by representatives of a foreign government moves into another country and sets up a new administration, this country should be considered as under occupation and *de facto* deprived of its political freedom.

No. 80

The U.S. Chargé D'Affaires in Estonia, Leonard, to the U.S. Secretary of State, Hull

TALLINN, June 16, 1940 — 11a.m.
[Received 8:04 p.m.]

62. I have just learned from a reliable official source that Estonia was confronted today by demands from the Soviet Union to permit Soviet troops to march into Estonia tomorrow, namely on June 17. The Government of Estonia is now in conference and it is believed it will accede to Soviet demands. I have also been informed that similar demands have been made on Latvia.

LEONARD

Editor's comment: The occupation of Lithuania was completed on June 15, 1940. On June 16, the Soviet Government presented similar ultimatums to Latvia and Estonia, and on June 17, the same day that France petitioned Germany for an armistice, Soviet troops occupied the two countries, completing the "final settlement of the entire Baltic complex" under the secret protocols of August 23 and September 28, 1939

No. 81

The U.S. Minister in Kaunas, Norem, to the U.S. Secretary of State, Hull

KAUNAS, June 16, 1940 — 1 p.m.
[Received 2:05 p.m.]

111. President Smetona together with various officials and civilians fled to Germany last evening. This morning the Lithuanian Government officially proclaimed his post vacant and asked Prime Minister Merkys to act *ad interim*. Mr. Bizauskas, Vice Prime Minister, is carrying on negotiations with the Soviet representatives. They met at midnight and this morning at 10 a.m. The Soviet representatives asked new instructions when told of President's fleeing. No definite conclusions have been reached since the Russians declare the provisions of the ultimatum are not as yet fulfilled. The two men named by the Soviets, former Minister of Interior Skucas and former Director of State Security, having fled, voluntarily gave themselves up and are now returning to Kaunas. Soviet informant declared that the new government must be completely pro-Russian. All strategic points are occupied by Soviet troops. Demands include free access routes from the Soviet Union to Lithuania and sufficient army reinforcements to be stationed at all important points to insure against incidents directed against the Russian troops.

Repeated to Moscow.

NOREM

Editor's comment: When Smetona, the President of Lithuania, was informed that a Soviet emissary had been sent from Moscow to take charge of the formation of a new cabinet, he knew that under the circumstances he could no longer perform his constitutional functions and would only be a prisoner of the Soviets, to be used as a tool in the destruction of the Lithuanian State. In order to fulfil his duties in exile, Smetona fled abroad on June 15, as Soviet troops were taking possession of Lithuania.

No. 82

The U.S. Minister in Kaunas, Norem, to the U.S. Secretary of State, Hull

KAUNAS, June 16, 1940 — 8 p.m.
[Received 11:50 p.m.]

112. The Acting President of Lithuania, Merkys, announced in a short talk at 4 p.m. today that all necessary steps are being taken to form new government. He urged the people to accept the fact of the military

occupation and to return to their normal work. One director of the Lithuanian Foreign Office has been in close touch with our Mission and stated this evening that nothing new was obtainable [at] 8 p.m. this evening although indications are that the results are sad for Lithuania. Evening sessions seem advisable and we may expect some announcements tomorrow morning. Talks are being conducted by Merkys, Bizauskas and certain Cabinet members for Lithuania and Dekanozov, Assistant Soviet Commissar for Foreign Affairs, Posdnyakov, Soviet Minister to Lithuania, and various advisers acting for Russia.

Editor's comment: The U. S. S. R. now tried by all possible means to provide legal continuity and a constitutional basis for the new administration. However, although the Lithuanian Government accepted the Soviet ultimatum, although Prime Minister Merkys, acting for the President, 'cooperated' in the formation of a new government, and Seimas 'elections' were held, all these steps occurred under the imminent threat of overwhelming force by the Soviet occupation troops backing up the instructions of the Soviet emissaries, Pozdniakov and Dekanozov, in the absence of the legal Lithuanian chief executive, President Smetona, who had left the country and the constitutional national parliament being dissolved and political parties suppressed. Under those circumstances, the actions of the interim administrative organs of Lithuania are, of course, legally null and void, that is to say, based on no known legal principle except *manu belli.*

No. 83

Memorandum of an Official of the German Foreign Ministry on a Communique of the German Supreme Military Command

BERLIN, June 16, 1940.

The High Command of the Wehrmacht (Colonel von Geldern) reports that it has received from the Counterintelligence Office in Königsberg, the following communication:

Tonight at 3 o'clock President Smetona with family and entourage crossed the "green frontier." He had given orders to the Lithuanian garrisons of Mariampole and Taurage to cross the frontier into Germany fully equipped and armed.

The High Command of the Wehrmacht requests instructions as to what action to take if the Lithuanian troops, which apparently have not yet arrived, should wish to cross the border.

VON KESSEL

No. 84

The German Foreign Minister, Ribbentrop, to the German Foreign Ministry and the Supreme Military Command

Teletype

Baumschule No. 56   June 16, 1940 — 11:15 a.m.

1. I have already given orders through the Gestapo to intern the Lithuanian President, Smetona, with family and other functionaries who have crossed the "green frontier." This will be done by the Secret State Police.

2. If Lithuanian troop contingents ask permission to cross the German border, this request may be granted. The troops are to be disarmed and likewise to be interned.

3. It is reported that a Lithuanian Colonel offered to have his regiment cross the border. It is requested that the disarming and interning of any Lithuanian soldiers who might cross the border be done by the Wehrmacht in collaboration with the Border Police. In agreement with the State Police please take the measures necessary so that the border posts concerned may be immediately informed.

It is again pointed out that border crossings are to be permitted only upon request of the Lithuanians and that we, for our part, must not do anything to encourage such requests.

This communication is to be transmitted at once by the fastest route, orally and in written form, to the OKW with the request for further action.

RIBBENTROP

BERLIN, June 16, 1940.

Minute:

The transmittal to the OKW was made immediately in accordance with instructions. At the same time, the OKW was asked to see to it that in every case of a border crossing of Lithuanian troop contingents a report be made immediately to the Foreign Ministry.

v. d. HEYDEN-RYNSCH

Editor's comment: President Smetona was allowed to leave Germany for Switzerland. He then went to the United States where he died tragically in a fire in Cleveland in 1944.

President Ulmanis of Latvia and President Päts of Estonia were deported to the U. S. S. R. Päts died in exile in the U. S. S. R. in 1943; the fate of Ulmanis is unknown.

No. 85

Memorandum by the Director of the Political Department of the German Foreign Ministry, Woermann

BERLIN, June 16, 1940.

The Lithuanian Minister called on me today to pass on information he had received. Compared with reports here at hand, the following facts are wholly or in part new:

1) Merkys is for the present still fulfilling the duties of Minister President. In consequence of President Smetona having crossed the frontier, he has likewise taken over the duties of President, in accordance with the terms of the constitution. Dekanosov, the People's Commissar now in Kaunas, has given no indication whether or not he acknowledges Merkys in this dual function for the interval.

Nothing is so far known as to the probability of a reconstruction of the Government.

2) A Lithuanian general is negotiating with the Russian Commanding General, Pavlov, the object being, on Lithuania's part, to find some sort of legal basis for the new military situation.

3) During the night the Minister was instructed by Kaunas to try to induce President Smetona to return to Lithuania. M. Škirpa then spoke by telephone to Smetona, who was in Eydtkuhnen. Smetona rejected the idea of returning because Russian interference in Lithuanian affairs is so far-reaching that his return would be useless. Besides this the President believes that he would be arrested at once on his return.

4) At first the Russians posted sentries in front of the Lithuanian ministries, but have withdrawn them; the radio, telegraph, and telephone services are quite free. It is true the Russians have been

interfering in the general management of affairs but not in day to day matters. The Minister was personally of the opinion that this, too, was only a temporary situation.

Speaking with great emotion, M. Škirpa then said that in the report by the German press which gave only the Russian version, he had missed any sign of sympathy for Lithuania, and asked again if an opinion by the Reich Government had not been expressed on these events. I told him that I must refrain from any comment on the situation, whereupon M. Škirpa burst into tears and could not recover for some time.

WOERMANN

Editor's comment: Škirpa, obviously, would attempt to discover the German attitude on the events in his country. For equally obvious reasons, Germany was so compromisingly involved that the German Government could only refrain from any comment.

No. 86

The German Minister in Latvia, Kotze, to the German Foreign Ministry

Telegram

MOST URGENT   RIGA, June 16, 1940 — 11:35 p.m.
No. 257 of June 16   Received June 17 — 2:30 a.m.

The Cabinet has been in session with the President since the delivery at 3 p.m. of the Russian ultimatum, the separate conditions of which are still unknown, but which certainly include the resignation of Ulmanis and complete military freedom of action for the Russians. Although the session has not yet ended, I have just received confidential information from a reliable source that the ultimatum was going to be accepted and the original idea of resistance abandoned. The entry of Russian troops will take place in the early hours of June 17, as in the case of Lithuania. It appears that the Russians are no longer using the reported frontier incident[1] as a pretext at all, but in general the alleged conspiracy by the Baltic States against the Soviet Union.

(3 groups garbled) openly-expressed fears of internal differences and conflicts between army and militia, as well as of a rising of the mob, died down after the state of alert for the army had been countermanded and

the call-up of the militia canceled. Pro-Russian circles are at the moment busily spreading the allegation that the action is directed exclusively against Germany and that before long it will develop into an offensive on German territory. As opposed to this I consider it more probable that while the action may be directed against Germany, it is due to growing anxiety in face of German superiority, and is of a defensive nature. They wish to have the territory of the Baltic States at their disposal for massing as large a number of troops as they desire and for the construction of defense works, but otherwise not to interfere with cultural individuality and to allow economic bodies useful to them for the supply of large cities to continue their activities as far as possible without interference. Please inform DNB and Europapresse (group garbled) of these contents as correspondents' reports are not getting through.

Please also inform OKH Attaché Department.

KOTZE

No. 87

The Director of Political Division VI of the German Foreign Ministry, Grundherr, to the Foreign Minister's Secretariat

Teletype

No. 285 to Baumschule   BERLIN, June 17, 1940 — 6:55 p.m.
e.o. Pol. VI 1759.

For Sonnleithner.

With reference to telegram Baumschule No. 57 of June 16, 1940.[1]

I. The cooperation between the Baltic States of Estonia, Latvia, and Lithuania is based on the Treaty of Mutual Understanding and Cooperation concluded for ten years by these three States on September 12, 1934.[2] In addition, Latvia and Estonia signed a mutual defense pact on November 1, 1923.[3] In practice, the political cooperation consisted mainly of semiannual conferences of Foreign Ministers and joint press conferences; on the other hand, there has often been an abundance of discord and rivalry within the Baltic Entente. Latvia and Estonia explicitly indicated their disinterestedness in the Memel and Vilna questions, which were important to Lithuania. The assertion, now made by Russia, that Lithuania had joined the Estonian-Latvian military pact, is, according to information available here, without any foundation. Because of the very similar economic structure of these countries, the economic cooperation between the three States, in spite of much effort during the last few years, made no appreciable progress. Since the conclusion of the Soviet Mutual Assistance Pacts with the Baltic countries in September-October 1939 there has been no closer cooperation in an anti-Russian sense among the Baltic States. In view of the occupation of their countries by Soviet Russian troops, the three Baltic Governments were aware of the dangers of such a policy.

II. For the same reason, there can be no question — during the last few months — of dependence in foreign policy on Germany by the Baltic States. The Lithuanian Government, to be sure, has probably not been quite certain until the last few days whether or not we were politically completely disinterested in Lithuania, so that in many circles, as for instance in the case of the Lithuanian Minister here, there was perhaps some hope that Germany would, in case of further Russian demands, put in a good word for Lithuania in Moscow, although there was never, of course, any occasion given on our part for such an assumption.

On the other hand, our economic relations with the Baltic States have been strengthened very much since the beginning of the war. Regarding the great importance of the Baltic States to the war economy of the Reich, please see the attached memorandum from Minister Schnurre.

GRUNDHERR

Editor's comment: Since the Soviet military bases had been introduced in October, 1939, the three Baltic States had been very careful not to antagonize the Soviet Union in any way. Even independent newspapers avoided saying anything against the U. S. S. R. Any alliance or line of foreign policy in the Baltic States directed against the Soviet Union was inconceivable. The accusation that secret military alliances had been formed after the conclusion of the Mutual Assistance Pacts was pure and simple fabrication. however firmly grounded in the traditional paranoia of the Kremlin. This was confirmed again and again by authoritative sources and the archives of the countries involved.

No. 88

Memorandum by the Chief of the Eastern European Section of the Economic Policy Department of the German Foreign Ministry, Schnurre

BERLIN, June 17, 1940.

The economic importance of the three Baltic States for our supply of food and of raw materials essential for war has become quite considerable as a result of the commercial treaties concluded with these three States during the last year. In the course of the last six months, we have furthermore concluded secret treaties with all three States whereby the entire export of these countries, except the small part going to Russia and another small portion which goes to neutral countries, will be sent to Germany. That means for all three States about 70 percent of their total exports. German imports from the three Baltic States will in the current year amount to a total of approximately 200 million reichsmarks — comprising grain, hogs, butter, eggs, flax, lumber, seeds, and in the case of Estonia, petroleum.

The consolidation of Russian influence in these areas will seriously endanger these imports which are necessary to us. For one thing, the Russians will do their utmost to keep the raw materials, and especially food, at home for their own use. On the other hand, if part continues to go to Germany, they will make quite different demands in regard to deliveries of German products from those made in the past by the Baltic States, so that in effect the previous exchange of goods will break down. We were able to make the deliveries desired by the Baltic States much more easily, and in many cases, under the stress of circumstances, we were able to put these States off till later.

In contrast, the economic interests of the Soviet Union in the three Baltic States are of minor importance. The Soviet Union was able to secure only about 10 percent of the export trade of these countries for itself by means of treaties it recently concluded.

SCHNURRE

Editor's comment: In view of the economic necessities of the conduct of the war, the Baltic region was of critical importance to Germany. If she could insure her agricultural supply from the Baltic States as had been provided for by military expansion into Poland and into Southeastern

Europe, Germany would have sufficient food supplies assured for a long war in the west.

The abandonment of the Baltic region to Russia was a considerable loss for the German war economy, and may have influenced the German decision to invade Russia in 1941.

No. 89

Circular by the State Secretary of the German Foreign Ministry, Weizsäcker, to all German Diplomatic Missions

Telegram

BERLIN, June 17, 1940.
Pol. VI 1673.

For information and orientation of your conversation.

The unresisted reinforcement of Russian troops in Lithuania, Latvia, and Estonia and the reorganization of the Governments of the Baltic States, sought by the Russian Government to bring about more reliable cooperation with the Soviet Union, are the concern of Russia and the Baltic States. Therefore, in view of our unaltered friendly relations with the Soviet Union, there is no reason for nervousness on our part, which some of the foreign press has tried to impute to us in only too transparent a manner.

Please refrain during conversations from making any statement which could be interpreted as partisan.

Please acknowledge receipt.

WEIZSÄCKER

Editor's comment: In view of the German-Soviet agreements of August 23 and September 28, 1939, to partition Poland and the Baltic area, the incorporation of Latvia, Lithuania and Estonia into the U. S. S. R. was a move not unexpected by the German Government, and could not, for the moment, change the relations between the two partitioning powers, even though the Baltic region was of great economic and strategic importance to Germany.

Nevertheless, the German Government was unpleasantly affected by the Soviet move. Old-line German diplomats, especially Wipert von Blücher, Minister in Helsinki, disapproved of abandoning the traditional German interests in the Baltic, and had to be sharply held in line. Secondly, the unseemly haste with which the Soviet Government rushed a massive army into the Baltic region while the German army was engaged in the West arroused German apprehensions. "Friendly" partitions of Eastern Europe did not preclude power politics between the two giants.

No. 90

The German Ambassador in Moscow, Schuienburg, to the State Secretary of the German Foreign Ministry, Weizsäcker

Telegram

VERY URGENT   Moscow, June 18, 1940 — 1:10 a.m.
No. 1167 of June 17   Received June 18, 1940 — 4 a.m.

Molotov summoned me this evening to his office and expressed the warmest congratulations of the Soviet Government on the splendid success of the German Armed Forces. Thereupon, Molotov informed me of the Soviet action against the Baltic States. He referred to the reasons published in the press and added that it had become necessary to put an end to all the intrigues by which England and France had tried to sow discord and mistrust between Germany and the Soviet Union in the Baltic States.

For the negotiations concerning the formation of the new Governments the Soviet Government had, in addition to the Soviet envoy accredited there, sent the following special emissaries:

To Lithuania: Deputy Commissar of Foreign Affairs Dekanosov; to Latvia: Vishinski, the representative of the Council of Ministers; to Estonia: Regional Party Leader of Leningrad Zhdanov.

In connection with the escape of Smetona and the possible crossing of the frontier by Lithuanian army units, Molotov stated that the Lithuanian border was evidently inadequately guarded. The Soviet Government would, therefore, if requested, assist the Lithuanian Government in guarding its borders.

SCHULENBURG

Editor's comment: The congratulations of the Soviet Government on German military successes in the west, even though the enthusiasm seems a trifle hollow, and the briefing on the recent Soviet actions in the Baltic States show how close relations between the two powers still were at the time. However, the Soviets, who had eagerly expected to watch the three imperialist powers, Germany, England and France, bleed themselves into slow exhaustion in a protracted confrontation on the Western Front, were shocked by the swift German victory. The German armies were now relieved from their immediate task in France, and the U. S. S. R., engaged in the militarization and annexation of the Baltic region, had to be especially careful not to strain its friendship with Germany.

No. 91

Memorandum by the German Minister in Kaunas, Zechlin

BERLIN, June 22, 1940.

The crisis in relations between the Soviet Union and Lithuania which has lasted for several weeks and during which the Soviet Union avoided making any kind of concrete demands on Lithuania, had caused a high degree of nervousness among leading Lithuanian politicians, which was heightened still more by the fruitless sojourn of Minister President Merkys and Foreign Minister Urbšys in Moscow. On the evening of June 14 the Soviet ultimatum regarding the reconstruction of the Lithuanian Government and the entry of an unlimited number of troops, was delivered to Lithuania. The majority of the Lithuanian Cabinet favored acceptance.

Complete panic broke out in Kaunas when, on June 15, the Lithuanian proposal to form a new cabinet under General Raštikis was turned down by the Russians, and at the same time there was announced the entry of Russian troops into Lithuania. A few hours later, when the entry of the Soviet troops into Kaunas was already imminent, President Smetona and Musteikis, the Minister for War, asked me for a visa as they were in utmost danger of their lives. Unfortunately it was no longer possible to consult Berlin. I issued the visa to Smetona and Musteikis — without prejudice to the complete freedom of action of the Reich Government — because there was the danger that they would be stood against a wall, and because then British propaganda would certainly have laid the blame at our door; furthermore because politically Smetona's flight was bound to be extremely welcome to the Russians as it provided them with the best opportunities for propaganda against his Government. The last few days have fully borne this out: The new Government has exploited Smetona's flight in every conceivable way for the purposes of propaganda against him and his adherents.

When it became known next day that Smetona had crossed the "green frontier" (without making use of the visa), I at once informed the Tass representative in Kaunas, who had a graphic description published in the Soviet press of how Smetona, with trousers turned up, had waded across the boundary stream.

Meanwhile the situation has developed in such a way that today Lithuania is already completely under the domination of the Soviet Union: Soviet commissars are installed in all government offices; the police, especially, is now in the hands of extreme Communists. One of the influential members of the new Cabinet is a Jew. Communist propaganda is developing with such speed and force that presumably already within the next few weeks elections to the Soviets will take place, which will then in all probability soon proclaim annexation by the Soviet Union. For this reason it is quite generally expected that Lithuania's formal independence will not last very much longer.

During this period, however, there are still very important German interests to be safeguarded in Lithuania. For one thing, the Reich Germans and Volksdeutsche living there in the midst of general unrest and a complete change in all conditions are now in very special need of the protection of the Legation. In this connection too, we must take into account the existence of the numerically very strong and anti-German Jewish element in Lithuania, which now plays an important part politically, and whose growing insolence can be distinctly felt. If the national group is to remain in Lithuania for some time yet, the presence of the Legation in full strength, would, for that reason, be especially important.

It would, however, in my opinion be better if preparations for the resettlement of the national group could be made in the near future. This would, of course, have to be preceded by an understanding on the matter with Moscow. I believe that resettlement of the national group could not but be welcome to the Soviets, because in Soviet circles in Kaunas there is a great inclination to regard all Germans in Lithuania as spies. In particular, however, the Russians will see in the re-settlement of the national group the strongest proof that Germany is finally disinterested in Lithuania. Therefore I recommend the re-settlement of the national group.

In view of the size of the German national group in Lithuania and the important German interests which would need to be protected in the event of their resettlement, and still more if they remain there, I recommend that the Legation be left at full strength, especially as the Lithuanian State cannot expect to remain in existence for long.

ZECHLIN

Editor's comment: This German memorandum clearly reveals the true political situation in Lithuania and confirms the basic fact that after June 15 Lithuania was under the complete control of the U. S. S. R.

As early as June 15, President Smetona could no longer freely cross the German frontier, but was stopped by guards acting on the orders of the Soviet Union and was forced to flee the country secretly, by wading across a stream. The refusal of Moscow to accept the candidacy of Raštikis for the post of Prime Minister indicated that Lithuania's government was being formed not in accordance with the constitution of the country, but in accordance with the orders of Dekanozov.

No. 92

The German Minister in Kaunas, Zechlin, to the German Foreign Ministry

Telegram

MOST URGENT   KAUNAS, July 5, 1940 — 12:40 a.m.
No. 127 of July 4   Received July 5 — 5:10 a.m.

I have learned in strict confidence from a good source that Molotov told Lithuanian Foreign Minister Krévé-Mickevičius, who returned to Kaunas yesterday evening, that Lithuania's incorporation in the Soviet Union is a settled decision. All attempts of Krévé-Mickevičius to modify this decision failed. Lithuania's incorporation is to be the first to be completed and will be followed by that of Latvia and Estonia. To Krévé-Mickevičius' question why Lithuania had to be the first, Molotov is reported to have replied that this was done on account of Germany.

The procedure apparently planned is to convoke a Seimas which is to agree that (apparently one group missing) is declared. Dekanosov, who also was in Moscow these last days, has returned with several officials in order to arrange the details of the proceedings.

ZECHLIN

Editor's comment: It is to be noted that the establishment of Soviet military bases in the Baltic States in 1939 began with Estonia and ended with Lithuania, while incorporation (1940) began with Lithuania and ended with Estonia. This special sequence was used for reasons of political strategy, taking into account potential intensity of resistance. The Soviets calculated that the country most resistant to the bases should be last, and the most westward, thus the most exposed for incidents, should be incorporated first.

As long as Germany was deeply involved in the West, the USSR could feel safe in the Baltic States, but now that German attention was once more disengaged, one never knew when Hitler might reconsider his attitude about abandoning the Baltic region to the USSR. A fait accompli would compel Germany to deal with Lithuania as an integral part of the USSR.

No. 93

The German Ambassador in Moscow, Schulenburg, to the State Secretary of the German Foreign Ministry, Weizsäcker

Tgb. No. A/3192/40.   Moscow, July 11, 1940.

The entire political interest in Moscow is now focussed on events in the Baltic States and what will happen in relation to Turkey and Iran.

Most people believe that the three Baltic States will be changed into entities completely dependent on Moscow, i.e., will be incorporated into the Soviet Union. The Legations of the three Baltic States here in Moscow expect to be completely dissolved and to disappear in a very short time. It is generally believed that the Soviet Government will demand the withdrawal of all foreign missions in Kaunas, Riga, and Reval (Tallinn). The excitement among Lithuanians, Latvians, and Estonians here is extremely great. However, actual developments will have to be awaited.

COUNT VON DER SCHULENBURG.

No. 94

The U.S. Minister in Kaunas, Norem, to the U.S. Secretary of State, Hull

Telegram

KAUNAS, July 12, 1940.
[Received July 12 — 4 p.m.]

150. I have the honor to inform the Department that the new Sejm to be elected on July 14 will most likely ask for immediate inclusion of Lithuania into the Union of Soviet Socialist Republics. Mr. Seja told me confidentially that the Lithuanian Minister for Foreign Affairs had been so informed on his recent visit to Moscow. The one list of candidates to be presented to the people includes laborers, farmers, soldiers, dancers, writers, and singers who have expressed radical views. The Minister of Finance resigned a few days ago and the Minister of Foreign Affairs is reported to have tendered his resignation for the second time.

NOREM

Editor's comment: The "Seimas" elections were illegal and invalid for the following reasons: a) They were held under the occupation of the country by foreign troops; b) The candidates were selected by only one party allowed and approved by the occupation authorities; c) The district Electoral Commissions submitted the lists of candidates to the Supreme Electoral Commission (Article 23 of the Electoral Law). Since the Supreme Electoral Commission was, infact, selected and approved by the Soviet emissaries, Dekanozov and Pozdniakov, it should be considered as an organ of the occupational forces, operating in the interests of the USSR, and its actions not binding on Lithuania and having no constitutional force.

No. 95

The Lithuanian Minister in Washington, Žadeikis, to the U.S. Secretary of State, Hull

No. 826 WASHINGTON, July 13, 1940.

SIR: Referring to my note of June 25. 1940 I have the honor to advise you further that, according to information available, H. E. Antanas Smetona, the President of Lithuania, before departing for abroad because of ill health, on June 15, 1940 officially requested Mr. Antanas Merkys, the Prime Minister, to substitute [for] him in the duties of the President, in accordance with Article 71 of the Constitution of the Republic of Lithuania.

On June 16, 1940, Mr. Antanas Merkys as Acting President of the Republic was replaced by Mr. Justas Paleckis, the new Prime Minister.

While President Antanas Smetona still remained abroad, Mr. Paleckis' government, which came into existence as a result of the Soviet Union ultimatum of June 14, 1940, dismissed the Seimas (Parliament) as of July 1, 1940 and on July 6 decreed that new elections be held on July 14, 1940, disregarding the fact that the whole of Lithuania is pervaded with numerous divisions of foreign troops, which is another result of the previously mentioned Soviet ultimatum of June 14, 1940.

From the information available, it appears that the scheduled elections will be carried out exclusively under the aegis of the Communist party which was legalized recently for this and other purposes by the Paleckis government.

Grave doubt and concern arises regarding the possibility of free expression of the true will of the Lithuanian nation through the impending elections under such circumstances.

Accept [etc.]

P. ŽADEIKIS

Editor's note: Jurgis Glušauskas viewed the Seimas elections from a slightly different perspective. In 1940, he was not only inside Lithuania, but police chief of Kaunas, soon to become People's Commissar of Social Maintenance and the Lumber Industry. We give here his reminiscences, written in Adelaide, Australia on November 15, 1953:

"On July 14, 1940 I was appointed to watch the voting to the 'People's Diet" in the district of Mariampole. At that time I was chief of police of the city of Kaunas and its district. The task assigned to me was to render help whereever necessary.

When I arrived at Mariampole, I found everything ready for the election. I learned that the supervisor of the election there was a high official of the Soviet secret polict (NKVD), a Russian, who had at his disposal a number of Russian soldiers and some army trucks. Therefore, all that was left for me to do was to observe what was going on.

Several hours before the closing of the polls, it was announced that only 5 or 10 percent of those eligible to vote had cast their ballots. The NKVD officer was greatly concerned over such a situation. Finally, the following orders were given: 1. All chairmen of electoral districts were ordered to record higher percentages of votes than were actually cast. As a result of this order, in an hour, all reports showed a 40 to 60 percent vote, and when the polls were about to close the percentage suddenly leaped to 99. 2. The NKVD personnel had instructions to tour villages and bring in voters by force. But because only a few trucks were available, this measure did not prove successful. Also, there was very little time left for voting.

I consider the elections to the 'People's Diet' were a deception for the following reasons:

, 1. Actually, only 5 to 15 percent of the electors voted, and therefore did not represent the will of the Lithuanian people.

2. Candidates for the 'People's Diet' were nominated by the Central Committee of the Communist Party without their knowledge or consent. The list of candidates was presented by the Working People's Union which was the Communist Party itself. There were exactly as many candidates as members of the 'Diet' to be elected. There was no choice but to vote for those nominated by the Communist Party.

3. No lists of electors had been prepared so that it was impossible to determine the percentage of the votes cast. This circumstance offered a good opportunity to falsify the results of the elections.

4. It was publicly made known that persons failing to appear at the polls will be regarded as 'enemies of the people'. Everybody knew that such a branding meant deportation to forced labor camps in Siberia or other remote places in Russia.

Conclusion: All decisions of the 'People's Diet are null and void as the 'Diet' itself could not and did not represent the will of the Lithuanian people."

No. 96

Memorandum by the Assistant Chief of the Division of European Affairs of the U.S. State Department, Henderson

[WASHINGTON,] July 15, 1940.

\s you are aware, on one pretext or another the Soviet Government.

by demands backed up with threats of force, has during the last six weeks forced the three Baltic countries of Estonia, Latvia, and Lithuania to permit the entrance of Soviet troops aggregating about 500,000 men. Under Soviet pressure the Governments in all three countries have been replaced by governments which are mere Soviet puppets. The President of Lithuania was successful in escaping to Germany; the President of Latvia appears to be a virtual if not an actual prisoner; the President of Estonia is also apparently without any power whatsoever.

Under Soviet pressure elections were ordered in these three countries for yesterday and today. It is clear from reports which reach us that these elections are merely a mockery. Only persons approved by the Soviet Government or the Communist International are permitted to stand as candidates. It appears likely that following these so-called elections it will be arranged for these three republics to be merged into the Soviet Union. Whether these arrangements will be put into effect at once or whether the Soviet Government will be satisfied for some time to come with having the three countries under its actual control, although fictitiously independent, remains to be seen.

On Saturday, July 13, shortly after noon, the Latvian Minister presented the attached not to Mr. Atherton after having endeavored unsuccessfully to obtain an appointment with the Secretary or Under Secretary. In this note he points out that in view of the circumstances surrounding the holding of the elections in Latvia he "reserves the right not to recognize the results of the coming elections and the acts emanating therefrom". The Minister also states that in United States banks there are deposits of the Latvian State and of Latvian banks, corporations and private citizens, and that there are a number of Latvian ships in the waters of the western hemisphere.

Editor's comment: The memorandum was addressed to Assistant Secretary of State Adolf A. Berle, Jr., and Adviser on Political Relations James C. Dunn, who added by hand: "I feel funds of all 3 of these countries should be blocked on the same basis as those of countries occupied by Germany." The memorandum is significant as an acknowledgement by a neutral state of the Soviet military occupation of the Baltic Republics and as consideration of the Baltic States in the same category as "countries occupied by Germany."

No. 97

The U.S. Minister in Kaunas, Norem, to the U.S. Secretary of State, Hull

KAUNAS, July 19, 1940 — 10 a.m.
[Received 7:38 p.m.]

158. The election results have been announced as one of 99% variety and indicates a total lack of true democratic expression. Indications point to complete absorption into the Soviet Union. The new Seimas is scheduled to meet on Sunday, July 21.*

The *Kulturverband* is completing its registration of all German-owned property. The actual transfer of some 36,000 of German blood and 400,000 mixed blood, many of whom joined the organization for protection, has been discussed in Berlin and local reports are to the effect that it will be effected within the next 5 weeks.

Former Government leaders Merkys and Urbšys are reported to be in Moscow as "guests" of the Soviet Government.

The Argentine Consul has shipped his effects and plans to leave for Berlin in a few days.

NOREM

Editor's comment: It should here be pointed out that Norem proved to be an unusually competent American diplomat gaining the friendship and confidence of many Lithuanians. All available comments on him are very complimentary, and the high regard of many of his Lithuanian friends survived the war and the emigration. Norem was recalled to the United States on July 30, 1940. He was not reappointed to another diplomatic post.

In 1943 Norem published a history of Lithuania, *Timeless Lithuania* (Chicago: Amlit Press), devoting a good deal of space to his own observations of the Soviet occupation and incorporation. The book is certainly an excellent narrative of the events of the occupation of Lithuania by the U. S. S. R., for he displays a sharp eye for detailed observation. Here are some of his more perceptive glimpses:

---

*This body met at noon on July 21 and "decided to petition the Soviet Union for incorporation into the Soviet Union as a republic with full status."

The trains deporting political prisoners to Siberia would leave carrying banners marked: "Enemies of the People". They would return, empty, carrying banners marked: "Food for starving Lithuanians."

Some American students who were in Lithuania during the elections to the People's Seimas arrived home with their American passports stamped "Balsavo" — voted.

During the early stages of the occupation it cost $10.00, American money, to half-sole a shoe. Eggs sold for $1.00 a piece. Norem estimates that commodity prices rose over 300%, while wages increased by 30%.

7,333 families were evicted from their homes and apartments to provide accomodation for the Soviet officials and their dependents who had been imported into Lithuania.

The street housing the Soviet Legation was renamed from Laisves Aleja (Freedom Boulevard) to Stalino Aleja (Stalin Boulevard).

No. 98

Counselor of the U.S. Embassy in Moscow, Thurston, to the U.S. Secretary of State, Hull

Telegram

Moscow, July 20, 1940 — 9 p.m.
[Received 9:30 p.m.]

885. I was requested by Assistant Commissar Lozovski to call at the Commissariat for Foreign Affairs this evening. Upon my arrival he stated that he had been directed to lodge a strong protest against the withholding from the Soviet State Bank by American banks of gold acquired by it from Estonian, Latvian and Lithuanian banks. He then handed to me the following memorandum stating that an early reply is desired and commenting that the American action is illegal and serious. I stated that I would bring the memorandum of protest to the attention of my Government and advise him promptly of such reply as I might be instructed to make to it. With respect to his comment on the illegality of our acts I stated that while there is room for differences of opinion regarding such matters I could not accept his employment of the term "illegal" as my Government does not engage in illegal activities:

"The Government of the U. S. S. R. directs the attention of the Government of the United States to the actions of the Federal Reserve

Bank, New York, a bank which has permitted an arbitrary suspension of the transfer of gold belonging to the Soviet state to the State Bank of the U.S.S.R.

The above-mentioned gold was acquired by State Bank of the U.S.S.R. from the Lithuanian, Latvian and Estonian banks on the basis of sale purchase agreements and was subject to transfer to the deposit of the State Bank of the U.S.S.R. by virtue of telegraphic orders of July 13, 1940 of the Lithuanian, Latvian and Estonian banks, orders which are unconditionally binding upon the Federal Reserve Bank. Nevertheless, instead of immediately fulfilling the above-mentioned instructions of the banks of Lithuania, Latvia and Estonia the Federal Reserve Bank after a completely unjustified delay of 3 days informed the State Bank of the U.S.S.R. by a telegram of July 16, 1940 that it was soliciting the permission of the Federal Treasury of the United States for transfer of the gold to the State Bank of the U.S.S.R. Along with this the Federal Reserve Bank referred to 'Executive Order No. 8484 of July 15, 1940 which prohibits operations involving property in which Latvia, Lithuania or Estonia or citizens of those countries, have an interest, from being conducted without permission.

No further communication concerning a change in the situation which has arisen of suspension of the transfer of the gold to the account of the State Bank of the U.S.S.R. have arrived from the Federal Reserve Bank up to the present time.

The Soviet Government considers the actions of the American institutions to be directed against the Soviet Union's realization of its legal property rights to the said gold as undermining the foundations of normal commercial relations and as contrary to the elementary principles of international law.

The Soviet Government in particular notes that:

1. The Federal Reserve Bank had no legal bases whatsoever for suspending the execution of the operations of transferring the gold to the State Bank of the U.S.S.R., operations with which the Bank was already commissioned on July 13, 1940 by the Banks of Lithuania, Latvia and Estonia. The references of the Federal Reserve Bank to the 'Executive Order No. 8484 of July 15, 1940' as a basis for nonfulfillment during the course of July 13th, 14th and 15th of the said instructions are absolutely unconvincing inasmuch as these instructions had already been received prior to the issue of the order.

2. With regard to the contents of 'Executive Order No. 8484,' contents cited in the communication of the Federal Reserve Bank, it is

necessary to point out that neither this nor any other order can limit the rights of the U. S. S. R. to the receipt of the property which it has purchased or to the disposal of this property as property of a sovereign state which possesses immunity by virtue of its sovereignty.

On the basis of the foregoing the Soviet Government makes to the Government of the United States of America a determined protest against the violation by the aforesaid institutions of the United States of America of the interests of the Soviet Union and of the latter's legal right to the gold purchased from the banks of Lithuania, Latvia, and Estonia for an appropriate equivalent.

The Soviet Government expects an immediate transfer of the gold which it has purchased from the Banks of Lithuania, Latvia and Estonia to the State Bank of the U.S.S.R. and charges the Government of the United States of America with all responsibility for the losses inflicted upon the U.S.S.R. by the actions of the American institution."

THURSTON

Editor's comment: The U. S. Government had frozen the funds of the Baltic States in Federal Reserve Banks on the same basis as the funds of countries under German occupation.

No. 99

Excerpts from a Speech by the First Secretary of the Central Committee of the Lithuanian Communist Party, Snieckus

July 13, 1940

At least 58 of the 79 members of the Diet were Communists. They knew upon whom the real authority rested. On July 13, the secretary of the Communist Party central committee stated openly:

Comrades. The People acquired their freedom not accidentally. During 22 years the working people of Lithuania struggled in the worst conditions of reaction. The best sons and daughters have lost their lives for freedom. *At all times, our best friend, the Soviet Union, has helped us * * * * [Italics furnished.]

Finally, *the Soviet Union helped us to overthrow the yoke of Smetonists* under which we suffered more than 13 years. For this paternal aid no gratitude would be too great * * * [Italics furnished.]

Today, the Communist Party, is a strong and decisive force in Lithuanian life. It became such because it was closely connected with the people and served them, because it always was led by the science of Marx-Engels-Lenin-Stalin, because it was under the leadership of the Comintern, and finally because the pilot of the Comintern was Comrade Dimitrov. It is a guarantee that the Communist Party will not stop halfway and will not deceive the people.

Editor's comment: It would be redundant to point out the many specific occasions on which the U.S.S.R., in international agreements or unilateral declarations, pledged not to interfere in the domestic affairs of Lithuania. Yet even these pledges were in a sense superfluous, since noninterference in the internal affairs of other States is one of the cornerstones of international law, as important as the principle of fidelity to treaty obligations. This is necessary for the existence of an international system composed of many hostile political ideologies, each of which rejects many of the premises on which the others are founded. The consensus seems to be that a stable international community requires that one's political religion be left at home. The U. S. S. R. fully participated in the international system, and, after the Soviet Government had established itself, benefited from the principle of noninterference in its domestic affairs.

However, it should be pointed out that the U. S. S. R. never really meant to observe the principle of noninterference in the domestic affairs of others. The Soviet Government was not only the ruling organ of a large and powerful country, but also the director of the world revolution. The dialectic between its duties as a government and revolutionary conspiracy to a large extent determined the course of Soviet foreign policy.

In this case, the interference in domestic affairs was only a means to an end, the violation of Lithuanian sovereignty. The Soviet Union thus doubly abused the concept of sovereignty, the foundation of the international legal system.

No. 100

Resolution of the People's Seimas of Lithuania

July 21, 1940

The regime of Smetona, indifferent to the real interests of the people, pushed the Lithuanian internal and external policy into a hopeless impasse. The vital interests of the Lithuanian toilers were sacrificed to the selfish interests of small groups of wealthy people and exploiters. The destiny of the toiling people of the cities and villages were: unemployment, uncertainty for the future, privations, and inequality of ethnic groups. For many years the people were oppressed by this reactionary regime.

The gang of Smetona kept our toiling people in the chains of despotism. The toiling people were deprived of the most elementary freedoms. The people could not have their own political, labor, and cultural organizations. Anyone who dared to voice his honest opinion was mercilessly oppressed.

The aim of the national policy of Smetona was to provoke collisions between the different ethnic groups and to instigate one ethnic group against another. Such national policy was the basis of the usurping Government of Smetona and his gang. This is the reason why for 8 months after the Union of Soviet Socialist Republics recognized the city of Vilnius and its region as a part of Lithuania, national discord in the Vilnius region did not abate but grew stronger.

The interests of the Lithuanian people required the building up of constant and close relations with the U. S. S. R. However, Smetona and his accomplices cultivated a hostile policy toward the U. S. S. R. They pushed our country into semicolonial dependence on individual capitalist robbers, causing great injury to the Lithuanian people and preparing the field for further aggression against the U. S. S. R.

The Lithuanian people could no longer tolerate such abitrariness and treachery in their relations with foreign governments. The people liquidated the hated Government together with the high administration and so cleared the way for the free elections of the People's Diet, which really could represent the interests of the toiling people and which was constructed by the people's own hands.

The days of July 14-15 were historic days in the life of the toiling people of Lithuania. In these days was born the alliance of workers, peasants, and working intelligensia. These days marked the victory of the platform of the Union of the Working People of Lithuania. This platform rallied all honest patriots of the country and all who cherished Lithuanian interests.

In these days the Lithuanian people expressed its will to abolish the political domination of landlords and capitalists forever, and also to form a real people's Government and with its own hands to begin the reorganization of the governmental structure of our country. The victory of the Union of the Working People of Lithuania is a historic turning point, granting to the toiling people all civic and political rights, guaranteeing a better future for them and future generations.

The People's Diet, as representative of the sovereign will of Lithuania, being called upon to strengthen its victories achieved in the struggle with plutocrats, considers its main task and duty to resolve the question of the form of the Lithuanian regime on a new basis.

From the great historic experience of the people of the U. S. S. R., we have learned that only the Soviet government is a real representative and defender of the interests of the toiling people, that only the Soviet government is a real people's government, where the country is governed by the people itself without capitalists and landlords. Only the soviets (council of workers) represent a real incarnation of the alliance between workers and peasants.

In the Soviet Union the exploitation of man by man is abolished forever. The guiding principle of all life in the U. S. S. R. is the concern for the well-being of the citizens-human-beings. All working people are granted the right to work, rest, free education, free medical care, and security in old age. The Soviet government is the most democratic government. From the experience of capitalist countries we have learned that every other form of government is the domination of a small group of exploiters and unlimited arbitrariness directed against the toiling people. All toiling people take part in the government through the soviets on an equal basis and contribute to the building up of a free and happy life for all. Only the Soviet system provides the proper conditions to bring up from among the people the necessary leaders and organizers of the state, and of economic and public life. It gives an opportunity for the people to exercise their own talents and abilities. In the U. S. S. R. there is no oppression of ethnical groups or inequality of those groups. This cursed inheritance is definitely abolished. The introduction of the soviet system in Lithuania, where the overthrown governing gang has initiated the struggle between ethnic groups, will be unique and the most effective guarantee of the equality of ethnic groups and national prosperity. Only the soviet system can assure us peace, work, and freedom and deliver the people of cities and villages from exploitation, misery, and despotism. Only the soviet system can assure us political, economic, and cultural prosperity. All this is proved by the example of the U. S. S. R.

The People's Diet, expressing the unanimous will of the toiling people, proclaims that the soviet system shall be introduced in Lithuania. Lithuania shall be proclaimed a Soviet Socialist Republic. Beginning today all power in the Lithuanian Soviet Socialist Republic shall belong to the toiling people of the cities and villages, represented in the soviets by their own representatives.

The People's Diet is firmly convinced that all inhabitants of Lithuania will rally around the Soviet Government to assure welfare, economic and cultural prosperity, to give our country freedom and happiness, and to lead the country towards final victcry of the people.

Long live the Lithuanian Soviet Socialist Republic!

Long live the representatives of the Soviets toiling peoples!

Long live the Soviet Union — fatherland of all toiling people of the world!

Long live comrade Stalin — the Leader and Teacher of all toiling people of the world!

J. PALECKIS,
The Prime Minister, Acting as President of the Republic.
Prof. V. KREVE-MICKEVICIUS,
Deputy Prime Minister.

Editor's comment: The declaration of Lithuania as a Soviet Socialist Republic is an obvious step toward incorporation. With the introduction of the Soviet system, there was no longer any possibility of maintaining Lithuania outside the Union. It should be pointed out, however, that the People's Seimas, even if one were to concede the validity of its election, would still be an ordinary legislative body, not elected for the purpose of changing the form of government, much less for changing sovereignty, and in introducing such drastic changes, it would still clearly exceed its constitutional mandate.

One might well ask why the Soviet Union, given its absolute preponderance of physical force and the docility of local Communists who had survived the great purges, did not pay more attention to the trappings of legality in conducting the incorporation. The change of government would have required a constituent Seimas. To begin with, the Soviets had enough trouble electing a docile legislature, ostensibly to conduct the daily necessities of government business, without risking a general election for a Constituent Seimas. Such an election would have revealed their future projects in full. At worst they could have been faced with a popular revolt. At best, some sort of referendum on the new order would have had to be staged, and it would have been impossible to eliminate the yes/no option and still maintain any sort of credit in the eyes of the world. In other words, whatever happened, the U.S.S.R. would be embarrassed, and the "spontaneity" of the petition of incorporation, meant to cover its irregularity, would have been lost.

Besides, all this would have taken a great deal of time, and after Germany's lightning victory in the West, the Soviet Union had no time to spare.

No. 101

Declaration of the People's Seimas of Lithuania

July 21, 1940

After a brief intermission following adoption of the resolution on the form of government, the People's Diet adopted the second resolution. Like the previous resolution, this second resolution was proclaimed as a declaration by the Prime Minister on July 21, 1940. This resolution stated:

The Lithuanian people, pitilessly exploited and raped, condemned to misery, and vanishing, have established a new governmental system, a system where the lawful master of the house is the people. This system is the Soviet system. Lithuania has become a Soviet Socialist Repbulic.

For a long time both labor and intelligentsia in Lithuania suffered from unemployment, and oppressed by misery and lawlessness, they could find no way out. The landless and small peasants of Lithuania were smothered, because the largest part of the land was robbed by landlords and other big owners. In the old Lithuania the only ones who had good living conditions were exploiters, manufacturers, bankers, landlords, and top employees, and those hunting for high profits and incomes have enslaved the toiling people of Lithuania.

Treacherous rulers-Smetonists promoted foreign capital in Lithuania, which raped insatiably and lacerated with rapacious claws the body of the Lithuanian people. The political and economic dependence of Lithuania upon imperialistic robbers and upon foreign capitalists and bankers increased more and more. *Now, the people helped by the mighty Red Army,* overthrew the yoke of slavery thrust upon them by

Smetonists, and established the Soviet system in their own country. [Italics furnished]

The existing Soviet Socialist Republics are not closed and separated one from another, but they constitute an indestructible union. They entered in the Union of Soviet Socialist Republics formed on an equal free basis.

From experience we have learned that collaboration between the Soviet republics gave them exceptional prosperity, huge economic and cultural development. In a short time they became the most progressive republics from a political, economic, and cultural point of view. Never would an individual republic achieve such results.

From experience we have learned that only united Soviet republics could oppose imperialistic efforts to enslave small people. Without a state's union of the Soviet republics, without gathering together their economic and military forces into a union it would be impossible to oppose the united forces of capitalists in either economic or in military fields.

The Lithuanian people know that the policy of the Soviet Union toward Lithuania was friendly at all times. If Lithuania was not seized by the landlords of Poland, if the old Lithuanian capital Vilnius was returned to Lithuania, if Lithuania could stay away from World War fire, *if the Lithuanian people could establish in their country the only just system of government — Soviet Government — it is all due to the Soviet Union.* Therefore, the Lithuanian people in all times have seen a better future in closer relationship with the Union of Soviet Socialist Republics. [Italics furnished.]

The reactionary criminal clique of former Lithuanian rulers obstructed by every means the fraternal relationship between Lithuania and the U. S. S. R.

Now, the Lithuanian people, freed from violence and lawlessness and having established a new state and social order, shall ratify by law a firm friendship and union between the Lithuanian Republic and the Union of Soviet Socialist Republics.

The Lithuanian People's Diet is convinced that only entrance in the Union of Soviet Socialist Republics will guarantee the true sovereignty of the Lithuanian State, the real development of industry and economy, the real blossom of national culture, and the complete development of material and spiritual forces of the people.

Obedient to the will of the people, who overthrew the old regime of oppression and lawlessness, the regime of exploitation of man, the People's Diet resolved:

To ask the Supreme Soviet of the U. S. S. R. to admit the Lithuanian Soviet Socialist Republic in the body of the Union of Soviet Socialist Republics as a union republic on the same basis as the Ukrainian, the Byelorussian, and other union republics.

Long.live the Lithuanian Soviet Socialist Republic.

Long live the great Union of the Soviet Socialist Republics.

J. PALECKIS,
Prime Minister, Acting as President of the Republic.
Prof. V. KREVE-MICKEVICIUS.
Deputy Prime Minister.

Editor's comment: Normally the procedure for a change of government, and especially for the transfer of sovereignty, requires something more than a routine legislative resolution — at least a plebiscite. For all the loud and frequent protestations about the dictates of the will of the people, the population of Lithuania was never consulted on the important questions facing Lithuania.

In fact, the incorporation procedure even differed significantly from all previous additions to the Union of Soviet Socialist Republics. The normal procedure for Republics applying for membership was to sign a bilateral treaty of federation with the Soviet Union. The Lithuanian S. S. R. was admitted by two legislative acts, one of its own Seimas, one of the Supreme Soviet. This way, the Soviets thought, no one could accuse them of forcing Lithuania to sign a treaty under duress.

No doubt Molotov and Stalin fully realized that the only law by which they would hold Lithuania was *vis et armis*. Had it not been for the overwhelming presence of the Soviet military, neither treaty nor puppet legislature could have secured the annexation — with the triumph of Soviet arms, nothing could be done to actively contest their conquests. Sniečkus, the first secretary of the LCP, knew that very well when he said: "Now the people, helped by the mighty Red Army . . . have established in their country the Soviet government. . . . If the people have established in their country the only just order — the Soviet order — it is all due to the Soviet Union."

No. 102

List of Delegates Elected by the People's Seimas to Present the Petition for Incorporation to the Supreme Soviet of the USSR

July 21-22, 1940

Justas Paleckis
Liudas Adomauskas
Matas Mickis
Antanas Venclova
Gen. Vincas Vitkauskas
Karolis Didžiulis
Liudas Gira
Motiejus Šumauskas
Petras Cvirka
Kazys Petrauskas
Pranas Zibertas
Stase Vaineikiene
Adomas (Icikas Meskupas)
Viktoras Ditkevičius
Pranas Petrauskas
Juozas Demskis
Marija Kutraite
Bijuré Abdulskaite
Salomeja Neris

Editor's comment: The incorporation of Lithuania was the ultimate achievement of the LCP, and the list of honors seems to have been made up carefully to spread the glory most efficiently throughout the Party. Certainly the list seems to be drawn with only the Party in mind, disregarding representation of Lithuanian society as a whole, or even of the People's Seimas, and it is likely that only the magnitude of the event justified the blatant clubbishness of the occasion.

As far as can be ascertained, the delegation was composed mostly of Party Members. Individual backgrounds can be checked in the Biographical Glossary at the back of the book, but in brief, all those for whom full information is available were in the Party, and the remainder would seem to have been from all the available evidence.

The delegates can be divided into three categories. There was the new power establishment, which had risen to prominence essentially only through holding State office after the occupation, that is: Paleckis, Adomauskas, Mickis, Venclova, Vitkauskas, Šumauskas. Next, we find a significant group of Party organizers who had guided the Party through the underground years, but did not actively participate in the higher State Government, but apparently remained in the provinces as organizers: Didžiulis, Kazys and Pranas Petrauskas, Zibertas, Adomas, Ditkevičius, Demskis, Abdulskaite, and Kutraite. These seem to represent a Party core which remains distinct from the State organs, headed by Adomas, the Second Secretary of the LCP. Finally, there is a group of leftist writers, whose Communist credentials are not particularly strong, but who have solid literary reputations, perhaps the genesis of a Lithuanian Revolutionary Inteligentsia. These are: Gira, Vainekiene, Neris, and Cvirka.

There seems to be very little overlap between these distinct categories. In fact several prominant Lithuanian Communists who held high offices in both Party and State, like Snieckus, First Secretary of the LCP and chief of the secret police, and Glovackas, Acting Foreign Commissar and member of the Central Committee, are absent, though their inclusion would seem obvious.

While it is not clear exactly why the list of delegates was so tailored, it seems obvious that the selection had more to do with the LCP Central Committee and Soviet Legation than with Seimas politicking. Every indication seems to point to the conclusion that the People's Seimas was a carelessly used rubber stamp of the Party machinery.

No. 103

Law on the Admission of the Lithuanian Soviet Socialist Republic into the Union of Soviet Socialist Republics

August 3, 1940

Law on the Admission of the Lithuanian Soviet Socialist Republic into the Union of Soviet Socialist Republics

Having heard the report of the Plenipotentiary Commission of the Seimas (Diet) of Lithuania, the Supreme Soviet of the Union of Soviet Socialist Republics has decided:

1. to grant the request of the Seimas (Diet) of Lithuania and to admit

the Lithuanian Soviet Socialist Republic into the Union of Soviet Socialist Republics as an equal Federal Soviet Socialist Republic;

2. to accept the proposal of the Supreme Soviet of the Byelorussian SRR on the cession of the rayon [District or County] of Svencionys and parts of the rayons of Vidzin, Godutiskiu, Ostroveckiu, Varonovskiu, and Rodunes of the Byelorussian SSR, territories with a predominantly Lithuanian population, to the Federal Lithuanian Soviet Socialist Republic;

3. to ask the Supreme Soviet of the Byelorussian Soviet Socialist Republic and the Supreme Soviet of the Lithuanian Soviet Socialist Republic to submit for consideration a draft of the exact delimitation of the frontiers between the Byelorussian Soviet Socialist Republic and the Lithuanian Soviet Socialist Republic;

4. to carry out elections, in accordance with sections 34 and 35 of the Constitution (basic law) of the U. S. S. R., to the Supreme Soviet of the U. S. S. R. in the Federal Lithuanian Soviet Socialist Republic;

5. to authorize the Presidium of the Supreme Soviet of the U. S. S. R. to set the day of elections.

The Chairman of the Presidium of the Supreme Soviet of the U. S. S. R. —

U. KALININ.

The Secretary of the Presidium of the Supreme Soviet of the U. S. S. R. —

A. GORKIN.

Editor's comment: The Lithuanian, Latvian and Estonian delegations presented their petitions for incorporation on the same day, at the same time. It was a golden day for the Soviet Union.

The annexation of Bessarabia and northern Bukovina was formalized soon afterwards with the creation of the Moldavian S. S. R. With the territorial gains in Poland and the land won in the Finnish war, the entire cordon sanitaire stretching from the Black Sea to the Baltic, which the statesmen of Versailles had erected as a barrier to the expansion of Communist Russia, became the forward bastion of the U. S. S. R. in Eastern Europe, greatly strengthening its strategic position vis a vis Germany.

The incorporation of Lithuania besides depriving it of its sovereign rights subjected the Lithuanian people to many obvious impositions.

The Soviet occupation forces brought the N. K. V. D. and the Stalinist terror with them. The confiscation of industrial plants and commercial establishments, and even bank accounts, greatly impoverished the rich and the middle classes; however, because the products of the Lithuanian economy were diverted for the benefit of the U. S. S. R., the poor gained nothing from the changes, and became even poorer themselves. The beginnings of collectivization already threatened the modicum of prosperity achieved by the small farmers who made up the bulk of the Lithuanian population.

Yet, the exploitation of Lithuania was more subtle and far reaching than these gross generalizations can show. For example, the Lithuanian litas had the buying power of four rubles before the war. The Soviets declared a new rate of exchange in which one litas equalled .9 rubles, withdrew 223,000,000 litai from circulation and reissued 200,000,000 rubles. Lithuania thus lost 800,000,000 litai, in effect, because of the more even distribution of wealth, or poverty, after the Soviet invasion, 250 litai for every Lithuanian. This is but one example of how thorough the exploitation of Lithuania proved to be, the new occupants not only taking the Lithuanians' homes and bank accounts, but pausing to pick their pockets.

CHAPTER III
AFTERMATH OF INCORPORATION
A. DIVIDING THE SPOILS

No. 104

Memorandum of the Director of the Political Department of the German Foreign Ministry, Woermann

BERLIN, July 22, 1940.

The Lithuanian Minister called on me today and stated the following:

In view of the important events in his country he considered it his duty not to let these events pass into history without taking action. He had summarized his attitude toward events in Lithuania in a letter to the Reich Foreign Minister. The presentation of this letter amounted to a unilateral act on his part, for which he alone assumed responsibility. He himself did not wish to cause any embarrassment to German policy by this act.

The matter arose in the following way: Some time ago, as a precaution, Foreign Minister Urbšys instructed all Lithuanian Ministers to take such a step in case of a transfer of sovereignty to the Soviet Union. On the basis of a communication between the Lithuanian Ministers he felt sure that a corresponding note would be presented today in all capitals in which Lithuania was represented. The Minister then handed me the enclosed letter, which contains "a most solemn and determined protest."

I told Herr Škirpa that for the time being I wanted to keep the document myself, and I assumed from his statements that he did not expect any comment on it. However, I could not tell him whether as the German Government we would be prepared to accept such a note at all, and we would therefore have to reserve the right to return it to him.

The Minister then stated that particularly in view of the known attitude of Germany he had omitted one point in the note, which the other Lithuanian Ministers would include in their notes to the governments to which they were accredited, namely, the request that the incorporation not be recognized. The Minister asked whether he could not at least orally present this request here. I rejected this, whereupon the Minister stated that the request was to be considered as not having been made. Finally, the Minister said that he intended to make known his action by an announcement from the Berlin office of the Elte Agency, since this appeared to him necessary for the assertion of his personal attitude toward events.

I requested the Minister to refrain from this, and he promised to comply.

Transmitted to the Reich Foreign Minister through the State Secretary with the request for instructions whether the note should be retained here. The Latvian and Estonian Ministers may be expected to present similar notes here. The Latvian Minister had already made an appointment with me for 5:30 p.m. today.

WOERMANN

No. 105

The Counselor of the U.S. Embassy in Moscow, Thurston, to the U.S. Secretary of State, Hull

Telegram   Moscow, August 11, 1940—6 p.m.
                                         [Received August 11—3:28 p.m.]

1001. I have just received a formal note from Molotov dated August 11th, which after citing the fact of the admission of Lithuania, Latvia and Estonia into the Soviet Union as component parts thereof having all the rights and obligations ensuing from their new status, stated that direct diplomatic relations between those states have in consequence ceased.

The note then states that

"The Soviet Government therefore expects that the missions of the United States of America in Kaunas, Riga, and Tallinn will complete the liquidation of their affairs by August 25th, 1940. Likewise, the exequaturs which were issued by the former Lithuanian, Latvian, and Estonian Governments to foreign consuls, lose their validity; and these consuls are to liquidate their consular offices by the same date.

"Furthermore the diplomatic and consular missions of Lithuania, Latvia and Estonia in other states cease to operate, and transfer their functions, as well as their archives and property, to the appropriate plenipotentiary representatives or consulates of the Union of Soviet Socialist Republics."

I shall appreciate instructions as to the reply to be made to this communication.

Repeat to Kaunas, Riga and Tallinn.

THURSTON

No. 106

The U.S. Charge in Kaunas, Gufler, to the U.S. Secretary of State, Hull

Telegram   KAUNAS, August 13, 1940—11 a.m.
                                                        [Received 4:15 p.m.]

205. Within the past 2 days all representatives of foreign countries in Lithuania have received notes dated August 10th requesting them to inform their governments that as a result of the entry of Lithuania into the Soviet Union the Lithuanian diplomatic and consular representations in their respective countries are liquidated as of August 8th. A note so dated and signed by the General Secretary of the Foreign Office, Glovackas, as Acting Foreign Minister, was received by this Legation this morning.

I have also received this morning a note dated August 12th signed by Professor Kreve-Mickevicius, the Minister for Foreign Affairs, requesting me to inform the Government of the United States that in view of the admission of Lithuania into the Soviet Union all direct diplomatic relations between Lithuania and the United States of America have ceased to exist.

The note continues:

"The Government of the Soviet Socialist Republic of Lithuania hopes that the Legation of the United States of America will liquidate its affairs in Lithuania by the 25th of this month. On its part it will undertake to extend to you and to the members of the Legation all necessary assistance in matters concerning the departure.

"On this same occasion, I have the honor to inform you that the activity of all foreign consulates in Lithuania must be stopped and that the consulates are equally obliged to liquidate their offices by the same date, the 25th of August 1940."

All of the other Legations here have received similar notes.

The Foreign Office has informed me orally that the words "liquidate its affairs in Lithuania by the 25th of the month" mean that we must be over the frontier in person and with our property by that date. In the course of repeating orally the offer of assistance made in the note, the Secretary General of the Foreign Office conveyed to me a strong intimation that if we did not get our personnel and property across the frontier in a hurry while he was still in a position to assist us we might experience some serious difficulties.

GUFLER

No. 107

The Acting U.S. Secretary of State, Welles, to the Counselor of the U.S. Embassy in Moscow, Thurston

Telegram   WASHINGTON, August 13, 1940—6 p.m.

437. The Department plans to make a statement along the following lines to the Soviet Ambassador today or tomorrow:

"The Commissar for Foreign Affairs has informed our Chargé d'Affaires at Moscow by note that the Soviet Government expects the missions and consulates of the United States in Kaunas, Riga, and Tallinn to complete the liquidation of their affairs by August 25, 1940. Our Chargé d'Affaires has been instructed to inform the Commissar by note that it is the intention of the American Government to close its offices in Kaunas, Riga, and Tallinn in the near future.

The presence of American Foreign Service officers in the cities above mentioned will be needed for a considerable time after August 25 in order to lend appropriate and necessary assistance to American nationals, to look after American interests, and to arrange the liquidation of the offices. While it expects to close the offices in all three cities as soon as possible, there is the possibility that it may be desirable for them to continue to perform consular functions even until October 1, 1940. It suggests that as a matter of comity the Soviet Government cooperate with it in working out an arrangement whereby it would be possible for American Foreign Service Officers, with the assistance of a competent staff, to continue performing work of a consular nature in Riga after October 1. The American Government, except during the years 1917-1919, has maintained a consular office in Riga for many years. It is important for the protection of American citizens and interests in the Baltic that such an office continue to function. In case Riga should later be used as a port for trade with the United States, the presence of American consular officers in that city would be particularly helpful. It is hoped that it will be possible for these officers to carry on their work in Riga without the question of exequaturs being raised. A plan might be evolved whereby the Foreign Service Officers in question be assigned to the American Embassy at Moscow but continue, as attached to the consular section of the American Embassy at Moscow, to perform consular work in the offices now maintained by the American Government in Riga. In the performance of their consular duties in Riga they could, if found desirable, use the seals of the consular section of the Embassy.

The American Government considers this suggestion as reasonable. Although it has been unable to recognize changes in the status of certain territories in other parts of the world, the governments which at present are in control of such territories in a number of instances have, as a matter of international comity, permitted it to maintain consular offices in those territories."

It is suggested that you also present proposals along these lines immediately to the appropriate officers of the Commissar [*Commissariat?*] for Foreign Affairs, pointing out that your Government should be informed at once of the Soviet attitude towards such proposals.

In case the question is raised as to the attitude of this Government with respect to the Soviet announcement that the Baltic States have been admitted into the Soviet Union, you may state that you have been given to understand that the views of your Government on this subject were set forth in the statement made by Mr. Welles on July 23, 1940.

WELLES

No. 108

The Soviet Ambassador in Washington, Oumansky, to the Acting U.S. Secretary of State, Welles

WASHINGTON, August 13, 1940

Dear Mr. Secretary: Upon instruction of my Government I have the honor to bring to your attention the following information:

1. Foreigners not in possession of Soviet entry or transit visas will hereafter not be allowed to enter or cross the territory of the Lithuanian, Latvian and Esthonian Soviet Socialist Republics. Exemption will be made only in the cases of those foreigners who are now in possession of Soviet transit visas or of transit visas issued prior to August 7, 1940 by the diplomatic missions of the former Lithuanian, Latvian and Esthonian Republics.

2. All visas other than those enumerated above and issued by the former Lithuanian, Latvian and Esthonian diplomatic and consular representatives are invalidated.

3. Visas permitting entry into, or transit across, the territory of the Lithuanian, Latvian and Esthonian Soviet Socialist Republics after August 7, 1940 will hereafter be issued only by the diplomatic and consular representatives of the Union of Soviet Socialist Republics.

Accept [etc.]   C. OUMANSKY

No. 109

The German Foreign Minister, Ribbentrop, to the German Ambassador in Moscow, Schulenburg

Telegram

MOST URGENT   BERLIN, July 9, 1940—1:05 a.m.
No. 1164 of July 8   Received July 9—9:00 a.m.

For the Ambassador.

Please inform Molotov orally of the following:

In accordance with evacuation plans announced by the Führer in his Reichstag speech of October 6, 1939, the Reich Government intends, now that resettlement of the German national group in Latvia and Estonia has been completed, to carry out resettlement in the Reich of the Germans from Lithuania. The Reich Government will accordingly submit to the Lithuanian Government, a proposal based on the principle of reciprocity and voluntary cooperation. A great many persons of Lithuanian nationality live in the Memel territory and the Suwalki district. The German minority in Lithuania numbers about 40,000.

Naturally the resettlement will not affect the strip of territory which, under the Moscow agreements of September 1939 is to be incorporated into Germany to rectify the German-Lithuanian boundary. As was stated in the exchange of letters between you and M. Molotov, we reserve the right to determine the time for the incorporation of this territory. We assume, however, that the military measures carried out by the Soviet Government in Lithuania do not include this district.

RIBBENTROP

On July 12 Schulenburg wired the following reply: "Instruction carried out today with Molotov. Molotov replied that he would study the situation and take up the question again soon" (telegram No. 1348: 104/112307).

No. 110

The State Secretary of the German Foreign Ministry, Weizsäcker, to the German Legation in Kaunas

Telegram

SECRET   BERLIN, July 11, 1940.
No. 185   e.o. Kult B. sper 68-05 (g) 8.7.

For the Minister personally.

For your personal information. Secret.

With reference to your telegram No. 135 of July 8.[1]

The Ambassador in Moscow has been instructed to inform Molotov orally, as follows:

[Here follow the instructions contained in telegram No. 1164 of July 8 from the Foreign Minister to the Ambassador in the Soviet Union, document No. 139.]

The Lithuanian Government will be notified of our proposed resettlement project only after Moscow's reaction has become known.[2]

Please convey to the executive of the national group, upon instruction from the Volksdeutsche Mittelstelle, the following directive: No panic sales of German property; no departures without orders; refrain as far as possible from taking sides on domestic political issues; wait calmly for directives from Berlin.

WEIZSÄCKER

---

[1] This telegram reported increasing anxiety among members of the German national group in Lithuania and suggested that this might be relieved by an announcement that their resettlement was envisaged (321/193327).

No. 111

The German Ambassador in Moscow, Schulenburg, to the German Foreign Ministry

Telegram

MOST URGENT
No. 1363 of July 13

Moscow, July 13, 1940 — 7:04 p.m.
Received July 13 — 9:10 p.m.

With reference to your telegram No. 1164 of July 8 and my telegram No. 1348 of July 12.

Molotov summoned me today and stated the following: Stalin had carefully re-examined the situation with respect to the strip of Lithuanian territory and has concluded that our claim to this strip of territory and the Soviet obligation to cede it are incontestable. In the present circumstances, however, the cession of this strip of territory would be extremely inconvenient and difficult for the Soviet Government. Therefore, Stalin and he himself earnestly request the German Government to consider whether, in conformity with the extraordinarily friendly relations between Germany and the Soviet Union, a way cannot be found which would leave this strip of territory permanently with Lithuania. Molotov added that we could of course at any time move the population of German origin out of Lithuania as well as out of this strip of territory. Molotov stressed again and again the difficulties which would at present result for the Soviet Union from the cession of this strip of territory, and he made his and Stalin's request seem very urgent by repeatedly expressing hope of a German concession. Request instructions by wire. Perhaps the Soviet request can be used to put through our economic and financial demands with respect to the Baltic States.

SCHULENBURG

Editor's comment: At the moment when the process of incorporation was beginning, ceding this most important province of Lithuania to Germany would have caused an uproar among Lithuanians, both Communist and non-Communist, directed against the U.S.S.R. A popular uprising would have seriously contradicted the myth of the introduction of the Soviet system by popular desire, and unnecessarily battered the already strained idealism of Communist sympathizers. Besides, there was always the chance that the secret dealings with Germany might come to light, embarrassing the Soviet Government in the eyes of the world, To preserve the secret, the U.S.S.R. had to have the Strip.

No. 112

The German Ambassador in Moscow, Schulenburg, to the German Foreign Minister, Ribbentrop

Telegram in code

Foreign Office
Berlin

MOST URGENT   Telegram no. 1398 of July 17
                                     In reference to Telegram no. 1363
                                              of July 13

During my conversation with Molotov today, he again came to the question of the strip of Lithuanian territory and emphasized [word crossed out: what] the great importance which the Soviet Government would attribute to leaving that piece of territory with Lithuania.

Schulenburg

No. 113
Memorandum by an Official of the Soviet Commissariat For Foreign Affairs

740/357754   *English translation*

To: Com. V.M. Molotov

Information   *Secret*

"On the number and national composition / of population / in the Lithuania's territory on which an agreement was made in the Protocol of September 28, 1939.

1) Lithuania's territory on which an agreement was made in the Protocol of September 28, 1939, is bounded in the southwest by the Lithuanian-German boundary and in the northeast is delimited by a line which unites the following populated places: Širvintai, Pilviškiai,

Marijampolě, Simnas, Zapockině. (Map of Lithuania, scale 1:750.000).

To it belongs: almost the whole district of Vilkaviškis, 1/3 District of Marijampolě, 1/5 District of Seinai, and 1/15 District of Alytus.

2) According to the data of the Lithuanian Statistical Bureau, communicated by comrade Pozdniakov, the number and national composition of inhabitants in that territory was as follows:

A. *Total population:*

1. According to census of 1923 — 151.394 people.
2. In December 1939   — 184.108 -"-

B. *According to nationalities:*

	1923	In % %	*December 1939*	In % %
Lithuanians —	124.036	81.8%	151.186 —	82.3%
Germans —	11.361	7.5%	13.475 —	7.3%
Poles —	2.710	1.8%	3.396 —	1.8%
Russians —	1.380	0.9%	1.659 —	0.9%
Jews —	11.583	7.8%	13.963 —	7.6%
Others —	329	0.2%	429 —	0.3%
TOTAL	151.394	100%	184.108	100%

Note: **Figures for December 1939** were computed using the following method: as a base were taken figures of the census of 1923 and corrections made based on the median yearly population increase in Lithuania.

Compiled by: (IVANOV)

/Marginal note in German:/

This notation was handed over to Mr. Ambassador by Molotov on July 17, calling attention to preponderance of Lithuanian population in the concerned strip of territory, and a low percentage of Germans (less than Jews).

Editor's comment: From the Lithuanian point of view, the territory of the Lithuanian Strip was the heart of the Lithuanian cultural movement from the very beginning of the Lithuanian national renaissance in the 19th Century. The dialect of the area became the literary language of modern Lithuania. Separation of the Strip from Lithuania would have been a serious blow to Lithuanian cultural homogeneity.

No. 114

The German Foreign Minister, Ribbentrop, to the German Embassy in Moscow

Telegram

No. 1339 of August 2   Berlin, August 2, 1940 — 4:24 p.m.
                              Received August 2 — 8:45 p.m.

With reference to your telegram No. 1363 of July 13.[1]

You are requested to inform M. Molotov that the Reich Government has taken cognizance of the wish of the Soviet Government that Germany leave to the Soviet Union that part of Lithuania allocated to Germany by the Moscow agreements. This would represent a rather considerable change in the Moscow Treaty to the disadvantage of Germany. Before the Reich Government can consider the matter in detail, therefore, I should be interested in hearing what quid pro quo the Soviet Government would propose.

RIBBENTROP

Editor's comment: Fully aware of the importance of the Strip to the U.S.S.R., which was by now irrevocably embroiled in the incorporation of Lithuania, Germany decided to reap the benefits of the Soviet predicament.

No. 115

The German Ambassador in Moscow, Schulenburg, to the German Foreign Ministry

Telegram

URGENT   Moscow, August 7, 1940 — 6:33 p.m.
No. 1590 of August 7   Received August 7 — 8:05 p.m.

With reference to your telegram No. 1339 of August 2.[1]

Carried out instruction today with Molotov regarding strip of Lithuanian territory. Molotov appeared satisfied and declared that since the German Government had declared its willingness to examine the matter more closely, the Soviet Government too is ready to discuss suitable compensation. In any event the Soviet Government will await notification of the German wishes.

SCHULENBURG

Editor's comment: The Soviets had no choice but to make a deal with the Germans. Having just accepted the Lithuanian SSR into the Soviet Union (August 3), they could not start carving up its territory for the sake of Germany.

No. 116

The German Foreign Ministry to the German Embassy in Moscow

CONFIDENTIAL   BERLIN, August 9, 1940.
                                                         W XII 5228

For personal information only.

The incorporation of Lithuania into the territory of the Soviet Union creates a completely new situation for the Memel Free Port Zone. The Free Port Zone represented an international obligation, made to facilitate the return by little Lithuania of her most important port to Germany. For Russia, which has expanded and has at her disposal a great number of Baltic Sea ports, it has lost its real significance; its continued existence would lead to politically dangerous Russian privileges on German territory. If Russia should demand the continuance of the Free Port Zone in Memel, the position taken here will be that the promises given in the German-Lithuanian Treaty of March 22, 1939, are no longer applicable to a Lithuania which has been incorporated into the Soviet Union. The competent offices will initiate the necessary steps for terminating the present state of affairs.

The question of handling Russian traffic via the German port of Memel will especially be kept in mind.

By order: Martius

Editor's comment: Germany considered that the rights and privileges of Lithuania in Memel under the German-Lithuanian Treaty of March 22, 1939 were not succeeded to by the U.S.S.R. It was a question of definitions; the Germans did not accept the fiction of Soviet federalism, but felt that with incorporation the Lithuanian State had been destroyed, like Poland, for instance, or Czecho-slovakia. The Soviets tried to reap the advantages of the Lithuanian SSR's theoretical quasi-sovereignty, by treating it as a succession state to the Lithuanian Republic. For their reply, see Document No. 121.

No. 117

The German Ambassador in Moscow, Schulenburg, to the German Foreign Ministry

Telegram

MOST URGENT   Moscow, August 13, 1940 — 12:25 a.m.

SECRET   Received August 13 — 4:25 a.m.

No. 1638 of August 12

With reference to my telegram No. 1590 of August 7.

Concerning the Lithuanian strip of territory Molotov today handed me a long memorandum stating that territorial compensation was unacceptable to the Soviet Union, but declaring readiness to pay 3,860,000 gold dollars within 2 years (i.e., half of the sum the U.S.A. paid to Russia for the cession of Alaska), either in gold or goods, as Germany may prefer, for the retention of the strip of territory by the Soviet Union.

The text of the memorandum will be sent Wednesday via courier by plane.

SCHULENBURG

Editor's comment: At this particular time the U.S.S.R. had no territory to dispose of. The eastern part of Poland had already been incorporated into the Ukrainian and Byelorussian S.S.R.'s, and, for the same reasons which made retention of the Lithuanian Strip so important, the U.S.S.R. could not carve up the territory of the Ukraine or Byelorussia to give to Germany. Thus, the only means of exchange available was gold.

No. 118

Memorandum of the People's Commissar
For Foreign Affairs of the USSR, Molotov,
to the German Government

Translation

German Embassy
Moscow   August 13, 1940

Secret
   Reference to Telegram No. 1638 of August 12.
Contents: Cession of a strip of Lithuanian territory.

   I have the honor to forward with a German translation a
memorandum which was handed to me yesterday by Mr. Molotov on
the subject of a strip of Lithuanian territory.
                         (signed) v.d. Schulenburg

To: Auswärtiges Amt
Berlin
Enclosure to Ag/3659/40.   *English translation*

   To the declaration by German Ambassador Count von der Schulen-
burg on August 7 this year concerning the compensation for the strip of
Lithuanian territory for which a clause was included in the German-
Soviet Protocol of September 28, 1939, the People's Commissariat for
Foreign affairs has the honor to make the following statement.

   1. It is impossible to give some kind of compensation by cession to
Germany of any part of the territory which according to the treaty with
Germany already came into the possession of the Soviet Union, because
it would inflict great moral loss to the Soviet Union; in the whole
territory which might be considered for compensation a new state order
has been established which corresponds to the regime of the Soviet
Union and which already has become stable, also a reshaping of the
mode of life of the rural and urban population has been accomplished.

   Otherwise the cession to Germany of any part of a territory which
came into possession of the Soviet Union would require at the present
time the unavoidable resettlement of that region's Russian, White
Russian, Ukrainian and Lithuanian population; all that would cause

great difficulties and would have undesirable political consequences.

On the contrary, the renunciation of the above mentioned part of Lithuanian territory would cause no similar difficulties to Germany, because that territory never was a part of the German State, therefore, a renunciation in the favor of the USSR would cause Germany no moral loss.

Not to mention that every new change of official borders between the German States and USSR would give hostile elements enough cause to speak about serious frictions between our countries and about the instability of our mutual relations.

2. The population of the above mentioned part of Lithuanian territory is in its preponderant majority of Lithuanian nationality (82.3 %), and only a negligible part of the population belongs to German nationality (7.3%), therefore, in case of transfer of that territory to Germany the majority of the population should be resettled in Lithuania.

According to the declaration given by the USSR Government, the material interests of persons of German citizenship or nationality who would want to resettle from Lithuania to Germany would not be hurt.

3. Further the Government of the Soviet Union considers it proper to point out that according to the Protocol of August 23, 1939, and following the demarcation line on the formerly Polish territory, agreed on September 22, 1939, the region of Suwalki fell to the USSR. Nevertheless, by the final drawing of the state boundary in that territory of the former Polish state, the Suwalki region was ceded to Germany without any compensation, merely answering a request by the German Government, although in that case the USSR had no obligation toward Germany whatsoever. It was done without doubt as a manifestation of good will shown by the Soviet Union toward Germany by satisfying its interests in the most generous way.

Notwithstanding all that and taking into consideration the requirements and necessities caused to Germany by the present war, the Soviet Government is ready to give Germany material compensation for cession of the strip of territory to the Soviet Union.

The Soviet Union could pay in two years three million 860 thousand gold dollars, i.e. one half of the sum which once was paid by the United States to Tsarist Russia for the Alaska Peninsula. The Soviet Union could pay that sum either in gold or in merchandise, according to the wish of German Government.

The Soviet Government hopes that the German Government will be attentive to the interests of the USSR and would accept the proposal.

August 12, 1940

Editor's comment: The reasons why the U.S.S.R. could not compensate for the Strip in territory are well stated: the preservation of moral, political and territorial integrity. The little Strip became a major problem between the two powers, a constant aggravation, and a readily available *casus belli* if no satisfactory solution was arrived at.

No. 119

The German Ambassador in Moscow, Schulenburg, to the German Foreign Ministry

To: Foreign Office
Berlin

Most urgent   Telegram no. 1676 of August 17, 1940
In connection with Telegram no. 1638 of August 12

Today Molotov delivered to me a notice of the following contents:

"The Soviet Government informs the German Government that as a result of the acceptance of the Lithuanian Republic into the structure of the U.S.S.R., as of August 20, 1940 the Soviet side will introduce the same order as exists on the whole Soviet-German border line to the new section of the state border between the U.S.S.R. and Germany from the Igorka river to the Baltic Sea, i.e. on the former German-Lithuanian border.

Soviet frontier authorities shall receive proper instructions on that matter.

The Government of the Soviet Union expects that the German Government on its part will give corresponding instructions to German frontier authorities."

Schulenburg

Editor's comment: The territory in question included the Lithuanian Strip. The introduction of Soviet troops into the Strip was a serious step.

Germany had been ceded the Strip by the secret protocol of September 28, 1939, and, though negotiating with the U.S.S.R. for another exchange, considered itself to have sovereignty over the area. The Soviet occupation of the Strip made retention by Germany impossible, forcing an exchange. At best, it would create ill will in the German Government, at worst, serve as a justification for denouncing the Non-aggression Pact, in fact, the Germans were sufficiently annoyed to raise their price.

No. 120

The German Ambassador in Moscow, Schulenburg, to the German Foreign Ministry

Urgent
To: Foreign Office   Telegram No. 1734 of August 23, 1940.
Berlin   In connection to telegram No. 1638 of August 12.
August 12.

Secret

Molotov reminded me today about the pending German attitude in the case of the strip of Lithuanian territory, and asked me insistently to get a quick answer

Schulenburg

No. 121

Note of the Soviet People's Commissariat for Foreign Affairs to the German Government

The People's Commissariat for Foreign Affairs has the honor to inform the German Embassy concerning the following matter:

The Government of the USSR calls the attention of the German Government to the activities of the German authorities in the Lithuanian Free Zone of Memel violating the rights and interests of the Lithuanian SSR

As it is known, according to the treaty between Germany and Lithuanian Republic of May 20, 1939, about the establishment for Lithuania of a free zone in the port of Memel for 99 years, the following rights were granted: the right of free use of the above mentioned zone, the free import, export and storage of merchandise, direct communication between Lithuania and the Free Zone of Memel, the keeping of a Lithuanian customs office in Memel, the undisturbed activity in the port territory of Lithuanian workers and employees who live on the Lithuanian territory outside the zone, also the right to economic and tax privileges.

Disregarding those rights, the German authorities on August 27 sent to the Free Zone a military detachment, stopped the activity of the customs office and requested that all Lithuanian merchandise stored in the zone should be taken away. In this way the German authorities subjected the Lithuanian Republic, which now belongs to the Soviet Union to a flagrant impairment of economic and trade conditions, compared to the conditions which existed previously for Lithuania.

The Government of the USSR considers that the Lithuanian SSR is entitled to all the rights and privileges which are based on the above mentioned German-Lithuanian treaty concerning the free zone and also the exchange of letters between Mr. Schnurre and Mr. Norkaitis on the same date which cannot loose its validity because of unilateral action.

> August 29, 1940
> (signed) M.

Note: German translation made by German Embassy in Moscow is also available: 740/357802-03.

Editor's comment: The question of mutual rights and privileges under the German-Lithuanian treaties of March 22, and May 20, 1939 was apparently dropped. Germany seems to have lost her rights in the Baltic region, and vice versa.

No. 122

Memorandum by an Official of Political Division V of the German Foreign Ministry

BERLIN, September 2, 1940

CONVERSATION BETWEEN THE FOREIGN MINISTER AND SOVIET AMBASSADOR SHKVARTSEV, SEPTEMBER 2, 1940

Ambassador Shkvartsev, accompanied by Secretary of Embassy Pavlov, started the conversation with an explanation of alleged frictions between the Soviet Union and Finland over the Aland Islands. This question, which was touched upon at his last visit, can now be answered: The rumors do not correspond in any way to the real situation. The Foreign Minister welcomed this news. Furthermore, the Ambassador referred to the conversation which took place on August 12, 1940, concerning compensation for part of Lithuania. The Foreign Minister explained that he had received the proposals through Count Schulenburg from Moscow. At this time German officials are dealing with this subject and their careful examination is not yet concluded. He could already say, however, that the proposal to pay the stated sum does not compensate for changing the agreements regarding this territory. The Foreign Minister believed that Soviet officials too would conclude that in regard to value their proposal in no way corresponded to the actual situation. After this proposal has been examined in principle and from the economic side once more, the Foreign Minister will ask the Führer for his views and will communicate the results to the Ambassador. Already, however, he could say that the proposal is not acceptable as it now stands. The Ambassador asked when he might expect an answer. The Foreign Minister regretted not being able to name a date, for various questions still had to be clarified. Count Schulenburg too had inquired by wire and he too had been asked to wait for an answer.

Editor's comment: Long and hard bargaining for the Strip now began. The fact that the Strip was already *de facto* an integral part of the U.S.S.R. and that Germany considered the territory under its sovereignty made the whole affair of the Strip very complicated.

No. 123

The German Foreign Minister, Ribbentrop, to the German Embassy in Moscow

Telegram

No. 1580 of September 3   BERLIN, September 3, 1940 — 6:20 a.m.
                                              Received September 3 — 1:50 p.m.

With reference to your telegram No. 1815.

Please call on M. Molotov again and reply in accordance with the following memorandum to his statement that Germany by her action in Vienna had violated the obligation to consult contained in article III of the Non-Aggression Pact, and afterwards hand him this n.⸱ ⸱o⸱a⸱dum as a summary of your instructions.

The Reich Government, moreover, believes itself the more justified in this view in that the Soviet Government itself, on the occasion of its various political moves in the recent past, by no means considered the fact of contiguity to Germany of the territories affected by its acts as a reason for prior consultation with the Reich Government. In this connection the Reich Government refers to Russian action in the Baltic countries, especially Lithuania. In the latter case, besides the fact that Lithuania is adjacent to Germany, an obligation existed to surrender to Germany a certain area in the southwest of Lithuania in the event that the Soviet Union should take special measures on Lithuanian territory for the safeguarding of her interests. Nevertheless, the Soviet Union effected a military occupation of that area although, as a result of the Russian measures, it should have been treated forthwith as territory belonging to Germany. Only after representations by the Reich Government was this question reopened.

In conclusion, the Government of the Reich would like further to observe, with reference to the statement that Germany had confronted the Soviet Union with accomplished facts, that while the moves of the Soviet Union were planned moves for the occupation of various territories in th neighborhood of Germany and were not previously announced to the Government of the Reich, the steps of the Reich Government in the case of Rumania and Hungary served the purpose of securing the peace in the Danube region, which was gravely threatened by the tension between the two countries, and this could only be accomplished by rapid diplomatic intervention. Moreover, the Government of the Reich is probably not mistaken in believing that by its campaign of pacification in the Danube area it has rendered a substantial service to all countries bordering on that area.

RIBBENTROP

Editor's comment: The "action in Vienna" referred to here was part of the German revision of the Versailles Treaty in the Balkan area. Having pressured Roumania into surrendering Bessarabia to Russia and Dubruja to Bulgaria, Ribbentrop summoned Roumanian and Hungarian representatives to Vienna in late August of 1940 and forced Roumania to cede northern Transylvania to Hungary (the Vienna

Award of August 30, 1940). The purpose of the German policy was to prevent war between the fiercely irredentist Balkan States and to secure them for the Axis; Roumania was probably selected as the victim in reprisal for her role in the Little Entente. The policy was successful. Hungary joined the axis on September 23, 1940, Roumania on September 30, and Bulgaria on March 1, 1941, causing the Soviets great anxiety. The occupation of the Lithuanian Strip by the Soviets had provided the Germans with grievances which they now had the occasion to use.

No. 124

The German Ambassador in Moscow, Schulenburg to the German Foreign Ministry

Telegram

VERY URGENT   Moscow, September 4, 1940 — 5:30 p.m.
No. 1841 of September 4
Reference your telegram No. 1580 of September 3.

Furthermore, my interview with Molotov would be substantially facilitated if I were enabled at the same time to communicate to him the position of the German Government, for which Molotov has in the meantime pressed several times, in the matter of the strip of Lithuanian territory as well as in the question of the Free Port Zone of Memel (see our telegrams No. 1799 and 1800 of August 30). The question of the Free Port Zone of Memel was taken up with Schnurre on September 2 by Mikoyan in a manner which leaves no doubt as to the resentment felt by the Soviet Government, and makes much more difficult the further pursuit of our interests in the Baltic States. (See telegram No. 1829 of September 3.)

Please wire instructions.

SCHULENBURG

Editor's comment: It is not clear of what German "interests in the Baltic States" Schulenburg is speaking in this document. All German interests in the area had been renounced by the secret protocols of August 23 and September 28, 1939. The Strip was the only Baltic territory left in the German sphere of interest by the Secret Protocol of September 28.

No. 125

The German Foreign Minister, Ribbentrop, to the German Ambassador in Moscow, Schulenburg

Telegram
VERY URGENT   BERLIN, September 6, 1940 — 4:35 a.m.
Received Moscow, September 6, 1940 — 10 a.m.
No. 1609 of September 5

For the Ambassador personally.

Reference your telegram No. 1841.

To your suggestions I state the following for your information:

I leave it to you whether or not you think it opportune to bring up on this occasion the question of the strip of Lithuanian territory. If you think it advisable, you may tell Herr Molotov that the Government of the Reich is prepared in principle, against adequate compensation, to forego the cession of the strip of Lithuanian territory which was agreed upon in Moscow. The compensation which the Soviet Union has offered is certainly not acceptable to us. At the moment we are engaged in drawing up a proposal for adequate compensation and we shall soon approach the Soviet Government with this proposal.

5) On the other hand, I request you not to broach the question of the Free Port of Memel on this occasion. We must persist in our view that we cannot grant the Soviet Government a free port zone in Memel. But this question will have to be discussed separately with the Soviet Government.

Please report by wire on the course of your interview with Herr Molotov.

RIBBENTROP

Editor's comment: Until this date, the U.S.S.R. did not have even Germany's agreement in principle to the transfer of the Strip to the Lithuanian S.S.R. Ribbentrop's instruction to Schulenburg to commit Germany, at least in principle, to the transfer of the Lithuanian Strip to the U.S.S.R. was a considerable relief to the Soviet Government, anxious as it was to terminate this delicate question.

No. 126

The German Ambassador in Moscow, Schulenburg, to the German Foreign Ministry

Translation   Telegram in code

URGENT

To: Foreign Office
BERLIN   TELEGRAM No. 1885 OF SEPTEMBER 9, 1940

During today's conversation Molotov asked again about the German attitude toward the strip of Lithuanian territory. I answered/crossed words: gave to M./accordingly to point 4) of telegram No. 1609 of September 5.

The question concerning free port of Memel was not raised.

SCHULENBURG

No. 127

The German Ambassador in Moscow, Schulenburg, to the German Foreign Ministry

Telegram
URGENT   Moscow, September 10, 1940 — 5:58 p.m.
                                Received September 11, 1940 — 8 p.m.
No. 1900 of September 11

Reference you telegram No. 1649 of the 10th.

Molotov displayed great interest in, and had me repeat several times, the statement that "the Government of the Reich is prepared in principle, against adequate compensation, to forego the cession of the strip of Lithuanian territory which was agreed upon in Moscow." I had the impression that Molotov was satisfied. The statement that the compensation offered was certainly not acceptable to us and that we were engaged in drawing up a counter-proposal, Molotov noted with interest, without any further comment.

SCHULENBURG

Editor's Comment: Germany's agreement in principle to sell the Strip was a great relief for Russia. She could thus preserve the territorial integrity of the new Lithuanian Soviet Republic, and at the same time remove the cause of probable tension with Germany, which at this time she was trying to avoid by all means.

No. 128

Memorandum by an Official of the German Foreign Minister's Secretariat

FüH. 33   BERLIN, November 15, 1940.

RECORD OF THE CONVERSATION BETWEEN THE FÜHRER AND THE CHAIRMAN OF THE COUNCIL OF PEOPLE'S COMMISSARS, MOLOTOV, IN THE PRESENCE OF THE REICH FOREIGN MINISTER AND THE DEPUTY PEOPLE'S COMMISSAR FOR FOREIGN AFFAIRS, DEKANOZOV, AS WELL AS OF COUNSELOR OF EMBASSY HILGER AND M. PAVLOV, WHO ACTED AS INTERPRETERS, IN BERLIN ON NOVEMBER 13, 1940.

The Führer referred to the remark of Molotov during yesterday's conversation, according to which the German-Russian agreement was fulfilled "with the exception of one point: namely, of Finland."

Molotov explained that this remark referred not only to the German-Russian agreement itself, but in particular to the Secret Protocols too.

The Führer replied that, in the Secret Protocol, zones of influence and spheres of interest had been designated and distributed between Germany and Russia. In so far as it had been a question of actually taking possession, Germany had lived up to the agreements, which was not quite the case on the Russian side. At any rate, Germany had not occupied any territory that was within the Russian sphere of influence.

Lithuania had already been mentioned yesterday.* There could be no doubt that in this case the changes from the original German-Russian agreement were essentially due to Russian initiative. Whether the difficulties — to avoid which the Russians had offered their suggestion — would actually have resulted from the partition of Poland, could be

---

* In his conversation with Molotov on November 12, Hitler was more courteous: (the Führer) had not been ready to make concessions, but he had realized that it was desirable to meet the needs of Russians half-way, as, for instance, in the case of Lithuania. From an economic point of view, Lithuania, it is true, had a certain importance for us, but from a political point of view, we had understood the necessity of straightening out the situation in this whole field in order thereby to prevent in the future the spiritual revival of tendencies that were capable of causing tension between the two countries of Germany and Russia.

left out of the discussion. In any case, the Voivodeship of Lublin was economically no compensation for Lithuania. However, the Germans had seen that in the course of events a situation had resulted which necessitated revision of the original agreement.

As to the question of the revision of the original agreement with regard to Lithuania and the Voivodeship of Lublin, Molotov pointed out that the Soviet Union would not have insisted on that revision if Germany had not wanted it. But he believed that the new solution had been in the interest of both parties.

At this point the Reich Foreign Minister interjected that, to be sure, Russia had not made this revision an absolute condition, but at any rate had urged it very strongly.

Molotov insisted that the Soviet Government would not have refused to leave matters as provided in the original agreement. At any rate, however, Germany, for her concession in Lithuania, had received compensation in Polish territory.

The Führer interjected here that in this exchange one could not, from the point of view of economics, speak of adequate compensation.

Molotov then mentioned the question of the strip of Lithuanian territory and emphasized that the Soviet Government had not received any clear answer yet from Germany on this question. However, it awaited a decision.

Regarding Bucovina, he admitted that this involved an additional territory, one not mentioned in the Secret Protocol. Russia had at first confirmed her demands to northern Bucovina. In the present circumstances, however, Germany must understand the Russian interest in southern Bucovina. But Russia had not received an answer to her question regarding the subject either. Instead, Germany had guaranteed the entire territory of Rumania and completely disregarded Russia's wishes with regard to southern Bucovina.

The Führer replied that it would mean a considerable concession on the part of Germany, if even part of Bucovina were to be occupied by Russia. According to an oral agreement, the former Austrian territories were to fall within the German sphere of influence. Besides, the territories belonging to the Russian zone had been mentioned by name: Bessarabia, for example. There was, however, not a word regarding Bucovina in the agreements. Finally, the exact meaning of the expression "sphere of influence" was not further defined. At any rate, Germany had not violated the agreement in the least in this matter. To the objection of Molotov that the revisions with regard to the strip of

Lithuanian territory and of Bucovina were not of very great importance in comparison with the revision which Germany had undertaken elsewhere by military force, the Führer replied that socalled "revision by force of arms" had not been the subject of the agreement at all.

Molotov, however, persisted in the opinion previously stated: that the revisions desired by Russia were insignificant.

Editor's comment: Hitler hinted here that while the secret protocols between Germany and the U.S.S.R. designated and distributed zones of influence and spheres of interest, but did not grant the right actually to take possession of these territories. It would seem that this comment by Hitler was only a convenient instrument in the "debate", while the actual truth was that the partition of the Baltic States contained the understanding that the Sovietization of the Baltic States, at any rate, would eventually result. The memorandum reveals the tensions arising between the two powers in Southeastern Europe, and also particularly in the Baltic area.

The interview between Hitler, Ribbentrop and Molotov in Berlin on November 13, 1940 was apparently a decisive factor in Hitler's decision to invade Russia in 1941.

No. 129

Memorandum by an Official of the German Foreign Ministry

RM 50   BERLIN, December 22, 1940

RECORD OF THE CONVERSATION BETWEEN THE REICH FOREIGN MINISTER AND THE RUSSIAN AMBASSADOR, DEKANOZOV, ON DECEMBER 21, 1940, FROM 7:45 TILL 8:30 P.M.

First of all, Ambassador Dekanozov congratulated the Foreign Minister on the birth of his son.

Ambassador Dekanozov then made the following statement: On August 28 last the People's Commissariat for Foreign Affairs had handed the German Embassy in Moscow a note verbale on the demarcation of the sector from the Igorka river to the Baltic Sea, i.e., the former German-Lithuanian boundary. In this note, a copy of which could be submitted, the People's Commissariat asked that the demarcation be undertaken by the Central Mixed German-Soviet Russian Commission in the same manner as on other sections of the common boundary and that it be completed if possible before the beginning of winter. Since Germany had not replied to this note of August 28 last, he had been instructed to express the dissatisfaction of the Soviet Government.

After Secretary of Embassy Pavlov had translated the text of the note, the Foreign Minister asked why this question had not been brought up before. To this question Dekanozov replied that this section of the boundary had been mentioned for the first time in the note verbale. Since he (Dekanozov) had taken part in the work of the Commission at the time, he was in a position to state in this connection that the time then seemed propitious, since the Commission would have been able to continue its work without interruption. No German reply had been received, however, and meanwhile the Central Commission had completed its work.

After a brief consultation with Under State Secretary Woermann the Foreign Minister replied to M. Dekanozov that the demarcation question was connected with that of the Lithuanian strip, which was to fall to Germany on the basis of the confidential agreement. The Russian Government had, to be sure, proposed cession of this strip in return for a monetary compensation, but the Reich Government had not considered that to be its equivalent in value. He (the Foreign Minister) had asked the domestic authorities to determine the value of the strip of territory to be ceded. He had not yet received the report regarding the matter. As soon as he had, it would be decided;

1) whether a cession could be made, and

2) if so, what compensation was to be demanded.

Since the question of the Lithuanian strip had not yet been settled, there had so far not been any definitive demarcation. Under State Secretary Woermann would report about this in the next few days to the Foreign Minister. But so long as the domestic authorities had not completed the assessment of the Russian proposal, the Foreign Minister could not make any decision in the question of the Lithuanian strip.

Dekànozov replied that the question of the Lithuanian strip had in his opinion remained unsettled on account of the compensation, but he did not know whether it had any direct relation to the demarcation question. Dekanozov stated that he wanted to report to his Government about it. It was a fact that;

1) The Soviet note of August 28 last had remained unanswered; and

2) the inquiry regarding the amount of the compensation for the Lithuanian strip had likewise remained unanswered, since its form had not been definitively settled;

3) the absence of a reply to the note verbale might delay the signing of the economic treaty.

The Foreign Minister emphasized in his reply that he had heard today for the first time that the demarcation had not yet been completed. Under State Secretary Woermann had further told him that since the definitive fixing of the boundary was connected with the question of the Lithuanian strip, the intention had been to avoid double work in that respect. As for the question of the Lithuanian strip itself, it had probably receded somewhat into the background as a result of the many things that had happened. The question of compensation would be studied from the point of view of value and he hoped that by the middle of next week he would be able to give Dekanozov a definitive statement from the Reich Government on the proposal which had been made.

After M. Dekanozov stated that he had no further questions, the Foreign Minister inquired in conclusion whether the Soviet Government still desired cession of the Lithuanian strip, to which M. Dekanozov replied in the affirmative.

DR. ERICH SOMMER

Editor's Comment: On December 18, 1940, Hitler gave the directives for Operation Barbarossa, the invasion of Russia. However, the Germans tried to conduct their relations with Russia with the appearance of willingness to negotiate agreements on points of conflict, which were already numerous.

No. 130

**The Head of the German Economic Delegation
to the USSR, Schnurre,
to the German Foreign Minister, Ribbentrop**

AT MOSCOW, December 25, 1940.

DEAR HERR MINISTER: The decisive significance which the new economic agreement, now ready for signature, has for the German war economy and the conduct of the war prompts me to call your attention in this direct way to the dangerous situation which will ensue if the signature is delayed for any length of time. The new economic agreement is the largest that Germany has ever concluded and goes considerably beyond the first agreement with the Russians. It obligates the Russians to make very extensive deliveries of raw materials in the very areas where we have shortages that we cannot cover in other ways. A central position is occupied by 2.5 million tons of grain, 1 million tons of mineral oil products, 100,000 tons of cotton, nonferrous and precious metals, manganese ore, etc. The economic agreement is suplemented by the agreement on the lump sum compensation of the German property claims in the Baltic States which is likewise almost ready for signature and assures us payments up to the amount of 150 million reichsmarks, beginning at once. The German counterdeliveries are calculated for precise deadlines and can only be made on schedule if the treaty enters into force in December and necessary measures inside Germany are undertaken at once. If signature of the economic agreement is postponed until January all of the deadlines will likewise be delayed. The German promises of delivery will be uncertain and we can start all over again in January to negotiate with the Russians. With this all the advantages which the agreement offers us would be rendered doubtful once more. In addition, my opposites in the negotiations here will in their Armenian-Caucasian way connect every question that comes up in the meantime with the economic agreement in order to obtain every possible advantage from the present situation. I am particularly concerned in this regard with the Petsamo question, which will enter a critical stage in 10 days to 2 weeks at the latest. The Finns will then have to decide whether they will capitulate and turn over the northern part of their country to Soviet Communist influence or whether they will continue to resist the unmistakable demands of the Russians. We have encouraged the Finns to do the latter. Should they continue to comply with our wishes the Russians will blame us for the Finnish resistance and combine this question, too, with the economic agreement. I should also like to point to the political effects of a further delay of the conclusion of the negotiations. It will not be possible to prevent news of the difficulties that have now arisen from getting out. There will be combinations that are highly undesirable to us.

For these reasons I wish to propose that we have the Lithuanian boundary agreement concluded at once in order to assure us of the great advantages of the economic agreement and to deprive the Russians of the opportunity of extorting further concessions from us. The compensation that we will receive for the strip of Lithuanian territory is in too great a disproportion to the treaty involving billions which is at stake. With the economic agreement and the Baltic agreement in their hands as a means of pressure, the Russians will no longer be willing to pay much more than they already have offered us. Therefore I should like to suggest that I be authorized to conclude the boundary treaty with the best compensation that can be obtained without losing more than 2 or 3 days time in that way. I sent the files to Minister Clodius today but am retaining my personal files here so that it can be assumed in the instruction to me that I am acquainted with the previous material.

I should like to add my most cordial wishes for the year 1941, that will bring you, dear Herr Minister, and your political work further historical success and thereby victory and peace for Germany.*

HEIL HITLER!

SCHNURRE

Editor's comment: Such a treaty, so economically advantageous to Germany, was contemplated by the U.S.S.R. in the hopes of pacifying its neighbor and at the same time obtaining a better deal on the Lithuanian Strip. In view of the German decision, taken in December 1940, to attack Russia in the spring of 1941, the trade treaty negotiations can be seen as a policy of taking every possible advantage of the still-continuing friendship with the U.S.S.R. to economically strengthen the German war potential.

No. 131

The German Foreign Minister, Ribbentrop, to the German Embassy in Moscow

Telegram

SECRET   BERLIN, December 29, 1940 — 2:30 a.m.
No. 2381 of December 28   Received December 29 — 8:15 a.m.
Special security handling. Reply by courier or in secret code.
For the Ambassador and Schnurre.
With reference to your telegram No. 2816.

---

* In a private letter of Jan. 2, 1941, Weizsäcker told Schnurre that he regretted Schnurre's being held on such a short leash, but that those who had the power of decision were acting on the assumption that Germany, in the last analysis, "held the longer arm of the lever." (124/123106)

I. Please inform the Soviet Government as follows concerning the question of the Lithuanian strip:

We are willing in principle to give up the Lithuanian strip in return for adequate compensation. We take the view that payment in gold or commodities is actually not an adequate compensation for relinquishment of an area. Nevertheless we are willing, in order to facilitate a quick settlement of the matter, to comply with the Russian proposal. However, the sum of 3,860,000 gold dollars offered by the Russians does not seem to us to be an adequate equivalent. We concede that it is difficult to find a proper criterion for evaluating an area. A comparison with payments made in other cases, however, especially when these other cases occurred many years ago, as is true of the cession of Alaska, does not at any rate seem to us to be a suitable criterion. A calculation of the real estate value according to Lithuanian prices would result in an amount of 13 million gold dollars. We are willing to consider this sum adequate compensation if the equivalent of this amount is made available in additional raw material deliveries.

II. Please make it absolutely clear in the negotiations that the deliveries of raw materials are entirely independent of the economic agreement and thus clearly represent additional deliveries. The corresponding written agreement must likewise be kept entirely separate from the economic agreement. Please adhere to the total amount of 13 million gold dollars.

The following come into question in first place as additional raw materials to be delivered: nonferrous metals, then possibly also naphtha products, cotton, flax, manganese ore. They are listed according to priority. Please.do not demand grain, since we are afraid that the amount of 2½ million tons agreed upon and the further deliveries contemplated for the occupied areas may exhaust the Russian capacity to deliver so that the special deliveries now designated as additional would in the end be charged to our contingent after all.

IV. The draft of an agreement between the German Reich and the USSR on the former German-Lithuanian border, along with explanatory remarks, is en route by courier. Please do not pass on this draft, however, without obtaining my consent in advance.

RIBBENTROP

Editor's Comment: $13,000,000 is a huge sum to be termed "adequate" for a small strip of territory which never belonged to either seller or buyer. Germany knew that under the political circumstances, Russia was forced to buy the Strip, and took full advantage of it.

No. 132

Most Urgent Telegram From The German Embassy in Moscow to the German Foreign Ministry

Telegram

MOST URGENT   Moscow, December 30, 1940 — 10:45 p.m.

SECRET   Received December 31 — 2:00 a.m.

No. 2838 of December 30

For the Foreign Minister

With reference to your telegrams No. 2381 of December 28 and No. 2385 of December 29.

There was a conference with Molotov yesterday evening lasting almost 2 hours concerning the question of compensation for the Lithuanian strip.

Molotov took the stand from the very start that the German demand for 13 million gold dollars was obviously greatly exaggerated and the method of calculating it was in contradiction to the agreement already reached regarding the lump sum payment of *mutual* property claims. Only 7.3 percent of the population in the area in question were of German stock, and their property was included in the lump sum of 200 million reichsmarks offered by the Soviet Government. If this area had come to Germany, then Germany would have had to pay compensation for the property of the Lithuanian majority (82.3 percent) according to the principles established for the lump sum settlement. Consequently one could not now talk of a property loss of the Reich, particularly since there was no government property in the Lithuanian strip. Therefore all the German property claims in the Lithuanian-German strip were taken care of in the generous lump sum payment.

In spite of our emphatic protests Molotov insisted with quite unusual stubbornness on his negative standpoint. He repeated again and again that the cession of the Lithuanian strip presented a purely political problem for the Soviet Government, that was not to be resolved with the aid of economic calculations. Also the compensation of 3.86 (a group evidently missing) gold dollars offered by the Soviet Government at the time had been considered an attempt at a political solution.

We protested that with its offer of gold and commodities the Soviet Government had itself wanted to solve the compensation question in an economic way. In order to be obliging we had complied with this form of compensation, although we had maintained the standpoint from the very start that gold or commodities were not an adequate means of compensation.

In the end Molotov said he was willing to report to his Government and to find out whether for political considerations and by expressly eliminating every other sort of calculation a sum could be proposed that would satisfy both sides. He assumed that today or tomorrow we would be in a position to communicate to him the German draft of the border agreement. Then he would also be able to communicate the final position of his Government in the compensation question.

In reply to our question whether, in view of the purely political character of the Lithuanian matter, which Molotov himself had emphasized, the trade agreement which had nothing to do with this matter could be signed, Molotov insisted on tying all of the agreements together.

In order to bring the matter to a close we request telegraphic authorization to communicate to Molotov the text of the boundary treaty which arrived here today and to settle the compensation question on the basis of a compromise. Every further delay endangers the economic and Baltic agreements, as Minister Schnurre has already explained in his letter to the Foreign Minister.

SCHNURRE

SCHULENBURG

Editor's Comment: Molotov's insistence on tying the economic and Strip agreements together represents pressure by Russia to influence Germany to compromise on the question of the Strip.

It is clear that Germany absolutely needed the trade agreement with the USSR, which promised essential materials for her war industry. A compromise, thus, was the solution to the delicate "Strip" question. The alternative would have been to get nothing from Russia. In this way, Germany got a tremendous economic advantage, both from the Strip arrangement and the economic treaty, before the crucial dates of May-June, 1941.

No. 133

The German Foreign Minister, Ribbentrop, to the German Embassy in Moscow

Telegram

MOST URGENT   BERLIN, January 1,1941.

SECRET

No. 1

For the Ambassador and Schnurre personally.

With reference to your telegram No. 2838.

1. I agree to the transmittal of the boundary treaty. Please state on that occasion that signature of the treaty is naturally dependent upon a satisfactory settlement of compensation for the Lithuanian strip.

2. In regard to Molotov's statements, we fully maintain our justified standpoint in the question of compensation for the Lithuanian strip. I am entirely in accord with your response to Molotov's statements. Please add that any connection between compensation for the Lithuanian strip and a lump sum to pay off private legal claims in the former Baltic States, such as Molotov is making, is entirely beside the point. The compensation is not a matter of monetary damages for private property interests, but is political compensation for renunciation of sovereignty over an area.

3. Please report at once on Molotov's new offer, so that a decision on acceptance can then be made here.

RIBBENTROP

Editor's Comment: There was no reason to believe that the "Strip deal was exclusively an economic problem. The exchange of Lithuania for the Lublin area was the beginning of political dealings for political and strategic advantages. By giving up Lithuania to Russia, in view of the coming events of June 1941, Germany gave up vital geographic approaches to Russia through the Baltic area. Germany tried to compensate for this economically through the Strip deal.

The German thesis differentiating between the title to real estate and political "sovereignty" is very interesting. According to the German thesis, "sovereignty" could not be compensated for in accordance with material values; thus, there was no objective way of determining "adequate compensation."

No. 134

The German Embassy in Moscow to the German Foreign Minister, Ribbentrop

Telegram

MOST URGENT   Moscow, January 2, 1941 — 9:55 p.m.
No. 4 of January 2   Received January 3 — 12:45 a.m.

For the Foreign Minister.

With reference to your telegram No. 1 of January 1.

Molotov received our communications with visible satisfaction.

1. Molotov agreed in principle with the draft boundary agreement. He suggested, however, investigating whether it would not be well to mention in article 1 of the boundary agreement the three boundary agreements of October 1, 1920, January 22, 1928, and March 22, 1939, concluded between Germany and Lithuania. Regarding article 4, Molotov remarked that the Soviet Government would probably prefer a *pactum de contrahendo*

2. In the question of compensation for the Lithuanian strip Molotov made a compromise proposal, stating that he was willing to double the Soviet offer of 3.86 million gold dollars; he requested that the German claim be correspondingly reduced. Thus the Soviet offer amounts to 32.4 million reichsmarks payable in 2 years in accordance with the previous Soviet proposal.

3. As regards the goods to be delivered, Molotov said the Soviet Government was willing to comply with the German wishes. However, he pointed out that the nonferrous metals already promised in the economic agreement had to be taken from national reserves and would create difficulties in the delivery of further quantities. Nevertheless he did not intend to exclude nonferrous metals. He would instruct People's Commissar Mikoyan to make concrete proposals tomorrow to Minister Schnurre concerning distribution of the compensation in goods.

Molotov said he agreed to our request to conclude an agreement on this entirely independent of the economic agreement.

Please authorize Minister Schnurre in an open telegram to conclude this special agreement; a neutral designation should be chosen in consideration of the secret character of the agreement.

4. Molotov said he was willing to make the entire agreement ready for signature by Monday, or Tuesday at the latest. He will likewise instruct the Soviet delegations in Riga and Kaunas to conclude their work by this time. In order on our part to be able to meet this deadline,

which is very desirable for us, we request instructions in the course of January 3. We propose accepting the offer of the Soviet Government. Minister Schnurre will try during tomorrow's discussion with Mikoyan to reduce the term of payment from 2 years and to obtain as favorable a distribution of commodities as possible.

5. A separate telegraphic report follows concerning treatment of the agreement in the press.

SCHNURRE
SCHULENBURG

Editor's Comment: Doubling the amount of compensation for the Strip indicates Russia's urgency to compromise. It was of primary importance to Russia to legitimize the new frontier between Germany and the USSR, thus obtaining the recognition that Lithuania, including the Strip, was part of the USSR.

No. 135

**The German Foreign Minister, Ribbentrop,
to the German Embassy in Moscow**

Telegram

MOST URGENT   SPECIAL TRAIN, FUSCHL, January 3, 1941

SECRET   Received Berlin, January 3 — 8:30 p.m.

No. 1 of January 3 from Fuschl

No. 9 of January 3 from the Foreign Ministry

For the Ambassador personally and Schnurre.

With reference to your telegram No. 4 of January 2.[1]

I agree to the Soviet Government's compromise proposal regarding the Lithuanian strip provided that the amount is paid, not after 2 years but at once, by immediate delivery of nonferrous metals, this to be entirely independent of the raw material deliveries envisaged in the economic agreement. In case delivery of nonferrous metals in the full amount of the sum causes difficulties, I authorize you to accept half of the sum as *immediate* payment in gold. The other half of the sum is to be delivered if possible entirely in the form of nonferrous metals.

RIBBENTROP

Editor's Comment: In view of the approaching crucial events in Eastern Europe in May-June, 1941, immediate payment made sense for Germany.

No. 136

The German Embassy in Moscow
to the German Foreign Ministry

Telegram

MOST URGENT   Moscow, January 7, 1941 — 10:50 p.m.
SECRET   Received January 8 — 1:45 a.m.
No. 44 of January 7

With reference to our telegram No. 33 of January 6.

We have been negotiating again with Molotov today regarding compensation for the strip of Lithuanian territory.

At the start Molotov asked whether the Reich Government's reply to his statement yesterday concerning the Soviet standpoint had been received. We replied that there was no change in the attitude of the Reich Government. We asked that we be informed of the Soviet Government's reply, as promised. Molotov stated that the Soviet Government was willing to comply with the German wishes in certain points, and he made the following final proposal:

The Soviet Government agreed to pay half of the compensation amount in nonferrous metals, the remainder in raw materials, and, in so far as these were not sufficient, in gold rubles. As regards the time limit Molotov said that in view of the burden of the obligations for delivery assumed toward Germany in the economic agreement the Soviet Government was unable to pay the compensation within the time limit of 3 months as requested by Germany. It was willing to shorten the time limit from 2 years to 1½ years with the condition that half of the entire compensation would be paid by the end of 1941 and the other half by July 1, 1942.

Molotov termed this the most the Soviet Union could do, and stated once more that this proposal of the Soviet Government was final. The Soviet Government did not want to assume any obligations which it could not fulfill, and it asked the Reich Government to regard the Soviet proposal in this light.

We request telegraphic instructions on whether we may accept Molotov's proposal, in order thereby to make possible the signing of the economic agreement, the Baltic agreement, and the resettlement agreement.

SCHNURRE
SCHULENBURG

Editor's Comment: In view of German plans for early summer, 1941, the Russian offer to pay half the amount of compensation for the Strip by the end of 1941 and the other half by July 1, 1942, was meaningless. It would have amounted to ceding the Strip for nothing, for the German-Russian war started on June 22, 1941.

No. 137

The German Ambassador in Moscow, Schulenburg, to the German Foreign Ministry

Telegram

MOST URGENT   Moscow, January 7, 1941 — 10:50 p.m.
No. 45 of January 7   Received January 8, — 12:20 a.m.

For the Reich Foreign Minister.

With reference to our telegram No. 44 of January 7.[1]

In the matter of the compensation for the strip of Lithuanian territory, I take the liberty of submitting to you the following consideration:

A rejection of the Soviet proposal will not only lead to serious political resentment on the part of the Soviet Government, but also thwart the realization of all other agreements in which we have a vital interest. Upon the conclusion of the resettlement agreements depends the fate of 55,000 resettlers, whose living conditions are deteriorating from day to day. The fact that the economic agreement, which was ready for signature by December 20, has not yet been signed, is already giving rise in wide circles to disagreeable comments on German-Soviet relations which, through the immediate conclusion of all agreements, could be successfully transformed into the opposite.

From my personal working relations with Molotov, I have the definite impression that the Soviet Government in making its offer has actually done its utmost, and that a further compliance with our wishes cannot be expected.

SCHULENBURG

Editor's Comment: It seems that Schulenburg, the German Ambassador in Moscow, at this date was not yet informed of Berlin's decision to attack Russia in the spring of 1941; thus, his willingness to accept the Russian compromise would be understandable. Schnurre and Schulenburg were mainly interested in the pending Russo-German trade treaty, and they saw in it, and in the Soviet offer for the "Strip," only a great advantage for Germany's hard pressed war economy.

No. 138

The German Embassy in Moscow to the German Foreign Ministry

Telegram

MOST URGENT   Moscow, January 8, 1941 — 4:45 p.m.
No. 47 of January 8   Received January 8 — 6:10 p.m.

With reference to our telegram No. 44 of January 7.[1]

After we, in speaking to Molotov yesterday, had strongly emphasized Germany's demand for *immediate* payment of compensation for the strip of Lithuanian territory, Molotov sent for us again at noon today, and informed us as follows:

The Soviet Government wishes to comply with the German request for the speediest liquidation of the entire matter, and therefore makes the following offers:

1) Immediate payment of the entire sum in gold, namely, through a charge against our gold payments, which are due after the signing of the commercial agreement.

2) Delivery of one-eighth of the amount of compensation in non-ferrous metals within the next 3 months, and payment of the remaining seven-eighths in gold at once, likewise through a charge against our gold payments.

Request instructions by telegram.

SCHNURRE
SCHULENBURG

No. 139

German-Soviet Secret Protocol

The German Ambassador, Count von der Schulenburg, Plenipotentiary of the Government of the German Reich, on the one hand, and the Chairman of the Council of People's Commissars of the USSR, V.M. Molotov, Plenipotentiary of the Government of the USSR, on the other hand, have agreed upon the following:

1. The Government of the German Reich renounces its claim to the strip of Lithuanian territory which is mentioned in the Secret Additional Protocol of September 28, 1939, and which has been marked on the map attached to this Protocol;

2. The Government of the Union of Soviet Socialist Republics is prepared to compensate the Government of the German Reich for the territory mentioned in Point 1 of this Protocol by paying 7.500,000 gold dollars or 31,500,000 million reichsmarks to Germany.

The amount of 31.5 million reichsmarks will be paid by the Government of the USSR in the following manner: one-eighth, that is, 3,937,500 reichsmarks, in nonferrous metal deliveries within 3 months after the signing of this Protocol, the remaining seven-eighths, or 27,562,500 reichsmarks, in gold by deduction from the German gold payments which Germany is to make by February 11, 1941, in accordance with the correspondence exchanged between the Chairman of the German Economic Delegation, Dr. Schnurre, and the People's Commissar for Foreign Trade of the USSR, M. A. I. Mikoyan, in connection with the "Agreement of January 10, 1941, concerning reciprocal deliveries in the second treaty period on the basis of the Economic Agreement between the German Reich and the Union of Soviet Socialist Republics of February 11, 1940."

3. This Protocol has been executed in two originals in the German language and two originals in the Russian language and shall become effective immediately upon signature.

Moscow, January 10, 1941.

For the Government	With full power of the
of the German Reich:	Government of the USSR:
SCHULENBURG	V. MOLOTOV
(SEAL)	(SEAL)

Editor's Comment: Thus ended the long and tortuous wrangling about the famous Lithuanian Strip, which seemed to be dragging the two powers to the brink of war. This settlement ended the destruction of Lithuania by Germany and Russia.

In addition to the Secret Protocol on the Lithuanian Strip, a series of other agreements between Germany and the USSR were signed in Moscow and Berlin on January 10, 1941:

1) A trade agreement, to supplement the economic treaty of 1940, which was expiring in February. The agreement provided for the exchange of German manufactured goods for Russian grain, raw

materials, and oil in a volume of over one billion marks. German radio stated that the USSR would supply Germany with "the largest quantity of grain ever shipped from one country to another."

2) A German-Soviet Boundary Treaty finalizing the Russo-German frontier from the River Igorka (Igara) to the Baltic Sea (Document No. 140). (The Russo-German frontier in Poland was finalized in Berlin on August 31, 1940.)

3). An agreement for the repatriation of nationals between Germany and the USSR. 30,000 German nationals in Northern Bucovina and 90,000 from Bessarabia (Moldavian SSR) were repatriated in November, 1940, by a treaty signed on August 29, 1940. 118,000 German nationals in the Soviet zone of Poland had been repatriated in December, 1939. There still remained 40,000 Germans in Lithuania and 10,000-15,000 in Latvia and Estonia, who were now exchanged for the Balts and Byelorussians in German territories.

4) An economic agreement arranging compensation for the property of German and Russian nationals affected by the repatriation agreement.

No. 140

German-Soviet Boundary Treaty

APPENDIX A

U.S.S.R. - Germany

Treaty Regarding the German-Soviet Frontier from the River Igorka to the Baltic Sea*

January 10, 1941

In view of the absorption of the Lithuanian Socialist Soviet Republic into the body of the Union of Socialist Soviet Republics which took place on August 3, 1940, the following treaty regarding the frontiers of the German Reich and the Union of Socalist Soviet Republics in the sector from the river Igorka to the Baltic Sea has been concluded between the German Reich Government, represented by the German Ambassador in Moscow, Count von der Schulenburg, and the Government of the

Wide World Photos

Very intensive negotiations between the Führer and Chancellor of the German Reich Adolf Hitler (r.) and Soviet Foreign Commissar V. Molotov (l.) took place in November, 1940 in Berlin. (See document # 128)

Wide World Photos

Signing of the Nazi-Soviet Pact and its additional secret protocol of September 23, 1939, in Moscow.

(L. to R.) German Foreign Minister Joachim von Ribbentrop, Head of the Soviet Communist Party Joseph Stalin, Undersecretary of State Gauss, Counsellor of the Legation Hilger, seated signing the pact Soviet Foreign Commissar V. Molotov, and German Ambassador to Moscow Count von Schulenberg. (See Documents Nos. 16 and 17)

Union of Socialist Soviet Republics, represented by the Chairman of the Council of People's Commissars of the U.S.S.R., W.M. Molotov.

Article I

The frontier of the German Reich and the Union of Socialist Soviet Republics, in the aforementioned sector, shall run from the point established with frontier sign No. I/I on the river Igorka in the demarcation of the national frontier and frontier of interest of the German Reich and the national frontier of the Socialist Soviet Republics in the year 1940 in an approximately northwesterly direction to the coast of the Baltic Sea. This frontier runs as follows:

(a) In the sector from point I/I on the river Igorka to the former junction of the frontiers of the German Reich, Lithuania, and Poland, along the line of the former national frontier between Lithuania and Poland as described in the resolution of the Conference of Ambassadors of March 15, 1923;

(b) In the sector from the junction mentioned under (a) above to the frontiers of the former Memel district, along the former national frontier between the German Reich and Lithuania as described in the treaty between the German Reich and the Lithuanian Republic of January 29, 1928;

(c) In the sector from the southernmost point of the frontier of the former Memel district to the Baltic Sea, along the former national frontier between the German Reich and Lithuania as laid down in Article I of the treaty between the German Reich and Lithuania of March 22, 1939.

Article II

The provisions of the German-Soviet Frontier Treaty of August 31, 1940, shall apply correspondingly to the legal status on the frontier described in ARTICLE I.

Article III

The two contracting parties agree to examine the question of the legal status on the frontier waterways in the course of subsequent negotiations.

Article IV

This Treaty is to be ratified. The exchange of the instruments of ratification will take place in Berlin in as short a time as possible.

The Treaty becomes effective on its signature.

Done in two original copies, one each in the German and Russian languages, both texts having equal validity.

Moscow, January 10, 1941

On behalf of the Government of the U.S.S.R.

For the German Reich Government

(Signed) Count von der Schulenberg

(Signed) W. M. Molotov

B. Resistance And Repression

No. 141

Note from the Lithuanian Minister in Berlin, Škirpa, to the Reich Foreign Minister, Ribbentrop

Lithuanian Legation in Germany
No. 3.991
Berlin July 21, 1940

His Excellency M. Von Ribbentrop
Minister of Foreign Affairs at Berlin

Dear Mr. Minister:

I have the honor to bring the following to your attention: As you are already well aware, the U. S. S. R., with absolutely no justifiable reason for so doing, dispatched on July 14, 1940, an ultimatum to Lithuania which demanded:

1. The abdication of the constitutionally formed government of Lithuania;

2. The rendition before the judicial authorities, without any legal basis for a claim of wrongdoing, of the Minister of the Interior and the Director of the Department of National Security;

3. The introduction into Lithuania of an unlimited number of Soviet troops.

The next day, the Red Army, after having attacked Lithuanian border positions and crossed the frontier, occupied the whole of Lithuania. Subsequently a high-ranking Soviet official was expressly dispatched into Lithuania to impose upon our country a so-called government, and the U. S. S. R. assumed complete administrative control.

In order to achieve definitively the incorporation of Lithuania into the U. S. S. R., elections were conducted last July 14 with a view to the formation of the Diet (Seimas); the holding of such elections ran completely opposite to the will of the Lithuanian people.

In order to suppress every manifestation of opposition, every Lithuanian association and political grouping was decimated. The more or less influential leaders of such groups were placed under arrest. There were placed at the head of every State bureau, and, in particular, of the Ministry of Defense, persons who formerly were classified as enemies of the Lithuanian state.

The Communist Party was the only political group permitted to function freely. It alone exercised decisive influence upon the elections. A single list of candidates was presented, a list which was viewed as acceptable to the Communist Party.

To assure the greatest possible participation in these elections, any non-participant was threatened with being denominated an "enemy of the people." The voters were then subjected to the most rigorous restrictions.

Elected in such circumstances, the Diet was completely in the hands of the Communists. As such, it was simply a tool of the Soviet Government. Today, July 21, 1940, the Diet determined to introduce the Soviet system into Lithuania and to incorporate Lithuania into the U. S. S. R.

All of these proceedings by the U. S. S. R. constitute a flagrant violation of each and every treaty signed by Lithuania and the U. S. S. R., and in particular:

1. The Treaty of Peace of July 12, 1920, in which the U. S. S. R., as successor state to the ancient Czarist Russia, granted unconditional recognition of the independence and sovereignty of Lithuania and renounced forever all rights of sovereignty, formerly enjoyed by Russia, over the Lithuanian nation.

2. The Non-Aggression Treaty of September 28, 1926, as maintained in force under dates of May 6, 1931, and April 4, 1934.

By virtue of this latter treaty, the U. S. S. R. bound itself to recognize, in every situation, the sovereignty of Lithuania as well as its political integrity and territorial inviolability (see Art. 2) and to renounce the use of force in any form (Art. 3).

3. The Treaty of Mutual Assistance of October 10, 1940, by virtue of

which the U.S.S.R. once again solemnly pledged itself not to interfere in any way with either the sovereign rights of the Lithuanian state or its internal political structure.

Given the circumstances described above, as Minister Plenipotentiary duly accredited to the German Reich by the proper constitutional authorities of the Republic of Lithuania, I feel it my indispensable duty to lodge a protest in the most serious and vigorous fashion possible against this rape of my country and against the abolition of the sovereignty and independence of the Lithuanian Republic. The afore-mentioned decision of the Diet, rendered under the pressure of the Russian invaders, is nothing but an outrageous distortion of the expression of the will of the Lithuanian people, contrary to the Constitution and interests of the Lithuanian state, as well as to the right of the Lithuanian people to self-determination. As such, this decision cannot be recognized as having any legal validity whatsoever.

I take this opportunity, Excellency, to extend to you the expression of my highest consideration.

K. ŠKIRPA
Minister Extraordinary and
Plenipotentiary of Lithuania

Editor's comment: Similar notes were presented by the Lithuanian missions in all countries with which Lithuania had diplomatic relations. No cases of Lithuanian diplomats defecting to the Soviets were recorded; the protests were unanimous. The diplomatic representatives of Latvia and Estonia took similar measures.

No. 142

The U.S. Minister of Kaunas, Norem, to the U.S. Secretary of State, Hull

KAUNAS, July 21, 1940 — 9 a.m.
[Received 12:10 p.m.]

164. I have the honor to report that in answer to an urgent request made at 10:30 p.m. last evening by the provisional Foreign Minister, I called upon him [*her*] to receive the formal protest against the freezing of credits. Miss Avetenaite after declining interpreter and, after translating the letter (full translation follows in gray), added very quietly: "Please disregard all of our protests. We do not act indepen-

dently any more. We appreciate what Washington is doing more than we dare tell. People are listening and I cannot say any more." I concluded that she had expressed the exact sentiments of all who count for the good of Lithuania and for the other two Baltic countries as well. While the Lithuanians would prefer to have their investments held safe until better times return, the Bolsheviks apparently are much annoyed and a trifle perplexed. They desire so earnestly to make the whole business of the transfer seem spontaneous on the part of these poor people. The freezing decree may possibly affect their instructions to the Seimas meeting today. . . . called informally also and explained that "advisers" in the Foreign Office could not understand our inability to accept the invitation to attend today's meeting of the Seimas. He himself expressed deep appreciation of our Government's understanding and treatment of the whole procedure. He added that the powers that be are considering the continuance of the three small countries as protectorates in order to better solve outstanding problems. Soviet control and direction is now almost complete. The text of the note presented is as follows:

The Lithuanian Government was greatly surprised when it learned that on July 15th, 1940 the Government of the United States of America issued an order No. 8484 by which all operations pertaining to the property of the Lithuanian State and citizens are prohibited without a permit.

On the basis of this order the Federal Reserve Bank of New York has up to this time not acted upon the request of the Lithuanian Bank of July 13th, 1940, to transfer to the account of the State Bank of the Soviet Union the gold which the Lithuanian Bank purchased from that Bank.

In depositing its capital with an American bank the Lithuanian Government showed confidence in the credit institutions of the United States of America. The Executive Order of the Government of July 15th, 1940 greatly injures Lithuania's rights and interests and likewise causes great losses to the Lithuanian Bank.

The Lithuanian Government is forced to express its categorical protest against this illegal and baseless order of the Government of the United State of America, which limits its rights to property which as property of a sovereign state enjoys immunity.

All responsibility for losses which may accrue to Lithuanian interests in connection with Executive Order No. 8484 of July 15th, 1940 will fall upon the Government of the United States of America.

The Lithuanian Government express, however, a strong conviction that the United States Government will annul the order of July 15th and assure that the gold which the Lithuanian Bank sold for an appropriate equivalent to the State Bank of the Soviet Union will be transferred to the latter.

Norem

Editor's comment: Anyone who delivered an official communication at this date acted on the orders of Dekanozov. Miss Avietenaite acted in behalf of the acting Foreign Minister of the People's Government, Pijus Glovackas. At this time Lithuania had not yet been formally incorporated into the Soviet Union, and the Soviets acted as if the Lithuanian Foreign Minister still represented a free government conducting normal foreign relations.

No. 143

The Lithuanian Minister in Berlin, Škirpa, to the Office of the Lithuanian Minister of Foreign Affairs

Telegram

Minister of Foreign Affairs — Kaunas

It is my considered opinion that the Diet, formed during the period of foreign occupation and under the oppression of a foreign power, stifling all other opinion save that of the Communist Party, is incapable of expressing the true will of the Lithuanian people concerning any matter whatsoever.

I herewith protest the steps taken by the Diet on July 21 to impose the Soviet regime upon Lithuania and to incorporate Lithuania into the Soviet Union, thereby suppressing the political independence of the country.

I deem the aforementioned steps taken by the Diet illegal, contrary to the provisions of the constitution now in force and to the interests of our country and our people and, for me, as legally constituted representative of an independent Lithuania, completely null and void.

July 22, 1944
Signed: Škirpa

No. 144

Note of the Lithuanian Minister to the Holy See, Girdvainis, to the Papal Secretary of State, Maglione

Lithuanian Legation
Holy See
No. 200

ROME, July 22, 1940

To His Eminence Cardinal LOUIS MAGLIONE
Secretary of State to His Holiness
Vatican City

Your Eminence,

An assembly meeting in Kaunas pre-empted the title of Parliament and decided on July 21 to request that the government of Moscow accept Lithuania into the U. S. S. R. That decision was taken under pressure from the Soviet government, whose army, as is known, invaded the territory of the Republic of Lithuania in considerable numbers on June 15, 1940; after this event proper functioning of the constitutional organs of the state became practically impossible. The Soviet Union thereupon took into its own hands control and direction of the entire administration of the Republic.

These acts were in effect a violation by the government of Moscow of the Peace Treaty of July 12, 1920, the Non-aggression Treaty of September 28, 1926, which was to remain in force until December 31, 1945, the Agreement of July 5, 1933, upon the definition of Aggression, and the Mutual Assistance Treaty of October 10, 1939, as well as other universally recognized international agreements.

In the circumstances outlined above, as duly accredited Lithuanian Minister to the Holy See, I have the honor:

1 - to state that the decision by the so-called Parliament, imposed by a foreign government, is illegal and in no way corresponds to the wishes of the Lithuanian people, who will never recognize this violation of their right to live as free, independent, and sovereign people on the land of their ancestors.

2 - to record my protest against the unprovoked aggression of the U. S. S. R., which has violated its treaties, the rights of nations, and Lithuanian sovereignty.

3 - to request that the Holy See refuse to recognize annexation of Lithuania by the U. S. S. R.

Respectfully yours,
GIRDVAINIS
Minister of Lithuania

No. 145

Note of the Lithuanian Minister in Italy, Lozoraitis, to the Italian Foreign Minister, Ciano

No. 200

LITHUANIAN LEGATION IN ITALY,
Rome, July 22, 1940.

To His Excellency Count GALEAZZO CIANO,
Minister of Foreign Affairs, Rome.

EXCELLENCE: On July 21 (1940), a gathering in Kaunas, assuming the name of the People's Seimas, passed a resolution, asking the Muscovite Government to accept Lithuania into the Union of the Soviet Socialist Republics. This Seimas has been constituted under direct pressure from the Soviet Government, which, on June 15, as we remember, ordered a very great number of troops to invade the whole territory of the Republic of Lithuania. Thus the carrying on of the administrative functions, provided for by the Constitution and the laws, became impossible. The Soviet Union took into its own hands control of the administration of the Republic.

Therefore, the Muscovite Government has flagrantly violated the Peace Treaty of July 12, 1920, the Non-aggression Pact of September 28, 1926, which was to remain in force until December 31, 1945, the Convention on Definition of the Aggressor of July 5, 1933, the Mutual Assistance Pact of October 10, 1939, and the universally recognized principles of international law.

Under such circumstances, I, as the duly accredited Minister to His Majesty the King of Italy and Albania and the Emperor of Ethiopia by the constitutional authorities of the Lithuanian state, deem it my honor

to protest publicly against the unprovoked aggression by the Union of the Soviet Socialist Republics, which had violated the treaties, the principles of the international law and the sovereignty of Lithuania;

to state that the resolution of the so-called Seimas, which has been imposed upon by a foreign government, is illegal and completely inconsistent with the will of the Lithuanian people, which will never recognize this violation of its right to be free, independent and sovereign in its own country;

I beg you, dear Minister, to accept the assurance of my highest consideration.

St. Lozoraitis.

No. 146

Note of the Lithuanian Minister in Argentina, Graužinis, to the Argentine Foreign Minister, Cantilo

No. 909

Lithuanian Legation,
Buenos Aires, July 22, 1940.

To His Excellency Mr. Jose Maria Cantilo,
Minister of Foreign Affairs, Buenos Aires.

Dear Minister: After the so-called Lithuanian Seimas had yesterday decided to ask for the incorporation of Lithuania into the Union of the Soviet Socialist Republics, it is my honor, as Minister of Lithuania to Argentina, to forward to the attention of the Government of Argentina the following statement:

(1) The so-called Seimas does in no way represent the will of the Lithuanian people;

(2) The elections to this Seimas and the resolution, passed by it, was made under the oppression of the Soviet Russian army which, as it may be remembered, had in advance occupied the territory of the Republic of Lithuania;

(3) Under such circumstances and following the true will of the Lithuanian people, I deem it my honor to express my most open and extremely urgent protest against the violation of the independence of Lithuania, perpetrated by the Soviet Union;

(4) All the ministers of Lithuania, accredited to foreign governments in accordance with the unquestionable will of the people, with all means in their possession, to preserve and to defend their own nation, refuse to recognize this illegal incorporation of Lithuania into

the U. S. S. R. I firmly believe that the Government of Argentina will graciously support our attitude.

In forwarding this statement to Your Excellency, I reserve my right to explain more precisely in which way the Union of the Soviet Socialist Republics had violated its treaties and solemn obligations with Lithuania.

Please accept, dear Minister, the assurance of my highest consideration.

Dr. KAZIMIERAS GRAUŽINIS.

NOTE. — On the same day similar notes were addressed to Mr. Alberto Guani, Minister of Foreign Affairs of Uruguay, Mr. Oswaldo Aranna, Minister of Foreign Affairs of Brazil and to many ambassadors and envoys in the capital of Argentina.

No. 147

Note of the Lithuanian Minister in Switzerland, Šaulys, to the Swiss Federal President

BERNE, July 23, 1940.

DEAR PRESIDENT: It is my honor to bring to the attention of the Federal Government of Switzerland the following:

On July 14, of this year, the so-called Government of Lithuania, imposed by the Muscovite army, which on June 15 of this year had invaded my country, held the "elections" to the Seimas.

These elections were a sad farce and a clear falsification of the intentions of the Lithuanian people. The Communist Party, legalized after the Red Army had invaded the country, was the only political party, which had monopolized all rights and liberties. Only a single candidate list of the "Union of Working Peoples of Lithuania," dominated by the Communists and their fellow-travellers, was permitted.

On July 21 of this year this "assembly," constituted under the armed terror of the Soviets and controlled and directed by the emissaries from the USSR, had voted to incorporate the Republic of Lithuania into the Union of the Soviet Socialist Republics.

By this action the government of the U.S.S.R. had flagrantly violated the following treaties, duly concluded with the Republic of Lithuania:

The Peace Treaty of July 12, 1920,

The Non-aggression Treaty of September 28, 1926,

The Convention on the Definition of Aggression of July 3, 1933,

The Mutual Assistance Pact and the Treaty on returning Vilnius and the Vilnius region to Lithuania of October 10, 1939.

In view of the foregoing, as a duly accredited Extraordinary Envoy and Minister Plenipotentiary of the Republic of Lithuania to the Federal Government of Switzerland, I deem it my honor to declare that the above-mentioned resolution of the so-called Seimas, imposed by the Soviet Government,

(1) is completely inconsistent with the will of the Lithuanian people,

(2) is unlawful and illegal and as such must be regarded as null and void.

The people of Lithuania will never recognize the violation of its most sacred and inalienable right to Independence and Sovereignty.

Thus, being faithful to the idea of national independence and to the duties of a qualified representative of his country, I voice my most solemn protest against the unprovoked and flagrant act of aggression on the part of the U.S.S.R., in violation of valid treaties, the formal obligations of international law and the sovereignty of the Republic of Lithuania.

Therefore I express my solidarity with all the representatives of Lithuania, accredited to the foreign governments, in their refusal to recognize this aggression and the violation of the sovereignty of the Republic of Lithuania, and I permit myself to express hope that the Swiss Federal Government will meet this attitude with sympathy.

I beg you, Mr. President, to accept the assurance of my highest consideration.

Dr. J. Šaulys.

Note. — Mr. Šaulys addressed a similar note to the Government of Hungary, and Mr. Turauskas to the Governments of Rumania and Yugoslavia.

No. 148

Note of the Lithuanian Minister in Sweden, Gylys, to the Swedish Foreign Minister

No. 657 5/4 A72

LITHUANIAN LEGATION,
Stockholm, July 23, 1940.

DEAR MINISTER: In connection with the declaration of the Lithuanian Soviet Socialist Republic and the resolution, asking that it be admitted into the Union of the Soviet Socialist Republics of July 21, 1940, I as the duly accredited Envoy of the constitutional and independent Republic of Lithuania to Sweden, deem it my duty to forward to the Swedish Government the following statement:

According to the Lithuanian-Soviet treaty of October 10, 1939. § 7, the Government of the Soviet Union had solemnly promised not to interfere in the internal affairs of Lithuania. On June 15 of this year the Government of the Soviet Union has disgracefully broken its promises, by occupying the whole territory of Lithuania, by forcing the legal government to resign and by forming in its place the puppet government, the members of which have been selected by the Soviet Union. From the legal point of view, this puppet government was unconstitutional because, after the elected President had left the country, the new government was appointed by the former chief of government, who had resigned and did not hold any constitutional powers.

This pro-Soviet government soon proclaimed elections to the Seimas, i.e., to the Representative Body of Lithuania. Only one political party was permitted in the pre-election campaign, and the single list of candidates, proposed by this party, was distributed to the election districts. By terror and force, the people of Lithuania were then pushed to the polls. Finally, by falsifying the election results, the Soviet Government succeeded in forming this prearranged Seimas, even by the so-called large participation of voters.

The fatal resolutions, passed by this so-called parliament on July 21, are inconsistent with the true will of the people, with their most sacred interests, and with the constitution of a free Republic. It is easy, even for a foreigner, to understand that a people, which for centuries fought for national, cultural, and political freedom, could not voluntarily accept the Russian yoke, being under no illusions of the consequences.

In the same manner, as the Czarist regime, which allowed our fighters for freedom to suffer the hardships in Siberia, its successor — the Soviet regime — embarked upon the same road, even more outrageously, by jailing and deporting for an unlimited term the leaders of free Lithuania.

My countrymen, living in an oppressed and sorrowful country, are deprived of the possibility to appeal to worldwide public opinion against the methods of violence, perpetrated by the Soviet government, methods which are unknown to the civilized world.

I respectfully ask Your Excellency to bring to the attention of his Majesty's Government of Sweden that —

(1) the Soviet Union, by occupying Lithuania, had outrageously broken its solemn obligations,

(2) the elections to the Seimas were carried out by terror,

(3) the resolution, passed by the pro-Muscovite people's representatives, establishing the Soviet regime in our country and incorporating it into the Soviet Union, is inconsistent with the will and interests of our people. In view of the foregoing, I voice my most vigorous protest.

I firmly hope that His Majesty's Government of Sweden will not recognize the change in the status of the Republic of Lithuania, which brought about by force, and I beg Your Excellency to accept the assurance of my most respectful consideration.

VYTAUTAS GYLYS.

NOTE. — A similar note was sent to His Majesty's Danish Government.

No. 149

Note of the Lithuanian Minister in London, Balutis, to H. M. Principal Secretary of State, Lord Halifax

23d July, 1940.

The Rt. Hon. VISCOUNT HALIFAX,K, G., P. C, G. S. C. I., G. C. I. E., G. C. I. E.,
His Majesty's Principal Secretary of State for Foreign Affairs, Foreign Office, London, S. W. I.

MY LORD: I consider it my painful duty to inform you that my country has become a victim of unprovoked aggression committed by the Soviet Government in violation of a series of treaties by which the Soviet Government in violation of a series of treaties by which the Soviet aggression against Lithuania.

2. As late as 10th October, 1939, a treaty was concluded between the Soviet Union and Lithuania, providing for the stationing of a limited number of Russian garrison troops in Lithuania, ostensibly for the mutual protection of both States. This treaty contains the following provision:

"The fulfillment of the present treaty shall not in any way affect the sovereign rights of the contracting parties, particularly their State organization, economic and social system, military methods, and generally, the principle of nonintervention in internal affairs. (Article VII)."

3. On June 14, 1940, on the pretext of entirely false charges, the Soviet Government abruptly confronted my Government with an ultimatum, presented at midnight of that day and expiring nine hours later; demanding unlimited occupation of Lithuania by Soviet military forces and the formation of a new Government acceptable to the U. S. S. R. while the entire country came under the rigid occupation of the Soviet military forces.

5. On July 14th and 15th, elections were staged for the return of a new Parliament which, on July 21st, decided unanimously, it is claimed, to surrender the independence of Lithuania and asked for incorporation into the U. S. S. R.

6. It must be obvious to any impartial and unprejudiced observer that neither the "elections" held under the pressure of foreign occupational troops nor the so-called Parliament constituted under such conditions can in any manner whatsoever reflect the will of the Lithuania people; they did not possess a shred of electoral liberty or the remotest possibility of expressing their true wishes.

7. In these circumstances, my duty as a representative of the Lithuanian people in this country, is to voice a most solemn protest against this wanton act of aggression against my country. At the same time, I wish to declare that I am unable to recognize as valid and binding any decision of the Parliament elected under foreign domination or any act of the Government formed and acting under duress.

8. Bringing the above to the notice of His Majesty's Government, I venture to hope that His Majesty's Government, themselves engaged in a struggle "till freedom for ourselves and others is secured" (to use your

Lordship's own inspiring words of yesterday) will decline to recognize the acts depriving Lithuania of her freedom.

I have the honour to be,

With the highest consideration,

My Lord,

Your obedient Servant,

B. K. Balutis.

No. 150

Memorandum by the Director of the Political Department of the German Foreign Ministry, Woermann

BERLIN, July 24, 1940.

I returned today in a friendly manner the notes regarding the incorporation of their countries into the Soviet Union to the Lithuanian and Latvian Ministers and justified this by stating that we could accept from Ministers only notes which they presented here in the name of their Governments. At the same time, in accordance with instructions, I did not indicate that they were returned by order of the Reich Foreign Minister.

The Estonian Minister likewise wished to hand me a similar note today. I requested him to refrain from doing so, giving the appropriate reasons.

The Lithuanian Minister informed me that of his own accord he had sent the Lithuanian Government a telegram of protest against the resolution of incorporation into the Soviet Union, stating among other things that he did not consider this resolution binding on the Lithuanian people, the nation or himself. The Lithuanian and Estonian Ambassadors told me that they had not sent a similar telegram and did not contemplate doing so.

Furthermore, I told the three Ministers that they and the other members of the Legation, including families, if they so desired, could remain in Germany. The three Ministers expressed their very great appreciation for this and also requested me to thank the Reich Foreign Minister.

WOERMANN

Editor's comment: Germany, conscious of her part in the incorporation of the Baltic States into the U. S. S. R., could not accept the protest notes of the Baltic diplomats for fear of antagonizing the Soviet Union — her partner in the partition.

No. 151

Note of the Lithuanian Minister in Washington, Žadeikis, to the U. S. Secretary of State, Hull

No. 1009

LITHUANIAN LEGATION,
Washington, D. C., August 3, 1940.

The Honorable CORDELL HULL,
Secretary of State, Washington, D.C.

SIR: According to information available, the supreme Soviet authority of the Union of the Soviet Socialist Republics on August 3, 1940 made a move to incorporate the Republic of Lithuania into the Soviet Union, thus not only completing a process whereby the Lithuanian nation has been deprived, temporarily at least, of her independence and the possibility of exercising her sovereignty rights, but also inflicting untold suffering and misery upon the innocent people.

The government of the Soviet Union, in order to camouflage its devious methods of aggression and to confuse world opinion, was eager to base this ignominious move against Lithuania's integrity on a resolution made in Moscow but adopted in Kaunas on July 21, 1940 by the Seimas (Parliament) which, in fact, was elected illegally and was one of the byproducts of the Soviet invasion. But the Soviet leaders for obvious reasons failed to mention the Lithuanian-Soviet treaties broken by them: the Treaty of Nonaggression, for example, extended to 1945; the Lithuanian-Soviet Russian Peace Treaty of July 12, 1920, the first Article of which reads as follows:

"Relying on the strength of a declaration made by the Federal Soviet Socialist Republic of Russia to the effect that all peoples of every nationality have the right of self-determination and complete separation from the State to which they belonged previously, Russia, without any reservation whatsoever, recognizes Lithuania as a self-governing and independent State with all juridical consequences that follow from such a recognition and in a spirit of free and good will renounces all sovereignty rights of Russia concerning the Lithuanian nation and Lithuanian territory which previously belonged to her. The fact that Lithuania for some time was under Russian sovereignty does not impose on the Lithuanian people and their territory any obligations towards Russia."

As the so-called Parliamentary elections of July 14 and 15, 1940, and the forced adoption of a resolution to join the Soviet Union were utterly void of legality, as referred to in my previous note of July 22, 1940, so is the incorporation of Lithuania, together with her historic capital Vilnius and the Vilnius District, into the Soviet system a lawless act, contrary to elementary rules of international conduct — an act that is in fact the final phase of veiled aggression and imposition by threat of force of the Soviet's will upon its weaker neighbor.

As the duly accredited representative of the Sovereign Republic of Lithuania near the Government of the United States of America I repeat my protest against the unprovoked aggression and illegal incorporation of Lithuania into the Soviet Union and at the same time express the hope of the Lithuanian nation that no State in the world will recognize this international outrage as having any legality or bona fide excuse.

I take this opportunity to express my most profound gratitude to the American Government for the stand taken in this matter as evidenced in the statement by the Honorable Acting Secretary of State on July 23, 1940, and hope that the American Government will continue to refuse legal recognition of the Soviet's aggressive acts against Lithuania's integrity and independence.

Accept, sir, the renewed assurances of my highest consideration.

P. ŽADEIKIS,
Minister of Lithuania.

No. 152

Note of the Lithuanian Minister in Vichy, France, Klimas, to the Foreign Minister, Baudouin

HOTEL DE LILAS,
VICHY, August 4, 1940.

To His Excellency Mr. Baudouin,
    Minister of Foreign Affairs.

DEAR MINISTER: According to the official Soviet News Agency, the

Supreme Soviet of the Union of the Soviet Socialist Republics, complying with the will, expressed by the so-called representatives of the Lithuanian people, elected on July 14 and 15 and assembled in Kaunas on July 21, had decided to incorporate the independent State of Lithuania into the U. S. S. R.

It is my honor to point out to Your Excellency, in addition to my verbal explanations, that these people's representatives were appointed, after the territory of the Republic of Lithuania had been occupied by the army of the U. S. S. R. which, in violation of every right, on June 15, 1940, had entered, in great numbers, into Lithuania. The elections were imposed by a single, specially selected, list of candidates. The people were deprived of the possibility to offer any other list of candidates. The freedom of assembly and discussions were abolished. There was no provision guaranteeing the regularity of voting and ballot counting. The desired results were published in advance, even before the elections were over.

It is clear that under such circumstances the elected body of representatives cannot be regarded as expressing the true will of the people. Neither the resolution passed by this body of the so-called people's representatives, and requesting the incorporation of Lithuania into the U. S. S. R., may in any way be regarded as consistent with the will of the Lithuanian nation, which for centuries had fought for freedom and independence.

From this viewpoint, the government of the U. S. S. R. had committed an act of aggression, by using military force and by violating the principles of international law and the obligations expressed in the Peace Treaty on July 12, 1920, the Non-aggression Pact of 1926, which had been reaffirmed many times hereafter, the Briand and Kellogg Pact of 1928, the Convention on Definition of Aggression of 1933, and, finally, the recently concluded Pact of Mutual Assistance and Non-interference in internal affairs of October 10, 1939.

I deem it my duty to bring to your attention this flagrant violation of international law perpetrated by the Government of the U. S. S. R. As the duly accredited Minister of the free and independent State of Lithuania to France which had recognized Lithuania de jure and with which Lithuania had always entertained the most cordial and friendly relations, I ask the French Government not to recognize this act of violence, by which the U. S. S. R. had occupied my country.

I firmly hope that the French Government will acknowledge the right of the Lithuanian people to live in freedom and independence, and I beg you, Sir, to accept the assurance of my highest and most cordial consideration.

P. KLIMAS,
Extraordinary Envoy and Minister Plenipotentiary of Lithuania.

N. B. A similar note was sent to the Government of Portugal.

No. 153

The German Ambassador in Moscow, Schulenburg to the German Foreign Ministry

Telegram

MOST URGENT   Moscow, August 12, 1940—2:33 p.m.
No. 1628 of August 12   Received August 12—5:00 p.m.

With reference to your telegram No. 1284 of July 25 (Pers. H 11163).[1]

Foreign Commissar Molotov communicated the following by a note of August 11:

Lithuania, Latvia, and Estonia have by decision of the Supreme Soviet been incorporated in the territory of the Soviet Union and therewith have become a part of the Soviet Union. The direct diplomatic relations of Lithuania, Latvia, and Estonia are terminated. The Soviet Union accordingly expects that the German Legations in Kaunas, Riga, and Tallinn will be liquidated on or before August 25. Consulates must likewise be liquidated on or before September 1. A portion of the staff of the German Legation in Kaunas may exercise consular functions during the resettlement. The Lithuanian, Latvian, and Estonian Diplomatic and Consular Missions will cease their activities and transfer their functions, archives, and property to the proper Soviet Mission.

SCHULENBURG

Editor's comment: Škirpa, the Lithuanian Minister in Berlin, refused to hand over the Lithuanian legation building in protest and was evicted by the German police. He also succeeded in raising the Lithuanian flag over the building in such a way that it was inaccessible. When the

---

[1] Not found.

Soviets did finally manage to occupy the building they found it impossible to remove, and were forced to call upon the Berlin fire department to remove the Lithuanian flag.

No. 154

Note of Protest of the Attaché of the Lithuanian Legation in Stockholm to the Swedish Foreign Ministry

Aug. 12, 1940

We are living through one most deeply sorrowful moment in Lithuanian history. Our legation in Sweden is being forced to interrupt its activity. Since, as we all know, Sweden is a land which always valued international justice and stood for the small nations' right to live. I hereby wish, charged with this duty by the Minister of the Republic of Lithuania, to make the following declaration:

1) If I transfer the Lithuanian legation to the representative of the Swedish Ministry of Foreign Affairs at this time, this is the consequence of the most treacherous occupation perpetrated in violation of the most solemnly given pledges. Thus, the legation is placed in a situation in which we have no choice whatsoever. It must submit to the consequences which follow from the toleration of force. Those consequences are a forcible act, and thus the transfer of the legation cannot in any way be understood as a voluntary action.

2) To avoid possible unpleasantries to the land with which free Lithuania always maintained most friendly relations, the Lithuanian Legation agreed to the present procedures of forcible transfer, however, only with the self-evident condition that this procedure does not alter the principles held by the Head of the Legation, that is, that this transfer is in no way to be interpreted to mean our agreement to transfer our legation to Soviet Russia.

3) To formalize the forcibly imposed obligation to stop the operation of the Legation, I now transfer the keys of the legation to the free disposal of the Swedish Government, while the flag of free Lithuania flies at half mast. Be assured that Lithuania will not long remain under the foreign yoke, but will rise again.

By this I have fulfilled the most sorrowful duty which can possibly be imposed on a civil servant, and in this hour of farewell it remains for me to express warm gratitude for the splendid relations which our Legation enjoyed with the Royal Ministry of Foreign Affairs. On behalf of

Minister Gylys and myself I request the employees of the Ministry, and you, monsieur Chef de Bureau, to accept my personal gratitude for your cooperation, interest, and the sympathy which you have shown to our unhappy fatherland.

Editor's comment: Sweden was the first country after Germany to recognize the Soviet incorporation of Lithuania. Žilinskas was selected to surrender the keys as the lowest ranking diplomat on the legation staff. The note was delivered orally and in writing by Žilinskas to Lennart Nilander, Chef de Bureau of the Swedish Foreign Ministry.

As it turned out, Latvia, Estonia, Finland, Denmark, and Norway also had their opportunity to thank Sweden for her friendship in better times. as Sweden proved to be one of the most notorious fair weather friends in recent diplomatic history.

No. 155

Lithuanian Activist Front Appeal; All Forward Together to Create a New Lithuania

July-Aug. 1940

Our fatherland, Lithuania, lost its political independence which had been reconquered with the blood of the best sons of our nation.

Lithuania has fallen again under the Russian yoke, but this time under the Red Army, the blind executioner of the Moscow Communist gangsters and their gangster designs.

But the Lithuanian nation, having known liberty, will never forsake it again. Such is the Lithuanian nation.

The Russian occupants have trampled our national flag, but they will not be able to uproot the feelings of liberty from the Lithuanian spirit, or the desire for the reestablishment of Lithuanian political independence.

This ideal has been a beacon in our nation's ancient past, when the Grand Dukes of Lithuania created a Lithuanian State from the Baltic to the Black Sea. This ideal has produced great spiritual heroes and sparked a national consciousness in the masses of the Lithuanian people. It produced thousands of volunteer hero fighters for the struggle for Lithuania's independence in the period 1918-1920. This ideal still gives the Lithuanian nation today indomitable will and the determination for new sacrifices for the restoration of Lithuania's political independence.

As long as this ideal remains in the hearts of Lithuanians, and certainly it will remain as long as the Lithuanian nation survives, our forces will remain invincible. They are unconquerable because we are fighting for our most sacred rights, based on pure justice, which is always more powerful than aggression, violence and injustice.

The Lithuanian Activist Front has undertaken the task of restoring the new Lithuania, and this Front has been known to our people for some time. It always appeared whenever the former rulers of Lithuania showed inability to care for the affairs of the Lithuanian nation and the Lithuanian State, thus placing Lithuanian independence in domestic and foreign jeopardy. For the courage they showed many activists suffered greatly. But persecutions, banishment to labor and concentration camps, imprisonment and other means of torture not only did not break down the determination of the activists, but hardened them even more for further struggle.

Engaging now in the grave struggle for the restoration of the new Lithuania, the Activist Front has no doubts that the entire Lithuanian nation will come to its aid. Thus we confidently address ourselves to our Lithuanian brothers and sisters, appealing to all to whom the freedom of Lithuania is dear to hasten into the honorable ranks of the activists.

Our ideal is the ideal of the entire Lithuanian nation: a free and independent Lithuania. We will no longer repeat the mistakes of the past. The so called nationalist regime of long standing deceived the Lithuanian nation exactly as the former parliamentary democratic laxity did. The new Lithuania is being created on the basis of national popular socialism, which so brightly shines in the skies of our neighbor Germany. This promises a happier picture for Lithuania too.

The loss of Lithuanian political independence is a very sorrowful blow to the Lithuanian nation, but let us not despair! The hour of deliverance is nearing. Only let us hasten our organization so that when the fateful hour comes we will show ourselves worthy of freedom.

Let us not waste time but start to create the links of a secret activist chain, groups and units in every Lithuanian village, town, office, factory, in the army and every other place wherever it is possible.

Do not expect any particular urging or directives from above. Under the present circumstances, when the leaders of the activists are specially shadowed and watched by the enemy, when they are arrested and imprisoned, the proper directions from above might not arrive. Each one should take independent initiative. Everyone who is determined must find around him some trustworthy friends of the same ideology and should stand at the head of them as their leader and establish contacts with the nuclei of the neighborhood shock organization.

In this way, all over Lithuania the network of Activist Front fighter will be formed, and thus altogether, blessed by Supreme Providence, we will deliver Lithuania.

The Supreme Command of the Activist Front reserves the right to appoint the commanders higher than battalion commanders; the Supreme Command also will give directives on how to conduct our common struggle.

Any Lithuanian, without distinction, regardless of his political persuasion, can become a member of the Activist Front if he is determined to fight for the deliverance of Lithuania, if he is worthy of the confidence, and if he agrees with the ideas of the activists. Each new member of the Activist Front must take an oath in the presence of the chapter or link of the shock troops to which he is accepted, to the effect that he will be faithful to the interests of the Lithuanian nation and the Lithuanian State. For perjury he will answer with his honor and his life.

Those who engage in the struggle without reservations and spare nothing to restore the freedom of Lithuania, who are determined to sacrifice all, even their lives for the freedom of Lithuania, these will also be the master of the new Lithuania. From these fighters will be formed the Government of the new Lithuania, and the social order of the new Lithuania will be based on them. The new Lithuania shall not be one of the lax ones and jellyfish, not one of the lackeys, of the party politicians, or led by the plutocrats, but one of the united will of determined men, the best sons of the nation, of those who risked their blood to deliver the new Lithuania. Generation after generation will remember them with honor as the memory of the heroes of the nation.

Thus, all hastily join the Activist Front for the deliverance of the fatherland!

Our oath is-unrelenting struggle against Communism and the Russian occupant, faithfulness unto death to the Lithuanian Activist Front, all freedom for the fatherland, and to the restoration of independence.

Our insignia is a tricolor triangle in enamel with the number of the member on the other side.

Our greeting is raising the right hand and saying: "Fight!"

We are not engaging in this struggle alone. Millions of our fighting comrades, German nationalists fighting for a just new European order, are stretching forth their helping hands. Thus, swift victory is assured! Let the trumpets of the struggle resound today across the entire land, let the spirit of our forefathers and our freedom fighters rise. This spirit will break the foreign yoke and will restore a free Lithuania.

signed: The Supreme Command of the Lithuanian Activist Front.

Editor's comment: In spite of the LAF's claim that "the movement of Lithuanian Activism is not a copying of Fascism or National Socialism," the reader cannot help but be struck by the Nazi tone sometimes evident in the appeals. A certain Nazi vocabulary is present, anti-Semitism makes a brief appearance, and the pre-war government is bitterly attacked. It is not our place or our concern to make apologies for the LAF; nevertheless, there are a number of external circumstances which place LAF movement in a different context and a different perspective.

In 1940-1941 the star of Germany was bright and growing brighter. In the circumstances of late 1940 it seemed obvious that Germany would be dictating the political order of post-war Europe, and the inescapable conclusion was that not even formal sovereignty would be possible for Lithuania without German consent. When the first appeal was written, war between Germany and the USSR was not yet certain; in fact, the possibility did not yet officially exist, and the German government would never have allowed the publication of the appeal. The appeal was not even written to be published; Škirpa delivered a copy to Peter Kleist, head of the Foreign Policy Bureau of the NSDAP, and that was it. Škirpa himself claims that the appeal was written specifically for official German consumption, and there is no reason to doubt him. He frankly admits the presence of Nazi phraseology but says that the appeal was written without any German influence. He claims it was successful since it aroused German interest in the LAF and its projects.

Thus, it would seem reasonable to conclude that the Nazi overtones of the appeals are more a question of Jesuitry than of any genuine ideological conviction. Subsequently, the LAF and the Germans conflicted as soon as their interests did not coincide, indicating that the LAF was not a Nazi puppet front. Škirpa himself claims that neither Kleist nor any other official "ever tried to force National Socialist Doctrine on us. On the contrary, they always liked to insist that National Socialism was not an export article." It seems obvious that one cannot have been a declared anti-Nazi and still have expected German aid, and it cannot be overemphasized that at the time only Germany was capable of driving the Soviets out of Lithuania.

The anti-Semitism may have been more than just Jesuitry however. It must be recalled that although there had been no anti-Semitism in Lithuania before the war and the conditions of the Jews were better in Lithuania than anywhere else in eastern Europe the Lithuanian Jewish population was compromised during the Soviet occupation, having contributed more than its proportional share of active Communists. Jewish minorities always seem more inclined to the left than the ethnic majority population, and Communism may very well have seemed the only hope of salvation from Hitler's notorious persecution of the Jews, but a certain residue of resentment was created among the ethnic Lithuania population. Though some may call this resentment anti-Semitism, anti-Semitism is not necessarily Nazism.

Finally, we must take the character of Škirpa himself into consideration. Škirpa was a Socialist-Populist whose popularly supported and constitutionally elected socialist government (in which he had been Chief of Staff) was overthrown by the right-wing Nationalist and Christian Democrat coup d'etat of 1926 (subsequently even the more centrists Christian Democrats were evicted from the ruling coalition as the government slipped farther to the right). So, it is easy to understand the undisguised gusto with which Škirpa, who wrote the LAF appeals, heaped abuse on the Smetona government. However, under the circumstances, the contention that Skirpa turned Nazi in 1941 becomes absurd, as absurd as would be the idea that he and the LAF turned Communist in 1941 when they refused to collaborate with German plans. The LAF, of course, was and remained nationalistic, not choosing sides in an ideological debate, but trying to rescue the freedom of Lithuania from two foreign occupants.

The reader would do well to bear in mind that these appeals represent the work of only the LAF leadership in Berlin. In fact, communication, not to speak of control, between Berlin and the rank and file in Lithuania was tenuous at best. In fact, the local leadership of the LAF operated quite independently of Berlin most of the time. Thus, while the credit for the original idea and organization of the LAF goes to the exiles in Berlin, the planning and execution of the June 23 insurrection and the proclamation of independence is almost exclusively the work of local activists, who, in extreme danger, raised a mass revolt against Soviet rule, in which the bulk of the insurgents probably never heard of the LAF.

No. 156

Resolution of the Lithuanian Diplomatic Conference in Rome

(Sept. 25, 1940)

In view of the Soviet aggression against Lithuania, the diplomatic envoys and ministers plenipotentiary of independent Lithuania, on the basis of the mandate, granted to them by the organs of independent Lithuania to represent the independent Lithuanian State, to speak in its name, to defend its independence, and to protect and preserve its interests, having protested against Moscow's act of aggression, not recognizing any legal effect or legal result of this act of aggression, executing the duty assigned to them by their country, decided:

To form a Lithuanian National Committee, whose supreme task shall be:

To coordinate the work of all Lithuanians in the restoration of the independence of the Lithuanian State, and in the duration of Lithuania's occupation to care for the interests of the Lithuanian State and Lithuanian nation;

To form the Lithuanian Committee of a president and two or three permanent members;

To charge the chairman of the Lithuanian National Committee if need be to, issue acts and act in the name of the whole Committee;

To invite the Lithuanians of the world to help the Lithuanian National Committee in its work and to request the Lithuanians of the United States to delegate their representatives with a deciding vote to the Committee.

It was decided further to invite Engineer Ernest Galvanauskas as president of the Lithuanian National Committee; Stasys Lozoraitis was appointed his deputy ipso jure. Selected as permanent members were Eduardas Turauskas and Kazys Škirpa. Also, it was provided for a second deputy to the chairman Povilas Žadeikis, the Lithuanian Minister in Washington.

Editor's Comment: In spite of the broad purposes set forth in the resolution, in practice, the Lithuanian National Committee set itself up for two aims: to maintain the diplomatic life of Lithuania in the community of nations, and to organize the large Lithuanian minority in the United States (394,811 registered on the 1940 census, unofficially perhaps more than a million) which had distinguished itself in the first Lithuanian struggle for independence during World War I. This is evident from the fact that in addition to the specific mention of the American immigration, Galvanauskas, the chairman, was instructed to visit the US as soon as possible. The LNC was not a government-in-exile. That they lacked even aspirations in that direction is shown by their delegation of the task of forming a provisional government to Škirpa and the LAF.

Galvanauskas had been the prime minister and minister of finances of Lithuania before the Smetonist coup. He was a well-known Lithuanian statesman without any overwhelming party identification. According to Škirpa, he was selected to be chairman mainly because he was not tied to any specific diplomatic post, and thus was free to travel wherever he was needed, especially to America.

No. 157

The Charter of the Lithuanian Activist Front

We, the undersigned Lithuanians, driven by fate to the Capital of Germany, Berlin, on November 17 of this year assembled at the residence of Kazys Škirpa in Achenbachstrasse and having heard his report on the causes of the destruction of Lithuanian independence and the possibilities and means of restoring the Lithuanian State, hereby express our agreement with this plan to gather all the most active energies of the Lithuanian nation into the Lithuanian Activist Front for the struggle for the deliverance of Lithuania from the Soviet Communist yoke;

Convinced that the management of the restored Lithuania on the foundations of the ideology of the Activist Front is the surest road for achieving the ideals of the Lithuanian nation, we are the first to enroll in the Lithuanian Activist Front and to assume all the duties and discipline assigned to the members.

For the wellbeing of the Lithuanian fatherland and the Lithuanian nation we invite Kazys Škirpa, the first creator-volunteer of the army of independent Lithuania and initiator of the Lithuanian Activist Front, to take over the duties of executing our determination, and to lead the Lithuanian Activist Front.

    Fight!   Forward courageously with firm steps.
               For the new Free Lithuania.
               Berlin, November 17, 1940

(signed:)

J. Viliušis, E. Galvanauskas, M. Kavolis, St. Puodžius, P. Skurauskas, J. Pyragius, J. Našliunas, J. Jurkunas, R. Skipitis, Jz. Dženkaitis, K. Brunius, B. Raila, A. Valiukenas, Jn. Dženkaitis, J. Čiuberkis, M. Kukutis, T. Dirmeikis, St. Yla, A. Maceina, Dr. P. Karvelis, A. Danta, Col. Ambraziejus, Rev. Barauskas, J. Katilius, M. Brakas, Dr. Pr. Ancevičius.

Agreed: K. Škirpa

Editor's Comment: For better or worse, the period of June 1940-June 1941 in the history of Lithuanian resistance is dominated by the sudden rise of Kazys Škirpa, brought to an end by his equally sudden fall when his project for cooperation with the Germans fell through and the German government isolated him in Berlin. The LAF was guided almost exclusively by his ideas, and the extent of his personal leadership is shown by the form of the charter. It should be noted that Galvanauskas, a former premier of Lithuania, in 1940 the chairman of the Lithuanian National Committee, signed, as did important Social Democrats, Christian Democrats, Populists, Nationalist Unionists (Tautininkai), academics, clergymen, military officers, and even members of the far-right Nationalist Voldemarininkai, whose idol and leader Professor Voldemaras had returned to Soviet Lithuania.

    Škirpa himself explained that the LAF did not consider itself a ruling party or coalition, but a united action group, since the recognized leaders of the pre-occupation political movements were still in Lithuania and any action which could be linked with a specific political group would serve as a pretext for Soviet reprisals against the Lithuanian intelligentsia. In all fairness to Škirpa, it must be said that the diversity of the charter membership of the LAF does make it seem highly unlikely that the organization was conceived of as the future ruling party (like the Nazi, Communist, Fascist, or Falange) of an authoritarian, one-party state.

No. 158

Draft Memorandum of the Lithuanian Minister in Berlin, Škirpa, for the German Foreign Ministry

(May 12, 1941)

Herr Foreign Minister of the Reich:

I have the honor to submit humbly to your Excellency the following: As it is already well known, the Union of Soviet Socialist Republics, on June 14, 1940 sent an ultimatum to Lithuania, under a nonexistent and unfounded pretext, demanding, among other things, that Lithuania allow an unrestricted number of Soviet armed troops into Lithuania and that it form a government acceptable to the Union of Soviet Socialist Republics. On the following day Lithuania was occupied by the strong armed forces of Soviet Russia.

This was accomplished in violation of all the treaties signed between Lithuania and the Union of Soviet Socialist Republics, and in gross offense of the universally recognized law of nations. Since the constitutional operation of the country was thus made impossible by a foreign occupation, the President of the Republic Lithuania felt compelled to leave the country on June 15, 1940 in protest against this act of violence of the Union of Soviet Socialist Republics.

By using the falsified and staged elections of July 14-15, for the so-called People's Seimas the government of the Union of Soviet Socialist Republics attempted to justify the fait accompli post factum, by forcing the so-called People's Seimas on July 21, 1940 to adopt a resolution to introduce a Soviet system into Lithuania and to incorporate the Lithuanian State into the Union of Soviet Socialist Republics.

This was a brutal falsification of the will of the Lithuanian nation. But the Lithuanian nation was certainly not inclined to give up its political independence, gained so dearly by the greatest sacrifices, to the foreign intruding masters.

For this reason all the diplomatic envoys and ministers accredited abroad, as well as all the organizations of Lithuanians residing abroad, being in a position to speak freely in the name of Lithuania, immediately expressed protests against the violence perpetrated on the Lithuanian nation and requested all the governments of the respective countries not to recognize the incorporation of Lithuania into the Union of Soviet Socialist Republics.

Until now, no State in the world justified this act of violence perpetrated by the Union of Soviet Socialist Republics. Thus, the political sovereignty of Lithuania is not negated by any other country. This circumstance gives not only an objective foundation to the ever growing movement of Lithuania to regain independence, but also shows that the domination of the Union of Soviet Socialist Republics in Lithuania is only a temporary and de facto occupation.

It is with great interest and deep satisfaction that the Lithuanian nation heard the repeated declarations of members of the Reich Government according to which, in the new Europe guided by Germany, the possibility of national and political self determination will be assured to all nations. Therefore, the Lithuanian nation thinks that it has reason to hope to regain its national freedom and to restore its political independence and its sovereignty. The Lithuanian nation further thinks that it may hope for recognition and support of these efforts in seeking her freedom, from the creative European powers, especially from the government of the German Reich, even more so for the reason that the temporary destruction of Lithuanian independence was one of the results of the political situation created by this war in Eastern Europe.

In view of all this, I allow myself humbly to inform you, Her Reichminister, that a new Lithuanian government has been formed, the structure of which is as follows:

Prime Minister
Minister of Foreign Affairs
Minister of Defense
Minister of the Interior
Minister of Agriculture
Minister of Education
Minister of Commerce, Industry and Finance
Minister of Communications
Minister of Justice
Minister of National Culture and Propaganda.

The essential objectives of this government are: deliverance of the Lithuanian Nation from Russian Bolshevism, restoration of Lithuanian Sovereignty in the territory determined by the treaty of peace between Lithuania and Soviet Russia of July 12, 1920, and its coordination within the framework of the new Europe, and the revival of the national economy.

This newly created government will be based on the Lithuanian

Activist Front, which amalgamates the most active and the most creative energies of the Lithuanian nation and is determined to spare no sacrifices to restore Lithuania.

I was charged by this government to request cordially the government of the Reich to grant Lithuania the aid necessary to her struggle against the Soviet Russian occupation and to its efforts to restore the sovereignty of Lithuania as well as her political independence.

I use this occasion to express to your Excellency my highest esteem.

Berlin   signed: Skirpa

Minister Plenipotentiary and Envoy Extraordinary of Lithuania

Clarifications: Added to this memorandum addressed to his Excellency the Reich Foreign Minister concerning the eventual formation of the new Lithuanian Government.

This memorandum would be delivered at a date agreed upon in advance. The delivery of this memorandum would be considered the formal beginning of the reestablishment of the Lithuanian State.

However, the deliverance of the Lithuanian State from Russian Bolshevism would proceed according to the following stages:

1. Secret preparatory work in Lithuania to take arms against the Russian occupation.

2. Discreet diplomatic preparatory work in Berlin.

3. The proclamation of the the newly formed Lithuanian government at the moment of the insurrection.

4. The takeover of the administration of the country by the newly formed government.

5. The proclamation of the platform of the government.

6. Organization of the structure of the new government.

This method for the restoration of Lithuanian political independence is based on the following considerations:

1. Each nation which seeks to regain its freedom must also be ready for the unavoidable sacrifices; the Lithuanian nation must do the same.

2. It is important that by the active participation of the Lithuanian nation in the struggle against the Russian Red Army the impression be given to the world that the restoration of Lithuania is not a German intrigue but natural objective sought by the Lithuanian nation using the eventual march of the Germans against the Russian Red Army.

3. From the point of view of international law, the present situation in Lithuania is only a temporary Soviet Russian occupation. No country

of the world ever justified Soviet Russia's act of violence against Lithuania.

4. The restoration of Lithuania would not signify the creation of some completely new State. It would be only the restoration of the political sovereignty which just recently existed, was fully independent, recognized by all the other States of the world as a member of the community of nations equal before the law.

5. From the point of view of foreign policy also it is important to emphasize as clearly as possible the continuity of the Lithuanian State, in order to deprive the enemy of grounds for suspecting that Germany is seeking to annex Lithuania on her own. Respect of the principle of continuity would place the enemies of Germany in a dilemma: either to agree with the fact of the restoration of Lithuania with German help, and thus recognize the credit due to Germany for it, or by denying the restitution, to show themselves as the enemies of Lithuanian independence and of the liberation of the Baltic nations from Soviet Russian Bolshevik slavery.

6. Continuity would be maintained if the new Lithuanian government were formed not by the Reich government, but according to the provisions of the Lithuanian constitution. In the case of Lithuania, this is fully possible, because the Lithuanian President successfully evaded falling into the hands of the Russian occupants.

7. The respect of legal principles would be important also in this sense: first, there would be no necessity in this case to seek the repeated recognition de jure of Lithuania; second, this would make it possible to automatically reconstitute Lithuanian diplomatic representation abroad, as well as to continue its functions.

8. From the point of view of domestic policy, respect for legal principles would contribute significantly to the consolidation of the internal situation in the country itself; this would be of great importance for the reorganization of the State and the development of the production of the country in peace and order.

Editor's Comment: Škirpa submitted the memorandum to the German military to sound out their attitudes. This was part of "Škirpa's doctrine" of exploiting every possibility for liberating Lithuania. Actually, Škirpa may not have known how precarious his position was. Rosenberg, the Reichsminister for Occupied Eastern Territories, was a Baltic German and as early as April 2, 1941, had produced a memorandum on colonizing the Baltic States with German, Dutch,

Norwegian, and Danish immigrants. The Nuremberg trials revealed that on May 8, 1941, four days before Škirpa submitted his memorandum, Rosenberg received a directive: "The aim of a Reichskomissar for Estonia, Latvia, Lithuania, and White Russia (in pencil) must be to ... transform the region into part of the Greater German Reich by germanizing racially possible elements, colonizing Germanic races, and banishing undesirable elements. The Baltic Sea must become a Germanic inland sea."

Still, Škirpa knew very well that in 1940, when "no state of the world justified this act of violence (against Lithuania) by the Union of Soviet Socialist Republics," Germany had recognized the incorporation. In his Lithuanian Activist Front Appeals he expressed the awareness that Germany might be "seeking to annex Lithuania on her own." Thus, submitting this draft memorandum to the O. K. W. was an act of great personal courage.

For a discussion of German ideology and policy in relation to the Baltic States, especially Lithuania, see Julius P. Slavenas: "Nazi Ideology and Policy in the Baltic States," Lituanus (Chicago), v. 11, no. 1, 1965: 34-47

No. 159

Lithuanian Activist Front:
Directives for the Liberation of Lithuania

Instruction 1: Directives for the liberation of Lithuania
March 24, 1941. — Excerpts

V "How to reach the goal?"

No nation gains freedom for nothing. Nations struggle for freedom with great sacrifices. Though not always successful, they cannot forsake this ideal, regardless of how long the struggle is and how much the nation suffers on its road of deliverance.

Lithuania lost her political liberty but no one can deny her the right to restore her freedom and to fight for it.

The Lithuanian diplomatic posts remaining abroad as well as Lithuanian organizations abroad invest all their efforts by all means possible to pursue the idea of liberation and to raise it wherever it is possible. But diplomatic efforts are not sufficient. They are only auxiliary means. If the nation itself does not fight for its own freedom the other efforts would be very little appreciated as the realistic efforts to restore the State. Thus, the ultimate factor in the deliverance of Lithuania is the battlefront of the fatherland.

It would also be erroneous to think that we can restore our political independence and the State only by using foreign aid, and therefore in this way would be no necessity in sacrificing the best sons of our nation in an unequal struggle with a more powerful enemy. Such thinking is the attribute of salon politicians who can never make up their minds. Lithuania reconstituted by foreign hands would not be close to our hearts. Besides, nobody will reestablish Lithuania if we ourselves do not undertake the work. Yes, for us, a small nation, aid is necessary and inescapable, but only as aid. The burden of the task we have to carry on our own shoulders. The greater part of this burden we carry ourselves, the more foreign aid will we receive, and the easier will we reach our ultimate goal. This foreign aid, because of the circumstances in Eastern Europe, will come to us naturally, only we have to know how we can rationally use it for our interests. Under the foreseeable circumstances, we will use it best if we ourselves seize weapons when the fatal hour comes, if we take over the rule of the country without waiting for somebody from the outside to grant us this favor.

Thus, activity and the determination to spare no sacrifices, and taking arms for active struggle against the enemy is exactly the road which we have to take in order to regain political independence and freedom for Lithuania.

Armed conflict between Germany and Soviet Russia, as we have already mentioned, is maturing very quickly and becoming inevitable. There are very serious indications that this conflict may break out in the very near future. This means that the moment and our occasion to free ourselves from the Russian occupation is nearing. Other nations enslaved by Russian Red imperialism, for example the Ukrainians, White Russians, the Caucasian nations, and our brothers in fate, the Latvians and Estonians, are preparing for this conflict. As it is already known, Germany is preparing to march into Eastern Europe as a liberator of the aforementioned nations, that is, Germany is determined to partition Soviet Russia into a series of States under German auspices. These nations which resist will be threatened by the German sword. Under these circumstances, the aforementioned nations have no choice but to embark on the road dictated to them by the circumstances of the present historical moment.

In the restoration of Lithuania we have to base ourselves on the following eventualities:

1. We succeed in advance in agreeing with Germany on the formation of a Lithuanian government, and in this way, on the formal reestablishment of Lithuanian sovereignty;

2. We do not succeed in agreeing on the formation of a Lithuanian government, but we succeed in seizing the actual administration of the country, so to speak, the apparatus for the operation of the country, by using the interregnum which would occur in Lithuania for a brief period while the German army was marching in and the Russian Red Army was withdrawing;

3. The Lithuanian Government is proclaimed in Lithuania by revolution as the result of an insurrection;

4. The Lithuanian government is formed post factum, finding an agreement with the Germans when the country is already in the hands of the German armies and factually liberated from the Bolsheviks.

The first eventuality would be most favorable for us, and we must do everything to make it succeed. There is reason to hope that we will succeed in finding agreement with the factors deciding German foreign policy. But, for the time being, it is not a sure thing, because Germany is behaving very carefully. Whether or not we will be allowed to form our government in advance, as we naturally want, will become clear only at the last moment, that is, before Germany starts its march against the Red Army, or after the march has, in fact, already begun.

The second eventuality is already clear to the point that we cannot confirm that we will be able to form an administrative apparatus from our own people. This is preferred even by the Germans themselves, and they are not preparing to obstruct this. By using the moment of interregnum, we would take over all the offices, factories etc., eliminating from them Soviet officials and Commissars.

The third eventuality would arise only if an agreement in advance with the Germans on the formation of the government failed, or if we were surprised by events. The proclamation of a government by revolution in Lithuania, for example in Vilnius, would not create any particular danger, bearing in mind the second eventuality that the Germans agree and consent to our plan to seize the government of the land in the interregnum period. The formation of a government in this way would compel the Germans to acknowledge the fait accompli and this would facilitate the legalization of the government thus formed.

The fourth eventuality would be least favorable to us. After the Germans occupied our country they would feel that they were masters there, and they would be able to confront us with a variety of conditions for the formation of the Government, if they allowed such a government at all. Besides, the formation of the government would then possibly be postponed, and thus the morale of the country would be undermined. For the time being, we are not negotiating with the Germans to form a government post factum because so far all our efforts are directed toward an agreement with the Germans on the advance formation of the government.

Whatever happens with the formation of the government, the most important task arising, while the Germans are advancing, is the seizure of the government apparatus of the country. This seizure would be the first realistic step towards the restoration of Lithuanian sovereignty. Therefore, it is necessary to dedicate all efforts in Lithuania to organizing secretly in such a way that when the German Army starts out against the Russian Red Army a universal insurrection breaks out spontaneously throughout the land. The purpose of this would be to take the apparatus of the administration of the country in our own hands, and to confront the Germans with a fait accompli which they are inclined to accept, and which they will have to take into consideration later on. Besides, this energetic act with great sacrifices would have not only factual but also moral political significance: by virtue of this insurrection Lithuania would strengthen her right to demand from the Germans that they place no obstacles in the way of the restoration of the Lithuanian State without waiting for the end of the war.

Moreover this would also have great international significance, because the whole world would learn that the Lithuanian nation is really determined to restore its freedom. This would everywhere provide our diplomacy with a very strong measure to intensify as much as possible the defense of the reconstitution of Lithuania.

VI Directives for Insurrection

The supreme task of this preparatory period is to organize as many chapters and battle units of the Lithuanian Activist Front movement as possible. It would be ideal if it were possible to reach the stage where such units were formed not only in the cities where most of our intellectuals and patriotic students live, but also everywhere in the provinces, in little towns and villages, no matter whether they have weapons or not, for there is hope that the weapons will be there when needed.

Each established unit should from the first have a concrete and clear strategic assignment which it will have to fulfil when the hour of insurrection strikes, for example, to take over the electric power stations or to disconnect electric lines, to raise panic by exploding grenades, to take over central post offices, to disrupt telephone and telegraph lines, cut railroad lines, take over county seats, free political prisoners in the jails or in houses of arrest, arrest Communist committees, disarm the Red militia in the police precincts, to gather reserves, etc.

Since the insurrection will have to start by using the attack of the German army, the direction of the attack and the strategic goals of which are not revealed to us by the Germans, to work out a common insurrection plan for all Lithuania is impossible. Thus, each unit taking a mission must prepare its own individual assignment and see how best to execute that assignment whenever the signal is given. The superior centers of the Lithuanian Activist Front will prepare insurrectional plans only for the far reaching and higher strategical purposes. The same assignments are to be prepared also by intermediate centers, each in his own area in accordance with the general directives given in advance. Thus, all the preparatory work is done on the basis of wide decentralization, trusting the initiative and good sense of the local activists.

Here are given only the most general directives:

1. to disarm the Red militia and GPU agents all over the country, and to arrest them and liquidate them if they dare to resist;

2. to arrest all Commissars, political leaders of the army, and other pillars of the Soviet regime;

3. to destroy Communist Party centers and their chapters, and to arrest all the more active Party members and more active members of the cells;

4. to free political prisoners from the jails, and to see to it that the Russians or our own Communists do not massacre them or deport them into the Soviet Union;

5. to take over the more important offices in the centers and provinces, the factories, railroad stations, post and telegraph stations in bigger cities, and the warehouses of merchandise etc.

6. to take precautions against arsonists and take measures that Bolsheviks, while withdrawing, do not destroy property and that there are no robberies;

7. to cut the railroad lines in various localities, also highways and roads, telegraph and telephone lines, electric cables having strategical importance. But see to it that the poles are not cut;

8. to create all possible obstacles to the withdrawal of Red Army units, to their convoys and transports, and make all efforts to disarm them and to attack them wherever possible with guerilla tactics:

9. if the proportions of forces allow it, try with the help of the National Corps to disarm Russian army units when they are panicking.

10. While making obstacles for the withdrawal of Red Army transports, greater explosions should be avoided, in order not to destroy more important bridges. On the contrary, the bridges should be protected wherever possible from being destroyed by the Reds, because they will be needed by the advancing German army, especially their motorized units, so that they do not waste time crossing rivers.

Liaison with the Supreme Command of the Lithuanian Activist Front should be maintained through liaison men on the border. For this purpose it is advised that the border district centers get in touch with these liaison men immediately, letting them know who are your liaison men on the other side of the border so that it will not be necessary to send agents deep into Lithuanian territory, this being connected with the great danger of falling into the hands of the GPU.

Editor's Comment: In complying with the request of the German General Staff, the Lithuanian Activist Front on May 1, 1941 communicated a summary of the planned insurrection to Colonel Graebe of the OKW (Supreme Command of the armed forces) withholding from this communication certain sections which the Front believed that the Germans should not know. This communication consisted mostly of the elements contained in the general directives to the organization of the Lithuanian Activist Front, excerpts from which are given in §4. The Communication was entitled: "General Directives for the Liberation of Lithuania" and signed by the Supreme Command of the Lithuanian Activist Front.

The German text of this communication was in the archives of the Lithuanian Legation in Berlin, subsequently transferred to the Hoover Library of Revolution and Peace in Stanford, California and is temporarily in the hands of the former Lithuanian Minister to Berlin, Kazys Škirpa. It will be returned to the Hoover Library for holding.

The documents are persuasive evidence that the Lithuanian Activist

Front pursued an essentially independent policy in reference to but not in subservience to the Reich. Škirpa was attempting to maneuver the great power conflict in eastern Europe to the benefit of Lithuania. However, his rational calculations 'were obsolete in the face of German geopolitical diplomacy, just as Urbšys' and Merkys' had been when confronted by Molotov in 1939. Škirpa underestimated Hitler's conceit of power, which made him ignore the potential advantages of securing Baltic military support for his Russian campaign, and the magnitude of Germany's land hunger, by now out of any proportion to reality, which led the German government to reject the principle of self determination for eastern European nations.

The passages cited are only excerpts from Sections V and VI of the extremely lengthy directives.

No. 160

Instructions of the Soviet Deputy Commissar for Public Security, Serov

I.—INSTRUCTIONS

Regarding the Procedure for carrying out the Deportation of Anti-Soviet Elements from Lithuania, Latvia and Estonia

STRICTLY SECRET

(Translated in London from the original Russian Text)

1. GENERAL SITUATION

The deportation of anti-Soviet elements from the Baltic Republics is a task of great political importance. Its successful execution depends upon the extent to which the district operative "troikas" and operative headquarters are capable of carefully working out a plan for implementing the operations and for anticipating everything indispensable. Moreover, care must be taken that the operations are carried out without disturbance and panic, so as not to permit any demonstrations and other troubles not only on the part of those to be deported, but also on the part of a certain section of the surrounding population hostile to the Soviet administration.

Instructions as to the procedure for conducting the operations are given below. They should be adhered to, but in individual cases the collaborators engaged in carrying out the operations shall take into account the special character of the concrete conditions of such operations and, in order correctly to appraise the situation, may and must adopt other decisions directed to the same end, viz., to fulfill the task entrusted to them without noise and panic.

2. Procedure of Instructing

The instructing of operative groups by the district "troikas"* shall be done as speedily as possible on the day before the beginning of the operations, taking into consideration the time necessary for travelling to the scene of operations.

The district "troika" shall previously prepare the necessary transport for conveyance of the operative groups in the village to the scene of operations.

On the question of allocating the necessary number of motor-cars and wagons for transport, the district "troikas" shall consult the leaders of the Soviet party organized on the spot.

Premises for the issue of instructions must be carefully prepared in advance, and their capacity, exits and entrances and the possibility of intrusion by strangers must be considered.

Whilst instructions are being issued the building must be securely guarded by operative workers.

Should anybody from among those participating in the operations fail to appear for instructions, the district "troika" shall at once take steps to replace the absentee from a reserve which shall be provided in advance.

Through police officers the "troika" shall notify those assembled of the Government's decision to deport a prescribed contingent of anti-Soviet elements from the territory of the said republic or region. Moreover, they shall briefly explain what the deportees represent.

The special attention of the (local) Soviet party workers gathered for instructions shall be drawn to the fact that the deportees are enemies of the Soviet people and that, therefore, the possibility of an armed attack on the part of the deportees cannot be excluded.

---

*"Troika"—a body consisting of three members.

3. PROCEDURE FOR ACQUISITION OF DOCUMENTS

After the general instruction of the operative groups, documents regarding the deportees should be issued to such groups. The deportees' personal files must be previously collected and distributed among the operative groups, by communes and villages, so that when they are being given out there shall be no delays.

After receipt of the personal files, the senior member of the operative group shall acquaint himself with the personal affairs of the families which he will have to deport. He shall, moreover, ascertain the composition of the family, the supply of essential forms for completion regarding the deportee, the supply of transport for conveyance of the deportee, and he shall receive exhaustive answers to questions not clear to him.

Simultaneously with the issuing of documents, the district "troika" shall explain to each senior member of the operative group where the families to be deported are situated and shall describe the route to be followed to the place of deportation. The roads to be taken by the operative personnel with the deported families to the railway station for entrainment must also be indicated. It is also essential to indicate where reserve military groups are stationed, should it become necessary to call them out during trouble of any kind.

The possession and state of arms and ammunition of the entire operative personnel shall be checked. Weapons must be in complete battle readiness and magazine loaded, but the cartridge shall not be slipped into the rifle breach. Weapons shall be used only in the last resort, when the operative group is attacked or threatened with attack or when resistance is offered.

4. PROCEDURE FOR CARRYING OUT DEPORTATIONS

If the deportation of several families is being carried out in a settled locality, one of the operative workers shall be appointed senior as regards deportation in that village, and under his direction the operative personnel shall proceed to the villages in question.

On arrival in the villages, the operative groups shall get in touch (observing the necessary secrecy) with the local authorities: the chairman, secretary or members of the village soviets, and shall ascertain from them the exact dwelling place of the families to be deported. After this the operative groups, together with the representatives of the local authorities, who shall be appointed to make an inventory of property, shall proceed to the dwellings of the families to be deported.

Operations shall be begun at daybreak. Upon entering the home of the person to be deported, the senior member of the operative group shall assemble the entire family of the deportee into one room, taking all necessary precautionary measures against any possible trouble.

After the members of the family have been checked in conformity with the list, the location of those absent and the number of sick persons shall be ascertained, after which they shall be called upon to give up their weapons. Irrespective of whether or not any weapons are delivered, the deportee shall be personally searched and then the entire premises shall be searched in order to discover hidden weapons.

During the search of the premises one of the members of the operative group shall be appointed to keep watch over the deportees.

Should the search disclose hidden weapons in small quantities, these shall be collected by the operative groups and distributed among them. If many weapons are discovered, they shall be piled into the wagon or motor-car which has brought the operative group, after any ammunition in them has been removed. Ammunition shall be packed and loaded together with rifles.

If necessary, a convoy for transporting the weapons shall be mobilized with an adequate guard.

In the event of the discovery of weapons, counter-revolutionary pamphlets, literature, foreign currency, large quantities of valuables, etc., a brief report of search shall be drawn up on the spot, wherein the hidden weapons or counter-revolutionary literature shall be indicated. If there is any armed resistance, the question of the necessity of arresting the parties showing such armed resistance and of sending them to the district branch of the People's Commissariat of Public Security shall be decided by the district "troikas."

A report shall be drawn up regarding those deportees in hiding or sick ones, and this report shall be signed by the representative of the Soviet party organization.

After completion of the search the deportees shall be notified that by a Government decision they will be deported to other regions of the Union.

The deportees shall be permitted to take with them household necessities not exceeding 100 kilograms in weight.

    1. Suit.

    2. Shoes.

    3. Underwear.
    4. Bedding.
    5. Dishes.
    6. Glassware.
    7. Kitchen utensils.
    8. Food—an estimated month's supply for a family.
    9. Money in their possession.
    10. Trunk or box in which to pack articles.

It is not recommended that large articles be taken.

If the contingent is deported from rural districts, they shall be allowed to take with them small agricultural stocks—axes, saws and other articles, which shall be tied together and packed separately from the other articles, so that when boarding the deportation train they may be loaded into special goods wagons.

In order not to mix them with articles belonging to others, the Christian name, patronymic and surname of the deportee and name of the village shall be written on the packed property.

When loading these articles into the carts, measures shall be taken so that the deportee cannot make use of them for purposes of resistance while the column is moving along the highway.

Simultaneously with the task of loading by the operative groups, the representatives of the Soviet party organizations present at the time shall prepare an inventory of the property and of the manner of its protection in conformity with the instructions received by them.

If the deportee possesses his own means of transport, his property shall be loaded into the vehicle and together with his family shall be sent to the designated place of entrainment.

If the deportees are without any means of transport, carts shall be mobilized in the village by the local authorities, as instructed by the senior member of the operative group.

All persons entering the home of the deportee during the execution of the operations or found there at the moment of these operations must be detained until the conclusion of the operations, and their relationship to the deportee shall be ascertained. This is done in order to disclose persons hiding from the police, gendarmes and other persons.

After verification of the identity of the detained persons and establishment of the fact that they are persons in whom the contingent is not interested, they shall be liberated.

If the inhabitants of the village begin to gather around the deportee's home while operations are in progress, they shall be called upon to disperse to their own homes, and crowds shall not be permitted to form.

If the deportee refuses to open the door of his home, notwithstanding that he is aware that the members of the People's Commissariat of Public Security have arrived, the door must be broken down. In individual cases neighboring operative groups carrying out operations in that locality shall be called upon to help.

The delivery of the deportees from the village to the meeting place at the railway station must be effected during daylight; care, moreover, should be taken that the assembling of every family shall not last more than two hours.

In all cases throughout the operations firm and decisive action shall be taken, without the slightest excitement, noise and panic.

It is categorically forbidden to take any articles away from the deportees except weapons, counter-revolutionary literature and foreign currency, as also to make use of the food of the deportees.

All participants in the operations must be warned that they will be held legally accountable for attempts to appropriate individual articles belonging to the deportees.

5. Procedure for Separation of Deportee's Family from Head of the Family

In view of the fact that a large number of deportees must be arrested and distributed in special camps and that their families must proceed to special settlements in distant regions, it is essential that the operation of removal of both the members of the deportee's family and its head should be carried out simultaneously, without notifying them of the separation confronting them. After the domiciliary search has been carried out and the appropriate identification documents have been drawn up in the deportee's home, the operative worker shall complete the documents for the head of the family and deposit them in the latter's personal file, but the documents drawn up for members of his family shall be deposited in the personal file of the deportee's family.

The convoy of the entire family to the station shall, however, be effected in one vehicle and only at the station of departure shall the head of the family be placed separately from his family in a car specially intended for heads of families.

During the assembling (of the family) in the home of the deportee the head of the family shall be warned that personal male effects must be packed in a separate suitcase, as a sanitary inspection of the deported men will be made separately from the women and children.

At the stations of entrainment heads of families subject to arrest shall be loaded into cars specially allotted for them, which shall be indicated by operative workers appointed for that purpose.

. 6. Procedure for Convoying the Deportees

The assistants convoying the column of deportees in horse-carts are strictly forbidden to sit in the said carts. The assistants must follow alongside and behind the column of deportees. The senior assistant of the convoy shall from time to time go the rounds of the entire column to check the correctness of movement.

When the column of deportees is passing through inhabited places or when encountering passers-by, the convoy must be controlled with particular care; those in charge must see that no attempts are made to escape, and no conversation of any kind shall be permitted between the deportees and passers-by.

7. Procedure for Entrainment

At each point of entrainment a member of the operative "troika" and a person specially appointed for that purpose shall be responsible for entrainment.

On the day of entrainment the chief of the entrainment point, together with the chief of the deportation train and of the convoying military forces of the People's Commissariat of Internal Affairs, shall examine the railway cars provided in order to see that they are supplied with everything necessary, and the chief of the entrainment point shall agree with the chief of the deportation train on the procedure to be observed by the latter in accepting delivery of the deportees.

Red Army men of the convoying forces of the People's Commissariat of Internal Affairs shall surround the entrainment station.

The senior member of the operative group shall deliver to the chief of the deportation train one copy of the nominal roll of the deportees in each railway-car. The chief of the deportation train shall, in conformity with this list, call out the name of each deportee, shall carefully check every name and assign the deportee's place in the railway-car.

The deportees' effects shall be loaded into the car, together with the deportees, with the exception of the small agricultural inventory, which shall be loaded in a separate car.

The deportees shall be loaded into railway-cars by families; it is not permitted to break up a family (with the exception of heads of families subject to arrest). An estimate of twenty-five persons to a car should be observed.

After the railway-car has been filled with the necessary number of families, it shall be locked.

After the people have been taken over and placed in the deportation train, the chief of the train shall bear responsibility for all persons handed over to him and for their delivery to their destination.

After handing over the deportees the senior member of the operative group shall draw up a report on the operation carried out by him and shall address it to the chief of the district operative "troika." The report shall briefly indicate the name of the deportee, whether any weapons and counter-revolutionary literature have been discovered, and also how the operation was carried out.

After having placed the deportees on the deportation train and having submitted reports of the results of the operations thus discharged, the members of the operative group shall be considered free and shall act in accordance with the instructions of the chief of the district branch of the People's Commissariat of Public Security.

DEPUTY PEOPLE'S COMMISSAR OF PUBLIC SECURITY
OF THE U.S.S.R.
Commissar of Public Security of the Third Rank.
(Signed) SEROV.

Editor's Comment: The instructions were dated October 11, 1939, i.e., one day after the signing of the Mutual Assistance Treaty between Lithuania and the USSR. They were received in Lithuania on June 7, 1941, and the deportations were carried out between June 14 and 22, probably in order to snuff out any anticipated Lithuanian resistance against Sovietization. The Lithuanian Red Cross, on the basis of incomplete information, positively certified 40,000. The most prominent statesmen deported were Stulginskis, president of Lithuania from 1920 to 1926, and Voldemaras, former professor and premier. Of the cabinet which signed the Mutual Assistance Treaty: Merkys, the Premier; Bizauskas, Deputy Premier; Urbšys, Foreign Minister; and Skučas, Minister of the Interior and many others were arrested and deported. The effects of this deportation on a small country like Lithuania were devastating and to a large degree explain the bitterness and bloodiness of the future resistance to the Soviets.

Winston Churchill, who, after all, got on famously with Stalin throughout the Second World War, was shocked. In his History of the Second World War, he wrote:

"A ferocious liquidation of all anti-Communist and anti-Russian elements was carried through by the usual methods. Great numbers of people who for twenty years had lived in freedom in their native land and had represented the dominant majority of the people disappeared. A large proportion of these were transported to Siberia. The rest went farther. This process was described as "Mutual Assistance Pacts".

As for the Soviet position on such actions:

CHARTER OF THE INTERNATIONAL MILITARY TRIBUNAL

II. Jurisdiction and General Principles

a) Crimes against peace: namely, planning, preparation, initiation, or waging of war of aggression, or a war in violation of international treaties, agreements or assurances, or participation in a common plan or conspiracy for the accomplishment of any of the foregoing;

b). War crimes: namely, violations of the laws or customs of war. Such violations shall include, but not be limited to, murder, ill-treatment or deportation to slave labor or for any other purpose of civilian population of or in occupied territory, murder or ill-treatment of prisoners of war or persons on the seas, killing of hostages, plunder of public or private property, wanton destruction of cities, towns or villages, or devastation not justified by military necessity.

c) Crimes against humanity: namely, murder, extermination, enslavement, deportation, and other inhumane acts committed against any civilian population, before or during the war; or persecution on political, racial or religious grounds in execution of or in connection with any crime within the jurisdiction of the Tribunal, whether or not in violation of the domestic law of the country where perpetrated.

. . . .

For the Government of the Union
of Soviet Socialist Republics
/s/ R. Rudenko

No. 161

Memorandum of the Head
of Political Division VI
of the German Foreign Ministry, Grundherr

SECRET   Berlin, June 19, 1941.

Pol. VI 3302 g.

As instructed, I received today the former Lithuanian Minister, Škirpa, who had requested an audience with the State Secretary. The purpose of his visit was to give me the enclosed "memorandum regarding the restitution of the political independence of Lithuania" and to explain to me what propagandistic advantages there would be for Germany, in the opinion of M. Škirpa, if the German Government would assent to the restitution of the national independence of Lithuania.

As instructed, I replied to the Minister that I did not see any basis for his train of thought in the political situation, to which the Minister responded with a smile. Of course, I could receive only in a private capacity his memorandum addressed to the Reich Foreign Minister. The Minister did not seem to have expected anything else.

The following developed from his further remarks:

The National Committee of Lithuania, in whose name M. Škirpa had signed the memorandum, consists of the former Lithuanian Prime Minister, Galvanauskas, who fled here, as chairman, M. Škirpa as vice chairman, the former Lithuanian Minister in Rome, Lozoraitis, the Counselor of Legation at the Lithuanian Legation in Bern, Dr. Turauskas, and several others. The Committee also maintains connections with the Lithuanians in the United States.

M. Škirpa stated that in recent months he had kept in contact with the Dienststelle Ribbentrop (Dr. Schuette and Herr Kleist), with the Abteilung Abwehr of the High Command of the Wehrmacht (Lieutenant Colonel Graebe and Dr. Markert), the Gestapo (Dr. Graefe), and with Dr. Leibrandt of the Aussenpolitisches Amt.

According to the statements of M. Škirpa, numerous armed partisan bands have been formed in Lithuania, which have already delivered valuable intelligence material to our counterintelligence and are willing, at the proper moment, to take up the fight against the Russians.

Naturally I maintained an entirely noncommittal attitude during the conversation and at the close repeated once more that I had received M. Škirpa's remarks only in a purely private capacity.

M. Škirpa gave copies of the memorandum to the Dienststelle Ribbentrop, Abteilung Abwehr, Dr. Leibrandt, and the Gestapo.

GRUNDHERR

No. 162

Memorandum of the Former Lithuanian Minister in Berlin, Škirpa, to the German Foreign Minister, Ribbentrop

[In a lengthy memorandum in seven sections addressed to the German Foreign Minister, Ribbentrop, Mr. Škirpa first emphasizes the seriousness of the question of the independence of Lithuania, submits a review of Soviet-Lithuanian relations, and presents the facts of the military occupation and incorporation of Lithuania into the Soviet Union in violation of a series of international treaties.

Stating that Lithuania still exists, Skirpa informs that measures for the liberation of Lithuania have already been initiated, and makes the following specific proposals to Germany:]

The Lithuanian National Committee has undertaken the liberation of Lithuania from Bolshevism and the restoration of an independent Lithuanian State. This committee is the offshoot of the diplomatic representatives duly accredited to foreign countries by the constitutional government of Lithuania, who protested against the Soviet Russian acts of force and the incorporation of Lithuania into the Union of Soviet Socialist Republics. Now, as it has been in the past, it is the task of the Lithuanian envoys to represent the independence of Lithuania and defend its interests against other States, as is expressly provided in their letters of accreditation.

The Lithuanian National Committee is composed of various members: of accredited · Lithuanian envoys, and of delegates of various Lithuanian organizations abroad. At the head, as president, of this National Committee stands a person who had several times formerly been Prime Minister of Lithuania. This committee amalgamates all Lithuanians residing abroad as well as those in Lithuania who have undertaken to save their land.

The practical work of reconstituting the Lithuanian State is based on the activities of the Movement of Lithuanian Activists. This is a political organization which comprises all former political parties of Lithuania, which have freely united themselves in this general movement, guided by one will, representing nationalist and socialist, but strictly anti-Communist attitudes, and which amalgamates all more active and more determined elements of the Lithuanian nation.

Based on the absolute unity of the nation, the Lithuanian Activist Front set itself a task of leading all national forces ready to stand in the struggle and to take the necessary steps so that the Lithuanian nation, in its struggle for the liberation of Lithuania from the Bolshevik occupation, would not stand aside but would actively and massively participate in it, and with its blood and sacrifices would throw off the yoke.

As the next task, the Lithuanian Activist Front intends to take the necessary preparations to lay sound foundations for reconstituting a reformed and liberated Lithuanian state, and its integration into the New Europe.

6. *The Foundations of Lithuanian Reconstitution*

In the case of Lithuania it is not a question of creating a new state, but of reconstituting the sovereignty of the state which just recently had been independent and recognized by all the states of the world as a member of the family of nations, and whose governmental administration, for the most part, is still in existence. Since Lithuania at present is temporarily under foreign rule of occupation, we may say that Lithuania could automatically return to the community of independent states of Europe as soon as she is delivered from the USSR and frees itself from the Bolshevism imposed upon her.

The rebuilding of the Lithuanian State would be easy to accomplish in view of the fact that the Bolshevik occupation is very recent and, as we have already stated, was not yet able to ruin what had been built during the independent period. It would only be necessary to free the country from the occupying power, return its political freedom and its administrative apparatus, and to clean it from Bolshevik commissars and agents of GPU, and the land would soon recover from the devastations of the Soviet system. Life would return to normal and economic development would go on.

From the foreign policy point of view it is very important to emphasize clearly the continuity of the Lithuanian State, in order that any suspicion, that someone else seeks to incorporate Lithuania, would be eliminated in advance. And if this principle of continuity is followed, enemies of the reorganization of Europe would be placed in a dilemma: either to agree with the reconstitution of Lithuania as the first example of the liberation of states recently occupied by the Soviet Union, and thus publicly acknowledge the merits of Germany, or to negate that and thus present themselves as enemies of Lithuanian independence, and also as enemies of the liberation of nations from Soviet Bolshevik subjugation.

On the same basis, it is important to emphasize the active resistance of the Lithuanian nation in its struggle against the Red occupants. This would clearly prove to the world and confirm by action the re-establishment of the independent Lithuanian State, as well as its integration into the new Europe, accomplished not by the intrigues of some other state, but achieved naturally by the Lithuanian nation itself as her national goal. All this would be a free and desirable contribution to the evolution of the new Europe.

These considerations are based on the principal realization that the interests of the Lithuanian nation are to be in close political, economic, and cultural relationship with Germany, as it was in 1918-1920 and in her cultural and political life during the independent period, and also in the Lithuanian struggle with Polonism.

Contrary to the former policy of Lithuanian neutrality in foreign policy, against which Lithuanian activists struggled for many years even before the loss of Lithuanian independence, the Movement of Lithuanian Activists today, emanating from the expression of the will of the entire Lithuanian nation, assures by the clear and friendly attitude towards Germany that the new Lithuania shall not deviate from the here-qualified road of her vital interests.

7. Practical Realization of Lithuanian Restoration

The Lithuanian nation, as we have already stated, is firmly determined in the first place to invest her own sacrifices for her freedom and the reestablishment of political independence. But, being a small nation as compared to overwhelming military forces of the Russian occupant, she will not have enough strength to defeat the enemy. Therefore, help from other sources is imperative and urgently needed.

The declarations of members of the Government of the Reich that in the New Europe, created by the great German Reich, the right of self-government in their political and national life will be assured to all nations were met by the Lithuanian nation with great interest and deep satisfaction. Thus, the Lithuanian nation hopes that in her struggle for liberation she will receive help from the Government of the Reich.

In order to receive this help and to make proper agreements to this effect with Germany as well as to make necessary preparations as to make ready Lithuanian integration into the new Europe and take over the government of the land after liberation from the Soviet occupation, it is necessary to take into consideration the consequences which would come about in the whole land under the present circumstances, favorable to Germany, if the absolute faith and hope of the Lithuanian nation to have its own government after liberation from Bolshevik occupation were not fulfilled.

This government would be based on the Movement of Lithuanian Activists, which is determined to spare no sacrifice to reestablish Lithuania and is determined to integrate the Lithuanian State as an equal member of the New Europe guided by Germany.

The formation of such a government at the proper time is important also in this respect when we take into account the possibility that such a government, if not formed in advance, might be proclaimed by the Lithuanian nation itself as the result of an uprising against the occupants while the liberating forces would be marching into Lithuania, and such a situation could provoke undesirable misunderstandings.

The formation of a Lithuanian Government should be left to the Lithuanians themselves. This could be accomplished by the principle of legality, that is, according to the constitution of the Lithuanian State.

The adoption of this principle of legality would be important in the sense that first, it would then be unnecessary to seek again the recognition of Lithuania *de jure* by other states; secondly, this would contribute considerably to the consolidation of the domestic situation and would greatly influence the political order and domestic peace and would also spur the industrial production of the country.

The Lithuanian nation does not assume any responsibility for the fact that it has become the victim of Bolshevik Muscovite acts of force in the general military-political situation in Europe. Thus, Lithuania feels that it has the moral right to hope and expect not only sympathy from the civilized world, but also the real support of other states.

Especially, it trusts that the nations and their leaders who have undertaken to reorganize the world on the foundations of justice, and to assure peace, justice and better conditions of life to the nations of the European continent, considering these as the goals of this war, will take into account the suffering of the Lithuanian nation and will erase this cultural disgrace perpetrated by Soviet Russia on Lithuania at the present time.

> Berlin
> June 19, 1941
> on behalf of the Lithuanian National Committee
>
> (signed) K. Škirpa
> Envoy Extraordinary and Minister
> Plenipotentiary of Lithuania

Addressed to His Excellency the Foreign Minister
of the Reich, in Berlin

Editor's comment: Kazys Škirpa emerges from this dark era of Lithuania as a diplomat statesman, one of the very few who rose to the occasion and surmounted the adversity of this almost hopeless situation. His ultimate failure has robbed him of the sanction of success, and his outspokenness and ambition made him many enemies among other Lithuanian emigres working for the cause of Lithuanian liberation, but this should not be allowed to detract from the admiration he so convincingly meritted.

Škirpa was thoroughly unsuited to work with the Western Powers, conducting high minded fantasies of diplomatic rhetoric amidst an atmosphere of well-bred futility which generally characterized Western promises about the status of post-War Europe. Fortunately, the War found him in Berlin, where the rules of civilized diplomacy only tenuously applied, and he was allowed to give free play to his remarkable, rather Nietschean talents.

However, while it is true that the circumstances suited the man, it would be unfair to neglect the adversity of these circumstances. Škirpa was a private citizen, deprived of any official status when Germany recognized the Soviet incorporation of Lithuania. Furthermore, he was in Germany only on sufferance. Soviet Lithuania had condemned him, and the Soviet Union was in close friendship with Germany. Thus only the shaky German offer of asylum, which could be withdrawn at any time, stood between him and extradition followed by liquidation. Yet Škirpa defied the German Government in a way that seems inconceivable even thirty years later.

The fact that Škirpa compromised with German sensibilities by frequently lapsing into Nazi terminology should not be misinterpreted by the reader as meaning any compromise on matters of substance. Certainly the Germans themselves were not thus misled. Škirpa persisted in demanding the (essentially unconditional) independence of Lithuania, and he never modified this crucial demand. On the question of the insurrection, he was willing to modify his plans in order to coordinate them with the German military planners, but when agreement proved unattainable, he did not cancel his plans. In his actions he flagrantly contradicted the announced foreign policy of Germany and in fact crossed its secret plans for the future. Eventually, he was thrown into a concentration camp. The evidence strongly suggests that Škirpa was aware of the basic disagreement between himself and the German policy makers and of the dangers he ran, yet there is no sign that this knowledge inhibited him in the least. On the contrary, he chides and reprimands the German Government from a position of moral rightness. The failure of his efforts cannot diminish the courage of his actions.

No. 163

Letter of the Chairman of the Lithuanian National Committee Galvanauskas, to the Supreme Commander of the Lithuanian Activist Front, Škirpa

To: Mr. Kazys Škirpa
   Berlin

Very Honorable Mr. Škirpa,

After the Soviet Union violated all her treaties with Lithuania and occupied our land, the Lithuanian National Committee took over the defense of the interests of the Lithuanian State and unified Lithuanian efforts to free our land from the Bolshevik occupation and to restore Lithuanian's political independence

Taking into consideration the political and military events in Eastern Europe, which vitally affect Lithuania, I address myself to you on behalf of the Lithuanian National Committee, in this hour so fateful for the Lithuanian nation and the Lithuanian State, to take over the heavy burden and form the government of the Lithuanian Republic, to lead her and represent her in accordance with the Lithuanian Constitution of February 12, 1938 (Official Journal No. 600).

Since the President of the Lithuanian Republic has departed to the United States of America and because of War conditions rapid communication with him is impossible, the formation of the Lithuanian government according to the Constitution is unrealizable. But the formation of the government is a vital and immediate necessity for Lithuania.

By inviting you, sir, to assume this great responsibility for the fate of our nation, the Lithuanian National Committee is firmly convinced that you will invest all your strength in this task, that you will value the freedom of the fatherland more highly than anything else and will defend the rights of the Lithuanian nation.

The Lithuanian National Committee wishes you the speediest possible reestablishment of the constitutional order and hopes that you will gather all Lithuanians into a fraternal unity and guide the Lithuanian nation and Lithuanian State on the road which will assure to Lithuania prosperity and well being.

The Lithuanian National Committee invites all Lithuanians to help you in the execution of this great task and to sacrifice everything to assure freedom of the fatherland and provide for the welfare of the Lithuanian nation.

Berlin June 22, 1941

(signed) E. Galvanauskas
Chairman of the Lithuanian
National Committee

No. 164

Proclamation of the Reestablishment of Independence by the Provisional Government of Lithuania

The formed Lithuanian Provisional Government of the newly-reborn Lithuania hereby proclaims Lithuania to be a free and independent state.

Before the entire world the young state of Lithuania enthusiastically promises to participate in a new constituent organization of Europe.

Having been tortured and terrorized by the Bolsheviks, the Lithuanian Nation is determined to build its future on the basis of national unity and social justice.

Signatures Follow

Vilnius, Kaunas June 23, 1941

No. 165

Memorandum of an Official of ABW. II/Military Intelligence Dr. Pactzold

Concerns: the former Lithuanian Minister, Skirpa. No. 779/6. 41ABW.II/AVERW, June 22, 1941

Within the framework of the collaboration of the ABW.II (intelligence section) with the Former Lithuanian Minister Skirpa, the latter, on June 22 at 4:30 FM delivered a list of Lithuanian translators which had been made up for the disposal of the Deputy Commander of the Military District of Königsberg.

On this occasion Minister Skirpa expressed his concern that that day, at about 1:00 PM he was informed by an employee of the police that from this day on he must register every day in the police precinct and not depart from Berlin.

Minister Skirpa sees in this measure taken by the authorities of the German Government the purpose of isolating him from the actual events of today. He expressed the fear that this might signify the desire to isolate him from the insurrection he organized in his native land. Minister Skirpa also let us understand that, in his opinion, the German authorities so it would seem are thus injuring mutual confidence. He said he prepared the Lithuanian forces for this action in a most loyal manner and in such a way that the insurrection cannot be held up, and will take place. He misses, first, the proper declaration of the Reich government about the reestablishment of the independence of the Lithuanian State and secondly, the possibility — as he expressed himself — to fight for the honor of his fatherland at the head of his comrades in arms.

Minister Skirpa today thrice requested the Ministry of Foreign Affairs for an audience with the Secretary of State, von Weizsäcker or the Undersecretary of State, Woermann, but in vain. He regretted that, as the head of the Lithuanian insurrectional organization, he is prevented from receiving any communications on the situation or any information on the progress of the struggle.

He declared with emphasis that if the promises about the restoration of Lithuanian independence given by the German authorities during the negotiations in Königsberg are not fulfilled by the German Government, his partizans would declare Lithuanian political independence on their own within the framework of the insurrection and declare him the head of the new state. Minister Skirpa said that he wants to state this clearly, because the Government of the Reich might eventually feel that it was confronted by a *fait accompli* which, then, would be impossible to change, and if suppressed would go down in history as a very great injustice.

Although it is not known what development is reserved for the former peripheral states, the reply was made to Minister Skirpa that the competent German authorities seemingly want to have him at their disposal in Berlin at all times for the necessary discussions. Finally, it was hardly proper to hope for a basic declaration by the Reich Government on the questions which concerned him less than twenty-four hours after the beginning of the events, or to seek to use his person within the framework of the insurrection.

(signed) Dr. Pactzold

No. 166

Proclamation of the Lithuanian Provisional Government

June 23, 1941

The independent state of Lithuania has been reestablished. In its flight, the Red Army took along the leaders of the so-called Soviet Lithuania which it had established. The history of Red Lithuania is finished; we are closing that chapter. We are closing this chapter as a nightmare, for this one year and eight days destroyed all that our best people built in twenty years. It ruined the welfare of the farmer and destroyed the balance between income and spending for the laborer and the white-collar worker. Industrial equipment was plundered and industrial plants, which had been constructed with such difficulty by workingmen, were destroyed. Tens of thousands of Lithuanian people were exiled. The remaining were forced to become implements of Russian imperialism and Bolshevik chauvinism.

The state of independence, which was regained in the last several days, was paid for by the great many sacrifices and deaths of innocent citizens and members of the resistance.

Today, we, together with the entire nation, bow our heads in reverence to those heroes and martyrs. In the name of our nation, we bow before the supreme sacrifice — the sacrifice for one's country.

The German march to the East made it possible for us to proclaim the independent state of Lithuania. This strengthened our confidence, that even small nations do not perish, even though they may temporarily succumb to a foreign yoke. This also made it possible for us to once again participate in the culture of the Western world.

When definite patterns of relations between the German Reich and Lithuania will be established, a permanent Lithuanian government will be formed and the difficult task of rebuilding the nation will begin once more. This task will not be as it was during the sadly remembered regime before June 15th, 1940, which ended in the dishonorable dissolution of the state. Neither will be as it was in Soviet Lithuania during the red regime, before June 23, 1941.

A new era, a new life, a new creative activity. The state will make every effort to enhance the welfare of not just one faction or one party, but of all the Lithuanian people having a heartfelt interest in the Lithuanian nation. This past year and especially the last several days showed which citizens are loyal to the nation, on whom the nation can depend in times of stress. These are the Lithuanian farmers, the laborers, and the students. Improvement of the moral and spiritual welfare of these majorities, their representation in the government, and due recognition for their personal initiative are the means to be used in establishing the proper basis for national existence.

Class struggle is not necessary to us. There is no need for a struggle between the laborer and the farmer, for both are working men. We are too small to afford the destruction of one another in battles. Let large nations permit themselves this extravagance; we cherish every loyal citizen with no discrimination as to creed or class.

Labor was never intended to be the means by which the capitalist or the state exploits the worker. The state as we have learned from the gruesome past, may exploit the worker just as badly as the private capitalist does — the state not only exploits the citizen but also destroys his entire life.

Labor is intended to be the means of bettering the standard of living for all who partake in it, whether on the farm, in an office, or in the arts and sciences. Labor is meant to show the worker and the majority of the citizens that the standard of living is rising, and, if it is not rising, to show that all in the independent nation are enduring the hardships equally and are forging ahead to a better life.

In truth, let us be prepared to endure many hardships. We were all robbed — the farmer, and the laborer, and the white-collar worker. Above all, however, we become free and independent. This thought alone will help — must help — us bear all hardships. This thought must encourage every Lithuanian who loves his country to fulfill his daily tasks with as much determination, with as much humble dedication as was shown by our heroes dying for our country. It is just as heroic to live and toil for one's country as it is to die for it.

The Provisional Government does not make any promises. It feels that even without promises the nation understands its goals and agrees with them. These goals are not determined by the Provisional Government; they are simply gathered by it from three million hearts and are formulated by it — we wish to remain independent, and are determined to sacrifice everything and give everything for Lithuania.

The Provisional Government of
Independent Lithuania

Editor's comment: For the composition of the government, see Doc. No. 173. At the time of the proclamation of July 25, there were some differences: Kazys Škirpa was Prime Minister and Rapolas Skipitis was Foreign Minister; both were detained in Berlin by the German government. Ambrazevičius, the Minister of Education and Deputy Prime Minister, took over the functions of Prime Minister. Vladas Nasevičius was the original Minister of Internal Affairs and Vytautas Statkus the Minister of Commerce. Both were arrested and deported by the NKVD. Nasevičius was replaced by Col. J. Šlepetys and Statkus by Vainauskas, originally the state comptroller.

No. 167

Associated Press Dispatch in the New York Times

Three Baltic States in Revolt, Lithuania 'Free', Finns Hear

by the Associated Press

HELSINKI, Finland, June 23 — Actual or impending revolt in Lithuania, Latvia and Estonia was declared by anti-Soviet sources today to be threatening Russia along her northwestern frontier.

Reports of revolt in Lithuania and a call for an uprising in Latvia were broadcasted to the Baltic area by the Lithuanian radio and the German station at Koenigsberg, East Prussia. Latvia was reported under rigid Soviet martial law.

[According to the United Press, in a dispatch from Stockholm, Sweden, a broadcast, purportedly from Kaunas, said that Lithuania had proclaimed her independence.]

Estonia, third of the little Baltic States absorbed by Russia last Summer, was expected by Baltic political exiles to revolt with the approach of Nazi armies.

First word of any uprising against Russia came in a broadcast by the Lithuanian radio station at Kaunas which proclaimed a revolt and said a "front of Lithuanian activists" had ordered the Red flag removed and the Lithuanian standard raised on official buildings.

New Regime Set Up

The broadcast said that Kazys Skirpa had assumed the premiership of the new anti-Russian Government, and that General Stasys Rastikis had returned as Defense Minister. Mr. Skirpa had fled to Germany, where he had been Minister to Berlin before the Russian occupation.

[Moscow radio broadcasts declared that people at scores of meetings in Estonia and Latvia yesterday pledged themselves to fight "for Comrade Stalin".]

Whether German troops or pro-German elements were in control in Kaunas was not known here, but fighting had been reported some ten miles within the Lithuanian border.

Shortly after the Lithuanian revolt was reported, a Latvian "government in exile" radioed from Koenigsberg a declaration of independence and resistance to the "Russian-British coalition".

Listeners here identified the voice as that of Karl Ulmanis, Nebraska-educated former Latvian President, who was deposed by Moscow. Swedish reports a year ago said he had been killed by political assassins.

From Riga, capital of Latvia, came a radio announcement of a proclamation of martial law.

Baltic political refugees said that Russia herself had expected revolts in Lithuania, Latvia and Estonia and pointed out that the main Russian defenses had been kept inside the original Soviet frontier. The Red Army was expected to retreat quickly according to planned strategy if the revolts threatened its position.

Insurgents put at 150,000

STOCKHOLM, Sweden, June 23 (AP) — Revolt against Russian control was reported spreading today through the three small Baltic States — Lithuania, Estonia and Latvia — and a radio broadcast, purportedly from Kaunas, proclaimed that Lithuania had declared her independence.

Well-informed quarters said the broadcast, heard at 10:25 A.M., declared Lithuania a "free and independent" country. The proclamation was followed by the playing of the Lithuanian national anthem.

Dispatches from Berlin in the Stockholm newspaper Aftonbladet inferred that the Baltic revolt against the Soviets embraces all three Baltic countries and was assuming sizable proportions, with 150,000 insurgents in the uprising.

The Berlin dispatches claimed also that widespread sabotage in the Baltic States was creating serious difficulties for the Russians.

Well-informed Russian quarters in Stockholm admitted the Baltic unrest but claimed the latest news indicated that the Red Army had succeeded in suppressing the rebellion in Estonia, which apparently was especially vigorous.

Berlin Denies Knowledge

BERLIN, June 23 (AP) — Lithuanians here said the Kaunas radio had proclaimed an uprising against Soviet Russia and establishment of a new government today, but German authorities professed to know nothing about an insurgent anti-Russian regime in Lithuania.

Emigres here from the Russian-absorbed Baltic republic, who have listened eagerly for broadcasts from Kaunas, said the Lithuanian station went off the air suddenly at about 2 P.M. today.

Previously it had named Kazys Skirpa, former Lithuanian Minister to Berlin, as the insurgent Premier, and said General Stasys Rastikis, former Defense Minister, had resumed that post in the new government.

But both Mr. Skirpa and General Rastikis were said to be in Berlin, although they could not be located immediately.

Lithuanian sources explained the Kaunas radio's silence as meaning either that the Germans have approached the city and taken over the radio or that Red Army troops sent to crush the rebellion have seized possession of it.

"The Lithuanian people, with all the means at their disposal, will fight for freedom and independence," declared a broadcast from Kaunas, capital of the independent Lithuanian Republic before it was absorbed by the Soviet Union last year.

The new government exhorted the people to take up arms "in order to assist the German Army in liberating Lithuania from the Bolshevik occupants" and admonished them to receive the Germans in the most friendly, helpful manner possible.

The new anti-Russian Cabinet includes eight other Lithuanians the broadcast reported.

The coup was said to have been engineered by "the front of Lithuanian activists", and its members were ordered to take local power into their own hands.

They were told to raise the Lithuanian flag on official buildings and assure uninterrupted work in Lithuanian industry.

Editor's comment: The Associated Press report, as any contemporary journalistic summary, contains a few inaccuracies: Škirpa and Raštikis were indeed announced as the Premier and War Minister of the Provisional Government. However, they were not allowed to leave Berlin to participate in the insurrection. Raštikis was eventually allowed to return to Lithuania. Škirpa was isolated in Berlin under close police surveillance; he remained the figurehead premier, however, while Juozas Ambrazevičius, the Provisional Minister of Education, took over the active duties of the prime ministry.

The Germans, of course, were highly embarrassed by the Lithuanian insurrection and declaration of independence, which added one more complication to their project to completely Germanize the Baltic coast. Thus, they adopted a policy of ignoring the existence of the revolt and of the Provisional Government which arose from it. At the time, it was reasonable to assume that the Germans would have an interest in fostering nationalistic revolts in the rear of the Red Army. No one, except the German and Soviet high commands, realized the totality of the rout of the Red Army. No one except the Germans themselves knew of the future plans for the Baltic region, which provided for the elimination of the Baltic peoples.

The "listeners" who identified the radio speaker as Karlis Ulmanis, the last President of Latvia, were engaging in wishful thinking. Ulmanis had been deported to the Soviet Union in 1940. He was last located in the vicinity of Voroshilovsk in 1942, and his subsequent fate is unknown.

No. 168

O.K.W. Directive to the Armed Forces in Lithuania
SECRET

Armee-Oberkommando 18   June 26, 1941
Ic/A.O. No. 1167/41 sec.

The new Lithuanian Government is not recognized. Such acts as might be construed as official recognition of it or would signify political relations with it are to be avoided.

Engagements in common with Lithuanian units are prohibited. If larger organized Lithuanian units, regiment size or larger, engage in common battle against the Red Army, then the Army Command must immediately take care to receive the decision of OKH [Supreme Command Land Army] for it. Smaller units must be amicably disarmed and assembled in camps. Attempts of Lithuanian units to detach themselves from the Red Army and their mutinies should be supported.

The formation of a Lithuanian police is prohibited.

The existing regular police, and the one formed by national organizations, is permitted to be used for cleanup operations. Reinforcing the regular police by auxiliary police and smaller military units is permitted. All active national organizations acting as police and

Lithuanians belonging to army units should be marked by special insignia.

For OKH
Officer of the General Staff

[signature illegible]

Editor's comment: The German military was not attuned to the Nazi policy for the Baltic States.* The German military commander in Kaunas, von Rocques, and his chief of staff, Kriegsheim were enthusiastic supporters of Lithuanian autonomy.

No. 169

Memorandum by an Official of the O.K.W., Litter

(June 24, 1941)

Pol. IM

Oberkommando der Wehrmacht — Ausland — Officer on Duty, Captain-Lieutenant Körber made the following telephone communication today at 1:30 AM: Northern Group Wehrmacht (Ic) requests a speedy directive on what attitude it should take toward the newly formed Skirpa government. O.K.W. Abwehr II proposes the following answer:

"The proclamation of Skirpa's government occurred without the support of German official authorities. Therefore, any support to that government is to be avoided. Military authorities must abstain from any interference with decisions which are within the exclusive competence of the political leadership."

Undersecretary of State Woermann, upon telephone inquiry, confirmed the proposed formulation of Abwehr II. Minister von Grundherr has been informed of this by telephone. O.K.W. — Ausland Officer on Duty has been informed of the decision taken.

signed: Dr. Litter
Temporarily in service of Pol. IM

---

*See the editor's comment on the following document.

Editor's comment: The tone of the reply with its sharp admonition at the end indicates that either there was a good deal of controversy in arriving at the decision or that it was anticipated that Northern Group, Wehrmacht would be dissatisfied with the reply.

No. 170

Appeal to the Lithuanian Nation by the Reichskomissar for Ostland, Lohse

Lithuanians! By the order of July 17, 1941, the Führer of the great German Reich, Adolf Hitler, appointed me "Reich Commissioner for the region of the East (Reichskomissar für das Ostland)".

By the order of the same day, the Führer appointed Dr. Adrian von Renteln as Generalkomissar for the territory of the former Lithuanian Republic. Generalkomissar Dr. von Renteln is responsible to me as the representative of the Reich's government for the Reichskomissariat for the East, for the execution of all the directive-orders of the Reich government, as well as mine. His (Renteln's) own orders and directives in that region are also binding in all cases.

I am inviting all the citizens residing in the territory of the former Lithuanian Republic and in the lands up to the river Dauguva to contribute in unity and with all strength to the fullfilment of the task assigned to me — to reconstitute order and normal working conditions in this region.

Bolshevism menaced all Europe. It was ready to commit aggression against Germany. It caused you too many sorrowful injuries. If this enemy of the world had remained master of your country for a few years, little would have been left of your values and your nation. The leaders of the Bolsheviks would have deported you to Siberia, would have robbed you and murdered you.

By sacrificing its blood, the armed forces of the German nation crushed Bolshevism, the enemy of the world. Thus, everyone will understand that by the same, the German nation took over the right and duty to create such conditions that a similar danger will never again threaten European culture and European nations.

Those who promised so much freedom to you during the last twenty years, thought that the purpose of their policy should be maintenance of the equilibrium between the Soviet Union and the German Reich. But in the moment when the German Reich, the victim of English aggression, had to give up the defense of its interests in the East, this pernicious policy showed its true face. The Soviet Union then had the opportunity, and could commit aggression against you without any resistance.

In spite of all the losses that Germanism then suffered here and in spite of all the assaults directed now against the National Socialist German Reich, the Reich Government is caring for your well being, so that all will have work, bread, and the conditions for further progress. However, the organs of the German government demand that all its orders be strictly obeyed, because they seek only one goal; to assure the security of the land and your daily life. The organs of the German government in the countries and cities will co-operate with your representatives. In case of need, they will invite trustees from the midst of your nation who will be able to submit your wishes to the Commissars of the districts, to the Generalkomissar, and to the Reichskomissar. They will organize security organs to safeguard your work and your life.

I trust that all the people will obey my directives so that we can more quickly heal the wounds inflicted on you by the enemy of the world, Bolshevism. Only then will culture and economic prosperity blossom and only then will all of you be able to live in peace. The German Reich grants you favorable conditions for this. Now all depends on you, to use these conditions.

signed: Lohse, Reichskomissar for Ostland.

Kaunas, July 28, 1941

Editor's comment: In case of victory, the German administration of the Lebensraum in the east was to be subdivided into four Generalkomissariats: Ostland, Russia, the Ukraine, and the Caucasus. Ostland was to include Estonia, Latvia, Lithuania, and Byelorussia, totalling 404,000 km² and 10.6 million inhabitants. The structure of the proposed German administration evolved from the work of the Ostbureau, headed by Alfred Rosenberg. The original plan had been to organize the Baltic territories into a single province to be called Baltenland but the administrative area was renamed Ostland after the inclusion of Byelorussia. For details, see Lietuvos Enciklopedija, v. 21, pp. 238-241, and the documents of the International Military Tribunal (Nuremburg, 1947).

Lohse had been Gauleiter of Schleswig-Holstein since 1925 and was also the president of the Nordic Society. Hitler had great confidence in his ability as an administrator and personally selected him to supervise the making of the Baltic into a German lake.

No. 171

Appeal to the Lithuanian Nation by the Generalkomissar for Lithuania, Von Renteln

(July 28, 1941)

Lithuanians!

Appointed by the Führer of the great German Reich, I assumed the Civil Government of the region of the former Republic of Lithuania.

As the district Komissars are appointed:

For the city of Kaunas-Gabietskomissar Krämer.

For the district of Kaunas-Gebietskomissar Lentzen.

For the city of Vilnius-Gebietskomissar Hingst.

For the district of Vilnius-Gebietskomissar Wulff.

For Siauliai-Gebietskomissar Gewecke.

Orders of the Gebietskomissars must be obeyed in all cases.

Directives for the civilian population in the future will be given only by the Civil Government and its organs.

The orders of the military authorities issued previously concerning civilian life are still valid.

Lithuanians!

The work of the reconstruction of the region entrusted to me must begin immediately. Your work in city and village will help this reconstruction. With all your strength help to eradicate the traces of bloody Bolshevik rule.

signed: von Renteln, Generalkomissar.

Editor's comment: Von Renteln and his assistants were hardly chosen from the elite of the German bureaucracy. For a succinct review of their administrative shortcomings see: Peter Kleist, Die Europäische Tragödie (Göttingen: Schütz, 1961), pp. 151, 159. Kleist, director of the foreign policy bureau of the NSDAP in 1941 was one of the more brilliant realists of the German Foreign Service, supporting autonomy of nations in this area. In fact, the German government was divided over Ostland. Goebels was for it, Himmler was for an autonomous Baltic area. Burmeister, Ministerialrat of the Ministry of the interior stationed in Riga was for autonomy. The local military commanders, General von Rocques in Kaunas and von Unruh in Riga, were for autonomy, and SS Gen. Berger, on Lohse's staff, considered the Zivilwerwaltung a mistake. See: Slavenas, "Nazi Ideology."

Among other faults the Ostland Zivilwerwaltung drastically over-estimated the Lithuanian's perception of the significant differences between German Nazi and Russian Soviet occupants. It never occurred to them that in view from the bottom, one group of Commissars had simply replaced another.

No. 172

Proclamation of the Generalkomissar for Lithuania, Von Renteln, to the Provisional Lithuanian Government

(Aug. 5, 1941)

After the introduction of the Civilian Government, your work as ministers must be considered as terminated. Thus, I appoint you my trustees and counsellors for the general services of the Commissariat. I am not undertaking to change the personnel, and I request you, the heads of the governmental offices to continue the work in my government and under my authority.

Editor's comment: The Ziwilverwaltung was hampered in its fight against the provisional government by the fact that it lacked the personnel to take over the effective administration of the country. For a first person account of the negotiations in the month before the dissolution see: Stasys Raštikis: "The Relations of the Provisional Government of Lithuania with the German Authorities June 23-August 5, 1941." Lituanus, v. VIII, No. 1/2, 1962: 16-22.

No. 173

Memorandum of the Lithuanian Insurrectional Government for the Government of the German Reich

[The lengthy memorandum first reviews the historical background of Soviet-Lithuanian relations, and incorporation of Lithuania into the U.S.S.R. The following excerpts concern only the period of the Provisional Government and its relationship to the German authorities in Lithuania.]

Taking cognizance of the appeals of the Reichskomissar for Ostland of July 28, and your appeal to Lithuanians of the same day, we have the honor, on behalf of the Provisional Government of Lithuania, to bring the following to your kind attention:

The de facto regime of the Soviet Union in Lithuania having disappeared, the forcible incorporation of Lithuania into the Soviet Union became null and void. It would be incomprehensible if any government friendly to Lithuania would be of the attitude that the aggression committed against Lithuania, that is its incorporation of Lithuania into the Soviet Union, was still valid and binding on Lithuania or having any binding significance to other countries. The de facto rule of the Soviet Union in Lithuania having disappeared, we have to consider that the legal status quo ante, that is, her independence has been reestablished in Lithuania, and thus it is understood, that to consider Lithuania as part of the Soviet Union is entirely without foundation. If there is no basis for considering Lithuania as having been a part of the Soviet Union, Lithuania can by no means be treated as occupied enemy territory.

If Lithuania at the present moment could be considered as being in a state of war, then it is in a state of war only with the Soviet Union. Units of the regular Lithuanian army, which had been forcibly incorporated into the Red Army, everywhere, where circumstances allowed engaged in battle against Communism and the Red Army. Those units, as it is well-known to the German Military commanders, have fulfilled useful operational tasks, especially in the battle for Vilnius.

Lithuanian guerilla warfare against the Red Army is also known to the leadership of the German Army.

It could also be noted that both units of the regular Lithuanian Army and Lithuanian guerillas joined the battle against the Red Army not accidentally but according to a plan prepared in advance in agreement with German military leadership. Under the circumstances, to consider Lithuania as occupied enemy territory would be wrong not only from the legal, but from the moral point of view.

In order to express its gratitude for the liberation of Lithuania and its desire to co-operate and determination to help the German army in its march to the East, the Provisional Lithuanian Government immediately took steps, in Berlin as well as in Kaunas, to contact and to establish relations with the German Government.

We have to state with regret that the Lithuanian Government did not succeed in this.

Regardless, in July there was created a situation in Lithuania in which the German military government considered the Lithuanian Provisional Government as existing de facto, and co-operated with it. Being encouraged by this, the Lithuanian Provisional Government revived the offices of the state and regional governments in a very short time and under very difficult circumstances; this government took steps to eliminate the abnormalities of the Soviet system and to return to the conditions normally existing in Lithuania. It began to revive the land economically, but could not, without a proper agreement with the German authorities, resolve other important problems. Therefore, conscious of the urgency of these problems, the Lithuanian Provisional Government anxiously awaited the moment when it would be able to enter into relations with the Government of the Reich.

To our greatest regret, we must state that the fact of the existence of the Lithuanian Provisional Government was not taken into consideration either by the appeal of the Reichskomissar for Ostland, or your appeal, Herr Generalkomissar, and also in general, the Lithuanian nation's aspirations of living its independent political life were silently bypassed.

Together with the entire Lithuanian nation we feel gratitude to the German nation for the liberation of our land from the Bolshevik yoke. However, at the same time, we feel it our duty to note that the national aspirations of the Lithuanian nation cannot be satisfied by satisfying only material questions, because the Lithuanian nation cannot forsake the developing of its culture in its own political state. We are firmly convinced that the future independent political existence of Lithuania fits completely into the new order of Europe if it is supported by the friendship of the great German Reich. On the other hand, we cannot conceal that the disappointment of Lithuanian expectations for a national and political restoration would create dismay in Lithuania.

Being determined always to maintain and strengthen the enthusiastic feelings of friendship of the Lithuanian nation for the German nation, we request you, Herr Generalkomissar, to transmit through Herr Reichskomissar for Ostland, to the Führer of the great German Reich, Adolf Hitler, and to the invincible German army, our nation's gratitude for its liberation, and at the same time explain to them the legal and factual status quo of Lithuania as presented above.

We trust that the government of the German Reich, keeping in mind the constant friendship of the Lithuanian nation for the German nation, will recognize the further political existence of Lithuania. Deeply convinced in the justice of the Führer and the German nation, the Lithuanian nation expects such recognition.

At the same time, we declare that the Lithuanian nation is sincerely determined to co-operate positively with the Great German Reich, especially in its endeavors for the liberation of nations from destruction by Bolshevism, and also in the creation of the new order in Europe.

Signed: J. Ambrazevičius, Deputy Prime Minister of Education.

Col. J. Slepetys, Minister of Internal Affairs

J. Matulionis, Minister of Finance

P. Vainauskas, Minister of Trade

Prof. B. Vitkus, Minister of Agriculture

Eng. V. Landsbergis-Zemkalnis, Minister of Communal Economy

Dr. A. Damušis, Minister of Industry

Dr. J. Pajaujis, Minister of Labor and Social Security

K. Vencius, Minister of Health

Eng. A. Novickis, Minister of Communications

S. Raštikis, Minister of Defense

Kaunas, August 5, 1941

Editor's comment: The Memel crisis, Lithuania's refusal to intervene militarily in Poland in September of 1939, and the influence of Rosenberg, a Baltic German, had convinced Hitler and Göbels that the Lithuanians were the least redeemable of all the Baltic nations. However, the feeling was not universal. It is possible that the reservations, often expressed in terms of unconcealed derision, of many high German officials about the policy in the Baltic States made Rosenberg, Lohse, and von Renteln even less flexible and uncompromising. The Lithuanians were not insensitive to the hostility at the top of the Nazi hierarchy. Thus, the emphasis in the memorandum is on the German nation rather than the Nazi government and army.

No. 174

Statement by the Deputy Prime Minister of the Provisional Government of Lithuania, Ambrazevičius

(Aug. 5, 1941)

Taking into consideration the appeal of the Reichkomissar and Generalkomissar to Lithuania, dated July 28, and also the subsequent official statement of the Generalkomissar For Lithuania to the members of the Lithuanian government on August 5, in which it was expressly stated that from now on the Lithuanian Government is considered as having ceased to operate, the Provisional Lithuanian Government states that the political leadership of Germany under the conditions of war gave orders to the German authorities to take over the entire Civil Government in Lithuania and this takeover of the Civil Government by the representatives of the German Ziwilwerwaltung is in process. In view of these facts, the Lithuanian Provisional Government considers its operations as suspended against its will.

No. 175

Letter of the Deputy Prime Minister of the Provisional Government of Lithuania, Ambrazevičius, to the Generalkomissar for Lithuania, Von Renteln

(Aug. 9, 1941)

[When letters for the dissolution of the Lithuanian Provisional Government were sent to its members for counter signature, Ambrazevičius replied to von Renteln: (Editor)]

The audience [of August 5] was arranged not by the Lithuanian General Counselors but by the Lithuanian Provisional Government, and the ministers were received by the Generalkomissar under this title. In view of the declaration of Herr Generalkomissar von Renteln that the operations of the Provisional Government are suspended, the Lithuanian Provisional Government has taken the decision to consider its operations suspended against its will, and to inform that the positions as General Counselors cannot be accepted, because the Deputy Prime Minister, and the majority of the other members of the government do not believe they would be able to enjoy the same support and confidence of the nation as they did when the sovereignty of the Lithuanian state was proclaimed.

Editor's comment: The "audience" referred to by Ambrazevičius was the August 5 meeting of von Renteln with the Provisional Government, at which von Renteln communicated to the Cabinet the dismissal of the government. The Germans organized the organ of German appointed trustees known as the Lithuanian General Counselors as a replacement.

Ambrazevičius (now Brazaitis) survived the war and wrote his memoirs under the nom de plume of N.E. Suduvis: Vienu Vieni (Alone, All Alone), Brooklyn: I Laisve Fondas Lietuviškai Kulturai Ugdyti, 1964. Also available in German as: Allein, ganz allein; Widerstand am Baltischen Meer (New Rochelle, New York: Freunde der Litauischen Front in Europa, 1964).

No. 176

Note of the Lithuanian Minister in Washington, Žadeikis, to the U.S. Secretary of State, Hull

No. 996.   September 3, 1941

Sir:

Referring to my statement, concerning the recent German invasion of Lithuania, submitted to the Department of State on June 25, 1941, I have the honor to inform you further as follows.

When practically all nations of present day dictator-dominated Europe are suffering from foreign oppression or threat of invasion, my country, Lithuania, is no exception from this grim reality. In fact, Lithuania's misfortune is even greater than that of some other European countries in that Lithuania within the period of one year was subjected twice to the horrors of foreign invasion.

On June 15, 1940 Lithuania was treacherously invaded by Soviet Russia. The Soviet regime of occupation with its terroristic administrative methods, with its compulsory Sovietization, characterized by the nationalization of all land and private property, mismanagement and plunder, mass imprisonments and mass deportations to Siberia, was a continuous nightmare to the people of all strata and aimed to annihilate the entire Lithuanian nation. Such ruthlessness of a foreign invader finally provoked a spontaneous uprising of the people in many localities.

This uprising of June 23, 1941, which resulted in heavy casualties among the insurgents, presented a hazardous opportunity to proclaim the restitution of Lithuania's independence just in advance of the approaching second invader. The spirit of the Lithuanian uprising was directed, fundamentally, against both the invaders: the retreating Soviet forces and the advancing German forces. This uprising was a desperate and determined effort to regain freedom. Under the circumstances the effort failed, but the spirit remains.

The second invasion of Lithuania began on June 22, 1941 when the German army marched into Lithuanian territory and engaged in pursuing the Red army division, and within a week succeeded in occupying the whole of Lithuania. Although the German Government disclaimed having any intention of occupying Lithuania, and insisted that the invasion of Lithuania by the German army was in line with the German self-appointed mission of protecting Europe, including self-protection against the Soviet menace, nevertheless two months of German occupation of my country already has convincingly proved that the German military occupation of Lithuania is but a step towards the realization of the general German policy of expansion commonly known as the Drang Nach Osten.

The German invasion of Lithuania, predetermined by the German-Soviet non-aggression pact of 1939, is in essence an act of aggression, and violation of Lithuania's integrity; it discarded the modus of normal relations between the two neighboring nations based on previously concluded treaties; it deprived my country of the sacred rights to self-determination and independence. The regime of German invasion abolished the provisional government born of the revolt of the Lithuanian people against the regime of the preceding Soviet occupation, and appointed Civil Commissars as Governors of the newly-invaded territory. In doing so, it failed to indicate that even in the future the elementary rights of the Lithuanian nation would be respected. Recently even the name of LITHUANIA, which several centuries ago successfully resisted Teutonic domination, is being avoided by the new crusaders as Lithuania is being merged into the newly-created Ostland.

As the duly accredited representative of the legitimate Government of Lithuania near the Government of the United States of America I protested last year, in my two notes of July 23 and August 3, 1940, against the unprovoked Soviet Russian aggression against Lithuania, and I requested the American Government to refuse recognition of

Soviet annexation of Lithuania, based on false pretexts and distorted results of mock parliamentary elections. At this instance, I am happy to recall the very definite stand taken in this matter by the American Government.

And now, when Soviet occupation has been replaced by German occupation, and Lithuania's opposition to foreign encroachments continues, I consider it my duty to register, in behalf of my Government, a protest against the German imperialistic invasion of my country and declare that any attempt by Germany to shape Lithuania's political future without due regard to the free will of the Lithuanian people, and any acts of the German regime of occupation of Lithuania incompatible with the spirit of international laws, will be considered void of any legality. Moreover, relying on the general attitude of the American people, I take this opportunity to express my full confidence that the American Government will not recognize that annexive German regime which Lithuanians believe will have to withdraw sooner or later and make way for a democratic and truly representative government of the Lithuanian people now suffering from two successive foreign invasions.

Until Soviet dictatorship, now itself a victim of aggression by its previous partner, renounces its annexation of Lithuania of 1940, or at least indicates a change in its aggressive policy towards the Baltic States, the Damocles Sword of Soviet threats will hang over the destiny of my country. Until German dictatorship's boundless appetite for conquest is checked there will be no security for any nation. But the hope of a brighter future was rekindled in the hearts of all oppressed nations, Lithuania among them, by the momentous declaration made somewhere in the Atlantic by the two greatest leaders of the democratic world. Those significant eight points of the declaration are bound to bring desirable results: the riddance of the despotic domination of all dictatorships.

Accept, Sir, the renewed assurances of my highest consideration.

Minister of Lithuania
P. Žadeikis

The Honorable Cordell Hull
Secretary of State
Washington, D.C.

No. 177

Letter of the Assistant Secretary of State, Berle, for the Secretary, to the Lithuanian Minister in Washington, Žadeikis

Washington, September 18, 1941.

SIR:

I have the honor to acknowledge the receipt of your note of September 3, 1941 protesting against the invasion of Lithuania by Germany and declaring that any attempt on the part of Germany to shape the political future of Lithuania without regard to the free will of the Lithuanian people and that any acts of the German regime of occupation imcompatible with the spirit of international law will be considered void of any legality.

You will recall that in the joint declaration agreed upon by the President of the United States and the Prime Minister of Great Britain during their historic meeting at sea it is stated that the United States and Great Britain respect the right of all peoples to choose the form of Government under which they desire to live and the United States and Great Britain wish to see self-government restored to those peoples who have been forcibly deprived of it.

Accept/etc./

For the Secretary of State:
A.A. Berle, Jr.

Editor's comment: Clemenceau said that Wilson talked like Jesus Christ and acted like Lloyd George; much the same can be said for Roosevelt. The dichotomy between lofty principle and mundane action is a traditional characteristic of American foreign policy, and the Atlantic Charter is one of the loftier enunciations of principles which American presidents have produced, but American governments have never implemented. Not even at the international conferences of Yalta and Potsdam did the United States attempt to give the principles of the Atlantic Charter practical application.

No. 178

Memorandum of the Lithuanian Activist Front for the Government of the Reich

The Lithuanian Activist Front was organized during the Bolshevik occupation as a military organization which undertook the task of reconstituting independent Lithuania by armed insurrection. For this purpose the Lithuanian Activist Front entered into contacts with the German military government. The basis of the Lithuanian Activist Front's co-operation with the German Military command consisted of the German military command's express recognition of the essential purpose of the Lithuanian Activist Front, namely the struggle for the freedom of Lithuania.

When the war began, the Lithuanian Activist Front with the residual Lithuanian army started the insurrection and fulfilled a number of military assignments, previously agreed on with the German military command. About 100,000 guerillas took part in this insurrection. Over 4,000 Lithuanian youths died in the battle with the Bolsheviks.

The Lithuanian Activist Front and the entire youth of Lithuania considered that the purposes of the Lithuanian and German nations in the struggle against Bolshevism were identical. The Lithuanian Activist Front and all the youth of Lithuania, respecting and highly valuing the dominant national principle in German policy, considered, and still considers that in the principle of the national idea, respect for foreign nationalities is also included.

The Lithuanian Activist Front, together with the entire Lithuanian nation lives through a very sorrowful time since the introduction of the German Civil Government in Lithuania.

The Lithuanian Activist Front requested to be allowed to explain its concern to the leader of the Great Reich, Adolf Hitler, and to his brave army, hoping that the blood of Lithuanian youth, shed in the battle against Bolshevism, enables them to say frankly what they could not under different circumstances

When the battle against the Bolsheviks began, the Lithuanian Activist Front formed the Lithuanian Government, which, in spite of great difficulties, succeeded in a series of organizing tasks; had these tasks not been accomplished, the German army's advance through Lithuania would have been more difficult. In spite of this, without any complaint of essence against the Lithuanian government, its operations were suspended against its own will. A Generalkomissar was appointed for Lithuania, and he immediately took the civil government into his own hands. In describing his territorial competence in his appeal to Lithuania of July 28, the Reichskomissar for Ostland declared that he was being appointed for "the territory of the *former* Lithuanian state".

The Lithuanian nation did not consider the incorporation of Lithuania into the Soviet Union as legal or imposing any obligation on her because that incorporation was accomplished with the aid of falsified elections and contrary to the will of the entire Lithuanian nation. However, if anybody even considered this incorporation of Lithuania into the Soviet Union as legal, even in this case, Lithuania had not lost its existence as a sovereign republic, because she had the right to secede from the Soviet Union at any time (see the constitution of the Soviet Union, articles 15 and 17). The Lithuanian Government on June 23 declared the restored independence of Lithuania, thus dissipating any doubts about Lithuania's independence. The Soviet Union did not protest against this act of the Lithuanian Government.

Since Lithuania cannot be considered a part of the Soviet Union, the independent Lithuanian Republic not having been suppressed by any international act, it is incomprehensible that the Reichskomissar for Ostland in his appeal to Lithuania of July 28 talks about "the territory of the former Lithuanian state". This means that the Bolsheviks, against whom the Lithuanians fought together with the German soldiers would seem to recognize that the Lithuanian Republic has seceded from the Soviet Union as a seperate state, while Germany, whom Lithuania helped to fight the Bolsheviks, considers Lithuania as a former state.

When the German Army marched into Lithuania, it found very friendly Lithuanian Government organs everywhere, not Bolshevik offices. Lithuanian army units and Lithuanian guerillas everywhere helped the German army marching through Lithuania as much as they could. Lithuanians fought with Germany, not against it, In spite of this, the organs of the German Government treat Lithuania as occupied enemy territory. Thus a situation has been created in which the Lithuanian Activist Front, who declared war on the Soviet Union, fought the Soviet Union with the entire Lithuanian youth, and now the result of that struggle is that Lithuania is considered the same enemy territory as the territory of that country which fights war against Germany . . . .

[The memorandum, having criticised German economic and agricultural policy in detail, passes to strictly national-cultural problems, and in its Item 9 continues:]

. . . One of the questions very closely related to the Lithuanian nation is the question of Lithuanian higher education. About 5,000 young people are registered in Lithuanian institutions of higher education. Lithuania has never been as much in need of physicians, teachers, jurists, etc. as she is now after the difficult year of Bolshevik occupation. But at the same time, when all Lithuania is waiting for intensive work from her higher educational institutions, the German Civil Government in Lithuania not only prohibits admission of new students into the schools-of higher education, but also suspends the operation of higher semesters, except the senior year. No one in Lithuania understands these measures of the German Civilian Government except as means of obstructing the cultural and economic development in Lithuania. It is difficult for Lithuanians to admit that the organs of the civil administration of Germany in Lithuania would seek to oppress the Lithuanian nation; however we have to state the fact that Lithuanian national and cultural life at the present time is hampered by the following means:

a) Lithuanians are not presently allowed to have in Lithuania even one daily newspaper published in the Lithuanian language, because the Lithuanian daily newspapers are ordered to publish news and articles in German;

b) from the beginning of the war, the German censorship has not allowed even one Lithuanian book to appear in Lithuania (not even a Lithuanian scientific dictionary, printed before the war, could appear on the market);

c) in Lithuanian radio broadcasts, the Lithuanian language is more and more being pushed aside, and is only allowed to be used with German;

d) Lithuanian radio stations are not allowed to play the Lithuanian national anthem;

e) in the Lithuanian military museum, one of the most honored places in all Lithuania, the bells used to ring the melody "We are born Lithuanian and we will remain Lithuanians". This song was prohibited by the government of the Tsar before the first world war. The music for this song was written by the well-known Lithuanian composer Stasys Šimkus, and the words were written at the end of the Nineteenth

Century by the German scientist Zauerwein, a great friend of Lithuania; the administration of the Lithuanian military museum was requested not to play this melody any more;

f) the Lithuanian national flag was removed from the most sacred place in Lithuania, the mountain of Gediminas in Vilnius;

g) Lithuanian national holidays are prohibited

The Lithuanian Activist Front thinks that if other organizations in Lithuania and certain representatives of the people feel obliged to inform the German Civil Government of the situation in Lithuania, then the Lithuanian Activist Front, the organization which was constantly in contact with the German military command, has the same obligation to inform the German military government and the leader of the Great German Reich, Adolf Hitler. At the same time, the Lithuanian Activist Front dares to direct the attention of the higher leadership to the abnormalities described in the memorandum, so that they may disappear. That the continued existence of the Lithuanian state be recognized and that a national government be the leader of the nations' political life is the warmest desire and request of the Lithuanian nation.

[The memorandum is followed by seven enclosures].

Kaunas, September 15, 1941.

signed: The Leadership of the Lithuanian Activist Front

    L. Prapuolenis
    Col. of the General Staff Mačiokas
    Division General St. Pundzevičius
    Dr. Eng. A. Damušis
    Col. Dr. Eng. J. Vebra
    Gen. Nagius Nagevičius
    Lt. Col. of the General Staff N. Tautvilas
    Dr. K. Vencius
    Col. Z. Talevičius
    Dr. J. Ambrazevičius
    Maj. A. Andriunas
    Atty. Dr. Toliušis
    Gen M. Mieželis
    M. Naujokas
    Dr. Pr. Padalskis
    Lt. Col. of the General Staff Iz. Kraunaitis
    J. Deksnys

St. Vainoras
Lt. Col. of the General Staff J. Jankauskas
J. Rudokas
P. Malinauskas
J. Žostautas
P. Žukauskas
Col. J. Bobelis
J. Katinauskas
P. Vilutis
J. Bagdanavičius
Capt. A. Tindžiulis
P. Baronas
M. Pečeliunas

Editor's comment: The German reaction to this memorandum was swift and harsh. The next day, September 21, the Gestapo occupied the headquarters of the Lithuanian Activist Front in Kaunas, made a detailed search, and having found nothing, arrested one of the leaders of the Lithuanian Activist Front and commander of the insurrection, Leonas Prapuolenis, and tried to arrest all the signatories of the memorandum. Praupuolenis was imprisoned in Tilsit, and later taken to the concentration camp at Dachau.

On September 22, Generalkomissar von Renteln officially proclaimed that the Lithuanian Activist Front was dissolved and its property was confiscated.

No. 179

Letter of the Reich Minister for Occupied Territories in the East, Rosenberg, to the Reichskomissar for Ostland, Lohse

Minister of the Reich for the occupied lands of the East no. 00318/41/R/H

To Gauleiter Heinrich Lohse, Reichskomissar for Ostland
Riga   Berlin, November 11, 1941
                                                        Secret
                      Concerns: Nationalist Party of Lithuania

From a report of the Generalkomissar for Lithuania I see that he had received a certain delegation of so-called Lithuanian nationalists; this group, composed of elements friendly to the Germans, clearly spoke in their conversation of an independent Lithuanian state, the creation of which they expect from Germany. The Generalkomissar did not attach any significance to those statements, and speaking in general, he remarked that he views this political party as a potential instrument, and that so far he has succeeded with it quite well. In fact, however, in the existence of such a political party lurks a danger for the future. In principle, no political party can be considered in any General-alkomissariat as an expression of the national and political designs of a nation. The desires arising among the inhabitants, if they appear just, and correspond to the interests of Germany, can be considered by the district and General Commissioners. The formation of the political party which, it is self-evident, would have its intellectual and political center in the capital of the Generalkomissariat, harbors in itself a danger of the formation of a centrally guided opposition, which should be eliminated in advance. In Latvia and Byelorussia there are no political parties, and there will be none in Estonia. The existence of a Lithuanian political party might arouse questions by Latvians and Estonians, why they are not allowed the same as the Lithuanians. Therefore, it is necessary to take proper means to dissolve the Lithuanian Party. I would request the question be considered without delay, and after consultation with the Generalkomissar in Lithuania, that the proper proposals be submitted to me for the creation of a certain directory, perhaps a Generaldirektorium, in Riga, or perhaps select a means even less obligating, namely a system of trustees (System von Vertrauensräten) who would be put in charge of certain assignments of a general character.

signed: Rosenberg

Editor's comment: Reichskomissar Lohse informed Rosenberg on January 15, 1942, that the Lithuanian Nationalist Party had been informed of its dissolution and that the closing of the party did not arouse much disappointment.

For detailed information on the Lithuanian Nationalist Party, see **Romuald Misiunas,** "Fascist Tendencies in Lithuania," Slavonic and **East European** Review (London), v. 48, no. 110, January 1970: 88-**109.**

No. 180

List of Underground Publications during the German Occupation of Lithuania

Underground Press. The underground press played a very great part in Lithuania's fight for freedom during the Nazi regime. It was difficult task to organize and publish various underground publications. The distribution of the underground newspapers and bulletins was even more difficult and dangerous. The entire country was infiltrated by a great number of Nazi spies. The following is a list of the leading newspapers and bulletins issued by the Lithuanian underground organizations during the Nazi occupation of Lithuania:

1. Nepriklausoma Lietuva (Independent Lithuania)
2. I Laisve (Toward Freedom)
3. Laisves Kovotojas (Champion for Freedom)
4. Lietuva (Lithuania)
5. Lietuvos Laisves Trimitas (Herald of Lithuanian Freedom)
6. Vieninga Kova (United Struggle)
7. Vardan Tiesos (in the Name of Truth)
8. Baltija (The Balticum)
9. Atžalynas (Saplings)
10. Jaunime, Budek! (Youth, Beware)
11. Pogrindžio Kuntaplis (Underground Slipper, satirical)
12. Lieiuvos Judas (Lithuanian Judas)
13. Tautos Žodis (Voice of the Nation)
14. Frontas (Front)
15. Apžvalga (Review)
16. Lietuvos Šauliu Sajungos Biuletenis (Bulletin of the Lithuanian Home Guard Association)
17. Užsienio Politikos Apžvalga (Review of Foreign Politics)
18. Naujas Žygis (New Undertaking)
19. Mūsu Zeme (Our Country)
20. Politines Naujo Žodzio Apžvalgos (Political Reviews of the New World)
21. Vytis (The Knight).*

---

* Originals available in the Library of the Hoover Institute of War, Revolution and Peace, Stanford, Calif.

No. 181

Declaration of Ten Former Members of the People's Government of Lithuania

"Meeting at Kaunas, on August 30, 1942, we, members of the former Lithuanian Government and the "People's Diet," state publicly:

"1. In violation, by use of force, of the solemn obligations given to the Republic of Lithuania to respect, in all circumstances, her 'sovereignty and also integrity and territorial inviolability' (paragraph 2 of the Treaty of Nonaggression of September 28, 1926, between the Republic of Lithuania and the U.S.S.R.), the Government of the Soviet Union, on June 15, 1940, occupied Lithuania by its armed forces.

"2. The Lithuanian Government which was created according to the provisions of the Moscow ultimatum and which had obtained assurances that the independence of Lithuania will be respected, later, under pressure from Moscow, was reorganized, without any knowledge or consent of the Acting Prime Minister, Prof. V. Kreve-Mickevičius, by securing its majority for the Communists, headed by M. Gedvila, for the purpose of making it a tool in Moscow's hands.

"3. The Moscow Government ordered the Lithuanian Government, thus reorganized to carry out elections to the 'People's Diet' in order that it should later on, request the incorporation of Lithuania into the Soviet Union.

"4. The 'People's Diet' could not and did not proclaim the will of the Lithuanian people because:

"(a) The composition of the 'People's Diet' was made up in advance by the Communist Party, directed by Moscow's representative, V.G. Dekanozov, and by the Soviet Minister to Lithuania, N.G. Pozdniakov. Only the Union of Working People of Lithuania was allowed to select candidates who were nominated by the Communist Party. The number of candidates was exactly the same as the number of members elected to the 'People's Diet.'

"(b) As the composition of the 'Diet' was made up in advance, it declared, in order to enhance the effect, that 95.51 percent of all the electorate had voted, while actually, as confirmed by the Supreme Election Commission and by the statement made by the former People's Commissar, M. Gedvila, and by the President of the L.S.S.R. Supreme Soviet, J. Paleckis, at secret meetings, only 16 to 18 percent of valid voting cards were submitted at the polls.

"(c) A number of members of the 'Diet,' who were not members of the Communist Party, were compelled by threats to become members of the 'Diet' and to vote for incorporation into the Soviet Union.

"(d) When the voting on the incorporation into the Soviet Union took place the votes of the members were not counted; all strangers present at the meeting voted together with them.

"5. Not a single member of the 'People's Diet' could express a protest against the use of force as, under the circumstances, such protest would have involved danger to his life. Moscow's representatives and the members of the Soviet Legation openly threatened all those members of the 'Diet' and their families who would have dared to announce their intention not to vote for incorporation into the Soviet Union.

"6. We, former members of the 'People's Diet,' raise a public protest against the methods of violence and of falsifications which were directed by the Bolshevik Government against the Republic of Lithuania and the Lithuanian nation during the elections to the 'Diet' as well as during its session. Neither we nor the other members of the 'Diet' could express and did not express the will of the Lithuanian nation for incorporation in the Soviet Union.

"7. The 'People's Diet' itself stated in its declaration of July 21, 1940, 'Now the people, helped by the mighty Red army, did away with the yoke of Smetona's oppressors and established in their own country the Soviet Government. If the people have been able to establish in their own country the only just order, the Soviet order, it is all due to the Soviet Union.' In this way the 'People's Diet' itself admitted the Red army's influence in its decisions and the decisions of other government authorities.

"Former Members of the People's Diet: Dr. A. Garmus, L. Dovydenas, H. Kačinskas, R. Juknevičius, V. Biržietis, P. Mickus, Mrs. S. Vainekiene, Miss P. Milančiute, the former Acting Prime Minister and Minister of Foreign Affairs of the People's government, Prof. V. Kreve-Mickevičius, the former Commissar for Social Care and Forest Industry of the L.S.S.R., Jurgis Glušauskas.

"KAUNAS, *August 30, 1942.*"

Editor's comment: Well established facts confirmed even by Soviet sources determine the fraudulent character of the elections:

    1) There was only one list of candidates, made up by the Communist Party and Dekanozov's delegation.

2) All other political parties and leaders and even newspapers were either suppressed or intimidated into silence.

3) The mandate of the Seimas to vote on incorporation was neither voted by the people nor even revealed to them.

4) The ballots were not officially counted.

No. 182

Appeal of the Supreme Committee of Lithuania: To the Lithuanian Nation

To the Lithuanian Nation!

The Lithuanian State has not ceased to exist legally. It was recognized de facto and de jure by almost all the States of the world; it was and still is a member of the League of Nations. It could change its legal status only by measures provided for in the constitution; this change would have to be recognized by the various individual states.

The intrusion of the Red Army into Lithuania and all the later reforms connected with this intrusion and the incorporation were nothing but acts of violence which are not recognized either by the Lithuanian nation, or by other states.

The German Reich, which, with the aid of Lithuanian guerillas, occupied Lithuania did not change the legal status either and rules Lithuania by right of conquest.

By using military power, the occupants are conducting policies and issuing directives in Lithuania which are not in accord with the sovereignty of Lithuania and which are often injurious to our nation and our state. A great task is set before us, to defend our rights and to reconstitute our independent state. We can accomplish this task only by organizing and gathering all the vital forces of the nation.

Heretofore, we had no organ which could speak and act in the name of the nation. The General Councillors are the employees of the occupation government, they have no right to act and pronounce important decisions in the name of the nation.

Under these circumstances, the people have found it necessary to create the Supreme Committee of Lithuania, in the formation of which the bulk of the Lithuanian people participated. The first task of this committee will be to coordinate the attitudes and actions of all the different currents of the nation in seeking the common goal — to reconquer the independence of the land. When freedom is restored the country will choose such a political order as it finds proper. The Supreme Committee for Lithuania desires that the future Lithuania be good and dear to all of us, especially to the farmers and workers, and that by our common efforts the standard of living of everyone and the country's material, cultural, and intellectual level be raised, and that the rights and freedoms of everyone be respected within the limits of common life.

The cruel war is approaching its end. Both belligerents are exhausting themselves, and they will not be able to continue the war for long. For us, the fateful hour is approaching. We must gather all the vital forces of our land, we must strengthen our deep conviction of a free future and determinedly prepare ourselves for events. Our fate depends on our success in achieving this. The basis of our future endeavors must be unity, a clear understanding of our goals and determined action.

The reestablishment of the freedom of Lithuania is the concern of all the inhabitants of Lithuania. We do not agree with violent means against the minorities living in Lithuania, and we wish to induce every citizen of sound attitudes to join in the recovery of independence and the government of the land.

Furthermore, the Supreme Committee of Lithuania proclaims that it is against all the methods which are not in accordance with international law, by which our people are destroyed and the economy and general wealth are ruined. The Committee speaks publicly now against the mobilization of men, as international law does not allow an occupant to do this. The Lithuanian nation is unanimously determined that, if need be, it will fight vigorously against the first occupant of our land — , the Eastern barbarian. However, only the legal sovereign government of Lithuania can call Lithuanians to war and conduct a mobilization for the protection of the interests of the nation.

The Committee vigorously pronounces itself against the deportation of Lithuanians abroad for forced labor, against the imposition of starvation on Lithuanian workers and city people, against requisitions from Lithuanian farmers above the normal potential of agriculture, against the robbery of the basic assets of Lithuanian agriculture, and against the ruin of industry and the robbing of industrial products.

The Committee invites all to unite, not to split into small groups in their activities, to forget mutual grudges, to help each other, and not to give in to the provocations of the enemy. We must be circumspect and determined. The administrators appointed by the Germans are invited to be sensible Lithuanians and to do only what is useful to our nation and its future.

> signed: the Supreme Committee of Lithuania
> March 1, 1943

No. 183

Appeal of Sixty-Five Swedish Intellectuals in Behalf of the Baltic States

> April, 1943

In an article recently published in newspapers in various countries, three prominent representatives of the culture of Estonia, Latvia and Lithuania appealed to the enlightened opinion of the world for support in the fight for the just national demands of their peoples. We the undersigned, who are in full agreement with this appeal, wish to state the following:

Estonians, Latvians and Lithuanians constitute completely distinct peoples, with independent languages and independent forms of culture, which have lived through centuries of oppression and thereby show their national vitality.

Estonians, Latvians and Lithuanians have, during their twenty years of peace between the two world wars, carried out work in various spheres — cultural, economic and political — which has gained for them the admiration of the world and clearly demonstrated their ability to build up a State, and at the same time given an example of the fact that culture can only flourish in condition of freedom.

The Baltic people's highest aim has been to work for the welfare of their nations in the best possible cooperation with their neighbors. Through no fault of their own they have been subjected to occupation by two great powers who have robbed them of their freedom and caused the people heavy suffering.

The world's conscience can never be at peace while small, peaceful states, which do beneficial work in the service of culture, are sacrificed to the imperialistic interests of great Powers. If they are robbed of their freedom for the future, right and justice will be given a wound which cannot be healed; and a crime will be committed against the highminded principles which are proclaimed in the Atlantic Charter, which promises freedom independence to all peoples who have been deprived of them by force.

We, the undersigned, assert the unassailable right of the Baltic peoples to live their own free life. Before the coming peace settlement, we appeal for freedom and independence for the sorely tried peoples of Estonia, Latvia and Lithuania.

(signed) A. Ahlenberg, Doctor of Philosophy; N. Ahlund, Professor; I. Anderson, Chief Editor, leader of the Upper House of the Swedish Riksdag; T. J. Arne, Professor; K. Asplund, Doctor of Philosophy; J. Bergman, Professor; N. Beskow, Doctor of Theology; M. Bjorkquist, Bishop; B. Boethius, Professor; Y. Brilioth, Bishop; B. Colliander, Professor; S. Curman, Curator; G. Danell, former Headmaster; S. Danell, Head of Ersta College for Social Workers; G. deGeer, Professor Emeritus; J.I.A. Dicson, Kammerherre, leader of the Lower House of the Riksdag; G. Eberstein, Professor; H. Eek, Doctor of Law; S. Erixon, Professor; Wera von Essen, Baroness; I. Fagraeus, former Consul General; A. Gauffin, former Curator of National Gallery of Stockholm; G. Hafstrom, M.A. of Philosophy, M.A. of Law; H. Hammar, Director; H.E. Henke, former Latvian Consul General; K. Hildebrand, Doctor of Philosophy; O. Holmdahl, Director General, leader of the Lower House of the Riksdag; Th. Jakobsson, Lt. Col.; B. Johnson, Bishop; O. Jarte, Departmental Chief; S. Karling, former Professor at the University of Tartu; H. Kjellin, Professor, Keeper of Archives; Y. Larsson, Town Counselor of Stockholm; A. Lindblom, Head of Nordiska Museet; J. Lindblom, Professor; C. Lindhagen, Mayor; C. Lindskog, Professor and Chief Editor; F. Loven; B. Nerman, Professor; A. Pers; A.C. Peterson, former Headmaster; von Post, Professor; G. Rudberg, Professor; Hanna Rydh, Doctor of Philosophy, leader of the Lower House of the Riksdag; A. Schuck, Reader; J.A. Selander, Chief Editor; Marika Stiernstecht, Authoress; N. Stjernberg, Professor Emeritus; G. Stridsberg, Writer; F. Strom, leader of the Upper House of the Riksdag, former Chairman of Stockholm Town Council; P. Socerback, Headmaster; Alice Tegner, Composer; T. Tegner, Chief Editor; R. Wagnsson, Official at Board of Education and leader of the Upper House of the Riksdag; Lydia Wahlstrom, Professor; R. Wallberg, Consul General; H. Wallin, teacher; C. Weibull, Professor; Greta Wieselgren, former professor at University of Tartu, Don.; K. Wistrand, Director, leader of the Upper House of the Riksdag; N. Wohlin, Director General; A. Orne, Director General.

Editor's comment: The Swedish government, however, denied asylum to Baltic refugees, who had fled to Sweden after being forcibly inducted into the German army, and returned them forcibly to Soviet authorities upon request.

No. 184

Joint Declaration of the Lithuanian Political Parties and Groups

As the end of this frightful war draws nearer, the Lithuanian nation, separated for more than three years from the outside world by a wall of bayonets, desires that the world should hear the true voice of the Lithuanian people.

The Lithuanian State was first established in the twelfth century. The Lithuanian nation lost its independence for the first time in 1795 when the Lithuanian State was incorporated in the Russian Empire. From 1795 the Lithuanians took advantage of every occasion to endeavor to restore the Lithuanian State (e.g., 1812 and 1863) until they were finally able to accomplish their desire in 1918. The Treaty of July 12th, 1920, between Lithuania and Russia states that "Russia without any reservation recognizes Lithuania as a separate and independent state with all the juridical consequences ensuing from such recognition and voluntarily renounces for all time the rights of sovereignty which it has exercised over the Lithuanian people and their territory" (Art. 1).

On September 28th, 1926, there was concluded between Lithuania and the Soviet Union a Non-Aggression Treaty, according to which both states "mutually promise to respect one another's sovereignty and territorial integrity and inviolability under all circumstances."

This Treaty was again confirmed on October 10, 1939, by the Treaty for the Restitution to the Lithuanian Republic of Vilnius and the Vilnius Territory and for Mutual Assistance between Lithuania and the Soviet Union. By the same Treaty Lithuania was forced to accept Soviet garrisons.

In a speech made to the Supreme Council of the U.S.S.R. on October 31st, 1939, the President of the Council of the Peoples' Commissars and Commissar for Foreign Affairs, speaking of this Mutual Assistance Treaty with Lithuania and similar treaties with the other Baltic States, stated: "We stand for the conscientious and exact observation of the treaties concluded, on the principle of entire reciprocity, and declare the idle talk about the sovietization of the Baltic States to be profitable only to our common enemies and to all kinds of anti-Soviet provocateurs."

Despite this, on June 15th, 1940, the Soviet Union carried out a military occupation of Lithuania and on July 21st the sovietization of Lithuania was proclaimed. In an act passed on the same day with the view of union with Soviet Russia, it was expressly stated that the sovietization of Lithuania had been accomplished with the help of the Red Army, "thanks to the Soviet Union alone" (Official Journal No. 719, Serial 5744). All this happened in spite of the fact that (according to data disclosed during the congress of the Lithuanian Communist Party, held in February, 1941) at the time of the entry of the Red Army, the Lithuanian Communist Party had barely 1,500 members (*see* "Tarybu Lietuva" of 1941, No. 35) out of a population of 3,000,000. And even of those 1,500 members the majority were not of Lithuanian origin. Upon the declaration of the sovietization of Lithuania (favored by 1,500, and it may be even fewer, Communists), the Lithuanian State was incorporated in the Soviet Union against the will of 3,000,000 people and contrary to international treaties.

As will be seen from the note of the German Foreign Office to the Soviet Government on June 21st, 1941, the incorporation of Lithuania in the Soviet Union came about as a result of agreements between the Soviet Union and Germany, according to which Lithuania was originally recognized as entering into the German sphere of interest. Later Germany renounced her interest in the greater part of Lithuania "waehrend ein Streifen des Gebietes noch in der deutschen Interessensphere verblieb" (while a strip of the territory still remained in the sphere of German interest). That "Streifen des Gebietes" comprised the districts of Sakiai and Vikaviskis, with parts of the districts of Mariampole and Seinai. Regarding the renunciation of its interest in this part of Lithuania also, the note of the German Government states: "Als dann spaeter an Deutschland dieserhalb herangetreten wurde ueberliess die Reichsregierung ... auch dieses Teil Litauens der Sovietunion' (when later Germany was approached on this subject, the German Government ... gave this part up also to the Soviet Union). This "giving up" of Lithuania to the Soviet Union is said to be correlated to the fact that Lithuania refused to take part in the war against Poland, the ally of Great Britain, on the side of Germany.

From the very beginning the Lithuanian nation has held the sovietization of Lithuania and her incorporation in the Soviet Union to be null and void.

The domination of the Soviets in Lithuania did not last long; it was ended by the outbreak of the German-Russian war and by the Lithuanian revolt against the Soviet Government at the beginning of that war. During this period the Lithuanians formed a Provisional Government, which was set aside by the German occupation authorities and Lithuania has since been living for over two years under German military occupation.

As the war enters its final phase the Lithuanian nation awaits with the greatest anxiety the decision to be made concerning the future of Lithuania. The Lithuanian people believe that this war may decide the question of their very existence; that as a result of the war they will either be left to live as a nation and a state or will be annihilated by the well-known methods for the destruction of nations, methods which have been already applied to the Lithuanian people for over three years. The Lithuanians see no third way out for them. The fact alone that Lithuania, which has taken no direct part in the war, has proportionately lost more people than any one of the belligerent states, explains the anxiety with which Lithuania awaits the morrow. According to approximate statistics, Lithuania, which at the end of 1939 had about 3,000,000 inhabitants has since the beginning of the war lost more than 250,000 people. About 45,000 were lost during the Soviet occupation, either killed in Lithuania or deported to die in distant Russian lands; among these were many of the flower of Lithuanian youth and of her intellectuals. Over 4,000 lost their lives bearing arms during the latter part of June, 1941, in the uprising against the Soviet Government. Over 200,000 have been put to death during the present existing German occupation. The greater number of those who perished during the German occupation were Lithuanian citizens of Jewish origin. Besides these, on the occupation of the country by the Red Army, tens of thousands fled from Lithuania to whatever lands were open to them. From the very beginning of the German occupation thousands of those who fled from Soviet occupation and of those forcibly taken to Germany, will never return to their homes. Since June 15th, 1940, the lives, liberty and property of the Lithuanians have been completely at the mercy of foreign rulers.

In the course of the war and under present circumstances, should Lithuania's occupation by an alien power again change hands, the Lithuanian nation may expect a new and still more terrible wave of extermination. Those who, according to the doctrine so foreign to the Lithuanian people, would be destroyed first have been dubbed "enemies of the people"; these "enemies of the people" are practically the whole of the more active, more vital element of the nation.

In calling the attention of the world to this critical situation, the Lithuanian people wish at the same time to emphasize that in this fourth year of their struggle against foreign occupation and for the national independence of Lithuania, they are fighting for their very existence; that they, too, even as other nations, great or small, await the establishment of "a peace which will afford to all nations, the means of dwelling in safety within their own boundaries, and which will afford assurance that all men in all lands may live out their lives in freedom from fear and want."

Signed by:

THE LITHUANIAN NATIONAL UNION	*(Balys Gaidžiunas)*
THE PEASANT POPULIST UNION OF LITHUANIA	*(Juozas Audėnas)*
THE UNION OF COMBATANTS FOR THE LIBERTY OF LITHUANIA	*(Jonas Deksnys)*
THE LITHUANIAN NATIONALIST PARTY	*(Klemensas Brunius)*
THE SOCIAL-DEMOCRATIC PARTY OF LITHUANIA	*(Steponas Kairys)*
THE LITHUANIAN CHRISTIAN-DEMOCRATIC PARTY	*(Stasys Lušys)*
THE LITHUANIAN FRONT	*(Juozas Ambrazevičius)*

KAUNAS
14th October, 1943

No. 185

Appeal of the Supreme Committee for the Liberation of Lithuania

(Dec. 1943)

The Lithuanian nation, keeping before its eyes the supreme goal of iberation of the Lithuanian state, and conserving its strength and vital orces for this reason, but taking, however, into consideration the approaching Bolshevik invasion which threatens to occupy Lithuania and the Lithuanian nation and to destroy them completely, and also considering the Bolshevik banditry growing in the country, unanimously decided that it was necessary to create a Lithuanian army.

The occupying German power, having denied this firm desire of Lithuania, and offering to organize Lithuanian units under German leadership instead of a Lithuanian army, proves that the Germans continue to seek only political advantages and to disregard the vital interests and needs of Lithuania.

Therefore, the Supreme Committee for the Liberation of Lithuania calls on the Lithuanian nation to adhere to its firm determination in unity, to obey the call to mobilize only when a Lithuanian army is organized by the Lithuanians themselves and led by Lithuanians to protect Lithuania's borders and to fight for independence. Any persons violating this united attitude of the Lithuanian nation will be considered by the Committee as a gross injury of the Lithuanian cause and Lithuanian interests.

At the same time, the Supreme Committee for the Liberation of Lithuania reminds our public that the mobilization proclaimed by the German occupation government or by persons consenting to the German administration would be contrary to our purposes and to the will of the people, and legally is not binding on the citizens of Lithuania. The use of violent means against resisters to mobilization will be an act of force contrary to international law.

The Supreme Committee for the Liberation of Lithuania invites the entire Lithuanian nation to continue to prepare speedily for the fateful battle against the threat of the Bolshevik invasion, even under illegal conditions. The Committee wishes the German occupation government would finally understand the attitude of the Lithuanian nation and recognize its designs.

signed: the Supreme Committee for the Liberation of Lithuania

The mobilization, incidentally, was a total failure. So few volunteers appeared that the German authorities dropped the project.

Editor's comment: This is the first appeal of the new Supreme Committee for the Liberation of Lithuania (known from its Lithuanian abbreviation as VLIK) formed in November of 1943. VLIK integrated all the political parties and groups of the Lithuanian nation. Without dissension, it became the leading force of Lithuanian resistance during the German occupation, the second Soviet occupation, and in exile. It is still active as an unofficial government-in-exile in New York, making diplomatic demarches wherever possible and dispensing information.

VLIK maintains short-wave radio hours in Madrid, Rome and the Philippines, and operates the New York-based Elta news and information agency, which issues news bulletins concerning Lithuania in English, French, Spanish, and Italian.

No. 186

Declaration of the Supreme Committee for the Liberation of Lithuania: To the Lithuanian Nation!

TO THE LITHUANIAN NATION:

The Lithuanian nation, seeking to liberate Lithuania from occupation and to restore the functioning of the sovereign organs of the Government of Lithuania, which was temporarily impeded by foreign forces, is in need of unified political leadership. For that purpose Lithuanian political groups, as the exponents and the executors of the political thought of the nations, have agreed to join all their forces for the common cause and have therefore created the VYRIAUSIAS LIETUVOS IŠLAISVINIMO KOMITETAS — VLIK (Supreme Committee for the Liberation of Lithuania).

In beginning its work, the Supreme Committee for the Liberation of Lithuania declares that:

1. The freedom of the Lithuanian nation and the independence of the Lithuanian State are absolute conditions of national existence, progress, and welfare.

2. The sovereign State of Lithuania has not ceased to exist because of its occupation by the Soviet Union, or because of its present occupation by the Reich; only the functioning of the sovereign organs of the State has been temporarily suspended. The functioning of the sovereign organs of Lithuania, which was interrupted by the occupation by the Soviet Union on June 15, 1940, and by acts of force and fraud committed under compulsion of that occupation, was temporarily reestablished by the uprising of the nation on June 23, 1941, and by the action of the Provisional Government.

3. After the liberation of Lithuania, the Lithuanian Constitution of 1938 shall remain in force until it is changed by legal methods.

4. The Government of the Republic will be formed at the right time within the Supreme Committee for the Liberation of Lithuania by agreement of the political groups on a coalition basis.

5. The democratic form of government of the Lithuanian State will be adapted to the interests of all strata of the population and to general postwar conditions.

6. Laws relating to the election of the President and of the Seimas will be modified in accordance with the principles of democratic elections.

7. Leading the nation in its struggles and efforts to liberate itself, to restore the functioning of the sovereign organs of the Lithuanian state, to re-establish democratic government, and to defend the land from communism and other factors threatening its life, the Supreme Committee for the Liberation of Lithuania will endeavor to bring about the greatest possible consolidation of the nation's active forces by eliminating strife among political groups.

8. Highly appreciating the importance of national armed forces in the struggle for Lithuania's liberation, the Committee will support by all means the re-establishment of the Lithuanian Army.

9. The Committee will maintain close relations with the legations and consulates of Lithuania, and will collaborate with Lithuanians living abroad, especially with those living in the United States, and with all nations which recognize the principles of national self-determination and the independence of Lithuania.

10. In order to hasten the cultural and economic progress of the nation and to speed the country's return to normal life, the Committee will assemble and prepare material for the administration of liberated Lithuania, for the organization of its economy and social life and its judicial and educational work.

In making known this Declaration to the Nation, the Supreme Committee for the Liberation of Lithuania calls on all Lithuanians of good will of all political viewpoints to cooperate in mutual understanding and in the spirit of unity in the relentless struggle for Lithuania's freedom.

For the cause of Lithuania
Let unity flourish!

Vilnius, February 16, 1944.

THE SUPREME COMMITTEE FOR
THE LIBERATION OF LITHUANIA.

No. 187

Appeal of the Supreme Committee for the Liberation of Lithuania: Compatriots

Compatriots!

Not once only has the occupation government of the Reich tried to subject the Lithuanian nation to its war machine against the interest of Lithuania. Only because of our unshakeable and united resistance have all the German efforts so far been unsuccessful. In spite of all the German failures, we are once again faced with a threat of the German occupational administration against Lithuania.

The German occupational administration, seeking to destroy the vital strength of the Lithuanian nation, prepared a plan to mobilize approximately 5,000 people per week for labor in the Reich, beginning March 5, 1944: men between 15 and 55 and women between 16 and 45, totalling 100,000 people. As always, so now, in this case, the execution of this plan against the Lithuanian nation is being enforced by the Germans through the apparatus of the Lithuanian administration. Kubiliunas, the first councellor, and Kupcikevičius, in charge of labor and social affairs, dared to set their signatures under this plan, thus committing the greatest crime against the Lithuanian nation.

Without mentioning that such an extortion of labor force from Lithuania would cause ruin and disintegration in the economy of our country and would undermine our capacity for defence against Bolshevism, from the point of view of the vital interests of Lithuania, the betrayal of 100,000 Lithuanian workers would signify the destruction of the Lithuanian nation.

Therefore, the Supreme Committee for the Liberation of Lithuania is warning all functionaries of the administration who allow themselves to be used to perform this cruel execution of our nation to decide for their nation, for Lithuania, even though German reprisals would threaten them. All the executors must know that they should suffer themselves or avoid their service duty by going into hiding rather than become the executioners of thousands and earn the condemnation of the nation.

The Committee appeals to all those who are called, not to submit to the fear of terror, and all Lithuanians must courageously and unanimously say — no! to all the evil designs of the occupants toward us, this time as in the past. All those who are called and pursued must not give up, but must hide to spare their strength and their life for the defense of Lithuania from the Bolshevik danger, and for the reestablishment of Lithuanian independence. The Supreme Committee for the Liberation of Lithuania obliges all compatriots to help those who are in hiding.

Let us live through this difficult trial too with immovable strength and united will.

Let unity blossom in Lithuania.

signed: the Supreme Committee for the Liberation of Lithuania
Vilnius, February 18, 1944

No. 188

Appeal of the Lithuanian American Council, United Latvian American Committee, and United Committee of Estonian American Organizations to the Government of the United States

August, 1944

APPEAL:

Whereas, the United States has declared that it opposes all forms of aggression and territorial changes made during the war; and

Whereas, it is in the interest of the United States to promote unity and harmony among the United Nations in accordance with the principles of the Atlantic Charter, the Declaration by United Nations, and the Moscow and Teheran Declarations, and

Whereas, it is in the interest of the United States to prevent chaos and disorder, and to ensure stability and legality, in the liberated countries of Europe, and

Whereas, the United States continues to recognize the sovereignty of the Republics of Lithuania, Latvia and Estonia; and

Whereas, the actions of the Soviet occupation regime in Lithuania, Latvia and Estonia in the years of 1940 and 1941 bode ill for these nations in the event of the imminent second occupation of the Baltic States by the Soviet forces, UNLESS such occupation proceed in accordance with the international laws of warfare and military occupational administration, and UNLESS this administration be placed under an effective Inter-Allied Military Control; and

Whereas, the Soviet diplomacy and propaganda since the adherence of the Soviet Union to the Declaration by United Nations are in direct violation of the letter and the spirit of the principles thereof; and

Whereas, it is in the interest of the United States, and pursuant to the declared and established principles of the United States to "see sovereign rights and self-government restored to those who have been forcibly deprived of them, to "afford assurance that all men in all the lands may live out their lives in freedom from fear and want," and to save human lives and alleviate the sufferings of the peoples being liberated from the German yoke,

THE UNDERSIGNED AMERICAN ORGANIZATIONS URGENTLY APPEAL, PENDING THE RE-ESTABLISHMENT OF NATIONAL REPRESENTATIVE GOVERNMENTS OF THE BALTIC REPUBLICS AND WITHOUT PREJUDICE TO THE SOVEREIGN RIGHTS OF THE PEOPLES OF LITHUANIA, LATVIA AND ESTONIA, TO INTERCEDE NOW WITH THE GOVERNMENT OF THE SOVIET UNION:

(1) That the military occupation of the territories of the Republics of Lithuania, Latvia and Estonia by the armed forces of the Soviet Union proceed in accordance with international law and rules of warfare and be placed under immediate Inter-Allied Military Control and under the supervision of the Inter-Allied European Advisory Committee:

(2) That the occupying military authorities of the Soviet Union do not interfere with and do fully respect the civil liberties, religious worship and instruction, freedom of the press and freedom of speech;

(3) That no Soviet civil administration be installed or be attempted to be imposed, promoted or preferred, and that the representative democratic local administration be assisted to restoration under the supervision of the Inter-Allied Military Control Commission;

(4) That the respective democratic constitutional laws, due processes of law, civil liberties and private property rights in effect prior to June, 1940, be reinstated in full force and effect, behind the immediate zone of military operations in Lithuania, Latvia and Estonia;

(5) That the temporary military administration proceed in accordance with rules of international law regarding administration of foreign territory under military occupation; that such administration attempt no reprisals nor methods of error against the inhabitants of the Baltic States; that all criminal prosecutions proceed under the respective national laws in effect prior to June, 1940, in local courts of

the respective countries and under the supervision of the Inter-Allied Military Control Commission;

(6) That there be no deportations, individually or en masse, of the citizens of Lithuania, Latvia and Estonia;

(7) That the citizens of Lithuania, Latvia and Estonia deported into the U.S.S.R. in 1940 and 1941 be released and permitted to return home under the supervision and with the assistance of the International and/or National Red Cross agencies of any of the United Nations;

(8) That the American Red Cross and American relief agencies be given full facilities to extend relief to the inhabitants of Lithuania, Latvia and Estonia, and to the Baltic deportees in Soviet Russia.

The Lithuanian American Council, Inc.
1739 So. Halsted Street, Chicago, Ill.

The United Latvian American Committee
157 E. 86th Street, New York, N.Y.

United Committee of Estonian American
Organizations
15 East 125th Street, New York, N.Y.

No. 189

Appeal of the Supreme Committee for the Liberation of Lithuania to the Governments of Great Britain and the United States

The following Appeal has reached London:

"In view of the situation newly arisen through the second occupation of the greater part of Lithuania by the Red Army, the Supreme Committee for Liberation of Lithuania makes the following declaration in the name of the entire Lithuanian Nation: —

The Powers Signatory to the Atlantic Charter solemnly proclaimed by that act that they "seek no aggrandisement, territorial or other" and that "they wish to see sovereign rights and self-government restored to those who have been forcibly deprived of them." The Soviet Union, in adhering to the Atlantic Charter, pledged itself to observe the principles set forth therein.

Speaking at the Inter-Allied meeting held in London on September

24, 1941, the Soviet Ambassador, Ivan Maisky, declared: "The Soviet Union has applied, and will apply, in its foreign policy the high principles of *respect for the sovereign rights of peoples* . . . the Soviet Union defends *the rights of every nation to independence and territorial integrity* of its country."

However, neither when the Red Army crossed the frontiers of Lithuania nor when the occupation of the greater part of the country was taking place last summer, did the Soviet Union give any assurance that it would respect the sovereign rights of the Lithuanian Nation and its territorial integrity.

On the contrary, while the occupation of Lithuania by the Red Army proceeds, Lithuania is being treated as part of the Soviet Union. The Soviet regime is being re-introduced, and general mobilization for the Red Army of all Lithuanians born in the years 1909 to 1926 has been decreed. Furthermore, the arrests and executions of Lithuanian political leaders, public men and members of their families, and mass deportations of Lithuanian men and women into the depths of the Soviet Union have begun.

The Lithuanian Nation has always maintained and continues to insist that *the so-called incorporation of Lithuania into the Soviet Union* was carried out in contravention of international engagements undertaken by the Soviet Union and in violation of the treaties entered into with Lithuania, and is *null and void.*

The Red Army first occupied Lithuania on June 15, 1940, in violation of the solemn declaration by Viacheslav Molotov, the Commissar for Foreign Affairs of the Soviet Union, made to the session of the Supreme Soviet on October 31, 1939, to wit: "The Soviet Union insists upon the honorable and correct execution of the treaties which it has signed, on the basis of absolute reciprocity, and declares that *all the talk about a sovietization of the Baltic States is only of use to our enemies* and to all possible anti-Soviet provocateurs."

The incorporation of Lithuania into the Soviet Union and the sovietization of the country were carried out when Lithuania had been completely occupied by the Red Army and with the latter's active intervention. This was carried out by violence, force and deceit, against the will of the Lithuanian Nation. The true will of our People is proved, inter alia, by the effective boycott of the "elections to the People's Diet," as well as to the Supreme Soviet of the U.S.S.R.; by the uprising of the Lithuanian People against the Soviet Union at the outbreak of the

German-Soviet war; and by the proclamation of the restoration of sovereignty of the Independent Lithuanian Republic.

The Supreme Committee for Liberation of Lithuania, representing the entire Lithuanian Nation, solemnly declares that *Lithuania does not hold herself to be a part of the Soviet Union,* and therefore categorically refuses to make any use of the rights of a member of the Soviet Union or to accept the obligations which membership in the Soviet Union would imply.

The Supreme Committee for Liberation of Lithuania further declares that *the so-called "Soviet Government of Lithuania,"* formed in 1940 after the occupation of Lithuania by the Red Army and since June, 1941, established in Moscow, *does not represent Lithuania.* It is merely a front for the so-called "Communist-Bolshevik Party of Lithuania" which, according to the official data published by the Soviet newspapers early in 1941, had barely 2,500 members and even these were mainly of non-Lithuanian extraction. The Lithuanian People have never considered and shall never consider any acts of that alleged "government" to be binding. The Lithuanian People regard the Red Army as *a foreign army of occupation* for which all the rules of International Law regulating the conduct of an army of occupation on foreign soil, are obligatory. Accordingly, *Lithuania must not be treated worse than an enemy territory.*

The Supreme Committee for Liberation of Lithuania *formally protests* on behalf of the People of Lithuania *against the general mobilization decreed by the foreign Soviet occupational authorities* and against all other violations on the part of the authorities of the Soviet Union of the rules which govern warfare and define the limits of power of the authorities of occupation in occupied territories.

The Supreme Committee for Liberation of Lithuania equally *protests against the forcible re-introduction of the Soviet regime in Lithuania* and regards this as a hostile act of pure physical violence and moral terror. *The Committee appeals to the conscience of the world against the extermination of the Lithuanian Nation which has already begun.*

During the entire period of German military occupation, the Lithuanian People fought for their most sacred cause — the restoration of an Independent State of Lithuania. Our People bravely faced the excessively severe repressive measures taken against it by the Germans, and there was no backing away from any sacrifice. *Our People refused to be involved in a war for Germany's interests and resisted all the German efforts to enforce an effective mobilization of Lithuanian manpower.*

Continuing its struggle for the restoration of sovereignty of Lithuania, *the Lithuanian People will resist to the utmost all endeavors of the Soviet Union to yoke Lithuania to Soviet interests.* The Lithuanian People will resist all attempts to re-introduce the undemocratic Soviet regime in Lithuania and will defend themselves against all attempts to deport the Lithuanian masses to the remotest regions of the U.S.S.R. This struggle of the Lithuanian People is a *fight for its liberty, for its right to an independent life, for its very survival.*

Lithuania is still a member of the International Community of independent sovereign states with all the rights and obligations ensuing therefrom. The free Democracies and the highest spiritual authorities of the world have never explicitly or implicitly recognized any attempted change in the international status of Lithuania. The Lithuanian People firmly believe that the principles set forth in the *Atlantic Charter* and the obligations thereby assumed by the United Nations are *applicable to Lithuania* as to all other nations, large and small, and that Lithuania will again enjoy full sovereign rights after the defeat of Nazi Germany.

However, the continuing hostilities of war against Germany may cause Lithuania to remain for some time under the Soviet military occupation. This occupation should not preclude the practical restoration of state functions of the sovereign Lithuanian authority.

The Supreme Committee for Liberation of *Lithuania urgently appeals* to His Majesty's Government of *Great Britain* and to the Government of *the United States of America to dispatch their missions to Lithuania,* without delay, in order to *safeguard the rights and the vital interests of the Lithuanian People and to save our nation from threatening extermination.*

VILNIUS-KAUNAS, *September 30, 1944."*

No. 190

Proclamation of the People's Commissariat of the Interior of the Lithuanian Soviet Socialist Republic

ORDER

Of the People's Commissar for Internal Affairs of the Lithuanian SSR

15th February 1946   *Vilnius*

The organs of the People's Commissariat for Internal Affairs and the army, succored by the inhabitants and the people's defenders, have performed a great task in smashing the bands of Lithuanian-German nationalists after the liberation of the Lithuanian SSR by the heroic Red Army from the German plunderers.

In most of the counties, nearly all of the bands and the illegal anti-Soviet bourgeois nationalist organizations had been crushed.

Leaders of the Lithuanian-German nationalists were, with few exceptions, detained or destroyed, and those who had been compelled to enlist in the bands by deception or threats — surrendered to the Soviet government organs and returned to peaceful work. A great many of them have expiated their crimes against the Fatherland by conscientious work.

It is known, nevertheless, that some bandits surrendered to the Soviet government organs not of their own will but by direction of the bands' leaders; it is likewise known that they had not surrendered their arms, that they maintain contacts with their leaders and are aiding Lithuanian-German nationalists in executing bestial deeds against peaceful inhabitants.

In view of the continuing existence of some remnants of Lithuanian-German nationalists who, by their acts of banditry, obstruct the quiet life of the inhabitants, and in order to liquidate those remnants of the Lithuanian-German nationalists, —

I ORDER:

1. County and township chiefs of the People's Commissariat for Internal Affairs, the armed forces of the People's Commissariat for Internal Affairs and the detachments of people's defenders, — to immediately take drastic measures to clear all the counties of the Lithuanian SSR from the remnants of the Lithuanian-German nationalists.

2. To apply no repressions, to release home and issue passports to bandits, including the bands' leaders, of the LLA *(Laisvu Lietuviu Armija* — The Army of Free Lithuanians) and participants of other bourgeois nationalist organizations who surrender of their own will, after they had surrendered and turned in their arms.

3. I order the participants of the bands whose leaders enjoin their voluntary surrender to the Soviet government organs — to kill such leaders and to report in an organized manner and with arms to the institutions of the People's Commissariat for Internal Affairs. None of the persons who had killed the leaders of the bandit gangs or the rank-and-file bandits obstructing such surrender, will be persecuted.

4. Bandits who had surrendered earlier but had not turned in their arms, also all other persons possessing arms, — must without delay turn the same over to the institutions of the People's Commissariat for Internal Affairs.

5. To arrest and exile members of the families of the bandits and participants of the bourgeois nationalist organizations who had not surrendered to the institutions of the People's Commissariat for Internal Affairs.

6. Inhabitants in whose homes or settlements are installed bunkers or other hiding places for bandits and persons in hiding from the government organs, — must w:.hout delay report the fact to the institutions of the People's Commissariat for Internal Affairs.

Persons who fail to surrender arms or to report the presence of bunkers and hiding places under their control, are to be arrested and tried as bandits.

7. Persons who know the location of bunkers and hiding places, regardless of the location of such hiding places, must report the fact without delay to the institutions of the People's Commissariat for Internal Affairs.

All those who, while knowing the location of bunkers and hiding places, failed to report the fact to the institutions of the People's Commissariat for Internal Affairs, are to be arrested and tried as accomplices of the bandits.

PEOPLE'S COMMISSAR FOR INTERNAL AFFAIRS OF THE
LITHUANIAN SSR
Major General BARTAŠIUNAS

Editor's comment: Juozas Bartašiunas (1895-1972) was Lithuanian born. He joined the Latvian Riflemen's Regiment in 1915 and remained in the Soviet Union until 1940 when he was appointed the political commissar of the 29th (Lithuanian) Corps of the Red Army. In 1944 Major General Bartašiunas was appointed the Minister of the Interior of the Lithuanian SSR, directing the counterinsurgency effort in Lithuania until his retirement in 1953.

Maj. Gen. Bartašiunas' evaluation of the situation in 1946 was optimistic to say the least. In 1946 Lithuanian guerrilla resistance was just beginning. The guerrilla war in Lithuania lasted until 1952 and cost the Soviets some 80,000 dead.

No. 191

List of Underground publications From the Second Soviet Occupation of Lithuania

Underground Press. The underground press played one of the major parts in Lithuania's struggle for freedom during the second Communist occupation. Newspapers, mimeographed bulletins, printed appeals and newssheets were widely distributed among the people. From 1944 until the crush of the revolt at the end of 1952 or the beginning of 1953, the underground press used to reach every family and each and every patriotic Lithuanian in the country. There were some 20 newspapers published regularly:

1. "Už Laisve" (For Freedom);
2. "Kova" (The Struggle);
3. "Ginkime Lietuva" (Defend Lithuania);
4. "Tėvynės Kovotojas" (The Patriotic Fighter);
5. "Laisvės Varpas" (The Liberty Bell);
6. "Laisvoji Lietuva" (Free Lithuania);
7. "Partizanas" (The Partisan);
8. "Už Tevu Žeme" (For the Land of Our Ancestors);
9. "Laisves Šauklys" (Herald of Freedom)
10. "Laisves Rytas" (Morning of Freedom);
11. "Kovos Kelias" (Path of Combat);
12. "Laisves Žvalgas" (Scout of Freedom);
13. "Aukstaičiu Kova" (Combat of Aukstaitis);
14. "Aukuras" (The Altar). *

Editor's comment: The number of newspapers successfully printed iₗ the country in spite of the Soviet's well known and very efficien methods of repression is indicative of the scale of Lithuanian resistance. In one respect, the underground editors were fortunate. The literacy rate in Lithuania was extremely high (92% in 1940 as opposed to only 81% in the USSR that year), so that for all practical purposes, the readership of the underground press included the whole adult population.

---

* These publications can be found at the Library of the Hoover Institute of War, Revolution and Peace, Stanford, Cal.

No. 192

Letter of the Lithuanian Minister in Washington, Žadeikis, to the President of the Paris Peace Conference

(July 29, 1946)

Mr. President:

At this moment, when the Peace Conference, in which 21 States are taking part and the goal of which is to resolve certain problems of the re-establishment of Peace, that is to say, to liquidate the consequences of acts of violence, is meeting in Paris on July 29, 1946, I have the honor of calling your attention to the situation in which the Republic of Lithuania, the victim of unprovoked aggressions, finds itself.

Lithuania is one of the first victims of Germany. On March 21, 1939 Germany seized the territory of Memel from Lithuania.

When the war began on September 1, 1939, Lithuania, like the other Baltic States, proclaimed its neutrality and adhered to this policy, despite the fact that the sympathies of the Lithuanian nation without exception were on the side of the Western democracies. In spite of extreme demands from Germany to make Lithuania enter the war against Poland on its side, the Lithuanian Government and the Lithuanian nation as one most energetically rejected these demands and accorded asylum to tens of thousands of Polish citizens, civilian and military.

On October 10, 1939, the U.S.S.R. forced Lithuania to sign a mutual assistance pact with it, by which the Government of Moscow expressly committed itself not to interfere in the internal affairs of Lithuania, and not to injure the independence of Lithuania.

On June 15, 1940, at a moment when the attention of the entire world was turned to the events of the war in Western Europe, the army of the Soviet Union, after an ultimatum, completely occupied Lithuania, which, when it refused to enter the war against Poland, was ceded by Germany to the Soviet Union by virtue of the secret pact of September 26 [sic] 1939 between these two powers, concerning Lithuania, a fact which was also revealed at the Nuremberg trial.

On June 17, 1940, a special plenipotentiary [delegate] of the Government of Moscow, M. Dekanosov, sent especially for this purpose, formed the so-called government of Lithuania, a puppet government, an instrument of the occupying power.

Under these conditions, on July 14-15, 1940, the instrument of the Government of Moscow, the so-called puppet Government of Lithuania, staged elections in Lithuania in which there was only one list of candidates, drawn up by the occupying power. From this was chosen the so-called "People's Diet", which, on July 21, 1940, was ordered by the authorities of the occupying power to take a decision asking for the incorporation of Lithuania into the U.S.S.R.

While the Lithuanian nation resisted this violation of its will by every means possible, the diplomatic representatives of Lithuania abroad, as well as the organizations of Lithuanian emigrants, protested most energetically against this act of violence of the Soviet Union and requested the foreign powers not to recognize it.

On June 22, 1941, when the German-Soviet campaign had begun, the Lithuanian nation, expressing its true will to be free and independent, revolted, formed the Provisional Government of Lithuania, restored the sovereign rights of the Republic of Lithuania and introduced its own administration before the arrival of German troops.

The Nazi Government of the Reich, after it occupied Lithuania, suppressed the Provisional Government of Lithuania and introduced an occupational administration.

The Provisional Government and the Lithuanian people protested against this act of violence and resisted, as a consequence, the German occupation.

The Lithuanian nation unanimously began the resistance, and conducted a struggle which lasted through the whole occupation with incredible perseverance in spite of great sacrifices. By this struggle the Lithuanian people constantly oriented themselves toward the Western democracies, and thus contributed to the war effort of those nations which were carrying on the struggle against totalitarianism without outside aid. The Lithuanian nation was sustained in this attitude by hope for the victory of the Western democracies and the certainty that this victory would bring it liberty and independence. But Lithuania fell again under the occupation of the Soviet Union, harsher yet than the first Soviet occupation.

Always, the legitimate representatives of the Lithuanian State and the Supreme Committee of Liberation, representing the will of the Lithuanian people, unifying all the political parties and all the combat organizations and directing the resistance struggle, protested against the occupation of Lithuania.

Today, when the world is in the process of repairing the damages inflicted on peoples, the Lithuanian nation firmly believes that its most sacred rights will not be violated, and expects that the free exercise of its sovereign rights and its political independence will be reestablished in conformity with the principles of the Charter of the United Nations, the Atlantic Charter, and International Law.

The Lithuanian people protest energetically against any attempt on the part of the Soviet Union to gain recognition on the international level for the consequences of the act of violence committed by it against the Republic of Lithuania.

They energetically contest the Soviet Union's right to speak on its behalf and to present the functionaries of the Soviet occupation authorities as representatives of Lithuania.

The Lithuanian nation has the firm hope that each time that questions concerning its country are examined, its legitimate representatives will be heard in conformity with the principle of justice and of law.

In bringing the preceding to the attention of Your Excellency, I have the honor to request in the name of my people, to kindly support the just cause of Lithuania.

Please accept, Mr. President, I pray, the assurance of my highest consideration.

P. Žadeikis

Editor's comment: The Paris Peace Conference of 1946 was convened to establish the conditions of peace between the Allies and the lesser Axis countries, Italy, Hungary, Roumania and Bulgaria.* The principal Axis belligerents, Germany and Japan, were not involved; this was by no stretch of the imagination another Versailles.

The delegation of the U.S.S.R. was composed of Molotov, Vyshinskii, the Soviet Ambassadors to London, and Paris, and the three so called "foreign ministers" of the Baltic S.S.R.'s, Messieurs Valeskaln of Latvia, Kruus of Estonia, and Rotomskis of Lithuania. These sought admission to the conference as the official representatives of their countries.

Povilas Rotomskis (1906-1962), had been the representative of the Lithuanian S.S.R. in Moscow from 1940 to 1944. In that year he was

---

*Also Finland, which was considered a co-belligerent, but not an ally of the Axis, and thus received different treatment from the others.

appointed both so called Lithuanian "Foreign Minister" and to a secondary post in the Soviet Consulate General in New York.

The Lithuanian diplomatic representations in the West and the Supreme Committee for the Liberation of Lithuania also sent an unofficial delegation to represent free Lithuania. The delegation, headed by Dr. Stasys Bačkis, Charge d'Affaires of Lithuania in Paris, made official and unofficial demarches and co-ordinated the protest against the seating of the Soviet Baltic delegations. Žadeikis also wrote a sharply worded protest to Dean Acheson, the U.S. Secretary of State; Bronius Balutis, Lithuanian Minister in London, protested to the British Foreign Office; Mykolas Krupavičius, Chairman of the Supreme Committee for the Liberation of Lithuania, sent a letter identical to this document, also to the President of the Peace Conference.

The Peace Conference admitted the Baltic "foreign ministers," but only as members of the Soviet delegation, not as representatives of their countries. Inasmuch as their only function at Paris had been to gain international recognition for the Soviet incorporation of the Baltic States, their mission was a failure.

No. 193

Letter of Kazys Grinius, Former President of Lithuania, to the Secretary General of the United Nations, Lie

Chicago, December 12, 1949

Your Excellency,

The crime of genocide is being systematically perpetrated against Soviet occupied Lithuania. Lithuanians are arrested, tortured, massacred and deported to Siberia by force, and colonists brought from the depths of Russia are installed in the homes and farms of the deportees. In occupied Lithuania there are neither civil rights nor fundamental liberties. If this extermination of Lithuania continues for some time, the greater part of the Lithuanian nation, endowed with civilization and open to progress, will be destroyed. This persecution is exposed in detail in the Memorandum of the Supreme Committee for the Liberation of Lithuania, which was transmitted to Your Excellency on October 31, 1949 by P. Žadeikis, Minister of the Republic of Lithuania in Washington.

I warmly support the aforementioned memorandum of the Supreme Committee for the Liberation of Lithuania, and ask that it be taken under consideration immediately, and that a commission of the United Nations be charged with the study of the crime of genocide committed by the Soviet Union in Lithuania and the other Baltic States; that all possible measures be taken to stop the persecution of the innocent Lithuanian population and to reestablish the liberty of Lithuania.

Respectfully,

(signed) Dr. Kazys Grinius

Former President of the Republic of Lithuania

His Excellency
M. Trygve Lie
Secretary General of the United Nations
Lake Success, New York

No. 194

Note of the Lithuanian Minister in Washington, Žadeikis, to the President of the General Assembly of the United Nations, Pearson

No. 1763 November 21, 1952

Excellency:

Diplomatic representatives of Lithuania, Latvia, and Estonia have submitted to the Presidents of previous General Assemblies of the United Nations, as well as to the Secretary General of the United Nations, various reports and memoranda on the conditions prevailing in their respective countries under Soviet Russian occupation.

I feel it my duty to call once again the attention of the United Nations to this intolerable situation and request that this problem be taken up in the United Nations with a view to bringing an end to the destruction of my people and restoring to them their freedom and independence for which they have struggled for centuries.

The distortion of truth, the flagrant misrepresentation of ideas, principles and facts by the Government of the Union of Soviet Socialist Republics and by its Delegation to the Assembly of the United Nations and their efforts to give an apparent literal legality to the aggressive acts of the U.S.S.R., has no precedent in the history of international relations. All the proposals and statements made by Mr. A. Vyshinsky, Foreign Minister of the Soviet Union, and by his substitutes in the United Nations, are marked by this stigma.

The Soviet Delegation to the Fifth General Assembly of the United Nations introduced — and this is only one example — a draft resolution proposing "to define the concept of aggression as accurately as possible . . ." which would serve as a guide for the Security Council in the Assembly when dealing with such matters.

What is the true significance of the Soviet initiative and what are its true intentions? Would the definition of aggression, as proposed by the Soviet Delegation, cover all the devious processes, including infiltration, intimidation, subversion, treachery, military threat and, even, outright recourse to force, unscrupulously used by the rulers of the Kremlin, to undermine the sovereignty, independence and freedom of the nations, which are still free and to pave the way for their enslavement?

The assertion made by Mr. Vyshinsky in his speech before the General Assembly of the United Nations on October 17, 1952, namely, that

"the Soviet Union respects the independence of other nations"

is outrageous and has the same value as the declaration made by Mr. V. M. Molotov before the Supreme Soviet of the U.S.S.R. in Moscow on October 31, 1939, with reference to the Mutual Assistance Pacts recently concluded with Lithuania, Latvia, and Estonia:

"We stand for scrupulous observance of pacts on a basis of complete reciprocity and we declare that all nonsense about sovietizing the Baltic countries is only to the interest of our common enemies and of all anti-Soviet provocateurs."

The question of defining aggression will be discussed within a few days by the Sixth Committee of the present Assembly of the United Nations. As Lithuania has already experienced Soviet practices in the above mentioned field and is the victim of the complete disregard by the Soviet Union of all its international commitments and pledges, I feel duty bound to present to you the enclosed memorandum showing the ways and means by which the Soviet Union, although bound by treaties of Non-aggression, the Definition of Aggression, and other commitments, destroyed the independence and freedom of Lithuania, as well as of Latvia and Estonia. By applying a slightly different, but nonetheless devious procedure, other states in Eastern and Central Europe — Poland, Rumania, Bulgaria, Hungary, Czechoslovakia,

Albania and Yugoslavia — and in Asia — China — have been enslaved by the Soviet Union.

It would serve the cause of justice and the liberation of the victimized nations if the record of the U.S.S.R. vis-a-vis Lithuania, as related in the enclosed memorandum, would be thoroughly scrutinized. I believe that this memorandum will cast additional light on the complexity of the problem of defining aggression and will permit the delegates of the Seventh General Assembly of the United Nations to look deeper into this new diplomatic maneuver of the Soviet Government.

Please accept, Excellency, the assurances of my highest consideration.

P. Žadeikis
Minister of Lithuania

Editor's comment: In 1950, and again in 1953, the U.S.S.R. introduced draft resolutions on the definition of aggression, similar to the London Conventions of July 3 and 5, 1933, in the United Nations. The draft resolutions were ultimately rejected because "any 'legal' definition of aggression would be an artificial construction, which could not, with the continuous expansion of methods of aggression, be adequately comprehensive for future application."

No. 195

Statement by the Supreme Committee for the Liberation of Lithuania to the United Nations Delegations

(June 17, 1967)

Honorable Delegates;

On the initiative of the Government of the USSR, the General Assembly of the United Nations has been called in an extraordinary session to deal with the Middle East crisis. In the General Assembly, the Delegation of the USSR will assume the role of a champion of national independence and territorial integrity of small states. She will propose to condemn the aggressor and to compel him to withdraw his troops from the invaded territories of other states.

This Soviet championship will carry weight and eventually have an effect if it would be endowed with sincerity and support by a corresponding policy of its promoter.

Yet it deems proper to recall to your memory that, before the outbreak of the Second World War the Government of the Soviet Union entered into a shameful deal with Hitler Germany and, after the outbreak of the war, committed a series of aggressive acts against the sovereign and independent state of Lithuania, as well as against the other Baltic States, invaded its territory with Soviet military forces. This Soviet occupation of Lithuania continues until the present day with all its sinister implications for the population.

We should be grateful to you if you would find it possible in your interventions from the rostrum of the World Organization to evoke the above-mentioned facts and to remind the Government of the USSR, member of the United Nations, of its international duty to withdraw its troops and administrative apparatus from Lithuania and thus restore political independence and territorial integrity of this state.

Hoping that you will give due consideration to this our request, I am

Sincerely yours,
J.K. Valiunas
President
Supreme Committee for Liberation of Lithuania

Editor's comment: The exposition of the Supreme Committee for the Liberation of Lithuania is well grounded in international law. In his address to the American Society of International Law, Quincy Wright cited the Soviet expansion into the Baltic States as one of the few cases in recent history in which territory was annexed by force of arms. The consensus among experts on international law still holds that acquisition of territory by force is illegal. See: Quincy Wright, "The Middle Eastern Crisis," address with comments and discussion, in the American Journal of International Law, (Washington, D.C.), v. 64, no. 4, September 1970: 71-87.

No. 196

Manifesto on the Fiftieth Anniversary of the Restoration of Lithuanian Independence

The Conference to mark the Fiftieth Anniversary of the Restoration of Lithuania's Independence, convened in Washington, D.C., on October twenty-first and twenty-second of the year of Our Lord one-thousand-nine-hundred-and-sixty-seven, in the seven-hundred-and-seventeenth year since the establishment of the Lithuanian Kingdom, and in the fiftieth year since the restoration of Lithuania's independence — announce a Manifesto on the Fiftieth Anniversary of the Restoration of Lithuania's Independence.

The Lithuanian nation, established since ancient times at the Baltic Sea, unified into a Kingdom by King Mindaugas in the year one-thousand-two-hundred-and-fifty-one, for centuries played a significant role in Europe.

The growth of Russian imperialist power led to Moscow's incursion into Lithuania's territories and to the occupation of Lithuania at the end of the eighteenth century. The foreign oppression has not broken down the spirit of the Lithuanian people. The pages of recent Lithuanian history have been filled with the blood and life-sacrifice of insurrectionists, book-smugglers, volunteers, and partisans.

In fulfillment of the Lithuanian nation's will to be free and independent, the Council of Lithuania issued the following declaration on February 16, 1918:

— The Council of Lithuania has unanimously decreed at its session of February 16, 1918, to present the following declaration to the governments of Russia, Germany and other states.

— The Council of Lithuania, as the sole representative of the Lithuanian nation, supporting its claims on the recognized principle of self-determination of nations and on the decisions of the Lithuanian National Assembly made at Vilnius on September 17-23, 1917, hereby proclaims the reestablishment of the independent State of Lithuania on a democratic basis with its capital at Vilnius, and announces the separation of that state from all political ties, which previously have linked it with other nations.

— Likewise, the Council of Lithuania declares that, in order to fix definitely the foundations of the state of Lithuania and its relations with other states, a Constituent Assembly, elected by the inhabitants in accordance with democratic principles, will be convoked as soon as possible.

The Declaration of February Sixteenth was unanimously confirmed on May 15, 1920, by the freely elected Lithuanian Constituent Assembly. The international community of nations, including Soviet Russia, recognized the restored Lithuanian independence. In its Peace Treaty with Lithuania, signed on July 12, 1920, Soviet Russia stated that it:

— recognizes without reservation the sovereign rights and independence of the Lithuanian State, with all the juridical consequences arising from such recognition and voluntarily and for all time abandon all sovereign rights of Russia over the Lithuanian nation and its territory . . .

The restoration of independent Lithuania and its return to the community of self-governing nations has been the most significant event of the century for the Lithuanian people. The period of independence is a graphic manifestation of the political maturity, economic progressiveness and cultural creativity of the Lithuanian nation.

During the Second World War Lithuania's independence fell victim to a conspiracy between the Soviet Union and Hitler's Germany. The Soviet Union, after having entered into secret agreements with Hitler's Germany, — dated August 23 and September 28, 1939, and directed against the independence of Lithuania, Latvia, Estonia, Finland, and Poland, — occupied Lithuania on June 15, 1940, and by the use of force and perfidy incorporated it into the USSR on August 3, thus violating all the treaties it had signed with Lithuania as well as other international obligations.

THE LITHUANIAN NATION, in commemorating the fiftieth anniversary of the restoration of Lithuania's independence:

Declares to the entire world, be they friends or foes, that it shall never agree with the enslavement of Lithuania, that the Act of February Sixteenth is a sacred and final determination to lead a free and independent life, and that national independence is a condition for the development of national culture and for the very survival of the nation;

Accuses the Soviet Union of the acts of aggression, destruction of Lithuania's independence, genocidal extermination and Russification of the Lithuanian people, colonial exploitation of Lithuania, denial of the basic human rights and freedoms to the Lithuanian people;

Demands that the Soviet Union withdraw its army, police, and administration from Lithuania;

Asks the governments and parliaments of the free world to use all their means to restore the independence of Lithuania;

Appeals to the United Nations for action to liquidate the Soviet aggression against Lithuania and to the conscience of mankind to support Lithuanian efforts to restore their independence.

LITHUANIANS LIVING IN FREEDOM, respectful and proud of the determination of their nation to resist the occupying power; bowing their heads before those who fell in the fight for freedom; paying honors to the patriarchs of the National Awakening and to the signatories of the Declaration of February; dutybound and favored by the liberty that surrounds them to speak and act on behalf of their unfree nation; are united in their effort to free Lithuania from Soviet occupation, and therefore declare the year one-thousand-nine-hundred-sixty-eight — the fiftieth anniversary year since the restoration of Lithuania's independence — the Year of Lithuania's Fight for Freedom.

Although Lithuania's struggle for liberty has been going on since the very first days of the Soviet occupation, the Year of Lithuania's Fight for Freedom should activate in a new and special way the forces of all free Lithuanians in their effort to restore the power of the Declaration of February Sixteenth. The united forces of the Lithuanian nation against Soviet Russian occupation will again make the Declaration of February Sixteenth a living reality.

Liberation of nations is advancing inexorably from west and east, south and north. The oppression of Russian bolshevism will not be able to prevent Lithuania's liberation, the living goal of the entire nation.

In the progress march of mankind, freedom is more powerful than oppression.

Long live free and independent Lithuania!

Washington, D.C.
October 22, 1967

THE DIPLOMATIC SERVICE OF THE LITHUANIAN REPUBLIC:
Min. Stasys Lozoraitis
Chief of Lithuanian Diplomats

LITHUANIAN COMMUNITY OF THE UNITED STATES:
Bronius Nainys
Chairman

COMMITTEE FOR A FREE
LITHUANIA:
Min. Vaclovas Sidzikauskas
  Chairman

LITHUANIAN AMERICAN
COUNCIL:
  Antanas Rudis
  Chairman

THE SUPREME COMMITTEE
FOR LIBERATION OF
LITHUANIA:
  Dr. J.K. Valiunas
  President

LITHUANIAN COMMUNITY
OF CANADA
  Antanas Rinkunas
  Chairman

THE WORLD LITHUANIAN
COMMUNITY:
  Juozas Bachunas
  Chairman

Editor's comment: One misconception which has been used by those
who would dismiss the existence of any Baltic question is the notion that
the Baltic States were artificial creations whose twenty years of
existence was some quirk of Wilsonian Democracy. The signatories
point out that Lithuania has a 664 year history of independence. This
not only exceeds most of the new countries of Asia and Africa but even
the not-so-new countries of the Americas, states whose right to exist
goes unquestioned.

No. 197

Memorandum on the Denial of Human Rights in Lithuania Occupied by the Soviet Union Presented to the Delegations at the United Nations

Before the outbreak of World War II Lithuania was an independent
democratic state. Profiting from the Ribbentrop-Molotov Agreements of
September 23 and October 28, 1939, dividing Eastern Europe into Nazi
German and Soviet spheres of influence, the Soviet Government forced
Lithuania and two other Baltic States, Estonia and Latvia, to sign the
so-called "Pacts of Mutual Assistance" providing for the establishment
of Soviet military bases. On June 14-16, 1940, the Kremlin presented an
ultimatum to the governments of the three independent Baltic States,
and next day Soviet armed forces invaded and occupied these countries.

The constitutional government of Lithuania was forced to resign and was replaced by Kremlin's emissaries with an illegal regime faithful to Moscow. Mock Soviet-style elections were held on July 15, 1940, under the strict control of the Soviet military troops and the secret police (NKVD). The formal incorporation of Lithuania into the Soviet Union was completed on August 3, 1940, when the Supreme Soviet of the USSR granted a "petition" to that effect by the puppet parliament created by Moscow. A political, economic, cultural, and social system patterned on that of Soviet Russia was forcibly imposed upon the subjugated nation. The Western Powers do not recognize this annexation.

In the course of the Second World War, the Soviet occupation of Lithuania was replaced by that of Nazi Germany which lasted until the fall of 1944 and cost about 300,000 lives. In 1944 the Soviet military occupation was returned bringing in its wake the totalitarian Soviet system. The Soviet occupation has lasted to this day with its continuing police terror, Russification, exploitation of the populace and of the natural resources of the country, and denial to the Lithuanian people of the basic human rights, enumerated in the Universal Declaration of Human Rights proclaimed by the General Assembly of the United Nations on December 10,1948.

Here are a few examples of life in occupied Lithuania illustrating the attitude and practices of the Soviet Union pertaining to the deprivation of the basic human rights.

1. As a result of the Soviet genocidal extermination and deportation practices, the total Lithuanian population declined from 3.2 million in 1939 to 2.7 million in 1959. Under normal conditions, taking into consideration the normal annual population growth of 1.2 percent, the population of Lithuania in 1959 should have been 4 million. In other words, the Soviet Russia through her genocidal practices is responsible for the loss of 940,000 inhabitants of Lithuania.

In spite of Soviet denials, people from captive Lithuania continue to be deported to the remote regions of the Soviet Union. In Lithuania, the Soviet authorities are still using compulsory labor and Russification methods deporting every year thousands of Lithuanians under the guise of the so-called "Corrective Labor Colonies" which is a new name substituting forced labor camps; the so-called "volunteers" and the competition of the so-called training in remote establishments of the Soviet Union (for the most part in Asian Russia) after graduating from various technical schools and institutions of higher learning, and to some degree — performing pre-university "practice" and "studying socialism."

2. Lithuania is the furthermost Catholic country in Eastern Europe. The Lithuanians are deeply religious and resist the Communist designs to eradicate religion in their country, in spite of the tremendous pressure from the Kremlin. By 1945, of the 14 Roman Catholic bishops in the country only one remained. At present there are only two bishops performing their functions: Juozapas Labukas-Matulaitis and Juozapas Pletkus. Both are newly consecrated, both are in their mid-seventies. Two previously consecrated bishops — J. Steponavičius and V. Sladkevičius — were not permitted to assume duties in their bishoprics. Both were exiled from their bishoprics and live under police surveillance. Over 50 percent of the Roman Catholic priests (741 out of 1546) were removed from their parishes (many of them deported to Siberia and some murdered). All monasteries and convents, over 50 churches and 3 priest seminaries were closed. The property and enterprises of the churches, monasteries and convents have been confiscated. The churches have been desecrated and converted into storage houses, art galleries, and atheistic museums. For the use of church buildings the churchgoers have to pay exhorbitant taxes to the government. There is only one priests seminary with approximately 20 seminarians which works under the strict control of the Soviet government. No religious periodicals and books are allowed to be published in occupied Lithuania. Propagation of religion and faith, pilgrimages and processions are forbidden. There are no parochial schools or religious education. Churchgoers are discriminated. Priests and laymen are arrested and sentenced by Soviet courts for teaching prayers or giving communion under a law which forbids "teaching religious exercises to minors."

Other churches and denominations have suffered equally at the hands of Lithuania's occupant, Soviet Russia.

3. The right to freedom of peaceful assembly and association never did exist and does not exist now in captive Lithuania. Thus, there is no possibility for Lithuanian people to exercise the right of self-determination. The Soviet occupation in Lithuania was followed by the dissolution of all political parties except the Communist. Any assembly or association whose purpose is not active support of the Communist regime is termed an act hostile to the established order and punished as a criminal offense. The voters in occupied Lithuania are offered no choice whatsoever. They are confronted with a Soviet-style electoral process, listing only one Communist-selected candidate for each vacant

seat or position. The voters do not have a right to change matters; they must vote to show their loyalty to the goals of the Communist Party.

In addition to denying the right of self-determination, the Soviet occupational regime in Lithuania denies the exercise of other basic human rights, to wit: freedom of speech, freedom of the press, and freedom to choose one's place of work and domicile. The practice of these and other fundamental freedoms spelled in the Universal Declaration of Human Rights is denied to the people of Lithuania to the present day.

April 16, 1968

SUPREME COMMITTEE FOR LIBERATION OF LITHUANIA

29 West 57th Street
New York, New York, USA

No. 198

Statement of the Joint Baltic American Committee on the Thirtieth Anniversary of the Molotov-Ribbentrop Pact and its Secret Protocols

(Aug. 1969)

On August 23, 1969 thirty years will have passed since the signing of the infamous Molotov-Ribbentrop Pact between the Soviet Union and Hitler Germany. A secret protocol attached to the so-called Non-Aggression Treaty entered into by these two countries on that day divided their spheres of interest in the Baltic States, Estonia, Latvia and Lithuania, giving Lithuania to Germany, and Estonia and Latvia to the Soviet Union. Another secret protocol, similarly signed by these two powers one month later, on September 28, 1939, somewhat changed the earlier demarcation line by allotting all three of the Baltic States to the Soviet Union. But the essence of the agreement remained the same: it allowed these two dictatorial powers a free hand to deal as they wished with the smaller democratic nations situated between them.

The three Baltic nations involved were not consulted at all. The fact that they wanted to maintain their independence, their freedom, absolute neutrality and peace did not matter. Peace treaties and non-aggression treaties at that time in existence between the three Baltic

States and the Soviet Union were disregarded. The principle of self-determination of nations and other principles of international law were utterly ignored.

The high-handed settlement by the two dictatorial powers of their potential differences in the territories between them made it possible soon thereafter for both of them to attack and divide Poland, and for Germany to risk entry into the war with the Western powers.

As to the Baltic countries, the events following the signing of the Molotov-Ribbentrop Pact clearly spelled out the intentions of the Soviet Union. Very soon thereafter, by the threat of force, it imposed on Estonia, Latvia and Lithuania so-called mutual-assistance pacts, which allowed the Soviet Union military bases on the territories of these independent states. On September 28 of the same year Estonia, on October 5 Latvia, and on October 10 Lithuania were forced to sign in Moscow their acquiescence to the establishment of such bases, and soon thereafter Soviet troops were stationed within their boundaries. At that time the Soviet Union still pretended to recognize the independence of the three Baltic countries, but in mid-June of 1940 ultimata were presented to them by the Soviet Union, demanding immediate admission of Soviet troops into their territories and radical changes in their governments. On June 15 Soviet troops in great numbers marched into Lithuania, and on June 17 the same fate befell Latvia and Estonia. Thus with the Western powers involved in a war with Germany, and with Germany having agreed to freedom of action for the Soviet Union in the Baltic area, the three small nations stood alone in the face of the Soviet military juggernaut and could not resist its brutal aggression.

In line with orders from the Kremlin and the Red Army in full military control of the three prostrate nations, the Soviet emissaries forced upon them new governments of their liking and staged fake "general elections" of puppet parliaments, which then in turn petitioned admission of the three countries to the Soviet Union. Thus the complete annexation of the three independent Baltic states was accomplished in less than two months after their military occupation and in less than a year after the signing of the Molotov-Ribbentrop Pact.

A number of great statesmen of the Western world in their memoirs, and many political scientists and historians in their books, have accurately described the actual happenings in the Baltic countries in the course of that fateful year and the true meaning of these events. Volumes of official documents, among them the reports of the United States diplomatic missions in the Baltic and nearby countries, have likewise unmasked the attempted disguises by the Soviet Union of this act of forcible military occupation and annexation. The Government of the United States has never recognized this wanton Soviet seizure of Estonia, Latvia and Lithuania and still recognizes the diplomatic representatives of the three republics as the lawful representatives of the Baltic peoples in Washington. As early as July 23, 1940 Under Secretary of State Sumner Welles, acting on behalf of the United States Government, branded the action of the Soviet Union in the Baltic as "devious processes" and spoke of the deliberate annihilation of the Baltic Republics. Those Estonians, Latvians and Lithuanians who escaped the Soviet occupation and are now scattered all over the free world will never cease — individually and through their respective national organizations — to protest the destruction of their native states and to demand their restoration.

It should never be forgotten that the beginning of the Baltic tragedy goes back to the Molotov-Ribbentrop Pact, the high-handed decision of two greedy dictatorial powers to impose their will on their smaller neighbors. It is our firm conviction that there can be no lasting peace in the world until the injustices perpetrated by these dictatorships are corrected; until freedom, independence and a democratic form of government are restored to Estonia, Latvia and Lithuania; and until the principles of international law are in general re-established in relations among all nations.

Therefore, on the thirtieth anniversary of the infamous Molotov-Ribbentrop Pact and its Secret Protocols we address to the United States Government and the American people, as well as to the governments and people of all the nations of the Free World, a plea that they raise their voices in protest and take action, by peaceful means, to remedy the injustice inflicted upon Estonia, Latvia and Lithuania.

For The Joint Baltic American Committee

Heikki A Leesment	Peter P. Lejins	Eugene A. Bartkus
President	*President*	*President*
Estonian National	American Latvian	Lithuanian American
Committee	Association	Council
in the United States	*Chairman*	

No. 199

Letter of the Supreme Committee for the Liberation of Lithuania to the President of the United States, Richard M. Nixon

His Excellency   April 14, 1970
Mr. Richard M. Nixon
President of the United States
The White House
Washington, D.C.

Your Excellency,

Lithuania became one of the first victims of Soviet aggression early in World War II, alongside with her neighbors, Estonia and Latvia, as well as other nations of East-Central Europe. Following the notorious Hitler-Stalin Pact (August 23 and September 28, 1939) by which the two totalitarian powers, Nazi Germany and Soviet Russia, divided Europe into "spheres of their influence," Soviet armed forces attacked and overran Lithuania. This act of aggression was followed by the incorporation of Lithuania into the Soviet Union in blatant violation of international law. Moscow's crimes were condemned throughout the world and the annexation of Lithuania is not recognized by the United States and many other states.

After the end of World War II, the Potsdam Conference (July 27 to August 2, 1945) preliminarily settled some territorial problems of East-Central Europe, leaving their final settlement to the future peace conference.

Almost twenty-five years have elapsed since, and no peace conference is in sight yet because the Soviet Union opposes it. Moscow is anxious to maintain its political and military stronghold over East-Central Europe, so that, at the first opportunity, the Soviets could use it as a springboard to renew their westward expansion.

Therefore, neither the solution of the problem of Berlin, nor the unification of Germany as provided by the Potsdam Conference, nor the restoration of independence of the at present occupied Lithuania, Latvia and Estonia, nor the exercise of self-determination of the Soviet-dominated parts of East-Central Europe, are acceptable and desirable to the Soviet Union. This is clearly shown by the Warsaw Pact, the objective of which is to facilitate Soviet aggression, as evidenced by the recent invasion of Czechoslovakia. To justify their aggression against

Czechoslovakia, the so-called Brezhnev doctrine was created, designed to permit the Soviets to pursue with impunity their willful political, economic and cultural oppression and exploitation of the captive countries. The Soviet Union's active support of North Vietnam is aimed at diverting the attention of the United States from European affairs and simultaneously preventing the establishment of peace in the Far East.

Universal peace is one of the greatest ideals of mankind and the main goal of the United States policy. However, peace is impossible as long as Europe remains divided into free and captive, as long as some of its nations are prevented from exercising their right to self-determination.

The East-Central European area, forcibly separated from Western Europe, cannot develop naturally and must subordinate its political, economic, and cultural aspirations to the alien ways and designs of Soviet Russia. It therefore will remain a constant source of tension and unrest. The Hungarian revolution, the uprisings in Poland, East Germany, Lithuania and the Ukraine, the ever growing underground resistance, and the Czechoslovak effort to shake off the foreign rule, are ample proof that a dentente is impossible until political independence is restored to Soviet-occupied countries.

Although the United States have very important peace commitments in other parts of the world, requiring enormous efforts and sacrifices, Europe should not be left alone to her fate and Soviet designs. In pursuit of a political detente, the restoration of independence to Soviet-occupied countries of East-Central Europe, including Lithuania, is a major task.

The Chief of the Lithuanian Diplomatic Service and the Supreme Committee for Liberation of Lithuania have been following with great interest last year's talks on Strategic Arms Limitations in Helsinki, to be continued in April of this year in Vienna. These talks will have much more far-reaching consequences than the mere limitation of strategic arms of the two great powers. They may turn into preliminaries to a European Security Conference, so eagerly advocated by the member states of the Warsaw Pact.

The Lithuanian people greatly appreciate the United States Government's continuing policy of non-recognition of the forcible incorporation of the Baltic States into Soviet Union and are pleased by the official assurances of the continuation of this policy periodically being received from the Government of the United States.

Keeping in mind the fact that the European Security Conference may be called in the near future, we deem it most important that the restoration of the independence and freedom of the Baltic States —

Lithuania, Latvia and Estonia — be included on the agenda of the Conference.

We would be very grateful to you, Mr. President, if you were to instruct the United States Delegation to the SALT Negotiations in Vienna accordingly.

Please accept, Mr. President, the renewed expression of our highest esteem.

Stasys Lozoraitis
Chief of the Lithuanian
Diplomatic Service

Dr. Juozas K. Valiunas
President of the Supreme
Committee for Liberation
of Lithuania

No. 200

Letter of the Surviving Members of the Lithuanian Constituent Assembly to the Legislative Assemblies of the World

TO THE MEMBERS OF UPPER HOUSES
AND THE SENATES OF RESPECTIVE COUNTRIES

TO THE MEMBERS OF COMMONS,
HOUSES OF REPRESENTATIVES,
PARLIAMENTS OR SIMILAR INSTITUTIONS OF
DEMOCRATIC REPRESENTATIONS
OF RESPECTIVE COUNTRIES

Gentlemen:

On the occasion of the fiftieth anniversary of the historic first meeting of the Lithuanian Constituent Assembly we, the undersigned, its former members living in the free world, submit the following to your kind attention:

The Lithuanian Constituent Assembly, elected in 1920 by popular vote and endowed with the mandate of the Lithuanian people, proclaimed on May 15, 1920, the accomplished fact of the restoration of an independent and sovereign Republic of Lithuania, free from any ties whatsoever with Russia or any other state. The Constituent Assembly also ratified the Lithuanian Peace Treaty with Soviet Russia, whereby the latter proclaimed that she "recognized without reserve the sovereignty and independence of the Lithuanian State with all of the juridical consequences resulting from such recognition, voluntarily and forever renouncing all sovereign rights possessed by Russia over the Lithuanian people and territory."

In 1939, however, the USSR joined with Nazi Germany in a conspiracy against Poland, Rumania, Finland, and the Baltic States. As a result of this Soviet-Nazi collusion, the so-called "mutual assistance pact" was imposed upon Lithuania, several Soviet military bases were established there and, on June 15, 1940, the armed forces of the Soviet Union invaded and occupied the country.

Seeking to camouflage these acts of unprovoked aggression against Lithuania the USSR, after banning all non-Communist parties and arresting over 2,000 prominent Lithuanian leaders in the political, cultural, and economic fields, staged on July 14, 1940, the so-called "elections to the People's Diet," whose candidates were selected by the Kremlin. With the Red Army omnipresent and non-voters exposed to overt threats, the electorate had no choice but to "vote" for the "proposed" slate of candidates.

On July 21, 1940, one hour and three minutes after the opening of its first session, the "People's Diet" adopted a resolution introducing the Soviet system into Lithuania and declaring Lithuania a Soviet Socialist Republic. After a brief intermission, to permit the translation of the next resolution from Russian into Lithuanian, the "People's Diet" adopted a second resolution petitioning the Supreme Soviet of the USSR to admit Lithuania into the USSR, as a constituent republic.

However, all the attempts by the USSR to disguise its aggression have not deceived the world. In its conclusion, the report of the Select Committee of the United States House of Representatives (83rd Congress, H. Res. 346) states:

Any claim by the USSR that the elections, conducted by them in July 1940, were free and voluntary or that the resolutions adopted by the resulting parliaments petitioning for recognition as a Soviet Republic were legal, — are false and without foundation in fact.

And in its Report on the Baltic States (August 23, 1960, Doc. 1173), the Council of Europe revealed that:

Moscow is trying to persuade the free world that the Lithuanian nation has joined the group of Soviet-enslaved peoples by its free

*volition and that the Lithuanian people have made appreciable
economic and cultural progress under Soviet domination ... In fact,
however, Soviet propaganda has failed to produce international legal
act or contractual provision in support of its contention. The
statements made by the Soviet rulers are misleading and contradict
the factual situation in Lithuania.*

We express our deepest gratitude to the Governments and the
parliamentarians of all those countries, which firmly adhere to the
policy of non-recognition of the forcible and illegal annexation, however
camouflaged, and which support the right of self-government of all
nations. We also extend our thanks to the Governments, parliamentarians, and individuals in the free world who support the
Lithuanian people in the defense of their human rights and in their fight
for Lithuania's freedom and independence.

At the same time we appeal to the Governments, parliamentarians, as
well as to all freedom loving people to exert their influence on every
appropriate occasion to:

(1) insure that no international institution, conference, or treaty
explicitly or implicitly lend recognition or international legality to the
Soviet acts of aggression;

(2) demand that the USSR withdraw its military and police forces as
well as its administrative apparatus from occupied Lithuania and the
other Soviet-occupied countries, enabling their respective peoples to
exercise their rights of self-determination and the free choice of
government.

MEMBERS OF THE LITHUANIAN CONSTITUENT ASSEMBLY:

ELIZIEJUS DRAUGELIS
Farmers' Union

JUOZAS PRONSKUS
Peasant Populist Union

MAGDALENA GALDIKIENE
Christian Democratic Party

KAZYS ŠKIRPA
Peasant Populist Union

MYKOLAS KRUPAVIČIUS
Christian Democratic Party

New York
May 15, 1970

ANTANAS MILČIUS
Labor Federation

JONAS PAKALKA
Social Democratic Party

CHAPTER IV

PRINCIPLE OF NON-RECOGNITION OF THE USE OF FORCE AND CONQUEST IN INTERNATIONAL RELATIONS

A. LAW AND PRINCIPLES

No. 201

Covenant Of The League Of Nations

The High Contracting Parties,
   by the acceptance of obligations not to resort to war,
   by the prescription of open, just and honorable relations between
      nations,
   by the firm establishment of the understandings of international law
      as the actual rule of conduct among Governments, and
   by the maintenance of justice and a scrupulous respect for all treaty
      obligations in the dealings of organized peoples with one another,
   Agree to this Covenant of the League of Nations.

Article 10

GUARANTEES AGAINST AGGRESSION

The Members of the League undertake to respect and preserve as against external aggression the territorial integrity and existing political independence of all Members of the League. In case of any such aggression or in case of any threat or danger of such aggression the Council shall advise upon the means by which this obligation shall be fulfilled.

Article 12

DISPUTES TO BE SUBMITTED FOR SETTLEMENT

1. The Members of the League agree that, if there should arise between them any dispute likely to lead to a rupture, they will submit the matter either to arbitration or *judicial settlement* or to inquiry by the Council, and they agree in no case to resort to war until three months after the award by the arbitrators or *the judicial decision* or the report by the Council.

2. In any case under this Article the award of the arbitrators *or the judicial decision* shall be made within a reasonable time, and the report

Article 13

ARBITRATION OR JUDICIAL SETTLEMENT

1. The Members of the League agree that, whenever any dispute shall arise between them which they recognize to be suitable for submission to arbitration *or judicial settlement,* and which can not be satisfactorily settled by diplomacy, they will submit the whole subject matter to arbitration *or judicial settlement.*

2. Disputes as to the interpretation of a treaty, as to any question of international law, as to the existence of any fact which if established would constitute a breach of any international obligation, or as to the extent and nature of the reparation to be made for any such breach, or declared to be among those which are generally suitable for submission to arbitration *or judicial settlement.*

3. *For the consideration of any such dispute, the court to which the case is referred shall be the Permanent Court of International Justice, established in accordance with Article 14, or any tribunal agreed on by the parties to the dispute or stipulated in any convention existing between them.*

4. The Members of the League agree that they will carry out in full good faith any award or *decision* that may be rendered, and that they will not resort to war against a Member of the League which complies therewith. In the event of any failure to carry out such an award or *decision*, the Council shall propose what steps should be taken to give effect thereto.

No. 202

BRIAND-KELLOGG PACT
GENERAL TREATY FOR THE RENUNCIATION OF WAR
PACT OF PARIS

Text of Kellogg-Briand Pact for the Renunciation of War, August 27, 1928

The President of the German Reich, the President of the United States of America, His Majesty the King of Great Britain, Ireland and the British Dominions beyond the Seas, Emperor of India, His Majesty the King of Italy, His Majesty the Emperor of Japan, the President of the Republic of Poland, the President of the Czechoslovak Republic;

Deeply sensible of their solemn duty to promote the welfare of mankind;

Persuaded that the time has come when a frank renunciation of war as an instrument of national policy should be made to the end that the peaceful and friendly relations now existing between their peoples may be perpetuated;

Convinced that all changes in their relations with one another should be sought only by pacific means and be the result of a peaceful and orderly process, and that any signatory Power which shall hereafter seek to promote its national interests by resort to war should be denied the benefits furnished by this Treaty;

Hopeful that, encouraged by their example, all the other nations of the world will join in this humane endeavor and by adhering to the present Treaty as soon as it comes into force bring their peoples within the scope of its beneficent provisions, thus uniting the civilized nations of the world in a common renunciation of war as an instrument of their national policy;

Have decided to conclude a Treaty and for that purpose have appointed as their respective Plenipotentiaries:

Article I

The High Contracting Parties solemnly declare in the names of their respective peoples that they condemn recourse to war for the solution of international controversies and renounce it as an instrument of national policy in their relations with one another.

Article II

The High Contracting Parties agree that the settlement or solution of all disputes or conflicts of whatever nature or of whatever origin they may be, which may arise among them, shall never be sought except by pacific means.

Article III

The present Treaty shall be ratified by the High Contracting Parties named in the Preamble in accordance with their respective constitutional requirements, and shall take effect as between them as soon as all their several instruments of ratification shall have been deposited at Washington.

This Treaty shall, when it has come into effect as prescribed in the preceding paragraph, remain open as long as may be necessary for adherence by all the other Powers of the world. Every instrument evidencing the adherence of a Power shall be deposited at Washington and the Treaty shall immediately upon such deposit become effective as between the Power thus adhering and the other Powers parties hereto.

It shall be the duty of the Government of the United States to furnish each Government named in the Preamble and every Government subsequently adhering to this Treaty with a certified copy of the Treaty and of every instrument of ratification or adherence. It shall also be the duty of the Government of the United States telegraphically to notify such Governments immediately upon the deposit with it of each instrument of ratification or adherence.

In faith whereof the respective Plenipotentiaies have signed this Treaty in the French and English languages both texts having equal force, and hereunto affix their seals.

Done at Paris, the twenty-seventh day of August in the year one thousand nine hundred and twenty-eight.

Editor's Comment: The treaty was binding on 63 nations, including Germany and U.S.S.R., at the outbreak of the war in 1939. In the opinion of the International Military Tribunal at Nuremburg, the Briand-Kellogg Pact made war of aggression illegal, and those who planned and waged such a war were criminals.

No. 203

The Stimson Doctrine

The Secretary of State to the Consul General at Nanking (Peck) *

WASHINGTON, January 7, 1932 — noon.

2. Please deliver to the Foreign Office, as through the Legation, on behalf of your Government as soon as possible the following note:

---

* The same, *mutatis mutandis*, to the Ambassador in Japan as telegram No. 7, *Foreign Relations*, Japan, 1931-1941, vol. I, p. 76; text of note repeated to the Consul at Geneva in telegram No. 4, January 7, 1 p.m., with instructions to transmit the note to the Secretary General of the League of Nations.

"With the recent military operations about Chinchow, the last remaining administrative authority of the Government of the Chinese Republic in South Manchuria, as it existed prior to September 18th, 1931, has been destroyed. The American Government continues confident that the work of the neutral commission recently authorized by the Council of the League of Nations will facilitate an ultimate solution of the difficulties now existing between China and Japan. But in view of the present situation and of its own rights and obligations therein, the American Government deems it to be its duty to notify both the Government of the Chinese Republic and the Imperial Japanese Government that it cannot admit the legality of any situation *de facto* nor does it intend to recognize any treaty or agreement entered into between those Governments, or agents thereof, which may impair the treaty rights of the United States or its citizens in China, or to the international policy relative to China, commonly known as the open door policy; and that it does not intend to recognize any situation, treaty or agreement which may be brought about by means contrary to the covenants and obligations of the Pact of Paris of August 27, 1928, to which Treaty both China and Japan, as well as the United States, are parties."

State that an identical note is being sent to the Japanese Government.
Repeat whole of above to Legation.

STIMSON

No. 204

Resolution Of The
Eighth Pan-American Conference

December 22, 1938

... the Buenos Aires Conference reaffirmed the principle of non-recognition in two instruments: The *"Declaration of Principles of Inter-American Solidarity and Cooperation,"*adopted on *December 21, 1936,* stated among the principles "accepted by the *American Community of Nations"* the *"proscription of territorial conquest, and that, in consequence, no acquisition made through violence shall be recognized."* The *"Convention to Coordinate, Extend and Assure the Fulfillment* of the Existing Treaties between the American States," signed on December 23, 1936, provided in Article 6 that the Contracting Parties reaffirmed their loyalty to the principles enunciated in the following five agreements: the Gondra Treaty of May 3, 1923; the Briand-Kellogg Pact of Paris of August 27, 1928; the Conventions of January 5, 1929, on Inter-American Conciliation and Arbitration; and the Argentine Anti-War Pact.

At the Eighth Inter-American Conference, *held at Lima* in 1938, no treaties or conventions were concluded; the principle of non-recognition, however, was again reaffirmed in the following resolution, adopted on December 22, 1938:

The ... Conference ... declares that it reiterates as a fundamental principle of the Public Law of America, that the occupation or acquisition of territory or any modification of territorial or boundary arrangement obtained through conquest by force or by non-pacific means shall not be valid or have legal effect.

No. 205

Resolution Of The
Assembly Of The League Of Nations

March 11, 1932

The Assembly

Considering that the provisions of the Covenant are entirely applicable to the present dispute, more particularly as regards:

(1) The principle of a scrupulous respect for treaties;

(2) The undertaking entered into by Members of the League of Nations to respect and preserve as against external aggression the territorial integrity and existing political independence of all the Members of the League;

(3) Their obligation to submit any dispute which may arise between them to procedure for peaceful settlement;

Adopting the principles laid down by the acting President of the Council, M. Briand, in his declaration of December 10, 1931;

Recalling the fact that twelve Members of the Council again invoked those principles in their appeal to the Japanese Government on February 16, 1932, when they declared that no infringement of the territorial integrity and no change in the political independence of any Member of the League brought about in disregard of Art. 10 of the

Covenant ought to be recognized as valid and effectual by Members of the League of Nations;

Considering that the principles governing international relations and the peaceful settlement of disputes between Members of the League above referred to are in full harmony with the Pact of Paris, which is one of the cornerstones of the peace organization of the world and under Art. 2 of which "the High Contracting Parties agree that the settlement or solution of disputes or conflicts, of whatever nature and whatever origin they may be, which might arise among them shall never be sought except by pacific means";

Pending the steps which it may ultimately take for the settlement of the dispute which has been referred to it;

Proclaims the binding nature of the principles and provisions referred to above and declares that it is incumbent upon the Members of the League of Nations not to recognize any situation, treaty or agreement which may be brought about by means contrary to the Covenant of the League of Nations or to the Pact of Paris.

No. 206

Resolution Of The
Council Of The League Of Nations

April 17, 1935

The Council,

Considering, (1) That the scrupulous respect of all treaty obligations is a fundamental principle of international life and an essential condition of the maintenance of peace;

(2) That it is an essential principle of the law of nations that no Power can liberate itself from the engagements of a treaty nor modify the stipulations thereof unless with the consent of the other contracting parties;

. . . .

I. Declares that Germany has failed in the duty which lies upon all the Members of the international community to respect the undertakings which they have contracted, and condemns any unilateral repudiation of international obligations . . .

League of Nations, *Official Journal* (1935) 551.

"No state can relieve itself of the obligations of a treaty or modify its stipulations except by the agreement, secured through peaceful means, of the other contracting parties."

"Whenever a treaty becomes impossible of execution through the fault of the party entering into the obligation, or through circumstances which at the moment of concluding it were under control of this party and unknown to the other party, the former shall be responsible for damages resulting from its non-execution."

Arts. 10 and 12, convention on treaties, adopted by the Sixth International Conferenke of American States, Feb. 20, 1928: *Final Act* (Habana, 1928) pp. 135, 139.

No. 207

Speech Of The Soviet Commissar For Foreign Affairs, Litvinov, To The Council Of The League Of Nations

May 12, 1938

His remarks on nonrecognition are highly significant. Said Maxim Litvinov:

Among the means for combating aggression and defending its Members which the League has at its disposal, non-recognition does not by any means play a conspicuous part. It is improbable that anyone would assert that the mere threat of non-recognition may avert aggression, or that non-recognition itself might free the victim of aggression from the grip of the conqueror . . . .

It would be quite wrong, however, to assert that resolutions on non-recognition are in themselves devoid of any particular value. While such resolutions have in every case a certain moral significance, and give satisfaction to public opinion, they also cause the aggressor some preoccupations and inconveniences, as is evidenced by the efforts which aggressors usually make to obtain recognition of their conquests, if only in an indirect way.

But, according to circumstances, non-recognition may be of vast importance, not only morally, but also politically — particularly when the victim of aggression itself continues to fight for its independence and for the integrity of its territory. In such cases, the recognition of the results of acts of violent aggression, or the abandonment of the policy of non-recognition, would be equivalent to abetting the aggressor directly, and to stabbing his victim in the back by discouraging and demoralising him. We have to reckon, not only with the question whether any struggle between the aggressor and his victims has come to an end, but also — should that have occurred for the time being — whether there are chances of the struggle being renewed, and likewise we have to reckon with other circumstances which may bring about a change in the situation created by aggressive acts of violence.[45]

Whatever the decision on the question before us, and whatever the conclusions which individual States will think it necessary to draw, on their own responsibility, from our discussion, one thing must be clear: The League of Nations has not changed its view of those actions which resulted in an Ethiopian problem arising within the League, and none of the condemnations of such activities adopted by the League is withdrawn. It must be made even more clear that the League of Nations has not changed its opinion on the general principle of non-recognition of the accomplished fact produced by aggression, and on the appropriate resolutions adopted by the League in other cases. The latter particularly applies in cases where the States which have been the victims of attack have aroused the amazement and admiration of the world by the valiance of their citizens who continue to fight the aggressor with unweakening energy, obstinacy and fortitude. It must be clear that the League of Nations has no intention of changing its attitude, whether to the direct seizure and annexation of other people's territory, or to those cases where such annexations are camouflaged by the setting-up of puppet "national" governments, allegedly independent, but in reality serving merely as a screen for, and an agency of, the foreign invader.

I have still to remark briefly on the other aspects of the question which I have mentioned. When the United Kingdom Government puts forward its motion to grant freedom of action to all League Members, it bases its principal argument on the fact that many Members of the League, in violation of League resolutions, have already taken steps towards recognizing the annexation of Ethiopia, and therefore the same opportunity should be afforded to others. This may be fair from the standpoint of equality of obligations, but equality at such a low level can hardly be an ideal of the League. If we once admit that principle, we may expect that it will be sufficient for one or a few Members of the League to break one of its decisions — and that may easily happen, in the present state of international morality — for all other Members of the League, one by one, to follow them.

We cannot admit that breaches of international obligations are examples to be followed. The League of Nations and its individual

Members have made mistakes, errors and blunders; they have not always fulfilled their obligations. We should recognize and condemn such failures and take measures to prevent their repetition in future, but on no account must we legalize them, or lower the collective responsibility of the League of Nations to their level. Of course, the League's decisions are not eternal, and can always be reviewed and corrected by the League, at the request of individual League Members, but it is the League collectively which has to recognize such decisions as being out of date and invalid, not the individual Members, when they think it required, or when it seems to be required, by their national interests at the time. The League Council should leave no room for doubt that it not only does not approve such anarchic activities, or erect them into a virtue, but severely condemns those of its Members who are the first to set the example of engaging in them.

Mr. Litvinov concluded:

If we had before us any resolution or résumé of our discussion, I should insist on its reflecting the considerations I have laid before you. To neglect them will not allow the League to remain in existence much longer, and I should like to think that its preservation answers to the interests of peace and to the wishes of the vast majority of States.

Editor's Comment: Litvinov delivered the speech on the occasion of Great Britain's recognition of the Italian annexation of Ethiopia.

No. 208

Resolutions Of The Assembly And Council Of The League Of Nations

December 12, the Soviet Government replied that it was not able to accept the invitation for reasons set out in the telegram of December 4 to the Secretary General. The Special Committee submitted to the Assembly a report culminating in the following resolution:

The Assembly

I

. . . .

Solemnly condemns the action taken by th U.S.S.R. against the State of Finland;

Urgently appeals to every Member of the League to provide Finland with such material and humanitarian assistance as may be in its power and to refrain from any action which might weaken Finland's power of resistance.

Authorizes the Secretary-General to lend the aid of his technical services on the organization of the aforesaid assistance to Finland;

And likewise authorizes the Secretary-General, in view of the Assembly resolution of October 4, 1931, to consult non-member States with a view to possible co-operation.

II

Whereas, notwithstanding an invitation extended to it on two occasions, the U.S.S.R. has refused to be present at the examination of its dispute with Finland before the Council and the Assembly;

And whereas, by thus refusing to recognize the duty of the Council and the Assembly as regards the execution of Article 15 of the Covenant, it has failed to observe one of the League's most essential covenants for the safeguarding of peace and the security of nations;

And whereas it has vainly attempted to justify its refusal on the ground of the relations which it has established with an alleged Government which is neither de jure nor de facto the Government recognized by the people of Finland in accordance with the free working of their institutions;

And whereas the U.S.S.R. has not merely violated the Covenant of the League, but has by its own action placed itself outside the Covenant;

And whereas the Council is competent under Article 16 of the Covenant to consider what consequences should follow from this situation;

Recommends the Council to pronounce upon the question.

The resolution of the Special Committee was adopted.

In the ensuing debate the delegates unanimously denounced the action of the Soviet Government.

The Council

Having taken cognizance of the resolution adopted by the Assembly on December 14th, 1939, regarding the appeal of the Finnish Government;

1. Associates itself with the condemnation by the Assembly of the action of the U.S.S.R. against the Finnish State; and

2. For the reasons set forth in the Resolution of the Assembly, in virtue of Article 16, paragraph 4, of the Covenant,

Finds, that, by its act, the U.S.S.R. has placed itself outside the League of Nations. It follows that the U.S.S.R. is no longer a Member of the League.

Editor's Comment: When Finland raised the question of Soviet aggression, the U.S.S.R. refused to participate in the discussion. The position of the U.S.S.R., stated by Molotov, was: a) the U.S.S.R. was not at war with Finland: b) the U.S.S.R. had sent its troops into

Finland in support of the legitimate government in order to help liquidate the holdovers from the former regime: c) the Finnish delegate to the League represented the former illegal regime, and thus his statements did not represent the Finnish people. The Soviet objections did not impress the members of the League, and on December 14, the U.S.S.R. was expelled.

No. 209

Address Of Franklin D. Roosevelt, President Of The United States To The American Youth Congress

February 10, 1940

More than twenty years ago, while most of you were very young children, I had the utmost sympathy for the Russian people. In the early days of Communism, I recognized that many leaders in Russia were bringing education and better health and, above all, better opportunity to millions who had been kept in ignorance and serfdom under the imperial regime. I disliked the regimentation under Communism. I abhorred the indiscriminate killings of thousands of innocent victims. I heartily deprecated the banishment of religion — though I knew that some day Russia would return to religion for the simple reason that four or five thousand years of recorded history have proven that mankind has always believed in God in spite of many abortive attempts to exile God.

I, with many of you, hoped that Russia would work out its own problems, and that its government would eventually become a peace-loving, popular government with a free ballot, which would not interfere with the integrity of its neighbors.

That hope is today either shattered or put away in storage against some better day. The Soviet Union, as everybody who has the courage to face the fact knows is run by a dictatorship as absolute as any other dictatorship in the world. It has allied itself with another dictatorship, and it has invaded a neighbor so infinitesimally small that it could do no conceivable possible harm to the Soviet Union, a neighbor which seeks only to live at peace as a democracy, and a liberal, forward-looking democracy at that.

It has been said that some of you are Communists. That is a very unpopular term these days. As Americans you have a legal and constitutional right to call yourselves Communists, those of you who do.

You have a right peacefully and openly to advocate certain ideals of theoretical Communism; but as Americans you have not only a right but a sacred duty to confine your advocacy of changes in law to the methods prescribed by the Constitution of the United States — and you have no American right, by act or deed of any kind, to subvert the Government and the Constitution of this Nation.

Editor's comment: Franklin D. Roosevelt was always amicably inclined toward the U.S.S.R. It will be recalled that he was the President who established diplomatic relations with the Soviet Union, and later, during the Big Three conferences of 1944-45, his relations to Stalin were those of personal friendship. Yet, in 1940, the blatancy of Soviet aggression against Finland was enough to fill even Roosevelt with distaste. The Soviet aggression against the Baltic States which occurred soon afterwards was no different from the attack on Finland — only more successful. It was a continuation of the same policy, by the same men, in implementation of the same secret protocols with Germany.

No. 210
Excerpts from the Judgement of the International Military Tribunal at Nuremberg

"It was contended before the Tribunal that the annexation of Austria was justified by the strong desire expressed in many quarters for the union of Austria and Germany; that there were many matters in common between the two peoples that made this union desirable; and that in the result the object was achieved without bloodshed.

These matters, *even if true,* are really immaterial, for the facts plainly prove that *the methods employed* to achieve the object were those *of an aggressor.* The ultimate factor was the armed might of Germany ready to be used if any resistance was encountered. . ."

Editor's comment: The Soviets justify their actions in the Baltic States by claiming that the Baltic peoples themselves cast off their government by spontaneous revolution and expressed the strong desire to be joined in political union with the working classes of the Soviet Union, for the common protection of the interests of the proletariat.

With a few changes of terminology, this is precisely the German defense against the charge of perpetrating aggression in the Austrian anschluss of 1938.

In fact, there was a great deal of popular support for the anschluss, a keen popular belief in the ties of teutonic aryan race which bound Austria to Germany and the common destiny of the Germanic people, and a strong pro-Nazi faction in the country. Nonetheless, German officials were convicted and executed because of the role of German agents within Austria and the explicit threat of the German army on Austria's borders, which constituted aggression regardless of internal political developments. The basis for this is the principle of non-interference in the domestic affairs of other States. The Soviet members of the tribunal were the harshest and most implacable in demanding the death penalty for the implicated German officials.

In the case of the Soviet Union and Lithuania, there were no Russian population in Lithuania; the massive Soviet garrisons inside the latter country, and the compromising supervisory roles of Dekanozov, the Special Emissary, and Pozdniakov, the Soviet Minister, in the downfall of the ancien regime are clear interference in Lithuanian domestic affairs. The parallelisms between the incorporation of the Baltic States into the U.S.S.R. and the Austrian anschluss are too exact. It would seem , then, the Soviet Union stands convicted by its own standards.

B. NONRECOGNITION OF THE INCORPORATION OF LITHUANIA INTO THE U.S.S.R.

No. 211

Executive Order No. 8389

27A. The War Spreads; the Funds in the
United States of Victims of Aggression Are
Protected. Executive Order 8389,
April 10, 1940.

By virtue of the authority vested in me by section 5(b) of the Act of October 6, 1917 (40 Stat. 411), as amended by section 2 of the Act of March 9, 1933 (48 Stat. 1), and by virtue of all other authority vested in me, I, FRANKLIN D. ROOSEVELT, PRESIDENT OF THE UNITED STATES OF AMERICA, do hereby amend Executive Order No. 6560, dated January 15, 1934, regulating transactions in foreign exchange, transfers of credit, and the export of coin and currency by adding the following sections after section 8 thereof:

"Section 9. Notwithstanding any of the provisions of sections 1 to 8, inclusive, of this Order, all of the following are prohibited, except as specifically authorized in regulations or licenses issued by the Secretary of the Treasury pursuant to this Order, if involving property in which Norway or Denmark or any national thereof has at any time on or since April 8, 1940, had any interest of any nature whatsoever, direct or indirect:

"A. All transfers of credit between any banking institutions within the United States; and all transfers of credit between any banking institution within the United States and any banking institution outside the United States (including any principal, agent, home office, branch, or correspondent outside of the United States, of a banking institution within the United States);

"B. All payments by any banking institution within the United States;

"C. All transactions in foreign exchange by any person within the United States;

"D. The export or withdrawal from the United States, or the earmarking of gold or silver coin or bullion or currency by any person within the United States; and

"E. Any transaction for the purpose or which has the effect of evading or avoiding the foregoing prohibitions.

"Section 10. *Additional Reports.*

"A. Reports under oath shall be filed, on such forms, at such time or times and from time to time, and by such persons, as provided in regulations prescribed by the Secretary of the Treasury, with respect to all property of any nature whatsoever of which Norway or Denmark or any national thereof has or had an interest of any nature whatsoever, direct or indirect, and with respect to any acquisition, transfer, disposition, or any other dealing in such property.

"B. The Secretary of the Treasury may require the furnishing under oath of additional and supplemental information, including the production of any books of account, contracts, letters or other papers with respect to the matters concerning which reports are required to be filled under this Section.

"Section 11. *Additional Definitions.* In addition to the definitions contained in Section 7, the following definitions are prescribed:

"A. The terms 'Norway', and 'Denmark', respectively, mean the State and the Government of Norway and Denmark on April 8, 1940, and any political subdivisions, agencies and instrumentalities thereof, including territories, dependencies and possessions, and all persons acting or purporting to act directly or indirectly for the benefit or on behalf of the foregoing. The terms 'Norway' and 'Denmark', respectively, shall also include any and all other governments (including political subdivisions, agencies, and instrumentalities thereof and persons acting or purporting to act directly or indirectly for the benefit or on behalf thereof) to the extent and only to the extent that such governments exercise or claim to exercise de jure or de facto sovereignty over the area which, on April 8, 1940, constituted Norway or Denmark.

"B. The term 'national' of Norway or Denmark shall include any person who has been or whom there is reasonable cause to believe has been domiciled in, or a subject, citizen or resident of Norway or Denmark at any time since April 8, 1940, but shall not include any individual domiciled and residing in the United States on April 8, 1940, and shall also include any partnership, association, or other organization, including any corporation organized under the laws of, or which on April 8, 1940, had its principal place of business in Norway or Denmark or which on or after such date has been controlled by, or a substantial part of the stock, shares, bonds, debentures, or other securities of which has been owned or controlled by, directly or indirectly, one or more persons, who have been, or whom there is reasonable cause to believe have been, domiciled in, or the subjects, citizens or residents of Norway or Denmark at any time on or since April 8, 1940, and all persons acting or purporting to act directly or indirectly for the benefit or on behalf of the foregoing.

"C. The term 'banking institution' as used in section 9 includes any person engaged primarily or incidentally in the business of banking, of granting or transferring credits, or of purchasing or selling foreign exchange or procuring purchasers and sellers thereof, as principal or agent, or any person holding credits for others as a direct or incidental part of his business, or brokers; and, each principal, agent, home office, branch or correspondent of any person so engaged shall be regarded as a separate 'banking institution.'

"Section 12. *Additional Regulations.* The Regulations of November 12, 1934, are hereby modified insofar as they are inconsistent with the provisions of sections 9 to 11, inclusive, of this Order, and except as so modified are hereby continued in full force and effect. The Secretary of the Treasury is authorized and empowered to prescribe from time to time regulations to carry out the purposes of sections 9 to 11, inclusive, of this Order as amended, and to provide in such regulations or by rulings made pursuant thereto, the conditions under which licenses may be granted by such agencies as the Secretary of the Treasury may designate."

Note: The executive order was issued immediately following the invasion by Germany of Norway and Denmark. At that time there were approximately $267,000,000 of Norwegian and Danish credits and other assets in the United States. The executive order prohibited transactions in them, except pursuant to licenses authorized by the Secretary of the Treasury.

This executive order was followed by similar executive orders after other nations were invaded or subjected to the domination of the aggressor nations.

On May 10, 1940, similar control was placed over $1,619,000,000 of the Dutch assets, $760,000,000 of Belgian assets, and $48,000,000 of Luxembourg assets. On later occasions the same control has been applied to $1,593,000,000 of French assets, $29,000,000 of the assets of the Baltic countries, $53,000,000 of Rumanian assets, as well as to the assets of Bulgaria, Hungary, Yugoslavia, and Greece. By October 10, 1940, this "freezing control" had been extended to more than $4,000,000,000 of foreign assets.

In June, 1941, the assets of Germany and Italy were also frozen.

In July, 1941, the assets of Japan were frozen; and also at the specific request of China, the freezing order was extended to Chinese assets in this country.

These exchange controls were somewhat similar to the exchange controls exercised by our Government during the first World War in 1917, and also during the banking crisis of 1933.

The purpose of using this power of government in 1940 was primarily to prevent the aggressor nations from using, for their own purposes, these billions of dollars of assets in the United States which really belonged to their victims. This vast sum of money would unquestionably have been used by the aggressors to carry on their program of world conquest and destruction of democratic nations and democratic principles. It would not only have been great weakness, but absolute foolishness, to permit these billions of dollars under our control, to be grabbed by the aggressor nations and used against our own national interest. Besides, as a matter of ordinary justice, it would have been a betrayal of the confidence which had been placed in the integrity and free institutions of our country. For these assets had been deposited by their owners in our establishments in order to protect them from confiscation by invading conquerors.

No. 212

Executive Order No. 8484

Amendment of Executive Order No. 8389
of April 10, 1940, As Amended

By virtue of the authority vested in me by section 5 (b) of the Act of October 6, 1917 (40 Stat. 411), as amended, and by virtue of all other authority vested in me. I, FRANKLIN D. ROOSEVELT, PRESIDENT of the UNITED STATES OF AMERICA, do hereby amend Executive Order No. 8389[1]of April 10, 1940, as amended, so as to extend all the provisions thereof to, and with respect to property in which Latvia, Estonia or Lithuania or any national thereof has at any time on or since July 10, 1940, had any interest of any nature whatsoever, direct or indirect; except that, in defining "Latvia", "Estonia", "Lithuania" and "national" thereof the date "July 10, 1940" shall be substituted for the dates appearing in the definitions of countries and nationals thereof.

FRANKLIN D. ROOSEVELT

THE WHITE HOUSE,

July 15, 1940.
[No 8484]
[F.R. Doc. 40-2938; Filed, July 16, 1940; 10:12 a.m.]

No. 213

Memorandum by the Assistant Chief of the European Affairs Division of the U. S. State Department, Henderson *

[WASHINGTON,] July 15, 1940.

As you are aware, on one pretext or another the Soviet Government,

---

* Addressed to the Assistant Secretary of State, Adolf A. Berle, Jr., and to the Adviser on Political Relations, James Clement Dunn. A note written by the latter, at the beginning of the memorandum, reads: "I feel funds of all 3 of these countries should be blocked on same basis as those of countries occupied by Germany."

by demands backed up with threats of force, has during the last six weeks forced the three Baltic countries of Estonia, Latvia, and Lithuania to permit the entrance of Soviet troops aggregating about 500,000 men. Under Soviet pressure the Governments in all three countries have been replaced by governments which are mere Soviet puppets. The President of Estonia is also apparently without any power whatsoever.

Under Soviet pressure elections were ordered in these three countries for yesterday and today. It is clear from reports which reach us that these elections are merely a mockery. Only persons approved by the Soviet Government or the Communist International are permitted to stand as candidates. It appears likely that following these so-called elections it will be arranged for these three republics to be merged into the Soviet Union. Whether these arrangements will be put into effect at once or whether the Soviet Government will be satisfied for some time to come with having the three countries under its actual control, although fictitiously independent, remains to be seen.

On Saturday, July 13, shortly after noon, the Latvian Minister presented the attached note to Mr. Atherton after having endeavored unsuccessfully to obtain an appointment with the Secretary or Under Secretary. In this note he points out that in view of the circumstances surrounding the holding of the elections in Latvia he "reserves the right not to recognize the results of the coming elections and the acts emanating therefrom". The Minister also states that in United States banks there are deposits of the Latvian State and of Latvian banks, corporations and private citizens, and that there are a number of Latvian ships in the waters of the western hemisphere. He asks that if attempts are made to alienate these deposits, vessels and other Latvian property and interests in the United States, the American Government safeguard and secure the said deposits and property. It is understood that the Lithuanian Minister has also prepared a note which he plans to hand to the Department within the next few days, if he has not already done so, in which he will point out the illegality of the elections in Lithuania. There is no Estonian Minister in this country. The only representative of that government in the United States is the Estonian Consul General in New York.

The recent events in the Baltic States have raised a number of rather important questions. The note of the Latvian Minister merely serves to render these questions more active. Among these questions are the following:

1. Is the Government of the United States to apply certain standards of judgment and conduct to aggression by Germany and Japan which it will not apply to aggression by the Soviet Union. In other words, is the Government of the United States to follow one policy with respect to, say, Czechoslovakia, Denmark, and German-occupied Poland, and another policy with respect to Latvia, Estonia, Lithuania, and Finland, which before the end of the year is likely to suffer the same fate as the other three Baltic States. Is the United States to continue to refuse to recognize the fruits of aggression regardless of who the aggressor may be, or for reasons of expediency to close its eyes to the fact that certain nations are committing aggression upon their neighbors. If our Government at this juncture desires to take no step which might arouse the displeasure of the Soviet Union it would possibly be wise for it to overlook the present Soviet aggressive acts in the Baltic States, as well as similar acts which will probably take place in Finland. On the other hand, our failure to recognize Soviet conquests just now, although not pleasant to the Soviet Government, may possibly place another card in our hands when, if ever, a conference regarding the future of Europe takes place.

2. Does the Government of the United States desire to take steps to restrain the export of funds in this country belonging to the States of Latvia, Estonia and Lithuania, as it has done recently in the case of countries taken over by Germany. If no restriction on the export of these funds is laid down, it seems almost certain that they will pass into the Soviet Treasury. It is impossible at the present time to estimate the full amount. It seems likely that the assets of all three countries in the United States will not amount to much more than 12 or 13 million dollars. In this connection it will be observed that if the three countries in question are absorbed into the Soviet Union, the United States will probably not receive one cent of the several million dollars which the governments of these three countries owe us. Furthermore, American interests in those three countries will probably be a total loss. It is estimated that these interests will not approximate more than two or three hundred thousand dollars, although it is difficult to obtain figures. It will be recalled that the Soviet Government announced some time ago that since the acts of nationalization of that part of Poland which has

been annexed to the Soviet Union took place prior to the entry of that territory into the Soviet Union, the Soviet Government could not be held responsible for losses incurred as a result of those acts. It is possible that in the interim before the incorporation of the three Baltic States into the Soviet Union, the new puppet governments of those States might denounce all public indebtedness and nationalize property, and that the Soviet Government, after their entry into the Soviet Union, will take the attitude that it is not responsible for the acts of such puppet governments.

At the suggestion of Mr. Berle, which I conveyed to Mr. Livesey last week, Mr. Livesey has informally asked the Treasury to investigate the holdings of Latvia, Estonia, and Lithuania in this country in American banks and to request the banks in which the holdings are extensive to inform the American Government, before any large withdrawals are permitted. It is probable that during the present week endeavors will be made by the Soviet Government to obtain possession of these funds. It is essential, therefore, that a decision with respect to them be made at once.

3. Are vessels of the Baltic States in American harbors to be permitted to depart freely or are they to be held up like the vessels of a number of countries which have been taken over by Germany. For some time the ability of the Soviet Union to handle its foreign trade has been suffering because of lack of ships. For the last several months the Soviet Embassy has been endeavoring to arrange for the charter of Latvian bottoms in order to transport material to Vladivostok. Apparently the Soviet plan now is to force the Latvian Government and private owners to permit Soviet organizations to charter Latvian and other Baltic ships and to call these ships into Soviet ports where they are to be nationalized. Some of the Latvian ships are excellent and have a high rating in Lloyds, according to information received from our Legation at Riga. The Latvian Minister states that at the present time a Latvian vessel is in Baltimore taking on cargo for Vladivostok in pursuance of a recent Soviet charter. The Maritime Commission is undoubtedly in a much better position than this Department to decide whether it would be advantageous to the American Government to retain these vessels or to permit them to depart.

LOY W. HENDERSON

No. 214

**Statement by Sumner Welles,
Acting U.S. Secretary of State,
to the American Press**

BALTIC REPUBLICS

Statement by the Acting Secretary of State, Mr. Welles

[Released to the press July 23, 1940]

During these past few days the devious processes whereunder the political independence and territorial integrity of the three small Baltic republics — Estonia, Latvia, and Lithuania — were to be deliberately annihilated by one of their more powerful neighbors, have been rapidly drawing to their conclusion.

From the day when the peoples of these republics first gained their independent and democratic form of government the people of the United States have watched their admirable progress in self-government with deep and sympathetic interest.

The policy of this Government is universally known. The people of the United States are opposed to predatory activities no matter whether they are carried on by the use of force or by the threat of force. They are likewise opposed to any form of intervention on the part of one state, however powerful, in the domestic concerns of any other sovereign state, however weak.

These principles constitute the very foundations upon which the existing relationship between the 21 sovereign republics of the New World rests.

The United States will continue to stand by these principles, because of the conviction of the American people that unless the doctrine in which these principles are inherent once again governs the relations between nations, the rule of reason, of justice, and of law — in other words, the basis of modern civilization itself — cannot be preserved.

Editor's comment: Sumner Welles' declaration was in conformity with the Stimson Doctrine of Non-Recognition of Military Conquest, expressed on January 7, 1932, in a note to the Government of Japan. Stimson stated that the U.S.: "does not intend to recognize any situation, treaty, or agreement which may be brought about by means contrary to the covenants and obligations of the Pact of Paris [Briand-Kellogg] of August 27, 1928."

No. 215

The U.S. Acting Secretary of State, Welles,
to the Counsellor of the U.S. Embassy in Moscow, Thurston

WASHINGTON, August 9, 1940 — 6 p.m.

423. Your 885, July 20, 9:30 [9] p.m.

Section 1. The reply to the Soviet memorandum handed you by Lozovsky is set forth in the memorandum comprising section 2 of this telegram. Section 3 contains the text of a first person note which is to be presented simultaneously with the memorandum.

Please examine both documents carefully in order to make sure that no statements contained in them are contrary to facts of which the Embassy may have special knowledge. If in your opinion certain alterations are advisable you should request authority to make them.

It is suggested that you request an appointment on Monday, if possible, to present these documents in person to the Commissar or Assistant Commissar for Foreign Affairs and that you inform the Department in advance of the day and hour of the interview * so that it may furnish copies to the Soviet Embassy immediately thereafter.

Section 2. The Government of the United States of America has given careful consideration to the memorandum handed to the American Chargé d'Affaires at Moscow on July 20, 1940, in which the Soviet Government protested because the Federal Reserve Bank of New York had not transferred to the account of the State Bank of the U.S.S.R. certain gold held in the Federal Reserve Bank of New York belonging to the Banks of Lithuania, Latvia, and Estonia.

The memorandum states in part that the gold in question "was acquired by the State Bank of the U.S.S.R. from the Lithuanian, Latvian, and Estonian Banks on the basis of sale purchase agreements and was subject to transfer to the deposit of the State Bank of the U.S.S.R. by virtue of telegraphic orders of July 13, 1940, of the Lithuanian, Latvian, and Estonian Banks, orders which are unconditionally binding upon the Federal Reserve Bank".

Under the Gold Reserve Act of 1934 and regulations published pursuant thereto which have been in effect since January 31, 1934, gold in any form in the United States may be acquired and held, imported,

---

* The Chargé in the Soviet Union reported in his telegram No. 1006, August 12, 3 p.m., that he had handed the memorandum and the first person note to Assistant People's Commissar Lozovsky at noon on that day, without discussion (840.51-Frozen Credits/446).

exported, earmarked or held in custody for foreign or domestic account only to the extent permitted by and subject to the conditions prescribed in regulations which the Secretary of the Treasury of the United States is authorized to issue. Under regulations issued in January 1934 pursuant to such Gold Reserve Act, transfers of the character referred to in the memorandum of the U.S.S.R. may be made only if specifically licensed by the Secretary of the Treasury.

The nature of the United States Government control over gold situated in this country has been known or should have been known to the banks of Lithuania, Latvia, Estonia and U.S.S.R. The agreements pursuant to which the gold is held by the Federal Reserve Bank of New York provide that such gold is to be held "within the authority of, and subject to the terms of" the gold license issued to the Federal Reserve Bank by the Secretary of the Treasury. Under the terms of such gold license the Federal Reserve Bank is required, before it may make transfers of the type here in question, to obtain a specific license from the Secretary of the Treasury. Accordingly, the Federal Reserve Bank of New York had no authority to make the transfers of gold which were requested of it until it first received a license from the Treasury Department. In recent months the Federal Reserve Bank of New York has effected transfers of gold between accounts of the Bank for International Settlements and accounts of the Banks of Latvia and Lithuania. The exchange of telegrams between the Federal Reserve Bank and the Banks of Latvia and Lithuania in connection with such transactions must have made it entirely clear to such banks that transfers of gold are made by the Federal Reserve Bank of New York only pursuant to a license issued by the Secretary of the Treasury.

No agreement for the transfer of gold situated in this country, regardless of who may be the parties thereto, may be considered as "unconditionally binding" on the Federal Reserve Bank of New York in cases where no license for transfer has been issued by the Secretary of the Treasury. The alleged sale, therefore, by the Banks of Lithuania, Latvia, and Estonia of gold held in the Federal Reserve Bank of New York to the State Bank of the U.S.S.R. was without binding force and effect in this country since no license authorizing the transfer of such gold has been issued by the Secretary of the Treasury. Title to the gold situated in this country cannot be considered to have passed by virtue of any arrangement made outside the country unless the transfer is authorized by a license issued by the Secretary of the Treasury of the United States.

The memorandum of the U.S.S.R. states that there was a "completely unjustified delay of three days" in the application by the Federal Reserve Bank for authority to transfer the gold to the State Bank of the U.S.S.R. The Government of the United States cannot agree with such a statement. On July 13 the Federal Reserve Bank of New York received a telegram dated July 12 from the Lithuanian Bank requesting the transfer of certain gold to the State Bank of the U.S.S.R., and also stating "You will receive instructions from beneficiary", meaning the State Bank of the U.S.S.R. On July 13, the Bank of Lithuania sent a further telegram to the Federal Reserve Bank of New York amending its telegram of July 12 and, on the same day, the Bank of Latvia sent a telegram to the Federal Reserve Bank of New York instructing that certain gold be transferred to the State Bank of the U.S.S.R. July 13 was a Saturday and the Federal Reserve Bank of New York is not open for business between noon on Saturday and the following Monday morning. The telegrams of July 13 were not received at the Federal Reserve Bank of New York until long after the close of business on Saturday, July 13, and too late for any action to be taken in connection therewith until Monday July 15. On July 15, the Federal Reserve Bank of New York also received for the first time telegraphic instructions dated July 13 and July 15 from the State Bank of the U.S.S.R. relative to such gold transfers. On the same day, namely July 15, the Federal Reserve Bank of New York applied to the Treasury Department for a license, pursuant to the Gold Regulations which had been in effect since 1934, to transfer the gold referred to in the telegrams from the Banks of Latvia, Lithuania, and the U.S.S.R. On the following day, July 16, the State Bank of the U.S.S.R. was advised by the Federal Reserve Bank of New York that application for such license had been made. There was, accordingly, no delay whatever on the part of the Federal Reserve Bank in dealing with this matter.

In this connection it should be pointed out that the Federal Reserve Bank of New York has not as yet received instructions from the Bank for International Settlements to transfer gold which it holds under earmark for the Bank for International Settlements and which apparently belongs to the Bank of Estonia. On July 18, the Estonian Bank advised the Federal Reserve Bank of New York that it had previously given instructions to the Bank for International Settlements concerning such transfer and asked the Federal Reserve Bank of New York to assist in obtaining the necessary license for the transfer. The Bank for International Settlements has never issued any instructions to the Federal Reserve Bank of New York to make such transfer. In view of the agreement between the Federal Reserve Bank and the Bank for

International Settlements, pursuant to which such gold is held, the Federal Reserve Bank of New York is not in a position to take any steps looking to the transfer of such gold until it receives appropriate instructions from the Bank for International Settlements. On July 20, therefore, the Federal Reserve Bank of New York informed the Bank of Estonia that it would apply for the necessary licenses as soon as it received instructions from the Bank for International Settlements. No such instructions have been received up to the present time.

On July 15, 1940, the President of the United States, pursuant to the authority conferred on him by the Act of October 6, 1917, as amended, issued Executive Order No. 8484. This Order amended Executive Order No. 8389 of April 10, 1940, as amended, so as to extend all the provisions of Executive Order No. 8389 to, and with respect to, property in which Latvia, Estonia or Lithuania, or any national thereof, has, at any time on or since July 10, 1940, had any interest of any nature whatsoever, direct or indirect. Executive Order No. 8389 of April 10, 1940, provides that certain transactions involving property in which Norway or Denmark, or any national thereof, has had any interest on or since April 8, 1940, may be carried out only pursuant to license issued by the Secretary of the Treasury.

On May 10, 1940, the provisions of Executive Order No. 8389 were extended to, and with respect to, property in which the Netherlands, Belgium or Luxembourg or any national thereof, has, at any time on or since May 10, 1940, had any interest. On June 17, 1940, the provisions of Executive Order No. 8389 were extended to, and with respect to, property in which France, or any national thereof, has, at any time on or since June 17, 1940, had any interest. Under Executive Order No. 8484 transactions of the character referred to in the memorandum of the U.S.S.R. involving property in which Latvia, Estonia, or Lithuania, or any national thereof, has, at any time on or since July 10, 1940, had any interest, may be carried out only pursuant to a license issued by the Secretary of the Treasury. Accordingly, on July 16, 1940, the day following the issuance of Executive Order No. 8484 and the day after it had received instructions from the banks of Lithuania, Latvia, and the U.S.S.R., the Federal Reserve Bank of New York applied for a license pursuant to Executive Order No. 8484, authorizing the transfers of the gold in question. This application was in addition to the application for a license under the Gold Reserve Act of 1934 which, as previously indicated, was made by the Federal Reserve Bank of New York on July 15.

The measures against which the Soviet Government protests are neither arbitrary nor isolated manifestations of national policy. They are acts of conservation and control fully within the rights of the Government of the United States and involve no infringement of international law. Similar measures have been applied with respect to property situated in the United States belonging to various countries, or nationals thereof, which have been occupied by the armed forces of a foreign Power or otherwise deprived of their freedom of action by force or threats of force, giving rise to practical problems of the appropriate protection of American institutions and nationals from adverse claims which might result from the making of payments by them on instructions issued under duress, and of the protection of the interests of the rightful owners.

The attempt to transfer the gold belonging to the Banks of Lithuania, Latvia, and Estonia was made at a time when it had become apparent that the governments and peoples of those countries were being deprived of freedom of action by foreign troops which had entered their territories by force or threats of force. The attitude of the Government and people of the United States with regard to the use of force or threats of force in the conduct of international relations is well known. In keeping with this attitude, it is proper that the authorities of the American Government, in administering the orders and regulations referred to, should not fail to take into consideration the special situation existing in the three Baltic countries.

References in the memorandum to legal property rights and to the elementary principles of international law prompt the Government of the United States to draw the attention of the Soviet Government to the fact that nationals of the United States have suffered heavy losses in territories under the control of Soviet civil or military authorities as the result of acts committed by, under the direction of, or with the active approval of, such authorities. Certain of these losses which have been suffered during more recent months and the responsibility of the Soviet Government therefor are, however, being made the subject of a note to be addressed by the American Embassy at Moscow to the Commissariat for Foreign Affairs.

Section 3 (First Person Note). I have the honor, upon instructions from my Government, to draw the attention of Your Excellency to the fact that American institutions and nationals have suffered considerable losses in territories under the control of Soviet civil or military authorities as the result of acts committed by, under the direction of, or with the approval of, such authorities.

In September 1939, Soviet armed forces entered and occupied certain territories in Eastern Poland. While these territories were under the control of such forces certain persons or groups of persons proceeded to nationalize or confiscate property, including the property of nationals of foreign countries. Nationals of the United States own, or have interests in, property situated in these territories. Although this Embassy has submitted numerous requests to the People's Commissariat for Foreign Affairs for information regarding the status of these properties, it has as yet received no indication from the Soviet Government with regard to the disposition thereof. Under cover of a note dated April 26, 1940, however, the People's Commissariat for Foreign Affairs transmitted to the Embassy a copy of an instruction of the People's Commissariat of Justice relating to the "nationalization of foreign properties in the territories of Western Ukraine and of Western White Russia." This instruction stated in effect that since measures nationalizing land of estate owners, banks, and large industries had been approved and proclaimed on October 28 and 30, 1939, before the formal incorporation of the territories in question into the Soviet Union, there are no bases for the presentation to the Soviet Union of claims arising from such measures even though the property with respect to which such claims are presented may subsequently have passed into the possession of organs of the Soviet Government.

In June 1940 Soviet armed forces entered and occupied Bessarabia and Northern Bukovina. Nationals of the United States own property in these provinces. Although inquiries have been made to the Soviet Government by the Embassy of the United States at Moscow no information has as yet been received with regard to the status of such property or property interests.

In the countries of Lithuania, Latvia, and Estonia nationals of the United States also own or have interests in certain properties. It is the understanding of my Government that steps have already been taken by certain persons or groups under the control of the authorities of the Union of Soviet Socialist Republics to nationalize or confiscate these properties and to take other actions injurious to American property or interests.

My Government instructs me to state that regardless of any disclaimers of responsibility therefor on the part of the Government of the Union of Soviet Socialist Republics, the Government of the United States hold, and will hold, the Government of the Union of Soviet Socialist Republics responsible for all losses to American nationals resulting from acts of confiscation, or other acts injurious to the property or interests of such nationals, committed in territories under Soviet control by, under the direction of, or with the approval of, the authorities of the Union of Soviet Socialist Republics.

My Government also directs me to bring to the attention of the Government of the Union of Soviet Socialist Republics the fact that the governments, institutions, and residents of certain of the countries which at present are wholly or in part under occupation by Soviet armed forces have debts aggregating large sums to the Government or nationals of the United States.

Accept, Excellency, the renewed assurances of my highest consideration.

Section 4. In case the Soviet official to whom the documents are presented intimates that they may have an adverse effect on American-Soviet relations you may state that in view of the contents of the Soviet memorandum of protest and of the attitude displayed by the Soviet authorities with regard to American property and interests in territory now under Soviet control, your Government, in spite of the fact it is hoping for an improvement in American-Soviet relations, has no choice in the matter. It would be lacking in frankness if it should fail to make a clear statement of its position.

For your information, it may be added, during the last week informal discussions of various problems of American-Soviet relations have been taking place between the Soviet Ambassador and members of the Department. Among these problems are those advanced by Mikoyan on July 30. A summary of these discussions will be sent you later.

WELLES

No. 216

Address of the President of the United States, Roosevelt, to the Lithuanian-American Council's Delegation to the White House

(October 15, 1940)

Lithuania Will Be Free Again

President Roosevelt on the 15th October, 1940, received in the White House, a delegation of American Lithuanians, who presented him an address regarding the occupation of Lithuania by Soviet Russia.

The President read the address and made the following observations:

"It pleased me to see that you, American citizens of Lithuanian origin, are so deeply concerned with the fate of your mother country. My ancestors came to this country long before you came. They were from Holland. Regardless of the fact that many years have passed, I still consider Holland as the land of my forefathers; the misfortune that befell Holland pains me deeply and I shall do everything in my power to make Holland a free country again. The ancestors of my wife came from Belgium, naturally, the fate of Belgium is in no less a degree a concern of mine. Therefore, I understand perfectly your feelings concerning the fate of Lithuania.

But let me tell you that you have made here two mistakes; the first mistake is in your address that you gave me. It is stated here that Lithuania has lost her independence. It is a mistake to say so. Lithuania did not lose her independence. Lithuania's independence was only temporarily put aside. Time will come and Lithuania will be free again. This will happen much sooner than you may expect. The other mistake as I observed was made by one of your speakers when he referred to Lithuania as a very small state. Look at the Latin American Republics and you will see that there are even smaller states than Lithuania, but they live a free and happy life. It is not fit even to talk about the smallness of Lithuania for even the smallest nation has the same right to enjoy independence as the largest nation."

No. 217

Memorandum by the Assistant Chief of the Division of European Affairs of the U.S. State Department, Henderson

February 27, 1941

The Ambassador said that he wished again to take up the question of the Baltic ships in this country. Mr. Welles said that he would like to take the initiative in the subject. As the Ambassador knew, he, together with Mr. Atherton and Mr. Henderson, for some time had been giving much thought and study to the Baltic questions. It had been his desire, as well as that of Mr. Atherton and Mr. Henderson, to see that this Government did all that was possible in order to surmount various obstacles which had arisen to the improvement of relations between the United States and the Soviet Union. A number of months ago he had told the Ambassador that in certain cases it would be preferable from a practical point of view to recognize the fact that certain problems exist in the relations between the two countries which did not appear to be solvable and that more could be achieved if such problems would be, so to speak, left standing for the time being in the midst of the stream. It was his belief that problems relating to the Baltic States should be considered to be in the class of unsolvable problems. These problems could not be approached without coming up against a basic principle of policy of this Government — a policy which had been maintained absolutely unaltered since 1931. There had been no deviation from it. As long as this Government adhered to that principle of foreign policy it could not agree to make decisions which would imply any infringement of it.

If the Ambassador desired, he was prepared to discuss these problems with him in detail and at length but that since their objective was to soothe, to consult, and to construct, he hoped that the matter could be dropped for the time being.

The Ambassador said that on January 8 he had given to Mr. Welles a statement from Mr. Molotov in which it was pointed out that the Soviet Government did not believe that a readjustment of relations could be attained as long as the Baltic problems stood between the American and Soviet Governments, or as long as the former Ministers or Consuls of the three Baltic States continued their activities in the United States. Property belonging to his country, including the former Baltic ships, was being held by persons who had no right to it. It had been pointed out to the American Government that from the point of view of his Government, which was based on the knowledge of American foreign policy and upon statements made by former Secretaries of State with regard to the Baltic problems, the principle of American foreign policy to which Mr. Welles had just referred was hardly applicable to the situation of the Baltic because in previous years the eventual reunion of the Baltic States with the Soviet Union had been explicitly recognized by the United States. The Ambassador therefore felt that Mr. Welles in making his statement had apparently reduced the scope and results of the conversations in which they had been engaging for the last few months. Translating Mr. Welles' statement into practice, it would appear that the United States Government would continue to consider as valid and operative in the United States its treaties with the three former Baltic republics and also that the United States Government would continue to recognize the former Ministers and Consuls of the

Baltic States who, in cooperation with officials of the Department of State, local Customs authorities, and police officials, were continuing to arrest Captains and members of the crews of what are now Soviet vessels only because such persons desired to go home. These Consuls, armed with certificates issued by the Department of State testifying to their official status, were also appearing in the American courts and through fictitious means were changing the registry of these vessels and directing their movements. Apparently the statement of Mr. Welles meant that the Soviet Ambassador would be unable to assist scores of his nationals in this country and to represent the interests of the legitimate owners of these vessels. The existence of such unsolved problems would result in adding for an indefinite period of time acid to the relations between the two countries, and in the meantime, the damage which was being done to Soviet national interests and Soviet nationals would continue to accumulate.

Mr. Welles stated that since the Ambassador had raised the question and since the attitude of the Soviet Government would seem to indicate that the position taken by the American Government with regard to the Baltic States was a departure from the policy of previous administrations in the United States, he felt that he should make a statement in the way of clarification. It was true that immediately after the termination of the World War, the United States Government, in view of the traditional friendship between the Russian people and the American people, had taken the attitude that it desired to take no action which could be regarded in any sense as determining the alienation of territory of the Russian people. The Ambassador, however, should recall the fact that even before the United States had recognized the independence of the three Baltic republics the Soviet Government itself had done so and had continued over a period of many years to recognize the Governments of these three countries as separate sovereign governments. The attitude of the United States had consequently been identical with the attitude of the Soviet Government itself until a few months ago. The American Government had hoped and it still hoped that the policy of the Soviet Government would be identical also with the policy of the United States with regard to the desirability of safeguarding the legitimate interests of the smaller countries of the world, a policy which would strengthen and fortify the rights of small countries to integrity and independence in every possible way. The Ambassador had just spoken of the former Ministers and Consuls in the United States of the Baltic republics. It should be made clear that as far as the American

Government was concerned these officials were still being recognized as Ministers and Consuls of these republics. The attitude of the American Government was based on its policy of not recognizing the conquest of territory by force. In this connection the Ambassador should not overlook the fact that for a number of months after the total occupation of Czechoslovakia by the German Reich the Soviet Government had continued to recognize the Czechoslovak Minister of that country in Moscow. Mr. Welles added that to summarize as briefly as possible, he might state that the American Government felt very strongly that the Governments of the United States and the Soviet Union still had an opportunity to cooperate for a continuation of the principles of peace. It seemed singularly unfortunate, in view of the efforts which the Ambassador and he had been making to bring the two countries closer together, that this question should be brought up at the present time, since such an action tended to impede the progress which was being made. He felt it important that both sides should adopt a policy, which he strongly urged, that when they came to problems which could not be solved, they pass over them for the time being and he recommended that that policy be followed at least with regard to questions pertaining to the Baltic. The Soviet Ambassador again insisted that on July 25, 1922 the American Government had recognized the independence of the Baltic States; that no force was involved in the Soviet absorption of the Baltic States, since the absorption had been brought about by peaceful and parliamentary methods; and that the analogy with the Czechoslovak situation was not applicable since Czechoslovakia had never in the past belonged to Germany whereas the Baltic States historically had belonged to Russia.

He said that he would probably be compelled to surrender with great reluctance to Mr. Welles' suggestion that when they met an obstacle of great magnitude they pass over it instead of endeavoring to overcome it. He regretted particularly dropping the subject of the Baltic States since such action implied that the problem was one that could not be solved. The failure of the solution of this problem, he stated, would reduce the possibility of an improvement in the relations between the two countries.

Mr. Welles said that from the standpoint of expediency it was merely a matter of passing around an obstacle until a time came when it could be discussed to a better advantage. Nothing could be gained from a conversation in which Mr. Oumansky would insist that black is white while Mr. Welles insisted that white is black. Conversations of this kind were likely to be exacerbating rather than soothing. Mr. Welles said that without arguing, he must again disagree with the statements which Mr. Oumansky had just made.

No. 218

Memorandum of the British Prime Minister, Churchill, to the British Foreign Secretary

I was much disturbed by the reports which Mr. Eden had brought back with him from Moscow of Soviet territorial ambitions, especially in the Baltic States. These were the conquests of Peter the Great, and had been for two hundred years under the Czars. Since the Russian revolution they had been the outpost of Europe against Bolshevism. They were what are now called "social democracies," but very lively and truculent. Hitler had cast them away like pawns in his deal with the Soviets before the outbreak of war in 1939. There had been a severe Russian and Communist purge. All the dominant personalities and elements had been liquidated in one way or another. The life of these strong peoples was henceforward underground. Presently, as we shall see, Hitler came back with a Nazi counter-purge. Finally, in the general victory the Soviets had control again. Thus the deadly comb ran back and forth, and back again, through Estonia. Latvia, and Lithuania. There was no doubt however where the right lay. The Baltic States should be sovereign independent peoples.

Prime Minister to Foreign Secretary 8 Jan 42

We have never recognised the 1941 frontiers of Russia except *de facto*. They were acquired by acts of aggression in shameful collusion with Hitler. The transfer of the peoples of the Baltic States to Soviet Russia against their will would be contrary to all the principles for which we are fighting this war and would dishonor our cause. This also applies to Bessarabia and to Northern Bukhovina, and in a lesser degree to Finland, which I gather it is not intended wholly to subjugate and absorb. * * *

7. You have promised that we will examine these claims of Russia in common with the United States and the Dominions. That promise we must keep. But there must be no mistake about the opinion of any British Government of which I am the head, namely, that it adheres to those principles of freedom and democracy set forth in the Atlantic Charter, and that these principles must become especially active

whenever any question of transferring territory is raised. I conceive, therefore, that our answer should be that all questions of territorial frontiers must be left to the decision of the Peace Conference.

Juridically this is how the matter stands now.

No. 219
No. 4065
United States of America

DEPARTMENT OF STATE

To all to whom these presents shall come, Greeting:

I Certify *That the absorption of Estonia by the Union of Soviet Socialist Republics is not recognized by the Government of the United States.*

In testimony whereof, I, JAMES F. BYRNES

Secretary of State, have hereunto caused the seal of the Department of State to be affixed and my name subscribed by the Acting Authentication Officer of the said Department, at the city of Washington, in the District of Columbia, this twelfth *day of* June , 1946.

No. 4066

United States of America

DEPARTMENT OF STATE

To all to whom these presents shall come, Greeting:

I Certify *That the regime now functioning in Estonia is not recognized by the Government of the United States.*

In testimony whereof, I, JAMES F. BYRNES ....

Secretary of State, have hereunto caused the seal of the Department of State to be affixed and my name subscribed by the Acting Authentication Officer of the said Department, at the city of Washington, in the District of Columbia, this .... *twelfth* .... *day of* .... *June* ...., *1946.*

No. 4064

United States of America

DEPARTMENT OF STATE

To all to whom these presents shall come, Greeting:

I Certify *That the legality of the so-called Nationalization laws and decrees or of any of the acts of the regime now functioning in Estonia is not recognized by the Government of the United States.*

In testimony whereof, I, JAMES F. BYRNES ....
Secretary of State, have hereunto caused the seal of the Department of State to be affixed and my name subscribed by the Acting Authentication Officer of the said Department, at the city of Washington, in the District of Columbia, this .... *twelfth* .... *day of* .... *June* ...., *1946.*

No. 220

Department of State

WASHINGTON

In reply refer to   August 1, 1946
PL

My dear Captain Peterson:

I have received your letter of July 22, 1946 addressed to Mr.

Llewellyn E. Thompson, Chief, Division of Eastern European Affairs, in which you inquire about the status of the Baltic States.

In answer to your question I think you would be interested in knowing that the United States does not recognize the incorporation of the Baltic States into the Union of Soviet Socialist Republics. The representatives of Estonia, Latvia and Lithuania accredited to this Government continue to be recognized.

Sincerely yours,

Walter Walkinshaw
Chief, Public Views and
Inquiries Section
Division of Public Liaison

Captain R.J. Peterson
308 East 134th Street,
Bronx, New York, New York.

No. 221

**Message of the President of the United States, Truman,
to the Baltic States Freedom Committee**

THE WHITE HOUSE

WASHINGTON

NIGHT LETTER

June 13, 1952

MR. VACLOVAS SIDZIKAUSKAS
PRESIDENT
Baltic States Freedom Committee
16 WEST FIFTY-EIGHTH STREET
NEW YORK, NEW YORK

On the occasion of the twelfth anniversary of the lawless invasion of the Baltic States by the Soviet Union, I send you warm greetings. The

Government and people of the United States feel an instinctive and profound sympathy for the enslaved people of *Estonia, Latvia* and *Lithuania* coupled with revulsion at the acts of the occupying power, whose forcible incorporation of the Baltic States we have never recognized. We pay tribute to the determined endeavors of the diplomatic and other representatives of Estonia, Latvia and Lithuania on behalf of their homelands. We shall not forget our Baltic friends. We extend through you to them, wherever they may be, our heartfelt hope that they may have the fortitude and the patience to live through the grinding tyranny now imposed upon them to enjoy once again independence and freedom within the community of free nations.

HARRY S. TRUMAN

No. 222

Joint Declaration of Basic Principles by the President of the United States, Eisenhower, and the Prime Minister of Great Britain, Churchill

June 29, 1954

As we terminate our conversations on subjects of mutual and world interest, we again declare that:

1. In intimate comradeship, we *will continue our united efforts to secure world peace based upon the principles of the Atlantic Charter, which we reaffirm.*

2. We, together and individually, continue to hold out the hand of friendship to any and all nations, which by *solemn pledge and confirming deeds show themselves desirous of participating in a just and fair peace.*

3. *We uphold the principle of self-government and will earnestly strive by every peaceful means to secure the independence of all countries whose peoples desire and are capable of sustaining an independent existence. We welcome the processes of development, where still needed, that lead toward that goal. As regards formerly sovereign states now in bondage, we will not be a party to any arrangement or treaty which would confirm or prolong their unwilling subordination.* In the case of nations now divided against their will, we

shall continue to seek to achieve unity through free elections supervised by the United Nations to insure they are conducted fairly.

4. We believe that the cause of world peace would be advanced by general and drastic reduction under effective safeguards of world armaments of all classes and kinds. It will be our persevering resolve to promote conditions in which the prodigious nuclear forces now in human hands can be used to enrich and not to destroy mankind.

5. We will continue our support of the United Nations and of existing international organizations that have been established in the spirit of the Charter for common protection and security. We urge the establishment and maintenance of such associations of appropriate nations as will best, in their respective regions, preserve the peace and independence of the peoples living there. When desired by the peoples of the affected countries we are ready to render appropriate and feasible assistance to such associations.

6. We shall, with our friends, develop and maintain the spiritual, economic and military strength necessary to pursue these purposes effectively. In pursuit of this purpose we will seek every means of promoting the fuller and freer interchange among us of goods and services which will benefit all participants.

(signed) DWIGHT D. EISENHOWER

(signed) WINSTON S. CHURCHILL

No. 223

Excerpts From the Third Interim Report
of the Select Committee on Communist Aggression
of the U.S. House of Representatives

Introduction, Basic Findings, Conclusions, Recommendations

Publ. October, 1954.

This is the third interim report of the Committee on Communist Agression (formerly the House Baltic Committee) on the subject of the illegal incorporation of Lithuania, Latvia, and Estonia into the U.S.S.R.

Basic Findings

(1) In 1939, the U.S.S.R., after concluding a secret pact with the Nazis which divided Eastern Europe into spheres of influence, did

impose so-called mutual assistance pacts upon Estonia, Latvia, and Lithuania.

(2) The mutual-assistance pacts so imposed upon the Baltic States called for the establishment of Soviet Russian military bases and airfields in each of those nations, at the same time guaranteeing that there would be no interference with their internal affairs, including their political structure and social and economic systems.

(3) Contrary to the provisions of those mutual assistance pacts and other existing treaties, the Soviet Union, without provocation, did in June 1940 invade and take military and political control over Lithuania, Latvia, and Estonia, thus committing an act of unprovoked aggression.

(4) Under the protection of the occupying Red army forces, political commissars of the Kremlin (Vishinsky, Dekanozov, and Zhdanov) did dissolve the legal governments of Estonia, Latvia, and Lithuania and arbitrarily established puppet governments to control the people.

(5) A network of political agents of the U.S.S.R. did on July 14, 1940, conduct elaborately staged mock elections in the Baltic States with the support of powerful Red military forces, the results of which were completely assured long before the first ballot was cast. Only one list of candidates, handpicked by the Kremlin representatives, was presented to the voters, and the exercise of the secret ballot was denied.

(6) By the process of mock elections the political commissars of the U.S.S.R. did install puppet parliaments in Lithuania, Latvia, and Estonia which on July 21-22, 1940, adopted a resolution prepared in Moscow, petitioning the Supreme Council of the Soviet Union for recognition as a Soviet Republic. This action by the puppet parliaments was in violation of the sovereign will be the Lithuanian, Latvian, and Estonian people and in violation of the legal constitutions of those nations which required a popular referendum on such an issue.

(7) The U.S.S.R. has been and is now engaged in a ruthless program of sovietization in Estonia, Latvia, and Lithuania, employing the well-known Communist tactics of arrest and detention without cause, torture chambers, mass deportations to slave-labor camps, population transfers, and wide-scale political murders.

Conclusions

(I) The evidence is overwhelming and conclusive that Estonia, Latvia, and Lithuania were forcibly occupied and illegally annexed by the U. S. S. R. Any claims by the U. S. S. R. that the elections conducted by them in July 1940 were free and voluntary or that the resolutions adopted by the resulting parliaments petitioning for recognition as a Soviet Republic were legal are false and without foundation in fact.

(II) That the continued military and political occupation of Lithuania, Latvia, and Estonia by the U.S.S.R. is a major cause of the dangerous world tensions which now beset mankind and therefore constitutes a serious threat to the peace.

Recommendations

(1) That the Secretary of State take such steps as are necessary to cause this threat to world peace to be brought to the urgent attention of the current session of the General Assembly of the United Nations.

(2) That the United States delegation to the United Nations take the initiative in removing this threat to world peace by sponsoring a resolution in the General Assembly calling for the full and rapid withdrawal of all the military, political, and administrative personnel of the Union of Soviet Sovialist Republics from the territories of Estonia, Latvia, and Lithuania.

No. 224

Address of the President of the United States, Eisenhower, to a Joint Session of Congress

January 6, 1957

EXCERPTS

. . . International Communism, of course, seeks to mask its purposes of domination by expressions of good will and by superficially attractive offers of political, economic and military aid. But any free nation, which is the subject of Soviet enticement, ought, in elementary wisdom, to look behind the mask.

Remember Estonia, Latvia and Lithuania. In 1939, the Soviet Union entered into mutual assistance pacts with these then independent countries; and the Soviet Foreign Minister, addressing the Extraordinary Fifth Session of the Supreme Soviet in October 1939, solemnly and publicly declared that "we stand for the scrupulous and punctilious observance of the pacts on the basis of complete reciprocity, and we declare that all the nonsensical talk about the Sovietization of the Baltic countries is only to the interest of our common enemies and all anti-Soviet provocateurs." Yet in 1940, Estonia, Latvia and Lithuania were forcibly incorporated into the Soviet Union.

Soviet control of the satellite nations of Eastern Europe has been forcibly maintained in spite of solemn promises of a contrary intent, made during World War II.

Stalin's death brought hope that this pattern would change. And we read the pledge of the Warsaw Treaty of 1955 that the Soviet Union would follow in satellite countries "the principles of mutual respect for their independence and sovereignty and non-interference in domestic affairs." But we have just seen the subjugation of Hungary by naked armed force. In the aftermath of this Hungarian tragedy, world respect for and belief in Soviet promises have sunk to a new low . . .

No. 225

Statement to the Press
by the U. S. Secretary of State, Dulles

February 15, 1958

This year marks the fortieth anniversary of the declaration of national independence of the peoples of Lithuania, Latvia and Estonia. Although in 1920 the Soviet Union recognized their independence, renouncing forever all sovereign rights in the Baltic States, in 1940 the Soviet Government forcibly incorporated Lithuania, Latvia, and Estonia into the Soviet Union. This action was quickly denounced by the United States Government.

The United States remains convinced that relations between all nations must be governed by the principle of equality and guided by justice and law. It believes that the peoples of Lithuania, Latvia, and Es.onia have a firm right to choose their own political, economic. and cultural systems. Determination, industry, and love of freedom characterize the peoples of these Baltic States. These qualities have enabled their kinsmen here to make a valuable contribution to the development of the United States. The United States Government is confident that the same qualities will carry the peoples of Lithuania, Latvia, and Estonia successfully through the present tragic days and enable them to regain the rights of which they have been unjustly deprived.

No. 226

Public Law 86-90, adopted by the 86th Congress of the United States of America, July, 1959

PUBLIC LAW 86-90

Providing for the designation of the third week of July as "CAPTIVE NATIONS WEEK"

Adopted by the 86th Congress of the United States of America in July, 1959.

Whereas the greatness of the United States is in large part attributable to its having been able, through the democratic process, to achieve a harmonious national unity of its people, even though they stem from the most diverse of racial, religious, and ethnic backgrounds; and

Whereas this harmonious unification of the diverse elements of our free society has led the people of the United States to possess a warm understanding and sympathy for the aspirations of peoples everywhere to recognize the natural interdependency of the peoples and nations of the world; and

Whereas the enslavement of a substantial part of the world's population by Communist imperialism makes a mockery of the idea of peaceful coexistence between nations and constitutes a detriment to the natural bonds of understanding between the people of the United States and other peoples; and

Whereas since 1918 the imperialistic and aggressive policies of Russian communism have resulted in the creation of a vast empire which poses a dire threat to the security of the United States and of all the free peoples of the world; and

Whereas the imperialistic policies of Communist Russia have led, through direct and indirect aggression, to the subjugation of the national independence of Poland, Hungary, Lithuania, Ukraine, Czechoslovakia, Latvia, Estonia, White Ruthenia, Rumania, East Germany, Bulgaria, mainland China, Armenia, Azerbaijan, Georgia, North Korea, Albania, Idel-Ural, Tibet, Cossackia, Turkestan, North Vietnam, and others; and

Whereas these submerged nations look to the United States, as the citadel of human freedom, for leadership in bringing about their liberation and independence and in restoring to them the enjoyment of their Christian, Jewish, Moslem, Buddhist, or other religious freedoms, and of their individual liberties; and

Whereas it is vital to the national security of the United States that the desire for liberty and independence on the part of the peoples of these conquered nations should be steadfastly kept alive; and

Whereas the desire for liberty and independence by the overwhelming majority of the people of these submerged nations constitutes a powerful deterrent to war and one of the best hopes for a just and lasting peace; and

Whereas it is fitting that we clearly manifest to such peoples through an appropriate and official means the historic fact that the people of the United States share with them their aspirations for the recovery of their freedom and independence:

Now, therefore, be it

Resolved by the Senate and House of Representatives of the United States of America in Congress assembled, that the President is authorized and requested to issue a Proclamation designating the third week of July, 1959, as "Captive Nations Week" and inviting the people of the United States to observe such week with appropriate ceremonies and activities. The President is further authorized and requested to issue a similar proclamation each year until such time as freedom and independence shall have been achieved for all the captive nations of the world.

No. 227

Proclamation of "Captive Nations Week" by the President of the United States of America

July 18, 1960

CAPTIVE NATIONS WEEK, 1960

BY THE PRESIDENT OF THE UNITED STATES
OF AMERICA

A PROCLAMATION

WHEREAS many nations throughout the world have been made captive by the imperialistic and aggressive policies of Soviet Communism; and

WHEREAS the peoples of the Soviet-dominated nations have been deprived of their national independence and their individual liberties; and

WHEREAS the citizens of the United States are linked by bonds of family and principle to those who love freedom and justice on every continent; and

WHEREAS it is appropriate and proper to manifest to the peoples of the captive nations the support of the government and the people of the United States of America for their just aspirations for freedom and national independence; and

WHEREAS by a joint resolution approved July 17, 1959, the Congress has authorized and requested the President of the United States of America to issue a proclamation designating the third week in July 1959 as "Captive Nations Week", and to issue a similar proclamation each year until such time as freedom and independence shall have been achieved for all the captive nations of the world:

NOW, THEREFORE, I, DWIGHT D. EISENHOWER, President of the United States of America, do hereby designate the week beginning July 17, 1960, as Captive Nations Week.

I invite the people of the United States of America to observe such week with appropriate ceremonies and activities and I urge them to study the plight of the Soviet-dominated nations and to recommit themselves to the support of the just aspirations of the peoples of those captive nations.

IN WITNESS WHEREOF, I have hereunto set my hand and caused the seal of the United States of America to be affixed.

DONE at the City of Washington this eighteenth day of July in the year of our Lord nineteen hundred and sixty, and of the independence of the United States of America the one hundred and eighty-fifth.

Signed

Dwight D. Eisenhower

No. 228

Resolution of the Consultative Assembly of the Council of Europe

September 29, 1960

TWELFTH ORDINARY SESSION

RESOLUTION 189 [1960][1]

---

1. *Assembly debate* on 28th September 1960 [19th Sitting][see Doc. 1173, Report of the Committee on Non-represented Nations].
   Text adopted by the Assembly on 29th September 1960 [20th Sitting].

on the situation in the Baltic States on the twentieth
anniversary of their forcible incorporation into the
Soviet Union

1. The Assembly,

2. On the twentieth anniversary of the occupation and forcible
incorporation into the Soviet Union of the three European States of
Estonia, Latvia and Lithuania,

3. Notes that this illegal annexation took place without any genuine
reference to the wishes of the people;

4. Expresses sympathy with the sufferings of the Baltic peoples and
assures them that they are not forgotten by their fellow Europeans;

5. Is confident that Communist oppression will not succeed in crushing
their spirit and faith in freedom and democracy;

6. Notes that the independent existence of the Baltic States is still
recognised *de jure* by a great majority of the Governments of the nations
of the free world;

7. Urges member Governments to support appropriate efforts of Baltic
refugees to maintain their natural culture traditions and languages, in
anticipation of the time when Estonia, Latvia and Lithuania will be
able to play their part as free nations in our democratic international
institutions.

No. 229

The U.S. Undersecretary of State, Ball,
to the Lithuanian Charge
Ad Interim
in Washington, Kajeckas

DEPARTMENT OF STATE
WASHINGTON

February 7, 1965

Dear Mr. Charge d'Affaires:

On the occasion of the forty-seventh anniversary of Lithuania's
National Day I am pleased to express to you the sincere good wishes of
the Government and people of the United States.

Nearly twenty-five years have elapsed since the sovereign Lithuanian
Nation lost its national independence in the wake of the illegal

annexation by the Soviet Union. But the indomitable spirit of the Lithuanian people and their yearning to live in freedom and independence have not been dimmed throughout these years.

In recognition of the right of a free people to national self-determination, the United States Government has firmly and consistently stood by its declared policy of non-recognition of the forcible incorporation of Lithuania into the Soviet Union. The United States thereby not only accords recognition to the Lithuanian people's devotion to the cause of freedom and national independence, but expresses its confidence that this cause will ultimately prevail.

Sincerely yours,
/s/ George W. Ball
Acting Secretary

Mr. Joseph Kajeckas,
Charge d'Affaires ad interim
of Lithuania

No. 230

U.S. Secretary of State, Rusk, to the Lithuanian Charge Ad Interim in Washington, Kajeckas

THE SECRETARY OF STATE
WASHINGTON

February 11, 1966

Dear Mr. Charge d'Affaires:

On the occasion of the forty-eighth anniversary of Lithuania's independence, it is my pleasure to extend to you the good wishes of the Government and people of the United States.

Our country has consistently espoused the principle that all peoples have the right to determine the form of their national existence. In Lithuania's case, we have applied this principle by refusing to recognize the forcible incorporation of that country into the Soviet Union. We fully support your continuing efforts to marshal world public opinion and to bring it to bear on the issue of self-determination for the people of Lithuania.

In view of the courage and fortitude shown by the Lithuanian people during these years of foreign domination, I am confident that their just aspirations for freedom and national independence will ultimately be realized

Sincerely yours,
Dean Rusk

Mr. Joseph Kajeckas,
    Charge d'Affaires ad interim
        of Lithuania.

No. 231

Statement of the Vice President of the United States, H.H. Humphrey, on the Occasion of Baltic Freedom Day, June 12, 1966

THE VICE PRESIDENT
WASHINGTON

STATEMENT BY
VICE PRESIDENT HUBERT H. HUMPHREY
FOR BALTIC FREEDOM DAY
JUNE 12, 1966

Freedom and nationhood are rightly prized throughout the world. The peoples of Estonia, Latvia and Lithuania cherish — with particular fervor — the ideals of liberty and sovereignty.

On the occasion of Baltic Freedom Day, 1966, Americans of every ancestry extend greetings to our fellow citizens of Baltic descent and to their kinsmen abroad.

The U.S. Government is committed now, as in the past, to the right of self-determination of the Baltic and all other peoples.

Our Government has soundly refused either to condone or to accept the forced illegal annexation of the Baltic Nations and their territories into the Soviet Union. To the contrary, throughout the forums of the world, including the United Nations, we have repeatedly reaffirmed the right of Baltic peoples to restoration of sovereignty.

So, too, we continue to recognize the diplomatic and consular representatives of the pre-World War II Baltic Governments.

Reliable reports confirm that the Baltic peoples do continue to revere their respective national and cultural traditions. Despite alien occupation, oppression and mass deportation, the love of liberty burns strongly in Estonian, Latvian and Lithuanian hearts. We Americans deeply respect these brave peoples for their steadfast devotion to freedom. The United States re-pledges itself to the universal principles of independence, personal liberty and human dignity.

At this very time, in another part of the world, the sovereignty of another small nation — Viet Nam — is crucially at stake. Brave American fighting forces, as well as civilians, are giving their all for Vietnam's freedom. In this spirit, we re-dedicate ourselves anew to the cause of freedom everywhere.

No. 232

Concurrent Resolutions No. 416 of the U.S. House of Representatives and the Senate of the United States

Calendar No. 1573

89th CONGRESS
2D Session

H. Con. Res. 416

[Report No. 1606]

IN THE SENATE OF THE UNITED STATES

June 23, 1966
Referred to the Committee on Foreign Relations

September 19 (legislative day, September 7), 1966
Reported by Mr. Fulbright, without amendment

Concurrent Resolution

Whereas the subjection of peoples to alien subjugation, domination, and exploitation constitutes a denial of fundamental human rights, is contrary to the Charter of the United Nations, and is an impediment to the promotion of world peace and cooperation; and

Whereas all peoples have the right to self-determination; by virtue of that right they freely determine their political status and freely pursue their economic, social, cultural, and religious developme ·: and

Whereas the Baltic peoples of Estonia, Latvia, and Lithuania have been forcibly deprived of these rights by the Government of the Soviet Union; and

Whereas the Government of the Soviet Union, through a program of deportations and resettlement of peoples, continues in its effort to change the ethnic character of the populations of the Baltic states; and

Whereas it has been the firm and consistent policy of the Government of the United States to support the aspirations of Baltic peoples for self-determination and national independence; and

Whereas there exist many historical, cultural, and family ties between the peoples of the Baltic States and the American people: Be it

Resolved by the House of Representatives (the Senate concurring), That the House of Representatives of the United States urge the President of the United States —
(a) to direct the attention of world opinion at the
United Nations and at other appropriate international
forums and by such means as he deems appropriate, to
the denial of the rights of self-determination for the
peoples of Estonia, Latvia, and Lithuania, and
(b) to bring the force of world opinion to bear
on behalf of the restoration of these rights to the Baltic
peoples.
Passed the House of Representatives June 21, 1965.
Attest:

RALPH R. ROBERTS
Clerk

House concurrent Resolution 416 was adopted by the House of Representatives by a record vote of 298 yeas to no nays on June 21, 1965, and unanimously passed by the United States Senate on October 22, 1966.

Congressional Record

PROCEEDINGS AND DEBATES OF THE 89th CONGRESS SECOND SESSION

Saturday, October 22, 1966

Senate

CONCURRENT RESOLUTION TO REQUEST THE PRESIDENT OF THE UNITED STATES TO URGE CERTAIN ACTIONS IN BEHALF OF LITHUANIA, ESTONIA, AND LATVIA

Mr. MANSFIELD. Mr. President, I ask unanimous consent that the Senate turn to the consideration of Calendar No. 1573, House Concurrent Resolution 416.

The PRESIDING OFFICER. The concurrent resolution will be stated.

The LEGISLATIVE CLERK. A concurrent resolution (H. Con. Res. 416) to request the President of the United to urge certain actions in behalf of Lithuania, Estonia, and Latvia.

The PRESIDING OFFICER. Is there objection to the present consideration of the concurrent resolution?

There being no objection, the Senate proceeded to its consideration.

Mr. KUCHEL. Mr. President, I wish to say that I am delighted that this matter is being taken up. It deserves attention in this session as a mark of our continuing concern for those peoples who have been deprived of their democratic institutions and are unable to speak for themselves.

The PRESIDING OFFICER. The question is on agreeing to the concurrent resolution.

The concurrent resolution (H. Con. Res. 416) was agreed to.

EXECUTIVE POSITION

The position of the executive branch with respect to the concurrent resolution is outlined in the correspondence which follows:

Department of State,
Washington, June 1, 1965.

Hon. Thomas E. Morgan,
Chairman, Committee on Foreign Affairs,
House of Representatives.

DEAR MR. CHAIRMAN: I am writing in reply to your letter of May 20, 1965, to the Secretary of State, requesting the Department's comments on House Concurrent Resolution 416, which has been favorably reported to the full Committee on Foreign Affairs. The resolution requests the President of the United States to urge certain actions in behalf of Estonia, Latvia, and Lithuania. The language of the resolution, as formulated, is not objected to by the Department of State.

The Department has been advised by the Bureau of the Budget that from the standpoint of the administration's program there is no objection to the submission of this report.

Sincerely yours,

Douglas MacArthur II,

Assistant Secretary for Congressional Relations

(For the Secretary of State).

No. 233

Statement by the U.S. Ambassador to the United Nations, Goldberg

August 31, 1967

"The United States Government is maintaining the uncompromising support for the cause of self-determination. On various occasions, the United States delegates at the United Nations have taken appropriate opportunities to remind the USSR, and the world community, that the peoples within the USSR have the same right to self-determination which the people of so-called 'colonial' countries possess, and we have urged the Soviet Union to permit the full exercise of this right. We shall continue to express this viewpoint emphatically as occasions rise.

"Concerning the Baltic States specifically, the United States regards with full sympathy and understanding the aspirations of the Baltic peoples for freedom and national self-determination and has consistently adhered to the policy of non-recognition of the forcible incorporation of Latvia, Lithuania and Estonia by the Soviet Union. The position of the United States in this regard has been publicly affirmed both through continued recognition of Baltic Diplomatic Representatives in the United States and, on appropriate occasions, through the public statements of ranking United States officials such as the statement of Vice President Humphrey on June 12, 1966."

—ELTA, New York, October 20, 1967

No. 234

The U.S. Secretary of State, Rusk, to the Lithuanian Charge D'Affaires Ad Interim in Washington, Kajeckas

THE SECRETARY OF STATE
WASHINGTON

February 8, 1968

Dear Mr. Charge d'Affaires:

On the occasion of the fiftieth anniversary of Lithuania's independence, I am very pleased to extend to you best wishes on behalf of the Government and people of the United States.

Throughout its long and proud history, the Lithuanian nation has endured with fortitude many periods of trial and alien rule. Unhappily, in our own time, Lithuania's re-establishment as an independent state was followed only twenty-two years later by its forcible incorporation into the Soviet Union. The Lithuanian people have responded to this situation through the years with unyielding courage and unfaltering hope for freedom and national independence. The firm purpose with which the Lithuanians both at home and abroad have struggled to preserve their national heritage is the best assurance of their survival as a nation.

Americans look with understanding and sympathy upon the just aspiration of the Lithuanian people to determine freely their own destiny. The United States Government, by its continued nonrecognition of the forcible incorporation of Lithuania, affirms its belief in Lithuania's right of self-determination.

Sincerely yours,
Dean Rusk

Mr. Joseph Kajeckas,
    Charge d'Affaires ad interim
       of the Legation of Lithuania,
          2622 Sixteenth Street, N.W.,
             Washington, D.C.

No. 235

Letter of the Secretary of State for External Affairs of Canada, Sharp

THE SECRETARY OF STATE FOR EXTERNAL AFFAIRS
CANADA

OTTAWA, May 3, 1968

Dear Mr. Jekste,

I should like to thank you for your letter of April 4, 1968, in which you request a statement on Canada's position with respect to the incorporation of Latvia into the USSR, which was referred to me by the Honourable Charles R. Granger.

Canada stands by its refusal to recognize the legality of the incorporation of Latvia and the other Baltic states into the Soviet Union and acknowledges the right of the Baltic peoples to self-determination.

At the same time I am sure you will agree that the right of self-determination must be restored by peaceful means and that this must inevitably be a slow process.

Yours sincerely,

(Sgd.)

Mr. A. Jekste,
　　Managing Director,
　　　　Atlantic Films & Electronics Ltd.,
　　　　　　22 Prescott St.,
　　　　　　　　St. John's, Newfoundland.

No. 236

Letter of the Acting Minister for External Affairs of Australia, Fairhall

Acting Minister for External Affairs

Canberra A.C.T. 2600

September 16, 1969

Dear Mr. Hennoste,

In the absence overseas of the Minister for External Affairs, I am writing to thank you for your letter of 31st August in which you enquired whether recognition of the incorporation into the U.S.S.R. of Estonia, Latvia, and Lithuania had been raised in the course of the discussions between the Australian and U.S.S.R. Governments to which Mr. Freeth referred in his statement to Parliament on 14th August.

I should like to confirm that this matter has not been raised in the discussions to which Mr. Freeth referred and to assure you that Australia does not recognise the validity of the incorporation of Estonia, Latvia and Lithuania into the Soviet Union. Indeed Mr. Freeth has just had occasion to reaffirm publicly the Government's position on this matter in answer to a question on notice in the House of Representatives from Mr. Hayden on 9th September, 1969. In replying to Mr. Hayden, Mr. Freeth also pointed out that Australia has never withdrawn recognition from the Governments of Estonia, Latvia, and Lithuania which were forced into exile by the U.S.S.R.'s invasion and occupation of those States in 1940.

Sincerely yours,
ALLEN FAIRHALL

Mr. M. Hennoste,
Chairman of the Baltic Council of Australia,
Estonian House,
200, Jeffcott Street
North Adelaide S.A. 5006.

No. 237

State Department Document

No. 70/10865

United States Of America

DEPARTMENT OF STATE

To all to whom these presents shall come, Greeting:

I certify *That the incorporation of Lithuania into the Union of Soviet Socialist Republics is not recognized by the Government of the United*

States and that Anicetas Simutis is recognized by the Government of the United States as Consul General of the Republic of Lithuania at New York, New York.

In testimony whereof, I, William P. Rogers, ...
*   Secretary of State, have hereunto caused the seal of the Department of State to be affixed and my name subscribed by the Authentication Officer of the said Department, at the city of Washington, in the District of Columbia, this . . . . ninth . . . . day of . . . . . November . , 1970.*

No. 238

Statement by the U.S. Department of State in the "Diplomatic Pouch"

December, 1970

Our policy with respect to the Baltic States supports the right of self-determination for their peoples. We have never recognized the forcible incorporation of these nations by the Soviet Union. Our attitude and actions have been consistent with this policy, which has been publicly affirmed by our continued accreditation in the United States of diplomatic and consular representatives of the last free governments of the three Baltic States and through statements made by U.S. Government officials in public correspondence and before various public forums, including the United Nations, on appropriate occasions.

No. 239

The U.S. Secretary of State, Rogers, to the Charge D'Affaires of Lithuania in Washington, Kajeckas

THE SECRETARY OF STATE

WASHINGTON

January 27, 1971

Dear Mr. Charge d'Affaires:

As the Lithuanian people commemorate the fifty-third anniversary of Lithuania's independence, it is my sincere pleasure to extend to you best wishes on behalf of the Government and people of the United States.

Lithuania's history is the record of a long struggle against foreign domination. In 1918, that struggle culminated in the bright flame of national independence when Lithuania took its rightful place among the nations of Europe. That flame was tragically extinguished only twenty-two years later when Lithuania was forcibly incorporated into the Soviet Union. Nevertheless, the spirit of the Lithuanian people has remained undaunted, and their hope for a restoration of national independence has never wavered. The courage and patriotic determination which have sustained this goal have been an inspiration to all who cherish freedom.

The American people understand and sympathize with the desire of the Lithuanian people to be masters of their own destiny. The United States Government, by its continued non-recognition of the forcible incorporation of Lithuania, affirms its support for Lithuania's right of self-determination.

Sincerely yours,

William P. Rogers

Mr. Joseph Kajeckas,
    Charge d'Affaires of Lithuania,
        2622 Sixteenth Street, N.W.,
        Washington, D.C.

C. PRINCIPLES OF INTERNATIONAL LAW AND ETHICS SINCE WORLD WAR II

No. 240

Message of the President of the United States, Roosevelt, to the U. S. Congress

(Jan. 6, 1941)

In the future days, which we seek to make secure, we look forward to a world founded upon four essential human freedoms.

The first is freedom of speech and expression—everywhere in the world.

The second is freedom of every person to worship God in his own way—everywhere in the world.

The third is freedom from want—which, translated into world terms, means economic understandings which will secure to every nation a healthy peacetime life for its inhabitants—everywhere in the world.

The fourth is freedom from fear—which, translated into world terms, means a world-wide reduction of armaments to such a point and in such a thorough fashion that no nation will be in a position to commit an act of physical aggression against any neighbor—anywhere in the world.

That is no vision of a distant millennium. It is a definite basis for a kind of world attainable in our own time and generation. That kind of world is the very antithesis of the so-callled new order of tyranny which the dictators seek to create with the crash of a bomb.

To that new order we oppose the greater conception—the moral order. A good society is able to face schemes of world domination and foreign revolutions alike without fear.

Since the beginning of our American history, we have been engaged in change — in a perpetual peaceful revolution — a revolution which goes on steadily, quietly adjusting itself to changing conditions — without the concentration camp or the quick-lime in the ditch. The world order which we seek is the cooperation of free countries, working together in a friendly, civilized society.

This nation has placed its destiny in the hands and heads and hearts of its millions of free men and women; and its faith in freedom under the guidance of God. Freedom means the supremacy of human rights everywhere. Our support goes to those who struggle to gain those rights or keep them. Our strength is our unity of purpose.

To that high concept there can be no end save victory.

No. 241

The Atlantic Charter

The Atlantic Charter. Official Statement on Meeting Between the President and Prime Minister Churchill. August 14, 1941

The President of the United States and the Prime Minister, Mr. Churchill, representing His Majesty's Government in the United Kingdom, have met at sea.

They have been accompanied by officials of their two Governments, including high ranking officers of their military, naval, and air services.

The whole problem of the supply of munitions of war, as provided by the Lease-Lend Act, for the armed forces of the United States and for those countries actively engaged in resisting aggression has been further examined.

Lord Beaverbrook, the Minister of Supply of the British Government, has joined in these conferences. He is going to proceed to Washington to discuss further details with appropriate officials of the United States Government. These conferences will also cover the supply problems of the Soviet Union.

The President and the Prime Minister have had several conferences. They have considered the dangers to world civilization arising from the policies of military domination by conquest upon which the Hitlerite Government of Germany and other Governments associated therewith have embarked, and have made clear the steps which their countries are respectively taking for their safety in the face of these dangers.

They have agreed upon the following joint declaration:

The President of the United States of America and the Prime Minister, Mr. Churchill, representing His Majesty's Government in the United Kingdom, being met together, deem it right to make known certain common principles in the national policies of their respective countries on which they base their hopes for a better future for the world.

First, their countries seek no aggrandizement, territorial or other;

Second, they desire to see no territorial changes that do not accord with the freely expressed wishes of the peoples concerned;

Third, they respect the right of all peoples to choose the form of government under which they will live; and they wish to see sovereign rights and self-government restored to those who have been forcibly deprived of them;

Fourth, they will endeavor, with due respect for their existing obligations, to further the enjoyment by all states, great or small, victor or vanquished, of access, on equal terms, to the trade and to the raw materials of the world which are needed for their economic prosperity;

Fifth, they desire to bring about the fullest collaboration between all Nations in the economic field with the object of securing, for all, improved labor standards, economic advancement, and social security;

Sixth, after the final destruction of the Nazi tyranny, they hope to see established a peace which will afford to all Nations the means of dwelling in safety within their own boundaries, and which will afford assurance that all the men in all the lands may live out their lives in freedom from fear and want;

Seventh, such a peace should enable all men to traverse the high seas and oceans without hindrance;

Eighth, they believe that all of the Nations of the world, for realistic as well as spiritual reasons, must come to the abandonment of the use of force. Since no future peace can be maintained if land, sea, or air armaments continue to be employed by Nations which threaten, or may threaten, aggression outside of their frontiers, they believe, pending the establishment of a wider and permanent system of general security, that the disarmament of such Nations is essential. They will likewise aid and encourage all other practicable measures which will lighten for peace-loving peoples the crushing burden of armaments.

No. 242

Joint Declaration of the United Nations

1 Joint Declaration of the United Nations Pledging Cooperation for Victory. January 1, 1942

DECLARATION BY UNITED NATIONS:

A JOINT DECLARATION BY THE UNITED STATES OF AMERICA, THE UNITED KINGDOM OF GREAT BRITAIN AND NORTHERN IRELAND, THE UNION OF SOVIET SOCIALIST REPUBLICS, CHINA, AUSTRALIA, BELGIUM, CANADA, COSTA RICA, CUBA, CZECHOSLOVAKIA, DOMINICAN REPUBLIC, EL SALVADOR, GREECE, GUATEMALA, HAITI, HONDURAS, INDIA, LUXEMBOURG, NETHERLANDS, NEW ZEALAND, NICARAGUA, NORWAY, PANAMA, POLAND, SOUTH AFRICA, YUGOSLAVIA.

The Governments signatory hereto,

Having subscribed to a common program of purposes and principles embodied in the Joint Declaration of the President of the United States of America and the Prime Minister of the United Kingdom of Great Britain and Northern Ireland dated August 14, 1941, known as the Atlantic Charter,

Being convinced that complete victory over their enemies is essential to defend life, liberty, independence, and religious freedom, and to preserve human rights and justice in their own lands as well as in other lands, and that they are now engaged in a common struggle against savage and brutal forces seeking to subjugate the world, DECLARE:

(1) Each Government pledges itself to employ its full resources, military or economic, against those members of the Tripartite Pact and its adherents with which such Government is at war.

(2) Each Government pledges itself to cooperate with the Governments signatory hereto and not to make a separate armistice or peace with the enemies.

The foregoing declaration may be adhered to by other Nations which are, or which may be, rendering material assistance and contributions in the struggle for victory over Hitlerism.

Done at Washington
January First, 1942

The United States of America
   by Franklin D. Roosevelt
The United Kingdom of Great Britain & Northern Ireland
   by Winston Churchill
On Behalf of the Government of the Union of Soviet Socialist Republics
   Maxim Litvinoff, Ambassador
National Government of the Republic of China
   Tse Vung Soong, Minister for Foreign Affairs
The Commonwealth of Australia
   by R.G. Casey
The Kingdom of Belgium
   by Cte R.v.d. Straten
Canada
   by Leighton McCarthy
The Republic of Costa Rica
   by Luis Fernandez
The Republic of Cuba
   by Aurelio F. Concheso
Czechoslovak Republic
   by V. S. Hurban

The Dominican Republic
   by J. M. Troncoso
The Republic of El Salvador
   by C. A. Alfaro
The Kingdom of Greece
   by Cimon P. Diamantopoulos
The Republic of Guatemala
   by Enrique Lopez-Herrarte
The Grand Duchy of Luxembourg
   by Hugues Le Gallais
The Kingdom of the Netherlands
   Al Loudon
Signed on behalf of the Govt. of the Dominion of New Zealand
   by Frank Langstone
The Republic of Nicaragua
   by Leon DeBayle
The Kingdom of Norway
   by W. Munthe de Morgenstierne
The Republic of Panama
   by Jaen Guardia
The Republic of Poland
   by Jan Ciechanowski

La Republique d'Haiti
  par Fernand Dennis
The Republic of Honduras
  by Julian R. Caceres
India
  Girja Shankar Bajpai

The Union of South Africa
  by Ralph W. Close
The Kingdom of Yugoslavia
  Constantine A. Fotitch

No. 243

Declaration on the Political Future of Liberated Europe

(Feb. 11, 1945)

II. Declaration on Liberated Europe

The following declaration has been approved:

"The Premier of the Union of Soviet Socialist Republics, the Prime Minister of the United Kingdom and the President of the United States of America have consulted with each other in the common interests of the peoples of their countries and those of liberated Europe. They jointly declare their mutual agreement to concert during the temporary period of instability in liberated Europe the policies of their three governments in assisting the peoples of the former Axis satellite states of Europe to solve by democratic means their pressing political and economic problems.

"The establishment of order in Europe and the re-building of national economic life must be achieved by processes which will enable the liberated peoples to destroy the last vestiges of Nazism and Fascism and to create democratic institutions of *their own choice*. This is a principle of the Atlantic Charter—the right of all peoples to choose the form of government under which they will live—the restoration of sovereign rights and self-government to those peoples who have been forcibly deprived of them by the aggressor nations.

"To foster the conditions in which the liberated peoples may exercise these rights, the three governments will jointly assist the people in any European liberated state or former Axis satellite state in Europe where in their judgment conditions require (a) to establish conditions of internal peace; (b) to carry out emergency measures for the relief of distressed peoples; (c) to form interim governmental authorities broadly representative of all democratic elements in the population and pledged to the earliest possible establishment through free elections of governments responsive to the will of the people; and (d) to facilitate where necessary the holding of such elections.

"The three governments will consult the other United Nations and provisional authorities or other governments in Europe when matters of direct interest to them are under consideration.

"When, in the opinion of the three governments, conditions in any European liberated state or any former Axis satellite state in Europe make such action necessary, they will immediately consult together on the measures necessary to discharge the joint responsibilities set forth in this declaration.

"By this declaration we reaffirm our faith in the principles of the Atlantic Charter, our pledges in the Declaration by the United Nations, and our determination to build in cooperation with other peace-loving nations world order under law, dedicated to peace, security, freedom and general well-being of all mankind.

"In issuing this declaration, the Three Powers express the hope that the provisional Government of the French Republic may be associated with them in the procedure suggested."

No. 244

The Charter of the United Nations

(June 26, 1945)

We the peoples of the United Nations determined to save succeeding generations from the scourge of war, which twice in our lifetime has brought untold sorrow to mankind, and

to reaffirm faith in fundamental human rights, in the dignity and worth of the human person, in the equal rights of men and women and of nations large and small, and

to establish conditions under which justice and respect for the obligations arising from treaties and other sources of international law can be maintained, and

to promote social progress and better standards of life in larger freedom,

and for these ends to practice tolerance and live together in peace and with one another as good neighbors, and to unite our strength to maintain international peace and security, and to ensure, by the acceptance of principles and the institution of methods, that armed force shall not be used, save in the common interest, and

to employ international machinery for the promotion of the economic and social advancement of all peoples,

have resolved to combine our efforts to accomplish these aims. Accordingly our respective Governments, through representatives assembled in the city of San Francisco, who have exhibited their full powers found to be in good and due form, have agreed to the present Charter of the United Nations and do hereby establish an international organization to be known as the United Nations.

Chapter I, Purposes and Principles

Article 1

The Purposes of the United Nations are:

1. To maintain international peace and security, and to that end: to take effective collective measures for the prevention and removal of threats to the peace, and for the suppression of acts of aggression or other breaches of the peace, and to bring about by peaceful means, and in conformity with the principles of justice and international law, adjustment or settlement of international disputes or situations which might lead to a breach of the peace;

2. To develop friendly relations among nations based on respect for the principle of equal rights and self-determination of peoples, and to take other appropriate measures to strengthen universal peace;

3. To achieve international cooperation in solving international problems of an economic, social, cultural, or humanitarian character, and in promoting and encouraging respect for human rights and for fundamental freedoms for all without distinction as to race, sex, language, or religion; and

4. To be a center for harmonizing the actions of nations in the attainment of these common ends.

Article 33

1. The parties to any dispute, the continuance of which is likely to endanger the maintenance of international peace and security, shall, first of all, seek a solution by negotiation, enquiry, mediation, conciliation, arbitration, judicial settlement, resort to regional agencies or arrangements, or other peaceful means of their own choice.

2. The Security Council shall, when it deems necessary, call upon the parties to settle their dispute by such means.

Article 76

The basic objectives of the trusteeship system, in accordance with the Purposes of the United Nations laid down in Article 1 of the present Charter, shall be:

a. to further international peace and security;

b. to promote the political, economic, social and educational advancement of the inhabitants of the trust territories, and their progressive development towards self-government or independence as may be appropriate to the particular circumstances of each territory and its peoples and the freely expressed wishes of the peoples concerned, and as may be provided by the terms of each trusteeship agreement;

c. to encourage respect for human right and for fundamental freedoms for all without distinction as to race, sex, language, or religion, and to encourage recognition of the interdependence of the peoples of the world; and

d. to ensure equal treatment in social, economic and commercial matters for all members of the United Nations and their nationals, and also equal treatment for the latter in the administration of justice, without prejudice to the attainment of the foregoing objectives and subject to the provisions of Article 80.

No. 245

Charter of the International Military Tribunal and the Affirmation of the Principles by the General Assembly of the United Nations

(Aug. 8, 1945)

Article 6.

The following acts, or any of them, are crimes coming within the jurisdiction of the Tribunal for which there shall be individual responsibility:

(a) CRIMES AGAINST PEACE: namely, planning, preparation, initiation or waging of a war of aggression, or a war in violation of international treaties, agreements or assurances, or participation in a common plan or conspiracy for the accomplishment of any of the foregoing;

(b) WAR CRIMES: namely, violations of the laws or customs of war. Such violations shall include, but not be limited to, murder, ill-treatment or deportation to slave labor or for any other purpose of civilian population of or in occupied territory, murder or ill-treatment of prisoners of war or persons on the seas, killing of hostages, plunder of public or private property, wanton destruction of cities, towns or villages, or devastation not justified by military necessity;

(c) CRIMES AGAINST HUMANITY: namely, murder, extermination, enslavement, deportation, and other inhumane acts committeed against any civilian population, before or during the war;[1] or persecutions on political, racial or religious grounds in execution of or in connection with any crime within the jurisdiction of the Tribunal, whether or not in violation of the domestic law of the country where perpetrated.

Leaders, organizers, instigators and accomplices participating in the formulation or execution of a common plan or conspiracy to commit any of the foregoing crimes are responsible for all acts performed by any persons in execution of such plan.

No. 246

Message of the
President of the United States, Truman,
To Congress

(Mar. 12, 1947)

EXCERPTS

the Truman Doctrine

One of the primary objectives of the foreign policy of the United States is the creation of conditions in which we and other nations will be able to work out a way of life free from coercion. This was a fundamental issue in the war with Germany and Japan. Our victory was won over countries which sought to impose their will, and their way of life upon other nations.

To insure the peaceful development of nations, free from coercion, the United States has taken a leading part in establishing the United Nations. The United Nations is designed to make possible lasting freedom and independence for all its members. We shall not realize our objectives, however, unless we are willing to help free peoples to maintain their free institutions and their national integrity against aggressive movements that seek to force upon them totalitarian regimes.

This is no more than a frank recognition that totalitarian regimes imposed upon free peoples, by direct or indirect aggression, undermine the foundations of international peace and hence the security of the United States.

The peoples of a number of countries of the world have recently had totalitarian regimes forced upon them against their will. The Government of the United States has made frequent protests against coercion and intimidation, in violation of the Yalta agreements, in Poland, Rumania, and Bulgaria. I must also state that in a number of other countries there have been similar developments.

At the present moment in world history nearly every nation must choose between alternative ways of life. The choice is too often not a free one.

One way of life is based upon the will of the majority, and is distinguished by free institutions, representative government, free elections, guaranties of individual liberty, freedom of speech and religion, and freedom from political oppression.

The second way of life is based upon the will of a minority forcibly imposed upon the majority. It relies upon terror and oppression, a controlled press and radio, fixed elections, and the suppression of personal freedoms.

I believe that it must be the policy of the United States to support free peoples who are resisting attempted subjugation by armed minorities or by outside pressures.

I believe that we must assist free peoples to work out their own destinies in their own way.

I believe that our help should be primarily through economic and financial aid which is essential to economic stability and orderly political processes.

The world is not static, and the status quo is not sacred. But we cannot allow changes in the status quo in violation of the Charter of the United Nations by such methods as coercion, or by such subterfuges as political infiltration. In helping free and independent nations to maintain their freedom, the United States will be giving effect to the principles of the Charter of the United Nations.

Editor's Comment: This address was the inauguration and policy statement of the so-called "Truman Doctrine".

No. 247

The Essentials of Peace

(b) Resolution of the General Assembly, December 1, 1949

The General Assembly

1. *Declares* that the Charter of the United Nations, the most solemn pact of peace in history, lays down basic principles necessary for an enduring peace; that disregard of these principles is primarily responsible for the continuance of international tension; and that it is urgently necessary for all Members to act in accordance with these principles in the spirit of co-operation on which the United Nations was founded;

Calls upon every nation

2. *To refrain* from threatening or using force contrary to the Charter;

3. *To refrain* from any threats or acts, direct or indirect, aimed at impairing the freedom, independence or integrity of any State, or at fomenting civil strife and subverting the will of the people in any State;

4. *To carry out* in good faith its international agreements;

5. *To afford* all United Nations bodies full co-operation and free access in the performance of the tasks assigned to them under the Charter;

6. *To promote*, in recognition of the paramount importance of preserving the dignity and worth of the human person, full freedom for the peaceful expression of political opposition, full opportunity for the exercise of religious freedom and full respect for all the other fundamental rights expressed in the Universal Declaration of Human Rights;

7. *To promote* nationally and through international co-operation, efforts to achieve and sustain higher standards of living for all peoples;

8. *To remove* the barriers which deny to peoples the free exchange of information and ideas essential to international understanding and peace;

Calls upon every Member

9. *To participate* fully in all the work of the United Nations;

Calls upon the five permanent members of the Security Council

10. *To broaden* progressively their co-operation and to exercise restraint in the use of the veto in order to make the Security Council a more effective instrument for maintaining peace;

Calls upon every nation

11. *To settle* international disputes by peaceful means and to co-operate in supporting United Nations efforts to resolve outstanding problems;

12. *To co-operate* to attain the effective international regulation of conventional armaments; and

13. *To agree* to the exercise of national sovereignty jointly with other nations to the extent necessary to attain international control of atomic energy which would make effective the prohibition of atomic weapons and assure the use of atomic energy for peaceful purposes only.

EPILOGUE A

No. 248

Soviet Practice in Observing Treaties ("Soviet Political Treaties and Violations"; Staff Study of the Committee on the Judiciary, United States Senate, 84th Congress)

FOREWORD

By Senator James O. Eastland
Chairman, United States Senate Internal Security Subcommittee

During the chairmanship of my predecessor, Senator William E. Jenner, of Indiana, the Subcommittee on Internal Security authorized a staff study of the Soviet treaty record from 1917, when a handful of Bolsheviks seized power over 150 million non-Communists in Russia, to the present, when 800 million people on two continents suffer under Red despotism. The project was part of the subcommittee's examination of The Strategy and Tactics of World Communism. It contemplated a scrutiny of treaties and agreements involving peace, accord and fraternity, collaboration, friendship and neutrality, diplomatic recognition, frontier disputes, nonaggression pacts, conferences of conciliation, mutual aid, renunciation of war, and international promises to the peoples of the entire world — such as the Atlantic Charter.

The staff studied nearly a thousand treaties and agreements of the kinds described above, both bilateral and multilateral, which the Soviets have entered into not only with the United States, but with countries all over the world. The staff found that in the 38 short years since the Soviet

Union came into existence, its Government had broken its word to virtually every country to which it ever gave a signed promise. It signed treaties of nonaggression with neighboring states and then absorbed those states. It signed promises to refrain from revolutionary activity inside the countries with which it sought "friendship," and then cynically broke those promises. It was violating the first agreement it ever signed with the United States at the very moment the Soviet envoy, Litvinov, was putting his signature to that agreement, and it is still violating the same agreement in 1955. It broke the promises it made to the western nations during previous meetings "at the summit" in Teheran and Yalta. It broke lend-lease agreements offered to it by the United States in order to keep Stalin from surrendering to the Nazis. It violated the charter of the United Nations. It keeps no international promises at all unless doing so is clearly advantageous to the Soviet Union.

I seriously doubt that if during the whole history of civilization any great nation has ever made as perfidious a record as this in so short a time.

On the basis of the record, this question inevitably arises: Is the Soviet record merely a series of individual and unrelated misdeeds, or has treaty breaking been an instrument of national policy since the U.S.S.R. itself came into existence? In our second report on the activities of United States Citizens Employed by the United Nations, the subcommittee showed that this had been answered as long ago as 1920 by Bainbridge Colby, who was Woodrow Wilson's Secretary of State.

FOREWORD

The existing regime in Russia is based upon the negation of every principle of honor and good faith

said Mr. Colby.

The responsible leaders of the regime have frequently and openly boasted that they are willing to sign agreements and undertakings with foreign powers while not having the slightest intention of observing such undertakings or carrying out such agreements.

At the time he uttered these historic words, Secretary of State Colby had available to him many examples of how Communist leaders "frequently and openly boasted" that their pledged word was worthless. Let me call attention to just one of those examples, given by Zinoviev, Lenin's lieutenant, as long ago as 1919.

We are willing to sign an unfavorable peace —

Zinoviev said.

It would only mean we should put no trust whatever in the piece of paper we should sign. We should use the breathing space so obtained in order to gather our strength so that the mere continued existence of our Government would keep up the worldwide propaganda which Soviet Russia has been carrying on for more than a year.[1]

On another occasion, Joseph Stalin expressed the Communist diplomatic philosophy even more bluntly.

Words must have no relations to actions — otherwise what kind of diplomacy is it? Words are one thing, actions another. Good words are a mask for concealment of bad deeds. Sincere diplomacy is no more possible than dry water or wooden iron.[2]

This brings me to the fundamental issues that face the peoples of the world in connection with any effort to arrive at a workable agreement with communism.

Is the signature of any Communist Government on any document worth the paper it is written on?

When a Communist Government does sign an agreement, what can non-Communist nations do to see that the agreement is kept?

Until we can find satisfactory answers to these questions, it is futile to direct our efforts toward adding to the accumulation of documents which have already been signed and violated by the U.S.S.R. and other Communist countries.

The signatories of the Atlantic Charter promised that —

First, their countries seek no aggrandizement, territorial or other;

Second, they desire to see no territorial changes that do not accord with the freely expressed wishes of the peoples concerned;

Third, they respect the right of all peoples to choose the form of government under which they will live; and they wish to see sovereign rights and self-government restored to those who have been forcibly deprived of them.

If the U.S.S.R. would just live up to that pact, the greatest obstacles to world peace would disappear.

Soviet Political Treaties [With the Baltic States and Poland] and Violations

CHRONOLOGY

(With Soviet violations shown in bold print.)

(Key to source of references in column 1)

REFERENCES* FOR SOVIET POLITICAL TREATIES AND VIOLATIONS

1	Department of State Publication 4245–General Foreign Policy Series 53.
2	Busby Testimony to Senate Internal Security Subcommittee.
3	Klemov Testimony to Senate Internal Security Subcommittee.

---

[1] Congressional Record, p. 7049, vol. 74

[2] The Real Soviet Russia, Yale University Press, p. 71.

4 .... Testimony Strategy and Tactics Senate Internal Security Subcommittee, Vol. 1.

5 .... World War II International Agreements — Foreign Affairs Committee, 1953.

6 .... U. N. World, November 1950.

7 .... The New Leader, May 3, 1954.

8 .... Trends in Russian Foreign Policy Since World War I, Legislative Reference Service, 1947.

9 .... Background Information on the Soviet Union in International Relations Committee on Foreign Affairs, 1950.

10 .... A Decade of American Foreign Policy, Senate Committee on Foreign Relations and Department of State, 1950.

11 .... The Soviet Union in International Relations, Foreign Affairs.

12 .... Bullitt, William C., The Great Globe Itself, New York, Scribners, 1946.

13 .... Establishment of Diplomatic Relations With the U.S.S.R., 81st Cong., Document No. 90.

14 .... Congressional Record, 74th Congress May 14, 1935, Representative Tinkham.

15 .... Francis O. Wilcox, and Thorsten V. Kalijarvi, Recent American Foreign Policy, Basic Documents, 1941-51, New York, Appleton-Century-Crafts, 1952.

16 .... Walters, F. P., A History of the League of Nations, Vols. I and II, Oxford University Press, 1952.

SD .... State Department.

LNTS ...... League of Nations Treaty Series.

UNTS ...... United Nations Treaty Series.

BFSP ...... British Foreign Series Papers.

KR .... Kirsten Report.

FF .... Facts on File.

SB .... State Department Bulletin

DW .... Daily Worker.

XA .... Executive Agreement Series.

EE .... State Department, Office of Eastern European Affairs.

CH .... Current History.

BS .... Baltimore Sun.

USN .... U. S. News & World Report.

NT .... New York Times.

DD .... Defense Department.

*Example: 6 p. 1 would indicate "U.N. World. page 1."

8 p. 2 .... 1917, Dec. 31 .... Bolshevik government officially recognized independence of Finland.

SD, 16 p. 804 ..... 1939, Dec. 3 ..... A pact of mutual assistance and friendship was concluded by Soviet Russia and the Democratic Republic of Finland, headed by a Finnish Communist who had been in exile in Russia for 20 years. It included the ceding of territory extending across the Isthmus of Karelia and the lease of the port of Hanko for 20 years.

8 p. 4 .... 1918, Aug. 27 .... Russia and Central Powers. Russia renounced sovereignty over Lithuania and Latvia in supplementary peace treaty.

8 p. 21 .... 1939, Oct. 5 ..... A mutual assistance pact was imposed on Latvia by Soviet Russia,

8 p. 21 .... 1939, Oct. 10 .... A mutual assistance pact was imposed on Lithuania by Soviet Russia.

12 p. 220 .... 1940, Aug. 3 ..... Lithuania was incorporated into Soviet Russia.

12 p. 221 .... 1940, Aug. 5 ..... Latvia was incorporated into Soviet Russia.

8 p. 4 .... 1920, Feb. 2 ..... Estonia and Russia signed the Peace Treaty of Dorpat (Tartu). It recognized Estonia's independence and defined their joint boundaries.

12 p.228	1939, Sept. 28 . . .	The Soviet Government imposed a Pact of Mutual Assistance, infringing upon Estonian sovereignty.
12 p. 220, 228	1940, June 16	Soviet troops invaded and occupied Estonia and incorporated Estonia into the U.S.S.R. on Aug. 6, 1940
SD	1920, Apr. 12	Lithuania and Soviet Russia reestablished diplomatic relations.
8 p. 5	1920, Apr. 12	Lithuania and Russia signed Peace Treaty of Moscow. It recognized Lithuanian independence and defined their joint frontiers.
8 p. 21 . . . . :	1939, Oct. 10	A mutual assistance pact was imposed on Lithuania.
12 p. 220, 227	1940, June 15	Soviet troops invaded and occupied Lithuania. It was incorporated into the U.S.S.R. on Aug. 3, 1940.
SD	1920, Aug. 11	Latvia and Soviet Russia established diplomatic relations.
8 p. 5	1920, Aug. 11	Latvia and Russia. The Peace Treaty of Riga was signed in which Russia recognized Latvia, her independence and their common frontiers were defined.
8 p. 21	1939, Oct. 5	A mutual assistance pact was imposed on Latvia by Soviet Russia.
12 pp. 224, 229, 230	1940, June 16	Soviet troops invaded and occupied Latvia. It was incorporated into U.S.S.R. on Aug. 5, 1940.
8 p. 5	1920, Oct. 14	Finland and Russia. Treaty of Dorpat ended hostilities and defined boundaries.
12 p. 221	1940, Mar. 12	Soviet Russia took over the city and region of Viipuri and other territories.
SD	1921, Mar. 18	Treaty of Riga between Poland and Russia, ended hostilities and defined boundaries.
8 p. 21	1939, Sept. 17	Soviet troops invaded Poland.
8 p. 21	1939, Sept. 29	Germany and Soviet Russia signed a treaty partitioning Poland.
12 p. 222	1939, Oct. 10	The city and region of Wilno was detached from Poland and on Aug. 3, 1940, incorporated into Lithuania.
12 p. 221	1939, Nov. 1	Southeastern Poland was incorporated into the Ukrainian Soviet Republic.
12 p. 222	1939, Nov. 2	Northeastern Poland was incorporated into the Byelorussian Soviet Republic.
LNTS, 16:318	1922, June 1	Finland and Russia concluded an agreement regarding protection and inviolability of frontiers.
12 p. 223	1939, Nov. 30	Finnish borders were crossed by Soviet troops.
SD	1925, Aug. 3	Poland and Soviet Russia signed an agreement which settled frontier disputes.
8 p. 21	1939, Sept. 17	Soviet forces crossed Polish frontiers at many points.
LNTS, 60:145	1926, Sept. 28	Lithuania and Soviet Russia concluded a nonaggression pact. Protocols of May 6, 1931 and Apr. 4, 1934, extended the life of the treaty until Dec. 31, 1945.
12 p. 222	1940, June 15	Soviet Russia invaded and occupied Lithuania.
LNTS, 70:401	1927, Aug. 8	Estonia and Soviet Russia concluded an agreement regarding settlement of frontier disputes.
16 p. 385	1928, Sept. 27	Soviet Russia adhered to the KELLOGG-BRIAND PACT for Renunciation of War of Aug. 27, 1928. It provided that: "War should be renounced as an instrument of

national policy, and that the settlement of disputes should never be sought except by peaceful means."

8 p. 10 . . . . , ... The pact was signed by the United States, Belgium, France, Great Britain and the British Dominions, Italy, Japan, Poland, Czechoslovakia, Germany.[1]

Following are violations by Soviet Russia of the Kellogg-Briand Pact:

12 p. 223	1939, Sept. 17	Poland invaded.
12 p. 223	1939, Nov. 30	Finland invaded.
8 p. 22	1940, June 15	Lithuania invaded.
12 p. 224	1940, June 16	Latvia invaded.
12 p. 225	1940, June 16	Estonia invaded.
12 p. 230	1940, June 27	Rumania invaded.

LNTS, 82: 63 . . . . . 1928, Sept. 24 . . . . Finland and Soviet Russia signed notes settling Karelian Isthmus difficulties.

8 p. 11 . . . . 1931, May 6 . . . . . Lithuania and Soviet Russia renewed their nonaggression pact of Sept. 28, 1926. (See violations below item dated Sept. 28, 1926).

8 p. 11 . . . . 1932, Jan. 21 . . . . Finland and Soviet Russia signed a treaty of nonaggression.

12 p. 224 . . . . 1939, Nov. 30 . . . . Soviet Russia invaded Finland.

LNTS, 143: 113 . . . 1932, Feb. 5 . . . . . Latvia and and Soviet Russia signed a nonaggression pact.,

SD . . . . 1939, Oct. 5 . . . . . A pact of mutual assistance, which provided for stationing of Soviet troops was forced on Latvia.

12 p. 224 . . . . 1940, June 16 . . . . Soviet Russia invaded Latvia.

12 p. 224 . . . . 1932, Apr. 22 . . . . Finland and Soviet Russia concluded a convention of conciliation.

12 p. 224 . . . . 1939, Nov. 30 . . . . Soviet Russia invaded and occupied parts of Finland.

LNTS, 131: 297 . . . 1932, May 4 . . . . . Estonia and Soviet Russia signed a nonaggression pact.

SD . . . . 1939, Sept. 28 . . . . A pact of mutual assistance, which provided for stationing of Soviet troops was forced on Estonia.

12 p. 225 . . . . 1940, June 16 . . . Soviet Russia invaded Estonia.

12 p. 225 . . . . 1932, June 16 . . . . Estonia and Soviet Russia concluded a convention of conciliation.

8 p. 20 . . . . 1939, Sept. 28 . . . . Soviet Russia imposed pact of mutual assistance on Estonia.

12 p. 225 . . . . 1940, June 16 . . . . Soviet Russia invaded Estonia.

12 p. 225 . . . . 1932, June 18 . . . . Latvia and Soviet Russia concluded a convention of conciliation.

8 p. 21 . . . . 1939, Oct. 5 . . . . . Soviet Russia imposed a pact of mutual assistance on Latvia.

12 p. 226 . . . . 1940, June 16 . . . . Soviet Russia invaded Latvia.

LNTS, 136: 41 . . . . 1932, July 25 . . . . . Poland and Soviet Russia signed a nonaggression pact.

12 p. 226 . . . . 1939, Sept. 17 . . . . Soviet Russia invaded Poland.

12 p. 226 . . . . 1932, Nov. 23 . . . . Poland and Soviet Russia concluded a convention for conciliation.

12 p. 226 . . . . 1939, Sept. 17 . . . . Soviet Russia invaded and occupied parts of Poland.

LNTS 142: 265 . . . . 1933, June 3 . . . . . Poland and Soviet Russia signed a frontier dispute agreement.

8 p. 21 . . . . 1939, Sept. 17 . . . Soviet forces crossed Polish borders at many points.

LNTS 147: 67 . . . . . 1933, July 3 . . . . . Convention defining aggression was signed in London by Afghanistan, Estonia, Lavia, Persia, Poland, Rumania, Turkey, and Soviet Russia. Finland acceded on Jan. 31,

1934. This convention defined aggression as follows:
1. Invasion by armed forces;
2. Declaration of war;
3. Attack on territory, vessels or aircraft;
4. Naval blockade;
5. Aid to armed bands invading another state.

8 p. 47	1946, June 14	Soviet Russia was ceded Kushka by Afghanistan in a forced agreement.
12 p. 227	1939, Sept. 17	Soviet Russia invaded Poland.
Do	1939, Nov. 30	Soviet Russia invaded Finland.
8 p. 22	1940, June 15	Soviet Russia invaded Lithuania.
12 p. 227	1940, June 16	Soviet Russia invaded Estonia.
Do	do	Soviet Russia invaded Latvia.
Do	1940, June 27	Soviet Russia invaded Rumania.
8 p. 13	1933, July 5	Lithuania and Soviet Russia concluded a convention defining aggression.
8 p. 22	1940, June 15	Soviet troops invaded Lithuania.
SD	1933, July 28	Spain extended de jure recognition to Soviet Russia.
8 p. 12	1933, Dec. 19	Finland and Soviet Russia extended nonagression pact of 1932.
8 p. 21	1939, Nov. 30	Russian troops invaded Finland.
8 p. 13	1934, Feb. 6	Hungary and Soviet Russia established diplomatic relations.
8 p. 14	1934, Apr. 4	Latvia and Soviet Russia extended their nonagression pact for 10 years.
12 p. 220	1940, Aug. 5	Latvia was incorporated into Soviet Russia.
8 p. 14	1934, Apr. 4	Estonia and Soviet Russia extended their nonagression pact for 10 years.
12 p. 220	1940, Aug. 6	Estonia was incorporated into Soviet Russia.
8 p. 14	1934, Apr. 4	Lithuania and Soviet Russia extended their nonagression pact for 10 years.
12 p. 220	1940, Aug. 3	Lithuania was incorporated into Soviet Russia.
8 p. 14	1934, Apr. 7	Finland and Soviet Russia extended their nonagression pact until end of 1945.
12 p. 220	1939, Nov. 30	Soviet Russia attacked Finland.
8 p. 14	1934, May 5	Poland and Soviet Russia renewed their nonaggression pact of 1932 for 10 years.
12 p. 223	1939, Sept. 17	Soviet Russia attacked Poland.
12 p. 230	1934, June 9	Soviet Russia recognized Rumania and guaranteed her sovereignty.
16 p. 65, 807	1934, Sept. 15	Soviet Russia entered the LEAGUE OF NATIONS. On Dec. 14, 1939, it was declared to be no longer a Member of the League, by council resolution. (This was the first and only time that a member had been excluded from the League for violating the covenant.)

The Covenant of the League of Nations (adopted Apr. 28, 1919), preamble:

The High Contracting Parties, in order to promote international cooperation and to achieve international peace and security

by the acceptance of obligations not to resort to war,

by the prescription of open, just and honourable relations between nations,

16 p. 43 ....

by the firm establishment of the understandings of international law as by the actual rule of conduct among Governments, and

by the maintenance of justice and a

scrupulous respect for all treaty obligations in the dealings of organized peoples with one another,

Agree to this Covenant of the League of Nations.

16 p. 48 . . . .   ART. 10. The Members of the League undertake to respect and preserve as against external aggression the territorial integrity and existing political independence of all Members of the League * * *

16 p. 51 . . . .   ART. 16. 1. Should any Member of the League resort to war in disregard of its covenants under Arts. 12, 13, or 15 (these articles concerned arbitration, judicial settlement, the Permanent Court of International Justice, and submission of disputes to the Council) it shall ipso facto be deemed to have committed an act of war against all other Members of the League * * *

12 p. 219 . . . .   1939, Aug. 23 . . . .   A nonaggression treaty was concluded with Germany. It was a joint conspiracy to deprive Poland, Estonia, Latvia, and Lithuania of their independence and their territorial integrity, and Finland and Rumania of their territorial integrity.

12 p. 223 . . . .   1939, Sept. 17 . . . .   Poland was invaded by Soviet troops,

12 p. 219-220 . . . . .   1939, Sept. 28 . . . .   Germany and Soviet Russia concluded a treaty partitioning Poland.

8 p. 21 . . . .   do . . . .   A mutual-assistance pact was imposed on Estonia by Soviet Russia.

8 p. 21 . . . .   1939, Oct. 5 . . . . .   A mutual-assistance pact was imposed on Latvia by Soviet Russia.

8 p. 21 . . . .   1939, Oct. 10 . . . .   A mutual-assistance pact was imposed on Lithuania by Soviet Russia.

12 p. 223 . . . .   1939, Nov. 30 . . . .   Finland was invaded by Soviet troops.

SD, 16 p. 804 . . . . .   1939, Dec. 3 . . . . .   A pact of mutual assistance and friendship was concluded by Soviet Russia and the Democratic Republic of Finland, headed by a Finnish Communist who had been an exile in Russia for 20 years. It included the ceding of territory extending across the Isthmus of Karelia and the lease of the port of Hanko for 20 years.

LNTS 185: 384 . . . .   1937, Apr. 9 . . . . .   Latvia and Soviet Russia concluded a frontier dispute agreement.

12 p. 224 . . . .   1940, June 16 . . . .   Latvia was invaded by Soviet Russia.

8 p. 18 . . . .   1938, Nov. 26 . . . .   Poland and Soviet Russia reaffirmed adherenece to their nonaggression pact of 1932.

8 p. 21 . . . .   1939, Sept. 17 . . . .   Soviet forces crossed the Polish frontier.

8 p. 21 . . . .   1939, Sept. 28 . . . .   Germany and Soviet Russia signed a treaty partitioning Poland.

8 p. 20 . . . .   1939, Sept. 28 . . . .   Estonia and Soviet Russia signed a mutual assistance pact.

12 p. 225 . . . .   1939, Sept. 28 . . . .   Soviet Russia invaded Estonia.

12 p. 225 . . . .   1940, June 16 . . . .   Germany and U.S.S.R. signed a treaty partitioning Poland, and providing:

8 p. 21 . . . .   1939, Sept. 28 . . . .   1. Demarkation of German and Russian "interest spheres;"

2. Joint resistance to interference from others on partition;

3. Acknowledgment of the supremacy of each power in its respective sphere.

8 p. 21 . . . .   1939, Oct. 5 . . . . . .   Latvia and Soviet Russia signed a mutual assistance pact.

12 p. 220	1940, June 17	Soviet troops invaded Latvia.
8 p. 21	1939, Oct. 10	Lithuania and Soviet Russia signed a mutual assistance pact.
8 p. 22	1940, June 15	Soviet forces occupied Lithuania.
12 p. 221	1940, Aug. 3	Lithuania was incorporated into the U.S.S.R.
12 p. 221	1940, Aug. 5	Latvia was incorporated into the U.S.S.R.
12 p. 220	1940, Aug. 6	Estonia was incorporated into the U.S.S.R.
8 p. 25	1941, July 30	The Polish government-in-exile and Soviet Russia concluded an agreement on war cooperation which provided for: (1) Invalidation of Polish territorial changes in the 1939 treaty; (2) establishment of diplomatic relations; (3) rendition of mutual aid in war against Germany; (4) authorization for the formation of a Polish army in Soviet Russia; (5) amnesty to Polish prisoners in Russia.
8 p. 28	1943, Apr. 25	**Soviet Russia broke relations with the Polish government in exile because of the Polish demand for a Red Cross investigation of the Katyn Forest massacre.**
5 p. 1	1941, Sept. 24	Soviet Russia pledged Adherence to the ATLANTIC CHARTER[1] which resulted from the meeting between Roosevelt and Churchill, Aug. 14, 1941. It provided that: First, their countries seek no aggrandizement, territorial or other; Second, they desire to see no territorial changes that do not accord with the freely expressed wishes of the peoples concerned; Third, they respect the right of all peoples to choose the form of government under which they will live; and they wish to see sovereign rights and self-government restored to those who have been forcibly deprived of them;
5 p. 1	1941, Sept. 24	Fourth, they will endeavor, with due respect for their existing obligations, to further the enjoyment by all states, great or small, victor or vanquished, of access, on equal terms, to the trade and to the raw materials of the world which are needed for their economic prosperity; Fifth, they desire to bring about the fullest collaboration between all nations in the economic field with the object of securing, for all, improved labor standards, economic advancement and social security; Sixth, after the final destruction of the Nazi tyranny, they hope to see established a peace which will afford to all nations the means of dwelling in safety within their own boundaries, and which will afford assurance that all the men in all the lands may live out their lives in freedom from fear and want; Seventh, such a peace should enable all men to traverse the high seas and oceans without hindrance; Eighth, they believe that all of the nations of the world, for realistic as well as spiritual reasons, must come to the abandonment of the use of force. Since

no future peace can be maintained if land, sea or air armaments continue to be employed by nations which threaten, or may threaten, aggression outside of their frontiers, they believe, pending the establishment of a wider and permanent system of general security, that the disarmament of such nations is essential. They will likewise aid and encourage all other practicable measures which will lighten for peace-loving peoples the crushing burden of armaments.

Soviet territorial expansions:

	1939	Polish Provinces
	1940-44	Finnish Provinces
	1940	Rumanian Provinces
	1940	Estonia
	1940	Latvia
	1940	Lithuania
	1945	Koenigsberg area (East Prussia)
	1945	Czechoslovakian areas
	1945	Tanna Tuva
	1946	Afghanistan territory

Soviet-dominated territories:

1. Occupied areas:

	1946	Eastern Germany
	1945	Austria.[1]

2. European satellites:

	1946	Albania
	1946	Bulgaria
	1946	Rumania
	1947	Hungary
	1947	Poland
	1948	Czechoslovakia

3. Asiatic satellites:

5 p. 1	1945	Peoples Republic of Korea
	1946	Mongolian People's Republic
	1949	China
	1949	Manchukuo
	1951	Tibet
	1954	Northern Vietnam
116,193, 8 p. 26	1941, Dec. 4	Soviet Russia and the Polish government-in-exile signed declaration of assistance and friendship.
12 p. 230	1943, Apr. 25	Soviet Russia severed relations with the Polish government-in-exile and substituted for it a group of agents of Soviet Russia, which, on Jan. 1, 1945, it recognized as the Polish Government.
8 p. 26	1942, Jan. 1	Soviet Russia signed the United Nations declaration in Washington.[1]

The signatories of the United Nations declaration also "subscribed to the Atlantic Charter."

Violations are listed below the Atlantic Charter, Sept. 24, 1941.

EPILOGUE B

No. 249

The U.S.S.R. and Colonialism
(Letter of the United States Delegate, Stevenson, to
the President of the United Nations General Assembly)

UNITED STATES DELEGATION
TO THE GENERAL ASSEMBLY

For Immediate Release

Press Release No. 3862
November 28, 1961

Following is the text of a letter dated November 25, 1961, from Ambassador Adlai E. Stevenson, United States Representative to the United Nations, addressed to the President of the General Assembly, transmitting the comments of the United States Delegation on the Soviet Memorandum regarding colonialism.

"I have the honour to request that the attached commemts be circulated as an official document under agenda item 88, entitled 'The situation with regard to the implementation of the Declaration on the granting of independence to colonial countries and peoples', which is being discussed at the present session of the General Assembly."

COMMENTS BY THE UNITED STATES DELEGATION ON THE SOVIET MEMORANDUM CIRCULATED AS DOCUMENT A/4889

The United States delegation regrets that the Soviet Union has been unable to resist utilizing the United Nations forum to attack a number of Member States in the most outrageous and misleading terms. Under the circumstances, however, the United States now has no choice but to reply, even though we had hoped to be able to continue to keep the cold war out of the "colonialism" debates during the current session.

Role of the United Nations

The United Nations was created to reaffirm faith in fundamental human rights, in the dignity and worth of the human person, in the equal rights of men and women and of nations large and small.

Anything which derogates from the inherent rights of mankind and of nations is a proper — and even essential — subject for study and discussion by the General Assembly. The relationship between peoples and nations which we have come to call colonialism or by its variants — neo-colonialism or imperialism — can constitute a denial of the rights of the individual, and of the principle of self-determination and as such has frequently been the subject of our deliberations.

Since the formation of our Organization, the world community has devoted much of its time, talent and energy to the search for a solution to the pressing colonial problems in the world. The Fourth Committee of the General Assembly, the Trusteeship Council and the Committee on Information from Non-Self-Governing Territories have debated and made useful recommendations on a multitude of specific and general colonial problems. Other problems have arisen and have been discussed by other Committees and United Nations organs.

Only a hostile propagandist could maintain that the United Nations has not done useful work in this field. Through careful, detailed study and sound recommendations on specific issues, the General Assembly and other United Nations organs have facilitated the movement of one people after another to full and untrammelled independence.

We have seen the evidence of this development in the most concrete and meaningful terms; in the form of our membership, which has now more than doubled in the short lifetime of our Organization.

This hopeful evolution should not be cited to disguise the fact that much remains to be done in the colonial and related human rights fields. There are some cases where repeated admonitions by the General Assembly have proved unavailing. A number of items in this general area have remained on our agenda from year to year to serve as a concrete indication of our failure to find solutions.

But we should not despair of our ability to find the answers to those problems. There are many difficult items on the agenda of the sixteenth session of the General Assembly; others will be inscribed in years to come. With patience, goodwill and skill we will be able to solve them all in good time.

United States position on colonialism

The United States is against colonialism — wherever and whenever it occurs.

As a nation, we believe that man — a physical, intellectual and spiritual being, not an economic animal — has individual rights, divinely bestowed, limited only by the obligation to avoid infringement upon the equal rights of others.

We do not claim perfection in our own society and in our own lives, only that we seek it honestly and that the direction we take is always that of greater liberty.

We believe that justice, decency and liberty, in an orderly society, are concepts which have raised man above the beasts of the field; to deny any person the opportunity to live under their shelter is a crime against all humanity.

Our Republic is the produce of the first successful revolution against colonialism in modern times. Our people, drawn from all the nations of the world, have come to these shores in the search for freedom and opportunity in a progressive society. We have never forgotten either our origins or the nature of the world we live in.

As President Kennedy said in his inaugural address:

> "We dare not forget today that we are the heirs of that first revolution. Let the world go forth from this time and place, to friend and foe alike, that the torch has been passed to a new generation of Americans — born in this century, tempered by war, disciplined by a hard and bitter peace, proud of our ancient heritage — and unwilling to witness or permit the slow undoing of those human rights to which this Nation has always been committed, and to which we are committed today at home and around the world.

> "Let every nation know, whether it wishes us well or ill, that we shall pay any price, bear any burden, meet any hardship, support any friend, oppose any foe to assure the survival and success of liberty . . ."

Soviet allegations against the United States

In its frenetic effort to cover up its own dismal record in the field of colonialism and human rights, the Soviet Union has levelled two principal charges against the United States: (1) the United States is allied with colonialists and finances colonialist wars; and (2) the United States is itself a colonial Power. The answer to both charges, for those willing to see the truth, is simple.

The United States is unalterably opposed to all wars, including of course colonialist wars. We are not now and we shall never become allied with any nation for the purpose of planning, financing or waging colonial wars. The military alliances we have formed with others serve no aggressive aims; they are defensive alliances created in fact as a shield and a deterrent to those who would not shrink from the use of force to impose their new brand of colonialist rule on other peoples and territories.

Secondly, we would hold no people against its will. We are prepared to take the necessary measures to consult any or all of the approximately 100,000 people whose destinies are still associated with ours any time they request it. The people of Puerto Rico are fully self-governing, as the General Assembly has found after careful examination, enjoy the status of American citizens, and are free to request a change of status at any time. The remaining territories for which the United States exercises sovereignty are in the process of becoming self-governing.

The United States' position is that "the subjection of peoples to alien subjugation, domination and exploitation constitutes a denial of fundamental human rights, is contrary to the Charter of the United Nations and is an impediment to the promotion of world peace and co-operation". This is the language of Bandung; it is also the language of the General Assembly in resolution 1514 (XV) on the granting of independence to colonial countries and peoples. But there is a higher authority and a more definitive formulation.

The Charter declares in effect that on every nation in possession of foreign territories, there rests the responsibility to assist the peoples of these areas "in the progressive development of their free political institutions" so that ultimately they can validly choose for themselves their permanent political status.

We have and we will continue to abide by the Charter.

The Soviet record of imperialism

But the question remains why the Soviet Union decided to launch such a reckless attack on those countries which oppose its drive for world conquest at this time. Every outstanding colonial question of real substance is to be found on the agenda of this session of the General Assembly. There are two major items on the agenda of the plenary alone which will make it possible to discuss all aspects of the general problem.

Why has the Soviet Union twice in the last two years attempted to seize the initiative on the colonial issue from the new States of Africa and Asia? Why has the Soviet Union attempted to inject East-West differences into the complicated and difficult North-South problems, thereby making it less likely that we will be able to find realistic and meaningful solutions? Why has the Soviet Union sought to distract the General Assembly from the tried and true procedures it has followed for fifteen years with such marked success, substituting a war of words for detailed discussion and specific recommendations of individual territories and problems?

There are at least two answers.

First, the Soviet Union does not wish the United Nations to operate successfully in this or any other field. The Soviet Union is fearful that the solution of outstanding colonial problems involving the West will impel the United Nations to focus attention on the situation in the vast Soviet empire.

Moreover, in the past fifteen years, as the process of self-determination in the ex-colonial areas of Asia and Africa was rapidly expanding the world community of free and independent nations, the contrary process was taking place within the periphery of the Soviet Union. Wherever the influence of the Soviet armed forces could be brought to bear, independent countries, many of which had just been liberated from Hitler's terror, were absorbed and their national aspirations savagely repressed by a State bent on the eradication of the national identity of all peoples within the Soviet domain.

This indicates the second "well spring" of Soviet interest in the colonial question in the United Nations. The Soviet memorandum and initiative is a diversionary move; an attempt to prevent the world organization from focusing on the serious deprivations of human rights in the Soviet world.

Many criteria have been developed over the years to determine whether or not a particular situation falls into the "colonial category". Surely the key, however, is the absence of self-determination for the dependent peoples concerned.

Because the world cannot long remain half-slave and half-free, the United States expects that the United Nations will focus its attention as carefully on the "colonialism" of the Soviet Union as it does on that of Portugal or any other nation. For if the Soviet Union comes to believe it can enforce a double standard in the world with complete impunity, no country in the world will be safe.

The record speaks for itself.

Self-determination in the Soviet empire

We are told that the peoples of the Soviet Union enjoy the right of self-determination. Indeed, the Soviet regime at its inception issued a Declaration of Rights which proclaimed "the right of the nations of

Russia to free self-determination, including the right to secede and form independent States".

How did this "right" work in practice? An independent Ukrainian Republic was recognized by the Bolsheviks in 1917, but in 1917 they established a rival Republic in Kharkov. In July 1923, with the help of the Red Army, a Ukrainian Soviet Socialist Republic was established and incorporated into the USSR. In 1920, the independent Republic of Azerbaidzhan was invaded by the Red Army and a Soviet Socialist Republic was proclaimed. In the same year, the Khanate of Khiva was invaded by the Red Army and a puppet Soviet People's Republic of Khorezm was established. With the conquest of Khiva, the approaches to its neighbour, the Emirate of Bokhara, were opened to the Soviet forces which invaded it in September 1920. In 1918, Armenia declared its independence from Russia and a mandate offered to the United States Government was refused by President Wilson. In 1920, the Soviet army invaded, and Armenian independence, so long awaited, was snuffed out. In 1921, the Red Army came to the aid of Communists rebelling against the independent State of Georgia and installed a Soviet regime.

This process inexorably continued. Characteristically, the Soviets took advantage of the turmoil and upheaval of the Second World War to continue the process of colonial subjugation at the expense of its neighbours. The Soviets' territorial aggrandizement included the Karelian province and other parts of Finland and the Eastern provinces of Poland, the Romanian provinces of Bessarabia and Bukovina, the independent States of Estonia, Latvia and Lithuania, the Koenigsberg area, slices of Czechoslovakia, South Sakhalin, the Kurile Islands, and Tanna Tuva.

These are outright annexations of territories whose peoples are as enamoured of freedom and as fully entitled to their rights as are the people of Africa, Asia and the Americas. But there is another category of Soviet colonial territory, where neo-colonialism in a form never dreamed of in other parts of the world is practised.

Soviet colonial practices

The Soviet system of coping with disaffected populations in Soviet colonies is simple and effective, but shocking in the twentieth century. During the war, the Soviets deported entire ethnic groups to the East, fearful that they would use the occasion to fight for their independence. These groups included the Volga Germans (405,000), the Crimean Tatars (259,000), the Kalmucks of the northwestern Caspian area

(130,000), the Ingush (74,000). These deportations were admitted by Chairman Khrushchev in his secret speech before the Congress of the Communist Party of the Soviet Union. In 1957, the Supreme Soviet, apparently in recognition of the crime committed against humanity, belatedly decreed the rehabilitation and eventual return of the remnants of some of these ethnic groups.

Even more shocking was the series of deportations undertaken by the Soviets following their ruthless subjugation of the independent nations of Estonia, Latvia and Lithuania. In June of 1941, more than 200,000 persons were deported from the Baltic States, and the total now approaches 700,000.

As another indication of the fate of annexed ethnic groups in the Soviet Union, the case of the Kazakhs is instructive. The Moslem Kazakhs are the largest Asian nation subject to the colonial rule of Soviet Russia. In 1920, the Soviet census listed 3,968,289 Kazakhs. In 1939, their numbers had dwindled to 3,098,164. They comprised less than 30 per cent of the population in what Mr. Khrushchev describes as their national republic. This suggests the human costs — to national groups — of the material advances which he claims.

Following the Second World War, whole nations and peoples were swallowed up behind the Iron Curtain in violation of agreements and without a free vote of the peoples concerned. These included Poland, Hungary, Romania, Bulgaria, Albania and then Czechoslovakia in *coups d'état*. The German and Korean people, divided as the result of the war, were held from unity by the failure of the Soviet Union to live up to the agreements it had signed and to permit the self-determination of these peoples through free elections. Viet-Nam was divided as the result of later expansionism by communist subversion and military expansion.

The consequences of Soviet imperialism

The disgrace, barbarity and savagery — to cite the words used by Chairman Khrushchev — of Soviet imperialist rule is indicated by the never ending flow of refugees from the countries made colonies by the Soviet Union. More than 12 million persons have escaped since the Second World War from the Soviet Union, Communist China and the areas they control: Albania, Romania, Estonia, Latvia, Lithuania, North Korea, North Viet-Nam and Tibet.

The greatest sustained movement of refugees in modern history continues for the fourteenth year out of Soviet East Germany. Since the end of the Second World War, more than 3 million Germans have fled from their homes and businesses in the Soviet-controlled zone and East Berlin in order to live and work in the free world. Despite the wall erected to hold the East German people from the freedoms they earnestly desire, East Berliners risk their lives daily to reach freedom in West Berlin.

When the Soviet imperialist regime in North Korea was established north of the 38th parallel in May 1948, another mass exodus began. Within two years, 1.8 million residents of the Communist zone, out of an estimated population of 9 million, migrated southward to the Republic of Korea. Within seven months after the Communist armies of North Korea invaded the Republic of Korea, an additional 800,000 North Korean prisoners of war refused repatriation to North Korea and 25,000 Chinese soldiers also refused to go home.

Within ten months after the partition of Viet-Nam, nearly a million Vietnamese had fled the Soviet-controlled North. This displacement of persons took place despite the most strenuous efforts, in violation of the Geneva Armistice Agreement, to stem the flow.

Perhaps the most dramatic instance was the flight of nearly 200,000 Hungarians after the revolt of October 1956 was crushed by Soviet troops. Since the first Communist takeover of Hungary in 1947, an additional 200,000 persons fled their homes to live and work in the West.

We are at present living through the most recent example of this general pattern. With the Chinese Communist subjugation of Tibet, more than 20,000 refugees were forced to leave their homes behind them and flee to other countries.

The right to self-determination has never been accepted for its own dependent areas by the Soviet Government. Stalin in 1923 explained that "there are instances when the right of self-determination comes into conflict with another, higher right; the right of the working class to fortify its own power. In such cases, the right of self-determination cannot be and must not serve as an obstacle to the realization of the right of the working class to its own dictatorship. The former must give way to the latter." In short, self-determination is a right which can only be upheld when the peoples concerned have not fallen under Communist domination.

On the contrary, rather than assisting the development towards greater independence and self-determination of the nations under their domination, the announced Soviet design is to eradicate all national (including linguistic) differences that exist between these diverse nationalities and the Great Russian model. The Soviet Communist Party programme states: "the obliteration of frontiers between the classes and development of communist socialist relations strengthens the socialist uniformity of the nations and favours the development of common communist features." The programme laments, however, that "the obliteration of national features, particularly of the language differences, is a considerably longer process than the obliteration of class differences". Khrushchev, in his 18 October 1961 speech to the 22nd Congress of the Soviet Communist Party left no question as to his design towards peoples dominated by the Soviet Union when he said; "It is essential that we stress the education of the masses in the spirit of proletarian internationalism and Soviet patriotism. Even the slightest vestiges of nationalism should be eradicated with uncompromising Bolshevik determination." This is the unique aspect of Soviet "colonialism" — an aspect that differentiates it from all other historical examples of one State's suppression of another's freedom. Through the total State controls of mass culture, propaganda, education and movement, the Soviets seek to wipe out for ever the national characteristics that differentiate the Turk from Ukrainian, the Kazakh from the Armenian, the non-Russian from the Russian. They not only seek the eradication of differences and the suppression of freedom, but the eradication of the desire for freedom.

The Soviet plan

In view of the Soviet Union's own dark record of imperialist oppression and exploitation, Soviet professions of devotion to the welfare of the peoples of colonial or former colonial areas outside the Soviet empire are hypocritical. But more than mere hypocrisy is involved. These professions mask a sinister design in so far as the future of the colonial and newly-independent peoples themselves are concerned.

Communist doctrine pretends to provide an all-embracing explanation of historical processes. It therefore discloses to those who study it the real intentions of Soviet policy.

It is Soviet doctrine that the political development of newly independent States is to proceed in two distinct phases. The first stage — as Academician Y.E. Zhukov puts it in *Pravda* of 26 August 1960 — is one in which "the majority of the new Asian and African national

States are headed by bourgeois politicians under the banner of nationalism"

At the same time, however, local Communists are instructed to prepare for the future day of direct action. In this initial period, Communists are to concentrate their efforts on infiltrating and obtaining key positions in political and social groups, especially trade-union and student movements, as well as organizing and participating in Communist-front organizations of all types.

The Soviets regard the present state of political orientation within the newly-developing countries as merely a phase, one clearly undesirable and unacceptable from the long-range point of view. As Academician Zhukov phrases it: "One cannot, therefore, term socialist those general democratic measures which to some degree are implemented in India, Indonesia, the United Arab Republic, Iraq and other independent countries of Asia and Africa." The policies and politics of these countries, Zhukov states, are "of a democratic and not a socialist character". At the appropriate stage, therefore, the Communist parties must come forth frankly and openly with their bid for power.

Soviet statements on colonialism are in themselves typical of the semantic perversion in Communist philosophy, by which "freedom" becomes "slavery" and "slavery" becomes "freedom." By means of this distortion of words, the Soviet Union hopes to distract attention from the real issues. But the peoples of the world can forget four fundamental facts only at their own peril:

First, the Sino-Soviet bloc today embraces the largest colonial empire which has ever existed in all history.

Second, the Communist empire is the only imperial system which is not liquidating itself, as other empires have done, but is still trying energetically to expand in all directions. With the growth of Soviet and Chinese Communist power, these expansionist efforts have now become more blatant and are now being attempted in areas outside the periphery of the bloc.

Third, the Soviet colonial system is one of the most cruel and oppressive ever devised. By the ruthless and brutal use of techniques of police control, and by the erection of artificial barriers to communication, the regimes of the Sino-Soviet bloc have harshly suppressed all movements in the direction of freedom, have instituted programmes to eradicate all national identity in the people, and have held their peoples in virtual isolation from the outside world.

Finally, the Soviet colonial empire is the only modern empire in which no subject people has ever been offered any choice concerning their future and their destiny.

President Kennedy summarized it in the following words in his general debate statement at this session of the General Assembly:

> "I do not ignore the remaining problems of traditional colonialism which still confront this body. Those problems will be solved, with patience, goodwill and determination. Within the limits of our responsibility in such matters, my country intends to be a participant, and not merely an observer, in the peaceful, expeditious movement of nations from the status of colonies to the partnership of equals. That continuing tide of self-determination, which runs so strong, has our sympathy and our support.

> "But colonialism in its harshest forms is not only the exploitation of new nations by old, of dark skins by light — or the subjugation of the poor by the rich. My nation was once a colony — and we know what colonialism means; the exploitation and subjugation of the weak by the powerful, of the many by the few, of the governed who have given no consent to be governed, whatever their comment, their class or their colour.

> "And that is why there is no ignoring the fact that the tide of self-determination has not yet reached the communist empire where a population far larger than that officially termed 'dependent' lives under governments installed by foreign troops instead of free institutions — under a system which knows only one party and one belief — which suppresses free debate, free elections, free newspapers, free books and free trade unions — and which builds a wall to keep truth a stranger and its own citizens prisoners. Let us debate colonialism in full — and apply the principle of free choice and the practice of free plebiscites in every corner of the globe."

Editor's comment: Adlai E. Stevenson, the United States Ambassador to the United Nations from 1961 to 1965, was noted for his intelligence, tact, objectivity, and moderation. Even Soviet propagandists hesitated to call him a warmonger or instigator of the Cold War. His opinions and conclusions in this document were expressed after long research and reflection.

EPILOGUE C

Nc. 250

A United Nations Prayer For Victory Over Tyrants (Radio Address of Franklin D. Roosevelt, President of the United States, on United Flag Day, June 14 1942)

"God of the free, we pledge our hearts and lives today to the cause of all free mankind.

"Grant us victory over the tyrants who would enslave all free men and Nations. Grant us faith and understanding to cherish all those who fight for freedom as if they were our brothers. Grant us brotherhood in hope and union, not only for the space of this bitter war, but for the days to come which shall and must unite all the children of earth.

"Our earth is but a small star in the great universe. Yet of it we can make, if we choose, a planet unvexed by war, untroubled by hunger or fear, undivided by senseless distinctions of race, color, or theory. Grant us that courage and foreseeing to begin this task today that our children and our children's children may be proud of the name of man.

"The spirit of man has awakened and the soul of man has gone forth. Grant us the wisdom and the vision to comprehend the greatness of man's spirit, that suffers and endures so hugely for a goal beyond his own brief span. Grant us honor for our dead who died in the faith, honor for our living who work and strive for the faith, redemption and security for all captive lands and peoples. Grant us patience with the deluded and pity for the betrayed. And grant us the skill and the valor that shall cleanse the world of oppression and the old base doctrine that the strong must eat the weak because they are strong.

"Yet most of all grant us brotherhood, not only for this day but for all our years — a brotherhood not of words but of acts and deeds. We are all of us children of earth — grant us that simple knowledge. If our brothers are oppressed, then we are oppressed. If they hunger, we hunger. If their freedom is taken away, our freedom is not secure. Grant us a common faith that man shall know bread and peace — that he shall know justice and righteousness, freedom and security, an equal opportunity and an equal chance to do his best, not only in our own lands, but throughout the world, And in that faith let us march, toward the clean world our hands can make. Amen."

Serial no.
of document   LIST OF REFERENCES

Abbreviations:

D. Ger. F. P. — Documents on German Foreign Policy, 1918-1945;
from the Archives of the German Foreign Ministry. Washington,
G.P.O. (Dept. of State Publication). Series D: (1937-1945), v.
VII (published 1956), v. VIII (1954), v. IX (1956), v. X (1957),
v. XI (1960), v. XII (1962). Also published: London: H.M.S.O.

L. N. T. S. — League of Nationsl Treaty Series, Geneva (vol.:
pages).

Lit. Ber. — Archives of the Lithuanian Legation in Berlin, in the
Library of the Hoover Institution on War, Revolution and Peace,
Stanford University. [The Hoover Library has asked us to print
the following clarification: Some files of the former Lithuanian
Legation in Berlin were deposited in 1945 with the Hoover
Institution on War, Revolution and Peace at Stanford University
for safekeeping. When unpacked, these papers showed heavy
water damage and rot, The entire material was later returned to
the Lithuanian Legation at their request.]

Lit. Wash. — Archives of the Lithuanian Legation in Washington

Micr. (+reel and frame no.) — Microcopies of Captured German
Documents in the Microfilm Reading Room of the National
Archives, Washington, D.C.

Nazi-Soviet Relations — Nazi-Soviet Relations; documents from
the Archives of the German Foreign Office. Ed. by Raymond
James Sontag and James Stuart Beddie. Washington: G.P.O.
(Dept. of State Publication), 1948.

T. V. — Tarybu valdžios atkurimas Lietuvoje 1940-1941 metais;
dokumentu rinkinys (Restoration of Soviet Power in Lithuania
in 1940-1941; a collection of documents). E. Jakovskis et al., ed.
Vilnius: Mintis, 1965.

U. S. Baltic — U.S. Congress. House. Select Committee on
Communist Aggression. Baltic States Investigation. Hearings
before the Select Committee to Investigate the Incorporation of
the Baltic States into the U.S.S.R. . . . Washington: G.P.O., 1954

U. S. Com. Ag. — U.S. Congress. House. Select Committee on
Communist Aggression. Report of the Select Committee to
Investigate Communist Aggression and the Forced Incorporation
of the Baltic States into the U.S.S.R. Third Interim Report.
Washington, G.P.O., 1954.

U. S. Decade — U. S. Congress. Senate. Committee on Foreign
Affairs. A decade of American foreign policy; basic documents,
1941-1949. Washington: G.P.O., 1950.

U. S. For. Rel. — U. S. Department of State. Foreign relations of
the United States. Washington: G.P.O. the Soviet Union,
1933-1939 (pub. 1952). Papers relating to . . . 1922, v. II
(1938). Diplomatic papers, 1932, v. III (1948); 1940, v. I
(1959); 1941, v. I (1958).

Lietuvos Istatymai. Sistematizuotas istatymu, instruckciju ir isa-
kymu rinkinys (Lithuanian Statutes. A systematized collection
of statutes, instructions and executive orders). Kaunas: Išleido
Merkys ir Petrulis, 1922. p. 7

Serial no.
of document   LIST OF REFERENCES

2   a) *Ibid.*, pp. 8-9; b) Lietuvos Enciklopedija (Lithuanian Encyclo-
        pedia). Boston, Lietuvos Enciklopedijos Leidykla. 36 vols.,
        1953-1969. v. 15, pp. 353-56; c) Lietuvos Istatymai, p. 8.

3   L. N. T. S. 3:122-137; (for the text in Russian and Lithuanian,
        see: Lietuvos sutartys su svetimomis valstybemis. Surinko ir
        sutvarke Pranas Dailide . . . Recueil des traites conclus par la
        Lithuanie avec les pays étrangers. Publié par le Ministère des
        Affaires Etrangères. Kaunas, 1930. v. 1, pp. 30-31.

4   Documents diplomatiques, conflict polono-lithuanien, question de
        Vilna, 1918-1924. Kaunas: Republique de Lithuanie, Ministère
        des Affaires Etrangères, 1924. p. 1RW.

5   Lithuanian Recognition. Washington: Lithuanian Information
        Bureau, 1921. p. 21

6   U.S. For. Rel., 1922, v. II, pp. 973-74.

7   Ladas Natkevičius. Aspect politique et juridique du differend
        polono-lithuanien. 4me ed. Paris: Chauny et Quinsac, 1930. pp.
        51-52, 55. Also: 1918-1928 metu Lietuvos politikos gyvenimo
        chronologija (A chronology of Lithuanian political life, 1918-
        1928). Kaunas: Ministry of Foreign Affairs, 1929.

8   L.N.T.S., 60:152-159; for attached protocol see: L.N.T.S., 125:
        261-63. (For text in Russian and Lithuanian see: Recueil des
        traites conclus par la Lithuanie avec les pays estrangers, v. 1, pp.
        429-31.)

9   U. S. Baltic, p. 484.

10   *Ibid.*

11   L. N. T. S., 186: 273-75.

12   *Ibid,* 89: 371-79.

13   Recueil des traités conclus par la Lithuanie avec les pays étrangers,
        v. II (1939), pp. 252-55; See also: U.S. Baltic, pp. 486-87.

14   U.S. Comm. Ag., pp. 443-44

15   Vyriausybes žinios (Official Journal of Lithuania). Kaunas, no.
        632, Jan. 25, 1939; See also: La documentation internationale
        (Paris), no. 57-58, March-April, 1939.

16   Nazi-Soviet Relations, pp. 76-77

17   *Ibid.,* p. 78.

18   D. Ger. F. P., VII, p. 404.

19   *Ibid.,* p. 411.

20   *Ibid.,* p. 429.

21   *Ibid.,* p. 450.

22   *Ibid.,* p. 467.

23   *Ibid.,* VIII, pp. 55-56.

Serial no.
of document   LIST OF REFERENCES

24   *Ibid.*, pp. 62-63.

25   *Ibid.*, p. 75.

26   *Ibid.*, pp. 76-77.

27   Archives of the Estonian Consulate General in New York.

28   *Ibid.*

29   D. Ger. F. P., VIII, p. 113.

30   *Ibid.*, p. 123.

31   *Ibid.*, p. 112.

32   U.S. Com. Ag., p. 444.

33   D. Ger. F.P., VIII, p. 121.

34   *Ibid.*, p. 130.

35   *Ibid.*, p. 169.

36   *Ibid.*, p. 166.

37   Nazi-Soviet Relations, pp. 105-06.

38   D. Ger. F. P., VIII, no. 161.

39   *Ibid.*, no. 193

40   *Ibid.*, p. 199.

41   *Ibid.*, p. 207.

42   *Ibid.*, pp. 212-13.

43   *Ibid.*, pp. 214-15.

44   *Ibid.*, p. 215.

45   *Ibid.*, p. 219.

46   *Ibid.*, p. 238.

47   *Ibid.*, p. 244.

48   U.S. Com Ag., pp. 315-16.

49   Jane Degras, ed. Soviet Documents on Foreign Policy. V.III:
        1933-1941. London: Oxford University Press, 1953. pp. 380-82.
        See also: Vyriausybes zinios (Official Journal of Lithuania), no.
        699.

50   Lietuvos žinios (Kaunas), no. 247, October 30, 1939.

51   Tiesa (Vilnius), Nov. 15, 1940.

52   U.S. For. Rel., Soviet Union, 1933-39, pp. 974-75

53   D. Ger. F. P., VIII, pp. 284-85.

Serial no.
of document   LIST OF REFERENCES

54   U.S. For. Rel., Soviet Union, 1933-39, pp. 974-75.

55   *Ibid.*, pp. 976-78.

56   Lit. Wash.

57   U.S. For. Rel., Soviet Union, 1933-39, p. 979.

58   Lithuanian Bulletin (New York), v. VI, no. 3-4, March-April, 1948: 11-13; see also: Pravda (Moscow), Nov. 1, 1939.

59   Baltic Review (New York), no. 1, Dec. 1953: 8-9.

60   U.S. Com. Ag., p. 319.

61   *Ibid.*

62   *Ibid.*

63   Lit. Wash.

64   U.S. Com. Ag., p. 327.

65   D. Ger. F. P., IX, pp. 474-75.

66   U.S. Com. Ag., pp. 320-21. See also: Izvestia (Moscow), no. 123/7195, May 30, 1940; and: Vneshnaia politika SSSR; sbornik dokumentov. Moscow, 1946, v. IV, pp. 507-08.

67   D. Ger. F. P., IX, pp. 548-50.

68   U.S. Com. Ag., p. 332. See also: Izvestia (Moscow), no 137/7209, June 16, 1940; and: Vneshnaia politika SSSR, v. IV, p. 511.

69   Lietuvos Telegramu Agentura (ELTA) Bulletin; appeared in XX Amžius (Kaunas), no. 135(1186), June 17, 1940.

70   Tėvynė (New York). No. 30 (Aug. 20, 1965), no. 31 (Aug. 27), no. 32 (Sept. 3).

71   Alfred Bilmanis, comp. Latvian-Russian Relations; documents. Washington: Latvian Legation, 1944. p. 202.

72   Library of the Hoover Institute on War, Revolution and Peace, Stanford University.

73   *Ibid.*

74   Revue baltique (Tallinn), v. I, no. 1, Feb. 1940: 29-31.

75   D. Ger. F. P., IX, p. 572.

76   *Ibid.*, p. 574.

77   *Ibid.*, p. 575.

78   U. S. Baltic, p. 540.

79   Micr. T-120/286/214884.

80   U.S. For. Rel., 1940, v. I, p. 369.

Serial no.
of document LIST OF REFERENCES

81   *Ibid.*, pp. 369-70.

82   *Ibid.*, p. 371.

83   D. Ger. F. P., IX, pp. 578-79.

84   *Ibid.*, p. 579.

85   *Ibid.*, pp. 582-83.

86   *Ibid.*, p. 583.

87   *Ibid.*, p. 593.

88   *Ibid.*, pp. 594-95.

89   *Ibid.*, pp. 595-96.

90   Nazi-Soviet Relations, p. 154

91   D. Ger. F. P., IX, p. 687.

92   *Ibid.*, X, p. 126.

93   Nazi-Soviet Relations, p. 165.

94   U.S. For. Rel., 1940, v. I, p. 386.

95   *Ibid.*, p. 387.

96   *Ibid.*, p. 389.

97   *Ibid.*, p. 393.

98   *Ibid.*, pp. 395-97.

99   U.S. Com. Ag., p. 361; for full text of speech see Lietuvos Aidas, July 15, 1940.

100   U.S. Com. Ag., pp. 359-60; for Lithuanian text see: T. V., pp. 114-16.

101   U.S. Com. Ag., pp. 360-61; for Lithuanian text see: T. V., pp. 116-19.

102   T. V., p. 125.

103   U.S. Com. Ag., pp. 362-63; for Lithuanian text see: T. V., p. 129.

104   Nazi-Soviet Relations, p. 168.

105   U.S. For. Rel., 1940, v. I, p. 416.

106   *Ibid.*, p. 417.

107   *Ibid.*, p. 420.

108   *Ibid.*, p. 419.

109   *D. Ger. F. P., X, p. 167.*

Serial no.
of document   LIST OF REFERENCES

110   *Ibid.*, p. 192.

111   *Ibid.*, no. 162.

112   Micr. T-120/740/357755.

113   Micr. T-120/740/357754.

114   D. Ger. F. P., X, pp. 396-97.

115   *Ibid.*, p. 429.

116   *Ibid.*, p. 450.

117   *Ibid.*, p. 470.

118   Micro. T-120/740/357775-78; for Russian text see: Micr. T-120/
        740/357772-74.

119   Micr. T-120/740/357779; for Russian text see: Micr. T-120/
        740/357780.

120   Micr. T-120/740/357790.

121   Micr. T-120/740/357798-99.

122   D. Ger. F. P., XI, p. 4.

123   *Ibid.*, p. 8.

124   Nazi-Soviet Relations, p. 184.

125   *Ibid.*, pp. 186-87.

126   Micr. T-120/740/357826.

127   Nazi-Soviet Relations, p. 188.

128   D. Ger. F. P., XI, pp. 550-53. See also: D. Ger. F. P., XI, p. 544.

129   *Ibid.*, pp. 922-24.

130   *Ibid.*, pp. 960-61.

131   *Ibid.*, pp. 971-72.

132   *Ibid.*, p. 979.

133   *Ibid.*, p. 1000.

134   *Ibid.*, pp. 1000-01.

135   *Ibid.*, p. 1010.

136   *Ibid.*, p. 1039.

137   *Ibid.*, p. 1040.

138   *Ibid.*, p. 1052.

139   *Ibid.*, p. 1068.

Serial no.
of document   LIST OF REFERENCES

140   Deutsche Allgemeine Zeitung (Berlin), no. 19, Jan. 11, 1941.
       Reprinted in: Robert Strausz-Hupé and Stefan T. Possony,
       International relations in the age of conflict between democracy
       and dictatorship. New York: McGraw-Hill, 1950. pp. 309-310.

141   Nazi-Soviet Relations, pp. 169-171.

142   U.S. For. Rel., 1940, v. I, p. 397.

143   Lith. Wash.

144   U.S. Com. Ag., p. 369. Also: Lith. Wash.

145   U.S. Com. Ag., pp. 369-70. Also: Lith. Wash.

146   U.S. Com. Ag., p. 370. Also: Lith. Wash.

147   U.S. Com. Ag., pp. 370-71. Also: Lith. Wash.

148   U.S. Com. Ag., pp. 371-72. Also: Lith. Wash.

149   U.S. Com. Ag., p. 367. Also: Lith. Wash.

150   Nazi-Soviet Relations, pp. 172-73.

151   U.S. Com. Ag., p. 366. Also: Lith. Wash.

152   U.S. Com. Ag., pp. 371-72. Also: Lith. Wash.

153   D. Ger. F. P., X, p. 466.

154   Library of the Hoover Institution on War, Revolution and Peace,
       Stanford University.

155   Lith. Ber.

156   Lietuvos Diplomatu Protestai (Lithuanian Diplomatic Protests).
       Vilnius, 1940.

157   Lith. Ber.

158   Ibid.

159   *Ibid.*

160   U.S. Com. Ag., pp. 464-68; original, U.S. House of Repre-
       sentatives, files of Baltic Committee, Exhibit 16-H of 12.X.53.

161   D. Ger. F. P., XII, no. 650.

162   Micr. T-120/321/193371-84.

163   Lith. Ber.

164   *Ibid.* English text in: Lituanus (Chicago), v. VIII, no. 1-2, 1962:
       47).

165   Micr. T-120/261/193387-88.

166   Lith. Ber. English text in: Lituanus (Chicago), v. VIII, no. 1-2,
       1962: 48.

Serial no.
of document   LIST OF REFERENCES

167   Associated Press dispatch in The New York Times, June 24, 1941.

168   Micr. T-312/786/8438072.

169   Micr. T-120/616/249810.

170   Nacionalistu talka hitlerininkams (The nationalists, accomplices of
             the Hitlerites). E. Rozauskas, ed. Vilnius: Mintis, 1970. p. 32.
             Cited from Amtsblatt des Generalkomissars in Kauen (Kaunas),
             Sept. 1, 1941.

171   Nacionalistu talka hitlerininkams, p. 30.

172   Lith. Ber.

173   *Ibid.*

174   Nacionalistu talka hilterininkams, pp. 40-41.

175   Lith. Ber.

176   National Archives, Washington.

177   U.S. For. Rel., 1941, v. I, p. 648.

178   Lith. Ber.

179   Micro. T-454/26/000921-22

180   Leonard Valiukas. Lithuania, land of heroes. Hollywood, Cali-
             fornia: Lithuanian Days Publishers, 1962. pp. 42-43. The
             newspapers can be found at the Library of the Hoover
             Institution on War, Revolution and Peace, Stanford University.

181   Freedom for Lithuania. Extension of the Remarks of the Hon.
             Thomas J. Dodd of Connecticut in the House of Representatives,
             June 1, 1955. Washington: G.P.O., 1955.

182   Nepriklausoma Lietuva (Independent Lithuania), v. II, No . 4(16).
             March 1, 1943 (in Library of the Hoover Institution). English
             text: Current News on the Lithuanian Situation (Washington)
             vol. II, no. 8(32), August, 1943: 10.

183   Nepriklausoma Lietuva (Independent Lithuania), v. II, no. 8(20),
             May 15, 1943.

184   E. J. Harrison. Lithuania's Fight for Freedom. New York:
             Lithuanian American Information Center, 1945. pp. 55-57.
             Also: Lituanus, v. III, no. 1-2, 1962: 49-50.

185   Nepriklausoma Lietuva (Independent Lithuania), v. III, no. 2(38),
             January 30, 1944.

186   Harrison, pp. 57-58. Also: Current news on the Lithuanian
             situation (Washington), v. III, no. 6(42), June, 1944; and:
             Lituanus, v. VIII, no. 1-2, 1962: 51.

187   Nepriklausoma Lietuva (Independent Lithuania), v. III, no. 4(40),
             February 18, 19..

188   An appeal New Y.. .. Lithuanian American Information Center,
             1944. pp. 15-16.

Serial no.
of document   LIST OF REFERENCES

189   Harrison, pp. 59-60.

190   Lithuanian Bulletin (New York), v. IV, no. 4, Nov. 1946: 14-15.
         Also: Lituanus, v. VIII, no. 1-2, 1962: 51-52.

191   Valiukas, p. 58. The publications can be found in the Library of
         the Hoover Institution.

192   Lith. Wash.

193   *Ibid.*

194   *Ibid.*

195   Archives of the Supreme Committee for the Liberation of
         Lithuania.

196   *Ibid.*

197   *Ibid.*

198   *Ibid.*

199   *Ibid.*

200   *Ibid.*

201   Official documents: texts of selected documents on U.S. foreign
         policy, 1918-1952. New York: Woodrow Wilson Foundation,
         1952. pp. 63-76.

202   The general pact for the renunciation of war; text of the pact as
         signed, notes and other papers. Washington: GPO, 1928.

203   U.S. For. Rel., 1932, v. III, pp. 7-8.

204   Robert Langer. Seizure of Territory. Princeton, N.J.: Princeton
         University Press, 1947. pp. 78-79.

205   *Ibid.*, pp. 62-63.

206   League of Nations, Official Journal (1935) 551. Cited in: Green
         Haywood Hackworth. Digest of international law, v. V. Washing-
         ton: G.P.O., 1943. p. 165.

207   League of Nations, Official Journal (1938), 343. Cited in: Langer,
         pp. 145-47.

208   League of Nations, Official Journal (1939) 506-08, 512, 540.
         Cited in: Langer, pp. 258-61.

209   The public papers and addresses of Franklin D. Roosevelt, 1940.
         New York: McMillan, 1941. pp. 92-93.

210   Nazi conspiracy and aggression: opinion and judgement. Washing-
         ton: G.P.O., 1947. p. 24

211   Public papers and addresses of Franklin D. Roosevelt, 1940. pp.
         130-33.

212   Federal Register (Washington), July 17, 1940.

Serial no.
of document   LIST OF REFERENCES

213   U.S. For. Rel., 1940, v. I, pp. 389-92

214   Department of State Bulletin (Washington), v. III, no. 57, 1940:48.

215   U.S. For. Rel., 1940, v. I, pp. 410-16.

216   Im Ausland—Abroad (Augsburg). No. 10-I, April, 1948: 1

217   U.S. For. Rel., 1941, v. I, pp. 708-11.

218   The New York Times, Feb. 28, 1950.

219   Archives of the Estonian Consulate General in New York.

220   *Ibid.*

221   Harry S. Truman Library, National Archives.

222   Department of State Bulletin (Washington), v. XXXI, July 12, 1954: 49.

223   *Ibid.,* v. XXXVI, no. 917, Jan. 21, 1957.

224   *Ibid.*

225   Department of State Press Release of February 15, 1958.

226   Public Law 86-90. See: Congressional Record, v. 105, 1959: 12-672, 13-117.

227   Archives of the Assembly of Captive European Nations.

228   A report of the Council of Europe. Document 1173, Report of the Committee on Non-represented Nations.

229   Lith. Wash.

230   *Ibid.*

231   *Ibid.*

232   Calendar no. 1573, 89th Congress, 2nd Session.

233   Lit. Wash.

234   *Ibid.*

235   *Ibid.*

236   *Ibid.*

237   Archives of the Lithuanian Consulate General in New York.

238   The Diplomatic Pouch (Washington), Dec. 1970.

239   Lit. Wash.

240   The public papers and addresses of Franklin D. Roosevelt, 1940. pp. 672-73.

241   The public papers and addresses of Franklin D. Roosevelt, 1941. New York: Harper, 1942. pp. 314-17.

Serial no. of document	LIST OF REFERENCES

242   The public papers and addresses of Franklin D. Roosevelt, 1942. New York: Harper, 1943. pp. 3-5.

243   U. S. Decade, p. 29.

244   The United Nations in the making; basic documents. Boston: World Peace Foundation, 1947. pp. 41-72.

245   U.S. Decade pp. 955-56. Also: Nazi conspiracy and aggression, v. I. Washington: G.P.O., 1946. p. 5.

246   U.S. Decade, pp. 1253-57.

247   *Ibid.*, pp. 951-54.

248   U.S. Congress. Senate. Committee on the Judiciary. Soviet political treaties and violations; staff study for the subcommittee to investigate the administration of the Internal Security Act and other internal security laws. Washington: G.P.O., 1955. pp. 1-3, 5-7, 9-16.

249   Archives of the United Nations.

250   The public papers and addresses of Franklin D. Roosevelt, 1942. pp. 287-89.

Selected Bibliography

Collections of Documents

Baltic States investigation. *See* U. S. Congress. House. Select Committee on Communist Aggression.

Degras, Jane, *ed.* Soviet documents on foreign policy. Vol. III: 1933-1941. London, Oxford University Press, 1953. xxii, 500 p.

Dokumentai. In: Lietuva (New York), no. 6, 1954: 140-154; no. 8, 1956: 70-86.
A selection of most important documents, translated into Lithuanian.

The Finnish blue book: the development of Finnish-Soviet relations during the autumn of 1939, including the official documents and the peace treaty of March 12, 1940. Philadelphia, New York. Pub. for the Ministry for Foreign Affairs of Finland by J. B. Lippincott Co. [c 1940] 120 p. maps.
London edition by G. G. Harrap & Co. Ltd. has title: "The development of Finnish-Soviet relations during the autumn of 1939." Issued also in French (Paris, E.

Flammarion with title: "Documents sur les relations finno-sovietiques" (automne 1939).

Foreign Policy of the United States. *See* U. S. Department of State.

General Pact for the Renunciation of War; text of the pact as signed, notes, and other papers. Washington: G. P. O., 1928.

Germany. Auswärtiges Amt. Akten zur deutschen auswärtigen Politik, 1918-1945. Aus dem Archiv des Deutschen Auswärtigen Amts. Baden-Baden. P. Keppler Verlag. Ser. D, 1937-1945: Bd. VII-VIII (pub. 1961), Bd. IX (pub. 1962), Bd. X (pub. 1963), Bd. XI, 1 (pub. 1964).

Germany. Auswärtiges Amt. Documents on German foreign policy, 1918-1945; from the archives of the German Foreign Ministry. Washington, U. S. Govt. Printing Office (Department of State publication). Ser. D (1937-1945): v. VII (pub. 1956), v. VIII (pub. 1954), v. IX (pub. 1956), v. X (pub. 1957), v. XI (pub. 1960), v. XII (pub. 1962).

Also published with imprint: London, H. M. Stationary Office.

Germany. Auswärtiges Amt. Nazi-Soviet relations; documents from the archives of the German Foreign Office. Ed. by Raymond James Sontag and James Stuart Beddie. [Washington] Dept. of State, 1948. xxxvii, 362 p.

Great Britain. Foreign Office. Documents on British foreign policy, 1919-1939. Third series, v. V-VII. London, H. M. Stationary Office, 1953-1954.

Krėvė-Mickevičius, Vincas. Report on conversation between Krėvė-Mickevičius and Molotov. In: Report of the Selected Committee to Investigate Communist Aggression and the Forced Incorporation of the Baltic States into the U.S.S.R. Third interim report. Washington, 1954: 450-463.

Previously published under the title "Plain talk in Moscow" in: East and West (London), no. 5, 1955: 16-27.

Latvian-Russian relations; documents. Comp. by Alfreds Bilmanis. Washington, D. C., The Latvian Legation, 1944. 255 p. illus., map.

League of Nations. Treaty Series (Geneva). various volumes.

Lithuania. Lietuvių archyvas; bolševizmo metai. Vilnius, Studijų biuras, 1942-1943. 4 v. illus. (v. 1-3 published in Kaunas).

Lithuanian archives; the years of Bolshevism. Also published a selected edition in one volume, edited by J. Prunskis, Brooklyn, 1952. 436 p.

Lithuania. Vyriausybes Žinios (Official Journal of Lithuania).

Lithuania, Ministry of Foreign Affairs. Documents diplomatiques, conflict polono-lithuanien, question de Vilna, 1918-1924. Kaunas, 1930, v. 1.

Lithuania. Treaties, etc. Lietuvos sutartys su svetimomis valstybemis. Surinko ir sutvarkė Pranas Dailidė . . . Recueil des traités conclus par la Lithuanie avec les pays étrangers. Publié par le Ministère des affaires étrangères . . . Kaunas, 1930-1939. 2 v.

Lietuvos įstatymai. Sistematizuotas istatymų, instrukcijų ir įsakymų rinkinys. (Lithuanian Statutes. A systematized collection of statutes, instructions, and executive orders.) Kaunas. Išleido Merkys ir Petrulis, 1922.

Lietuvos TSR istorijos Šaltiniai. IV t. (1919-1940). [Sources for Lithuania's history. v. 4, 1919-1940] Vilnius, Valstybinė politinės ir mokslinės literatūros leidykla, 1961. 861 p.

Selection and abbreviation of documents were done with the aim to present the Soviet point of view. However, several documents are authentic and not easily available elsewhere.

Lithuanian Information Bureau. Lithuanian recognition. Washington, 1921.

Nacionalistų talka hitlerininkams (The nationalists, accomplices of the hitle-rites—collection of documents) E. Rozauskas, ed. Vilnius: Mintis, 1970.

Microcopies of captured German documents, section T-120 in Microfilm Reading Room, National Archives, Washington, D. C. (Abbr.: Micr.)

Miglinas, Simas. Lietuva sovietinės agresijos dokumentuose. [Memmingen, Ger.] Tremtis [1958] 86 p.

   Lithuania in the documents of Soviet aggression.

Nazi conspiracy and aggression: opinion and judgment. Washington, G. P. O., 1947.

Nazi-Soviet relations. *See* Germany. Auswärtiges Amt.

Official Documents: texts of selected documents on U. S. foreign policy. New York: Woodrow Wilson Foundation, 1952.

Rei, August, *comp.* Nazi-Soviet conspiracy and the Baltic States; diplomatic documents and other evidence. London, Boreas Pub. Co. [1948] 61 p.

Report of the Council of Europe with preface and supplementary comments. Stockholm: Estonian Information Center, 1962.

Seidl, Alfred, *ed.* Die Beziehungen Zwischen Deutschland und der Sowjetunion 1939-1941. Dokumente des Auswärtigen Amtes; aus den Archiven des Auswärtigen Amtes und der Deutschen Botschaft in Moskau. Tübingen, H. Laupp, 1949. xxxix, 414 p.

Selected documentary material on the Lithuanian resistance movement against total-itarianism 1940-1960. Lituanus (Brooklyn), v. 8, no. 1-2, 1962: 41-64.

Die Sowjetunion und die baltischen Staaten. [Berlin, Deutsche Informationsstelle, 1942] 75 p. facsims.

   "Dokumententeil:" p. 25-75. Als Manuscript gedruckt.

Tarybų valdžios atkūrimas Lietuvoje 1940-1941 metais; dokumentų rinkinys. [Red. kom.: E. Jacovskis ir kiti] Vilnius, Mintis, 1965. 345 p. illus.

   Restoration of Soviet power in Lithuania in 1940-1941; a collection of documents.
   — Documents are mostly authentic; however, selection and comments entirely biased. Summaries, lists, and contents of documents -' ɔ given in Russian and English.

The United Nations in the making; basic documents. Boston: World Peace Foundation, 1947.

U. S. Congress. Calendar no. 1573, 89th Congress, 2nd Session.

U. S. Congress. Senate. Committee on Foreign Affairs. A decade of American foreign policy; basic documents, 1941-1949. New York, Arno Press, 1971. xiv, 1381 p. maps. (Reprint from the 1950 edition.)

U. S. Congress. Senate. Committee on the Judiciary. Soviet political treaties and violations; staff study for the subcommittee to investigate the administration of the Internal Security Act and other internal security laws. Washington: G. P. O., 1955.

U. S. Congress. Senate. Committee on the Judiciary. Soviet political agreements and results. Revised to January 1, 1964. Staff study for the Subcommittee to Investigate the Administration of the Internal Security Laws. Third rev. ed. Washington, Govt. Print. Off., 1964. 2 v.

U. S. Congress. House. Select Committee on Communist Aggression. Baltic States investigation. Hearings before the Select Committee to Investigate the Incorporation of the Baltic States into the USSR. . . . Washington, U. S. Govt. Print. Off., 1954. 2 pts. (xii, 1448 p.) illus., ports., fold. maps.

U. S. Congress. House. Select Committee on Communist Aggression. Report of the Select Committee to Investigate Communist Aggression and the Forced Incorporation of the Baltic States into the USSR. Third interim report. Washington, U. S. Govt. Print. Off., 1954, ix, 537 p.

A reprint edition: Baltic States: a study of their origin and national development; their seisure and incorporation into the U. S. S. R. ... Editors: Igor I. Kavass and Adolph Sprudzs. Buffalo, N. Y., William S. Hein & Co., 1972. 537 p. (History reprint series, 4).

U. S. Department of State. Diplomatic Pouch. Washington, Dec. 1970.

U. S. Department of State. Foreign relations of the United States. Diplomatic papers. The Soviet Union 1933-1939. Washin͓ᵗon, 1952.

—"— Diplomatic papers 1940, v. I (pub. 1959); 1941 v. I (pub. 1958).

U. S. Department of State. Foreign relations of the United States, 1932, v. III. Washington: G. P. O.

U. S. Department of State. Papers relating to the foreign relations of the United States, 1922, v. II. Washington: G. P. O.

Memoirs, Memorandums, Comments, and Studies

Anderson, Edgars. Die militärische Situation der Baltischen Staaten. Acta Baltica (Königstein im Taunus), v. 8, 1968 (pub. 1969): 106-155.

Aspaturian, Vernon V. The Union Republics in Soviet diplomacy; a study of Soviet federalism in the service of Soviet foreign policy. Geneve, E. Droz, 1960. 228 p. illus.

Audėnas, Juozas. Paskutinis posėdis; atsiminimai. [Reminiscences about the last meeting of Independent Lithuania's Government in the night of June 14-15, 1940] New York, Romuva, 1966. 277 p.

Balys, Jonas. Sovietų ir nacių byla dėl Užnemunės ruožo [The talks between Soviets and Nazies concerning the Lithuanian strip] Į Laisvę (Los Angeles), no. 46(83), Oct. 1969: 24-41. map.

Barghoorn, Frederick Charles. Soviet Russian nationalism. New York, Oxford University Press, 1956. ix, 330 p.

Berzinš, Alfreds. The unpunished crime. New York, R. Speller [1963] xviii, 314 p. illus.

Bielinis, Kipras. Teroro ir vergijos imperija Sovietų Rusija [The realm of terror and slavery—Soviet Union] New York, Amerikos lietuvių soc.—dem. sąjunga, 1963. 309 p. illus., maps.

Bilmanis, Alfᵣ ᵢ ᵢs. Baltic essays. Washington, D.C., The Latvian Legation, 1945. 267 p. map. Bibliography: p. 222-256.

—"— Baltic problem and United Nations; facts in review. Washington, D. C., The Latvian Legation, 1947. 64, iv 1. map.

—"— Baltic problem and United Nations; facts in review. Washington, D.C., The Latvian Legation, 1947. 64, iv 1. map.

—"— Baltic States and world security organization. [Washington, The Latvian Legation, 1945] 67 p.

—"— The Baltic States in post-war Europe. Washington, D. C., The Latvian Legation, 1943. 86 p. maps.

Second revised printing, Sept. 1944. 45 p. illus., maps.

Brakas, Martynas. The Baltic question in international law. Lituanus (Chicago), v. 6, no. 2, Sept. 1960: 90-95.

A review article of works by K. Marek and B. Meissner.

—"— Lithuania's international status; some legal aspects (1). Baltic Review (N.Y.), no. 37, Oct. 1970: 43-59.

—"— Lithuania's international status—some legal aspects (2). Baltic Review (N.Y.), no. 38, August 1971: 8-41.

Budreckis, Algirdas Martin. The Lithuanian national revolt of 1941. [Boston] Lithuanian Encyclopedia Press [1968] xvi, 147 p. maps. Bibliography: p. 140-147.

—"— Lithuanian resistance, 1940-1952. In: Lithuania: 700 years (ed. by A. Gerutis, 2nd ed., New York, Manyland Books, 1969): 313-377.

—"— Soviet attempts to eradicate Lithuanian sovereignty. Baltic Review (N.Y.), no. 34, Nov. 1967: 36-42.

—"— Soviet occupation and annexation of the Republic of Lithuania, June 15 - August 3, 1940. New York. Amerikos Lietuvių Tautinė Sąjunga, I-sis skyrius, 1968. 31 p

Bullitt, William Christian. The great globe itself, a preface to world affairs. New York, Scribner, 1946. vii, 310 p.

Čeginskas, Ebba. Die Baltische Frage in den Grossmächteverhandlungen 1939. Commentationes Balticae (Bonn), v. 12-13, 1967: 31-103.

Chambon, Henry de. La tragédie des nations baltiques. Paris, Editions de la Revue parlementaire [1946] 226 p.

Chevrier, Bruno (pseud.) *See* Kaslas, Bronis J.

Čibiras, Kazimieras. Lituania y la URSS, la invasión soviética desde la perspective de un quindenio, 1940-1955 [por] Casimiro Verax [pseud.] Medellin, Colombia, Comité Católico Lituano, 1955. 62 p.

Congressional Record (Washington). V. 105, 1959: 12-672, 13-117.

Council of Europe. The Baltic States and the Soviet Union. Reprinted from a report of the Council of Europe, with a pref. and supplementary comments. Stockholm [Estonian Information Centre, 1962] 52 p.

Current News on the Lithuanian Situation (Washington). V. II, no. 8 (32), Aug. 1943: 10.

Dallin, David L. Soviet Russia's foreign policy 1939-1942. New Haven, Yale University Press, 1947. xx, 452 p.

Daulius, Juozas [pseud., real name: Yla, Stasys] Komunizmas Lietuvoje [Communism in Lithuania] Kaunas [1937] 259 p.

Daumantas, J. (Pseud.) *See* Lukša, Juozas.

Daunys, Stasys. The development of resistance and the national revolt against the Soviet regime in Lithuania in 1940-1941. Lituanus (Chicago), v. 8, no. 1-2, 1962: 11-15.

Dilks, David, *ed.* The diaries of Sir Alexander Cadogan, O. M., 1938-1945. New York, G. P. Putnam's Sons, 1972. 881 p.

[Dirmeikis, Bronius *and* Vincas Rastenis] Lietuva tironų pančiuose. [By] Jonas Audrūnas ir Petras Svyrius [pseud.] T. I. Bolševikų okupacija. Cleveland, Lietuvai vaduoti sąjunga, 1946-1947. 312 p. illus., ports.
    Lithuania in shackles of tyrants. Vol. I. Bolshevik occupation. (Vol. II never published.)

Dodd, Thomas J. "Freedom of Lithuania;" extension of the remarks of the Hon. Thomas J. Dodd of Connecticut in the House of Representatives, June 1, 1955. Washington, G. P. O., 1955.

Dovydėnas, Liudas. Mes valdysime pasaulį [We shall rule the world] New York, Romuva, 1971. 2 v. Also available in English.

Dulong, Gustave. Comment la Lituanie devint une Républic Soviétique Socialiste. Revue des deux mondes (Paris), avril 1, 1955: 521-527.

Elkin, Alexander. The Baltic States. In: Survey of international affairs 1939-1946, pub. 1958 [v. 11] p. 42-58.

Fabry, Philipp W. Der Hitler-Stalin Pakt, 1939-1941; ein Beitrag zur Methode sowjetischer Aussenpolitik. Darmstadt, Fundus Verlag [1962] 535 p.

—*"*— Die Sowjetunion und das Dritte Reich: eine dokumentierte Geschichte der deutsch-sowjetischen Beziehungen von 1933 bis 1941. Stuttgard, Seewald Verlag, 1971. 485 p.

Federal Register (Washington), July 17, 1940.

Gautherot, Gustave. Derière le rideau de fer. Paris, Hachette, 1946. "Le Calvaire des Pays Baltes: en Lithuanie." p. 67-76.

Gerutis, Albertas. Occupied Lithuania. In his: Lithuania: 700 years. (2d ed., New York, Manyland Books, 1969): 257-312.

Ginsburgs, George. Soviet views on the law of state succession with regard to treaties and acquired rights. The case of the Baltic Republics. In: Res Baltica (Leyden, 1968): 191-229.

Graham, Malbone W. What does non-recognition mean? Baltic Review (Stockholm), v. 1, no. 4-5, 1946: 171-174.

Gsovski, Vladimir *and* K. Grzybowski, *eds.* Government, law and courts in the Soviet Union and Eastern Europe. New York, F. A. Praeger [c 1959] 2 v. (2067 p.)
    Includes chapters on Lithuania: v. 1, p. 135-160, 628-633; v. 2, p. 1703-1724.
    Also chapter of general survey: "The Baltic States," v. 1, p. 588-611.

Hackworth, G. H. Digest of International Law, v. 5. Washington, G. P. O., 1943.

Harrison, Ernest J. Lithuania's fight for freedom. New York, Lithuanian American Information Centre, 1945. 63 p. (1st ed. London, 1944. 66 p.)

Hull, Cordell. The memoirs of Cordell Hull. New York, Macmillan, 1948. 2 v.
    About Lithuania and other Baltic States see: v. 1, p. 701, 810-819, v. 2, p. 1165-1173, 1266.

Ivinskis, Zenonas. Lietuvos ir Sovietų Sąjungos santykių dvidešimtmetis [Twenty years of relations between the Soviet Union and Lithuania] Aidai (Brooklyn), 1969, no. 6, p. 254-260; no. 7, p. 290-293.

—*"*— Lithuania during the war: resistance against the Soviets and the Nazi occupants. In: Lithuania under the Soviets (New York, 1965): 61-84.

—*"*— The Lithuanian revolt against the Soviets in 1941. Lituanus (Chicago), v. 12, no. 2, 1966: 5-19.

Jonaitis, B., *pseud.* Paskutinės nepriklaus-)mos Lietuvos dienos. Ką pasakoja 1939-1940 metų dokumentai. [The last days of independent Lithuania; the testimony of documents, 1939-1940.] Naujoji Viltis (Chicago), no. 1, 1970: 5-65. maps, facsims.

Jurkūnas, Ignas. Den röda floden stiger [The red deluge is rising] Stockholm, A. Bonnier [1941] 298 p. illus.
    Author's pseud., Ignas J. -Scheinius, at head of title.
    Lithuanian edition: "Raudonasis tvanas," New York [Talka] 1953. 327 p.
    Also published in Finnish (1942)

—*"*— Den röda floden swämmar över [The red deluge inundates] Stockholm, Natur och Kultur [1945] 257 p.

Kajeckas, Joseph. The story of captive Lithuania. Washington, The Lithuanian Legation, 1964. 12 p. mimeo.

Kalniņš, Kārlis. Baltic States. In: East Central Europe and the World: developments in the post-Stalin era (ed. by Stephen D. Kertesz, Univ. of Notre Dame Press, 1962): 21-44.

Kaslas, Bronis J. Baltic geopolitics. Baltic Review (N.Y.), no. 25, Oct. 1962: 49-57.

—*"*— The international status of the Baltic States. Baltic Review (Stockholm), v. 1, no. 6, 1946: 270-276, facsims.
    Signed: Bruno Chevrier (pseud.)

—*"*— Lietuva tarptautinių santykiu sūkuriuose [Lithuania in the whirlwind of international relations] Aidai (Brooklyn), no. 3, 1971: 97-101.

—"— La silence n'est pas une solution. Cahiers du monde nouveau (Paris), no. 9, Nov. 1946: 14-21.

Article signed: N. N.

—"— Le sort des Etats Baltes. Revue generale belge (Bruxelles), no. 29, March 1948: 702-716.

Signed: Bruno Chevrier (pseud.) and P. Chantier (pseud.)

Kazlauskas, Bronius. L'Entente baltique. Paris, Recueil Sirey, 1939. 327 p. map.

Kieseritzky, H. von. Die Bolschewisierung Litauens, 1940/41; ein Tatsachenbericht. Berlin, F. Eher Nachf., 1945. 104 p. illus.

Kleist, Peter. Zwischen Hitler und Stalin, 1939-1945; Aufzeichnungen. Bonn, Athenäum-Verlag, 1950. 344 p.

Klesment, Johannes. The Crime: seizure and forced "incorporation". Baltic Review (N. Y.), no. 1, Dec. 1953: 5-14.

Klimas, P. Le Développement de l'Etat Lithuanien (Development of Lithuanian State. See also German edition.) Paris, 1919.

—"— Der Werdegang des Litauischen Staates. Berlin, Druck, Pass u. Garleb G.m.b.H., 1919.

Klive, A. Pacts of mutual assistance between the Baltic States and the USSR. Baltic Review, no. 18, Nov. 1959: 31-40.

Kolarz, Walter. Russia and her colonies. [3d ed., reprinted] New York, Praeger [1955] xiv, 334 p. maps.

Krivickas, Domas. The international status of Lithuania. Lituanus (Brooklyn), v. 4, no. 4, Dec. 1958: 99-104.

—"— Soviet efforts to justify Baltic annexation. Lituanus (Brooklyn), v. 6, no. 2, Sept. 1960: 34-39.

—"— Soviet-German pact of 1939 and Lithuania. Hamilton [Ont., Federation of Lithuanian-Canadians, Hamilton Branch] 1959. 14 p. illus.

Krummacher, F. A. *and* Helmut Lange. Krieg und Frieden. Geschichte der deutsch-sowjetischen Beziehungen. Von Brest-Litovsk zum Unternehmen Barbarossa. München, Bechtle Verlag, 1970. 567 p.

Langer, Robert. Seizure of Territory. Princeton, Princeton University Press, 1947. 313 p.

Lietuvos diplomatų protestai (Lithuanian diplomatic protests). Vilnius, 1940.

Lithuania, Ministry of Foreign Affairs. 1918-1928 metų Lietuvos politikos gyvenimo chronologija (A chronology of Lithuanian political life, 1918-1928). Kaunas: 1929.

Lithuania. Pasiuntinybė. U. S. Lithuania's occupation by the Soviet Union. Washington, The Lithuanian Legation, 1960. 28 p.

Lithuanian American Information Center, New York. An appeal to fellow Americans on behalf of the Baltic States by united organizations of Lithuanian, Latvian, and Estonian descent. New York, 1944. 54 p. illus. (facsims.) Includes Supplements.

Lozoraitis, Stasys. Some juridical and moral aspects of the occupation of Lithuania. East and West (London), v. 2, no. 7, 1956: 29-37.

Loeber, Dietrich A. Baltic gold in Great Britain. (A legal opinion). Baltic Review (N.Y.), no. 36, Oct. 1969: 11-39.

A look behind the Iron Curtain. Exhibition of Genocide in Lithuania. [USA] 1951 [32] p. illus.

Lukasiewicz, Juliusz. Diplomat in Paris—Papers and Memoirs of Juliusz Lukasiewicz. New York, Columbia University Press, 1970.

Lukša, Juozas. Partizanai [The partisans behind the Iron Curtain. 2d enl. ed.] Chicago, I Laisve Fondas, 1962. 510 p. illus.

Author's pseud. Juozas Daumantas, at head of title. 1st ed. 1950.

Marek, Krystyna. Identity and continuity of states in public international law. Geneve, E. Droz, 1954.
"The Baltic States:" p. 369-416.

Mačiulis, Petras. Trys ultimatumai. [Brooklyn, Darbininkas, 1962] 134 p.
Three ultimatums: Polish (March 18, 1938), German (March 20, 1939), and Russian (June 14, 1940).

Meissner, Boris. Die Beziehungen zwischen der Sowjetunion und den baltischen Staaten von der deutsch-sowjetischen Interessenabgrenzung bis zum sowjetischen Ultimatum. Zeitschrift für Ostforschung (Marburg, Lahn), Jg. 3, Heft 2, 1954: 161-179.

—"— Die Grossmächte und die baltische Frage. Osteuropa (Stuttgart), Jg. 2, Heft 4, Aug. 1952: 241-249; Heft 5, Oct. 1952: 341-346.

—"— Die kommunistische Machtübernahme in den baltischen Staaten. Vierteljahreshefte für Zeitgeschichte (Stuttgart), Jg. 2, Heft 1, 1954: 95-114.

—"— Die Sowjetunion, die baltischen Staaten und das Völkerrecht. [Köln] Verlag für Politik und Wirtschaft [1956] 377 p.

Merkelis, Aleksandras. Antanas Smetona; jo visuomeninė, kūlturinė ir politinė veikla. New York, ALTS-gos leidinys, 1964. 740 p.
A monograph about President Antanas Smetona, his social, cultural, and political activity. — Several documents are included.

Mid-European Law Project. Legal sources and bibliography of the Baltic States ... New York, published for Free Europe Committee, by Praeger [c 1963] 197 p.

Musteikis, Kazys. Prisiminimų fragmentai. [Fragments of reminiscences] London, Nida, 1970. 126 p.

Navickas, Konstantinas. TSRS vaidmuo ginant Lietuvą nuo imperialistines agresijos 1920-1940 metais. [The role of the Soviet Union in protecting Lithuania against the imperialistic aggression in 1920-1940.] Vilnius, Mintis, 1966. 335 p.
Strictly pro-Soviet bias was the guide for interpretation of foreign relations between the independent Lithuania and the Soviet Union. Documentation is selective, biased, and incomplete.

Olberg, Paul. Die Tragödie des Baltikums; die Annexion der freien Republiken Estland, Lettland, und Litauen. Zürich, New York, Europa Verlag [1941] 87 p.
Also published in Swedish: "Tragedin balticum. . ." Stockholm [1941] 102 p.

Pakštas, Kazys. Lithuania and World War II. Chicago [Lithuanian Cultural Institute] 1947. 80 p. map.

—"— The Lithuanian situation. [Chicago] Lithuanian Cultural Institute, 1941. 61 p. illus.

Pelėkis, K., *pseud.* Genocide; Lithuania's threefold tragedy. Edited by Rumšaitis [pseud. W. Germany] "Venta," 1949. 286 p. illus., maps, facsims.

Pennar, Jaan. Nationalism in the Soviet Baltics. In: Ethnic minorities in the Soviet Union (ed. by Erich Goldhagen, New York, 1968): 198-217.

Petrov, Vladimir. Missing page in Soviet historiography: the Nazi-Soviet partnership. Orbis (Philadelphia), v. 11, no. 4, 1968: 1113-1137.

Petruitis, Jonas. Lithuania under the sickle and hammer. Cleveland, The League for the Liberation of Lithuania [1945?] 78 p. illus.
Condensed from the original Lithuanian "Kaip jie mus sušaudė" [W. Germany, 1952] 221 p.
Also published in Italian, translated by Vincenta Lozoraitis (1968).

Pick, F. W. 1939: the evidence re-examined. Baltic Review (Stockholm), v. 1, no. 4-5, 1946: 154-160.

Les problemes de la Baltique. [Par] Kaarel R. Pusta [et al.] Paris [1934] viii, 206 p. (Conciliation internationale. Bulletin, no. 8-9.)

Pusta, Kaarel R. The Soviet Union and the Baltic States. [2d printing] New York, John Felsberg [1943] 79 p. map.

Račkauskas, Konstantinas. Changes in policy toward the non-Russian nationalities in the Soviet Union. Baltic Review (New York), no. 18, Nov. 1959: 58-64.

—"— Power politics vs. international law. Baltic Review (New York), no. 14, August 1958: 61-79.

Raštikis, Stasys. Kovose dėl Lietuvos; kario atsiminimai. [In battles for Lithuania; memoirs of a soldier] Los Angeles, Lietuviu Dienos, 1956-1957. 2 v.

Rauch, Georg von. Die baltischen Staaten und Sowjetrussland 1919-1939. Europa-Archiv (Frankfurt a.M.), 1954, 9. Jahr, 17. Folge: 6859-6868, 20. Folge: 6965-6972, 22. Folge: 7087-7094.

Rei, August. The Baltic question at the Moscow negotiations in 1939. East and West (London), no. 4, 1955: 20-29.

—"— The drama of the Baltic peoples. [Stockholm] Kirjastus Vaba Eesti [1970] 383 p.

Remeikis, Thomas. The armed struggle against the Sovietization of Lithuania after 1944. Lituanus (Brooklyn), v. 8, no. 1-2, 1962: 29-40.

Res Baltica. A collection of essays in honor of the memory of Dr. Alfred Bilmanis (1887-1948). Edited by Adolf Sprudzs and Armins Rusis. Pref. by Loy W. Henderson. Leyden, A. W. Sijthoff, 1968. 304 p.

Riismandel, Väino J. The continued legal existence of the Baltic States. Baltic Review (New York), no. 12, Nov. 1957: 48-68.

Rimscha, Hans von. Die Baltikumpolitik der Grossmächte. Historische Zeitschrift (München), Bd. 177, 1954: 281-309.

—"— Zur Frage der Garantierung der Baltischen Staaten. Jahrbücher für Geschichte Osteuropas (München), Bd. 5, Heft 3, 1957: 396-398.

Rossi, Angelo (pseud.), See Tasca, Angelo.

Rothfels, Hans. Das Baltikum als Problem internationaler Politik. In: Zur Geschichte und Problematik der Demokratie, Festgabe für Hans Herzfeld (Berlin, 1958): 601-618.

Royal Institute of International Affairs, London. The Baltic States: a survey of the political and economic structure and the foreign relations of Estonia, Latvia and Lithuania. London [etc.] Oxford University Press, 1938. 194 p. map. Reprinted by Greenwood Press, Westfort, Conn. [1970]

Ruland, Bernd. Deutsche Botschaft Moskau. 50 Jahre Machtkämpfe und Intrigen auf dem heissen diplomatischen Parkett der russischen Hauptstadt. München, Heine (c 1964). 239 p. illus.

Rutenberg, Gregor. Die baltischen Staaten und das Völkerrecht. Riga, G. Loeffler, 1928. xvi, 156 p.

—"— Der litauisch-russische Freundschafts-und Neutralitätsvertrag und die Wilnafrage im Lichte des Völkerrechts. Zeitschrift für Völkerrecht (Breslau), 1928, Bd. 14, Heft 3: 370-385, Heft 4: 548-558.

Sabaliūnas, Leonas. Lithuania in crisis. Nationalism to Communism 1939-1940. Bloomington, Ind. [etc.] Indiana University Press [1972] 293 p.

—"— Prelude to aggression. Lituanus (Brooklyn), no. 3(12), Sept. 1957: 2-8.

Savasis, J., *pseud.* The war against God in Lithuania. New York, Manyland Books [1966] 134 p. illus., map.

    Translation of Lithuanian original "Kova prieš Dievą Lietuvoje" (Putnam, Conn., Immaculata Press, 1963. 91 p.)

    Also published in Spanish: "La lucha contra Dios en Lituania" (Mexico, Editiones Ascoala, 1964. 141 p.)

Schnorf, Richard A. The Baltic States in U.S.-Soviet relations. Lituanus (Chicago), v. 12 & 14, Spring 1966: 33-53, Winter 1966: 56-75, Fall 1968: 43-60.

Schram, Stuart R. L'Union Soviétique et les Etats Baltes. In: Foundation nationale des sciences politiques, Paris. Cahiers, no. 85, 1957: 25-166.
    A section of "Les frontières européennes de l'USSR. 1917-1941."

Schultz, Lothar. The Soviet concept of the occupation and incorporation of the Baltic States. Baltic Review (New York), no. 10, March 1957: 3-18.

Schwabe, Arvid. Baltic States. In: The Fate of East Central Europe (ed. by István Kertész, Notre Dame, Ind., 1956): 103-128.

Šeinius, Ignas J. (pseud.) *See* Jurkūnas, Ignas.

[Selter, Karl] Minutes of the Soviet-Estonian negotiations for the Mutual Assistance Pact of 1939. Lituanus (Chicago), v. 14, no. 2, 1968: 62-96.

Selter, Karl. Die Sowjetpolitik und das Baltikum. Monatshefte für auswärtige Politik (Berlin), Jg. 11, Heft 4, April 1944: 197-216.

Senn, Alfred E. Die bolschewistische Politik in Litauen, 1917-1919. Forschungen zur osteuropäischen Geschichte (Berlin), Bd. 5, 1957: 93-116.

—"— Soviet views of Lithuanian independence. Baltic Review (New York), no. 19, March 1960: 11-22.

Seraphim, Hans Günther. Die deutsch-russischen Beziehungen 1939-1941. Hamburg, Nölke, 1949. 94 p.

Sidzikauskas, Vaclovas. A review of Soviet policy toward the Baltic States. Baltic Review (New York), no. 8, Sept. 1956: 55-63.

—"— Thirty years of infamy: Soviet-Nazi secret deals of 1939. Baltic Review (New York), no. 36, Oct. 1969: 2-10.

Sinha S. Prakash. Self-determination in international law and its applicability to the Baltic peoples. In: Res Baltica (Leyden, 1968): 256-285.

Škirpa, Kazys. Apie Lietuvių Aktyvistų Fronto veiklą [About the activity of the Front of Lithuanian Activists] Lituanistikos Darbai (Chicago), v. 2, 1969: 77-123.

—"— 1941 metų vyriausybės kelias [The road of the Government of 1941] Aidai (Brooklyn), no. 6, June 1971: 242-250.

Slavėnas, Julius P., Nazi ideology and policy in the Baltic States. Lituanus, v. 11, no. 1, 1965: 34-37.

Slusser, Robert M. *and* Jan F. Triska. A calendar of Soviet treaties, 1917-1957. Stanford, Calif., Stanford University Press, 1959. xii, 530 p. (Hoover Institution. Documentary series, no. 4).

Smetona Antanas. Pro memoria. Margutis (Chicago), nos. 7-8, 1955.
    Reminiscenses by President Smetona about events of 1939-1940; written in Switzerland, July 1-25, 1940.

Smogorzewski, K. M. The Russification of the Baltic States. World affairs (London), v. 4, no. 4, Oct. 1950: 468-481.

Šmulkštys, Julius. The incorporation of the Baltic States by the Soviet Union. Lituanus (Chicago), v. 14, no. 2, Summer 1968: 19-44.

Strausz-Hupé, Robert *and* Stefan T. Possony. International relations in the age of conflict between democracy and dictatorship. New York: McGraw-Hill, 1950.

Suduvis, N. E., (*pseud.*) Allein, ganz allein; Widerstand am Baltischen Meer. [New Rochelle, New York, Freunde der Litauischen Front in Europe] 1964. 134 p.
    Condensed from the original Lithuanian "Vienų vieni; 25 metų rezistencijoje" [Brooklyn, 1954] 424 p.

Supreme Lithuanian Committee of Liberation. Appeal to the United Nations on genocide. [n.p.] Lithuanian Foreign Service [1950?] 80 p.

Supreme Lithuanian Committee of Liberation. Memorandum on the restoration of

Lithuania's independence. [West Germany] Lithuanian Executive Council, 1950. 93 p. illus., fold. maps.

Also published in French (1950. 87 p.) The memorandum was submitted to the secretaries for foreign affairs of the United States of America, France, and Great Britain.

Supreme Lithuanian Committee of Liberation. 20 years' struggle for freedom of Lithuania [by] Juozas Audėnas. New York, 1963. 149 p. illus., map.

Swettenham, John A. The tragedy of the Baltic States. New York, Praeger [1954] xi, 216 p.

Tarulis, Albertas N. A heavy population loss in Lithuania. Journal of Central European Affairs (Boulder, Colo.), v. 21, no. 1, Jan. 1962: 452-464.

—"— Soviet policy toward the Baltic States, 1918-1940. [Notre Dame, Ind.] University of Notre Dame Press, 1959. xii, 276 p. maps.

—"— Unused springboard and insecure safety zone: a look at Soviet strategic arguments. Baltic Review (New York), no. 21, Dec. 1960: 42-57.

Tasca. Angelo. The Russo-German alliance, August 1939-June 1941 [by] A. Rossi [pseud. Translated by John and Micheline Cullen] London, Chapman & Hall, 1950. xiii, 218 p.

Also published in French (1949), German (1954), Italian (1951), and Norwegian (1954).

Tauras, K. V., *pseud.* Guerilla warfare on the Amber Coast. Introduction by Leo Cherme. New York, Voyages Press, 1962. 110 p.

Toynbee, Arnold *and* Veronica, *eds.* Survey of international affairs 1939-1946. [v. 10] The eve of war, 1939. London, Oxford University Press, 1958. 744 p.

Triska, Jan F. *and* Robert M. Slusser. The theory, law, and policy of Soviet treaties. Stanford, Calif., Stanford University Press, 1962. xi, 593 p.

Turauskas, Eduardas. Communist diplomacy exposed; Lithuanian experiences in appeasement. In: Lithuanian Information Service, New York. Bulletin, no. 2, Feb. 1941: 1-6.

U. S. Congress. House. Select Committee on Communist Aggression. Communist takeover and occupation of Lithuania. Washington, 1955. 20 p. (Its special report, no. 14).

Vahter, Leonhard. Molotov-Ribbentrop Pact of August 23, 1939. Baltic Review (New York), no. 18, Nov. 1959: 58-64.

Vaitiekūnas, Vytautas. A survey of developments in captive Lithuania in 1965-1968. New York, Committee for a Free Lithuania [1969?] 160 p.

Valiukas, Leonard. Lithuania, land of heroes. Hollywood: Lithuanian Day Publishers, 1962.

Valters, Nikolaus. Ein Versuch, die baltische Zukunft zu deuten. Acta Baltica (Königstein, Ger.), v. 1, 1962: 180-214.

Vardys, Vytas Stanley. Aggression, Soviet style, 1939-1940. In: Lithuania under the Soviets (New York, 1965): 47-58.

—"— How the Baltic Republics fare in the Soviet Union. Foreign affairs (New York), v. 44, no. 3, April 1966: 512-517.

—"— *ed.* Lithuania under the Soviets; portrait of a nation, 1940-1965. New York, Praeger [1965] ix, 299 p. illus.

—"— The partisan movement in postwar Lithuania. Lituanus (Chicago), v. 15, no. 1, 1969: 8-40.

See also two articles by the same author and on the same subject published earlier in: Slavic Review (Seattle, Wash.), v. 22, no. 3, Sept. 1963: 499-522; and in: Lithuania under the Soviets (New York, 1965): 85-108.

—"— Recent Soviet policy toward Lithuanian nationalism. Journal of Central European Affairs (Boulder, Colo.), v. 23, no. 3, Oct. 1963: 313-332.

—"— Soviet colonialism in the Baltic States: a note on the nature of modern colonialism. Lituanus (Chicago), v. 10, no. 4, Summer 1964: 5-23.

—"—Soviet colonialism in the Baltic States 1940-1965. Baltic Review (New York), no. 29, June 1965: 11-26.

—"— Sovietinio kolonializmo 25 metaii [25 years of Soviet colonialism] Aidai (Brooklyn), no. 6, June 1965: 249-257.

Venster, Steven. Bolshevik elections in Lithuania; terror and forgery to produce 99% majority. Baltic Review (Stockholm), v. 2, no. 2, 1948: 52-60.

Verax, Casimiro (pseud.) *See* Čibiras, Kazimieras.

Vizulis, Jazeps. Die baltischen Länder—Opfer sowjetischer Aggression. Acta Baltica (Königstein im Taunus), Bd. 8, 1958: 74-105.

Waltari, Mika Toimi. Totuus Virosta, Latviesta, ja Liettuasta [The truth about Estonia, Latvia, and Lithuania. Malmö] Förlaget Balticum [1941] 172 p.
    Author's pseud., Nauticus, at head of title.

Weinberg, Gerhard L. Germany and the Soviet Union, 1939-1941. Leiden, E. J. Brill, 1954. 218 p. (Studies in East European History, 1)

Weiss, Helmuth. Die baltischen Staaten; von der Moskauer Verträgen bis zur Eingliederung der baltischen Staaten in die Sowjetunion (1939-1940). In: Die Sowjetisierung Ost-Mitteleuropas, Bd. 1, hrag. von Ernst Birke (Frankfurt a.M., 1959): 21-64.

Woodward, Llewellyn. British Foreign Policy in the Second World War. Vol. I., London, 1970.

Wrangell, Wilhelm. Die deutsche Politik und die Baltischen Staaten im Schicksalsjahr 1939. Baltische Hefte (Hannover-Döhren), Jg. 5, Heft 4, Juli 1959: 209-234.

Yla, Stasys. *See* Daulius, Juozas.

Biographical Glossary

Abbreviations:

A.A.—Auswertiges Amt [German Foreign Ministry]
Amb.—Ambassador
C.P.S.U.—Communist Party of the Soviet Union
D.O.S.—United States Department of State
F.M.—Foreign Minister
Ger.—German
LCP—Communist Party of Lithuania
Lith.—Lithuanian
Min.—Minister
NSDAP—Nationalsozialistische Deutsche Arbeiterpartei [Nazi Party]
OKW—Oberkommando der Wehrmacht [German Supreme Military Command]
P. Comm.—People's Commissar
Sec.—Secretary
Sov.—Soviet, pertaining to the U.S.S.R.
U.S.—United States

Abdulskaitė, Birutė 1913-   , Sec., Kretinga District, LCP, 1939-1940; Deputy, People's Seimas, 1940.

Adomas (Icikas Meskupas) 1907-1942, Second Sec., LCP, 1940-1941; Deputy, People's Seimas, 1940.

Adomauskas, Liudas 1880-1941, Lith. Chief of State Control, June 15-Aug. 3, 1940; Deputy, People's Seimas, 1940.

Aleksa, Jonas 1879-1954, Lith. Min. of Agriculture, 1920-1923.

Aleksandrovskiy, Sergei (Sergeevich) 1889-1945, U.S.S.R. Envoy to Lithuania, 1925-1927.

Ambrazevičius (Brazaitis), Juozas 1903-   , Educator; Min. of Education and Acting Prime Min., Lith. Provisional Government, 1941; Chairman, Political Commission, Supreme Committee for the Liberation of Lithuania, 1942-1944.

Ancevičius, Pranas 1895-1964, Correspondent of Lietuvos Žinios in Berlin, 1938-1945.

Atherton, Ray 1883-   , Chief, Division of European Affairs, D.O.S., 1940-1943.

Audenas, Juozas 1898-   , Vice-President of the Supreme Committee for Liberation of Lithuania, 1961.

Avietėnaite, Magdalena 1892-   , Director, Press & Information Department, Lith. Foreign Ministry, 1929-1940.

Bačkis, Stasys Antanas 1906-   , Counselor of the Lith. Legation in Paris and Secretary General of the Lith. Delegation at the League of Nations, 1938-1940.

Bachunas, Juozas 1893-1969, Pres., The World Lithuanian Community; Publisher, Resort Owner.

Ball, George W. 1909-   , U.S. Undersecretary of State, 1961-1966.

Baltrušaitis, Jurgis 1873-1944, Lith. Min. in Moscow, 1920-1939.

Balutis, Bronius 1879-1967, Lith. Min. in London, 1934-1967.

Banaitis, Saliamonas 1866-1933, Member, Lith. National Council, 1917-1920; Signatory of the Lith. Declaration of Independence.

Barauskas, Rev. Kazimieras 1904-   , Signed Charter of the LAF; Editor & Author

Bartašiunas, Juozas 1895-1972, Major General; Political Commissar, 27 (Lithuanian) Corps, Red Army, 1940-1941; P. Comm. of the Interior, Lith. S.S.R., 1944-1953; Member, Politburo LCP.

Basanavičius, Jonas 1851-1927, Member, Lith. National Council, 1917-1920; Signatory of the Lith. Declaration of Independence.

Baudouin, Paul 1894-   , F.M. of France (Vichy), June-October, 1940; Member, Council of Ministers, 1940-1944.

Beneš, Eduard 1884-1948, Czechoslovak F.M., 1918-1935.

Berle, Adolf A., Jr. 1895-   , U.S. Assistant Sec. of State, 1938-1944.

Bielskis, Jonas Julius 1891-   , Chief of the Lith. Information Bureau, Washington, 1917-1919; President, American-Lithuanian Council, 1917-1919; Consular service 1924-

Bilmanis, Alfred 1887-1948, Latvian Min. in Washington, 1945-1948.

Biržiška, Mykolas 1882-1962, Member, Lith. National Council, 1917-1920; Signatory of the Lith. Declaration of Independence.

Bizauskas, Kazys 1893-1941, Member, Lith. National Council, 1917-1920; Signatory, Lith. Declaration of Independence; Director of the Legal & Administrative Department of the Lith. Foreign Ministty, 1932-1939; Deputy Prime Min., March 1939-June 1940; Min. for Vilnius, Oct. 1939-June 1940.

Bobelis, Jurgis 1895-1954, Colonel; Commandant, Military District of Kaunas, 1936-1940; Provisional Commandant, 1941.

Bonch-Bruyevich, Vladimir Dimitrievich 1873-1955, Executive Sec. of the Council of People's Commissars, 1917-?.

Brakas, Martynas 1907-   , Director, Lith. Free Port of Klaipeda (Memel), 1939-1940; Assistant District Attorney of Siauliai, 1941-1942.

Brazinskas, Juozas 1891-1966, District Attorney of Vilnius, Oct. 1939-June 1940.

Briand, Aristide 1862-1932, French F.M., 1925-1932.

Cantilo, Jose Maria 1877-1953, Argentine F.M., 1938-1941.

Černius, Jonas 1898-   , General; Lith. Prime Min., March-Nov. 1939.

Chicherin, Georgi Vasilyevich 1872-1936, P. Comm. for Foreign Affairs (U.S.S.R.), 1918-1930.

Ciano Di Cortellazzo, Conte Galeazzo 1903-1944, Italian F.M., 1936-1943.

Čiuberkis, Jonas 1914-   , Signed Charter of the LAF; Sec. of the City of Vilnius; Head of the Chancellory of the Ministry of the Interior.

Clodius, Karl   , Deputy Chief, Economic Policy Department, A.A., 1937-1943.

Cosgrave, William T. (Liam McCosgair) 1880-1965, President of the Executive Council of the Irish Free State, 1922-1932.

Cvirka, Petras 1909-1947, Deputy, People's Seimas, 1940; Chairman of the Lith. Writers' Association, June 15, 1940-1947.

Cushendun, Roland Lord 1861-1934, British Acting Sec. of State for Foreign Affairs, 1929.

Damušis, Adolfas 1908-   , Educator: Docent of the Institute of Technology in Kaunas, 1940; Min. of Industry, Lith. Provisional Government, 1941.

Davila, Charles   , Roumanian Min. in Warsaw, 1929.

Dekanozov, Vladimir Georgevich 1898-1953, Sov. Deputy, P. Comm. for Foreign Affairs, 1939-1940; Sov. Amb. in Berlin, 1940-1941.

Deksnys, Jonas 1914-   , Leader of the LAF

Demskis, Juozas 1883-1943, Member, LCP, 1932-1943; Deputy, People's Seimas, 1940.

Didžiulis (Grosmanas), Karolis 1894-1958, Member, Secretariat & Politburo, LCP, 1927-1958; Member, Central Committee, LCP, 1934-1958; Deputy Chairman, Presidium of the Supreme Soviet, People's Republic of Lithuania, June-July 1940, Lith. S.S.R., 1940-1941, 1944-1958; Deputy, People's Seimas, 1940.

Ditkevičius, Viktoras 1917-   , Organizer, LCP, 1932-   ; Secretary, Simnas district, LCP, 1932-   , also founded eight other LCP branches; Deputy, People's Seimas, 1940; Member, Prosecutor's office, Lith. S.S.R., 1940-1941, 1944-

Dobkevičius, Jonas 1866-1934, Lith. Min. of Finance, Commerce & Industry, Feb.-Aug. 1922.

Dörnberg, Alexander, Freiherr von   , Chief of Protocol, A.A.

Dovydaitis, Pranas 1886-1942, Member, Lith. National Council, 1917-1920; Signatory of the Lithuanian Declaration of Independence.

Draugelis, Eliziejus 1888-   , Member of the Lithuanian Constituent Assembly for Farmer's Union.

Dženkaitis, Jonas   -1941, Signed the Charter of the LAF; Leader of Lithuanian Guerillas.

Galdikiene Draugelyte, Magdalena 1891-   , Member of Constituent Assemby for Christian Democratic Party.

Galvanauskas, Ernestas 1882-1967, Lith. Prime Min., 1922-1923; Chairman, Lith. National Committee, 1941.

Gaus, Friedrich   , Director, Legal Department, A.A., 1923-1945.

Gira, Liūdas 1884-1946, Poet, Deputy, People's Seimas, 1940; P. Comm. for Education, Lith. S.S.R., 1940-1941.

Girdvainis, Stasys 1890-1970, Lith. Min. to the Holy See, 1939-1970.

Glovackas, Pijus 1902-1941, Sec. General of the Lith. Foreign Office (Acting F.M.), July-Aug. 1940; Deputy Chairman of the Council of People's Commissars of the Lith. S.S.R., Aug. 1940-June 1941.

Glušauskas, Jurgis 1909-   , P. Comm. of Social Maintenance and Lumber Industry, Lith. S.S.R., July 1940-June 1941.

Gorkin, Aleksander   , Sec. of the Praesidium of the Supreme Soviet of the U.S.S.R., 1939-1952.

Graebe, Horst   , Lieutenant Colonel; chief of Baltic States section of the Abwehrabteilung (counterintelligence) of the OKW.

Graefe, (?)   , Chief of East Prussian Gestapo, headquarters at Tilsit, 1939-1940.

Graužinis, Kazimieras 1898-   , Lith. Min. in **Buenos Aires, 1939-1947**.

Grinius, Kazys 1899-1950, President of Lithuania, April-Dec. 1926.

Grundherr, Werner von   , Director of Political Division VI (Scandinavia, the Baltic States) of the A.A.

Gufler, Bernard 1903-   , U.S. Consul and 2nd Sec. of the Legation in Kaunas, 1938-1940.

Gylys, Vytautas 1886-   , Lith. Min. in Stockholm, 1937-1940; Lith. Min. to Denmark and Norway, 1937-1949.

Halifax, Edward Viscount 1881-1959, British Sec. of State for Foreign Affairs, 1938-1940.

Henderson, Loy W. 1892-   , Assistant Chief of the Division of European Affairs, D.O.S., 1938-1942.

Heyden-Rynsch, Bernd Otto, Freiherr von der   , Official, Political Division I, A.A., 1936-1940.

Hilger, Gustav   , Counselor to the German Embassy in Moscow, 1939-1941.

Hitler, Adolf 1889-1945, Chancellor and Fuehrer of the German Reich, 1933-1945.

Hughes, Charles E. 1862-1948, U.S. Sec. of State, 1921-1925.

Hull, Cordell 1871-1955, U.S. Sec. of State, 1933-1944.

Humphrey, Hubert H. 1911-   , U.S. Vice-President, 1965-1969.

Hymans, Paul 1865-1941, Belgian F. M., Min. of State, 1927-1935.

Ioffe (Joffe), Adolf Abramovich 1883-1927, Sov. Amb. in Berlin, 1918-1922.

Jakobas, Antanas 1895-   , Legal Adviser to the Lith. Ministry of the Interior, 1927-1940.

Jankauskis, Jurgis 1902-   , Leader of the LAF.

Juodakis, Petras 1872-1940, Lith. Min. of Education, 1922.

Jurgutis, Vladas 1885-1966, Lith. F.M., Feb.-Nov. 1922.

Jurkūnas, Jonas 1915-   , Chairman of the Presidium of the Union of Freedom Fighters

Kairys, Steponas 1878-1964, Member, Lith. National Council, 1917-1920; Signatory, Lithuanian Declaration of Independence

Kajeckas, Juozas 1897-   , Lithuanian Chargé D'Affaires in Washington, 1940-.

Kalinin, Mikhail Ivanovich 1875-1946, Chairman of the Presidium of the Supreme Soviet of the U.S.S.R., 1938-1946.

Kallas, Oskar Phillipp 1868-1946, Estonian Min. in London, 1922-1934.

Karakhan, Lev Mikhailovich 1889-1937, Deputy P. Comm. for Foreign Affairs, 1917-1923; Member, Central Committee, C.P.S.U., 1917-1920.

Karoblis, Vincas 1866-1939, Lith. Min. of Justice, 1920-1925.

Karvelis, Petras 1897-   , Lith. Min. of Finance, 1926-1927; industrialist.

Katilius (Vaitiekūnas), Juozas   , attorney; Leader of the Lith. Federation of Labor.

Kavolis, Martynas 1897-   , Rev.; Deputy Attorney General, Lith. Supreme Court, 1940-1944.

Kellogg, Frank B. 1856-1937, U.S. Sec. of State, 1925-1929.

King, William L. Mackenzie 1874-1950, Canadian Prime Min. and F.M., 1926-1930.

Kleist, Peter 1904-   , Specialist for Eastern Europe in the Dienstelle Ribbentrop (Foreign Office of the NSDAP).

Klimas, Petras 1891-1969, Member, Lith. National Council, 1917-1920; Signatory, Lithuanian Declaration of Independence; Lith. Deputy F.M., 1919-1923; Lith. Min. to France, 1925-1942.

Kotze, Hans Ulrich von   , Ger. Min. in Riga, Dec. 1938-1940.

Kraunaitis, Izidorius 1900-   , Colonel; commanding officer, Lith. hussars, 1939-1940.

Kreewinsch, Edgar 1884-   , Latvian Min. in Berlin, 1938-1940.

Krevė-Mickevičius, Vincas 1882-1954, Lith. Deputy Prime Min., June, 1940; Prime Min., F.M. and Min. of Education, June-July, 1940

Krievins, Edgars (see Kreewinsch).

Krupavičius, Mykolas 1885-1970, Member of Constituent Assembly for Christian Democrats.

Kukutis, Mykolas 1900-1950, Signed Charter of the LAF; Captain in Lith. Army; Leader of Lith. Sea Scouts.

Kutraitė, Marija 1911-   , Member, LCP, 1934-   ; official, Biržai District Administration, June 1940-June 1941; Deputy, People's Seimas, 1940.

Landsbergis-Žemkalnis, Vytautas 1893-   , Chief Engineer of the City of Vilnius, 1939-1944.

Lansing, Robert 1864-1928, U.S. Sec. of State, 1915-1920.

Legat, (?)   , Polizeikomissar; Director of the Foreign Section of the Gestapo (Geheime Staatspolizei—German secret police), 1940.

Lenin (Ulyanov), Vladimir Ilyich 1870-1924, Chairman of the Council of People's Commissars of the R.S.F.S.R., 1917-1922, U.S.S.R., 1922-1924.

Leonas, Atty. Petras 1864-1938, First Min. of Justice.

Lie, Trygve 1896-1968, Sec. General of the United Nations, 1946-1953.

Litvinov, Maksim Maksimovich 1876-1951, Sov. P. Comm. for Foreign Affairs, 1930-1939.

Lohse, Heinrich 1886-(?), Gauleiter of the Schleswig-Holstein NSDAP, 1925-1945; Oberpräsident of Schleswig-Holstein, 1933-1945; President of the Nordic Society; Reichskomissar for Ostland, 1941-1944.

Loktionov, Aleksander Dmitriyevich   , General; Sov. Deputy P. Comm. for National Defense, 1940.

Lozoraitis, Stasys 1898-   , Lith. Min. in Rome, 1939-Aug. 1940; Chief of Lith. Diplomatic Service, 1940-

Lozovskii, Solomon Abramovich 1878-1949, Sov. Deputy P. Comm. for Foreign Affairs, 1940-1944.

Maceina, Antanas 1908-   , Lith. philosopher; Dean, Faculty of Philosophy and Theology, University of Kaunas, 1935-1940.

Mačiokas, Mykolas 1899-   , Col. of the General Staff of the LAF.

Mackenzie-King, William L., (see King).

Mackevičius, Mečislovas 1906-   , Judge-candidate, Kaunas District, 1939-1940; Minister of Justice in the Provisional Government, 1941.

Maglione, Louis Cardinal 1877-1944, Papal Sec. of State, 1939-1944.

Malinauskas, Donatas 1869-(?), Member, Lith. National Council, 1917-1920; Signatory of the Lithuanian Declaration of Independence.

Manzoni, Conte Gaetano   , Italian Amb. in Paris, 1928.

Markhlevskiy (Karskiy), Iulian Iuzefovich   , Sov. diplomat, ca. 1918-1922.

Martius, Georg   , Ger. Min. in Riga, 1940; Director, Division W-XIIa (Maritime Transportation), A.A., 1940-1945.

Matulionis, Jonas 1898-   , Director of pre-war Land Bank, finance minister of provisional government.

Maysky, Ivan Mikhailovich 1884-   , Sov. Amb. in London, 1932-1943.

McCosgair, Liam, (see Cosgrave).

McLachlan, Alexander J. 1872-1965, Vice-President of the Executive Federal Council of the Commonwealth of Australia, 1932-1934; Min. of Science, Industry, & Development, 1932-1934; Min. of Scientific & Industrial Research, 1934-1948; Postmaster General, 1934-1948.

Merkys, Antanas 1887-1955, Colonel; Mayor of Kaunas, 1934-1939; Lith. Prime Min., Nov. 1939-June 1940.

Mickis, Matas 1896-   , Lith. P. Comm. of Agriculture (Min., June 15-July), June 15, 1940-July 1940.

Miežhelis, Gen. Vladas 1894-   , Leader of the LAF.

Mikoyan, Anastas Ivanovich 1895-   , Deputy Chairman, Council of People's Commissars of the U.S.S.R., 1937-1949; P. Comm. for Foreign Trade, 1937-1949.

Milčius, Antanas 1895-   , Member of Constituent Assembly for the Labor Federation.

Mironas, Vladas 1880-1953, Rev.; Member, Lith. National Council, 1917-1920; Signatory of the Lithuanian Declaration of Independence.

Molotov (Skryabin), Yvacheslav Mikhailovich 1890-   , Chairman, Council of People's Commissars of the U.S.S.R., 1930-1941; P. Comm. for Foreign Affairs, 1939-1949.

Monroe, James 1758-1831, President of the U.S.A., 1817-1825.

Munters, Vilhelms 1898-   , Latvian F.M., 1936-1940.

Musteikis, Kazys 1894-   , Lith. Min. of Defense, Dec. 1938-June 1940.

Nagevičius (Nagius), Vladas 1881-1954, General; Surgeon-General of the Lith. Armed Forces, 1920-1940.

Naruševičius, Tomas 1871-1927, Chairman of the Lith. Delegation to Moscow, Apr.-July 1920; Lith. Delegate to the League of Nations, 1920-1921.

Narutavičius, Stanislovas 1862-1932, Member, Lith, National Council, 1917-1920; Signatory of the Lith. Declaration of Independence.

Našliunas, Jonas 1900-   , Member of the Supreme Council of the Tautininkai (Lith. Nationalist Union).

Natkevičius (Natkus), Ladas 1893-1945, Lith. Min. in Moscow, 1939-1940.

Naujokas, Matas 1901-   , Leader of the LAF.

Neris, Salomeja 1904-1945, Lith. poetess; Deputy to People's Seimas, 1940; Lith. Deputy to the Supreme Soviet of the U.S.S.R., 1941-1945.

Norem, Owen 1902-   , U.S. Min. in Kaunas, 1937-1940.

Norkaitis, Jonas 1892-   , Director of the Economic Section of the Lith. Foreign Ministry, 1936-June, 1940.

Novickis, Antanas 1894-   , Lith. Director of Highway Construction, 1940; Min. of Communication, Lith. Provisional Government, 1941.

Obolenskiy, Leonid Leonidovich   , Sov. Delegate in Riga, 1920; Representative of the Government of the R.S.F.S.R. for the peace negotiations with the Baltic States; Sov. Min. in Warsaw, 1922-1924.

Oleka, Kazimieras 1880-   , Lith. Min. of the Interior, 1920-1923.

Ozols, Charles   , Latvian envoy extraordinary and minister in Moscow, 1929.

Packer, Earl Lenvin 1894-   , U.S. Consul and First Sec. of Legation in Riga, 1936-1940.

Padalskis (Padalis), Pranas 1911-1971, Educator; Docent at the University of Kaunas, 1935-1939, Vilnius, 1939-1940; Vice-Min. of Commerce in the Lith. Provisional Government, 1941.

Pajaujis-Javis, Juozas 1894-   , Lith. economist, publicist, Social-Democratic politician; Docent at the Lith. Institute of Commerce, 1941-1944.

Pakalka, Jonas 1894-   , Member of Constituent Assembly for Social Democrats.

Pakarklis, Povilas 1902-1955, Lith. Minister of Justice, June-July, 1940; P. Comm. of Justice, July 1940-June 1941.

Paleckis, Justas 1899-   , Lith. Prime Min., June 16-1940; Acting President of Lithuania, June-Aug. 1940; Chairman of the Presidium of the Supreme Soviet of the Lithuanian S.S.R., Aug. 1940-

Patek, Stanislaw   , Polish envoy extraordinary and Minister in Moscow, 1929.

Päts, Konstantin 1874-1943 (?), President of Estonia, 1934-1940.

Pavlov, Vladimir   , Sec. of the Sov. Embassy in Berlin, 1940-1941.

Pearson, Lester B. 1897-   , President of the General Assembly of the United Nations, 1952.

Petrauskas, Kazys 1914-   , Member, LCP, 1931-   ; Sec., Panevežys District, LCP, 1938-1940; Deputy to People's Seimas, 1940; President, Panevežys Agricultural Commission, 1940-1941.

Petrauskas, Pranas 1898-1941, Member, LCP, 1924-1941; Deputy, People's Seimas, 1940; Member, Presidium of the Supreme Soviet of the Lithuanian S.S.R., 1940-1941.

Petrulis, Alfonsas 1873-1928, Rev.; Member, Lith. National Council, 1917-1920; Signatory of the Lith. Declaration of Independence.

Potemkin, Vladimir Petrovich 1878-1946, Sov. First Deputy P. Comm. for Foreign Affairs, 1937-1940.

Povilaitis, Augustinas 1900-1940 (?), Director of the Security Department of the Lith. Ministry of the Interior, 1934-1940.

Pozdniakov, Nikolai Georgevich   , Sov. Min. in Kaunas, Nov. 1939-June 1940.

Prapuolenis, Leonas 1913-1972, Lith. industrialist; Colonel, Lithuanian Activist Front, 1941; Commander in Chief of the June 1941 insurrection.

Pronskus, Juozas 1893-   , Member of Constituent Assembly for Peasant Populist Union.

Pulaski, Casimir 1748-1779, General, U.S. Cavalry, 1778-1779.

Pundzevičius, Stasys 1893-   , General; Chief of Lith. General Staff, 1939-1940.

Puodžius, Stasys 1896-1942, Major; General Councilor in Ger. Ziwilverwaltung, 1941-1943.

Pyragius, Jonas 1902-   , Major, Lith. Air Force; noted Voldemarininkas, dismissed from service after attempted coup d'etat in 1934.

Račkauskas, Vytautas 1881-1956, Lith. Delegate to the Moscow Peace Conference, 1920; Director, Bureau of Land Reclamation, Lith. Ministry of Agriculture, 1920-1922.

Raila, Bronis 1909-   , Lith. journalist; Member, editorial board, *Lietuvos Aidas,* 1940-1941.

Raštikis, Stasys 1896-   , Chief of Lith. General Staff, 1935-Jan. 1940; Min. of Defense, Lith. Provisional Government, 1941.

Rei, August 1886-1963, Envoy extraordinary and Minister Plenipotentiary of Estonia in Moscow, 1938-1940.

Renteln (Theodore), Adrian von   , Director of NSDAP student organization, 193?-1941; Generalkomissar for Lithuania, 1941-1944.

Ribbentrop, Joachim von 1893-1946, German F. M., 1938-1945.

Rintelen, Emil von   , Director of Political Division II (Western Europe), A.A., (?) -1940; Deputy Director, Political Department, A.A., 1940-1945.

Rogers, William P. 1913-   , U.S. Sec. of State, 1969-.

Roosevelt, Franklin D. 1882-1945, President of the U.S.A., 1933-1945.

Rosenberg, Alfred 1893-1946, Editor in Chief, *Völkischer Beobachter* 1921-1945; Reichsminister for Occupied Eastern Territories, 1941-1945.

Rotomskis, Povilas 1906-1962, F. M. of the L. S. S. R., 1944-1948.

Rozenbaumas, Simanas 1859-1935, Lith. Min. for Jewish Affairs, 1919-1924.

Rudenko, Roman Andrejevic 1907-   , Russian Prosecutor at Nuremburg, 1946.

Rudokas, Juozas   -1945, Leader of the LAF.

Rusk, Dean 1909-   , U.S. Sec. of State, 1961-1969.

Salnais, Valdemars 1886-1948, Latvian F.M., 1933-1934.

Sapieha, Eustace 1881-   , Polish F.M., 1920-1921.

Šaulys, Jurgis 1879-1948, Member, Lith. National Council, 1917-1920; Signatory, Lith. Declaration of Independence; Lith. Min. in Berne, 1939-1948.

Šaulys, Kazimieras 1872-1964, Member, Lith. National Council, 1917-1920; Signatory, Lith. Declaration of Independence.

Schmidt, Paul Otto   , Interpreter with ministerial rank in A.A., 1923-1945; attached to F.M.'s Secretariat, 1939-1945.

Schnurre, Karl   , Head of Group East in Economic Policy Department, A.A., 1936-1945.

Schulenburg, Freidrich Werner Graf von der 1875-1944, Ger. Amb. in Moscow, 1934-1941.

Seljamaa, Julius Friedrich 1883-1936, Estonian Min. in Moscow, 1928-1933.

Šernas, Jurgis 1888-1926, Member, Lith. National Council, 1917-1920; Signatory of the Lith. Declaration of Independence.

Serov, Ivan Aleksandrovich 1905-   , Sov. Deputy P. Comm. for State Security, 1940-1945.

Shkvartsev, Aleksander A.   , Sov. Amb. in Berlin, Sept. 1939-Nov. 1940.

Shuette, Ehrenfried   , Deputy to Dr. Peter Kleist at the Dienstelle Ribbentrop.

Sidzikaukas, Vaclovas 1893-   , Lithuanian Minister in London, 1931-1934.

Siemaška, Domininkas 1878-1932, Lith. Min. without portfolio for Byelorussian Affairs, 1920-1922.

Skipitis, Rapolas 1887-   , Member, Lith. Council of the Bar, 1932-1940; F.M. of Lith. Provisional Government, 1941.

Škirpa, Kazys 1895-   , Chief of Lith. General Staff, 1926; Lith. Min. in Berlin, Feb. 1939-June 1940; Founder, Lith. Activist Front, 1940; Prime Min., Lith. Provisional Government, 1941.

Škučas, Kāzys 1894-1941, General; Lith. Min. of the Interior, March 1939-June 1940.

Šlepetys, Jonas 1894-   , Colonel; Prefect of the City and District of Vilnius, 1939-1940; Min. of the Interior, Lith. Provisional Government, 1941.

Sleževičius, Mykolas 1882-1939, Lith. Prime Min., Min. of Justice, Acting F.M., June-Dec. 1926.

Smetona, Antanas 1874-1944, Member of the Lith. National Council, 1917-1920; Signatory of the Lith. Declaration of Independence; President of Lithuania, 1919-1923, Dec. 1926-June 1940.

Sniečkus, Antanas 1903-   , First Sec., LCP, 1936-   ; Director, Department of Security, Lith. Ministry of the Interior, June 1940-June 1941.

Soloveičikas, Maksas 1883-   , Lith. Min. without portfolio for Jewish Affairs, 1919-1923.

Sommer, Erich   , Official, A.A., 1939-1941.

Sonnleithner, Franz   , Senior Counsellor in the Secretariat of the Ger. F.M.

Stalin (Dzhugashvili), Joseph (Iosif) Vissarionovich 1879-1953, Sov. P. Comm. for Nationalities, 1921-1923; General Sec. of the Central Committee of the C.P.S.U., 1922-1953; Chairman of the Council of People's Commissars of the U.S.S.R., 1941-1949.

Stašinskas, Atty, Vladas 1879-1944, First Min. of the Interior and Min. of Public Works & Welfare.

Staugaitis, Justinas 1866-1943, Member, Lith. National Council, 1917-1920; Signatory of the Lith. Declaration of Independence.

Streseman, Gustav 1878-1929, Ger. F.M., 1923-1929.

Stulginskis, Aleksandars 1885-1970, Member, Lith. National Council, 1917-1920; Signatory of the Lith. Declaration of Independence; President of the Lith. Constituent Seimas, 1920-1922; President of Lithuania, 1923-1926.

Šumauskas, Motiejus 1905-   , Member, LCP, 1924-   ; Deputy, People's Seimas, 1940; Lith. P. Comm. for Industry, 1940-1941; Chairman of Gosplan and Deputy Chairman of the Lith. Council of People's Commissars, 1944-1956.

Talevičius, Zigmas 1895-1956, Lt. Col.; hero of the Lithuanian War of Independence. 1918-1920.

Tamošaitis, Antanas 1894-1940, Minister of Justice; head of special commission on the kidnapped Russian soldiers.

Tautvilas, Narcizas 1903-   , Lt. Col of the General Staff of the LAF.

Thomson, Erik. Baltic tragedy. Central Europe journal, v. 19, no. 9/10, Sept./Oct. 1971: 310-318.

Thurston, Walter 1895-   , Counselor to the U.S. Embassy in Moscow, 1939-1943.

Tippelskirch, Werner von   , Counselor to the Ger. Embassy in Moscow, 1935-1941, with rank of Min., 1940-1941.

Titulesku, Nikolae 1883-1941, Roumanian F.M., 1932-1936.

Toliušis, Atty. Zigmas 1889-1971, Prominent attorney and leader of the resistance against the Germans; Leader of the LAF.

Tomaševičius, Benediktas 1879-(?), Lith. Vice-Min. of Communications, 1922-1923.

Tubelis, Juozas 1882-1939, First Min. of Agriculture & Min. of Natural Resources, 1918.

Turauskas, Edvardas 1896-1967, Lith. Representative at the League of Nations, 1940-1946; Counselor to the Lith. Legation in Berne, 1940-1946.

Uchida, Viscount Yasuya 1865-1936, Privy Councilor to the Emperor of Japan, 1924-1929.

Ulmanis, Karlis 1877-(?), President of Latvia, 1936-1940.

Umansky, Konstantin Aleksandrovich   , Sov. Amb. in Washington, 1939-1941.

Urbšys, Juozas 1896-   , Lith. F. M., Dec. 1938-June 1940.

Vailokaitis, Juozas 1880-1953, Member, Lith. National Council, 1917-1920; Signatory of the Lith. Declaration of Independence; President of the Lith. Bank of Agriculture, 1919-1941.

Vainauskas, Pranas 1899-   , Director, Free Port of Memel, 1939-1940; Min. of Commerce, Lith. Provisional Government, 1941.

Vaineikienė, Stasė 1884-1946, Lith. author; Deputy, People's Seimas, 1940; Member, Supreme Soviet of the Lithuanian S.S.R., 1940-1941.

Vainoras, Stasys 1909-1964, Editor of *Jūra*, 1935-1940; Liaison for Lithuanian, Latvian, and Estonian undergrounds, 1941-1944.

Valiūnas, Juozas Kestutis 1923-   , President, Supreme Committee for the Liberation of Lithuania.

Valiukėnas, Mecys 1910-   , Lith, banker; prominent member of Lith. underground, 1941-1944.

Vėbra, Juozas 1901-   , Lith. educator; docent at the University of Kaunas, 1940-1944.

Velykis, Col. Mykolas 1884-1956, Min. of Defense, 1918.

Vencius, Ksaveras 1906-1945, Min. of Health in Lith. Provisional Government, 1941; resistance leader, 1941-1944.

Venclova, Antanas 1906-1971, Lith. Min. of Education, June-July 1940, P. Comm. for Education, July 1940-June 1941.

Vileišis, Jonas 1872-1942, Member of the Lith. National Council, 1917-1920; Signatory of the Lith. Declaration of Independence.

Viliušis, Jonas 1896-   , Nationalist Deputy to Lith. Seimas, 1935-1940; First Sec. of the Presidium of the Seimas.

Vitkauskas, Gen. Vincas 1890-1965, Chief of Staff of the Lith. Army, Jan.-June 1940;

Min. of Defense, June-Aug. 1940; Commander, Soviet **XXIX Territorial Corps**, Aug. 1940-1945.

Vitkus, Balys 1898-   , Lith. educator; Professor of the Academy of Agriculture at Dotnuva, 1925-1940, Vice-Rector, 1940, Rector, 1941-1944.

Voldemaras, Prof. Augustinas 1883-1944 (?), Prime Min. & F.M. from 1918-1920, 1926-1929.

Voronko, Juozas 1891-(?), First Min. of Byelorussian Affairs.

Vygodskis, Jokubas 1857-(?), Min. of Jewish Affairs, 1918-

Vyshinskiy, Andrei Yanuarevich 1883-1954, Vice-Chairman of the Council of People's Commissars of the U.S.S.R., 1938-1940; Deputy, P. Comm. for Foreign Affairs, 1940-1949; Sov. F.M., 1949-1953; Sov. Amb. to the United Nations, 1953-1954.

Weizsäcker, Ernst Freiherr von 1882-1951, State Sec. of the A.A., 1938-1943.

Welles, Sumner 1892-   , U.S. Undersecretary of State, 1937-1943.

Wilson (Thomas), Woodrow 1856-1924, President of the U.S.A., 1913-1921.

Woermann, Ernst   , Director of the Political Department of the A. A., with the title of Undersecretary of State, 1938-1943.

Yčas, Jonas 1880-1931, Min. of Education, 1918.

Yčas, Atty. Martynas 1885-194 , Min. of Finance & Min. of Communications, 1918.

Yla, Stasys 1908-   , Rev.; Adjunct Professor of Theology, Faculty of Philosophy and Theology, University of Kaunas, 1935-1940.

Young, Evan E. 1878-1946, American Commissioner to Baltic States, 1920-1922; Chief of the Division of Eastern European Affairs, 1923-1925; Minister Plenipotentiary.

Žadeikis, Povilas 1887-1957, Lith. Min. in Washington, 1935-1957.

Zaleski, August 1883-   , Polish F.M., 1926-1932.

Zechlin, Erich 1883-1,954, Ger. Min. in Kaunas, 1933-1940.

Želigowski, Gen. Lucjan 1865-1946, Polish general occupied Vilnius, 1920.

Zhdanov, Andrei Aleksandrovich 1896-1948, Member, Central Committee, C. P. S. U., 1930-1948; Member, Politburo, C. P. S. U., 1939-1948.

Zibertas, Pranas 1895-1942, Deputy, People's Seimas, 1940.

Žilius, Jonas 1870-1932, Member of the Lith. National Council, 1917-1920; Agent of Lithuania in Washington, 1917-1918.

Žilinskas, Vladas 1912-   , Secretary at the Lithuanian Legation in Stockholm, 1939-1940.

INDEX

A

Abdulskaitė, Birutė: 244-245
Adomas (Icikas Meskupas): 244-245
Adomauskas, Liūdas: 244-245
Aggression, definition of: 100-101
Aleksandrovskiy, Sergei: 90,91
Alexander I of Russia: 14
Alexander, Grand Duke of Lithuania: 7
Ambrazevičius, Juozas: 347, 350, 359, 360-361
Andrusovo, Treaty of: 8
Anne, Tsarina: 9
Atlantic Charter: 474-476, 487
Audėnas, Juozas: 205
Augustus II of Pol-Lith: 8, 9
Augustus III of Pol-Lith: 9
Avietėnaitė, Magdalena: 292-294

B

Ball, George W.: 462-463
Baltic Entente: 188, 207-208
Baltic Union: 18
Baltrušaitis, Jurgis: 81, 89, 91, 92, 96
Banaitis, Saliamonas: 65
Bank Deposits: 76
Bartašiūnas, Juozas: 393
Basanavičius, Jonas: 66
Berle, A. A.: 364, 437
Biržiška, Mykolas: 66
Bizauskas, Kazys: 66, 114-115, 117, 142-143, 161-163, 165, 168-169, 216, 334
Blucher, Wipert von: 223
Brazinskas, Juozas: 178-179, 191-203, 192-204
Brezhnev, Leonid: 1, 16, 29
Briand-Kellogg Pact: 18, 97, 100, 117, 190, 418-420, 438
Bulgaria: 267-268
Butaev: 177, 185, 187-188, 193-203

C

"Captive Nations Week": 459-461
Catherine II (the Great): 9, 10, 12
Central Lithuanian Republic: 83

Č

Černius, Jonas: 108, 116, 118, 127, 168, 169-170, 193-203
Charles XII of Sweden: 8
Chicherin, Georgi V.: 81, 83, 90, 91, 93-95
Churchill, Winston: 335, 450, 454-455, 474-476
Citizenship: 72-73
Coalition Cabinet of 1918: 67
Colby: 486
Confederation of Targowica: 12
Constituent Seimas: 16, 65, 66, 67, 68, 84, 414-416
Consultative Assembly of the Council of Europe: 461-462
Convention for the Definition of Aggression Between Lithuania and the USSR: 100 ff
Council of Lithuania: 65, 66, 403-404
Council of State (Lith): 66
Cvirka, Petras: 244-245

D

Davila, Charles A.: 98, 99
Debts: 73-74
Dekanozov, Vlahimir G.: 22, 23, 212, 213-214, 216, 224, 227, 271-275, 294, 373, 395, 430, 456
Demskis, Juozas: 244-245
Deportation: 327-335
Didžiulis, Karolis: 244-245
Dimavičius: 197
Diplomatic Relations (Lith-Rus): 79
Ditkevičius, Viktoras: 244-245
Dolgoruki: 8, 23
Dovydaitis, Pranas: 66
Dulles, John Foster: 458
"Dumb Diet:" 8-9, 23
Dunn, James C.: 232

E

Eisenhower, Dwight D.: 454-455, 457-458, 461
Fairhall, Allen: 470-471
Finland: 426-429
France: 16, 19, 83, 86, 89, 118, 132, 139, 172, 225
Frederick II of Prussia: 9, 10

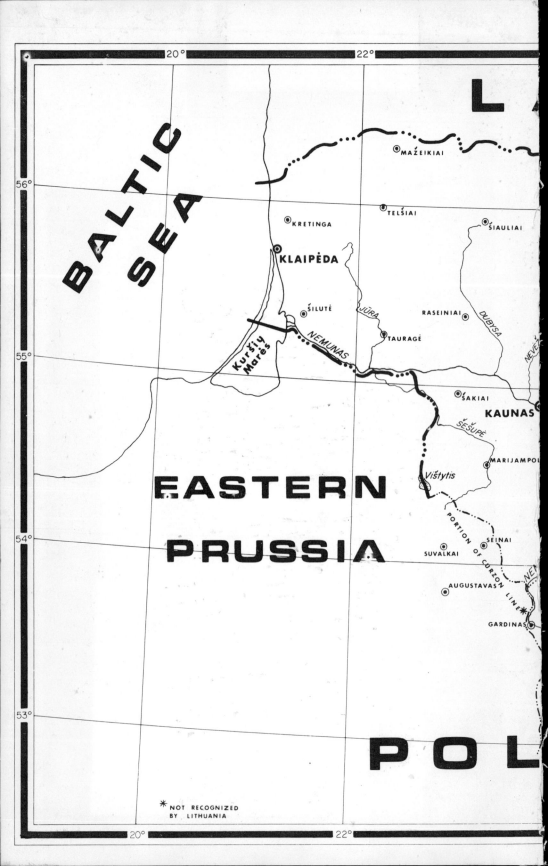

BALTIC
SEA

20° 22°

L A

MAŽEIKIAI

56°

TELŠIAI

KRETINGA

ŠIAULIAI

KLAIPĖDA

ŠILUTĖ

JŪRA

RASEINIAI

DUBYSA

TAURAGĖ

NEMUNAS

NEVEŽ

Kuršių
Marės

55°

ŠAKIAI

KAUNAS

ŠEŠUPĖ

MARIJAMPOL

Vištytis

EASTERN

PORTION OF CURZON LINE

SEINAI

54°

PRUSSIA

SUVALKAI

AUGUSTAVAS

NEM

GARDINAS

53°

P O L

* NOT RECOGNIZED
BY LITHUANIA

20° 22°